KARL MARX
FREDERICK ENGELS

COLLECTED WORKS

INTERNATIONAL PUBLISHERS

NEW YORK

K
FRED

FRE
CO

KARL MARX
FREDERICK ENGELS

Volume
8

MARX AND ENGELS: 1848-49

INTERNATIONAL PUBLISHERS
NEW YORK

This volume has been prepared jointly by Lawrence & Wishart Ltd., London, International Publishers Co. Inc., New York, and Progress Publishers, Moscow, in collaboration with the Institute of Marxism-Leninism, Moscow.

Editorial commissions:
GREAT BRITAIN: Jack Cohen, Maurice Cornforth, Maurice Dobb, E. J. Hobsbawm, James Klugmann, Margaret Mynatt.
USA: James S. Allen, Philip S. Foner, Dirk J. Struik, William W. Weinstone.
USSR: for Progress Publishers—N. P. Karmanova, V. N. Sedikh, M. K. Shcheglova, Y. V. Yeremin; for the Institute of Marxism-Leninism— P. N. Fedoseyev, L. I. Golman, A. I. Malysh, A. G. Yegorov, V. Y. Zevin.

Library of Congress Cataloging in Publication Data

Marx, Karl, 1818-1883.

Karl Marx, Frederick Engels: collected works.

1. Socialism—Collected works. 2. Economics—Collected works. I. Engels, Friedrich, 1820-1895. Works. English. 1975. II. Title.
HX39.5.A16 1975 335.4 73-84671
ISBN 0-7178-0508-5 (v. 8)

Contents

KARL MARX AND FREDERICK ENGELS

ARTICLES FROM THE *NEUE RHEINISCHE ZEITUNG*
November 8, 1848-March 5, 1849

1848

November

December

1849

January

February

March

FROM THE PREPARATORY MATERIALS

APPENDICES

NOTES AND INDEXES

ILLUSTRATIONS

TRANSLATORS

GREGOR BENTON: Articles 5, 6, 15, 25-30, 38-40, 44-49

RICHARD DIXON: Article 19

CLEMENS DUTT: Articles 2, 7, 10-12, 14, 17, 18, 20-22, 24, 31-37, 41, 43, 54, 55, 58, 60, 61, 65, 66, 69, 70, 74, 75, 80, 85-89, 91, 94, 96-98, 101, 103, 105, 107-09, 115, 116, 122, 126; From the Preparatory Materials 3

W. L. GUTTSMAN: Articles 120, 121, 123, 124

FRIDA KNIGHT: Articles 50, 51, 57, 62, 64, 67, 72, 76-79, 81, 82, 84

BARBARA RUHEMANN: Articles 52, 53, 63, 68, 90, 92, 106, 112, 114, 125, 127-30; Appendices 2, 3, 6-13, 17, 19, 20, 24

SALO RYAZANSKAYA: Articles 1, 3, 4, 8, 9, 13, 16, 23, 42, 56, 59, 71, 73, 83, 95, 113

BARRIE SELMAN: Articles 117-19

CHRISTOPHER UPWARD: Article 104

JOAN AND TREVOR WALMSLEY: Articles 93, 99, 100, 102, 110, 111; From the Preparatory Materials 1, 2; Appendices 1, 4, 5, 14-16, 18, 21-23

Preface

Volume Eight of the *Collected Works* of Marx and Engels contains their writings from November 8, 1848,to March 5, 1849. This is the second of three volumes (Vols. 7-9) covering the period of revolutions in 1848 and 1849.

The bulk of the volume consists of articles written by Marx and Engels for the *Neue Rheinische Zeitung*, organ of the revolutionary-proletarian wing of German and European democracy. These articles, like the rest of the contents of this volume—the letters written by Engels on behalf of the workers' organisations of Switzerland, the accounts (published in the Appendices) of Marx's and Engels' speeches at the meetings of workers and democrats in Cologne, and so on—demonstrate the part which Marx and Engels played in the revolutionary events of those days. Edited by Marx and Engels, the *Neue Rheinische Zeitung* was a fearlessly revolutionary journal. It consistently exposed the manoeuvres of the monarchist-aristocratic circles and of the liberal bourgeoisie whose connivance they enjoyed; it was the genuine organiser of the people's struggle. Through this newspaper, Marx and Engels directed the activity of Communist League members in various parts of Germany, influenced the German working-class and democratic movement as a whole, and promoted the unity and mobilisation of all the country's revolutionary forces.

These articles by Marx and Engels show the continuous, dialectical change in class forces during the revolution, the real meaning of the events taking place in Germany and other countries and the social background to the acute political conflicts. The conclusions they then drew have made a major contribution to the

Marxist teaching on the class struggle, explaining in detail working-class strategy and tactics at each new stage of the bourgeois-democratic revolution.

In the period covered by this volume the counter-revolutionary forces were fighting hard against the people's gains in the first months of the 1848 revolution. The defeat of the Paris proletariat in June was the signal for a general counter-attack by monarchist-aristocratic and Right-wing bourgeois circles whose aim was the complete or partial restoration of the old order.

The bourgeois-democratic revolutions in France and Germany were, indeed, largely in a stage of decline—yet the masses everywhere continued the struggle to defend their achievements. Police persecution notwithstanding, the democratic and proletarian organisations did not abandon their activity.

In these conditions, Marx and Engels concentrated their efforts on explaining the real situation to the broad masses, the real threat of defeat for the revolution, and on mobilising resistance against the counter-revolution. The *Neue Rheinische Zeitung* editors did everything in their power to unite the workers and revolutionary democrats, urging them to make use of parliamentary as well as other methods to bring about a turn of the tide in favour of the revolution.

Marx and Engels realised that if the revolutionary struggle was to succeed, it must not be confined within a national framework but become international; the international solidarity of the democratic and proletarian movement in all the major European countries should be counterposed to the bloc that was being formed by the internal and external counter-revolutionary forces. They saw in every revolutionary centre in any part of Europe an integral element of the general European revolutionary movement. They devoted particular attention to Italy and Hungary, where, despite the general downward trend of the European revolution, an upsurge of popular revolutionary energy was evident—a fact justifying their hopes that the reactionaries' attempts at restoration would yet be finally frustrated and the revolution be renewed with greater depth and scope.

The volume begins with Marx's article "The Crisis in Berlin". This, together with his series of articles "Counter-Revolution in Berlin", came as the immediate response to the counter-revolutionary coup d'état which had taken place in Prussia. The *Neue Rheinische Zeitung* had already in September 1848 warned that a coup d'état was imminent, and had pointed out that unless the

Prussian National Assembly took steps to rally the support of the masses, it would first be turned out of Berlin and then dissolved (see present edition, Vol. 7, p. 429). The prognosis proved correct. Early in November 1848, Frederick William IV charged the reactionary General Brandenburg with forming a government, and the provincial city of Brandenburg was declared to be the new seat of the Assembly. Marx saw this coup as a direct result of the suppression of the uprisings of the Paris proletariat in June and of the masses in Vienna in late October and November 1848.

At the moment of political crisis Marx proposed what should be done. His tactical platform of struggle against the counter-revolutionary forces envisaged not only active defence but also a counter-offensive to carry forward and consolidate the revolution. As an immediate reply to the coup d'état, he put forward on November 12, 1848, the slogan of refusal to pay taxes (see this volume, p. 21). This move would not only weaken the counter-revolution by undermining its financial resources, but — most important of all — would draw the masses of the people into action. At the same time, he adapted his tactical proposals to the actually developing conditions of the struggle. Thus the appeal of the Rhenish District Committee of Democrats of November 14, 1848, which was written by Marx, advised, for the time being, against any violent resistance to the collection of unpaid taxes under a writ of execution. While the Prussian National Assembly had as yet not decided to call on the masses to refuse to pay taxes and this slogan was not supported in the other provinces, such resistance could only have developed into premature and sporadic acts of rebellion. The situation changed when, under the influence of numerous local appeals, the National Assembly adopted on November 15 a decision on the refusal to pay taxes which was to come into force on November 17. Non-payment of taxes had now acquired nation-wide significance and the authority of the National Assembly. Marx immediately called on the masses and the workers' and democratic organisations to resist the collection of taxes by all means, including violence. On November 17 he wrote in the *Neue Rheinische Zeitung*: "It is high treason to pay taxes. Refusal to pay taxes is the primary duty of the citizen!" (see this volume, p. 36). From November 19 to December 17 the *Neue Rheinische Zeitung* carried in large type on its front page the slogan "No More Taxes!!!"

The Rhenish District Committee of Democrats' appeal of November 18, written by Marx, called for the organisation of a people's militia everywhere, the re-election of municipal councils that had refused to obey the decision of the National Assembly, the setting up of committees of public safety. Marx saw such committees as embryos of provisional revolutionary organs of power to replace Prussian officialdom. And he was himself a member of the People's Committee in Cologne, which played a considerable role in organising the campaign against tax payments in the Rhine Province. The Second District Congress of Democratic Associations of the province, held on November 23 with Marx as one of the delegates, approved Marx's programme of action (see this volume, p. 46).

Meanwhile, the liberal-democratic majority in the Prussian National Assembly confined itself to passive resistance. Many local democrats also remained irresolute. And Marx warned that their tactics of passive resistance were dooming the movement to failure. Such tactics, he wrote, "resemble the vain struggle of a calf against its slaughterer" (see this volume, p. 38). Profiting by their opponents' weakness, the Prussian counter-revolutionaries carried the coup d'état to its conclusion: on December 5, 1848, the Prussian National Assembly was dissolved.

Marx analysed the causes of the counter-revolutionary victory in Prussia in a series of articles, "The Bourgeoisie and the Counter-Revolution", in his articles "Montesquieu LVI", "The Berlin *National-Zeitung* to the Primary Electors" and "Camphausen", and in his speech at the trial of members of the Rhenish District Committee of Democrats on February 8, 1849. The first of these works was particularly important. It contained a general account of the German revolution and in what respects it differed from the previous battles waged against feudalism by the European bourgeoisie. Contrasting the events of 1848 in Germany with the English revolution of the seventeenth century and the French revolution of the eighteenth, Marx concluded that there were different types of bourgeois revolutions and that the differences between them were determined primarily by historical conditions—the specific features of the different stages in the emergence of bourgeois society, the degree of development of the class contradictions between the bourgeoisie and the oppressed classes, the proletariat above all.

The revolution in Germany, Marx pointed out, was, like the preceding revolutions in England and France, the result of an acute contradiction between the dominance of the feudal ruling class, whose bulwark was the monarchy, and the bourgeois relations which were taking shape. However, as distinct from the English bourgeoisie of the seventeenth century and the French bourgeoisie of the eighteenth, when the proletariat and the other exploited sections of the urban population "did not yet constitute independent classes or class sub-divisions", the Prussian bourgeoisie was already being challenged by an emerging working class which was beginning to fight for its own interests. And it could see in the example of France what a menacing turn the class struggle of the proletariat could take. That is why "from the first it was inclined to betray the people and to compromise with the crowned representative of the old society.... It stood at the helm of the revolution not because it had the people behind it but because the people drove it before them; it stood at the head not because it represented the initiative of a new social era but only because it represented the rancour of an old one" (see this volume, pp. 161, 162-63).

Whereas in England and France the bourgeois revolutions had led to a radical change in the political system corresponding to the requirements of the capitalist mode of production, the March revolution of 1848 in Prussia left intact "the old bureaucracy, the old army, the old boards of prosecuting magistrates" (see this volume, p. 317). The Prussian bourgeoisie decided to make its way to power, not with the help of revolution but by a deal with the aristocracy and the monarchy. Hence the "theory of agreement with the Crown" which was put forward by the Prussian liberal constitutionalists and which covered up, as Marx and Engels repeatedly stressed, the bourgeoisie's betrayal of the revolutionary cause. The opposition to the revolution by considerable sections of the Prussian, mainly big, bourgeoisie and their fear of the masses thus dictated their efforts to remain on "a legal basis", their renunciation of resolute struggle against the forces of feudal-monarchist reaction. Fearing for their own property, they nipped in the bud every encroachment on feudal property and thereby alienated the peasantry, their natural ally in the struggle against feudalism. This cowardly and essentially treacherous stand of the bourgeoisie doomed the bourgeois-democratic revolution to defeat in conditions when the working class was not yet itself ready to lead a revolutionary-democratic movement of the whole nation and had not yet achieved sufficient class consciousness and organisation.

The coup d'état in Prussia, Marx stressed, was the logical result of the policy of the Prussian so-called liberal governments which succeeded one another after March 1848 and surrendered position after position to the counter-revolutionary monarchists and aristocrats. And so, during the November crisis in Prussia, far from energetically supporting the Prussian National Assembly in its conflict with the Crown, the liberal majority of the Frankfurt National Assembly declared the Berlin decision on the refusal to pay taxes to be illegal and thus actually helped the Brandenburg

Government to implement its counter-revolutionary designs. In his article "The Frankfurt Assembly" Marx branded this as an act of treachery. Subsequently, too, the *Neue Rheinische Zeitung* continually exposed the Frankfurt Assembly's connivance at counter-revolution (see the article "Report of the Frankfurt Committee on Austrian Affairs" and others).

In 1848-49 Marx and Engels became finally convinced that the bourgeoisie was step by step losing its effectiveness as an advanced opponent of feudalism. The counter-revolutionary degeneration of the European bourgeoisie—even though in certain sectors of the struggle and in certain countries (Hungary, Italy) it was still acting in a revolutionary way—made it necessary drastically to reassess the disposition of class forces in the bourgeois-democratic revolution and the conditions for its victory. Since the bourgeoisie was losing the ability to carry through bourgeois-democratic reforms by means of revolution, it fell to the working class to head the people's struggle for total liquidation of the remnants of feudalism. Thus changes in the position of the various classes by the middle of the nineteenth century led Marx and Engels to the idea of the hegemony of the working class in the bourgeois-democratic revolution—an idea which was elaborated by Lenin in the new historic conditions of the twentieth century. During the 1848-49 revolution, Marx and Engels were already directing their efforts to preparing the working class for this role by accelerating the growth of its class consciousness and the creation of a revolutionary working-class party.

At the trial of the Rhenish District Committee of Democrats, Marx told the bourgeois jury that the bourgeoisie was in duty bound to fight to abolish feudal relations and absolutism. And yet, he said, by their appeals to preserve "a legal basis" the Prussian liberals were merely seeking to perpetuate the old laws and to impose them on the new social system which had arisen during the revolution. Society, he continued, was not founded on the law but, on the contrary, "the law must be founded upon society, it must express the common interests and needs of society... which arise from the material mode of production prevailing at the given time" (see this volume, p. 327). The preservation of old laws in despite of new needs of social development, the striving to impose on society an obsolete political system already doomed by the new conditions, led to social crises only to be resolved by revolution. He accused Prussia's ruling circles of conspiring against the people, against the law and order established as a result of the popular revolution in March 1848. He emphasised that, having in effect violated all legality, the Crown had no right to accuse the revolutionary movement's leaders of illegal activity. Refusal to pay taxes was a natural and legitimate means of self-defence for the people. "If the Crown makes a counter-revolution, the people has the right to reply with a revolution" (see this volume, p. 339).

Analysing the events in Prussia and Germany, Marx concluded that there was no middle way between the complete victory of the feudal absolutist forces, with the abolition of freedom of assembly, association and the press, and a new upsurge of the revolution, as a result of which the proletariat, the peasantry and the urban petty bourgeoisie would establish a democratic republic and proceed to carry out social measures to prepare the ground for transition to the proletarian revolution. Marx pointed out that "a purely *bourgeois revolution* and the establishment of *bourgeois rule* in the form of a *constitutional monarchy* is impossible in Germany, and that only a feudal absolutist counter-revolution or a *social republican revolution* is possible" (see this volume, p. 178).

Marx and Engels saw the German revolution as part of the European revolution, the course and prospects of which they followed closely in the *Neue Rheinische Zeitung*. It was to these problems that Marx devoted his articles "The Revolutionary Movement in Italy" and "The Revolutionary Movement", in which he noted that the triumphant progress of the European revolution in February and March 1848 had been followed by a reactionary counter-offensive. The prevention of the workers' demonstration of April 10 in London had weakened the revolutionary impetus of Chartism, and the June defeat of the French proletariat was a heavy blow for the European revolutionary movement as a whole. On August 6, Milan was retaken by Austrian troops; on November 1, revolutionary Vienna fell. This was followed by the counter-revolutionary coup d'état in Berlin.

Soberly assessing the consequences of the defeat of the revolution, Marx emphasised the importance of these lessons for the masses who at the beginning of the revolution had been prey to illusions, fine phrases about universal brotherhood and so on. "The chief result of the revolutionary movement of 1848 is not what the peoples won, but what they lost—the *loss of their illusions*" (see this volume, p. 197).

As regards the prospects of the revolution in Europe in 1849, Marx placed his hopes on the imminence of a new victorious rising of the French proletariat which would provide the impulse for a revolutionary upsurge in other countries of Europe, including Germany.

Marx saw in bourgeois-aristocratic England, with its enormous industrial and commercial might, a serious threat to the French proletariat and the cause of the revolution. He compared the England of that time to "the rock against which the revolutionary waves break.... A revolution of the economic relations in any country of the European continent," he stressed, "in the whole European continent without England, is a storm in a teacup" (see this volume, p. 214). That is why, taking account of the actual situation, Marx predicted that a victorious move by the French proletariat would call forth a military clash on a European and even on a world-wide scale—inasmuch as the involvement of England, as a colonial power, was inevitable. But in the course of this armed struggle between the revolutionary and the counter-revolutionary forces, the preconditions could again mature for a Chartist rising in England itself. "England will head the counter-revolutionary armies, just as it did during the Napoleonic period, but through the war itself it will be thrown to the head of the revolutionary movement and it will repay the debt it owes in regard to the revolution of the eighteenth century" (see this volume, p. 215).

This volume contains a large group of articles and reports written by Engels during his forced stay in Switzerland from November 1848 to the middle of January 1849. While living in that country of "classical" bourgeois federalism, Engels used every opportunity to disabuse of their illusions the South-German petty-bourgeois democrats who rejected the slogan of a centralised German democratic republic and saw the Swiss state system as a model for Germany. Engels' reports on the sittings of the Federal Assembly and its chambers show up the provincial limitations of political life in Switzerland, the narrow-mindedness, pettiness and prejudices of most of the politicians there. At the same time, Engels did not overlook progressive aspects of the struggle against aristocratic reaction and clericalism, the eradication of patriarchalism, the implementation of certain centralising reforms. His article "The German Central Authority and Switzerland" and his reports on the Swiss conflict with Austria and the so-called Imperial Government formed by the Frankfurt National Assembly defended the right of the Swiss to repulse the attempts of the reactionaries to interfere in their internal affairs, in particular the demands for the extradition or expulsion of revolutionary refugees.

Engels followed closely the development of the working-class movement in the Swiss Republic. In his reports "The Ex-Principality", "The New Institutions.—Progress in Switzerland", "Elections.—Sydow" and others, he emphasised ·that "the actual revolutionary forces of the people are among the Swiss and German workers" (see this volume, p. 59). He himself took part in the First Congress of the German Workers' Associations of Switzerland held from December 9 to 11, and was able to ensure that many of its decisions stressed the need for drawing the workers into the political struggle, and not merely into the struggle for limited economic demands. This point of view was constantly defended by the *Neue Rheinische Zeitung* against some of the leaders in the German working-class movement who were inclined, like Stephan Born, to see the tasks of the proletarian struggle only in terms of economic reforms. Elected by the Congress to the Central Commission of the newly created Union of German Workers' Associations in Switzerland, Engels worked hard to promote international links between the Swiss workers and the proletarian and democratic organisations of Germany (see "Address of the Central Commission of the Workers' Associations of Switzerland to the Executive of the March Association in Frankfurt am Main" and the "Letter of the Central Commission of the Workers' Associations in Switzerland to the Association in Vivis").

In the middle of January 1849, when he was no longer in danger of arrest if he appeared in Germany, Engels, who was eager to engage in active revolutionary work in his own country, returned to Cologne and continued, in association with Marx, to work with great energy on the editorial board of the *Neue Rheinische Zeitung*. This was when the newspaper published a number of his articles on the Hungarian revolution, on the national contradictions and conflicts in the Slav regions of the Austrian Empire, and on the national question as one of the most important problems of the revolution in Europe.

The struggle of oppressed nations for freedom and independence had Marx's and Engels' firm support. In a number of articles, they stressed the high importance for European democracy of the Polish people's national liberation movement. The *Neue Rheinische Zeitung* wrote with keen sympathy about the Italians' struggle for liberation from Austrian oppression and for national unification. A new wave of revolutionary events in a number of Italian states (the Papal states, Tuscany, Sicily etc.), the fall of the counter-revolutionary and moderate liberal governments there under pressure from the masses, and the prevailing republican influence were all welcomed as portents of possible change in general European revolutionary development in the interests of the working class and democracy. "After six months of almost uninterrupted defeats for democracy, after a series of unprecedented triumphs for the counter-revolution, there are at last indications of an approaching victory of the revolutionary party," wrote Marx about the turn of events in Italy at the end of November 1848 (see this volume, p. 101). The *Neue Rheinische Zeitung* greeted the proclamation of a republic in Rome on February 7, 1849, as an important revolutionary act (see this volume, p. 414).

In Hungary, too, the liberation struggle was entering upon a new phase which Marx and Engels believed could help rekindle the flame of general European revolution. Led by Kossuth's revolutionary Government, the Hungarian people were heroically repulsing the Austrian counter-revolutionaries, who, after the suppression of the Vienna uprising, had hurled heavy armed forces against them. Taking advantage of the contradictions between the Hungarian landowner and bourgeois top crust and the national minorities, the Austrian ruling classes dragged into the war against revolutionary Hungary national formations recruited in the Slav lands of the Austrian Empire and Transylvania—Serbs, Croats, Rumanians and others. They were able to direct the national movements of these peoples against the Hungarian revolution largely also because Kossuth's Government had long refused to grant these peoples autonomy and satisfy other national demands.

Marx and Engels stressed that the Hungarian people's national liberation war against the Habsburg monarchy was a genuinely revolutionary war, part of the revolutionary-democratic struggle of the people of Europe. They saw the fighters for the independence of Hungary, and also of Poland, as allies of the European proletariat and revolutionary democracy, part of the forces undermining such bulwarks of international counter-revolution as the Austrian Empire, the Prussian monarchy and Tsarist Russia. By shaking the might of the Habsburg Empire, the Hungarian revolution, wrote Marx and Engels, was having a big influence on the course of the European revolution.

As early as November 1848, Marx was devoting close attention to the revolutionary events in Hungary and asked Engels, who was then in Switzerland, to write an article about them. In January 1849, this article appeared in the *Neue Rheinische Zeitung* under the title "The Magyar Struggle". It was followed by a series of articles and reports in which the course of military operations in Hungary was analysed.

These articles refuted the reports of the "brilliant successes" of the Austrian army and the hopeless predicament of the Hungarians, spread by the official Austrian news bulletins and seized on by a number of German newspapers, liberal ones included. Engels noted that the German press as a whole adopted an attitude of open hostility and nationalist arrogance towards the Hungarians' struggle. Sifting and comparing the forced admissions contained in Austrian bulletins and local newspapers, he pieced together the true picture of the successful defensive battles being fought by the Hungarian army, which in fact possessed resources sufficient not only for defence but also for a counterblow. Subsequent events confirmed the accuracy of Engels' military forecasts (see the articles "European War Inevitable", "From the Theatre of War" and others). He pointed out that on the Hungarian side it was a genuinely revolutionary and popular war, and showed itself to be such in the very methods of warfare being used—mobilisation of all the forces of the people to repulse the invading enemy and the combination of regular army operations with widespread guerilla warfare. Despite the Austrian advantage in numbers and arms, the Hungarian army was superior in its fighting qualities, its revolutionary enthusiasm, its high morale, and in the support of the people and the unity of the rear and the front. The rear of the Austrian army of occupation was, as Engels constantly noted in his articles, extremely unreliable and the rebel movement occasionally flared up behind the lines. He gave a high appraisal of the political and military leaders of the Hungarian revolution, including the Polish revolutionaries who had joined Hungary's liberation struggle, and of the Hungarian Government's energy and resolution and its anti-feudal reforms. He spoke of Lajos Kossuth as a revolutionary leader "who for his nation is Danton and Carnot in one person" (see this volume, p. 227).

Engels saw danger, not only for the Hungarian but also for the European revolution, in the Austrian reactionaries' appeal for military aid from Tsarist Russia. The appearance of the first Tsarist detachments in Transylvania was interpreted by him, on the one hand, as testifying to the weakness of the Habsburg monarchy, which had proved incapable of suppressing the Hungarian revolutionary movement with its own forces, and, on the other hand, as the danger signal of an impending union of the counter-revolutionary states, a rebirth of the policy of the Holy Alliance, a policy of brutally imposing monarchist counter-revolutionary governments on the nations.

The use by the counter-revolutionary forces of a number of Slav peoples against Hungary, and also what was known as Austro-Slavism, a programme for uniting the Slavs under the aegis of the Habsburgs, provoked Engels to a violent attack on pan-Slavism. The denunciation of pan-Slavism was, for him, an integral part of the struggle against the bourgeois-landowner nationalist ideology. This campaign was vigorously fought by the editors of the *Neue Rheinische*

Zeitung, who also condemned other forms of nationalism—pan-Germanism, pan-Scandinavianism and the like.

In their entire approach to the national question, Marx and Engels invariably asked which class forces were playing the leading role in the national movements, to what extent they were helping to weaken the reactionary states, and whether they were reserves of the revolution or were, on the contrary, playing into the hands of counter-revolution. The class criterion was for them decisive in assessing any national movement. For in the course of the revolution, the entire character of a national movement may change depending on the preponderance of the various classes in it. In 1848-49, when the struggle against absolutism and the remnants of feudalism was complicated by violent national conflicts, the ruling classes deliberately sought to fan the flames of national hatred still higher, by deceit or violence to involve individual nations in predatory and counter-revolutionary wars, and to incite them against those peoples who were fighting for the victory of the bourgeois-democratic revolution and for truly national liberation. It was in this sense that Engels spoke in 1848-49 of revolutionary and counter-revolutionary peoples (see his article "The Magyar Struggle", "Democratic Pan-Slavism" and others).

In those years, owing to a number of historical causes, the development of the national movement of some of the Austrian Slav peoples was complicated and rife with contradictions. When the representatives of revolutionary-democratic trends had been defeated or pushed into the background, the leadership of these movements fell into the hands of monarchistic bourgeois and landowner elements who in effect subordinated them to the interests of the Habsburg monarchy and Russian Tsarism. Just before the 1848 revolution, Marx and Engels had sympathised with the independence struggle of the Slav peoples in the Austrian Empire (see Engels' article "The Beginning of the End in Austria", Vol. 6 of the present edition); and in June 1848 they expressed complete solidarity with the popular uprising in Prague (see Vol. 7 of the present edition, pp. 92 and 119). But after the defeat of the uprising, as the character of the national movements of a number of Slav peoples changed and reactionary Austro-Slavism showed its hand, they condemned these movements, describing them as counter-revolutionary and hostile to the cause of democracy and the working class.

Nor did Engels forget that the Austrian Slavs themselves were in many respects victims of the cunning and provocative policy of the Austrian reactionaries, who were only too free with their demagogical promises of autonomy. The Slav peoples, he wrote, would have to pay dearly for this deception: when they had finished with the Hungarians, the Habsburgs would trample on the illusions of a "Slav Austria", of a "federative state of nations with equal rights", and in particular of "democratic institutions" for the Austrian Slavs. These peoples "will have to suffer the same military despotism which they helped to impose on the Viennese and Magyars" (see this volume, pp. 375 and 376). In "War.—Discord between the Government and the Southern Slavs", "The War in Hungary", "Croats and Slovaks in Hungary" and other articles, Engels cited numerous facts showing how the Slav peoples had become painfully aware that they had been deceived and were being used for purposes contrary to their real interests. He noted with satisfaction the emerging sympathy for revolutionary Hungary among some of the Austrian Slavs, for instance in Slovakia (see this volume, pp. 442 and 469).

However, it must be evident to us today that the articles "The Magyar Struggle" and "Democratic Pan-Slavism" contain some erroneous judgments on the past and future of the small Slav peoples incorporated into Austria. Contrary to the picture of the predatory, oppressive policy of the German states in the east of Europe which Engels gave in his series of articles "The Frankfurt Assembly Debates the Polish Question" (see Vol. 7 of the present edition) and other works, in these articles he represented the subjugation of some of the Slav peoples as having been connected exclusively with the spread of civilisation and culture. History has not confirmed Engels' opinion that the small Slav peoples of Central Europe were doomed to be absorbed and assimilated by their larger and more highly civilised neighbours. The tendency towards political centralisation which resulted from the development of capitalism and caused the small peoples to lose their national independence, concealed from Engels another tendency which was not sufficiently manifest at the time, namely, the sharpening of the oppressed peoples' struggle for independence, for setting up their own states.

In these pronouncements, Engels was probably influenced by the gravity of the political situation at the time, and this accounted for the sharp polemical tone of his articles, all the heat of which was directed against the counter-revolutionary forces then going over to the offensive. A certain part was played in this by the idea which Marx and Engels entertained at that time of the nearness of a simultaneous victory of the proletarian revolution in the developed countries, a revolution which would have put an end to both social and national oppression and for which more favourable conditions would have been provided by capitalism drawing into its orbit the

backward peoples still in the stage of feudalism. As for the
tendencies towards decentralisation, including those which took the
form of national demands, Marx and Engels regarded them often
enough as a factor slowing down the development of the favourable
conditions.

This point of view was not final. Later on, substantial corrections
were made which took into account the liberation struggle of the
oppressed peoples in Europe and in the colonial countries against
national enslavement, a struggle which was developing with ever
growing vigour. Thus already at the period when the Crimean war
of 1853-56 was looming ahead, Engels supported the demand of
national independence for the small Slav and other peoples in the
Balkan Peninsula who were oppressed by the reactionary Turkish
Empire.

Yet Engels' opinion in 1848-49 that the small Slav peoples of the
Austrian Empire would hardly play a progressive role in the future
was not expressed without reservations. "If at any epoch while they
were oppressed the Slavs had begun a *new revolutionary history*, that by
itself would have proved their viability," he wrote (see this volume,
p. 371). Subsequent developments have shown that the Slav
peoples who were oppressed and enslaved under the Austrian
Empire proved entirely viable in the national sense, succeeded in
creating their own statehood, and later, as a result of the victorious
socialist revolution, set about establishing a highly advanced social
system, greatly contributing to human progress.

Much of the material in this volume reflects the struggle waged by
Marx and Engels to rally the revolutionary-democratic forces in
Germany after the counter-revolutionary coup d'état in Prussia, as
well as their efforts to develop the class consciousness of the German
proletariat and to prepare the ground for the creation of a mass
independent proletarian party. An important place in this struggle
was occupied by the defence of the German people's democratic
rights and liberties against the reactionaries, in particular against
their encroachments on the revolutionary press, one of their main
targets being the *Neue Rheinische Zeitung*. The article "Three State
Trials against the *Neue Rheinische Zeitung*", the speeches for the
defence by Marx and Engels at the trial of the newspaper's editors on
February 7, 1849, and other writings, administered a body blow
against the initiators of these reactionary moves. They bore witness
to the effectiveness of the revolutionary press in forming progressive
public opinion, exposing the arbitrariness of counter-revolutionary

power and organising the struggle against a reactionary political system (see this volume, pp. 316-17).

In the *Neue Rheinische Zeitung,* Marx and Engels defended members of the democratic movement in general who were victims of police persecution. The articles "The Prussian Counter-Revolution and the Prussian Judiciary", "The Tax-Refusal Trial", "Lassalle" and others informed the public of the lawlessness of the Prussian police authorities and showed up the whole Prussian police and judicial system.

During preparations for the elections for the Second Chamber of the Prussian Diet, which replaced the dissolved National Assembly, Marx and Engels worked to unite all the democratic forces without, however, glossing over the disagreements existing in the democratic camp. They punctured the parliamentary illusions associated with the Constitution imposed by the King, which not only the liberals but also certain democrats represented as a guarantee that democratic reforms would be carried out by peaceful and constitutional means.

In his articles "The Berlin *National-Zeitung* to the Primary Electors" and "The *Kölnische Zeitung* on the Elections", Marx exposed the vain belief that this Constitution would be a means of solving the social question, and also the attempts of the liberals to comfort themselves and the people with hopes of its revision in a progressive spirit. He foretold that it would indeed be revised, but only "insofar as it suits the King and the Second Chamber consisting of country squires, financial magnates, high-ranking officials and clerics" (see this volume, p. 257).

In opposition to the liberals and some of the democrats, Marx considered broad popular participation in the elections not as a means of directly achieving political and social aims by constitutional methods, but primarily as a means of politically activating the masses and preparing them for future revolutionary battles. The successes of the democrats at the electoral meetings and in the Chamber itself, he thought, would provide them with additional opportunities to influence the masses in this direction and resist the reactionaries. But he never ceased to emphasise that the pressing political and social problems could be solved only by a new revolution carried out by the working class, the urban petty bourgeoisie and the peasantry. "Are not precisely these classes the most radical, the most democratic, of society as a whole?" Marx wrote. "Is it not precisely the proletariat that is the specifically *red* class?" (see this volume, p. 289).

Marx and Engels also defended their tactical line in the revolutionary struggle in heated arguments with sectarians in the working-class movement. In particular, the adherents of Gottschalk in the Cologne Workers' Association were arguing against taking any part in the parliamentary elections, and trying to convince the workers that it would make no difference to them whether Germany was a monarchy or a republic. The *Neue Rheinische Zeitung* pointed out that this could lead only to the isolation of the proletariat from the other democratic forces, and that the democratic republic was the form of state which corresponded most closely to the interests of the working class and its allies and was best adapted to the tasks of their future revolutionary struggle. Under the influence of Marx and his supporters it was decided at committee meetings of the Workers' Association in January 1849 "to take part in the general electoral committees ... and to represent the general democratic principle there" (see this volume, p. 514).

While calling on the workers to take an active part in the democratic movement, Marx and Engels at the same time tried to help them become aware how much their own interests were politically and socially opposed to those of the bourgeoisie. Characteristic in this respect is Marx's article "A Bourgeois Document" which describes the Prussian bourgeoisie crawling "in the most servile reverence before throne, altar, army, bureaucracy and feudalism" and its "*shameless maltreatment of the working class*" (see this volume, p. 219).

The section "From the Preparatory Materials" contains the rough drafts of two of Marx's articles and also the draft of the judiciary part of his speech at the trial of the *Neue Rheinische Zeitung* on February 7, 1849.

The Appendices include reports on the meetings of the Committee of the Cologne Workers' Association and on the general meeting of its members. Although these reports are extremely brief and resemble minutes, they give a vivid picture of the ideological, educational and organisational work carried out by Marx and Engels in a mass workers' association which they were striving to transform into the foundation on which the future party of the German proletariat was to be built. The Cologne Workers' Association of which Marx was elected President *pro tem.* in the autumn of 1848 was becoming, due to the influence of Marx and other members of the Communist League, more and more a proletarian class organisation which took an increasingly active part in the political struggle.

Also included in the Appendices are reports on the "democratic banquets", or people's meetings, which took place in February 1849. Such banquets became a recognised form of political work among the masses and were held to commemorate the anniversaries of the

February and March revolutions. A number of the documents in this section convey the extent of official harassment and police persecution to which the *Neue Rheinische Zeitung* and its editors were subjected.

* * *

In compiling this volume, account has been taken, not only of the contents of Volume 6 of the German and Russian editions of Marx's and Engels' *Works*, but also of the results of research carried out in recent years in the Soviet Union and the German Democratic Republic to establish the authorship of articles in the *Neue Rheinische Zeitung*. Newly discovered articles by Marx, "Decision of the Berlin National Assembly", "Tax Refusal and the Countryside", "Position of the Left in the National Assembly", together with Engels' reports from Switzerland and his articles on the revolutionary war in Hungary—in all 52 articles and reports—have been included in this volume. Of the 130 works in the main section, 114 are being published in English for the first time, as is noted on each occasion at the end of the translation. Articles previously translated into English are accompanied by editorial notes giving the date of the first English publication. All the items in "From the Preparatory Materials" and the Appendices are being published in English for the first time.

Account has also been taken of the latest conclusions of German and Soviet research concerning the insufficiently justified inclusion in previous editions of certain articles attributed to Marx.

Wherever it has been impossible, on the basis of the materials available, to ascertain to which of the two authors — Marx or Engels — an article or item in the *Neue Rheinische Zeitung* belongs, the author's name is not included at the end of the translation. If such data are available, the author's name is given.

The titles of articles published in the *Neue Rheinische Zeitung* are taken from the table of contents in the newspaper. Titles provided by the editors of the present edition have been printed in square brackets. When newspaper sources quoted by Marx or Engels are not available, references are given to reproductions of the corresponding items in other newspapers.

The volume is provided with Notes, a Name Index, an Index of Quoted and Mentioned Literature, an Index of Periodicals and a Subject Index. For the reader's convenience, there is a Glossary of Geographical Names occurring in the text in the form customary in the German press of the time, but now archaic or Germanised.

Explanatory footnotes are provided for Swiss geographical names
still current in a German, French or Italian form.

The volume was compiled and the Preface and Notes written by
Vladimir Sazonov and edited by Lev Golman (Institute of Marxism-
Leninism of the CC CPSU).

Albina Gridchina and Yuri Vasin (Institute of Marxism-Leninism
of the CC CPSU) prepared the Name Index, the Index of Quoted
and Mentioned Literature, the Index of Periodicals and the Glossary
of Geographical Names, and Vladimir Sazonov the Subject Index.

The translations were made by Gregor Benton, Clemens Dutt,
W. L. Guttsman, Frida Knight, Barbara Ruhemann, Barrie Selman,
Christopher Upward, Joan and Trevor Walmsley (Lawrence &
Wishart), and Richard Dixon and Salo Ryazanskaya (Progress
Publishers), and edited by Maurice Cornforth, Clemens Dutt, Frida
Knight, Christian Maxwell and Margaret Mynatt (Lawrence &
Wishart), Richard Dixon, Lydia Belyakova, Tatyana Grishina and
Natalia Karmanova (Progress Publishers), and Larisa Miskievich,
scientific editor (Institute of Marxism-Leninism of the CC CPSU).

The volume was prepared for the press by Lyudgarda Zubrilova
(editor) and Nadezhda Korneyeva (assistant editor) for Progress
Publishers.

KARL MARX
and
FREDERICK ENGELS

ARTICLES FROM THE *NEUE RHEINISCHE ZEITUNG*

November 8, 1848-March 5, 1849

Neue
Rheinische Zeitung
Organ der Demokratie.

№ 138.   Köln, Donnerstag den 9. November.   1848.

THE CRISIS IN BERLIN[1]

Cologne, November 8. The situation looks very complicated, but it is very simple.

The *King,* as the *Neue Preussische Zeitung* correctly notes,[a] stands "*on the broadest basis*" of his "*hereditary*" rights "*by the grace of God*".

On the other side, the *National Assembly* has *no basis whatever,* its purpose being to constitute, to lay the basis.

Two sovereign powers.

The connecting link between the two is *Camphausen,* the *theory of agreement.*[2]

When these two sovereign powers are no longer able to agree or do not want to agree, they become two hostile sovereign powers. The *King* has the *right* to throw down the gauntlet to the Assembly, the *Assembly* has the *right* to throw down the gauntlet to the King. The *greater right* is on the side of the *greater might.* Might is tested in *struggle.* The test of the struggle is *victory.* Each of the two powers can prove that it is right only by its *victory,* that it is wrong only by its *defeat.*

The King until now has not been a *constitutional* king. He is an *absolute* monarch who decides for or against constitutionalism.

The Assembly until now has not been *constitutional,* it is *constituent.* It has so far attempted to constitute constitutionalism. It can continue or discontinue its *attempts.*

Both the King and the Assembly temporarily acquiesced in the constitutional ceremonial.

---

[a] In the article "Ministerium Brandenburg" published on November 5, 1848.—*Ed.*

The King's demand that a Brandenburg Ministry which is to his liking be appointed in defiance of the majority in the Chamber, is the demand of an *absolute monarch.*

The Chamber's presumption, by means of a deputation *straight* to the King, to forbid the formation of a Brandenburg Ministry is the presumption of an *absolute Chamber.*

The King and the Assembly have sinned against constitutional convention.

The King and the Assembly have both retreated to their original sphere, the King deliberately, the Chamber unwittingly.

The King is at an advantage.

Right is on the side of *might.*

Legal phrases are on the side of *impotence.*

A *Rodbertus* Ministry would be a cipher in which plus and minus neutralise each other.

Written by Marx on November 8, 1848   Printed according to the newspaper

First published in the *Neue Rheinische Zeitung* No. 138, November 9, 1848

First page of the *Neue Rheinis*
"The

THE EX-PRINCIPALITY[3]

From the Republic of Neuchâtel, November 7. You will be interested to hear something also from a little country that until recently enjoyed the blessings of Prussian rule, but which was the first of all the lands under the Prussian Crown to raise the banner of revolution and drive out the Prussian paternal Government. I am speaking of the former "principality of Neuenburg and Vallendis",[4] in which Herr Pfuel, the present Prime Minister, performed his first administrative exercises as Governor and was deposed by the people in May of this year, even before he could win laurels in Posen[5] and gather votes of no confidence as Prime Minister in Berlin. This little country has now assumed the prouder title of "République et Canton de Neuchâtel", and the time is probably not far off when the last Neuchâtel guardsman brushes his green tunic in Berlin. I must confess it gave me an amusing feeling of satisfaction five weeks after my flight from the Prussian Holy Hermandad[6] to be able once more to walk about unmolested on what is *de jure* still Prussian soil.

Incidentally, the Republic and Canton of Neuchâtel evidently finds itself in much more comfortable circumstances than the late principality of Neuenburg and Vallendis; for at the recent elections to the Swiss National Council the republican candidates received over 6,000 votes, whereas the candidates of the royalists, of the *bédouins,*[a] as they are called here, hardly mustered 900 votes. The Great Council,[7] too, consists almost entirely of republicans, and only Les Ponts, a small mountain village dominated by the aristocrats, sent

---

[a] This nickname of the Swiss royalists is an allusion to the fact that the old Swiss cantons preserved patriarchal relations similar to those found in the social organisation of an Arab nomadic tribe, the Bedouin.—*Ed.*

Calame, ex-State Councillor of the royal Prussian Neuenburg principality, as its representative to Neuchâtel, where a few days ago he had to swear an oath of loyalty to the Republic. Instead of the old royalist *Constitutionnel Neuchâtelois*, there is published now—in La Chaux-de-Fonds, the largest, most industrialised and most republican place in the canton—a *Républicain Neuchâtelois*, written it is true in very bad Swiss-French of the Jura, but otherwise not at all badly edited.

The clock- and watch-making industry of the Jura and the lace manufacture of Traverstal, which are the main sources of livelihood of this little country, are beginning to prosper again, and the Montagnards,[a] in spite of the snow here being already a foot deep, are gradually regaining their old cheerfulness. Meanwhile the *bédouins* go about looking very dejected, displaying uselessly the Prussian colours on their breeches, blouses and caps, and sighing in vain for the return of the worthy Pfuel and the decrees that began: "*Nous Frédéric-Guillaume par la grâce de Dieu.*" High up in the Jura, 3,500 feet above sea-level, the Prussian colours, black caps with white edging, have the same dejected look and are as ambiguously smiled at as among us on the Rhine; if one did not see the Swiss flags and the big placards with the words "République et Canton de Neuchâtel", one might think one was at home. Incidentally, I am glad to be able to report that in the Neuchâtel revolution, as in all the revolutions of 1848, the *German workers* played a decisive and very honourable role. For that reason, too, they are allotted the fullest measure of the aristocrats' hatred.

Written by Engels on November 7, 1848

First published in the *Neue Rheinische Zeitung* No. 140, November 11, 1848

Printed according to the newspaper

Published in English for the first time

---

[a] i.e. the revolutionary-minded population of the mountain canton of Neuchâtel who were engaged mainly in clock- and watch-making. They were given the name by analogy with the representatives of the revolutionary Montagne—the Jacobins—in the French Convention of 1792-93.— *Ed.*

THE NEW INSTITUTIONS.—PROGRESS IN SWITZERLAND[8]

Berne, November 9. The new legislative Federal Assembly, consisting of the Swiss National Council and the Council of States, has been gathered here since the day before yesterday. The city of Berne has done its utmost to give them as brilliant and seductive a reception as possible. There has been music, festive processions, illuminations, the boom of cannon and the peal of bells—nothing has been forgotten. The sessions began the day before yesterday. In the National Council, which is elected by universal suffrage and according to the number of inhabitants (Berne has returned 20 deputies, Zurich 12, the smallest cantons two or three each), the overwhelming majority of deputies are liberals of a radical hue. The decidedly radical party is strongly represented, and the conservatives have only six or seven seats out of over a hundred. The Council of States, which is made up of two deputies from each canton and one deputy from each demi-canton, on the whole resembles the last Diet[9] as regards composition and character. The *Ur*-cantons have once again returned several true separatists,[10] and as a result of the indirect elections, the reactionary element, though definitely in a minority, is nevertheless more strongly represented in this Council than it is in the National Council. As a matter of fact, by abolishing binding mandates[a] and invalidating half votes, the Council of States has been turned into a rejuvenated version of the Diet and has been

---

[a] i.e. the instructions which the deputies of the Swiss Diet received from their cantonal governments and which greatly impeded the adoption of general decisions.— *Ed.*

pushed into the background by the creation of the National Council. It plays the thankless role of a Senate or a Chamber of Peers, of a drag on the assumed excessive desire for innovation of the National Council, the role of heir to the mature wisdom and careful reflection of the forefathers. This dignified and sedate institution already shares the fate of similar bodies in England and America, and the now defunct one in France. Even before it has shown any signs of life it is looked down upon by the press and overshadowed by the National Council. Practically no one talks about the Council of States, and if it does make itself talked about it will be so much the worse for it.

Although the National Council is supposed to represent the entire Swiss "nation", it has already at its first sitting given proof of typically Swiss disunity and absorption with trifles, if not of petty cantonal spirit. Three votes had to be taken to elect a President, although there were only three candidates with any serious chances, and moreover all three of them from Berne. The three gentlemen in question were Ochsenbein, Funk and Neuhaus; the first two represent the old radical party of Berne, the third the old liberal, semi-conservative party. In the end Herr Ochsenbein was elected by 50 votes out of 93, that is, with a very narrow majority. One can understand the Zurich and other *Moderados*[11] preferring the wise and very experienced Herr Neuhaus to Herr Ochsenbein, but the fact that Herr Funk, who has exactly the same political colouring as Herr Ochsenbein, should have been put forward as a competing candidate and received support in two votings, shows how unorganised and undisciplined the parties still are. At any rate the election of Ochsenbein means that the radicals gained a victory in the first contest of the parties. In the subsequent election of a Vice-President, five votes had to be taken to produce an absolute majority. On the other hand, the staid and experienced Council of States almost unanimously elected the *Moderado* Furrer from Zurich as its President in the first round of voting. These two elections amply illustrate how different a spirit reigns in the two Chambers and that they will soon take different courses and enter into conflict with each other.

The choice of a federal capital will be the next interesting issue to be debated. It will be interesting for the Swiss because the financial interests of very many of them are involved, and interesting for people abroad because precisely this debate will reveal most clearly to what extent the old parochial patriotism, the petty cantonal narrow-mindedness has been discarded. The competition is most intense between Berne, Zurich and Lucerne. Berne would like to see

Zurich satisfied with the federal university, and Lucerne with the federal court of law, but in vain. Berne at any rate is the only suitable city, being the point where German and French Switzerland merge, the capital of the largest canton and the emerging centre of the whole Swiss movement. But in order to become a real centre, Berne must also possess the university and the federal court. But try and explain that to the Swiss whose fanaticism for their cantonal town has been roused! It is quite possible that the more radical National Council will vote for radical Berne, and the sedate Council of States for sedate, wise and prudent Zurich. An extremely difficult situation will then arise.

There has been considerable unrest in *Geneva* during the last three weeks. The reactionary patricians and bourgeois, who, from their villas, keep the villages around Geneva in almost feudal dependence, managed with the help of their peasants to push through all their three candidates in the elections to the National Council. But the committee declared the elections invalid, as more ballot-papers were returned than had been issued. Only this measure was able to pacify the revolutionary workers of Saint-Gervais, crowds of whom were already marching through the streets and shouting "*Aux armes!*" The attitude of the workers in the course of the week that followed was so menacing that the bourgeois preferred not to vote at all rather than provoke a revolution with the inevitable scenes of horror of which there had already been warning, especially since the Government threatened to resign if the reactionary candidates were once more elected. The radicals meanwhile altered their list of candidates, to which they added some more moderate names, made up for lost canvassing time, and obtained 5,000 to 5,500 votes in the new elections, that is almost a thousand more than the reactionaries had received in the previous round. The three reactionary candidates obtained hardly any votes; General Dufour, who received the highest number, managed to poll 1,500 votes. Elections to the Great Council were held a week later. The city elected 44 radicals, and the countryside, which had to elect 46 councillors, returned almost exclusively reactionaries. The *Revue de Genève* is still arguing with the bourgeois newspapers as to whether all 46 are reactionary or half a dozen of them will vote for the radical Government. We shall soon know. The confusion in Geneva may increase; for if the Government, which is here elected directly by the people, is forced to resign, then during the new elections the same thing might easily happen as during the second elections to the National Council, and a radical government could be confronted with a reactionary majority in the Great Council. It is moreover certain that the workers of

Geneva are only waiting for an opportunity to safeguard the threatened gains of 1847[12] by a new revolution.

On the whole, compared with the early forties, Switzerland has made considerable progress. This is nowhere so striking as among the working class. Whereas the old spirit of parochial narrow-mindedness and pedantry still holds almost undivided sway among the bourgeoisie and especially in the old patrician families, or has, at best, assumed more modern forms, the Swiss workers have developed to a remarkable degree. Formerly, they kept aloof from the Germans and displayed the most absurd "free Swiss" national arrogance, complained about the "foreign rogues" and showed no interest whatever in the contemporary movement. Now this has changed. Ever since working conditions have deteriorated, ever since Switzerland has been democratised, and especially since the minor riots have given place to European revolutions and battles such as those waged in Paris in June and in Vienna in October[13]—ever since then the Swiss workers have participated more and more in the political and socialist movements, have fraternised with the foreign workers, especially the German workers, and have abandoned their "free Swiss attitude". In the French part of Switzerland and in many of its German districts, Germans and German Swiss are members of the same workers' association on an equal footing, and associations consisting mainly of Swiss workers have decided to join the proposed organisation of German democratic associations which has partly come into being. Whereas the extreme radicals of official Switzerland dream at best of a Helvetian republic,[14] one and indivisible, Swiss workers often express the view that the whole of little Switzerland's independence will soon perish in the impending European storm. And this is said quite calmly and indifferently, without a word of regret, by these proletarian traitors! All the Swiss I have met expressed great sympathy for the Viennese, but among the workers it amounted to real fanaticism. No one speaks about the National Council, the Council of States, the riot of the priests in Freiburg,[15] but Vienna was on everybody's lips all day long. One would think that Vienna were again the capital of Switzerland as it was in the days before William Tell, that Switzerland belonged again to Austria. Hundreds of rumours were bruited about, debated, called in question, believed, refuted, and all possible aspects were thoroughly discussed. And when, at last, the news of the defeat of the heroic Viennese workers and students and of Windischgrätz's superior strength and barbarity was definitely confirmed, the effect on these Swiss workers was as though their own fate had been decided in Vienna and their own country had succumbed. Though this feeling is not yet a universal one, it is steadily gaining ground among the Swiss proletariat, and the fact that it already exists in many localities is, for a country like Switzerland, a tremendous advance.

Written by Engels on November 9, 1848   Printed according to the newspaper

First published in the *Neue Rheinische Zeitung* No. 143, November 15, 1848

COUNTER-REVOLUTION IN BERLIN[16]

[*Neue Rheinische Zeitung* No. 141, November 12, 1848]

Cologne, November 11. The *Pfuel Ministry* was a "*misunderstanding*"; its real meaning is the *Brandenburg Ministry.* The Pfuel Ministry was the *table of contents,* the Brandenburg Ministry is the *content* itself. *Brandenburg in the Assembly and the Assembly in Brandenburg.*[17] **Thus runs the epitaph of the House of Brandenburg.**[a]

The Emperor Charles V was admired because he had himself buried while still alive [18] To have a bad joke engraved on one's tombstone is to go one better than the Emperor Charles V and his penal system, his criminal code.[19]

Brandenburg in the Assembly and the Assembly in Brandenburg!

A King of Prussia once put in an appearance in the Assembly. That was not the real Brandenburg. The Marquis of Brandenburg who appeared in the Assembly the day before yesterday was the real King of Prussia.

The guardroom in the Assembly, the Assembly in the guardroom—that means: *Brandenburg in the Assembly, the Assembly in Brandenburg!*

Or will the *Assembly in Brandenburg*—Berlin, as is well known, is situated in the Province of Brandenburg—be master ... of the *Brandenburg in the Assembly?* Will Brandenburg seek the protection of the Assembly as a Capet once did in another Assembly?[20]

Brandenburg in the Assembly and the Assembly in Brandenburg is an expression with many meanings, ambiguous and portentous.

As we know, it is much easier for the peoples to cope with *kings* than with *legislative assemblies.* History gives us a whole list of abortive revolts of the people against national assemblies. It knows only two important exceptions to this rule. The English people in the person

---

[a] This refers to the Hohenzollerns, who became hereditary margraves of Brandenburg in 1417.—*Ed.*

of *Cromwell* dissolved the *Long Parliament,* and the French people in the person of *Bonaparte* dissolved the *Corps legislatif.* But the Long Parliament had long ago become a *Rump,* and the *Corps legislatif* a *corpse.*

Are the *kings* more fortunate than the peoples in their *revolts against legislative assemblies?*

Charles I, James II, Louis XVI and *Charles X* are hardly promising ancestral examples.

There are luckier ancestors in *Spain* and *Italy* however. And recently in *Vienna?*

But one must not forget that a *Congress of Nations* was in session in Vienna and that the *representatives of the Slavs,* except for the Poles, went over to the imperial camp with bands playing.[21]

The struggle of the camarilla in Vienna against the Imperial Diet was at the same time a struggle of the *Slav* Diet against the *German* Diet. It was not *Slavs,* however, who seceded in the Berlin Assembly, it was only *slaves,* and slaves do not constitute a party; at best they are camp-followers of a party. The members of the Right who left the Berlin Assembly[22] have not strengthened the enemy camp, they have infected it with a fatal malady—with *treason.*

The *Slav* party *was victorious* in Austria together with the camarilla. It will now *fight* the camarilla over the spoils. If the Berlin camarilla is victorious it will not have to share the victory with the *Right* or to defend it against the *Right;* the Right will be given a *tip*—and *kicks.*

The Prussian Crown is within its *rights* in confronting the Assembly as an *absolute Crown.* But the Assembly is in the *wrong* because it does not confront the Crown as an *absolute assembly.* To begin with it should have had the Ministers *arrested* as *traitors, traitors to the sovereignty of the people.* It should have *proscribed* and *outlawed* all officials who obey orders others than those of the Assembly.

But the *political* weakness characterising the actions of the National Assembly in *Berlin* may become a source of *civic* strength in the *provinces.*

The bourgeoisie would have liked so much to transform the *feudal monarchy* into a *bourgeois monarchy* in an *amicable* way. After depriving the feudal party of armorial bearings and titles, which are offensive to its civic pride, and of the dues appertaining to feudal property, which violate the bourgeois mode of appropriation, the bourgeoisie would have liked so much to unite with the feudal party and together with it enslave the people. But the old bureaucracy does not want to be reduced to the status of a servant of a bourgeoisie for whom, until now, it has been a despotic tutor. The feudal party does not want to see its marks of distinction and interests burnt at the altar of the bourgeoisie. Finally, the Crown sees in the elements of the old feudal society—a society of which it is the crowning excrescence—its true, native social ground, whereas it regards the bourgeoisie as an alien, artificial soil which bears it only under the condition that it withers away.

The bourgeoisie turns the intoxicating *"grace of God"* into a sober *legal title*, the rule of blood into the rule of paper, the royal sun into a civic astral lamp.

Royalty, therefore, was not taken in by the bourgeoisie. Its reply to the partial revolution of the bourgeoisie was a full-fledged counter-revolution. It drove the bourgeoisie once more into the *arms of the revolution, of the people*, by crying out to it:

Brandenburg in the Assembly and the Assembly in Brandenburg.

While admitting that we do not expect the bourgeoisie to answer in a manner befitting the occasion, we must not omit to remark, on the other hand, that in its rebellion against the National Assembly the Crown, too, resorts to hypocritical half measures and hides its head under the constitutional veil at the very moment when it tries to cast off this irksome veil.

Brandenburg makes the *German Central Authority*[23] *give* him the *order* for his *coup d'état. The regiments of the guards marched into Berlin by order of the Central Authority.* The Berlin counter-revolution is carried out by order of the German Central Authority. Brandenburg orders Frankfurt to give him this order. It denies its sovereignty at the very moment when it wants to establish it. Herr Bassermann of course eagerly seized the opportunity to play the servant as master. But he has the satisfaction that the master in his turn plays the servant.

Whatever the outcome in Berlin may be, the *dilemma* is: either the *King* or the *people*—and the people will be victorious with the cry, *Brandenburg in the Assembly and the Assembly in Brandenburg.*

We may have to go through a hard school, but it is the preparatory school for a **complete revolution**.

[*Neue Rheinische Zeitung* No. 141, November 12, 1848, second edition]

Cologne, November 11. The *European revolution* is describing a *circle*. It started in Italy and assumed a European character in Paris; the first repercussion of the February revolution took place in Vienna; the repercussion of the Viennese revolution followed in Berlin; European *counter-revolution* struck its first blow in Italy, in Naples; it assumed a European character in Paris in June; the first repercussion of the June counter-revolution followed in Vienna; it comes to a close and discredits itself in Berlin. *The crowing of the Gallic cock in Paris will once again rouse Europe.*[24]

But in *Berlin the counter-revolution is bringing itself into disrepute. Everything becomes disreputable in Berlin, even counter-revolution.*

In *Naples* the *lazzaroni*[25] are leagued with the monarchy against the bourgeoisie.

In *Paris* the greatest struggle ever known in history is taking place. The bourgeoisie is leagued with the *lazzaroni* against the working class.

In *Vienna* we have a whole swarm of nationalities who imagine that the counter-revolution will bring them emancipation. In addition—the secret spite of the bourgeoisie against the workers and the Academic Legion; strife within the civic militia itself[26]; finally, attack by the people supplying a pretext for the attack by the Court.

Nothing like that is happening in Berlin. The bourgeoisie and the people are on one side and the drill-sergeants on the other.

Wrangel and *Brandenburg*, two men who have no head, no heart, no opinions, nothing but mustachios [a]—such is the antithesis of this querulous, self-opinionated, irresolute National Assembly.

Will—be it even that of an ass, an ox, a moustache [a]—is all that is needed to tackle the weak-willed grumblers of the March revolution. And the *Prussian Court, which has just as little will as the National Assembly,* seeks out the *two most stupid men* in the monarchy and tells these lions: *represent will.* Pfuel still had a few grains of brain. But *absolute stupidity* makes even the grumblers of the March achievements flinch.

"With stupidity the gods themselves struggle in vain", [b]

exclaims the perplexed National Assembly.

These Wrangels and Brandenburgs, these blockheads who can *want* because they have no will of their own, because they want what they are *ordered,* and who are too stupid to question the orders they are given with a faltering voice and trembling lips—they, too, *discredit* themselves because they do not get down to *skull-cracking,* the only job these *battering-rams* are good for.

Wrangel does not go beyond confessing that he recognises only a National Assembly that obeys orders. *Brandenburg* is given a lesson in parliamentary behaviour, and after having shocked the Chamber with his crude, repulsive jargon appropriate to a drill-sergeant, he

---

[a] In the original *Schnurrbart* in both cases.— *Ed.*
[b] Schiller, *Die Jungfrau von Orleans,* Act III, Scene 6.—*Ed.*

allows the "tyrant to be tyrannised" and carries out the orders of the National Assembly by humbly *begging* for permission to speak, though he had just attempted to *take* this right.[27]

> *"I had rather be a tick in a sheep*
> *Than such a valiant ignorance."*[a]

Berlin's calm attitude *delights* us; the ideals of the Prussian drill-sergeants prove unavailing against it.

But the National Assembly? Why does it not pronounce the *mise hors de loi*[b]? Why does it not outlaw the Wrangels? Why does not one of the deputies step into the midst of Wrangel's bayonets to outlaw him and address the soldiers?

Let the Berlin National Assembly leaf through the *Moniteur*, the *Moniteur* for 1789-95.

And what should *we* do at the present time?

We should refuse to pay taxes. A Wrangel and a Brandenburg understand—for these creatures learn Arabic from the Hyghlans[28]—that they wear a sword and get a uniform and a salary. But *where* the sword, the uniform and the salary come from—that they do not understand.

There is only one means of defeating the monarchy, and that is to do it before the *advent of the anti-June revolution,* which will take place *in Paris* in December.[29]

The monarchy defies not only the people, but the bourgeoisie as well.

Defeat it therefore in a bourgeois manner.

And how can one defeat the monarchy in a bourgeois manner?

By starving it out.

And how can one starve it out?

By refusing to pay taxes.

Consider it well. All the princes of Prussia, all the Brandenburgs and Wrangels produce no *bread for the army.* It is you who produce even the bread for the army.

[*Neue Rheinische Zeitung* No. 142, November 14, 1848]

Cologne, November 13. Just as once the French National Assembly, on finding its official meeting place closed, had to continue its session in the *tennis-court,* so now the Prussian National Assembly has to meet in the *shooting-gallery.*[30]

---

[a] Shakespeare, *Troilus and Cressida,* Act III, Scene 3.—*Ed.*
[b] Outlawing.— *Ed.*

A decision adopted in the shooting-gallery declares *Brandenburg a traitor.* The text, as received from our Berlin correspondent (who signs his articles ☉), is contained in our special edition issued this morning, but it is not mentioned in the report published in the *Kölnische Zeitung.*[a]

However, we have just received a letter from a **member of the National Assembly** which we quote *word for word*:

"**The National Assembly has unanimously (242 members) declared that by introducing this measure (dissolution of the civic militia) Brandenburg has committed high treason, and any person who actively or passively co-operates in the implementation of this measure is to be regarded as a traitor.**"[31]

Dumont's trustworthiness is well known.

Since the National Assembly has declared *Brandenburg a traitor*, the **obligation to pay taxes** ceases **automatically**. *No taxes are to be paid to a government guilty of high treason.* Tomorrow we shall inform our readers in greater detail **how in England, the oldest constitutional country,** a **refusal to pay taxes** operated during a similar conflict.[32] Incidentally, the *traitorous Government itself* has shown the people the right way **when it immediately refused to pay taxes** (allowances etc.) **to the National Assembly** in order to **starve it out.**

The aforementioned deputy writes further:

"**The civic militia will not hand over its arms.**"

A fight therefore seems inevitable, and it is the **duty of the Rhine Province to hasten to the assistance of the Berlin National Assembly with men and weapons**.

Written by Marx on November 11 and 13, 1848

First published in the *Neue Rheinische Zeitung* Nos. 141, 141 (second edition) and 142, November 12 and 14, 1848

Printed according to the newspaper

---

[a] On November 12, 1848 (special supplement).—*Ed.*

[DECISION OF THE BERLIN NATIONAL ASSEMBLY][33]

Berlin, November 11, 7.45 p.m.

About 6 o'clock news came that Rimpler had been ordered to hand over all arms of the civic militia by 4 o'clock tomorrow. In the meantime the Assembly had adopted the following decision:

1) That General Brandenburg is **guilty of high treason**; 2) that the civic militia shall not give up its arms and, if necessary, shall repel **force by force**; 3) that any officer who gives the order to fire against citizens shall be charged with **high treason**.—In addition, a commission was appointed to discuss the question of **tax refusal**.

At its morning sitting the Assembly had already appointed a commission *to discuss tax refusal.*

When the National Assembly reached the playhouse, they found the entrance barred. Inside a company of soldiers was bivouacking. Their captain refused to allow Herr von Unruh to enter. The National Assembly then proceeded from there to the assembly hall, where they were likewise refused admittance. They then met in the Hotel de Russie.

Evening of November 11. The National Assembly transferred its afternoon sitting to the shooting-gallery in Lindenstrasse. On Monday it will move into the Köllnische Rathaus.[34] From what I hear, the Stock Exchange has offered credit and the city councillors are willing to guarantee the deputies' allowances. Several deputations from Spandau, Magdeburg and Pomerania have arrived here to acknowledge the authority of the Assembly.

During the course of the day a "*proclamation*" of the *King* was published, countersigned by the Ministers. This proclamation, which is reminiscent of similar proclamations by *Dom Miguel*, seeks to justify the prorogation of the National Assembly. A second royal decree disbands the civic militia; and a third appoints *Rintelen,* chief presiding judge of the Court of Appeal at Naumburg, to be Minister of Justice.[a]

---

[a] *Neue Rheinische Zeitung* No. 142, November 14, 1848.— *Ed.*

The royal *Supreme Court,* asked by Herr Bornemann whether the Crown had the right to prorogue, to transfer or to close down the National Assembly convened here in the name of the whole country, replied with a unanimous "No!"

In Berlin the rumour was circulating that at *Breslau* the troops have been driven out of the town and Brandenburg's hotel destroyed.

We cannot give credence to this rumour, for a letter which has just reached us from Breslau, dated 1 o'clock in the morning of November 11, contains no mention of this. The main contents of this letter are as follows:

At its sitting on November 10 the Central Committee of the civic militia decided to request that the City Council (and the City Councillors) take steps for the immediate general arming of all men capable of bearing arms and declare that it will recognise and protect the National Assembly under all circumstances and acknowledge it as the only seat of government. The *Oberpräsident*[a] declared to a deputation sent to meet him that he would not go beyond the law, but that he would never undertake any action against the National Assembly, nor lend his hand to such action. He would resign from office immediately if he was asked to do anything contrary to the law. He did not recognise the necessity for prorogation of the National Assembly.

The Chief of Police,[b] who was also present, gave his support to these declarations. He did not recognise any right to dissolve the Chamber and would immediately resign from office if anything of the sort were to happen.

The Central Committee of the Breslau civic militia has declared itself a permanent body.

Since the National Assembly **has declared** Prime Minister Brandenburg **guilty of high treason, the obligation to pay taxes automatically ceases,** for it would be impermissible to support his treasonable administration with taxes.—**Therefore, to pay taxes is now tantamount to high treason and refusal to pay taxes is the primary duty of the citizen.**

Written by Marx on November 11, 1848

First published in the *Neue Rheinische Zeitung* No. 141 (special edition), November 12, 1848

Printed according to the newspaper

Published in English for the first time

---

[a] Eichmann.— *Ed.*
[b] Minutoli.— *Ed.*

[SITTING OF THE SWISS CHAMBERS]

Berne, November 12. In the sittings held so far, the two Swiss Chambers have not yet debated any of the more important questions. Last week the main business was the constituting of the two Councils; the debate on the publication of proceedings (which, as is known, has been dropped for the present without any conclusion being reached); the recall of deputies elected with reservations regarding the new Constitution.[35] During yesterday's sitting the oath for the federal authorities was finalised and the salaries of the Federal Council fixed (6,000 Swiss francs for the President, 5,000 for each of the councillors, and 4,000 and free residence for the Chancellor). It will now no longer be possible to delay the choice of the federal capital and the appointment of the Federal Council. In addition the *Vorort*[a] yesterday informed both Councils of the measures taken with regard to Tessin.[36] Tessiners have appealed against the *Vorort* to the new federal authorities; however, it is not to be expected that the latter will modify or revoke altogether the decisions taken by their predecessors.

Written by Engels on November 12, 1848

First published in the *Neue Rheinische Zeitung* No. 147 (second edition), November 19, 1848

Printed according to the newspaper

Published in English for the first time

---

[a] Berne.—*Ed.*

[CAVAIGNAC AND THE JUNE REVOLUTION][37]

E. Girardin is pitiable in his apologia for the imperialistic cretin *Louis Napoleon*, the *"little constable"*[38]; he is likeable in his attacks on *Cavaignac*, the warrior hero of M. Marrast. Since November 7 he has been publishing in consecutive issues a philippic against the *hero of the European bourgeoisie*, which has fallen in love with his Arabian nightcap.[39] Perfidious as this bourgeoisie is, it has sacrificed him to the *Sipehsalar*[a] *Jellachich*, who is now the *lion* of the European hucksters.

We give our readers in full the *acte d'accusation* made by *La Presse*. In contrast to all European newspapers of great or small format, we have conceived the *June revolution* in a way that history has confirmed.[b] We insist on coming back from time to time to its chief factors and chief *dramatis personae*, since the *June revolution* is *the centre* around which the European revolution and counter-revolution revolve.[c] The distance from the June revolution, as we stated at the time when it was taking place, marked the zenith of counter-revolution, which had to make its tour of Europe. The return to the June revolution is the real beginning of the European revolution. Therefore, back to *Cavaignac*, to the *inventor of the state of siege*.

Written by Marx on November 13, 1848

First published in the *Neue Rheinische Zeitung* No. 142 (second edition), November 14, 1848

Printed according to the newspaper

Published in English for the first time

---

[a] Supreme commander.—*Ed.*

[b] See Karl Marx, "The June Revolution" (present edition, Vol. 7, pp. 144-49).—*Ed.*

[c] See Karl Marx, "The Victory of the Counter-Revolution in Vienna" (present edition, Vol. 7, pp. 503-06).—*Ed.*

APPEAL
OF THE DEMOCRATIC DISTRICT COMMITTEE
OF THE RHINE PROVINCE[40]

APPEAL

Cologne, November 14. The Rhenish District Committee of Democrats calls upon all democratic associations in the Rhine Province immediately to convene their associations and organise everywhere in the neighbourhood popular meetings in order to encourage the entire population of the Rhine Province to refuse to pay taxes, since this is the most effective means to oppose the arbitrary acts committed by the Government against the assembly of Prussian people's representatives.

It is necessary to advise against any violent resistance in the case of taxes collected under a writ of execution, but it can be recommended that at public sales people should refrain from bidding.

In order to agree on further measures, the District Committee is of the opinion that a congress of deputies from all associations should be held, and herewith invites them to meet on Thursday, November 23, at 9 a.m. (in the Eiser Hall, Komödienstrasse).

Cologne, November 14, 1848

For the District Committee

Karl Marx   **Schneider II**

Written by Marx on November 14, 1848

First published in the *Neue Rheinische Zeitung* No. 143, November 15, 1848

Printed according to the newspaper

IMPEACHMENT OF THE GOVERNMENT[41]

The city of Brandenburg refuses to have anything to do with the Brandenburg Ministry and sends an address of thanks to the National Assembly.

In its addresses the whole country recognises only the government of the National Assembly.

The Ministry has committed a further act of high treason by defying the Habeas Corpus Act[42] *and proclaiming a state of siege without the assent of the National Assembly and by expelling the National Assembly itself from the shooting-gallery at the point of the bayonet.*

The National Assembly has its seat in the people and not in the confines of this or that heap of stones. If it is driven out of Berlin it will meet elsewhere, in Breslau, Cologne, or any other place it thinks fit. It has declared this in the decision it adopted on the 13th.[a]

The Berliners scoff at the state of siege and will not allow themselves to be in any way restrained by it. Nobody is handing over his arms.

Armed men from various parts of the country are hurrying to the assistance of the National Assembly.

The guards refuse to obey orders. More and more soldiers are fraternising with the people.

Silesia and Thuringia are in full revolt.

We, however, appeal to you, citizens—send money to the democratic Central Committee in Berlin. But pay no taxes to the counter-revolutionary Government. The National Assembly has

---

[a] This decision was adopted at the evening sitting of November 12, 1848.— *Ed.*

declared that refusal to pay taxes is justified in law. It has not yet adopted a decision on this out of consideration for the officials. A *starvation diet* will make these officials realise the power of the citizenry and will make them also good citizens.

Starve the enemy and refuse to pay taxes! Nothing is sillier than to supply a traitorous government with the means to fight the nation, and the means of all means is *money*.

Written by Marx on November 15, 1848   Printed according to the newspaper

First published in the *Neue Rheinische Zeitung* No. 143 (special edition), November 15, 1848

Extra-Blatt

zu Nr. 143 der Neuen Rheinischen Zeitung.

Mittwoch, den 15. November.

Das Ministerium ist in Anklage= zustand versetzt.

Die Stadt Brandenburg will nichts wissen von dem Ministerium Brandenburg und schickt eine Dank-Adresse an die Nationalversammlung.

Das ganze Land erkennt in seinen Adressen nur die Regierung der Nationalversammlung an.

Das Ministerium begeht neuen Hochverrath, indem es im Gegensatze zu dem Habeas-Corpus-Act ohne Genehmigung der Nationalversammlung den Belagerungszustand ausgesprochen und die Nationalversammlung selbst mit Bajonnetten aus dem Schützenhause vertrieben hat.

Die Nationalversammlung hat ihren Sitz im Volke, nicht in dem Umkreis dieser oder jener Steinhaufen. Vertreibt man sie aus Berlin, so wird sie in einem andern Orte tagen, in Breslau, Köln oder wo es ihr gutdünkt. Sie hat in ihrer Sitzung vom 13. diesen Beschluß gefaßt.

Die Berliner moquiren sich über den Belagerungszustand und lassen sich in keiner Weise durch denselben einschränken. Niemand liefert die Waffen ab.

Von verschiedenen Gegenden sind Bewaffnete der National-Versammlung zur Hülfe geeilt.

Die Garden verweigern den Gehorsam. Die Soldaten fraternisiren immer mehr mit dem Volke.

Schlesien und Thüringen sind in vollem Aufstande.

Wir aber, Bürger, rufen euch zu: Schickt Geld dem demokratischen Centralausschusse nach Berlin. Zahlt dagegen keine Steuern an die contrerevolutionäre Regierung. Die National-Versammlung hat erklärt, daß die Steuerverweigerung rechtlich begründet sei. Sie hat sie noch nicht beschlossen aus Rücksicht für die Beamten. Die Hungerkur wird diese Beamte die Macht des Bürgers kennen lehren, und sie selbst zu guten Bürgern machen.

Hungert den Feind aus und verweigert die Steuern! Nichts thörichter als einer hochverrätherischen Regierung Mittel zum Kampfe gegen die Nation zu bieten und das Mittel aller Mittel ist — Geld.

Das Vaterland in Gefahr.

Heute Mittwoch den 15. November Mittags halb 1 Uhr

Versammlung

der Landwehrmänner und Reservisten aller Waffengattungen einschließlich deren Offiziere im Eiser'schen Saale.

Der Gerant: Korff.
Druck J. W. Dietz, unter Hutmacher 17.

Special edition of the *Neue Rheinische Zeitung* with Marx's article "Impeachment of the Government"

STATEMENT

Cologne, November 16. The *Kölnische Zeitung* in its issue of November 16 draws a wholly invented connection between the "Appeal of the Rhenish District Committee of Democrats"[a] and an *"Assurance"* about the refusal to pay taxes[43] alleged to have been sent to the provinces by the extreme Left of the Prussian National Assembly. Nothing is known to the undersigned of a news report spread by members of the extreme Left concerning a refusal to pay taxes already decided on by the National Assembly.

Karl Marx   **Schneider II**

Written by Marx on November 16, 1848

First published in the *Neue Rheinische Zeitung* No. 145, November 17, 1848

Printed according to the newspaper

Published in English for the first time

---

[a] See this volume, p. 24.— *Ed.*

CONFESSIONS OF A NOBLE SOUL[a]

Cologne, November 16. We predicted to the Right what would await them if the camarilla was victorious—a *tip* and *kicks*.[b]

We were mistaken. The struggle has not yet been decided, but they are already being given *kicks* by their chiefs, without receiving any *tip*.

The *Neue Preussische Zeitung*, Dame of the Army Reserve Cross "with God for King and Fatherland", *the official organ of those now in power*, states in one of its recent issues that the deputies *Zweiffel* (Chief Public Prosecutor in Cologne) and *Schlink* (Counsellor of the Court of Appeal in Cologne) are—let the reader guess—"*revolutionary stomachs*" [*Magen*] (the *Neue Preussische Zeitung* writes "*Mägen*"[c]). It speaks of these gentlemen's "*inexpressible emptiness of thought and absence of thought*". It finds even "*Robespierre's fantasies*" far superior to the ideas of these "*gentlemen of the central section*". *Avis à*[d] *Messieurs Zweiffel et Schlink!*

In the same issue of this newspaper *Pinto-Hansemann*[44] is declared to be a "*leader of the extreme Left*",[e] and according to the same newspaper there is only one remedy for leaders of the extreme Left—*summary justice*—the *rope*. *Avis à M. Pinto-Hansemann, ex-Minister of action and of the constabulary*.[45]

---

[a] This is the title of the sixth book of Goethe's novel *Wilhelm Meisters Lehrjahre*.—*Ed.*

[b] See this volume, p.15.—*Ed.*

[c] "Der Bericht der Zentralabteilung über Kirche und Schule", *Neue Preussische Zeitung* No. 115 (supplement), November 11, 1848.—*Ed.*

[d] Take notice.—*Ed.*

[e] In the leading article of the *Neue Preussische Zeitung* No. 115, November 11, 1848.—*Ed.*

For an *official news-sheet*, the *Neue Preussische Zeitung* is too naively frank. It tells the various parties too explicitly what is locked in the files of the Santa Casa.[46]

In the Middle Ages, people used to open Virgil at random in order to prophesy. In the Prussian Brumaire of 1848, people open the *Neue Preussische Zeitung* to save themselves the trouble of prophesying.[47] We shall give some new examples. What has the camarilla in store for the *Catholics*?

Listen!

No. 115 of the *Neue Preussische Zeitung* states:

"*It is equally untrue that the state*" (namely the royal Prussian state, the state of the Army Reserve Cross in its pre-March period) "*has assumed a* **narrow denominational** *character and has guided religious affairs from this one-sided standpoint.* **Admittedly this reproach, if it were true, would be an expression of definite praise.** *But it is untrue;* for it is *well known* that our Government has expressly abandoned the **old and good standpoint** of an **evangelical government**."

It is well known that *Frederick William III* made religion a branch of *military discipline* and had dissenters[48] thrashed by the police. It is well known that *Frederick William IV*, as one of the twelve minor prophets, wanted through the agency of the *Eichhorn-Bodelschwingh-Ladenberg* Ministry to convert the people and men of science forcibly to the *religion of Bunsen*. It is well known that even under the *Camphausen* Ministry the *Poles* were just as much plundered, scorched and clubbed because they were *Poles* as because they were *Catholics*. The *Pomeranians* always made a point of *thrusting their bayonets* through images of the Virgin Mary in Poland and *hanging* Catholic priests.

The persecution of *dissenting Protestants* under *Frederick William III* and *Frederick William IV* is equally well known.

The former immured in fortresses the Protestant pastors who repudiated the ritual and dogmas that he himself had invented. He was a great inventor of soldiers' uniforms and rituals. And the latter? The *Eichhorn* Ministry? It suffices to mention the name of the Eichhorn Ministry.

But all that was a mere nothing!

"**Our Government had expressly abandoned the old and good standpoint of an evangelical government**." Await therefore the *restoration* of Brandenburg-Manteuffel, you *Catholics of the Rhine Province* and *Westphalia* and *Silesia*! Previously you were punished with *rods*, you will be scourged with *scorpions*.[a] *You will get to know* "*expressly the old and good standpoint of an* **evangelical** *government*"!

---

[a] Paraphrased words of Rehoboam, King of Judah. See 1 Kings 12:11.—*Ed.*

And as for the *Jews*, who since the emancipation of their sect have everywhere put themselves, at least in the person of their eminent representatives, at the *head of the counter-revolution*—what awaits them?

There has been no waiting for victory in order to throw them back into their ghetto.

In *Bromberg* the Government is renewing the old restrictions on freedom of movement and thus robbing the Jews of one of the first of Rights of Man of 1789, the right to move freely from one place to another.

That is "*one*" aspect of the government of voluble **Frederick William IV** under the auspices of *Brandenburg-Manteuffel-Ladenberg*.

In its issue of November 11ᵃ the *Neue Preussische Zeitung* threw out *well-being* as bait to the "liberal-*constitutional* party". But it was already shaking its head doubtfully over the *constitutionalists*.

"For the time being at any rate, our *constitutionalists* are still *exceedingly shy of admitting*, when together in their clubs or in their public press, that they are *reactionaries*."

However, it adds soothingly and pertinently:

"*Every single one*" (*of the liberal-constitutionalists*) "*has long ago ceased to conceal* that at the present time there is no salvation except in *legal reaction*,"

that is to say, in making the *law reactionary* or *reaction legal, elevating reaction to the level of law*.

In its issue of November 15ᵇ the *Neue Preussische Zeitung* already makes short work of the "*constitutionalists*" who want *reaction* elevated to the level of *law*, but are opposed to the Brandenburg-Manteuffel Ministry because it wants *counter-revolution sans phrase.*ᶜ

"The *ordinary constitutionalists*," it says, "must be *left to their fate.*"

Captured together! Hanged together!

For the information of the ordinary constitutionalists!

And wherein lies the *extraordinary constitutionalism of Frederick William IV* under the auspices of Brandenburg-Manteuffel-Ladenberg?

The official government organ, the Dame of the Army Reserve Cross with God for King and Fatherland, betrays the secrets of *extraordinary constitutionalism.*

ᵃ "Aus Breslau, den 8. November", *Neue Preussische Zeitung* No. 115, November 11, 1848.—*Ed.*

ᵇ "Ob Königtum, ob Republik", *Neue Preussische Zeitung* No. 118, November 15, 1848.—*Ed.*

ᶜ Without mincing the matter.—*Ed.*

The "simplest, most straightforward and least dangerous remedy", of course, is "to remove the Assembly to another place", from a capital to a guardroom, from Berlin to Brandenburg.

However, this removal is, as the *Neue Preussische Zeitung* reveals, only an "*attempt*".

"*The attempt must be made*," it says, "*to see whether the Assembly by removal to another place regains internal freedom along with the re-achievement of external freedom of movement.*"

In Brandenburg the Assembly will be *externally free*. It will no longer be under the influence of the blouses,[a] it will only still be under the influence of the sabres of moustached cavalrymen.

But what about *internal freedom?*

Will the Assembly in Brandenburg *free* itself from the prejudices and reprehensible revolutionary sentiments of the nineteenth century? Will *its soul* be *free* enough to proclaim once more as *official articles of faith* feudal hunting rights, all the musty lumber of former feudal burdens, social estate distinctions, censorship, tax inequalities, aristocracy, absolute monarchy and the death penalty, for which Frederick William IV is so enthusiastic, the plundering and squandering of national labour by

> "the pale canaille who are looked upon
> as faith, love and hope"[b]

by starved country junkers, guard lieutenants and personifications of good conduct records? Will the National Assembly even in Brandenburg be *internally free* enough to proclaim once more all these items of the old wretchedness to be *official articles of faith?*

It is known that the counter-revolutionary party put forward the constitutional watchword: "*Completion of the work on the Constitution!*"

The organ of the Brandenburg-Manteuffel-Ladenberg Ministry *scorns* to wear *this mask* any longer.

"The state of affairs," the *official organ* admits, "has reached a point at which *even the long desired completion of the work on the Constitution can no longer help us.* For who can any longer conceal from himself that a legal document which has been dictated to the people's representatives, *paragraph by paragraph*, under threat of the wheel and the gallows, and which has been *wrung from the Crown* by these same representatives, *will be considered binding only as long as the most direct compulsion is capable of maintaining it in force.*"

Therefore, to *abolish* once again, *paragraph by paragraph*, the meagre rights of the people achieved through the National Assembly in Berlin—such is the task of the National Assembly in Brandenburg!

---

[a] That is workers.—*Ed.*

[b] Heinrich Heine, *Deutschland. Ein Wintermärchen*, Caput VIII.— *Ed.*

If it does not completely *restore* the old lumber, *paragraph by paragraph*, that just proves that while it is true that it has regained "*external freedom of movement*" in Brandenburg, it has not regained *internal freedom* as claimed by Potsdam.[49]

And how should the Government act against the spiritual obduracy, against the *internal lack of freedom* of the Assembly that has migrated to Brandenburg?

"*Dissolution ought to follow*," exclaims the *Neue Preussische Zeitung*.

But the idea occurs to it that perhaps the *people* is *internally still less free* than the Assembly.

"It would be possible," it says, shrugging its shoulders, "for *doubt* to arise *whether new primary elections might not produce a still more pitiful result than the first*."

In its primary elections the people is said to have *external freedom of movement*. But what about *internal freedom*?

That is the question![a]

The statutes of the Assembly resulting from new primary elections could exceed the old ones in their iniquity.

What is to be done then against the "old" statutes?

The Dame of the Army Reserve Cross strikes an attitude.

"*The fist gave birth to them*" (the old statutes of the Assembly after March 19), "*the fist will overthrow them—and that in the name of God and right*."

The *fist* will restore the "good old government".

The *fist* is the ultimate argument of the Crown, the *fist* will be the ultimate argument of the people.

Above all, let the people ward off the mendicant hungry fists which take out of their pockets civil lists—and cannon. The boastful fists will become emaciated as soon as they are no longer fed. *Above all, let the people refuse to pay taxes* and—later it will be able to count on which side is the *greater number of fists*.

All the so-called March achievements *will be considered binding only as long as the most direct compulsion is capable of maintaining them in force. The fist gave birth to them, the fist will overthrow them*.

That is what the *Neue Preussische Zeitung* says, and what the *Neue Preussische Zeitung* says, Potsdam has said. Therefore, let there be no more illusion! *The people must put an end to the halfway measures of March, or the Crown will put an end to them*.

Written by Marx on November 16, 1848   Printed according to the newspaper

First published in the *Neue Rheinische Zeitung* No. 145, November 17, 1848   Published in English for the first time

---

[a] Shakespeare, *Hamlet*, Act III, Scene 1; these words are written by Marx in English.— *Ed.*

THE *KÖLNISCHE ZEITUNG*

Cologne, November 16. The editorial board of the *Kölnische Zeitung* in its issue of November 16 describes itself brilliantly as follows:

"In *our wavering* between fear of anarchy today and fear of reaction tomorrow one is forcibly reminded of Luther's words: 'Man is like a drunken peasant; if he mounts a horse on one side, he falls off on the other.'"

Fear is the emotion of the *Kölnische Zeitung*.

Written by Marx on November 16, 1848

First published in the *Neue Rheinische Zeitung* No. 145, November 17, 1848

Printed according to the newspaper

Published in English for the first time

NO MORE TAXES!!![50]

Cologne, November 16. All the Berlin newspapers, with the exception of the *Preussische Staats-Anzeiger, Vossische Zeitung,* and *Neue Preussische Zeitung,* have failed to appear.

The civic militia has been disarmed in the Privy Councillors' quarter,[51] but only there. It is the same battalion that dastardly murdered the engineering workers on October 31.[52] The disarming of this battalion strengthens the popular cause.

The National Assembly has again been driven out of the Köllnische Rathaus by force of arms. It assembled then in the Mielentz Hotel, where finally it unanimously (by **226 votes**) adopted the following decision on the *refusal to pay taxes:*

"*So long as the National Assembly is not at liberty to continue its sessions in Berlin, the Brandenburg Ministry has no right to dispose of government revenues and to collect taxes.*

"*This decision comes into force on November 17.*

The National Assembly, November 15."

From today, therefore, taxes are abolished!!! It is high treason to pay taxes. Refusal to pay taxes is the primary duty of the citizen!

Written by Marx on November 16, 1848   Printed according to the newspaper

First published in the special supplement
to the *Neue Rheinische Zeitung* No. 145,
November 17, 1848

A DECREE OF EICHMANN'S

Cologne, November 18.

"The calls which are to be heard for a refusal to pay taxes make it my duty to utter a serious warning against them to the province entrusted to my care.

"After the King has publicly set out the weighty reasons for the removal of the National Assembly from Berlin, after a large part of the deputies has acknowledged the right of the Crown, and the German National Assembly equally with the Central Authority in Frankfurt has concurred with this acknowledgement, it cannot be my intention to add my voice to the verdict on this act of the Government which is being arrived at by the inhabitants of the Rhine Province.

"My official position alone obliges me to oppose with all the means at my disposal every attack against the laws and their implementation, without which no state can exist. Such an attack is to be seen in the calls to stop paying taxes, which are the indispensable means for maintaining law and order, taxes which have been legally imposed and can only be altered through a law.

"After my experience of the respect which the inhabitants of the province have for the law, I cannot envisage its violation by them, which would have serious consequences. On the contrary, I am confident that they will unshakeably resist such temptations directed against their honour and the common weal. As regards those unexpected cases where this confidence should nevertheless prove mistaken, I expect from all provincial and local authorities that they will ensure the payment of taxes by employing all the powers conferred on them by the laws and that they will do their duty without hesitation.

Cologne, November 17, 1848

Oberpräsident of the Rhine Province
(signed) Eichmann"

Such is the text of the reply of ex-Minister and *Oberpräsident Eichmann* to the appeal of the Rhenish Committee of Democrats.[a]

---

[a] See this volume, p. 24.— *Ed.*

When Herr Eichmann wrote this, his Epistle to the Thessalonians,[a] did he already know of the *decision of the National Assembly on the refusal to pay taxes?*

Eichmann previously represented the Brandenburg-Manteuffel elements within the Pfuel Ministry. He represents them now at the head of the Rhine Province. Eichmann embodies the *counter-revolution of the Government* in the Rhine Province.

Herr Eichmann's decrees, therefore, have the same value as those of Herr Brandenburg. *Arraignment for high treason* will sooner or later be the most fitting termination of the career of Herr Eichmann, this worthy man who in his youthful years with indefatigable zeal dispatched "traitors to the state" to imprisonment in fortresses.

In the above decree, Herr *Oberpräsident* Eichmann declares himself an *open enemy of the National Assembly*, in complete contrast to Herr *Oberpräsident Pinder* in Silesia, who is known to be a royalist. Herr Eichmann has *therefore ceased to be Oberpräsident*, just as his master, Brandenburg, has ceased to be a Minister. *Herr Eichmann has dismissed himself.* Officials who carry out his counter-revolutionary orders do so at their risk.

If the inhabitants of the Rhine Province wish to support the National Assembly in a more effective way than by mere addresses, if they are not prepared to kneel stupidly and unresistingly before the knout, they must compel *all authorities,* in particular *the Regierungspräsidenten, Landräten, burgomasters* and urban authorities, to make a *public* declaration as to whether *they* recognise the National Assembly and are willing to carry out its decisions, *oui ou non?* In case of refusal, and especially of direct contravention of these decisions, such officials are to be declared 1. *dismissed from office,* 2. *guilty of high treason,* and provisional *committees of public safety* appointed in their place, whose orders are alone to be regarded as valid. Where counter-revolutionary authorities seek forcibly to frustrate the formation and official activity of these committees of public safety, *force must be opposed by every kind of force. Passive* resistance must have *active* resistance as its basis.[53] *Otherwise it will resemble the vain struggle of a calf against its slaughterer.*

Written by Marx on November 18, 1848

First published in the *Neue Rheinische Zeitung* No. 147, November 19, 1848

Printed according to the newspaper

Published in English for the first time

---

[a] An allusion to the Epistles of St. Paul to Thessalonians.— *Ed.*

[TAX REFUSAL AND THE COUNTRYSIDE]

Cologne, November 18. Lack of space prevents publication today of the numerous fresh messages of support for the National Assembly in Berlin. They will be published in one of our next issues.[54]

There are reports that barricades have been erected in *Wittlich* (Trier administrative district) to prevent the entry of the 27th Regiment. We have an eyewitness report that townsmen in *Berncastel* are sharpening up old lances and manufacturing scythes with which they mean to hasten to Wittlich.

It is reported that in *Bonn* force was used at the gates to bring in flour and cattle *tax-free* and that this led to a conflict.

Today the new acting Chief Burgomaster of this city, Herr *Gräff,* Counsellor of the Court of Appeal, protected by a body of armed men who occupied the entrance to the Town Hall, first attended a sitting of the Municipal Council. In order to prevent possible conflicts in case of refusal to pay the slaughter tax on the *oxen* to be brought in in the next few days by the cattle-dealers, the Municipal Council is said to have decided to send a deputation to meet the dealers at the gate and come to an *agreement* with them.

The following report has reached us from Westphalia:

"The *Neue Rheinische Zeitung* has already succeeded in having the tax-collector who was sent the day before yesterday from Arnsberg to Neheim forced to leave almost empty-handed, since the peasants refused to pay any taxes at all."

We have received similar reports from various country places in the Rhine Province.

Berlin can only be safeguarded through the revolutionary energy of the provinces. The larger provincial towns, in particular the provincial capitals, can only be safeguarded through the revolutionary energy of the countryside. The **refusal to pay taxes** (whether *direct* or *indirect* taxes) gives the *countryside* the best opportunity to serve the revolution.

Written by Marx on November 18, 1848

Printed according to the newspaper

First published in the *Neue Rheinische Zeitung* No. 147 (second edition), November 19, 1848

Published in English for the first time

APPEAL[55]

Cologne, November 18. The Rhenish District Committee of Democrats calls upon all democratic associations in the Rhine Province to have the following measures decided upon and carried out:

1. Since the Prussian National Assembly itself has ruled that taxes are not to be paid,[a] their forcible collection must be resisted everywhere and in every way.

2. In order to repulse the enemy a people's militia must be organised everywhere. The cost of weapons and ammunition for impecunious citizens is to be defrayed by the community or by voluntary contributions.

3. The authorities are to be asked everywhere to state publicly whether they recognise the decisions of the National Assembly and intend to carry them out. In case of refusal committees of public safety are to be set up, and where possible this should be done with the consent of the local councils. Local councils opposed to the Legislative Assembly should be elected afresh by a universal vote.

Cologne, November 18

For the Rhenish District Committee
of Democrats

Karl Marx   Karl Schapper   Schneider II

Written by Marx on November 18, 1848

First published in the *Neue Rheinische Zeitung* No. 147 (second edition), November 19, 1848

Printed according to the newspaper

---

[a] See this volume, p. 36.— *Ed.*

ELECTIONS TO THE FEDERAL COURT.—
MISCELLANEOUS

Berne, November 18. Yesterday I gave you the names of the eight members of the Federal Court just elected.[56] In the course of yesterday's joint sitting the following were also appointed: *Jolly* from Freiburg (one of the local National Councillors, whose election had been annulled), Dr. Karl *Brenner*, editor of the *Schweizerische National-Zeitung* in Basle, and the lawyer *Jauch* from Uri, thus bringing the membership of the Federal Court up to the full complement of eleven judges. *Kern* was appointed President and Dr. K. *Pfyffer* Vice-President.

As you know, the National Council annulled the elections in the Freiburg canton because only those electors who were prepared to swear allegiance to the new Federal Constitution were allowed to vote.[57] The next day it confirmed its decision by rejecting almost unanimously (73 against 13) Funk's motion for the matter to be decided by *both* Councils. Apart from the local gossip which this decision evoked in Berne, it gave rise also to very bitter discussions between the radicals of German and French Switzerland. The matter stands as follows: according to the Federal Constitution, the first National Council is to be elected by all Swiss citizens of at least 20 years of age who are in other respects qualified to vote in their canton. For the rest, all arrangements, regulations and more detailed provisions are left to the individual cantons. The oath of allegiance demanded by the Freiburg administration is a condition for the suffrage in many other cantons as well; in these cantons every Swiss citizen who exercises his right to vote for the first time must swear allegiance to the cantonal Constitution. Clearly, the *intention* of the authors of the new Constitution was to ensure universal suffrage for the elections; but according to the *wording* of the Constitution the Freiburg administration is in the right, and in the circumstances in which it finds itself confronted by a compact hostile majority dominated by the priests, it had either to demand the oath or resign. The German radicals stand by the intention of the legislators, whereas the French, with Waadt[a] at their head, base themselves on the letter of the Constitution in order to rescue the Freiburg administration and the five radical votes in the National Council which they so much desire. They declare the decision of the National Council to be an indirect approval of the rebellion of the Bishop of Freiburg,[b] which—and in this they are quite correct—is bound to bring about the overthrow of the Freiburg radical administration and the establishment of a Sonderbund government in this canton.[58] They call the Berne and other German radicals "theoreticians", "makers of empty abstractions", "doctrinaires" etc. It is true that the German-Swiss radicals, most of whom are lawyers, often adhere too closely to their legalistic standpoint, whereas the men of Waadt and Geneva, who have been trained in the revolutionary French school, are better politicians and sometimes make light of questions of law.

The most forthright newspaper of this French-Swiss trend is the *Nouvelliste Vaudois* of Lausanne, the "organ of the revolution declared permanent", as the conservatives and even the moderate liberals call it. This newspaper, which moreover is written not without wit and a light hand, hoists the banner of the red republic without reservation, declares its support of the June insurgents in Paris, calls the death of Latour in Vienna "a mighty act of justice of the sovereign people" and with bitter irony ridicules the pietistic-reactionary *Courrier Suisse*, which rolled its eyes and howled at such an abomination. Yet this *Nouvelliste* is the organ of a powerful party in the Waadt administration, indeed one can almost say the organ of the majority in this administration. Nevertheless in Waadt absolutely everything goes on in an orderly way, the people are calm and enthusiastically support their Government, as the elections to the National Council prove once again.

According to a semi-official report of the *Revue de Genève*, the decisions of the diocesan conference about the Bishop of Freiburg (you will have learnt of them long ago[59]) will be ratified by Geneva, with a few small reservations due to previous concordats. The other cantons in the diocese have already ratified them. The newspaper further reports that as soon as all ratifications have been received Bishop Marilley will be set free, since the Freiburg canton has stated that it is ready to put a stop to the criminal proceedings begun

---

[a] The French name is Vaud.—*Ed.*
[b] Marilley.—*Ed.*

against him for participation in the recent attempt at an uprising.

People are very excited over the choice of the federal capital. If Berne is not going to be chosen—and it is regarded as a portent of this that no one from Berne has been appointed either as President[a] or Vice-President[b] of the Federal Council—a movement will break out here which would result in the overthrow of Ochsenbein, a majority for the radical trend (Stämpfli, Niggeler, Stockmar etc.) and the revision of the Federal Constitution which has only just been adopted. For, according to the Constitution, both Councils must be dissolved and new ones elected for a revision of the Constitution, if 50,000 enfranchised Swiss citizens demand it. Berne by itself can easily collect this number of signatures, without counting the masses who would come from the leading Romance-speaking cantons, stimulated by the prospect of a one-Chamber system and greater centralisation. However, all suppositions about the votes of the Swiss Councils are guesswork; the unlimited fragmentation, that inevitable consequence of the historical federative republic, the indescribable confusion of interests, and the inconceivable medley of determining motives must render futile all talk about probabilities and possibilities.

Written by Engels on November 18, 1848

First published in the *Neue Rheinische Zeitung* No. 150, November 23, 1848

Printed according to the newspaper

Published in English for the first time

---

[a] The President was Furrer.—*Ed.*
[b] The Vice-President was Druey.—*Ed.*

THE CITY COUNCIL

Cologne, November 20. The Cologne Municipal Council has sent a petition to Berlin in which it urgently begs the King[a] to dismiss the Ministry in order to save the monarchy.[b]

The Cologne City Council, or Herr Dumont and Co., addresses itself to the King at a time when the entire Rhine Province is turning away from the King in order to turn towards the Constituent Assembly. Herr Dumont, or the City Council, wants to save the King, whereas the Rhine Province is thinking only of saving itself. As if the salvation of the King had any connection with the salvation of the Rhine Province! At a moment when the kings and emperors are trying to save themselves by means of martial law and bombardments, the City Council wants to save the King. Who has authorised the City Council to save the King and issue a petition which is a most servile product of Cologne good-for-nothings? Judging from previous relations between the King and the Cologne City Council, the latter is begging for nothing more than to be kicked.

If the City Council had paid more attention to the decision of the Berlin deputies[c] than to the King's autocratic will and his salvation, it would long ago have ordered the Cologne city gates to be manned in order to prevent the levying of taxes and to emphasise the will of the Chamber. The Cologne City Council, therefore, must be dismissed without delay. All judicial and tax authorities that do not exert the utmost energy to hinder the levying of taxes must be treated as guilty of high treason.

If the city of Cologne does not dismiss its City Council and at once send two new deputies to Berlin in place of the two who ran away,[d] it deserves—the *knout.*

Written by Marx on November 20, 1848

First published in the *Neue Rheinische Zeitung* No. 148, November 21, 1848

Printed according to the newspaper

Published in English for the first time

---

[a] Frederick William IV.—*Ed.*

[b] "Petition des Kölnes Gemeinderates", *Kölnische Zeitung* No. 311 (second edition), November 19, 1848.— *Ed.*

[c] See this volume, p. 36.— *Ed.*

[d] The reference is to Haugh and Wittgenstein who left the Assembly—together with other Right-wing deputies—after hearing the King's order transferring its sitting from Berlin to Brandenburg.—*Ed.*

APPEAL

Cologne, November 20.
Democrats of the Rhine Province,

Instead of summoning *Oberpräsident* Eichmann, the well-known Chief Public Prosecutor **Zweiffel** has, through Examining Magistrate **Leuthaus**, summoned your Committee to appear tomorrow on a charge of public incitement to rebellion.

A scandal is expected; the Cologne Garrison Headquarters has made all preparations; in accordance with the order issued by a treacherous Ministry, on this occasion Cologne is to be declared in a state of siege.

Frustrate this hope. Whatever may befall us, conduct yourselves calmly.

The Congress is going to take place under any circumstances.[60]

The Rhine Province will sooner shed its last drop of blood than submit to the rule of the sword.

Karl Marx Karl Schapper Schneider II

Written by Marx on November 20, 1848

First published in the *Neue Rheinische Zeitung* No. 148 (second edition), November 21, 1848

Printed according to the newspaper

Published in English for the first time

ON THE PROCLAMATION
OF THE BRANDENBURG-MANTEUFFEL MINISTRY
ABOUT TAX REFUSAL

Cologne, November 21. The Brandenburg-Manteuffel Ministry has issued an order to all royal administrative authorities to employ forcible measures to collect taxes.[a]

The Brandenburg-Manteuffel Ministry, whose position is illegal, recommends coercion against the recalcitrant and mildness towards the propertyless.

It thus establishes two categories of non-payers: those who refuse to pay in order to comply with the will of the National Assembly, and those who do not pay because they are unable to pay. The intention of the Ministry is only too clear. It wants to divide the democrats; it wants to make the peasants and workers count themselves as non-payers owing to lack of means to pay, in order to split them from those not paying out of regard for legality, and thereby deprive the latter of the support of the former. But this plan will fail; the people realises that it is responsible for solidarity in the refusal to pay taxes, just as previously it was responsible for solidarity in payment of them.

The struggle will be decided between the force that pays and the force that is paid.

Written by Marx on November 21, 1848

First published in the *Neue Rheinische Zeitung* No. 149, November 22, 1848

Printed according to the newspaper

Published in English for the first time

---

[a] "An sämtliche königlichen Regierungen", *Preussischer Staats-Anzeiger* No. 200, November 20, 1848.— *Ed.*

THE CHIEF PUBLIC PROSECUTOR
AND THE *NEUE RHEINISCHE ZEITUNG*

Cologne, November 21. Who takes a legal stand, *Oberpräsident* Eichmann or the editors of the *Neue Rheinische Zeitung*? Who ought to be put in prison, the editors of the *Neue Rheinische Zeitung* or *Oberpräsident* Eichmann? This question is at present awaiting decision by Chief Public Prosecutor Zweiffel. Will the Public Prosecutor's office, which Zweiffel represents, side with the Brandenburg Ministry or will he, as an old contributor to the *Neue Rheinische Zeitung*,[61] take the side of his colleagues? This question is at present awaiting decision by the public.

The *Neue Rheinische Zeitung* was pressing for cessation of payment of taxes prior to the decision of the National Assembly[a]; it upheld legality before the legislative power did so. And if this anticipation of legality is an illegality, then for six whole days the editorial board of the *Neue Rheinische Zeitung* had been taking an illegal stand. Six days Herr Zweiffel could have instituted proceedings, but on the seventh day he would have had to give up his inquisitorial zeal.

On the seventh day, however, when the work of creation had been completed and Herr Zweiffel had celebrated the Sabbath, and the National Assembly had elevated the refusal to pay taxes to the level of law, *Präsident* Eichmann proposed to Herr Zweiffel to institute proceedings against those who had provoked the refusal to pay taxes. Who provoked the refusal to pay taxes? The editorial board of the *Neue Rheinische Zeitung* or the National Assembly in Berlin? Whom should Herr Zweiffel arrest: his old colleagues, the deputies in Berlin, or his old co-workers, the editors of the *Neue Rheinische*

---

[a] See this volume, pp. 20-21, 24 and 25-26.— *Ed.*

Zeitung, or the Prefect, Herr Eichmann? So far Herr Zweiffel has not arrested anyone.

We propose, therefore, that some other Zweiffel should arrest Herr Zweiffel because before the Sabbath he did not arrest the editors of the *Neue Rheinische Zeitung*, and after the Sabbath he did not arrest Herr Eichmann.

Written by Marx on November 21, 1848

First published in the *Neue Rheinische Zeitung* No. 149, November 22, 1848

Printed according to the newspaper

Published in English for the first time

THE PUBLIC PROSECUTOR'S OFFICE
IN BERLIN AND COLOGNE

Cologne, November 21. In Berlin the Public Prosecutor's office has capitulated to a *traitor to the state*. The Chief Public Prosecutor, Herr Sethe, instead of complying with the National Assembly's demand that he should do his duty in respect of the traitor Brandenburg, has resigned.

The Rhenish District Committee of Democrats, which is endeavouring to make the legal decision of the National Assembly as widely known as possible, and which therefore demands that the plans of a *traitor to the state* should be frustrated,[a] is being prosecuted by the Cologne Public Prosecutor on a charge of — *rebellion* (?!).

"He who has might, has right." — The representatives of the *right* are everywhere on the side of *might*.

Written by Marx on November 21, 1848

First published in the *Neue Rheinische Zeitung* No. 149, November 22, 1848

Printed according to the newspaper

Published in English for the first time

---

[a] See this volume, p. 41.—*Ed.*

THE FRANKFURT ASSEMBLY [62]

Cologne, November 22. The Frankfurt Parliament has declared the decision of the Berlin Assembly regarding the refusal to pay taxes null and void as being illegal. It has thereby sided with Brandenburg, with Wrangel, with specific Prussianism. Frankfurt has moved to Berlin, and Berlin to Frankfurt. The German Parliament is in Berlin, and the Prussian Parliament in Frankfurt. The Prussian Parliament has become a German Parliament, and the German one has become a Brandenburg-Prussian Parliament. Prussia was to be merged into Germany, now the German Parliament at Frankfurt wants Germany to be merged into Prussia!

German Parliament! Whoever spoke of a German Parliament after the grave events in Berlin and Vienna. After the death of Robert Blum no one gave another thought to the life of the noble Gagern. After the setting up of the Brandenburg-Manteuffel Ministry no one thought any more about a Schmerling. The professors who "made history" for their own amusement had to allow the shelling of Vienna, the murder of Robert Blum and the barbarity of Windischgrätz! The gentlemen who were so greatly concerned about the cultural history of Germany left the practical management of culture in the hands of a Jellachich and his Croats! While the professors were evolving the theory of history, history ran its stormy course without bothering about the professorial history.

The decision taken the day before yesterday has destroyed the Frankfurt Parliament. It has driven the Frankfurt Parliament into the arms of the traitor Brandenburg. The Frankfurt Parliament is guilty of high treason, it must be brought to trial. If a whole people rises to protest against an act of royal tyranny, and if this protest is made in an entirely legal way — by refusing to pay taxes — and an assembly of professors declares — without being at all competent to do so — that the refusal to pay taxes, this revolt of the whole people, is illegal, then this assembly places itself outside the law, it commits high treason.

It is the duty of all members of the Frankfurt Assembly who voted against this decision to resign from this "deceased Federal Diet".[63] It is the duty of all democrats to elect these resigned "Prussians" to the German National Assembly in Berlin in place of the "Germans" who have left. The National Assembly in Berlin is not a "fragment", it is a complete entity, for it has the right to take decisions. But the Brandenburg Assembly at Frankfurt will become a "fragment", for the inevitable resignation of the 150 deputies will surely be followed by that of many others who do not wish to set up a Federal Diet at Frankfurt. The Frankfurt Parliament! It fears a red republic and decrees a *red monarchy*! We do not want a *red* monarchy, we do not want the crimson Crown of Austria to extend its sway over Prussia, and we therefore declare that the German Parliament is guilty of high treason! Nay, we do it too much honour; we impute to it a political importance which it has long since lost. The severest judgment has already been passed upon it — disregard of its rulings and total oblivion.

Written by Marx on November 22, 1848   Printed according to the newspaper

First published in the *Neue Rheinische Zeitung* No. 150, November 23, 1848

[STATE OF SIEGE EVERYWHERE]

Cologne, November 22. We predicted that the Cologne City Council would receive kicks in answer to its petition to the King.[a] We were mistaken. It is true that the Municipal Council did receive kicks, although not from the King, but from Manteuffel-Brandenburg.[64] *Tant pis!*[b] We said further that after the decision of the Frankfurt Parliament, it was the duty of the Left to withdraw from it.[c] According to what we hear, not only the Left, but also the Left Centre has withdrawn in order to form a democratic Central Committee. *Tant mieux!*[d]

States of siege everywhere, such are the achievements of the March revolution. Düsseldorf in a state of siege! A town is besieged in order to be conquered. All Prussian towns are being gradually declared in a state of siege, in order to be reconquered. The whole of Prussia has to be reconquered because the whole of Prussia has become disloyal to Prussia. How is the state of siege put into effect? By disarming the citizens. How can a city like Cologne, which is already disarmed, be declared in a state of siege for a second time? By first of all being given back its arms. To put Cologne in a state of siege for a second time means putting weapons in its hands. Long live the state of siege!

Written by Marx on November 22, 1848

First published in the *Neue Rheinische Zeitung* No. 150 (special edition), November 23, 1848

Printed according to the newspaper

Published in English for the first time

---

[a] See this volume, p. 45.— *Ed.*
[b] So much the worse! — *Ed.*
[c] See this volume, p. 52.— *Ed.*
[d] So much the better!—*Ed.*

54

[POSITION OF THE LEFT IN THE NATIONAL ASSEMBLY]

Cologne, November 22. We have heard from private sources that the **Left** and the **Left** Centre of the National Assembly in Frankfurt decided yesterday evening at a closed sitting ***to withdraw, to constitute themselves a democratic committee for Germany, and at the same time to issue an appeal to the German people.***

In publishing this information, we do not guarantee its authenticity, but we are convinced this is the only course open to the Left and the Left Centre. Were they not to take it, they would be signing their own death warrants.

Written by Marx on November 22, 1848

First published in the *Neue Rheinische Zeitung* No. 150 (special edition), November 23, 1848

Printed according to the newspaper

Published in English for the first time

NEWS FROM SWITZERLAND

Berne, November 20. I have just heard from officials of the Federal War Department that the *German Central Authority is reported to have declared war on Switzerland.*[65] The courier arrived yesterday evening, and the *Vorort* was said to have gone into session at 11 o'clock the same evening. Measures had already been taken for serious war preparations. It was stated further that *50,000 imperial troops were concentrating on the Swiss frontier* to begin hostilities.

I am passing this news to you exactly as I heard it. I myself do not believe it, although the source is reliable. I would not credit even the Imperial Government with *such* lunacy.

Written by Engels on November 20, 1848

First published in the supplement to the *Neue Rheinische Zeitung* No. 151, November 24, 1848

Printed according to the newspaper

Published in English for the first time

[RESULT OF THE ELECTIONS
TO THE NATIONAL COUNCIL]

Berne, November 21. Here is the result of the elections to the National Council which took place the day before yesterday: ex-member of the Great Council Fischer (conservative), 1,793 votes, elected. Weingart 1,315, Matthys 1,266, Blösch (conservative) 1,256 votes. As none of the last three has an absolute majority, the two radicals Weingart and Matthys still remain in the ballot and Weingart will probably be elected. The fact that the radicals are having at least one of their candidates returned is due to the participation of the Berne militia battalion which happened to be on service in Freiburg and voted to a man for the radicals.

Written by Engels on November 21, 1848

First published in the *Neue Rheinische Zeitung* No. 152, November 25, 1848

Printed according to the newspaper

Published in English for the first time

ELECTIONS.—SYDOW

Berne, November 21. At yesterday's sitting the *Federal Assembly* (the two Councils in joint session) dealt with the Freiburg elections.[a] Earlier, the *Vorort* had announced that it intended to come to an agreement with Tessin and therefore desired the withdrawal of the troops that had been ordered there.[66] Further (because of the complications with the Imperial Government), the *Vorort* wants the Federal Diet to constitute itself as soon as possible.

Herr Escher wishes to resign as representative of the Confederation in Tessin.

Herr Furrer declares that for the time being, until the next session, he accepts the position of Federal Councillor and Federal President. This means that four members (Furrer, Ochsenbein, Frei-Herose and Näff) are present; Herr Ochsenbein declares the Federal Council to be constituted, and leaves the chair of the Assembly, which Herr Escher takes over, and the four Federal Councillors are sworn in.[67]

Proceeding to the agenda, Herr Brugisser proposes a motion in the name of the majority of the commission concerned calling for the revocation of the decision by which the National Council annulled the Freiburg elections.[68] The minority demands that the decision of the National Council be confirmed. Messrs. Kopp, Anton Schnyder, Pottier, Eytel, Pittet, Castella (Freiburg), Weder (St. Gallen), Ochsenbein and Fazy spoke in support of the majority motions and Messrs. Tanner, Trog, Escher, Frei, Streng and Imobersteg in support of the minority. The arguments were mostly of a legal nature, but the defenders of the Freiburg elections laid tremendous

---

[a] See this volume, pp. 42-43.— *Ed.*

emphasis on the political necessity to retain the Freiburg Government and to avoid exposing the canton once again to the intrigues of the clergy. The majority motion of the commission was finally adopted by 68 votes to 53, which meant that the decision of the National Council annulling the Freiburg elections was revoked.

The *Suisse* and the *Verfassungsfreund* are jubilant, for this decision ensures them five votes for Berne as the federal capital. The *Nouvelliste Vaudois* will also rejoice, for the radical Freiburg Government and the five radical votes on the National Council are for the time being guaranteed. The *Berner Zeitung*, although much closer in its principles to the *Nouvelliste* than to the two above-mentioned Ochsenbein newspapers, nevertheless declares that the decision of the Federal Assembly is the first victory for cantonal sovereignty in the new Confederation. In our opinion, the *Berner Zeitung* is wrong. Most speakers for the majority were certainly not serious about the issues of principle which were advanced during this debate, least of all Herr Eytel, who even went so far as to speak against the supporters of unity. With them it was purely a matter of practical interests; this is clear from the newspapers mentioned above, which pay homage to diametrically opposed parties and whose followers nevertheless used the same arguments in support of the same side. Most members of the minority, on the other hand, and especially the Berne radicals, were serious about the principles involved. But it is open to question whether these gentlemen did not allow themselves to be carried rather too far by their legal conscience.

To everyone's surprise, His Excellency Herr von Sydow, the Prussian envoy, returned here the day before yesterday after a year's absence. It is known that after the Sonderbund war[69] he took up residence in worthy Basle—birds of a feather etc. The significance of his sudden return is not yet known. Probably it has none at all. At least he has made no communication to the *Vorort*[70] or to the Federal Council. Besides, his whole staff has for the time being remained in Basle.

So my report yesterday[a] about disagreements with the Imperial Government did have some truth in it.—To be sure, there is no question of a declaration of war, nor has any new Note arrived from the Empire. But news of the 50,000 imperial troops said to be concentrating on the Swiss frontier and forming a cordon between Constance and Basle was certainly received the day before yesterday in the evening by the *Vorort* which, as I wrote to you, thereupon went

---

[a] See this volume, p. 55.— *Ed.*

into session the very same evening. We shall soon learn what sort of counter-measures it and the now constituted Federal Council have decided on.

The day before yesterday elections took place in the Mittelland district (Berne and vicinity) for two National Councillors to take the places of Dufour, who was elected in three constituencies and opted for Seeland, and of Ochsenbein, who on account of his election to the Federal Council loses his title of National Councillor. The conservative (i. e. reactionary) candidates Fischer and Blösch obtained 1,059 and 893 of the city's votes respectively, the two radicals Weingart and Matthys, 559 and 540.[a] Fischer's election is certain, while that of Blösch, who is the object of greater antipathy, is less so. The considerable conservative majority in the city of Berne is mainly due to the influence exercised on the elections by the rich and long established patrician families here. By far the greater part of the electorate is dependent on them and only breaks away from their tutelage in moments of crisis or when a candidate presents himself who, like Ochsenbein, has popular antecedents and has managed to achieve a respected position in Switzerland. Here, as in most places in Switzerland, the actual revolutionary forces of the people are among the Swiss and German workers, but since they have no permanent residence in the city, they only very rarely have the right to vote, even if they are citizens of the canton.[71] This circumstance, together with the fact that as soon as things become quieter the influence of the patricians once more begins to spread, explains the conservative elections which never fail to come about a few years after each liberal or radical revolution.

At today's sitting of the National Council, Dr. Steiger of Lucerne was elected President in place of Ochsenbein. The Assembly is debating the Tessin affair. In the course of a long and, for an Italian, very lifeless speech, Pioda (of Tessin) made numerous accusations against the representatives and troops of the Confederation in Tessin. Escher of Zurich, however, strove to refute these charges. If possible I shall send an additional report on the outcome of the sitting.[b] It looks as though this will be unqualified approval for the *Vorort* and the representatives, and at best simply an agenda based on the *Vorort's* announcement yesterday (see above) that everything has been settled.

---

[a] See this volume, p. 56. The difference in the number of votes is explained by the fact that in the previous report Engels quoted the preliminary result of the voting.— *Ed.*

[b] See this volume, pp. 142-53.— *Ed.*

There were several more speeches, including a final one from Colonel Ziegler. In this he supplemented the majority motions approving the steps taken by the *Vorort* with a motion ordering the Government of Tessin to pay at least a part of the costs and to express its appreciation of the representatives. The discussion was then adjourned until tomorrow on a motion from the President.

Written by Engels on November 21, 1848

First published in the supplement to the
Neue Rheinische Zeitung No. 153,
November 26, 1848

Printed according to the newspaper

Published in English for the first
time

[DEBATE IN THE NATIONAL COUNCIL]

Berne, November 22. At today's sitting of the National Council, there was a long debate in which General Dufour made an excellent speech in support of Tessin. All the other military men in the Council — Ziegler, Michel, Benz etc.— bitterly opposed Tessin and after Pioda had made an admirable reply to all the attacks, a motion of the minority on the commission

"to intern the Italian refugees who took part in the recent uprising and to leave the execution of this decision to the Government of Tessin"

was rejected on a roll-call by 62 votes to 31. On the other hand, the majority motions

"1) to expel *all* Italian refugees from the canton of Tessin into the Swiss interior, taking into account humanitarian considerations, on which the representatives of the Confederation shall decide",

and

"2) to forbid the canton of Tessin until further notice to allow Italian refugees to remain there",

were adopted by 62 votes to 31 and 50 votes to 46 respectively. The two Zurich deputies, Escher and Furrer, decided the issue by skilfully influencing the German Swiss; Furrer threw his whole weight as President of the Federal Council onto the scales against Dufour's noble gentlemanliness and almost brought the matter to a vote of confidence. The 31 votes for Tessin were, with five or six exceptions, all French Swiss. During the roll-call one heard nothing but "*oui*" and "*nein*", not one "*non*", and only five or six "*jas*". Romance Switzerland was hopelessly overwhelmed by the Germans.

The remaining points in the majority motion, to which the minority (Herr Pioda) also agreed, are just being adopted. The sitting and the post-office close at the same time. More details of this interesting debate tomorrow.[72]

Written by Engels on November 22, 1848

First published in the *Neue Rheinische Zeitung* No. 153 (second edition), November 26, 1848

Printed according to the newspaper

Published in English for the first time

[RAVEAUX'S RESIGNATION.— VIOLATION
OF THE SWISS FRONTIER]

Berne, November 23. Raveaux's resignation from his embassy post[a] is causing quite a sensation here and is unanimously approved. But great indignation has been caused by the German troops' violation of the frontier at Sulgen, and still more by their commander's cavalier apology. What! Thirty-five soldiers enter Swiss territory, weapons in hand, and force their way into a village. They surround a pre-selected house where a pre-selected refugee, Herr Weisshaar, is supposed to be hiding, and make as if to search it. They persist in their purpose despite being told repeatedly that they are on Swiss soil, threaten to use force and finally have to be driven off by peasants wielding cudgels and throwing stones. And despite those incontestable circumstances which prove beyond doubt that the attack was premeditated, the commander maintains that the troops did not know that they were on Swiss soil.

How then can we explain the strange fact that such a large detachment was commanded only by a non-commissioned officer, not at least by a lieutenant, as is otherwise invariably the case, particularly in Germany, which is teeming with lieutenants? How can we explain this, if not by the fact that the presence of an officer, who *would* certainly know that much geography, would have been far too compromising? The Swiss Government will certainly not rest content with an apology flung down so cavalierly after an insult so lightly committed. The Zurich authorities have already instituted an inquiry and the affair will probably end not with an apology from

---

[a] Imperial commissioner in Switzerland.—*Ed.*

Switzerland to the Barataria's Reich,[73] but with the Barataria's Reich apologising to Switzerland.

Written by Engels on November 23, 1848

First published in the supplement to the *Neue Rheinische Zeitung* No. 154, November 28, 1848

Printed according to the newspaper

Published in English for the first time

MANTEUFFEL AND THE CENTRAL AUTHORITY

Cologne, November 24. *The Minister Manteuffel declared yesterday to the imperial commissioners*[a] *at present in Berlin that the Prussian Government would not submit to the decision of the Frankfurt Assembly to form a popular Ministry*[74] *because this was an* **internal** *matter.*

Hence *Manteuffel* agrees with us that the decision of the Frankfurt Assembly on the **refusal to pay taxes**[b] is also null and void, because it concerns only an **internal** matter.

It is possible, of course, that the Brandenburg-Manteuffel Ministry will help to convert the *Rhine Province into an external matter for Prussia.*

Written on November 24, 1848

First published in the *Neue Rheinische Zeitung* No. 153, November 26, 1848

Printed according to the newspaper

Published in English for the first time

---

[a] Simson and Hergenhahn.—*Ed.*
[b] See this volume, pp. 51-52.— *Ed.*

THE GERMAN CENTRAL AUTHORITY
AND SWITZERLAND

Cologne, November 24. In the comedies of last century, notably
the French, there never failed to be a servant who amused the public
because he was continually being cudgelled, cuffed and, in especially
effective scenes, even kicked. The role of this servant is certainly a
thankless one, but still it is enviable compared with a role which is
being continuously performed at our Frankfurt imperial theatre:
compared with the role of the Imperial Minister of Foreign Affairs.
The servants in the comedy at least have a means of avenging
themselves—they are witty. But the Imperial Minister!

Let us be fair. The year 1848 is no year of roses for any Minister
of Foreign Affairs. Up to now Palmerston and Nesselrode have
been glad to be left in peace. Eloquent Lamartine, who with his
manifestos moved even German old maids and widows to tears, has
had to slink away in shame with broken wings and bedraggled
feathers. His successor, Bastide, only a year ago in the *National* and
the obscure *Revue nationale,* as official trumpeter of war, gave vent to
the most virtuous indignation at Guizot's cowardly policy. Now he
sheds silent tears every evening on reading his *œuvres complètes de la
veille*[a] and at the bitter thought that day by day he is sinking more
and more to the level of Guizot of the respectable republic.
Nevertheless all these Ministers have one consolation: if things have
gone badly for them in big matters, they have been able to take their
revenge in small matters, on Danish, Sicilian, Argentinian, Wallachian and other remote questions. Even the Prussian Minister of

---

[a] Collected works of the day before.—*Ed.*

Foreign Affairs, Herr Arnim, when he concluded the unpleasant armistice with Denmark,[75] had the satisfaction not only of being duped, but also of duping someone, and this someone was—the Imperial Minister!

In fact, the Imperial Minister of Foreign Affairs is the only one of them all who played a completely passive role, who received blows, but did not deal a single one. From the first days of his entry into office he has been the predestined scapegoat on whom all his colleagues of neighbouring states vented their spleen, on whom they all took reprisals for the petty sufferings of diplomatic life, a share of which they too had to bear. When he was beaten and tortured, he remained silent, like a lamb being led to the slaughter. Where is there anyone who can say that the Imperial Minister ever harmed a hair of his head? Truly the German nation will never forget Herr Schmerling for having dared with such determination and consistency to resume the traditions of the old Holy Roman Empire.[76]

Need we give further confirmation of Herr von Schmerling's courageous patience with a list of his diplomatic successes? Need we return to the journey of Herr Max Gagern from Frankfurt to Schleswig, that worthy parallel to the old story of *Sophia's Journey from Memel to Saxony*?[77] Need we again rake up the whole edifying history of the Danish armistice? Need we dwell on the unsuccessful offer of mediation in Piedmont and on Herr Heckscher's diplomatic study trip at the expense of the Empire? There is no need to do so. The facts are too recent and too striking for it to be necessary even to mention them.

But there is a limit to everything, and in the end even the most patient man must show his teeth, as the German philistine says. True to this maxim of a class which our worthy statesmen declare to be the great, well-meaning majority in Germany, Herr von Schmerling at last also felt the need to show his teeth. The sacrificial lamb looked for a scapegoat and believed it had finally found one in the shape of Switzerland. Switzerland—with scarcely two and a half million inhabitants, republicans into the bargain, the refuge from which Hecker and Struve invaded Germany[78] and seriously alarmed the new Holy Roman Empire—can one find a better and, at the same time, a less dangerous opportunity of proving that "great Germany" has teeth?

An "energetic" Note was immediately dispatched to the *Vorort* Berne because of the machinations of the refugees. The *Vorort* Berne, however, being conscious of its rights, replied no less energetically to "great Germany" in the name of "little Switzerland". But this did not at all intimidate Herr Schmerling. His capacity to bite grew with astonishing rapidity, and already on October 23, a new, still "more energetic" Note was drafted and on November 2 handed to the *Vorort*.[79] In it Herr Schmerling now threatened naughty Switzerland with the birch. The *Vorort,* even swifter in its actions than the Imperial Minister, replied two days later with the same calm and determination as before, and therefore Herr Schmerling will now put into effect his "provisions and measures" against Switzerland. He is already most busily engaged in this, as he has stated in the Frankfurt Assembly.[a]

If this threat was the usual imperial farce such as we have seen so many times this year, we would not waste a single word on it. Since, however, one can never sufficiently credit the stupidity of our imperial Don Quixotes, or rather imperial Sanchos, in administering the Foreign Office of their Barataria island,[80] it may easily happen that owing to this Swiss conflict we shall be involved in all kinds of new complications. *Quidquid delirant reges* etc.[b]

Let us then examine somewhat more closely the imperial Note to Switzerland.

It is well known that the Swiss speak German badly and are not much better at writing it. But the Note in reply from the *Vorort* is, as regards style, a perfect masterpiece worthy of Goethe compared with the schoolboyish, clumsy German of the Imperial Ministry, which is always at a loss for the right expressions. The Swiss diplomat (Federal Chancellor Schiess, it is said) seems to have deliberately used a specially pure, limpid and refined language in order in this respect too to form an ironical contrast to the Note of the Imperial Regent,[c] which could certainly not have been written in a worse style by one of Jellachich's red-coats.[81] In the imperial Note there are sentences which are quite incomprehensible, and others which are extremely clumsy, as we shall see later. But are not these sentences written precisely "in the *straightforward language* which the Government of the Imperial Regent will always consider it its duty to use in international intercourse"?

Herr Schmerling does no better in respect of the content. In the first paragraph he recalls

"the fact that in regard to the German Note of June 30 of this year for several weeks before any reply followed, proceedings took place in the Diet[82] in a tone which at that time would have made it impossible for a representative of Germany to stay in Switzerland".

---

[a] At its sitting on November 18, 1848.—*Ed.*

[b] First words of the line from Horace: "*Quidquid delirant reges, plectuntur Achivi.*" — *Ed.*

[c] Archduke John of Austria.— *Ed.*

(This is also a sample of the style.)

The *Vorort* is good-natured enough to prove to the "Government of the Imperial Regent" from the minutes of the Diet that these debates "for several weeks" were limited to a single brief session on *one single* day. It is clear, that our Imperial Minister, instead of looking up the documentary records, prefers to trust to his own confused memory. We shall find still further proofs of this.

Incidentally, the Government of the Imperial Regent could regard this obligingness of the *Vorort*, its readiness to come to the assistance of the Government's poor memory, as a proof of the "good-neighbourly attitude" of Switzerland. Indeed, if the Government of the Imperial Regent had taken into its head to speak in a Note in such a fashion about the debates of the English Parliament, the dry arrogance of Palmerston would have dealt with it in quite a different way! The Prussian and Austrian ambassadors in London can tell it what was said in public proceedings about their respective states and Notes, without anyone thinking that their stay in London was thereby rendered impossible. These tyros want to teach Switzerland international law and do not even know that the only thing that concerns them in the proceedings of sovereign assemblies is what is decided, but not what is said! These logicians assert in the same Note, "Switzerland should know that attacks on freedom of the press could not emanate from Germany" (it suffices to print these lines in the *Neue Rheinische Zeitung* to make them bitterly ironical!) — and they even want to meddle with the freedom of debate of the highest organ of authority in Switzerland at that time!

"There is no conflict here over principles. It is not a question of the right of asylum or of freedom of the press. Switzerland should know that attacks on these rights cannot emanate from Germany. Germany has repeatedly stated that it will not tolerate their abuse, it has recognised that the right of asylum must not become an industry for Switzerland" (what does that mean?), "a state of war for Germany" (the right of asylum a state of war—what German!), "that there must be a difference between shelter for the persecuted and a hiding-place for highway robbers."

"A hiding-place for highway robbers"! Have Rinaldo Rinaldini and all the robber chieftains who made their appearance with Gottfried Basse in Quedlinburg descended with their bands from the Abruzzi Mountains to the Rhine in order at a suitable time to plunder Upper Baden? Is Karl Moor on the march from the Bohemian forests? Has Schinderhannes also left behind a brother's son, who as the "nephew of his uncle" [a] wants to continue the dynasty from Switzerland? Far from it! Struve, now in the Baden

---

[a] An allusion to Louis Bonaparte.—*Ed.*

prison, Madame Struve, and a few workers who crossed the frontier *unarmed*—these are the "highway robbers" who had their "hiding-place" in Switzerland, or allegedly still have it there. The imperial authority, not satisfied with the prisoners on whom it can take revenge, is so lost to all decency that it hurls abuse across the Rhine at those who were lucky enough to escape.

"Switzerland knows that it is not being asked to persecute the press in any way, that it is not a question of newspapers and leaflets, but of their authors, who at the very frontier day and night wage a base contraband war against Germany by the mass smuggling in of inflammatory writings."

"Smuggling in"! "Inflammatory writings"! "Base contraband war"! The expressions become ever more elegant, ever more diplomatic—but has not the Government of the Imperial Regent "considered it its duty to use straightforward language"?

And, in fact, its language is remarkably "straightforward"! It does not demand from Switzerland any persecution of the press; it is not speaking about "newspapers and leaflets", but about "their *authors*". The activities of the latter must be put a stop to. But, worthy "Government of the Imperial Regent", when proceedings are instituted in Germany against a newspaper, e.g. the *Neue Rheinische Zeitung*, is it a question of the newspaper which is in everyone's hands and can no longer be withdrawn from circulation, or of the "authors", who are put in prison and brought before the court? This worthy Government does not demand any persecution of the press, it merely demands persecution of the *authors* of the press. Well-meaning persons! Wonderful "straightforward language"!

These authors "wage a base contraband war against Germany by the mass smuggling in of inflammatory writings". This crime of the "highway robbers" is truly unpardonable, the more so since it goes on "day and night", and the fact that Switzerland tolerates it is a flagrant violation of international law.

From Gibraltar whole shiploads of English goods are smuggled into Spain, and the Spanish priests declare that the English "by smuggling in evangelical inflammatory writings", e.g. the Spanish Bibles published by the Bible Society, wage a base contraband war against the Catholic Church. Barcelona manufacturers also curse the base contraband war waged from Gibraltar against Spanish industry by the smuggling in of English calico. But were the Spanish ambassador to complain about it just once, Palmerston would reply to him: Thou blockhead,[a] that is just what we took Gibraltar for!

---

[a] Engels wrote these two words in English.—*Ed.*

Hitherto all other governments have shown too much tact, taste and consideration to complain in Notes about smuggling. But the naive Government of the Imperial Regent speaks in such "straightforward language" that it most artlessly declares that Switzerland has violated international law if the Baden customs officials do not display the appropriate vigilance.

"Switzerland, finally, cannot be unaware also that the right of foreign countries to resist such *iniquity* cannot depend on whether the Swiss authorities lack the strength or desire to prevent it."

The Government of the Imperial Regent seems completely "unaware that the right" of Switzerland to leave in peace everyone who obeys the laws of the land, even if he wages a base contraband war etc. by smuggling in etc., "cannot depend on whether the *German* authorities lack the strength or desire to prevent" this smuggling. The Government of the Imperial Regent should take to heart Heine's reply to the Hamburger who moaned to him about a big fire:

Get yourselves better laws
And better fire-hoses [a]—

and then it would no longer need to make itself ridiculous by its straightforward language.

"The conflict is only over the facts," it goes on to say, and therefore we shall at last hear about some other significant facts besides the base contraband war. We are eager for them.

"The eminent *Vorort* demands, on the grounds of its lack of information, that it be supplied with definite proof of actions which could confirm the accusations made against the Swiss authorities."

Obviously, a very reasonable demand on the part of the eminent *Vorort*. And will the Government of the Imperial Regent most willingly accede to this just demand?

By no means! Just listen:

"But a controversial procedure between governments on generally known matters is not customary among nations."

That is a rough lesson in international law for arrogant little Switzerland, which believes itself entitled to be as impertinent towards the Government of the Imperial Regent of great Germany as little Denmark was at one time. It should take note of the example of the Danish armistice and be more modest. Otherwise the same thing might happen to it.

---

[a] Heinrich Heine, *Deutschland. Ein Wintermärchen*, Caput XXI.— *Ed.*

When the extradition of a common criminal is demanded from a neighbouring state, a controversial procedure is involved, however "generally known" the crime. But the controversial procedure, or rather the mere proof of guilt which Switzerland demands before taking measures — not against common criminals who have crossed the border, nor against refugees, no, against its *own officials*, elected on the basis of a democratic popular vote — such proof "is not customary among nations"! Truly, the "straightforward language" cannot be denied even for a moment. It could not be *more straightforwardly* confessed that there are no proofs to put forward.

There now follows a hail of questions in which all these generally known facts are enumerated.

"Does anyone doubt the activity of the German agitators in Switzerland?"

Of course no one does, just as no one doubts the activity of Herr Schmerling in Frankfurt. It is clear that most of the German refugees in Switzerland pursue some "activity". The only question is *what* their activity is, and obviously Herr Schmerling himself does not know, otherwise he would tell us.

"Has anyone any doubt about the refugee press?"

Of course no one has. Yet Herr Schmerling himself states that attacks on freedom of the press could not emanate from Germany. And if they were to come from there, Switzerland would certainly know how to repulse them. What then does this question mean? If we translate it from "straightforward language" into plain German, it can only mean: Switzerland should abolish freedom of the press for the refugees. *A un autre,*[a] *Monsieur de Schmerling!*

"Has Germany to give Europe proof of the pilgrimage to Muttenz?"

Of course not, cunning "Government of the Imperial Regent"! But to prove that these pilgrimages were the cause of Struve's invasion or possibly of some other enterprise giving greater grounds for complaint against Switzerland — to prove that would bring no discredit to the Government of the Imperial Regent, but would be all the more difficult.

Once again the *Vorort* is obliging enough to do more than "is customary among nations", and to remind Herr Schmerling that the pilgrimages to Muttenz[83] directly concerned *Hecker*, that Hecker was *against* the second invasion, that he even went to America in order to dispel all doubts about his intentions, that among the pilgrims there

---

[a] Tell that to somebody else.—*Ed.*

were prominent members of the German National Assembly. The *Vorort* is tactful enough, even in presence of the tactless Note of Herr Schmerling, not to mention the final and most striking reason: namely, that the "pilgrims" after all returned to Germany, where at any moment they could be called to account by the Government of the Imperial Regent for any punishable action, for all their "activity" in Muttenz. That this did not happen is the best proof that the Government of the Imperial Regent possesses no data incriminating the pilgrims, and that therefore it is still less able to reproach the Swiss authorities in this respect.

    "Or the meetings in Birsfeld?"

"Straightforward language" is a fine thing. Anyone who, like the Government of the Imperial Regent, "has considered it his duty in international intercourse" to use this language, has merely to prove that meetings in general, or even meetings of refugees, took place in Birsfeld to be able to accuse the Swiss authorities of gross violation of international law. Other mortals, of course, would first of all have had to show what occurred at these meetings that was contrary to international law. But, of course, they are "generally known facts", so generally known that I am prepared to bet that among the readers of the *Neue Rheinische Zeitung* there are not three to be found who have any idea what meetings Herr Schmerling is talking about.

    "Or the warlike preparations of the malefactors, who are able to pursue their activity along the frontier, in Rheinfelden, Zurzach, Gottlieben and Laufen?"

Praise God! At last we learn something more definite about the "activity" of the refugees! We did Herr von Schmerling an injustice in expressing the opinion that he did not know what the refugees were doing. He knows not only *what* they are doing, but also *where* they are doing it. *Where* do they do it? In Rheinfelden, Zurzach, Gottlieben and Laufen along the frontier. *What* do they do? "Pursue their activity"!

    "*They pursue their activity*"! Monstrous violation of all international law — their activity! What then does the Government of the Imperial Regent do in order not to violate international law? Is it perhaps "its excesses" [a]?

But Herr von Schmerling speaks of "warlike preparations". And since among the towns where, to the terror of the whole Empire, the refugees pursue their activity there are several that belong to the Aargau canton, the *Vorort* takes it as an example. It again does

_____

[a] A pun: the German *Wesen* here means "activity", *Unwesen* "excesses".— *Ed.*

something more than is necessary, it once again does more than "is customary among nations", and offers to prove by means of a "controversial procedure" that at that time only 25 refugees were living in the Aargau canton, that of these only ten took part in Struve's second expedition of volunteers,[84] and that even they entered Germany *unarmed*. That is all there was of "warlike preparations". But what does that mean? The other fifteen, who remained behind, were the most dangerous. They obviously only remained behind in order to continue to "pursue their activity" without interruption.

These are the weighty accusations of the "Government of the Imperial Regent" against Switzerland. More than this it is unable to put forward, nor does it need to do so, since it "is not customary among nations" etc. But if Switzerland is so shameless as still not to be shattered by these accusations, the "decisions" and "provisions" of the Government of the Imperial Regent will not fail to have a shattering effect. The world is curious to know what these decisions and provisions will consist of, and is all the more curious because Herr Schmerling is preparing them in the greatest secrecy and does not want to communicate any details even to the Frankfurt Assembly. Meanwhile the Swiss press has already shown that all reprisals Herr Schmerling might take are bound to have a more harmful effect on Germany than on Switzerland and, according to all reports, the Swiss regard the "provisions and decisions" of the Government of the Imperial Regent with the greatest equanimity. Whether the Ministers in Frankfurt will be of the same mind, especially if English and French Notes intervene, remains to be seen. One thing is certain: the affair will end, like the Danish war, in a new disgrace, which on this occasion, however, will fall on *official* Germany alone.

Written by Engels on November 24, 1848

First published in the *Neue Rheinische Zeitung* No. 153, November 26, 1848

Printed according to the newspaper

Published in English for the first time

DRIGALSKI—LEGISLATOR,
CITIZEN AND COMMUNIST[85]

Cologne, November 24. Düsseldorf has been declared in a state of siege; the Brandenburg-Wrangel Ministry has found worthy representatives in Herren *Spiegel-Drigalski.* The first of these gentlemen is a simple *Regierungspräsident,* but the second combines various qualities. He is not only a lieutenant-general and commander of a division—as such he figures in the army lists and as "supreme" legislator of the city and entire municipality of Düsseldorf—he is also an author and says of himself that he is at the same time a "citizen" and—a *communist,* and all that with God for King and Fatherland.[a] These two gentlemen, the simple as well as the multicoloured one, have discovered that the state of law in Düsseldorf can only be maintained by *extraordinary* measures; hence they have found themselves "compelled" to declare the entire municipality of Düsseldorf in a state of siege "for the protection of law and order".[86]

We have known for a long time that the Brandenburg Government can only preserve itself by *extraordinary* means; we know that its existence would have come to an end long ago if the country were not in a state of siege. The state of siege is the *state of law* of the Brandenburg Government.

"A state of siege, gentlemen, means a *state of war,*" declared Prime Minister von *Pfuel* at the agreement sitting[b] of September 29.[87] At that time the matter concerned the city and fortress of Cologne, at

---

[a] The words "with God for King and Fatherland" are from Frederick William III's decree of March 17, 1813, on organising the army reserve.— *Ed.*

[b] The reference is to the sitting of the Prussian National Assembly held to draw up a Constitution by agreement with the Crown.—*Ed.*

that time it was a question of an uprising, the decisions of the courts could not be carried out, the lawful force — the civic militia — could not ensure tranquillity, barricades had been erected; force could only be opposed by force. Such was the assertion at least of those who defended the state of siege, at least they still made an effort to save external appearances by relying on allegedly established facts. Now, however, the matter is regarded much more lightly; Düsseldorf is not in revolt, the activity of the courts has not been prevented for a single moment, the civic militia has always been ready to execute lawful orders; indeed one cannot appeal even to the obsolete *instructions* of the year 1809, on which the main stress was laid at that time, for Düsseldorf is not a fortress. But Düsseldorf with rare energy has declared itself *in favour of the tax refusal*; that sufficed for the two supporters of Brandenburg to establish the state of law, that is to say, to declare the city *outside the law*.

We shall not go into the accusations which are intended to serve as a pretext for proclaiming the state of siege; we recommend them to the attention of the judicial authorities as being *false* accusations, for nowhere has legal proof been adduced to support them; they are calumnies which come under Articles 367 et seq. of the Penal Code.[88] We desire here merely to set out the illegalities of which Herren *Spiegel* and *Drigalski* have made themselves guilty for the purpose of protecting law and order.

After these two gentlemen had proclaimed the state of siege and "*thereby* supreme power passed to the military authorities", "communist and citizen" Drigalski issued the following decrees:

1. The legally existing authorities remain in office and will be given the most energetic support in the measures undertaken by them.

That means that the legally existing authorities, insofar as they have a *legal* basis of existence, are dismissed, but they remain in office in order to support Herr von Drigalski.

> "I expect," says Drigalski to his "co-citizens", "that all well-intentioned inhabitants will facilitate *the application of the laws* for me, and that *the authorities will support me in this with complete determination*."

Herr Drigalski not merely makes the laws, he also applies them; the legally existing authorities are his henchmen. And the "independent" judges of the Düsseldorf district court and the Chief Public Prosecutor and his colleagues calmly put up with all that! They see no violation of the law in their being removed from office, they pay homage to the legislator Drigalski and rejoice at being allowed at this price to continue to draw their salaries. Fie! Are you not ashamed, gentlemen, under the rule of the sword, to issue orders for arrests and institute criminal proceedings? Or perhaps the arrest of Herr *Lassalle*, who, trusting unfortunately all too boldly in his good right and the protection of the judicial authorities, did not want to evade the state of siege, is only an act of private revenge on the part of Herr *Drigalski*? Perhaps proceedings against this man and his helpers based on Articles 114, 123 and 124 have already been instituted secretly and are in process?

The *second* law of Herr Drigalski states:

"All associations having political and social aims are abolished."

What does Herr Drigalski care about the law of April 6, Paragraph 4![89] If, in accordance with that law, "all Prussians are entitled without previous police permission to unite in societies for purposes which do not contravene the existing laws", that is obviously one of those "achievements" which must be annulled as quickly as possible, that is to say, are incompatible with Drigalski's legislation.

Third and *fourth* laws. Herr von *Drigalski* controls street traffic and business hours of public houses. As if Düsseldorf had become Paris, he issues a law against *attroupements*.[a] But he is not merely a big figure as a policeman, he betrays also special talent as a nightwatchman: he imposes a curfew.

Fifth law.

"In view of its impending reorganisation, the civic militia is disbanded and must surrender its arms as from today."

This law is a complex of illegalities. We distinguish the following:

a) The civic militia is *disbanded*. According to the ordinary laws, specifically the Civic Militia Law of October 17,[90] the militia can be disbanded only by a royal Cabinet Order. Has Herr von Drigalski perhaps a secret Cabinet Order *in petto*? Well then, why does he not publish it, as he published the statement of the Chief Postmaster, Maurenbrecher?[91] Of course, this statement was at once repudiated as a lie by the Düsseldorf militia. Herr von Drigalski has no Cabinet Order, he acts on his own assumption of plenipotentiary powers and assumes royal prerogatives, although he is a *royal*-minded "*citizen* and *communist*".

b) The civic militia is not *merely removed from its duties*. Herr von Drigalski is not satisfied with merely seizing for himself the official power of the *Regierungspräsident*. As far as illegality is concerned, he

---

[a] Gatherings.—*Ed.*

would have already done quite enough by merely removing the militia from its duties. Paragraph 4 of the law of October 17 states:

"If the civic militia of a municipality or district refuses to obey the orders of the authorities or interferes in the activities of municipal, administrative or judicial authorities, then the *administrative head of the governmental area* may provisionally remove it from its duties, provided he gives the grounds for so doing."

Hence removal from duties could be pronounced only by the *Regierungspräsident*, but not by a lieutenant-general or divisional commander, nor by a citizen, nor finally by a communist, even a "royal Prussian communist".

But Herr Drigalski has his own good reasons for at once acting as royalty without regard for the regular instances. If he had dealt with the militia merely as a *Regierungspräsident* he could not have *disarmed* it. But

c) "the civic militia must surrender its arms as from today". Mere removal from duties in no way justifies the taking away of arms. Otherwise officers who have been suspended would also have to give up their swords. But Herr Drigalski is right; if the militia had been allowed to keep its arms, it would probably not have allowed itself to be removed from duties by *him*; it would have fulfilled its function as Paragraph 1 of the law prescribes.

d) Herr von Drigalski orders the arms to be handed over *to him*. Since he feels himself called upon to act as if he were royalty, he is not concerned about the royal order on compliance with the law on the institution of the civic militia. Here Paragraph 3 states:

"The arms supplied by the state to the municipalities remain *in the possession of the latter in any case* until the time indicated above."

The "city administration and Municipal Council" of Düsseldorf raise no objection to this order. Instead of protesting against this illegality and standing up for the rights of the municipality, they exhort the citizens to adopt a "calm, legal attitude" towards their new dictator.

Sixth law.

"Anyone found engaging in open and armed resistance to the orders of the legal authorities, or who exposes the troops to danger or disadvantage by treacherous behaviour, *shall be brought before a military tribunal.*"

According to the law safeguarding personal freedom, [92] *no one may be brought before any judge other than the one designated by the law. Special courts and extraordinary commissions are inadmissible. No punishment can be threatened or imposed other than in accordance with the law.* According to the same law, this provision can *never* be suspended for any time or area, *even in case of war or insurrection.* For even then, according to Paragraph 8, only Paragraphs 1 and 6 can be suspended, but only *by decision and under the responsibility of the Ministry of State.* Yet Herr von Drigalski decrees that civilians are to be tried by a military tribunal. It can no longer be a matter for surprise that he orders arrests to be made and for this purpose violates the sanctity of the home. These provisions can at least still be suspended, although not by Herr von Drigalski. For the rest, it is a matter of indifference whether one believes the assertion of the *Düsseldorfer Zeitung*[a] that Lassalle's arrest was carried out in a wholly irregular manner or the assurance given by the *Kölnische Zeitung* that the arrest occurred by order of the examining magistrate.[b] The *Kölnische Zeitung*, of course, takes the side of the military commandant in order to put the blame on the examining magistrate. In any case, the arrest is illegal; for in an illegal situation no legal actions can be undertaken. In a state of war, civil justice ceases to be operative. If the examining magistrate continues to function, he assumes the position of a member of a *military tribunal*; the *articles of war* become his code of law. The Düsseldorf Public Prosecutor's office is well aware of its new situation; for if it still considered its competence to be that laid down in the Rhenish Penal Code it would have intervened long ago, if only on the basis of Paragraph 9 of the Habeas Corpus Act, which states:

> "No *preliminary permission of the authorities is necessary for taking legal action against public officials, civil or military, for violating the above-mentioned provisions by exceeding their official powers.*"

In order to become fully acquainted with the power of our Rhenish institutions, the question still remains whether the Prosecutor-General, Herr *Nicolovius,* under whose supervision are all officials of the judicial police, even the examining magistrates, will approve the attitude of the Düsseldorf Public Prosecutor's office. To a deputation which visited him yesterday in order to demand that he should exercise his official powers in relation to the Düsseldorf events, Herr *Nicolovius* is said to have replied that he did not have at his disposal any legal provisions on the basis of which he could intervene. We say only that Herr Nicolovius is said to have made that reply, although this utterance was communicated to us in a most trustworthy way. Nevertheless we cannot believe it, for otherwise we

---

[a] "Düsseldorf, vom 22. November", *Düsseldorfer Zeitung* No. 311, November 24, 1848.—*Ed.*

[b] "Neueste Nachrichten. Düsseldorf, 23. November", *Kölnische Zeitung* No. 315, November 24, 1848.— *Ed.*

would have to assume that Herr Nicolovius has completely forgotten the *Code pénal* together with all the laws that have been promulgated since March of this year.

Written by Marx on November 24, 1848

First published in the *Neue Rheinische Zeitung* No. 153, November 26, 1848

Printed according to the newspaper

Published in English for the first time

[THREE STATE TRIALS
AGAINST THE *NEUE RHEINISCHE ZEITUNG*]

Cologne, November 24. At this moment three state trials against the *Neue Rheinische Zeitung* are impending — we do not include the judicial proceedings against *Engels, Dronke, Wolff* and *Marx* for alleged "unnewspaperlike" political offences.— We are assured from well-informed sources that at least a dozen more inquisitions have been instituted against the **"scurrilous sheet"**— the official expression of the *ci-devant*[a] Public Prosecutor and actual Chief Public Prosecutor *Hecker* (*c'est du Hecker tout pur*[b]).[93]

First crime. Violent attack on the maidenly "*delicacy*" of six royal Prussian police officers and of the king of the Cologne Public Prosecutor's office, Herr Chief Public Prosecutor *Zweiffel*[94]— people's representative *in partibus infidelium*[95] who carries out his duties for the time being neither in Berlin nor in Brandenburg, but in *Cologne* on the Rhine. On the Rhine! on the Rhine! there our vines do grow![c] We, too, prefer the Rhine to the Spree and the Disch Hotel to the Mielentz Hotel.[96]

Va pour la délicatesse des gens d'armes![d] As far as the "delicacy" of Herr *Zweiffel* is concerned, for us it is a "*noli me tangere!*"[e] We were morally incensed at the indelicate vote of non-confidence by which his electors are said to have caused him to beat a retreat. As true guardians of the maidenly "*delicacy*" of Herr *Zweiffel*, we request him *to refute publicly* the statement of Herr *Weinhagen* of Cleve. Herr

---

[a] Former.—*Ed.*
[b] It's genuine Hecker.—*Ed.*
[c] Matthias Claudius, "Rheinweinlied".— *Ed.*
[d] So much for the delicacy of the police! — *Ed.*
[e] Not to be touched! — *Ed.*

Weinhagen stated in the *Neue Rheinische Zeitung* over his signature that he could communicate facts injurious to the "honour and delicacy" of Herr Zweiffel. He could even provide *proof* of these facts, he wrote, but he was compelled to refrain from publishing them as long as Herr Zweiffel could take refuge in the article of the *Code pénal*, by which every denunciation, even the most well-founded, is prosecuted as *calumny* unless it can be proved by a judicial verdict or authentic documents. We appeal therefore to the "honour and delicacy" of Herr *Zweiffel!*

Second crime. The simple Hecker and the dichotomous Hecker.

Third crime. This crime, which took place in 1848, is being prosecuted on the demand of the *Imperial Ministry.* The *crime —Schnapphahnski!* A *feature article as a criminal!*[97]

In its indictment, the Imperial Ministry is said to have described the *Neue Rheinische Zeitung* as the worst newspaper of the "bad press". For our part, we declare the imperial authority to be the most comic of all comic authorities.

Written by Marx on November 24, 1848   Printed according to the newspaper

First published in the *Neue Rheinische*   Published in English for the first
Zeitung No. 153 (second edition),   time
November 26, 1848

PERSONALITIES OF THE FEDERAL COUNCIL

Berne, November 24. It will not be unwelcome to the readers of the *Neue Rheinische Zeitung* to learn something about the personalities who are now called upon to rule Switzerland under the control of the two Councils,[a] and who have now just begun their work. Five members of the Federal Council accepted their election without reservation, another, Herr Furrer, has accepted provisionally until the spring, and about acceptance by the seventh (Munzinger) there can be no doubt.

The President of the Federal Council, Herr *Furrer*, is a typical Zuricher. He has, as the French would say, *l'air éminemment bourgeois*.[b] Clothes, demeanour and features, including his silver-mounted spectacles, reveal at the very first glance the "citizen of the imperial free town", who, as President of the *Vorort* and the Diet[98] respectively, has, it is true, become somewhat civilised, but has yet remained "every inch a provincial".[c] The chief merit of Herr Furrer, one of the most important lawyers of the "Swiss Athens" (as the Zurich philistine likes to call his little town of 10,000 inhabitants), is that by his consistent efforts and moderate liberalism the September regime in Zurich[99] was overthrown and the canton was won back to the party of progress. As President of the Diet he remained true to his principles. Moderate progress in internal affairs and the strictest neutrality in external affairs was the policy he

---

[a] The National Council and the Council of States which made up the Federal Assembly of Switzerland.— *Ed.*

[b] An eminently bourgeois appearance.— *Ed.*

[c] A paraphrase of Lear's words in Shakespeare's tragedy *King Lear*, Act IV, Scene 6.— *Ed.*

pursued. That he has now become President of the Federal Council is more a matter of accident than of design. People would have preferred a man from Berne; but then there was only the choice between Ochsenbein, against whom there was great antipathy, and Neuhaus, who now in 1848 has been just as conservative in his activity as five or six years ago and for that reason was not elected at all to the Federal Council. Owing to this difficulty a Zuricher was chosen, and in that case Furrer was of course the most suitable. Thus Furrer by no means represents quite exactly the majority of the Federal Assembly, but at any rate he is the representative of the majority of German Switzerland.

The Vice-President, *Druey*, is in all respects the opposite of Furrer and the best representative that French Switzerland could send. Whereas Furrer is too moderate for the majority and particularly for the radical minority, Druey on the other hand is far too radical for most. Whereas Furrer is a moderate bourgeois liberal, Druey is a resolute supporter of the red republic. The prominent role played by Druey in the recent revolutionary events in his canton is well known; less well known but all the greater for that are the multifarious services he has rendered his canton (Waadt). Druey, a socialist democrat of the Louis Blanc shade, a first-class authority on constitutional law, and the quickest and most industrious worker in the whole of Switzerland, is an element in the Federal Council which in time is bound to win more and more influence and have the most beneficial effect.

Owing to his antecedents, *Ochsenbein*, leader of the volunteer bands against Lucerne, President of the Diet which decided on the war against the Sonderbund,[100] colonel of the Berne reservists in that campaign, has become well known and popular not only in Switzerland, but throughout Europe. Less well known, however, is his attitude since the February revolution. The partially socialist character of that revolution, the measures of the Provisional Government in France, and the whole movement of the French proletariat, served to no small extent to intimidate him, the *démocrate pur*, whom the French would count as belonging to the party of the *National*.[101] He gradually drew closer to the moderate trend. Especially in external policy, in which he had shown so much energy before and during the war against the Sonderbund, he became more and more inclined to the old system of so-called strict neutrality, which in reality is nothing but the policy of conservatism and connivance with reaction. Thus as President of the *Vorort*, he delayed in recognising the French Republic, and behaved ambiguously, to say the least, in regard to the Italian affair. In addition, the unrestrained passion which he displayed in presiding over the Diet, and which often caused him to take a biassed attitude towards the radicals, made him many enemies among these, and especially among the French Swiss. If any other choice had been possible for the Berne member of the Federal Council than between him and Neuhaus, Ochsenbein would have obtained far fewer votes.

Colonel *Frey-Hérosé* from Aargau is considered one of the most capable of Switzerland's military men. He was Chief of the General Staff during the campaign against the Sonderbund. Like most Swiss staff officers, he too for a fairly long time played a political role in his canton, and in consequence became familiar also with civil administration. In any case, in his new post he will perform excellent work for the Military Department. As regards his political views, he is one of the stauncher liberals of his canton.

State Councillor *Franscini* from Tessin is certainly one of the most respected public figures in the whole of Switzerland. For many years he has worked tirelessly in his canton. It was mainly he who in 1830, already *before* the July revolution, succeeded in bringing the despised Tessin, which was considered politically backward, to be the first in all Switzerland, and without a revolution, to replace the old oligarchic Constitution by a democratic one. It was he again who headed the 1840 revolution, which for the second time overthrew the surreptitiously restored domination of the priests and oligarchs.[102] Furthermore, it was Franscini who, after that revolution, organised afresh the administration, which had fallen into complete disorder in the hands of the reactionaries, put a stop to the innumerable occurrences of theft, fraud, bribery and squandering and, finally, as far as the means of a poor mountain region allowed, once more organised education in the schools, which had completely gone to ruin under the direction of the monks. He thereby deprived the priests of one of their chief means of influencing the people, and the results[a] become more evident each year by the increasing confidence of the Tessiners in their Government. In addition, Franscini is regarded as the most expert economist in Switzerland and is the author of the best books on Swiss statistics (*Statistica della Svizzera*, Lugano, 1827, *Nuova Statistica della Svizzera*, 1848). He is a staunch radical and in the Federal Council will side with Druey rather than with Ochsenbein and Furrer. The people of Tessin especially value him, the leader of their Government for many years, for his "honourable poverty".

---

[a] In the *Neue Rheinische Zeitung* there is an editorial note: "To be continued in the supplement."—*Ed.*

Government Councillor *Munzinger* from Solothurn is the most influential man in his canton, which he has represented in the Diet almost continuously since 1830, and which he has actually ruled for several years. As a semi-radical newspaper of French Switzerland, the *Gazette de Lausanne,* puts it, he is said to *cacher sous les apparences de la bonhomie un esprit fin et pénétrant,*[a] which means that concealed beneath the outward appearance of a good-natured fellow he possesses that petty cunning which in the imperial free towns is regarded as diplomatic ability. As for the rest, he is a moderate man of progress *à la* Furrer and he demands that Switzerland should concern itself with its own affairs and leave the high politics of Europe to God and Lord Palmerston. Hence he speaks extremely unfavourably of the foreign refugees, who so far have always been a source of unpleasantness for Switzerland. Together with the Swiss Athenian, Dr. Escher, he has recently in Tessin again given proofs of his attitude in this respect.[103] In general, Furrer and Munzinger in the Federal Council perfectly represent the prejudices and narrow-mindedness of the "enlightened" German Swiss.

Finally, Herr *Näff* from St. Gallen, about whom I can say very little. He is said to have done much to improve the administration in his canton, and has also distinguished himself in other respects. The canton of St. Gallen, one can read in Swiss newspapers, is in general one containing the richest and most excellent men; but these excellent men suffer from the misfortune that not much is heard about them, and in any case they seem to lack initiative. Nevertheless, in his special capacity as administrator, Herr Näff is apparently not without merit. As regards his political views, he stands midway between Furrer and Ochsenbein; he is more resolute than the former, but does not go as far as could perhaps be expected of the latter judging by his antecedents.

In view of this composition of the Federal Council, there is no doubt about the policy Switzerland will pursue in the immediate future. It is the same policy as the old Diet and the *Vorort* Berne pursued under the leadership of Ochsenbein, and later of Funk (who without Ochsenbein is a nonentity). In internal affairs — strict implementation of the new Federal Constitution which still leaves too much scope to the sovereignty of the cantons; in external affairs — strict neutrality, of course stricter or milder according to circumstances, in particular stricter in relation to Austria. The moderate party definitely has the upper hand, and it is probable that Herr Ochsenbein will vote with it on most questions.

---

[a] Conceal a shrewd, penetrating mind under a kind-hearted appearance.— *Ed.*

But in order to understand how in such circumstances a minority, like Druey and Franscini, could agree to be elected and expose themselves to the prospect of being continually outvoted, how such a collegium can rule jointly — to understand this one must either be a Swiss or have seen how Switzerland is governed. Here, where all the executive authorities deliberate jointly, the principle followed is: Just accept the position; true, you are in the minority today, but perhaps you may still be of some use; and who knows whether in a year or two, owing to deaths, resignations etc., you will not find yourself in the majority. That is the natural consequence of the fact that governing collegiums are formed by means of elections. Then, just as in the legislative assemblies, each party tries at least to consolidate its position by securing the entry of one or several candidates to the collegium, and to ensure a minority for itself, as long as it cannot achieve a majority. If its candidates wished to refuse election, as would certainly happen in larger countries, the party would not take it amiss. But the Federal Council is no *commission du pouvoir exécutif*, [104] and Druey's position is infinitely remote from that of Ledru-Rollin.

The Swiss press as a whole asserts that the Federal Council consists of men of first-class talents. I doubt, however, whether a single one of its members apart from Druey and Franscini would ever play an outstanding role in a larger country, and whether any of the three other members, with the exception of Frey-Hérosé and Ochsenbein, would manage to achieve even an important *secondary* role.

Written by Engels on November 24, 1848

First published in the *Neue Rheinische Zeitung* No. 155, November 29, 1848, and in the supplement to No. 155

Printed according to the newspaper

Published in English for the first time

REPORT OF THE FRANKFURT COMMITTEE ON AUSTRIAN AFFAIRS

Cologne, November 27. Some forty years ago there were people who described *Germany in Its Deepest Humiliation.*[105] It is as well that they have already been gathered *ad patres.*[a] They could not now write such a book; they would not know what title to give it, and if they chose the old one they would contradict themselves.

Because for Germany there is always, as the English poet says, "beneath the lowest deep a lower still".[b]

We believed that the conclusion of the Danish armistice[106] signified the utmost depths of shame. It seemed to us that after the activity of the imperial envoy Raumer in Paris, of Heckscher in Italy, and of the Commissioner Stedtmann in Schleswig-Holstein, and after the two Notes to Switzerland,[c] the humiliation of Germany could not go farther. The actions of the two imperial commissioners in regard to *Austrian* affairs prove that we were mistaken. How incredibly far the German imperial commissioners go in their disregard for the honour of Germany, what stupid incapacity, cowardice or treachery can be inherent in the men of the old liberalism, is abundantly evident from the recently issued "Report of the Committee for Austrian Affairs etc.,"[107] and especially from the 20 documents it contains.

On October 13, Herren Welcker and Mosle travelled from Frankfurt on the orders of the Central Authority "to mediate in *Vienna* affairs". Persons not conversant with the new central

---

[a] To their fathers.—*Ed.*

[b] John Milton, *Paradise Lost.* The quotation is in English in the German original.— *Ed.*

[c] See this volume, pp. 67-68.— *Ed.*

diplomacy expected news of their arrival in Vienna within a few days. It was not known at the time that imperial commissioners have their own itineraries. The Imperial Regent's[a] Eisele and Beisele[108] took the most direct route to *Vienna*—via *Munich*. With the well-known travel map from the *Jobsiade*[109] in their hands, they arrived there in the evening of October 15. Until noon of October 17 they studied the Vienna events in cosy company with the Bavarian Ministers and the Austrian chargé d'affaires. In their first letter to Herr Schmerling they gave an account of their preliminary studies. In Munich the pair had a moment of illumination. They passionately desired the arrival of a "third colleague", if possible a Prussian, "because we would then be better able to cope with our great mission". The Herr "colleague" did not appear. The hope of a trinity was wrecked; the poor couple had to go out into the world alone. What then will become of the "great mission"? The great mission travels in the pockets of Herren Welcker and Mosle to Passau. Before crossing the Austrian Rubicon, the "great mission" sends out a proclamation in advance. It was frightful over there on the other side![b]

"Here, too," Welcker writes to Schmerling, "on the Austrian frontier the population is by no means free from revolutionary and terrorist symptoms." Indeed, "only by the intervention of a military occupation of the bridge was even the national guard of Krems rendered incapable of depriving their Emperor of it and therefore to some extent of making him a prisoner".

What reader would be so hard-hearted as not to appreciate fully these feelings of the fine soul of a political encyclopaedia [*Staatslexikonseele*]![c] After the two gentlemen had gathered strength in Passau from midday on the 18th to early on the 20th, they betook themselves to Linz.

They had left Frankfurt on October 13; in the evening of the 20th they were already in Linz. Is not this tremendous speed proof enough of the importance of their "great mission"? Were they perhaps spurred on by special instructions to this enormous haste? It suffices to say that after seven full days the gentlemen arrived in Linz. This town, which with its "big factory population already influenced by emissaries from Vienna" had aroused anxious

---

[a] Archduke John of Austria.—*Ed.*

[b] Paraphrase of a line from Schiller's ballad "Der Taucher": "Da unten aber ist's fürchterlich."— *Ed.*

[c] An allusion to the *Staats-Lexikon oder Encyklopädie der Staatswissenschaften, in Verbindung mit vielen der angesehensten Publicisten Deutschlands*, hrsg. von Carl von Rotteck und Carl Welcker, Bd. 15, Altona, 1843.—*Ed.*

forebodings in Herr Welcker during his stay in Passau, showed absolutely no signs of the gallows which he and his Herr colleague had probably envisaged in their imagination. On the contrary:

"The entire national guard with its officers and musicians ... received us in ceremonial formation with the German flag flying, and together with the surrounding people welcomed us with repeated cheers."

Therefore Linz—the revolutionary Sodom—turns out to be a well-disposed town, having sufficient *bonhomie* to welcome our excellent imperial commissioners with due ceremony. All the more dreadful does Vienna appear in the Welcker-Mosle reports to Herr Schmerling as the most godless Gomorrah, as a bottomless pit of anarchy etc.

On the 21st the gentlemen embarked on a steamship and went to Krems. On the way they reported to Frankfurt that they had been met with a guard of honour in Linz, that the main guard had paraded before them under arms, and other equally important matters. At the same time they prepared three letters: to Windischgrätz, to Minister Krauss, and to the Presidium of the Imperial Diet.

Should anyone still not be completely satisfied with the more than eight days activity of our imperial commissioners, let him now accompany them during the night of October 21-22 to the headquarters of Windischgrätz in Stammersdorf. Here the Central Authority in the shape of its commissioners appears before us in all its glory.

"Windischgrätz," say Welcker-Mosle, "rejected every attempt at influence on our part with a *certain harshness*."

In other words, they were received with kicks and had to make themselves scarce. "Indeed, he would not even see our credentials," Welcker complains to his Minister Schmerling. And to fill the cup of bitterness to overflowing: Windischgrätz did not offer a drop of wine to the personifications of the Central Authority confronting him, not even a tot of brandy.

Our commissioners therefore once more seated themselves in their carriage, sadly humming the words " *O du Deutschland etc.*",[a] and continued their journey to—Vienna? Heaven forbid! To Olmütz, "to the imperial residence". And they did well to do so. Otherwise the whole imperial joke would have lost its point, the last act would

---

[a] These words are from a German folk song well known in Ernst Moritz Arndt's adaptation under the title "Ausmarsch des Jahrs 1815".— *Ed.*

be missing from the mediation farce. If they were treated like stupid schoolboys by Windischgrätz, they found in Olmütz

"*a much more obliging reception* on the part of the Emperor and the imperial family" (cf. p. 11 of the report, letter No. 6).

They were invited to a meal and, as they write further to Herr Schmerling, "we had the pleasure of the *most gracious* reception". It is not at all the German lackey character that is expressed here, but the most sincere thankfulness which finds its appropriate expression in the song: "After so much suffering etc." [a]
After all the dining and wining the famous "great mission" still remains to be fulfilled. Our two commissioners address themselves in writing to Minister Baron von *Wessenberg*.

"Your Excellency" (begins the letter of October 25), "we humbly request you to *be so good* as to fix a time at which it will be convenient for you to receive our thanks for the benevolent reception which has been accorded our mission and ourselves by His Royal Imperial Majesty and Your Excellency, and to inform us of your views and decisions in respect of the following points concerning the fulfilment of our mission."

The "following points" say in a great many words that the commissioners wish to be allowed to go to Vienna for the purpose of mediation.
The whole letter, as also the second one to Wessenberg, is drafted in such a complicated last-century government office style, and is so full of excessive politeness and servility that it really does one good to be able to read Wessenberg's replies immediately after it. Compared with the Austrian Minister, the two commissioners give the impression in this correspondence of being two loutish peasants confronting a highly cultured nobleman, before whom they bow and scrape in a comical fashion and try to make use of really select expressions.
Wessenberg replied to the above-mentioned letter as follows:

"Your Excellencies, I must apologise for being so late in replying to your letter of today.... As regards your well-meant intention to make one more attempt in Vienna to settle the dissension there, it seems to me necessary first of all to acquaint you with the state of affairs there at the present time. It is not a question of negotiating with a party, but solely of suppressing an insurrection etc." (cf. p. 16 of the report).

Together with this reply, he returned them their credentials.
They repeated their request on October 27.

"We must regard it as our urgent duty," they say, "once more *most humbly to request* Your Excellency and through you the Imperial Government to send us as quickly as possible to Vienna under safe escort with lenient and conciliatory instructions and conditions, so that in this terrible crisis we can make use of the assuaging and personal influence embodied in us and our mission."

---

[a] From Rossini's opera *Tancredi.—Ed.*

We have seen how this "assuaging and personal influence" operated in the fourteen days after they left the gates of Frankfurt.

It exerted such a powerful effect on Wessenberg that in his reply he gave no answer to their request. He gave them some items of news from Vienna, half untrue at that, and remarked ironically:

"Furthermore, that revolts like that of the proletarians in Vienna cannot easily be suppressed without the use of means of coercion has been confirmed recently by the events in Frankfurt!" [110]

It was impossible for Herren Welcker and Mosle to withstand such arguments; hence they desisted from further attempts and waited with their "assuaging and personal influence" for the events that would come about.

On October 28 they again reported to Schmerling about their "great mission". In response to an offer by Wessenberg they handed their message to a courier whom the former was sending to Frankfurt. The courier departed, but not the message, which only arrived in Frankfurt on November 6. If they had not dined at the imperial table, if the imperial family, and especially Archduke Karl, had not spoken to them in such a friendly way — the commissioners must have gone out of their minds at such bad luck.

There now followed two days of silence. The "assuaging influence" was resting on the Sabbath after so much labour.

Then, on October 30, Wessenberg gave them official news of the surrender of Vienna. Their decision was taken. True, on October 28 they still expressed the opinion (p. 14 of the report),

"It seems that he" (Windischgrätz), "like the influential persons here" (in Olmütz), "is *all too greatly* dominated by the idea not only of subjugating Vienna but of inflicting a revengeful punishment for previous wrong-doing."

However, since then Wessenberg has assured them — and how should an imperial commissioner dare to doubt it — that

"the Austrian Government, in making use of this victory, will be guided by principles suitable for ensuring the sympathy of its subjects".

"We can therefore assume," exclaim Welcker-Mosle in a tone of imperial pathos, "that *nevertheless* our proposals have had some influence." Therefore, nevertheless? O certainly! For eight days you have most magnificently amused Wessenberg, Archduke Karl, Sophia & Co. You were an aid to the royal imperial digestion, *Welcker-Mosle*!

"After that assurance of the Minister, we regard our task as having been accomplished and we shall tomorrow" (October 31) "begin our return journey via Prague."

Such is the conclusion of the last message of Herren Welcker-Mosle.

And, in fact, you are right; your "great mission" of conciliation and mediation was fulfilled. Why should you now go to Vienna? Were not those apostles of humanity, Windischgrätz and Jellachich, masters of the city? Have not the red-coats[111] and the royal imperial troops by means of plunder, arson, murder and rape preached the gospel of peace and constitutional liberty in a way comprehensible to all?

How effective your "assuaging influence" has been, how splendidly you have carried out your task — is evident from the death-rattles of the murdered, the desperate cries of the ravished, it is testified by the thousands in the prisons, it is taught us by the blood-stained shade of *Robert Blum.*

Your task was to supplement the trilogy staged by Windischgrätz, Jellachich and Wessenberg by helping to perform a farce in Olmütz. That task has been worthily carried out; with great virtuosity you have played to the end the role of the *"bamboozled uncle"*, if not something worse.

Written on November 27, 1848

First published in the *Neue Rheinische Zeitung* No. 154, November 28, 1848

Printed according to the newspaper

Published in English for the first time

NEWS

Cologne, November 28. In its issue of November 17 the *Neue Rheinische Zeitung* stated:

"And as for the *Jews*, who since the emancipation of their sect have everywhere put themselves, at least in the person of their eminent representatives, at the *head of the counter-revolution*—what awaits them? There has been no waiting for victory in order to throw them back into their ghetto." [a]

At the time, we quoted government decrees from *Bromberg*. Today we have a still more striking fact to report. The big "Three Crowns" masonic lodge in Berlin—it is well known that the *Prince of Prussia* is the supreme head of the Prussian freemasons, just as *Frederick William IV* is the supreme head of the Prussian religion—has put a stop to the activity of the *Minerva* lodge in Cologne. Why? *Because it has Jews among its members. Let the Jews take note of this!*

A circular of the Brandenburg Ministry to all administrative bodies, which we came upon by chance, calls upon them to carry out *mass arrests of the leaders of the clubs.*

We are assured from a trustworthy source that *Cologne, Düsseldorf, Aachen etc.* will be given imperial troops, in fact *Austrians*, as a Christmas present from our most gracious sovereign. Probably they will include *Croats, Serezhans, Czechs, Raizes, Serbs etc.*,[112] so that "order and calm" will be established in the Rhine Province as in Vienna. By the way, people say that the Rhine Province borders not on *Russia* but on *France. Let the most gracious sovereign take note of this!*

Written on November 28, 1848

First published in the *Neue Rheinische Zeitung* No. 155, November 29, 1848

Printed according to the newspaper

Published in English for the first time

---

[a] See this volume, p. 32.— *Ed.*

SITTINGS OF THE FEDERAL COUNCIL
AND THE COUNCIL OF STATES

Berne, November 25. Yesterday's sitting of the National Council did not come any nearer to solving the question of the federal capital and, if anything, it made the solution even more remote. It was decided, against the majority, to choose the federal capital not by secret ballot at a joint sitting of the two Councils, but through a law to be deliberated by each Council separately. If this happens a conflict will ensue, as I conjectured earlier [a]; the National Council will choose Berne and the Council of States will choose Zurich. This is admitted by members of both Councils. Unless the Council of States revokes this decision, it is impossible to see how the conflict is to be resolved. In addition, the federal capital that is to be chosen was placed under obligation to procure and furnish the necessary quarters for the legislative federal assemblies and the Central Government and likewise to provide a mint. After that, unlimited credit facilities were granted to the Federal Council by a large majority. Similar credit was simultaneously granted by the Council of States, and therefore has the force of law.

Today there was first a sitting of the Council of States, then of both Councils jointly, and afterwards of the National Council. At the joint sitting Druey and Franscini were sworn in as Federal Councillors. Since I was prevented from attending the sittings, I shall report any further developments of importance tomorrow.

Written by Engels on November 25, 1848

First published in the *Neue Rheinische Zeitung* No. 155, November 29, 1848

Printed according to the newspaper

Published in English for the first time

---

[a] See this volume, p. 44.— *Ed.*

[LETTERS OPENED]

Cologne, November 28, 11 p.m. Two of the items of correspondence that have reached us this evening, one postmarked *Berne* and the other *Paris*, have clearly been *opened* by an official or semi-official hand. The seal was missing. The wafers with which the letters had been re-sealed *were not yet dry*. *Sedlnitzky*, too, is making propaganda with *Windischgrätz*.

Written by Marx on November 28, 1848

First published in the *Neue Rheinische Zeitung* No. 155 (special edition), November 29, 1848

Printed according to the newspaper

Published in English for the first time

JOINT SITTING OF THE COUNCILS.—
THE FEDERAL COUNCIL

Berne, November 26. Contrary to the intention and declared purpose that the Federal Councillors Druey and Franscini were both to be sworn in at yesterday's joint sitting of the Councils,[a] only the former was sworn in. Franscini had not arrived as heavy snow had held up the stage-coach over the St. Gotthard. The Federal Council was then empowered to swear in those Federal Councillors and Federal Judges who did not arrive until after the eventual adjournment of the two legislative Councils.

A sitting of the Council of States had taken place earlier to discuss the draft Bill adopted two days ago by the National Council on the question of the federal capital. This question, which had already been posed in a complicated manner by the National Council, was here made even more complicated. Fazy of Geneva proposed a motion to keep the seat of government in Berne for a provisional period of one year, and in the meantime to work out a more detailed law which would also include the obligations to be imposed on the canton with regard to the security of the federal authorities. The question was being treated much too lightly. The Swiss people should also first be given an opportunity to express its wishes. Briatte of Waadt, President of the Council of States, shared this opinion. Other members proposed further amendments: that the seat of the Federal Government should be determined by a vote at a joint sitting; that like the old *Vorort* it should be changed, but only every six years, at least until the federal university is established etc. The debate had to be broken off because the time allocated for the joint

---

[a] See this volume, p. 95.— *Ed.*

sitting had expired; it will be resumed today. Rüttimann (Zurich) proposed to refer the draft back to the commission together with the amendments.

After the joint sitting, the National Council remained assembled to discuss the draft Bill submitted by the Federal Council on taking over all the Swiss postal establishments by the Confederation as from January 1, 1849, with the individual cantons continuing meanwhile to administer them until the postal system is finally settled, but the federal authorities having full powers to alter the rounds etc., etc. The draft was adopted *séance tenante*[a] with slight changes by Druey and others. Today the National Council is discussing the law proposed by the radical Dr. Emil Frei (Baselland) on responsibility of the executive officials of the Swiss Confederation; and, time permitting, the draft Bill proposed by Ochsenbein on the establishment of a federal university.

The Federal Council, the executive authority, has already sat several times. Provisionally, Furrer has taken over external affairs, Ochsenbein military affairs and Frei-Herose finance. The Federal Council of War has been accordingly thanked for its services and suspended from activity. The Federal Council has further decided to announce to the cantons, to Switzerland's diplomatic agents abroad and to the foreign powers that it has been constituted. It has likewise decided to lodge a complaint with the Imperial Government regarding the territorial violation in the canton of Zurich,[b] and at the same time to make inquiries, in the relevant cantons, as to the behaviour of the refugees and the truth of the facts published by the imperial authorities in the *Oberpostamts-Zeitung.*[113]

Written by Engels on November 26, 1848	Printed according to the newspaper
First published in the *Neue Rheinische Zeitung* No. 156, November 30, 1848	Published in English for the first time

---

[a] On the spot.—*Ed.*

[b] See this volume, pp. 63-64.— *Ed.*

THE ORGAN OF MANTEUFFEL AND JOHANN—
THE RHINE PROVINCE AND THE KING OF PRUSSIA

Cologne. The *Neue Preussische Zeitung* confirms *Manteuffel's* statement which we have already published[a] concerning the Frankfurt
Central Authority and Assembly. Manteuffel's organ says:

**"The proclamation of the Imperial Regent[b] may be very well meant. We
Prussians, however, must decisively reject it, the people no less than the Crown."[c]**

Manteuffel's organ has guessed our inmost thoughts.

The same official newspaper instructs us as follows about the
validity of the Frankfurt decisions[114]:

*"We Prussians have no other master than our King. And only what he approves in the
Frankfurt decisions, only that will be binding for us, because* **He***"* (Prussian style!) *"finds
it good and for no other reason."*

We *"Prussians"*!!! In the great haggling over human beings in
Vienna, we *Rhinelanders* had the good fortune to win an *"Archduke"*
of the Lower Rhine, who has not fulfilled the conditions on which he
became *"Archduke"*.[115] A *"King of Prussia"* exists for us only
through the Berlin *National Assembly*, and since no Berlin *National
Assembly* exists for our *"Archduke"* of the Lower Rhine, no *"King of
Prussia"* exists for us. We fell to the lot of the Archduke of the Lower
Rhine owing to the haggling over nations! As soon as we have got so

---

[a] See this volume, p. 65.— *Ed.*

[b] Archduke John of Austria. The reference is to the "Proklamation des
Reichsverwesers an das deutsche Volk, den Konflikt zwischen der Krone und der
Nationalversammlung in Preussen betreffend", November 21, 1848.— *Ed.*

[c] *Neue Preussische Zeitung* No. 129, November 28, 1848.—*Ed.*

far that we no longer recognise the selling of human souls, we shall ask the "Archduke of the Lower Rhine" about his **"title to ownership"**.

Written on November 29, 1848

First published in the *Neue Rheinische Zeitung* No. 156, November 30, 1848

Printed according to the newspaper

Published in English for the first time

THE REVOLUTIONARY MOVEMENT IN ITALY[116]

Cologne, November 29. After six months of almost uninterrupted defeats for democracy, after a series of unprecedented triumphs for the counter-revolution, there are at last indications of an approaching victory of the revolutionary party. Italy, the country whose uprising was the prelude to the European uprising of 1848 and whose collapse was the prelude to the fall of Vienna — Italy rises for the second time. Tuscany has succeeded in establishing a democratic government, and Rome has just won a similar government for itself.

London, April 10; Paris, May 15 and June 25; Milan, August 6; Vienna, November 1[117] — these are the four important dates of the European counter-revolution, the four milestones marking the swiftly accomplished stages of its latest triumphal march.

Not only was the revolutionary might of the Chartists *broken in London on April 10*, but the *revolutionary propaganda impact of the February victory* was also for the first time *broken*. Those who correctly assess England and the role she plays in modern history were not surprised that the continental revolutions passed over her without leaving a trace for the time being. England, a country which, through her industry and commerce, dominates all the revolutionary nations of the Continent and nevertheless remains relatively independent of her customers because she dominates the Asian, American and Australian markets; a country in which the contradictions of present-day bourgeois society, the class struggle of the bourgeoisie and the proletariat, are most strongly developed and most acute, England more than any other country pursues her own, independent, course of development. The fumbling approach of continental provisional governments to the solution of problems and the abolition of contradictions is not required in England, for *she* is more competent in dealing with and solving them than any other country. England does not accept revolution from the Continent; when the time comes England will *dictate revolution to the Continent.* That was England's position and the necessary consequence of her position, and hence the victory of "order" on April 10 was quite understandable. But who does not remember how this victory of "order", this first counterblow to the blows of February and March, gave fresh support to the counter-revolution everywhere and raised daring hopes in the hearts of those who were called conservatives! Who does not remember how throughout Germany the action of London's special constables was immediately accepted as a model by the entire civic militia! Who does not remember the impression made by this first proof that the movement which had broken out was not unconquerable!

On May 15, Paris promptly provided its counterpart to the victory of the English conservative party. The outermost waves of the revolutionary flood were stemmed on April 10; on May 15 its force was broken at its very source. April 10 demonstrated that the February movement was not irresistible; May 15 demonstrated that the insurrection could be checked in Paris. The revolution defeated at its centre was of course bound to succumb at the periphery as well. And this happened to an increasing extent day by day in Prussia and the smaller German states. But the revolutionary current was still strong enough to ensure two victories of the people in Vienna, the first also on May 15, the second on May 26, while the victory of absolutism in Naples, likewise won on May 15, acted because of its excesses rather as a counterbalance to the victory of order in Paris.[118] Something was still missing, though. Not only had the revolutionary movement to be defeated in Paris, but armed insurrection had to be divested of the spell of invincibility in Paris itself; only then could the counter-revolution feel safe.

And that happened at *Paris* in a battle lasting four days, from *June* 23 to 26. Four days of gun-fire put an end to the impregnability of the barricades and the invincibility of the armed people. What did Cavaignac demonstrate by his victory if not that the laws of warfare are more or less the same in a street and in a defile, whether faced by a barricade or by an entanglement or bastion? That 40,000 undisciplined armed workers, without guns or howitzers and without deliveries of ammunition, can withstand a well-organised army of 120,000 experienced soldiers and 150,000 men of the national guard supported by the best and most numerous artillery and abundantly supplied with ammunition for no more than four days? Cavaignac's victory was the sheerest suppression of the smaller force by a force numerically seven times as big; it was the most inglorious victory ever won, the more inglorious for the blood that it cost despite the overwhelmingly superior forces. Nevertheless the world regarded it with amazement as if it were a miracle, for this victory won by superior forces divested the people of Paris and the Paris barricades of the aura of invincibility. By defeating 40,000 workers, Cavaignac's 300,000 men defeated not only the 40,000 workers, but, without realising it, defeated the European revolution. We all know what an impetuous storm of reaction set in from that day. There was nothing now to restrain it; the people of Paris were defeated with shell and grape-shot by conservative forces, and what could be done in Paris could be repeated elsewhere. Nothing remained to democracy after this decisive defeat but to make as honourable a retreat as possible and at least defend foot by foot in the press, at public meetings and in parliaments, the ground which could no longer be held.

The next great blow was the *fall of Milan.*[a] The recapture of Milan by Radetzky was indeed the first European event following the June victory in Paris. The double-headed eagle on the spire of the Milan Cathedral signified not only the fall of Italy as a whole, it signified also the restoration of *Austria,* the restoration of the stronghold of European counter-revolution. Italy crushed and Austria resurrected—what more could the counter-revolution demand! Indeed, with the fall of Milan there was an immediate slackening of revolutionary energy in Italy, Mamiani was overthrown in Rome, the democrats were defeated in Piedmont; and simultaneously the reactionary party raised its head again in Austria and from its centre, Radetzky's headquarters, it began with renewed courage to spread the net of its intrigues over all provinces. Only then did Jellachich assume the offensive, only then was the great alliance of the counter-revolution with the Austrian Slavs completed.

I say nothing of the brief intermezzi in which the counter-revolution gained local victories and conquered separate provinces, of the setback in Frankfurt,[119] and so on. They are of local, perhaps national, but not European significance.

Finally, the work that was begun on the day of Custozza[120] was completed on November 1—just as Radetzky had marched into Milan so did Windischgrätz and Jellachich march into Vienna. Cavaignac's method was employed, and employed successfully,

---

[a] In August 1848.—*Ed.*

against the largest and most active focus of German revolution. The revolution in Vienna, like that in Paris, was smothered in blood and smoking ruins.

But it almost seems as if the victory of November 1 also marks the moment when the retrogressive movement reaches the turning-point and a crisis sets in. The attempt to repeat the bold exploit of Vienna bit by bit in Prussia has failed. Even if the country should forsake the Constituent Assembly, the most the Crown can expect is merely a partial victory which will decide nothing, and at any rate the first discouraging effect of the Viennese defeat has been nullified by the clumsy attempt to copy it in every detail.

While Northern Europe has either been forced back again into the servitude of 1847 or is laboriously defending the gains won during the first months against the attacks of the counter-revolution, Italy is suddenly rising again. Leghorn, the only Italian city which the fall of Milan spurred on to a victorious revolution, Leghorn has at last imparted its democratic *élan* to the whole of Tuscany and has succeeded in setting up a radically democratic government, more radical than any that ever existed under a monarchy, and more radical than most formed in a republic. This Government responded to the fall of Vienna and the restoration of Austria by proclaiming an Italian Constituent Assembly. The revolutionary fire-brand which this democratic Government has thus hurled into the midst of the Italian people has kindled a fire: in Rome the people, the national guard and the army have risen as *one* man, have overthrown the evasive, counter-revolutionary Government and secured a democratic government, and first among the demands they suc-ceeded in putting through is a government based on the principle of Italian nationality, that is to say, the sending of delegates to the Italian Constituent Assembly as proposed by Guerazzi.[121]

That Piedmont and Sicily will follow suit is beyond doubt. They will follow just as they did last year.

And then? Will this second resurrection of Italy within three years — like the preceding one — herald the dawn of a new upsurge of European democracy? It almost looks as if it will. The measure of the counter-revolution has been filled to overflowing. France is about to throw herself into the arms of an adventurer[a] in order to escape the rule of Cavaignac and Marrast; Germany is more divided than ever; Austria is overwhelmed; Prussia is on the eve of civil war. All the illusions of February and March have been ruthlessly crushed

---

[a] Louis Bonaparte.—*Ed.*

beneath the swift tread of history. Indeed, the people have nothing more to learn from any further victories of the counter-revolution!

It is up to the people, when the occasion arises, to apply the lessons of the past six months *in good time* and *fearlessly*.

Written by Marx on November 29, 1848   Printed according to the newspaper

First published in the *Neue Rheinische Zeitung* No. 156, November 30, 1848

GERMAN PROFESSORIAL BASENESS

Cologne, November 29. The lackey nature of German professors finds its ideal surpassed in the learned gentlemen of Berlin and Halle. Such a servile frame of mind would shame a Russian serf. The pious Buddhist who credulously swallows the excrement of his Dalai Lama hears with astonishment about the Berlin and Halle Buddhists whose prostitution before royalty "by the grace of God" seems to him like a fable. He only believes in its reality when he is shown the addresses of the Berlin and Halle professors to the King of Prussia dated November 24 and 21 respectively, with the original signatures. [a]

"Freedom of discussion was abolished, the lives of the deputies menaced, the dignity of the Assembly and the honour of the nation besmirched, and the most well-intentioned and just proposals for putting an end to this reign of terror were frustrated by the resistance of those whom it was to benefit."

With these and other such brazen lies, and with the most servile assurances of inborn loyalty, 80 Berlin professors—including Hengstenberg, Schönlein, Ehrenberg, Böckh, the two Grimms etc.—have concocted an address to the King in which they bray in chorus their learned applause for the coercive measures of the Brandenburg Ministry.

The address of 19 Halle professors has a similar sound, but they go so far in their comicality as to speak incidentally of the "seriousness of their profession".

---

[a] "Adresse der Berliner Professoren an den König von Preussen", November 24, 1848; "Erklärung von Prorektor und Senat der Königlichen vereinten Friedrichs-Universität" in Halle, November 21, 1848 (*Preussischer Staats-Anzeiger*, November 25 and 26, 1848).— *Ed.*

The central feature in both addresses is an indescribable fury at the *refusal to pay taxes*. This is very easy to understand! No more taxes — and privileged erudition goes bankrupt. This money-greedy race of professors needs only the remotest threat to its purse for all science to be engulfed in fire and flames. Their monopoly is rooted in royalty "by the grace of God". They write addresses to the King expressing their devotion, that is to say, they are devoted until death to their own monopoly. If the people achieves final victory, these gentlemen will quickly, in spite of all the "seriousness of their scientific profession", manage to put themselves on the side of popular sovereignty, now so greatly condemned by them. The people, however, will cry out to them "too late" [122] and put a speedy end to the whole evil of privileged erudition.

Written on November 29, 1848

First published in the *Neue Rheinische Zeitung* No. 156, November 30, 1848

Printed according to the newspaper

Published in English for the first time

SITTING OF THE NATIONAL COUNCIL.—
THE COUNCIL OF STATES.—
PROTEST OF THE POPE.— IMPERIAL
GRAIN EMBARGO.— THE VALAISAN GREAT COUNCIL

Berne, November 26. At yesterday's sitting the National Council dispatched both items on the agenda (Emil Frei's motion on the law of responsibility and Ochsenbein's on the federal university) by referring them to the Federal Council. During the discussion on the university some strange remarks were made. Lusser from Uri saw in the project the ruin of his canton's finances. Hungerbühler from Berne similarly resisted the idea of a university with all his might: he said it was a luxury expenditure and that there were already enough people whose heads had been turned through too much learning. The Alcibiades of the Swiss Athens, Herr Escher from Zurich, also thought it necessary to wait first for the financial means. Alcibiades had good reason to press for an ordinary agenda; he was well aware that the Berne deputies intended to grab the seat of the Federal Government for themselves and let Lucerne be satisfied with the Federal Court and Zurich with the "Federal Higher School". But the ambition of the Athenians of Switzerland goes beyond that, and all but two of them voted, although to no avail, for an ordinary agenda.

In the Council of States the law on the seat of the Federal Government was approved in the draft proposed by the National Council and only one addendum was made, by Rüttimann, concerning the security of the federal authorities. Thus, it has now been decided that the seat of the Federal Government be chosen separately in each Council, and not by ballot, but according to the usual voting procedure. We shall see what comes of this.

A few days ago the canton of *Neuchâtel* witnessed scenes of great confusion. News arrived that all the State Councillors except one (Herr Steck) had tendered their resignations. All the members of the Republic's National Council and Council of States immediately went home in great consternation. From what we have heard, the dispute resulted from a violent attack on the part of Herr Steck and was settled by a commission of the Great Council appointed specially for the purpose. At the sitting the day before yesterday the State Councillors withdrew their resignations amidst loud cries of *vive la république* from the Great Council.

The Pope[a] has protested against the decisions of the five cantons of the Freiburg diocese, which are relieving Bishop Marilley of his episcopal duties and taking steps to set up a provisional administration of the bishopric.[123] If these measures are not revoked, he is threatening to issue "other decrees to which his conscience commits him towards the Catholic world". The *Schweizerischer Beobachter*, the local reactionary newspaper, consoled itself two nights ago with the hope that since a republic had now been proclaimed in Rome (the worthy paper was made to believe this), the papacy was finished with[124] and the Catholic world had regained its freedom, which meant that the confused situation in Freiburg would also be resolved!

There are conflicting reports from the German frontier as to whether or not a grain embargo has been introduced. It is known for sure that so far it has at the most been introduced at Lake Constance; for on the 24th, the day before yesterday, as many Swabian corn growers as ever before came to the market in Zurich.

The Valaisan Great Council has taken the decision to levy the taxes necessary to pay the Sonderbund war reparations not, as elsewhere, on the enormously rich monasteries, but on the municipalities. The proportion that Valais has to pay amounts to 1,600,000 Swiss francs. So, instead of the monks who were the original instigators of the insurrection, it is the poor people of the canton who will have to pay this tax. In the meantime, the reverend fathers are carting away more and more of their property to Piedmont, just as the *patres* of the Great St. Bernhard have already done. These priestlings, famous in school books and sentimental stories for their dogs and for their alleged selfless devotion to travellers dying in the snow, are in reality tremendously rich and live extremely comfortably. They have taken all their riches, their cattle, their money and their effects to Aosta, where they are also now staying and partaking copiously of Piedmontese wine. When Radetzky marched into Milan,[b] these philanthropists celebrated the happy event with banqueting and cannon-fire, for which they were brought before the Piedmontese

---

[a] Pius IX.—*Ed.*
[b] On August 6, 1848.— *Ed.*

courts. This *ecclesia pressa*[a] left nothing behind in their wintry monastery but a little bread and bacon, with which a few servants entertain travellers. However, the *Suisse* doubts whether the above decision was actually taken, even though it was printed in the *Journal du Valais.*

Written by Engels on November 26, 1848

Printed according to the newspaper

First published in the supplement to the *Neue Rheinische Zeitung* No. 157, December 1, 1848

Published in English for the first time

---

[a] Persecuted church.— *Ed.*

[SITTING OF THE NATIONAL COUNCIL]

Berne, November 27. At today's sitting of the National Council the question of publishing a bulletin of proceedings was once again taken up, but owing to the small number of members present it was very soon adjourned until tomorrow.

Written by Engels on November 27, 1848

First published in the supplement to the *Neue Rheinische Zeitung* No. 157, December 1, 1848

Printed according to the newspaper

Published in English for the first time

BERNE DECLARED FEDERAL CAPITAL.—
FRANSCINI

Berne, November 28. At today's sitting of the National Council *Berne was declared the federal capital* by 58 votes to 42. All that is now needed is the ratification of the Council of States, which in the opinion of the Berne public is a foregone conclusion. There will be a sitting of the Council of States at 4 o'clock this afternoon, when it will take a decision on this matter. As the post goes at half past four, it will be impossible for me to send a report today on the outcome of this sitting.

At yesterday's sitting the Council of States ratified the National Council's decision on the Tessin question [a] without amending it, which means that it has force of law. In the debate, which was somewhat long drawn out, Federal Councillor Franscini, who arrived the day before, particularly distinguished himself with a speech in support of the Tessiners. Carteret of Geneva also spoke out energetically in support of the Italian refugees and protested against their being referred to as "culprits" in this assembly, whereas they deserved the sympathy of all Swiss people for their aspirations and their struggles. It was indeed by demonstrating such active sympathy that the Tessiners proved that they were genuinely Swiss. In spite of this and several other vigorous protestations, especially against Article 2, which deprives Tessin of the right to grant asylum, the decision of the National Council was, as I have said, ratified in its entirety by a sizeable majority. Here too the German cantons were the decisive factor, even though a few German deputies also supported the Tessiners in the Council of States.

Written by Engels on November 28, 1848

First published in the *Neue Rheinische Zeitung* No. 158, December 2, 1848

Printed according to the newspaper

Published in English for the first time

---

[a] See this volume, pp. 61-62.— *Ed.*

[NEWS FROM SWITZERLAND]

Berne, November 29. At yesterday's sitting of the Council of States the law centralising the control of the posts in the hands of the federal authorities as from January 1, 1849,[a] was debated and approved without amendments. It had already received the approval of the National Council. The decision on the seat of the Federal Government was on the agenda. However, since the National Council was debating this decision at the same time and had already taken the initiative, the sitting was adjourned until four o'clock. At four o'clock the Council proceeded to the vote. At the first vote Berne received 21 votes, Zurich 13 and Lucerne 3, which gave an absolute majority to Berne. *Berne is therefore definitively the seat of the Swiss federal authorities.*

This morning both Councils came together to swear in Federal Councillor Franscini. Franscini delivered a longish speech in Italian which was applauded by all. Thereupon the Federal Assembly adjourned indefinitely. It was left to the Federal Council to reconvene the Assembly at the appropriate time.

The Federal Council made the following distribution of departments among its members: Furrer, as President, was put in charge of external affairs and general direction of federal policies; Druey, justice and police; Ochsenbein, war; Franscini, internal affairs; Munzinger, finance; Frei-Herose, taxes on commerce and turnpike money (*péages*); Näff, posts and public works.

The two recent elections in Berne for the National Council[b] resulted in victories for the liberals; in Mittelland Weingart was elected and in Emmenthal, governor Karrer.

---

[a] See this volume, p. 98.— *Ed.*
[b] See this volume, pp. 56 and 59.— *Ed.*

It goes without saying that the people of Berne are jubilant at their elevation to citizens of the capital of Switzerland. Last night there were any number of torchlight processions and serenades; in addition, the inevitable roar of cannon; bell-ringing seems to be left to the "imperial authority". There was naturally quite a serenade in front of the Erlacher Hof, where the Federal Council has its seat, and Steiger and Furrer made speeches.

I have just heard that Luvini fought a duel with Colonel Berg because of the latter's provocative remarks during the Tessin debate. It appears that no one was hurt; however, I cannot yet say anything definite on that score.

Written by Engels on November 29, 1848

Printed according to the newspaper

First published in the *Neue Rheinische Zeitung* No. 159 (second edition), December 3, 1848

Published in English for the first time

DUEL BETWEEN BERG AND LUVINI

Berne, November 30. In the duel yesterday between Herren Berg and Luvini, Herr Berg sustained fairly severe wounds in the arm and in the side. The weapon chosen was the officer's broadsword (*briquet d'ordonnance*). When Herr Berg left yesterday he had to be carried to the carriage.

Written by Engels on November 30, 1848

First published in the *Neue Rheinische Zeitung* No. 160, December 5, 1848

Printed according to the newspaper

Published in English for the first time

THE CLOSING OF THE GERMAN FRONTIER.— THE EMPIRE.— THE COUNCIL OF WAR

Berne, December 1. Thank God! At last it *appears* that the official news of the closing of the German frontier has reached the Federal Council and we shall now know what the position is. It was high time, considering how long their worships in the Central Authority have been taunting us Swiss and making fools of us. The Federal Council is said to have decided not to put even a single company of Swiss troops in the field against the mighty formation of 50,000 imperial troops. The imperial authorities can judge from this how much Switzerland fears their decisions, precautionary measures, threats and troop formations. Of course, the "Empire" does not have the same military system as Switzerland, which has no standing army at all but within a week can raise 150,000 trained and battle-ready troops—that is twice as many as the classical land of the military parade with its celebrated Scharnhorstian system of military organisation.

Even though the conflicting rumours about the closing of the frontier are threatening to dry up as a source of merriment for the Swiss, we can still rely on the "Empire" for something to laugh at. Yesterday the German and especially the Frankfurt imperial newspapers presented us in all seriousness with yet another fat canard: the recent invasion of Lörrach by refugees—or rather bandits—and the battle in which four real live Badenese dragoons succumbed! There is no need to tell you that the whole ridiculous story, which provoked the greatest hilarity here, is pure mystification. However, I can tell you that the Empire citizens' fear of the couple of volunteers who may still be prowling about on the border makes a hilarious impression on every Swiss. The newly coined phrase, "Scared as six Empire citizens by one volunteer", has permanently entered the language. The latest article in the *Frankfurter Oberpostamts-Zeitung* about the continuing subversive activities of the refugees along the frontier has greatly helped to keep up the laughter at the expense of the Empire.[a] What important revelations Herr Schmerling's spies have made! Metternich [b] is in Muttenz and has been seen in Birsfeld, where Neff too is residing and writing and receiving many letters. Siegel and Katzenmaier are staying in Emmishofen — and they say the Empire need not tremble! Even more terrifying, the Swiss Government tolerates the presence in Dornach, close to the German frontier, of — "a few *canteen-keeper stragglers* from Lörrach and the vicinity" !!! In addition to that, "it is generally believed" that fresh "predatory incursions" *would* have taken place *if...* etc., etc. And was there not sniping across the Rhine from Gross-Laufenburg? When, how and by whom the imperial newspaper has of course no idea. In short, if the Empire is in such a bad state that it shakes to its foundations just because Metternich is seen in Birsfeld and a few canteen-keeper stragglers are wasting away in Dornach, Switzerland will certainly have no part in propping up such a rotten building! What is more, these confused reports strung together by Empire *mouchards*[c] contradict themselves in every line: for example, Metternich is said to be the *only* refugee in Muttenz, and yet three lines further on "there are reports from Muttenz that *they* (!!) are once more *arming* there" !! "They" — means Metternich, all on his own! And it is for this — for making them the laughing-stock of the whole world with such clumsy contradictions — that the imperial authorities pay their *mouchards* in Switzerland! *Trema, Bisanzio,*[d] Metternich has been seen in Birsfeld and "several canteen-keeper stragglers" in Dornach have sworn your destruction!

But let us leave the Empire aside. The Federal Council of War has been dissolved *pro forma*, but immediately reconstituted as a military commission, Herr Ochsenbein, as head of the Federal War Department, taking over as chairman. The *Berner Zeitung* sharply criticises this reconstitution or retention of the most cumbersome and costly item of the old Federal Government. In its opinion, the Military Council has never achieved anything but the appointment of a few aristocratic officers and the birth, after protracted labour

---

[a] "Die Fortdauer der Überstände an der Schweizergrenze", *Frankfurter Oberpostamts-Zeitung* No. 314 (supplement), November 24, 1848.— *Ed.*

[b] Germain Metternich.— *Ed.*

[c] Informers.— *Ed.*

[d] Tremble, Byzantium! (Donizetti, *Belisario.*) — *Ed.*

pains, of federal drill regulations [*Kamaschenreglement*]. These regulations proved so expensive that for the same price the whole army might have been equipped with puttees [*Kamaschen*] and boots. For the rest, the Military Council restricted itself to drawing its daily allowance of sixteen francs per head and because of all the difficulties and hair-splitting has long since given up all hope of ever achieving anything.

Besides the duel between Luvini and Berg, there were prospects of a second one—between Pioda and Michel from Graubünden—as a result of the Tessin debate in the National Council. Colonel Michel had expressed himself in an unbecoming manner and ended up angrily declaring Pioda to be a downright liar. Pioda answered extremely calmly and properly, but afterwards called the old federal war-horse to account. Thereupon Michel made statements that gave complete satisfaction to Pioda and his friends and with that the affair was allowed to rest.

Written by Engels on December 1, 1848

First published in the *Neue Rheinische Zeitung* No. 160, December 5, 1848

Printed according to the newspaper

Published in English for the first time

THE FEDERAL COUNCIL AND THE FOREIGN AMBASSADORS.—
THE FEDERAL COUNCIL IN TESSIN.—
CENTRALISATION OF POSTS.—
GERMAN ARMY COMMANDER'S APOLOGY

Berne, December 2. Since announcing the constitution of the new federal authorities and the simultaneous expiry of the 1815 treaty,[125] the Federal Council has already received the assurance from all the foreign ambassadors that they believed they could promise in advance their governments' recognition of the new authorities and the new Constitution. Only the British ambassador, Master[a] Peel, made no mention of recognition, and merely stated tersely that he had communicated the announcement to his Government. As Russia has no representative here, no statement has, of course, come from that power.

The Federal Council has appointed as its representatives in Tessin Colonel Stehlin from Basle and Colonel Briatte from Waadt, both of them members, and the latter President, of the Council of States. The radical Briatte will, it is hoped, act differently from Herr Escher and Herr Munzinger.[126] Incidentally, all Italian refugees of military age have been removed from Tessin into the interior of Switzerland.

Further, the Federal Council has started to apply the law on the centralisation of posts. Herr Laroche-Stehelin from Basle has been appointed acting Postmaster-General of Switzerland, and two commissions have been set up, the first to assess the materials to be taken over from the cantons and private individuals, the second to draft a law on the organisation of the Swiss posts.

The German army commander concerned has made the appropriate apology in a letter to the Federal Council[b]; he declares himself ready to give the satisfaction required, and announces that those concerned have already been handed over for punishment.

Written by Engels on December 2, 1848

First published in the *Neue Rheinische Zeitung* No. 161, December 6, 1848

Printed according to the newspaper

Published in English for the first time

---

[a] This word is given in English in the original.— *Ed.*
[b] See this volume, pp. 63 and 98.— *Ed.*

SWISS EVIDENCE
OF THE AUSTRIAN ARMY'S HEROIC DEEDS
IN VIENNA

Cologne, December 5. While the Augsburg *Allgemeine Zeitung* and other bought newspapers exalt a Windischgrätz and a Jellachich to heaven for restoring law and order, crown the valiant Austrian troops with laurels and never tire of recounting the horrors of the democratic reign of terror, a new source of information has suddenly appeared in the Swiss press to serve the chronicling of the latest Viennese events. This source consists of the Swiss citizens who with difficulty and in mortal danger, and after maltreatment, escaped from the myrmidons of "order", and having returned to their homeland, publish their experiences during the "days of terror" and the "war of order". And indeed not raging "proletarians", but big capitalists, people who owned enormous factories in Vienna, most trustworthy bourgeois of conservative convictions — and a Swiss conservative is well known to be the equivalent of a German "wailer" [127] raised to the second power — and their reports are not appearing in radical scandal sheets but in the most serious conservative newspapers. We have taken the following details from one such description in the *Basler Intelligenzblatt*:

Herr *Specker* of St. Gallen was director of a big machine factory which stood quite isolated on the Tabor, the extreme customs boundary of Vienna. He, like his workers and foremen, all of them Swiss, had neither taken part in the fighting, nor had weapons in the house. Only 15 workers had remained on duty with the factory's fire-pump set up in the yard. At the approach of the military, General *Wyss*, patrician of Berne and chief of the Austrian General Staff, gave Herr Specker his word of honour that nothing would happen to his building if he had no weapons and if no shots were fired from the factory. The house was searched by the troops and nothing was found. In spite of this another detachment of riflemen asserted that shots had been fired from the house (very understandably, as they had permission to loot any house from which shots were fired). The "Swiss dogs", who had trusted the word of their compatriot General Wyss so implicitly that they had even left their wives and children in the factory, were most brutally mishandled by these soldiers, and only saved by the intervention of another officer. The latter took them to the guardroom. A neighbour pointed at one of the workers passing by and said: "He, too, was at the dismantling of the Tabor bridge." Immediately, without being allowed to say a word, the worker was put up against a wall and shot. In the guardroom guns were pointed at the "Swiss dogs" and only a loaded pistol brought out by the officer held the soldiers back. Director Specker was stood up against the wall, three soldiers set on him, one cocked his gun, put the barrel to Specker's mouth and fiddled about with the trigger. One of the officers took out his watch and said: "You have a quarter of an hour, Swiss dog, then you'll be shot, so say your prayers!" Before the time was up, the officer who had previously saved them returned, and took him to General Wyss, who reproached him for "breaking his word"! The general obstinately maintained that shots had been fired from the factory, although Herr Specker proved that this was physically impossible. At last he obtained a pass for himself and his people to Florisdorf. On returning to the factory they found everything in wrack and ruin and looted bare. Herr Specker's family had been chased around the house with rifle-shots; the book-keeper, a Swiss, riddled with bullets, rolled in his death throes in the garden and anyone who approached him was shot at, so that the unfortunate man was left till late at night to lie there and die. His name was *Kunz.* In the end the survivors succeeded in getting away safely to Florisdorf.

The machine manufacturer Bollinger, also a Swiss, who made himself famous by his work on the spire of St. Stephen's, succeeded with the help of fire-pumps in protecting his factory from being burned down. But here too the Austrians broke in under the false pretence that shots had been fired from the factory, and they plundered and demolished the whole building, set fire to it, and stabbed Bollinger's brother to death as he tried to escape from the flames. Another Swiss resident in Vienna, Madame Bodener, had her child shot in her arms by the Croats.

The report holds out prospects of still further information about the heroic deeds of the brave Austrian army as soon as other Swiss citizens return. At the same time, it depicts in most moving terms the assurance and calm of the armed proletarians, and the courteousness and decency with which the Swiss were treated during the so-called reign of terror of the Vienna proletariat and students.

We repeat: the originators of these reports are not radicals, not proletarians and malcontents, but big capitalists and true full-blooded Swiss aristocrats. Will the Augsburg *Allgemeine Zeitung* not let its various correspondents $\zeta\rho$, MW, ♯, △ , and others in Vienna collect information as to whether this is not word for word true? We have given names, locality, and all other details as exactly as the paper can wish. But it will of course be wary.

Written by Engels on December 5, 1848   Printed according to the newspaper

First published in the *Neue Rheinische Zeitung* No. 161, December 6, 1848   Published in English for the first time

[THE FRENCH WORKING CLASS AND THE PRESIDENTIAL ELECTIONS][128]

Paris. Raspail or Ledru-Rollin? Socialist or Montagnard? That is the question which is now splitting the party of the red republic into two hostile camps.[129]

What is this dispute really all about?

Ask the journals of the Montagnards, the *Réforme*, the *Révolution*, and they will tell you that they themselves cannot make it out; that the socialists have drawn up the same programme,[a] word for word, as the Mountain,[b] a programme of permanent revolution, of progressive taxes and death duties, and of organisation of labour; that there is no dispute on principles, and that the whole untimely scandal has been instigated by a few jealous and ambitious men who are deceiving the "religion and the good faith" of the people and out of egotism casting suspicion on the men of the people's party.

Ask the journal of the socialists, the *Peuple*, and you will be answered with bitter expletives about the ignorance and empty-headedness of the Montagnards, with endless legal, moral and economic treatises, and finally with the mysterious hint that at bottom it is all about Citizen Proudhon's new panacea, which they say is going to outdo the old socialist phrases of Louis Blanc's school.[c]

---

[a] A reference to "Manifeste électoral du Peuple", *Le Peuple* No. 4, November 8-15, 1848.— *Ed.*

[b] A reference to "Declaration au peuple", *La Réforme* No. 310, November 9, 1848.— *Ed.*

[c] [P.-J. Proudhon,] "Argument à la Montagne", *Le Peuple* No. 5, November 15-21, 1848.— *Ed.*

Finally, ask the socialist workers, and they will answer you shortly: Ce sont des *bourgeois*, les montagnards.[a]

Once again, the only ones who hit the nail on the head are the workers. They will have nothing to do with the Mountain because the Mountain consists only of *bourgeois*.

The socialist-democratic party, even before February, consisted of two different factions; first, of the spokesmen, deputies, writers, lawyers etc., with their not inconsiderable train of petty bourgeois who formed the party of the *Réforme* proper; secondly, of the mass of Paris workers, who were not at all unconditional followers of the former, but, on the contrary, were very distrustful allies, and adhered more closely to them or moved farther away from them, according to whether the *Réforme* people acted with more resolution or with more vacillation. In the last months of the monarchy the *Réforme* acted with great resolution in consequence of its polemic with the *National,* and the relationship between it and the workers was very close.

The *Réforme* people therefore also entered the Provisional Government as representatives of the proletariat.

There is no need to go into details here about how they were in the minority in the Provisional Government and hence, incapable of asserting the workers' interests, only served the pure republicans[130] to put off the workers until the pure republicans had re-organised public power, which was now *their* power over against the workers; how Ledru-Rollin, the leader of the *Réforme* party, was persuaded by Lamartine's phrases of self-sacrifice and by the lure of power to enter the Executive Commission[131]; how he thereby split and weakened the revolutionary party, partially putting it at the disposal of the Government, and so caused the failure of the insurrections of May and June, nay, even fought against them himself. The facts are still too fresh in the memory.

Enough said; after the June insurrection, after the overthrow of the Executive Commission and the rise of the pure republicans to exclusive domination[132] in the person of Cavaignac, the party of the *Réforme,* of the democratic-socialist petty bourgeoisie, lost all illusions about the development of the Republic. It was pushed into opposition, it was free again, acted again as opposition and resumed its old connections with the workers.

As long as no important questions were raised, as long as it was only a question of exposing the cowardly, treacherous and reaction-

---

[a] They are *bourgeois,* those Montagnards.— *Ed.*

ary policy of Cavaignac, so long the workers could put up with being represented in the press by the *Réforme* and the *Révolution démocratique et sociale*. The *Vraie République* and the real working-class papers had anyway already been suppressed by the state of siege, by tendentious trials and surety payments. They could equally well put up with being represented in the National Assembly by the Mountain. Raspail, Barbès and Albert were under arrest, Louis Blanc and Caussidière had had to flee. The clubs were in part closed, in part under strict supervision, and the old laws against freedom of speech continued and still continue in operation. Enough examples of how these laws were used against the workers were given in the newspapers every day. The workers, faced with the impossibility of having their own representatives speak, had again to be content with those who had represented them before February, with the radical petty bourgeois and their spokesmen.

Now the question of the Presidency arises. There are three candidates: Cavaignac, Louis Napoleon and Ledru-Rollin. For the workers Cavaignac was out of the question. The man who shot them down in June with grape-shot and incendiary rockets could only count on their hatred. Louis Bonaparte? They could only vote for him out of irony, to raise him by the ballot today and overthrow him again by force of arms tomorrow, and with him the honourable, "pure" bourgeois republic. And finally, Ledru-Rollin, who recommended himself to the workers as the only red, socialist-democratic candidate.

Really, after the experiences of the Provisional Government, of May 15 and June 24, could the workers be expected once again to give a vote of confidence to the radical petty bourgeoisie and Ledru-Rollin? To the same people who on February 25, when the armed proletariat ruled Paris, when they could have obtained everything, had only lofty, reassuring phrases instead of revolutionary action, only promises and vain hopes instead of quick and decisive measures, only the flag, the fine phrases and the styles of 1793, instead of the energy of 1793? To the same people who shouted with Lamartine and Marrast: First and foremost the *bourgeois* must be *reassured*, and who in doing so forgot to carry on the revolution? To the same people who on May 15 were undecided and on June 23 had artillery fetched from Vincennes and battalions from Orléans and Bourges?

And yet, the people might have voted for Ledru-Rollin so as not to split the votes. But then came his speech of November 25 against Cavaignac in which he once again took the side of the victors, reproached Cavaignac for not having acted with sufficient energy against the revolution, for not having had more battalions in readiness against the workers.

This speech deprived Ledru-Rollin completely of all credit with the workers. Even now, after five months, after having had to suffer all the consequences of the June battle so to speak on his own body, even now he still sides with the victors against the vanquished, he is proud of having demanded more battalions against the insurgents than Cavaignac could supply!

And the man who considers the June fighters were not vanquished quickly enough wants to be the head of the party which has entered upon the heritage of the June martyrs?

After that speech the candidature of Ledru-Rollin was lost for the Paris workers. The opposing candidature of Raspail, already put forward earlier and already having earlier enjoyed the sympathy of the workers, was victorious in Paris. If the ballot papers of Paris had decided, Raspail would now be President of the Republic.

The workers know very well that Ledru-Rollin is not yet played out, that he still can and will render great service to the radical party. But he has forfeited the confidence of the workers. For his weakness, his petty vanity, his dependence on high-sounding phrases, through which even Lamartine mastered him, *they*, the workers, have had to suffer. No service he can render will make them forget that. The workers will always know that when Ledru-Rollin becomes energetic again, his energy will only be that of the armed workers standing behind him and driving him on.

By giving Ledru-Rollin a no-confidence vote, the workers also gave a no-confidence vote to the whole of the radical petty bourgeoisie. The indecision, the dependence on the traditional phrases of *dévoûment*[a] etc., the forgetting of revolutionary action over revolutionary reminiscences, are all qualities which Ledru-Rollin shares with the class he represents.

The radical petty bourgeois are only socialistic because they clearly see before their eyes their ruin, their transition into the proletariat. They are enthusiastic for the organisation of labour and revolution in the relationship between capital and labour not as petty bourgeois, as possessors of a little capital, but as future proletarians. Give them political domination, and they will soon forget the organisation of labour. Political domination gives them, of course, at least in the intoxication of the first moment, the prospect of the acquisition of capital, of salvation from threatening ruin. Only when the armed proletarians stand behind them with bayonets at the ready, only then

---

[a] Devotedness.—*Ed.*

will they remember their allies of yesterday. That is how they acted in February and March, and Ledru-Rollin, as their leader, was the first to act like that. If they are now disappointed, does that alter the workers' attitude to them? If they come back in sackcloth and ashes, does that entitle them to demand that the workers now, under quite different circumstances, shall fall into the trap again?

By voting not for Ledru-Rollin but for Raspail, the workers give them to understand that they will not do so, that they know how they stand in relation to the radical petty bourgeoisie.

But Raspail—what services has Raspail rendered the workers? How can *he* be placed in opposition to Ledru-Rollin as a socialist *par excellence*?

The people know full well that Raspail is no official socialist, no system-maker by profession. The people want none of the official socialists and system-makers, they are fed up with them. Otherwise, Citizen Proudhon would be their candidate, and not the hot-blooded Raspail.

But the people have a good memory and are not nearly so ungrateful as it pleases certain unappreciated reactionary celebrities, in their modesty, to maintain. The people still remember very well that Raspail was the first to reproach the Provisional Government for its inactivity, for its preoccupation with mere republican stuff and nonsense. The people have not yet forgotten the *Ami du Peuple, par le citoyen*[a] Raspail, and since Raspail was the first to have the courage—and it did require courage—to speak out in revolutionary fashion against the Provisional Government, and since Raspail represents not any particular socialist *couleur*, but only the social *revolution*, the people of Paris vote for Raspail.

It is not at all a question of a few petty measures solemnly proclaimed in the manifesto of the Mountain as the salvation of the world. It is a question of the social revolution which will give the French people something very different from these incoherent, already stale phrases. It is a question of the energy to carry through this revolution. It is a question whether the petty bourgeoisie will have this energy, after it already once proved powerless. And the proletariat of Paris, by voting for Raspail, replies "*No!*"

Hence the amazement of the *Réforme* and the *Révolution* that one can accept their phrases and yet not vote for Ledru-Rollin, although he proclaims these phrases. These worthy papers, which think of themselves as working-class papers and yet are now more

---

[a] By Citizen.—*Ed.*

than ever before papers of the petty bourgeoisie, cannot, of course, realise that the same demand which on the lips of the workers is revolutionary, is on *their* lips a mere phrase. Otherwise they would not have their own illusions.

And Citizen Proudhon and his *Peuple?* More of them tomorrow.

Written by Engels at the beginning of December 1848

Printed according to the manuscript

First published, in German, in: Marx/Engels, *Gesamtausgabe*, Abt. 1, Bd. 7, 1935

Published in English for the first time

[PROUDHON]

Paris. Yesterday we spoke of the Montagnards and the socialists, of the candidatures of Ledru-Rollin and of Raspail, of the *Réforme* and the *Peuple* of Citizen Proudhon. We promised to return to Proudhon.

Who is Citizen Proudhon?

Citizen Proudhon is a peasant from the Franche-Comté who has done a variety of jobs and engaged in a variety of studies. He first drew public attention to himself by a pamphlet published in 1842: *What Is Property?*[a] The reply was: "Property is theft."

The surprising repartee startled the French. The Government of Louis Philippe, the austere Guizot, who has no sense of humour, was narrow-minded enough to take Proudhon to court. But in vain. In the case of such a piquant paradox any French jury can be relied on for acquittal. And so it came to pass. The Government disgraced itself and Proudhon became a famous man.

As to the book itself, it corresponded throughout to the above résumé. Every chapter was summed up in a curious paradox in a manner which is new to the French.

For the rest, it contained partly legal and moral, partly economic and moral treatises, each of which sought to prove that property amounts to a contradiction. As to the legal points, these can be admitted, inasmuch as nothing is easier than to prove that the whole of jurisprudence amounts to nothing but contradictions. As to the economic treatises, they contain little that is new, and what is new in them is based on wrong calculations. The rule of three is everywhere most disgracefully mishandled.

---

[a] P.-J. Proudhon, *Qu'est-ce que la propriété?—Ed.*

The French, however, were unable to cope with the book. For the jurists it was too economistic, for the economists too legalistic and for both too moralistic. *Après tout, c'est un ouvrage remarquable,*[a] they said finally.

But Proudhon was hankering after greater triumphs. After various long-forgotten minor writings, there appeared at last in 1846 his *Philosophie de la misère,* in two enormous tomes. In this work, which was to establish his fame for ever, Proudhon applied a badly mishandled Hegelian philosophical method to a curiously misunderstood political economy and sought by all kinds of transcendental leaps to found a new socialist system of a free association of workers. This system was so new that in England, under the name of Equitable Labour Exchange Bazaars or Offices,[133] it had already gone bankrupt ten times ten years earlier in ten different towns.

This ponderous, pseudo-learned, bulky work, in which eventually not only all previous economists but all previous socialists too were told the rudest things, made absolutely no impression on the easy-going French. This way of speaking and reasoning was new to them and much less to their taste than the curious paradoxes of Proudhon's earlier work. Similar paradoxes were not lacking here either, it is true (as when Proudhon declared himself quite seriously a "personal enemy of Jehovah"[b]), but they were, so to speak, buried under the allegedly dialectical lumber. The French again said: *C'est un ouvrage remarquable,* and put it aside. In Germany, the work was of course received with great reverence.

Marx at the time issued a pamphlet in reply, which was as witty as it was thorough (*Misère de la philosophie. Réponse à la Philosophie de la misère de M. Proudhon.* Par Karl Marx, Bruxelles et Paris, 1847), and which in thought and language is a thousand times more French than Proudhon's pretentious monstrosity.

As to the real content of Proudhon's two works in criticism of the existing social relationships, one can, after reading them both, say with a clear conscience that it amounts to zero.

As to his proposals for social reforms, they have, as already mentioned, the advantage of having been brilliantly proved in England a long time ago by multiple bankruptcy.

That was Proudhon before the revolution. While he was still engaged in efforts to bring out a daily newspaper, *Le Représentant du Peuple,* without capital but by means of a calculation unequalled in its contempt for the rule of three, the Paris workers be-

---

[a] After all, it is a remarkable work.— *Ed.*
[b] Heinrich Heine, *Deutschland. Ein Wintermärchen,* Caput XXIII.— *Ed.*

stirred themselves, chased out Louis Philippe and founded the
Republic.

Proudhon first became a "citizen" by virtue of the Republic;
afterwards by virtue of the Paris workers' vote, given on the strength
of his honest socialist name, he became a representative of the
people.

So the revolution flung Citizen Proudhon out of theory into
practice, out of his sulking corner into the forum. How did this
obstinate, high-handed, self-taught man, who treats all previous
authorities — jurists, scholars, economists and socialists — with equal
contempt, who declares all previous history to be drivel and
introduced himself, so to speak, as the new Messiah; how did he
behave now that he himself was to help make history?

We must say to his credit that he began by taking his seat on the
extreme Left, among the same socialists, and voting with the same
socialists whom he so deeply despised and had so vehemently
attacked as ignorant, arrogant dolts.

It is put about, of course, that in the party meetings of the
Mountain he renewed his old violent attacks on his former
opponents with fresh vehemence, that he declared them one and all
to be ignoramuses and phrase-mongers who did not understand the
ABC of what they were talking about.

We readily believe it. We even readily believe that the economic
paradoxes which Proudhon uttered with all the dry passion and
confidence of a doctrinaire caused no small embarrassment to
Messieurs les Montagnards. Very few among them are theoreticians of
economics and they rely more or less on little Louis Blanc; and little
Louis Blanc, though a much more significant brain than the infallible
Proudhon, is all the same too intuitive a nature to be able to cope
with his learned economic pretensions, odd transcendence and
seemingly mathematical logic. Moreover, Louis Blanc soon had to
flee, and his flock, helpless in the field of economics, remained
unprotected, exposed to the merciless claws of the wolf Proudhon.

We need hardly repeat that in spite of all these triumphs
Proudhon is still an extremely weak economist. Only his weakness
does not happen to lie within the grasp of the mass of French
socialists.

Proudhon won the greatest triumph of his life on the rostrum of
the National Assembly. On one occasion, I do not remember which,
he took the floor and angered the bourgeois of the Assembly for an
hour and a half with an endless string of truly Proudhonist
paradoxes, each crazier than the other, but all calculated to shock the
listeners most rudely in their dearest and most sacred feelings. And

all this was delivered with his dry academic indifference, in a toneless, academic Franche-Comté dialect, in the driest, most imperturbable style in the world — the effect, the St. Vitus's dance of the enraged bourgeois, was not at all bad.[134]

But this was the highlight of Proudhon's public activity. In the meantime he continued to belabour the workers, both through the *Représentant du Peuple* — which, after bitter experiences with the rule of three, had gradually materialised and soon was transformed into the *Peuple* pure and simple — as well as in the clubs, in favour of his theory of happiness for all. He was not without success. *On ne le comprend pas*, the workers said, *mais c'est un homme remarquable.*[a]

Written by Engels at the beginning of December 1848

First published, in German, in: Marx/Engels, *Gesamtausgabe*, Abt. 1, Bd. 7, 1935

Printed according to the manuscript

Published in English for the first time

---

[a] You can't understand him, but he is a remarkable man.—*Ed.*

HERR RAUMER IS STILL ALIVE

Cologne, December 6. Recently we mentioned the addresses of loyalty sent by the Halle and Berlin professors to the King.[a] Today we have to announce that Herr von Raumer, imperial envoy *in partibus*,[b] who at the present time is to be found in the antechambers of Bastide and Cavaignac, has fully joined in the professors' ignominy by stating his agreement with those addresses. As a matter of fact, nothing else was to be expected of an imperial envoy like Herr Raumer. But there seems to be yet another reason for his statement. For months past Herr Raumer has been entirely forgotten in Germany. In his longing to be rescued somehow from that oblivion, he eagerly seized the opportunity offered him by his fellow bonzes in Berlin and promptly published the above-mentioned statement. This production of Raumer's is to be found in the latest issue of the *Preussischer Staats-Anzeiger*.[c]

Written by Marx on December 6, 1848

First published in the *Neue Rheinische Zeitung* No. 162, December 7, 1848

Printed according to the newspaper

Published in English for the first time

---

[a] See this volume, pp. 106-07.— *Ed.*
[b] See Note 95.— *Ed.*
[c] Issue No. 215, December 5, 1848.— *Ed.*

[SECOND STAGE OF THE COUNTER-REVOLUTION]

Cologne, December 6. The counter-revolution has reached its second stage. The National Assembly has been dissolved. An imposed Constitution has been proclaimed by the "grace of the All-Highest" without more ado.[135]

All the hypocrisy over the "agreement"[136] which has been going on since May has been stripped of its last mask.

The March revolution is declared null and void and royal power "by the grace of God" celebrates its triumph.

The camarilla, the junkers, the bureaucracy, and the entire reaction, with and without uniform, are jubilant because the stupid people is at last to be driven back into the stall of the "Christian-Germanic" state.

Written by Marx on December 6, 1848

First published in the *Neue Rheinische Zeitung* No. 162 (special edition), December 7, 1848

Printed according to the newspaper

Published in English for the first time

THE COUP D'ÉTAT
OF THE COUNTER-REVOLUTION [137]

Cologne, December 7. *The National Assembly has been dissolved. The representatives of the people have been dispersed "by the grace of God".*

The reason given by the Government for this act of violence adds bitter contempt to the coup d'état carried through 'with such insolence.[138]

The National Assembly now reaps the fruits of its chronic weakness and cowardice. For months it allowed the conspiracy against the people to carry on its work unmolested, to grow strong and powerful, and hence has now become its first victim.

The people, too, is now suffering for its sins, committed out of magnanimity, or rather stupidity, in March and again in April and May, and finally through so-called passive resistance. It has now been taught a lesson which it will probably put to profit. Its next victory will put an end to "agreement" and to all other phrases and hypocrisies.

Written by Marx on December 7, 1848

First published in the *Neue Rheinische Zeitung* No. 163, December 8, 1848

Printed according to the newspaper

MEASURES CONCERNING THE GERMAN REFUGEES

Berne, December 5. The Federal Council has now taken measures to deal with the German refugees, partly in order to deprive the imperial authority of the pretext for hostile measures, partly to show its impartiality towards Tessin and to carry through in practice also in the northern cantons the triumph of the policy of strict neutrality which was won in the Tessin debate.[a] The policy of Furrer-Munzinger-Ochsenbein is being pursued everywhere. A circular of the Federal Council addressed to the border cantons concerned repeats the basic principles expressed by the *Vorort*, and again insists on the internment of all refugees who took part in the Struve campaign[139]; and in order to give weight to this demand the President of the Federal Assembly, Dr. Steiger, already left yesterday as representative of the Confederation to visit the northern cantons.

There can be no objection to the measure in itself. Nobody will blame Switzerland for not wanting to get involved in unpleasantness because of a few volunteer insurgents who are thirsting for adventure and heartily bored in their exile. But why then the previous bold talk against Germany, the positive assurance that the Swiss had done their duty, when it is now indirectly admitted that they did not do it, when they are only now seeking to satisfy themselves how far the cantons have obeyed the orders of the *Vorort*?— It is not to be denied that this decision of the Federal Council, an act of justice towards Tessin, is a complete *démenti* of the last official act of the *Vorort*, and though the Note[b] received unanimous applause, this beginning of disavowal in the Note will cause little joy.

---

[a] See this volume, pp. 61-62 and 112.— *Ed.*

[b] Sent to the Imperial Government on November 4, 1848. See this volume, pp. 67-68.— *Ed.*

Nothing has been heard about the closing of the German frontier, except that the whole of Swabia is protesting against it. Whether it will take place or not is again left to God to decide. In any case, the Federal Council has decided for the present not to range any troops opposite the imperial division.

The Federal Military Council has now concluded its current business and has been definitely disbanded. In its place there will be a War Office which Ochsenbein, as head of the Military Department, will organise and direct.

The new Spanish ambassador, Herr Zayas, who arrived here a few days ago with credentials for the *Vorort,* has now presented these to the Vice-President of the Federal Council, Herr Druey, and thereby made immediate contact with the new authorities.

The press is much incensed over the treatment of the Swiss in Vienna, of which I recently gave you some examples.[a] It insists on the Federal Council demanding satisfaction and compensation from Austria. In particular the behaviour of the Bernese General Wyss arouses general indignation here. This general's brother is a master builder here in Berne.

Written by Engels on December 5, 1848

First published in the *Neue Rheinische Zeitung* No. 165, December 10, 1848

Printed according to the newspaper

Published in English for the first time

---

[a] See this volume, pp. 120-22.— *Ed.*

THE NATIONAL COUNCIL

[*Neue Rheinische Zeitung* No. 165, December 10, 1848]

, *Berne*, December 6. Who in this period of European storms is concerned about Switzerland? Certainly almost no one apart from the imperial authority, which suspects there is a volunteer insurgent lying in ambush behind every bush on the left bank of the Rhine from Constance to Basle. And yet Switzerland is an important neighbour for us. Today constitutional Belgium is the official model state,[a] but who in these stormy days will guarantee us that tomorrow a republican Switzerland will not be an official model state? Already I know more than one *farouche*[b] republican who wishes nothing more than to transfer the Swiss political system with its large and small councils—federal, national, council of states, and other councils—across the Rhine, i. e. to transform Germany into a large-scale Switzerland, and then lead a calm and peaceful life in all godliness and honour as a member of the Great Council or a *Landammann*[c] of the Baden, Hesse or Nassau canton.

At any rate, therefore, we Germans should be concerned about Switzerland, and what the Swiss think, say and do may very soon be held up to us as a model. Hence it can do no harm if in advance we acquaint ourselves to some extent with the kind of customs and people the twenty-two cantons of the "Confederation" have produced in their Federative Republic.

It is reasonable for us first of all to consider the cream of Swiss society, the men whom the Swiss people themselves have appointed as their representatives; I am referring to the National Council which meets in the Town Hall in Berne.

---

[a] See present edition, Vol. 7, pp. 333-36 and 482-84.— *Ed.*
[b] Fierce.— *Ed.*
[c] President of a canton.— *Ed.*

Anyone who comes to the public gallery of the National Council is bound to be surprised at the variety of figures the Swiss people has sent to Berne to deliberate on matters common to the whole nation. One who has not already seen a good deal of Switzerland will hardly understand how a small country of a few hundred square miles and of less than two and a half million inhabitants can produce such a colourful assembly. But it is not at all surprising. Switzerland is a country in which four different languages are spoken—German, French, Italian (or rather Lombardian) and Romansh—and which combines all stages of culture, from the most advanced machine industry down to the most unadulterated pastoral life. The Swiss National Council combines the cream of all these nationalities and stages of culture and therefore looks anything but national.

There cannot be any question of definite seats, of separate parties in this semi-patriarchal assembly. The radicals have made a feeble attempt to seat themselves on the extreme left, but they do not seem to have been successful. Each member sits where he likes and often changes his place three or four times during one sitting. But most members have certain favourite seats which finally they always occupy, so that after all the assembly is divided into two rather sharply separated parts. On the three front semicircular benches one sees men with sharply defined features, many with beards, with well-kept hair and modern clothes of Parisian cut. Seated here are the representatives of French and Italian Switzerland, or the "Welch" members as they are called here; on these benches it is rare for anything but French to be spoken. But behind the Welch members sits a curiously motley society. True, no peasants in Swiss national costumes are to be seen; on the contrary, these are all people whose clothing bears the stamp of a certain degree of civilisation; here and there one even sees a more or less modern frock-coat, the owner usually possessing decorous features; then half a dozen Swiss officer types in civilian dress, looking very much alike, more solemn than military, their faces and clothing somewhat old-fashioned and to some extent reminiscent of Ajax in *Troilus and Cressida*[a]; lastly the bulk of the assembly, consisting of more or less elderly, old-fashioned gentlemen with features and costumes that defy description, each one different, each one a distinct type and in the main also a type for caricature. All varieties of the petty bourgeois, the *campagnard endimanché*,[b] and the oligarchy of the cantons are here represented, but all equally respectable, all terribly serious, all

---

[a] A drama by Shakespeare.—*Ed.*
[b] Peasant in his Sunday best.—*Ed.*

wearing equally heavy silver-rimmed spectacles. These are the representatives of German Switzerland, and this bulk of the assembly is sent by the smaller cantons and outlying areas of the larger ones.

The presidential chair facing this assembly is occupied by the famous Dr. Robert Steiger from Lucerne, who a few years ago was sentenced to death under the Siegwart-Müller administration, and is now the President of the Swiss Federal Assembly. Steiger is a small thickset man with clear-cut features, to which his grey hair, brown moustache, and even the inevitable silver-rimmed spectacles, provide a not unpleasant background. He carries out his duties with great calm and perhaps somewhat excessive restraint.

The discussion corresponds to the physiognomy. Only the Welch members, and not even all of them, speak a fully civilised, rhetorical form of language. The Bernese, who among the German Swiss have most of all adopted Romance customs, most closely resemble them. Some temperamental fire, at least, is still to be found among them. The Zurichers, these sons of the Swiss Athens, speak with the gravity and precision appropriate to someone halfway between a professor and a factory foreman, but always "educatedly". The officers speak with solemn slowness, without much skill or content, but always decisively as though their battalion stood behind them ready for action. Finally, the main body of the assembly provides orators who are more or less well-meaning, cautious and conscientious, and who weigh up the arguments on one side and the other but nevertheless in the end always come down on the side of their cantonal interests; almost all of them speak very clumsily and in some places according to their own rules of grammar. When the discussion turns on a question of cost, it always starts from them, particularly from the representatives of the *Ur*-cantons. In this respect the Uri canton has already a well-deserved reputation in both Councils.

Consequently, on the whole the discussion is dull, calm, mediocre. The National Council has very few talented orators who would be successful also in larger assemblies; so far I know only of two, Luvini and Dufour, and perhaps Eytel. True, I have not yet heard several of the more influential members; but neither their successes in the assembly nor the newspaper reports of their speeches are such as to justify great expectations. Only Neuhaus is said to be a brilliant orator. How indeed could oratorical ability develop in assemblies which represent at most a few hundred thousand people and have to concern themselves with the most petty local interests? At any rate, the defunct Diet[140] was a diplomatic rather than a legislative assembly; in it one could learn how to distort instructions and find a plausible way out of a situation, but not how to rouse an assembly and dominate it. Hence the speeches of the National Council members are mostly limited to motives for voting, with every speaker setting out the facts which induce him to vote in this way or that, and so without the slightest embarrassment he calmly repeats again what has already been repeated *ad nauseam* by previous speakers. Especially the speeches of the bulk of the representatives display this patriarchal sincerity. And once one of these gentlemen has the floor, as a matter of course he uses the opportunity also to voice his opinion at length on all the incidental points raised in the discussion, although they may have been disposed of long ago. Amidst this friendly chatter of the decent old fellows, a few main speeches laboriously keep the threads of the discussion together, and when the sitting ends one confesses to have seldom heard anything more boring. Philistinism, which lends a certain originality to the *physique*[a] of the assembly because it is rarely seen in this classical form, here too remains *au moral*[b] flat and tedious. There is little passion and no question at all of wit. Luvini is the only one who speaks with rousing, forceful passion, Dufour the only one who impresses by genuinely French clarity and precision. Frey from the Basle canton represents humour, which at times Colonel Bernold also attempts with some success. The French Swiss totally lack French wit. Throughout the existence of the Alps and the Jura not a single tolerable pun has been produced on their slopes, nor any quick, trenchant repartee heard there. The inhabitant of French Switzerland is not merely *sérieux*, he is *grave*.

The discussion which I will describe in some detail here concerns the Tessin affair and the Italian refugees in Tessin.[c] The circumstances are well known: the so-called intrigues of the Italian refugees in Tessin gave Radetzky the pretext for taking unpleasant measures; the *Vorort* Berne sent to Tessin federal representatives with extended powers[d] and also a brigade of troops; the uprising in Veltlin and in Valle Intelvi prompted a number of refugees to return to Lombardy, which they succeeded in doing in spite of the vigilance of the Swiss frontier posts; they crossed the frontier, without arms however, took part in the uprising and after the defeat of the insurgents, again unarmed, returned from Valle Intelvi to the Tessin area, and from there they were deported by the Tessin Government. Meanwhile Radetzky intensified his reprisals in the frontier area and redoubled his protests to the federal representatives.

---

[a] Outward appearance.—*Ed.*
[b] In essence.—*Ed.*
[c] See this volume, pp. 59-60, 61-62 and 112.— *Ed.*
[d] Escher and Munzinger.— *Ed.*

The latter demanded the deportation of all refugees without distinction; the Tessin Government refused; the *Vorort* confirmed the measure of the representatives; the Tessin Government appealed to the Federal Assembly, which in the meantime had begun its session. The National Council had to decide on this appeal and on the factual assertions put forward by both sides, concerning especially the behaviour of the Tessiners towards the representatives and the Swiss troops.

The majority of the commission appointed on this matter proposed the deportation of *all* the Italian refugees from Tessin, their internment in the interior of Switzerland, a ban on the entry of new refugees into Tessin, and in general that the measures taken by the *Vorort* should be confirmed and adhered to. The report of the commission was given by Herr Kasimir Pfyffer from Lucerne. But long before I had made my way to the public gallery through the crowded audience, Herr Pfyffer ended his rather dry report, and Herr Pioda was given the floor.[a]

[*Neue Rheinische Zeitung* No. 165, December 10, 1848, second edition]

Herr Pioda, Secretary of State in Tessin, who was the sole representative of the minority in the commission, proposed the deportation of only those refugees who had taken part in the last uprising and against whom, therefore, there were positive grounds for action to be taken. Herr Pioda, a major and battalion commander during the war against the Sonderbund,[141] despite his mild, blonde appearance, displayed great courage at the time at Airolo, and held his ground for a week against more numerous, better-trained and better-armed enemy troops which, in addition, had occupied a more advantageous position. Pioda's speech is as mild and full of feeling as his outward appearance. Since he speaks French perfectly, both as regards accent and fluency, I would at first have taken him for a French Swiss and was astonished to learn that he was an Italian. However, when he came to speak of the reproaches levelled against the Tessiners, when in contrast to these reproaches he described the actions of the Swiss troops, who behaved almost as if they were in enemy country, when he began to get heated, he revealed if not passion, at any rate that lively, thoroughly Italian eloquence which resorts at times to antiquated forms and at others to a certain modern, sometimes exaggerated, magniloquence. To his credit I

---

[a] The newspaper here has an editorial note: "To be continued."—*Ed.*

must say that in this last respect he knew how to keep within bounds, and these passages in his speech had a very good effect. On the whole, however, his speech was too long and too emotional. The German Swiss possess Horace's *aes triplex*,[a] and all the fine phrases, all the noble sentiments of the good Pioda made no impression on their breasts, which are as hard as they are broad.

The next to speak was Herr Doctor Alfred Escher from Zurich. *A la bonne heure*[b]—he is a man *comme il en faut pour la Suisse*.[c] Herr Doctor Escher, federal representative in Tessin, Vice-President of the National Council, the son—if I am not mistaken—of the well-known machine-builder and engineer Escher who canalised the Linth and founded a huge engineering works near Zurich. Herr Doctor Escher is not so much a Zuricher as a "Swiss Athenian". His frock-coat and waistcoat have been made by the best *marchand tailleur*[d] in Zurich; one sees the praiseworthy and partly successful effort to meet the demands of the Paris fashion magazine; but one sees also the influence of the town's original sin, which compelled the cutter to go back to the age-old, customary, petty-bourgeois lines. Like the frock-coat, so the man. The fair hair is very carefully cut, but in a horribly bourgeois manner, as also the beard—for our Swiss Alcibiades wears a beard, of course, a caprice of the Zuricher from a "good family" that strongly reminds one of the first Alcibiades. When Herr Doctor Escher takes the presidential chair to replace Steiger for a short time, he carries out this manoeuvre with a mixture of dignity and elegant nonchalance of which M. Marrast could be envious. One sees clearly that he is taking advantage of those few moments in the soft upholstery of the arm-chair to rest his back, weary from sitting on a hard bench. In a word, Herr Escher is as elegant as it is only possible to be in the Swiss Athens; moreover, he is wealthy, handsome, strongly built, and not more than 33 years old. The ladies of Berne need to beware of this dangerous Alcibiades of Zurich.

Herr Escher, in addition, speaks very fluently and in such good German as is only possible for a Swiss Athenian: an Attic idiom with a Doric accent, but without grammatical mistakes, and not every member of the National Council from German Switzerland is capable of that; like all the Swiss he speaks with the most terrifying solemnity. If Herr Escher were 70 years of age he could not have

---

[a] "*Illi robur et aes triplex circa pectus erat*". (Horace, *Carminum*, Ode 3.)—*Ed.*
[b] Excellent.—*Ed.*
[c] Such as Switzerland needs—*Ed.*
[d] Merchant tailor.—*Ed.*

adopted a more solemn tone than he did the day before yesterday—yet he is one of the youngest members of the assembly. Moreover, he has another quality not typical of the Swiss. The point is that every German Swiss has only a single gesture for all his speeches, in all circumstances and throughout his life. Herr Doctor Kern, for instance, stretches out his right arm to the side at right angles with his body; the various officers have exactly the same gesture, the only difference being that they hold the arm straight out in front of them instead of to the side; Herr Tanner from Aarau makes a bow after every third word; Herr Furrer bows first to the front, then in a half-turn to the right and then to the left; in short, if all the German-speaking members of the National Council were assembled, a fairly complete signalling code would result. Herr Escher's gesture consists in stretching out his arm in front of him and making a movement with it exactly like that of a pump-handle.

As for the content of Herr Doctor Escher's speech, there is no need for me to repeat his list of the complaints of the federal representatives, since almost all these complaints have reached most of the German newspapers through the *Neue Zürcher-Zeitung*. There was absolutely nothing new in the speech.

Zurich solemnity was succeeded by Italian passion: after Herr Dr. Escher came Colonel Luvini. Luvini is an excellent soldier, to whom the Tessin canton owes its whole military organisation; as the military leader he led the 1840 revolution. In August 1841, when the overthrown oligarchs and priests launched an attack from Piedmont and tried to make a counter-revolution, Luvini by his swift and energetic action suppressed the attempt in a single day. During the war against the Sonderbund he was the only one to be taken prisoner solely because the Bündeners left him in the lurch. Luvini very quickly leapt from his seat to defend his fellow countrymen against Escher. The fact that Herr Escher's reproaches were couched in the stilted but outwardly calm language of a schoolteacher did not make them any the less bitter; on the contrary, everyone knows that doctrinaire wisdom is in itself sufficiently intolerable and wounding.

Luvini replied with all the passion of an old soldier and Tessiner, who is Swiss by accident but Italian by nature.

"Are not the people of Tessin here being strongly reproached because of their 'sympathy with Italian freedom'? Yes, it is true that the Tessiners sympathise with Italy, and I am proud of the fact, and I shall not cease to pray to God every morning and evening for the liberation of this country from its oppressors. Yes, despite Herr Escher, the Tessiners are a calm and peaceful people, but if daily and hourly they have to watch the Swiss soldiers fraternise with the Austrians, with the police detachments of a man whose name I can never pronounce without a bitterness that comes from the depths of my soul, with Radetzky's hirelings — how can they fail to be embittered, they before whose very eyes, as it were, the Croats commit the most shocking atrocities? Yes, the Tessiners are a calm and peaceful people, but when they are sent Swiss soldiers who take sides with the Austrians, and in some places behave like the Croats, then, of course, they cannot be calm and peaceful!" (There follows an enumeration of facts about the behaviour of the Swiss troops in Tessin.) "It is already hard and sad enough to be oppressed and enslaved by foreigners, yet this is tolerated in the hope that the day will come when the foreigners will be driven out; but when my own brothers and members of the Confederation enslave me, when they, as it were, put a rope round my neck, then truly...."

The President's bell interrupted the speaker. Luvini was called to order. He said a few more words and ended his speech rather abruptly and irritably.

The fiery Luvini was followed by Colonel Michel from Graubünden. The Bündeners, with the exception of the Italian-speaking inhabitants of Misox, have always been bad neighbours to the Tessiners, and Herr Michel remained true to the traditions of his homeland. Speaking in the highly solemn tone of a man of worth, he tried to cast suspicion on the statements of the Tessiners, launched into a series of uncalled-for denunciations and slanders against the Tessin people, and was even tactless and ignoble enough to reproach the Tessiners because they (rightly) laid the blame for their defeat at Airolo on Michel's fellow countrymen, on the Bündeners. He concluded his speech by kindly proposing that part of the frontier occupation costs should be imposed on the Tessin Government.

On a motion by Steiger, the debate was then adjourned.

The following morning the first to speak was Herr Colonel Berg from Zurich. I shall not describe his appearance for, as I have pointed out, the German-Swiss officers all look alike. Herr Berg is the commander of the Zurich battalion stationed in Tessin, the insolent behaviour of which was described by Luvini with numerous examples. Herr Berg, of course, had to defend his battalion, but as he soon came to the end of the factual assertions put forward for this purpose, he launched into a series of the most unrestrained personal attacks on Luvini.

"Luvini," he said, "ought to be ashamed to talk about the discipline of the troops and moreover to cast suspicion on the discipline of one of the finest and most orderly battalions. For if what happened to Herr Luvini had happened to me I would long ago have resigned. What happened to Herr Luvini was that in the war against the Sonderbund he was defeated in spite of his army being numerically superior, and on being given the order to advance, replied that it was impossible, as his troops were demoralised etc. Incidentally, I should like to have a word with Herr Luvini on this matter, not here but somewhere else; I like to look my opponent in the eye."

All these and numerous other provocative statements and insults were uttered by Herr Berg in a tone that was in part dignified, in part blustering. He obviously wanted to imitate Luvini's *fougueuse*[a] rhetoric, but his effort was a complete fiasco.

As the story of Airolo has already cropped up twice in my report and has now come up again, I shall briefly recall the main circumstances. Dufour's plan in the war against the Sonderbund was as follows: while the main army attacked Freiburg and Lucerne, the Tessiners were to advance over the St. Gotthard, and the Bündeners over the Oberalp into the Urserental, liberate and arm the liberal-minded population there, and by this diversion cut off Wallis from the *Ur*-cantons[142] and compel the main Lucerne army of the Sonderbund to divide into two. The plan failed, firstly because the men of Uri and Wallis had already occupied the St. Gotthard before hostilities began and secondly because of the half-heartedness of the Bündeners. The latter totally failed to mobilise the Catholic militia, and even the troops that were mobilised let themselves be dissuaded from further advance by the Catholic population at a meeting in the Disentis High Court. Hence Tessin was quite alone, and bearing in mind that the military organisation of this canton was still very immature and that the entire Tessin army numbered only about 3,000, the weakness of Tessin compared with the Sonderbund is easily grasped. Meanwhile the men of Uri, Wallis and Unterwalden had been reinforced by more than 2,000 men with artillery and on November 17, 1847, they descended the St. Gotthard with their entire force and broke into Tessin. The Tessin troops were deployed in echelons up the Leventinatal from Bellinzona to Airolo; their reserves were in Lugano. The Sonderbund troops, concealed by a dense mist, occupied all the heights around Airolo, and when the mist dispersed Luvini saw that his position was lost before a shot had been fired. Nevertheless he assumed the defensive and after a battle lasting many hours, in which the Tessiners fought with the greatest courage, his troops were thrown back by the numerically stronger enemy. At first the retreat was covered by some army units, but the Tessin recruits, attacked on the flanks from the heights and fired on by artillery, were soon in total disorder and could only be brought to a halt at eight hours' distance from Airolo, behind the Moesa. Anyone who knows the St. Gotthard road will understand the huge advantages of an army coming down from above, especially if it has artillery, and the impossibility for an army retreating down the mountain to make a stand anywhere and deploy its forces in the

---

[a] Fiery.—*Ed.*

narrow valley. Moreover the Tessiners who were actually involved in the battle by no means outnumbered the Sonderbund troops, on the contrary. For this defeat, therefore, which incidentally had no further consequences, it was not Luvini who was to blame but, firstly, his numerically weak and untrained troops, secondly, the unfavourable terrain, thirdly and mainly, the absence of the Bündeners, who allowed themselves to quaff Veltlin wine in Disentis instead of being on the Oberalp, and who at last came to the help of the Tessiners over the St. Bernard, *post festum*, with two battalions. And this victory of the Sonderbund, at the only place where it was superior in numbers, is used to reproach the Tessiners by those who shamefully left them in the lurch or who won cheap laurels at Freiburg and Lucerne, fighting three against one!

As you know, these attacks by Berg against Luvini resulted in a duel in which the Welch man severely disabled the Zuricher.[a]

But let us return to the debate. Herr Dr. Kern from Thurgau rose to support the proposals of the majority. Herr Kern is a typical Swiss, tall, broad-shouldered, with not unpleasant clear-cut features and somewhat theatrical hair, such as perhaps an honest Swiss would imagine Olympian Jupiter; he is dressed somewhat like a man of learning, his look, tone of voice and bearing indicate unshakeable determination. Herr Kern is considered one of the most accomplished and shrewdest lawyers in Switzerland. "With his characteristic logic" and highly declamatory manner of speaking, the President of the Federal Court began to expound on the Tessin question, but soon I was so bored that I preferred to go to the Café italien and drink a glass of Wallis wine.

When I returned, Kern had already been followed by Almeras from Geneva, Homberger, Blanchenay from Waadt and Castoldi from Geneva—more or less important local figures whose fame in the Confederation is only just beginning. Eytel from Waadt was speaking.

In Switzerland, where people are proportionately as large as ordinary cattle, Herr Eytel may be considered delicately built, although in France he would pass for a *jeune homme fort robuste*.[b] He has a handsome, delicate face, fair moustache and fair curly hair, and like the Waadt people in general he reminds one of a Frenchman more than do the other inhabitants of Welch Switzerland. It goes without saying that he is one of the main supporters of the ultra-radical, red-republican trend among the Waadt people.

---

[a] See this volume, pp. 114, 115.— *Ed.*

[b] Quite robust young man.— *Ed.*

Moreover, he is still young and certainly not older than Escher. Herr Eytel spoke with great vehemence against the federal representatives.

"They behaved in Tessin as though Tessin were not a sovereign state, but a province which they had to administer as pro-Consuls; truly, if these gentlemen had acted in that way in a French canton, they would not have been allowed to remain there long! Yet these gentlemen, instead of thanking God that the Tessiners put up so calmly with their lust for domination and their fantastic ideas, even complain of being badly received!"

Herr Eytel speaks very well but is somewhat too long-winded. Like all the French Swiss, he fails to come to the point.

Old Steiger also said a few words from his presidential chair in favour of the majority proposals and then our Alcibiades Escher took the floor for the second time in order to repeat once more the account he had already given. But this time he attempted a rhetorical conclusion in which his schoolboy's exercise was evident three miles away.

"Either we are neutral or we are not neutral, but whatever we are, that we must wholly be, and old Swiss loyalty demands that we should keep our word, even if given to a despot."

From this new and striking idea, Herr Escher's tireless arm pumped out the broad stream of a solemn peroration, and when he had completed it Alcibiades, obviously pleased with himself, sat down again.

Herr Tanner from Aarau, President of the Supreme Court, was the next speaker. He is a lean, puny man of medium height who speaks very loudly about very uninteresting matters. Basically his speech was nothing but the hundredfold repetition of one and the same grammatical mistake.

He was followed by Herr Maurice Barman from French Wallis. To look at him no one would believe that he fought so bravely at Pont de Trient in 1844, when the men of Upper Wallis led by the Kalbermattens, Riedmattens and other Mattens[a] attempted a counter-revolution in the canton.[143] Herr Barman's outward appearance is that of a tranquil bourgeois but is by no means unpleasant; he speaks thoughtfully and rather disjointedly. He repulsed Berg's personal attacks on Luvini and supported Pioda.

Herr Battaglini from Tessin, who looks rather bourgeois and could remind a malicious observer of Dr. Bartholo in *Figaro*, read out a rather long discourse in French about neutrality in favour of

---

[a] *Matten* also means "meadows".— *Ed.*

his canton, a statement which contained perfectly correct principles but was listened to with only very superficial attention.

Suddenly the conversations and moving about in the assembly ceased. There was complete silence and all eyes turned to a beardless, bald old man with a big aquiline nose, who began to speak in French. This little old man, who in his simple black suit and with his completely civilian appearance was more like a professor than anything else, and who struck one only by his expressive face and lively, penetrating glance, was General *Dufour,* that same Dufour whose far-sighted strategy crushed the Sonderbund almost without bloodshed. What a distance separated him from the German-Swiss officers of that assembly! Those Michels, Zieglers, Bergs etc., those narrow-minded fire-eaters, those pedantic martinets, cut a very characteristic figure in comparison with the small unpretentious Dufour. One could see at a glance that it was Dufour who was the brain behind the whole war against the Sonderbund, whereas these Ajaxes full of a sense of their own worth were only the fists he needed for carrying out his decisions. The Diet had truly chosen correctly and found the necessary man.

But when one hears Dufour speak one becomes really astounded. This old officer in the Engineers, who has spent his whole life only organising artillery schools, drawing up regulations and inspecting batteries, who has never taken part in parliamentary proceedings, never spoken in public, spoke with an assurance and with a fluency, elegance, precision and clarity that is admirable and unique in the Swiss National Council. This maiden speech[a] of Dufour's on the Tessin question, as far as its form and content are concerned, would have created the greatest sensation in the French Chamber; in every respect it far surpasses Cavaignac's[b] three-hour speech which made him the leading lawyer in Paris—if one can judge from the text published in the *Moniteur.* As for beauty of language, it is doubly deserving of recognition in someone from Geneva. The national language of Geneva is a Calvinistically reformed French, broad, flat, poor, monotonous and colourless. Dufour, however, did not speak in the language of Geneva, but in real, genuine French. Moreover, the sentiments which he expressed were so noble, so soldierly in the *good* sense of the word, that they made the petty professional jealousies and petty cantonal narrowness of the German-Swiss officers stand out in glaring contrast.

---

[a] The words "maiden speech" are in English in the original.— *Ed.*
[b] This refers to Éléonore Louis Godefroy Cavaignac.—*Ed.*

"I am glad that everyone is talking about neutrality," said Dufour. "But what is neutrality? It consists in our not undertaking or allowing to be undertaken anything by which the state of peace between Switzerland and neighbouring states would be endangered. Nothing less, but also nothing more. We have the right, therefore, to grant asylum to refugees from abroad, it is a right of which we are proud. We regard it as a duty which we owe to misfortune. But on one condition: that the refugee submits to our laws, that he does not undertake anything that could endanger our security at home or abroad. That a patriot driven from his country by tyranny endeavours, from our territory also, to win back the freedom of his homeland, I can understand. I do not reproach him in any way on that account, but then we also have to see what we must do. If, therefore, a refugee takes up his pen or his musket to oppose the neighbouring Government—all right, we shall not deport him for it, that would be unjust, but we shall remove him from the frontier, intern him. That is demanded by our own security and by our regard for neighbouring states; nothing less but also *nothing more.* If, on the other hand, we take steps not only against the insurgent volunteer who has penetrated into foreign territory, but also against the brother or the father of that volunteer, against one who has remained in peace, then we are doing more than we are obliged to do, then we are no longer neutral, we take the side of a foreign government, the side of despotism against its victims." (General applause.) "And precisely now when Radetzky, a man for whom certainly no one in this assembly has any sympathy, is already demanding from us this unjust removal of *all* refugees from the frontier zone, when he is backing up his demand by threats, indeed, by hostile measures, precisely now it is least of all fitting for us to accede to the unjust demand of a more powerful opponent, because it would look as if we were bowing to superior force, as if we had taken this decision because a stronger opponent demanded it." (Bravo!)

I regret that I cannot give more of this speech and more word-for-word extracts from it. But there are no stenographers here, and I have to write from memory. Suffice it to say that Dufour astonished the entire assembly both by his oratorical skill and by the unpretentiousness of his speech as well as by the weighty arguments he put forward, and that after declaring he would vote for Pioda's proposal, he returned to his seat amid general applause. I have never on any other occasion heard applause during debates in the National Council. Dufour's speech decided the matter; after it there was nothing more to be said, and Pioda's proposal was carried.

However, this did not suit the knights of the small cantons whose consciences had been shaken, and to the call for an end to the debate they replied by casting 48 votes for its continuance. Only 42 voted for ending the debate, which therefore continued: Herr Veillon from Waadt proposed that the whole matter be referred to the Federal Council. Herr Pittet from Waadt, a handsome man with French features, spoke in favour of Pioda, fluently but verbosely and in a doctrinaire tone, and it seemed that the discussion was petering out when, finally, Herr Furrer, President of the Confederation, rose to speak.

Herr Furrer is a man in the prime of life, a counterpart of Alcibiades Escher. If the latter represents the Swiss Athens, Herr Furrer represents Zurich. If Escher tends to look like a professor, Furrer tends to look like a factory foreman. Together they are a complete representation of Zurich.

Herr Furrer, of course, is a man who favours the most absolute neutrality and since he saw his system seriously threatened as a result of Dufour's speech, he had to employ the most extreme measures to ensure himself a majority. It is true that Herr Furrer has only been Federal President for three days, but in spite of that he proved that he understands the politics of no-confidence questions despite Duchâtel and Hansemann. He declared that the Federal Council was extremely eager for the decision of the National Council, because this decision would be a decisive turning-point in the entire policy of Switzerland etc. After a little embellishment of this *captatio benevolentiae*,[a] he gradually proceeded to expound his own opinion and that of the majority of the Federal Council, namely, that the policy of neutrality must remain and that the view of the majority of the commission was also the view of the majority of the Federal Council. He said all this with such solemn dignity and in such an insistent tone that there was a hint of the no-confidence question in every word of his speech. One must bear in mind that in Switzerland the executive power is not an independent power alongside the legislative, as in a constitutional monarchy or in the new French Constitution, but only the derivative and instrument of the legislative power. One must bear in mind that it is not at all the custom for the executive power to resign if its wishes are disregarded by a decision of the legislative assembly; on the contrary, it is accustomed to carry out this decision most obediently and wait for better times. And since the executive power likewise consists of an elected council in which there are also various shades of opinion, it is of no great importance if the minority in the executive council has a majority on some questions in the legislative council. And here at least two members of the Federal Council, Druey and Franscini, were for Pioda and against Furrer. Consequently, from the point of view of Swiss customs and views, Furrer's appeal to the assembly was quite unparliamentary. But what does that matter? The weighty voice of the Federal President gave new courage to the knights of the small cantons, and when he returned to his seat, they even attempted a "bravo" which faded away without any response, and demanded an end to the debate.

---

[a] Attempt to win goodwill.—*Ed.*

But old Steiger was fair enough to give the floor first to Herr Pioda—as the reporter for the minority. Pioda spoke with the same calm and decorum as before. He again refuted all the accusations while briefly summing up the debate. He warmly defended his friend Luvini, whose *fougueuse* eloquence had perhaps somewhat carried him away but who, and this should never be forgotten, on a previous occasion had saved his canton for Switzerland. Finally, he touched upon Airolo and expressed his regret that this word had been mentioned here and, moreover, mentioned by the side from which he least of all expected it.

"It is true that we suffered a defeat at Airolo," he said. "But how did it come about? We stood there alone, our little, sparsely populated canton against the whole weight of the *Ur*-cantons and Wallis, which hurled themselves upon us and crushed us, although we defended ourselves bravely. It is true, we were defeated. But is it seemly for you" (turning to Michel) "to reproach us for it? You, gentlemen, you are to blame for the fact that we were defeated; you should have been on the Oberalp and have struck the Sonderbund forces in the flank, and it was you who were not there and who left us in the lurch, and that was why we were defeated. Yes, you did arrive, gentlemen, but when it was too late, when it was all over—then at last you arrived!"

Colonel Michel leapt up in a fury and with a face red as a lobster and declared that it was a lie and a slander. Called to order by loud murmurs and the President's bell, he continued somewhat more calmly. He said he knew nothing about having been supposed to be on the Oberalp. All he knew was that after getting the order he came to the aid of the Tessiners and in fact was the first to arrive.

Pioda replied as calmly as before: it had not entered his mind to attack Herr Michel personally, he had merely spoken of the Graubündeners in general, and it was a fact at any rate that they should have supported the Tessiners by descending from the Oberalp. If Herr Michel did not know that, it was easily explained by the fact that at the time he commanded only a battalion, and therefore the general plans of the campaign could very well have remained unknown to him.

With this intermezzo, which further led to private discussions of various kinds between these gentlemen outside the assembly hall and was finally settled by mutually satisfactory statements, the debate came to an end. The voting was by roll-call. The Frenchmen and four or five Germans voted with the Tessiners, the mass of the German Swiss voted against them. Tessin was deprived of the right to afford asylum, Radetzky's demands[144] were agreed to, neutrality at any price was proclaimed, and Herr Furrer could feel satisfied with himself and the National Council.

Such is the Swiss National Council, where the flower of the statesmen of Switzerland meet. I find that they are distinguished from other legislators by only one virtue, greater *patience*.

Written by Engels on December 6, 1848

First published in the *Neue Rheinische Zeitung* No. 165 and in the second edition of No. 165, December 10, 1848

Printed according to the newspaper

Published in English for the first time

THE BOURGEOISIE
AND THE COUNTER-REVOLUTION[145]

[*Neue Rheinische Zeitung* No. 165, December 10, 1848]

Cologne, December 9. We have never concealed the fact that ours is not a *legal basis*, but a *revolutionary basis*. Now the Government for its part has abandoned the false pretence of a legal basis. It has taken its stand on a revolutionary basis, for the *counter-revolutionary* basis, too, is *revolutionary*.[146]

§ 6 of the law of April 6, 1848, lays down:

"The right to approve all *laws* as well as to determine the national budget and the *right to grant taxes* must in any case belong to the future representatives of the people."

§ 13 of the law of April 8, 1848, reads:

"The Assembly convened on the basis of this law is called upon to *establish* the *future Constitution* by agreement with the Crown and during the period of its existence to exercise the prerogatives of the former imperial estates, in particular regarding the granting of taxes."

The Government sends this Agreement Assembly to the devil, most autocratically imposes a *soi-disant*[a] Constitution[147] upon the country and grants itself the taxes which the representatives of the people had refused it.

The Camphausen epic, a sort of pompous *legal Jobsiade*,[148] has been brought to an abrupt end by the Prussian Government. In retaliation the great *Camphausen*, the author of this epic, continues coolly to deliberate in Frankfurt as envoy of this same Prussian Government, and goes on scheming with the Bassermanns in the interests of this same Prussian Government. This Camphausen, who invented the theory of agreement in order to preserve the legal basis, that is in order first of all to cheat the revolution of the respect that is

---

[a] Self-styled.— *Ed.*

Neue Rheinische Zeitung

Organ der Demokratie.

№ 170. Köln, Samstag den 16. Dezember. 1848.

Keine Steuern mehr!!!

Uebersicht.

Deutschland. Köln. (Die Bourgeoisie und die Contrerevolution. Fortsetzung. — Der Belagerungszustand.) Wesslingen. (Verhaftungen. — Belagerungszustand.) Dortmund. (Mirbachs Verhaftung.) Bielefeld. (Die Verhaftungen und ihr Motiv. — Tumult zu Paderborn.) Münster. (Die Reactionswirthschaft.) Berlin. (Die Nachrichten aus Paris und die Russen. — Verbot der Nationalzeitung. — Polizeiwirthschaft. — Dowiats Prozeß. — Das Ministerium Brandenburg und die englische Presse. — Kladderadatsch.) Darmstadt. (Die Centralgewalt. — Standrechtliches.) Mainz. (Ein Beschluß des hiesigen Bezirksraths.) Eßlingen. (Adresse an einen Reichstagsdeputirten.)

Belgien. Lüttich. (Gründung eines demokratisch-socialen Vereins).

Französische Republik. Paris. (Die Wahl Louis Napoleons. — Volksauftritte. — Stimmung der Mobilen. — Napoleon, Raspail, Ledru Rollin. — Die Wahlurne. — Girardin. Lamartine. — Die Wahllisten. — Verbindung der Rothen mit den Napoleonisten. — Vermischtes. National-Versammlung.)

Italien. Oestreichische Truppenbewegungen. — Neue Schinderei Radetzky's. — Neapel. — Venedig. (Eindruck der römischen Nachrichten. — Papiergeld).

Portugal. Lissabon. (Das Saldanha'sche Kabinet und die Finanzen).

Großbritannien. London. (Fleming der Prophet. — Louis Philippe als Kläger vor dem Polizeigericht. — Der Morning Advertiser über die octroyirte preußische Verfassung. — Chartistische Parlamentskandidaten. — An die Wähler von Leicester. — Chartistenprozesse. — Lügen der reaktionären deutschen Journale über die englische Presse). Manchester. (Der Markt).

Amerika. (Neueste Nachrichten aus den Vereinigten-Staaten, Mexiko, Yucatan, Hayti, Havannah, Venezuela und Bogota. — Das californische Eldorado). Rio-Janeiro. (Rosa's Rüstungen).

Afrika. (Zustand am Cap der guten Hoffnung).

Deutschland.

* **Köln**, 15 Dezember. (Fortsetzung.) Die Vereinbarungstheorie, welche die im Ministerium Camphausen zur Regierung gelangte Bourgeoisie sofort als »breiteste« Grundlage des preußischen contrat social proklamirte, war keineswegs eine hohle Theorie; sie war vielmehr gewachsen auf dem Baume des »goldnen« Lebens.

Die Märzrevolution hat den Souverän von Gottes Gnaden keineswegs dem Volkssouveräne unterjocht. Sie hat nur die Krone, den absolutistischen Staat, gezwungen, sich mit der Bourgeoisie zu verständigen, sich mit ihrem alten Rivalen zu vereinbaren.

Die Krone wird der Bourgeoisie den Adel, die Bourgeoisie wird der Krone das Volk opfern. Unter dieser Bedingung wird das Königthum bürgerlich und die Bourgeoisie königlich werden.

Nach dem März giebt es nur noch diese zwei Mächte. Sie dienen sich wechselseitig als Blitzableiter der Revolution. Alles natürlich auf »breitester demokratischer Grundlage«.

Das war das Geheimniß der Vereinbarungstheorie.

Die Oel- und Wollhändler, welche das erste Ministerium nach der März-Revolution bildeten, gefielen sich in der Rolle, die blosgestellte Krone mit ihren plebejischen Fittigen zu decken. Sie schwelgten in dem Hochgenusse, hoffähig zu sein und widerstrebend, von ihrem rauhen Römerthum aus reiner Großmuth ablassend — von dem Römerthum des vereinigten Landtags — die Kluft, welche den Thron zu verschlingen drohte, mit dem Leichnam ihrer ehemaligen Popularität zu schließen. Wie spreizte sich der Minister Camphausen als Wehmutter des konstitutionellen Thrones. Der brave Mann war offenbar über sich selbst, über seine eigne Großmuth gerührt. Die Krone und ihr Anhang duldete widerstrebend diese demüthigende Protektorschaft, sie machte bonne mine à mauvais jeu in Erwartung bess'rer Tage.

Die halb aufgelöste Armee, die für ihre Stellen und Gehalte zitternde Bureaucratie, der gedemüthigte Feudalstand, dessen Führer sich auf konstitutionellen Studienreisen befand, übertölpelten leicht mit einigen süßen Worten und Knixen den Bourgeois Gentilhomme.

Die preußische Bourgeoisie war nomineller Besitzer der Herrschaft, sie zweifelte keinen Augenblick, daß die Mächte des alten Staats ohne Hinterhalt sich ihr zu Gebot gestellt und in eben so viele devote Ableger ihrer eignen Allmacht verwandelt hätten.

Nicht nur im Ministerium, in dem ganzen Umfang der Monarchie war die Bourgeoisie von diesem Wahn berauscht.

Die einzigen Heldenthaten der preußischen Bourgeoisie nach dem März, die oft blutigen Chikanen der Bürgerwehr gegen das unbewaffnete Proletariat, fanden sie nicht in der Armee, in der Büreaucratie und selbst in den Feudalherrn willig unterwürfige Helfershelfer? Die einzigen Kraftanstrengungen, wozu sich die lokalen Vertreter der Bourgeoisie aufschwangen, die Gemeinderäthe — deren zudringlich servile Gemeinheit von einem Windischgrätz, Jellachich und Welden später in angemessener Weise befußtrittet wurde — die einzigen Heldenthaten dieser Gemeinderäthe nach der Märzrevolution, ihre patriarchalischernsten Warnungsworte an das Volk, wurden sie nicht angestaunt von den verstummten Regierungspräsidenten und den in sich gegangenen Divisionsgeneralen? Und die preußische Bourgeoisie hätte noch zweifeln sollen, daß der alte Groll der Armee, der Bureaucratie, der Feudalen, in ehrfurchtsvoller Ergebenheit vor dem sich selbst und die Anarchie zügelnden großmüthigen Sieger, der Bourgeoisie, erstorben sei?

Es war klar. Die preußische Bourgeoisie hatte nur noch eine Aufgabe, die Aufgabe, sich ihre Herrschaft bequem zu machen, die störenden Anarchisten zu beseitigen, »Ruhe und Ordnung« wieder herzustellen und die Zinsen wieder einzubringen, die während des Märzsturms verloren gegangen waren. Es konnte sich nur noch darum handeln, die Produktionskosten ihrer Herrschaft und der sie bedingenden Märzrevolution auf ein Minimum zu beschränken. Die Waffen, welche die preußische Bourgeoisie in ihrem Kampfe gegen die feudale Gesellschaft und deren Krone unter der Firma des Volks in Anspruch zu nehmen sich gezwungen sah, Assoziationsrecht, Preßfreiheit &c., mußten sie nicht zerbrochen werden in den Händen eines bethörten Volks, das sie nicht mehr für die Bourgeoisie zu führen brauchte und gegen sie zu führen bedenkliche Gelüste kund gab?

Der Vereinbarung der Bourgeoisie mit der Krone, davon war sie überzeugt, dem Markten der Bourgeoisie mit dem alten, in sein Schicksal ergebenen Staate, stand offenbar nur noch ein Hinderniß im Wege, ein einziges Hinderniß, das Volk — *puer robustus sed malitiosus*, wie Hobbes sagt. Das Volk und die Revolution!

Die Revolution war der Rechtstitel des Volkes; auf die Revolution gründete es seine ungestümmen Ansprüche. Die Revolution war der Wechsel, den es auf die Bourgeoisie gezogen hatte. Durch die Revolution war die Bourgeoisie zur Herrschaft gelangt. Mit dem Tage ihrer Herrschaft war der Verfalltag dieses Wechsels angebrochen. Die Bourgeoisie mußte gegen den Wechsel Protest einlegen.

Die Revolution — das bedeutete im Munde des Volks: Ihr Bourgeois seid das Comité du salut public, der Wohlfahrtsausschuß, dem wir die Herrschaft in die Hand gegeben, nicht damit ihr euch über eure Interessen mit der Krone vereinbart, sondern damit ihr gegen die Krone unsere Interessen, die Interessen des Volks durchsetzt.

Die Revolution war der Protest des Volkes gegen die Vereinbarung der Bourgeoisie mit der Krone. Die mit der Krone sich vereinbarende Bourgeoisie mußte also protestiren gegen — die Revolution.

Und das geschah unter dem großen Camphausen. Die Märzrevolution wurde nicht anerkannt. Die Berliner Nationalrepräsentation konstituirte sich als Repräsentation der preußischen Bourgeoisie, als Vereinbarerversammlung, indem sie den Antrag auf Anerkennung der Märzrevolution verwarf.

Sie machte das Geschehene ungeschehen. Sie proklamirte es laut vor dem preußischen Volke, daß es sich mit der Bourgeoisie nicht vereinbart, um gegen die Krone zu revolutioniren, sondern daß es revolutionirt, damit sich die Krone mit der Bourgeoisie gegen es selbst vereinbare! So war der Rechtstitel des revolutionären Volkes vernichtet und der Rechtsboden der konservativen Bourgeoisie gewonnen.

Der Rechtsboden!

Brüggemann, und durch ihn die „Kölnische Zeitung," haben so viel geplaudert, gefabelt, gewimmert vom „Rechtsboden," so oft den „Rechtsboden" verloren, wiedergewonnen, den Rechtsboden durchlöchert, geflickt, von Berlin nach Frankfurt, von Frankfurt nach Berlin geschleudert, verengt, ausgedehnt, aus einem einfachen Boden in einen getäfelten Boden, aus einem getäfelten Boden in einen Doppelboden, — bekanntlich ein Hauptwerkzeug der schauspielernden Escamoteurs — aus einem Doppelboden in eine bodenlose Fallthüre verwandelt, daß der Rechtsboden sich für unsre Leser mit Recht schließlich in den Boden der „Kölnischen Zeitung" verwandelt hat, daß sie das Schiboleth der preußischen Bourgeoisie mit dem Privatschiboleth des Herrn Joseph Dumont, einen nothwendigen Einfall der preußischen Weltgeschichte mit einer willkührlichen Marotte der „Kölnischen" Zeitung verwechseln können und im Rechtsboden nur noch den Boden sehn, auf dem die „Kölnische Zeitung" wächst.

Der Rechtsboden und zwar der preußische Rechtsboden!

Der Rechtsboden, auf dem sich nach dem März der Ritter der großen Debatte Camphausen, das wiedererweckte Gespenst des Vereinigten Landtags und die Vereinbarerversammlung bewegen, ist er das Konstitutionsgesetz von 1815, oder das Landtagsgesetz von 1820, oder das Patent von 1847, oder das Wahl- und Vereinbarungsgesetz vom 8. April 1848?

Nichts von alledem.

Der „Rechtsboden" bedeutete einfach, daß die Revolution ihren Boden nicht gewonnen und die alte Gesellschaft ihren Boden nicht verloren habe, daß die Märzrevolution nur ein „Ereigniß" sei, welches den „Anstoß" zu der längst innerhalb des alten preußischen Staats vorbereiteten „Verständigung" zwischen dem Throne und der Bourgeoisie gegeben, deren Bedürfniß die Krone selbst in frühern allerhöchsten Erlassen schon ausgesprochen und nur vor dem März für nicht „dringlich" erachtet habe. Der „Rechtsboden" bedeutete mit einem Worte, daß die Bourgeoisie nach dem März mit der Krone auf demselben Fuße unterhandeln wolle wie vor dem März, als ob gar keine Revolution stattgefunden, und der Vereinigte Landtag ohne die Revolution sein Ziel erreicht hätte. Der „Rechtsboden" bedeutete, daß der Rechtstitel des Volkes, die Revolution, in dem contrat social zwischen Regierung und Bourgeoisie nicht existire. Die Bourgeoisie leitete ihre Ansprüche aus der altpreußischen Gesetzgebung her, damit das Volk keine Ansprüche aus der neupreußischen Revolution herleite.

Es versteht sich, daß die ideologischen Cretins der Bourgeoisie, ihre Zeitungsschreiber u. dgl., diese Beschönigung des Bourgeoisinteresses für das eigentliche Interesse der Bourgeoisie ausgeben und als solches sich und andern einbilden mußten. Im Kopfe eines Brüggemann verwandelte sich die Phrase des Rechtsbodens in eine wirkliche Substanz.

Das Ministerium Camphausen hatte seine Aufgabe gelöst, die Aufgabe der Vermittlung und des Uebergangs. Es bildete nämlich die Vermittlung zwischen der auf den Volks-

Die heilige deutsche Reichsarmee.

Die heilige deutsche Reichsarmee
Ist auf den Strumpf gekommen:
Sie hat aus Schwaben und Hessen sich
Die besten Jungens genommen.

Die heilige deutsche Reichsarmee
Die sollte die Schweiz berücken:
Schon rückte sie aus, da mußte sie, ach
Die verfluchten Hosen noch flicken.

Die heilige deutsche Reichsarmee
Die sollte ganz Limburg fressen:
Schon rückte sie aus, da hatte sie, ach
Das verfluchte Pulver vergessen.

Die heilige deutsche Reichsarmee
Die war zum Kampfe entschlossen:
Da haben die Preußen und Dänen, ach
Den verfluchten Frieden geschlossen.

Die heilige deutsche Reichsarmee,
Die sollte auch Wien erlösen:
Da ist, ach Gott, der Herr Windisch-Grätz
So verflucht bei der Hand gewesen.

Die heilige deutsche Reichsarmee
Die lebt ohn' viele Sorgen:
Die Landsknechte traun auf den lieben Gott —
Kommst du heute nicht, kommst du morgen.

Wien. Ein kaiserl. kgl. Soldat schickt der »Red. der N. Rh. Ztg.« die folgende Skizze zu. Wir nehmen sie mit Rücksicht auf den Absender trotz ihres Pathos auf:

Die nächtliche Schildwache im Belagerungsheer vor Wien.

Schaurig rückt die Mitternachtsstunde herauf, die Stunde meiner Ablösung. Sie werden kommen mich abzulösen — doch wer kann mich erlösen von der innern Unruh, die mich ängstigt und foltert. Es schwindelt der Kopf mir vom ewigen Auf- und Abschreiten der müden Füße. Halt! Halt! Doch in mir tobt ein Höllenruf: Marsch! Marsch!

Was ist es denn, was mir keine Ruhe läßt? Ach, es ist der heiße Kampf des Tages, der mir noch mit allen seinen Schrecknissen vor Augen steht, und dort im Hintergrunde die steigenden Feuersäulen der brennenden Kaiserstadt drohen wie zischende Schlangen den Schleuderern des Brandes, und rufen: Fluch den Brandstiftern! Fluch den Brüder- und Vatermördern! . . .

Wild und furchtbar ist der Krieg in seinem Toben, aber schrecklich ist der Moment des Austobens. Der Mensch hört auf Thier zu sein und er übersieht mit einem Blicke die Masse seiner Greuelthaten. Die Wunden, die er mit bestialischer Wuth seinen Nebenmenschen geschlagen, starren ihn klaffend an und er frägt sich, warum dies Alles geschah? . . .

Ach, warum, warum war ich heute ein wildes Thier? Und wer war denn das Wild, gegen das wir wie Jagdhunde gehezt wurden? Waren es etwa Feinde des Landes, die wir mit grimmiger Wuth zerfleischten? . . . Ach, es waren ja die Söhne des Landes wie wir selbst, es waren ja die Bürger der ersten Stadt des Reichs. Welch' eine Satansmacht hat uns gegen unsere Brüder, gegen unsere Väter gehetzt?

Wehe! Mein Blick verwirrt sich — das Schlachtfeld mit den Gefallenen wird regsam — die Todten mit ihren klaffenden Wunden richten sich auf — kommen auf mich zu — Marsch! Marsch! . . .

Ha, Geister meiner Erschlagenen, was wollt Ihr von mir? Wollt Ihr den Kampf von neuem beginnen? Kehrt um! Kehrt um! . . . Doch, was seh' ich! O, gräßlich, gräßlich! die Erschlagenen sind ja meine Brüder, meine wirklichen Brüder, meiste leiblichen Brüder! . . .

Max und Karl! — o Gott! — seid ihr es denn wirklich, die ich heute im blinden teuflischen Kampf erschlagen? Ha, wie sie ihre starren Häupter bejahend schütteln — Weh' mir, sie sind es, es sind meine leiblichen Brüder, die ich erschlagen — ach, sie eilten in den Kampf für Freiheit, für Vaterstadt — Und ich? — Und ich? — ich folgte dem starren Kommando: gegen Freiheit, gegen Vaterland, gegen Vaterstadt! . . . Fluch! ewiger Fluch! diesem Kommando zum Brudermord!

Wohin winkt Ihr mir, Ihr theuren Erschlagenen? Wollt Ihr, daß ich euch folge in die flammende Kaiserstadt, auf den Kirchhof der Freiheit? Aber dort kommen schon die Söldner um mich abzulösen — Gewehr an! . . Ha, wie sie winken, die geliebten Erschlagenen . . . Wohlan, ich folge eurem Bruderwink — Keine Ablösung durch die Feinde des Vaterlands! Nur Erlösung suche ich durch den Tod für's Vaterland! L. M.

Theater in Köln.

Jeder Mensch hat seine Nachtheile und seine Vortheile — so auch Herr Barth. Herr Barth hat alle Nachtheile, aber leider nur den Vortheil, daß die guten Kölner eine wahrhaft himmlische Geduld mit ihm haben. Herr Barth muß sich nicht wundern, daß wir weniger nachsichtig mit ihm sind als andere Leute; wir gestehen es grade heraus, wir tadeln ihn in unserm eignen Interesse, denn wir gönnen uns gern einen erträglichen Abend. — Gehen

A page of the *Neue Rheinische Zeitung* containing Marx's article "The Bourgeoisie and the Counter-Revolution" and the slogan "No More Taxes!!!"

due to it, at the same time invented the mines which were later to blow up the legal basis together with the theory of agreement.

This man introduced the *indirect* elections that produced an assembly to which, at a moment of sudden revolt, the Government could shout: **Trop tard!**[149] He recalled the Prince of Prussia, the head of the counter-revolution, and did not disdain an official lie to turn the Prince's flight into a study trip.[150] He let the old Prussian laws dealing with political crimes and the old courts continue to function. Under his government the old bureaucracy and the old army gained time to recover from their fright and to reconstitute themselves completely. All the leading personalities of the old regime were left untouched in their positions. Under Camphausen the camarilla carried on a war in Posen,[151] while he himself carried on a war in Denmark. The Danish war was intended as an overflow for the superabundant patriotism of the German youth, against whom also after their return the police took the appropriate measures. This war was intended to give some popularity to General Wrangel and his notorious Guards regiments and to rehabilitate the Prussian soldiery in general. This purpose achieved, the sham war had to be ended at any price by a disgraceful armistice, which was once again agreed on at Frankfurt am Main by the same Camphausen with the German National Assembly. The outcome of the Danish war was the appointment of the "*Commander-in-Chief of the two Marches*"[152] and the return to Berlin of the Guards regiments which had been driven out in March.

And the war which the Potsdam camarilla waged in *Posen* under the auspices of Camphausen!

The war in Posen was more than a war against the Prussian revolution. It was the fall of Vienna, the fall of Italy, the defeat of the heroes of June. It was the first decisive victory gained by the Russian Tsar over the European revolution. And all this was done under the auspices of the great *Camphausen*, the thinking friend of history,[a] the knight of the great debate, the champion of agreement.

Under *Camphausen* and with his help the counter-revolution seized all important positions; it prepared an army ready for action while the Agreement Assembly debated. Under *Hansemann-Pinto*,[153] the Minister of action, the old police force was fitted out with new uniforms, and the bourgeoisie waged a war—as bitter as it was petty—against the people. The conclusion from these premises was

---

[a] An ironical allusion to *Allgemeine Geschichte vom Anfang der historischen Kenntniss bis auf unsere Zeiten*, by Karl von Rotteck, a well-known work at the time. Its subtitle was: *Für denkende Geschichtsfreunde* (For Thinking Friends of History).—*Ed.*

drawn under *Brandenburg's* rule. The only things needed for this were a moustache and a sword instead of a head.

When Camphausen resigned we exclaimed:

He has sown reaction as interpreted by the bourgeoisie, he will reap reaction as interpreted by the aristocracy and absolutism.[a]

We have no doubt that His Excellency, the Prussian envoy *Camphausen*, at this moment considers that he himself is a feudal lord and will have come to a peaceable agreement with this "misunder-standing".

One should not, however, commit the error of ascribing initiatives of world-historic significance to such mediocrities as a Camphausen or a Hansemann. They were nothing but the mouthpieces of a class. Their language, their actions, were merely the official echo of the class which brought them to the forefront. They were simply the big bourgeoisie placed in the forefront.

The representatives of this class formed the *liberal opposition* in the blissfully deceased *United Diet*, which Camphausen resurrected for a moment.

The gentlemen of this liberal opposition have been reproached with having betrayed their principles after the March revolution. This is a fallacy.

The big landowners and capitalists, who were the only ones represented in the United Diet, in short the money-bags, became wealthier and more educated. With the development of bourgeois society in Prussia, in other words, with the development of industry, trade and agriculture, the old estate distinctions had, on the one hand, lost their material basis.

The aristocracy itself was largely bourgeoisified. Instead of dealing in loyalty, love and faith, it now dealt primarily in beetroot, liquor and wool. Its tournaments were held mainly on the wool market. On the other hand, the absolutist state, which in the course of development had lost its old social basis, became a restrictive fetter for the new bourgeois society with its changed mode of production and its changed requirements. The bourgeoisie had to claim its share of political power, if only by reason of its material interests. Only the bourgeoisie itself could secure legal fulfilment of its commercial and industrial requirements. It had to wrest the administration of these, its "most sacred interests", from the hands of an antiquated bureaucracy which was both ignorant and arrogant. It had to demand control over the national wealth, of which it considered itself the creator. Having deprived the bureaucracy of the monopoly

---

[a] See present edition, Vol. 7, pp. 108.— *Ed.*

of so-called education and conscious of the fact that it possessed a far superior knowledge of the real requirements of bourgeois society, the bourgeoisie had also the ambition to secure for itself a political status in keeping with its social status. To attain this aim it had to be able freely to debate its own interests and views and the actions of the Government. It called this *"freedom of the press"*. The bourgeoisie had to be able to *enter* freely *into associations*. It called this *"freedom of association"*. As a necessary consequence of *free competition*, it had likewise to demand *religious liberty* and so on. Before March 1848 the Prussian bourgeoisie was well on the way to realising all its aims.

The Prussian state was in financial difficulties. Its borrowing power was exhausted. This was the secret behind the convocation of the United Diet. Although the Government struggled against its fate and ungraciously dissolved the United Diet, lack of money and of credit facilities would inevitably have driven it gradually into the arms of the bourgeoisie. Those who are kings by the grace of God have always bartered their privileges for hard cash, as did the feudal barons. The first great act of this world-historic deal in all the Christian-Germanic states was the emancipation of the serfs; the second great act was the constitutional monarchy. *"L'argent n'a pas de maître"*,[a] but the *maîtres* cease to be *maîtres* as soon as they are demonetised.

And so the liberal opposition in the United Diet was nothing else than the opposition of the bourgeoisie to a political form that no longer corresponded to its interests and needs. In order to oppose the Court, the bourgeoisie had to court the people.

It may have really imagined that its opposition was *for* the people.

Obviously, the rights and liberties which the bourgeoisie sought *for itself* could be demanded from the Government only under the slogan: *popular rights* and *popular liberties*.

This opposition, as we have said, was well on the way to its goal when the *February storm* broke.

[*Neue Rheinische Zeitung* No. 169, December 15, 1848]

Cologne, December 11. When the March deluge — a Biblical deluge in miniature — subsided, it left on the surface of Berlin no prodigies, no revolutionary giants, but traditional creatures, thickset bourgeois figures — the liberals of the United Diet, the representatives of the

---

[a] "Money has no master."—*Ed.*

conscious Prussian bourgeoisie. The main contingents for the new Ministries were supplied by the *Rhine Province* and *Silesia,* the provinces with the most advanced bourgeoisie. Behind them came a whole train of Rhenish lawyers. To the same extent that the bourgeoisie was pushed into the background by the feudal aristocracy, the Rhine Province and Silesia were replaced in the Ministries by the old Prussian provinces. The only link of the Brandenburg Ministry with the Rhine Province now is through a single Elberfeld Tory. *Hansemann* and *von der Heydt!* These two names represent for the Prussian bourgeoisie the whole difference between March and December 1848!

The Prussian bourgeoisie reached the highest positions in the state, not, however, by means of a *peaceful deal with the Crown,* as it had desired, but as the result of a *revolution.* It was supposed to defend, not its own interests, but *those of the people* — for a *popular movement* had prepared the way for the bourgeoisie — against the Crown, in other words, against *itself.* For the bourgeoisie regarded the Crown simply as a cloak provided by the grace of God, a cloak that was to conceal its own profane interests. The inviolability of *its* own interests and of the political forms corresponding to these interests, when translated into constitutional language, was supposed to read: *inviolability of the Crown.* Hence the enthusiasm of the German bourgeoisie and in particular of the Prussian bourgeoisie for the *constitutional monarchy.* Therefore, although the Prussian bourgeoisie welcomed the February revolution together with its repercussions in Germany because it had placed the helm of state in their hands, it also upset their plans, because their rule was thus bound by conditions which they neither wanted nor were able to fulfil.

The bourgeoisie did not raise a finger; they simply allowed the people to fight for them. Hence the rule that was transferred to them was not the rule of a general who has defeated his adversary, but the rule of a committee of public safety to which the victorious people entrusts the protection of its interests.

Camphausen was still clearly aware of this embarrassing situation, and the weakness of his Ministry was entirely due to this feeling and the circumstances that gave rise to it. Even the most shameless actions of his Government are therefore tinted by a sort of shamefaced blush. Open *shamelessness* and *insolence* were Hansemann's privilege. The red *colouring* is all that distinguishes these two painters one from the other.

The *March revolution in Prussia* should not be confused either with the *English* revolution of 1648 or with the *French* one of 1789.

In 1648 the bourgeoisie was allied with the modern aristocracy against the monarchy, the feudal aristocracy and the established church.

In 1789 the bourgeoisie was allied with the people against the monarchy, the aristocracy and the established church.

The revolution of 1789 (at least in Europe) had as its prototype only the revolution of 1648; the revolution of 1648 only the revolt of the Netherlands against Spain.[154] Both revolutions were a century in advance of their prototypes not only in time but also in content.

In both revolutions the bourgeoisie was the class that *really* headed the movement. The *proletariat* and the *non-bourgeois strata of the middle class* had either not yet any interests separate from those of the bourgeoisie or they did not yet constitute independent classes or class sub-divisions. Therefore, where they opposed the bourgeoisie, as they did in France in 1793 and 1794, they fought only for the attainment of the aims of the bourgeoisie, even if not *in the manner of* the bourgeoisie. *All French terrorism* was nothing but a *plebeian way* of dealing with the *enemies of the bourgeoisie*, absolutism, feudalism and philistinism.

The revolutions of 1648 and 1789 were not *English* and *French* revolutions, they were revolutions of a *European* type. They did not represent the victory of a *particular* class of society over the *old political order*; they *proclaimed the political order of the new European society.* The bourgeoisie was victorious in these revolutions, but the *victory of the bourgeoisie* was at that time *the victory of a new social order*, the victory of bourgeois ownership over feudal ownership, of nationality over provincialism, of competition over the guild, of the division of land over primogeniture, of the rule of the landowner over the domination of the owner by the land, of enlightenment over superstition, of the family over the family name, of industry over heroic idleness, of bourgeois law over medieval privileges. The revolution of 1648 was the victory[a] of the seventeenth century over the sixteenth century; the revolution of 1789 was the victory of the eighteenth century over the seventeenth. These revolutions reflected the needs of the world at that time rather than the needs of those parts of the world where they occurred, that is England and France.

There has been nothing of all this in the *Prussian March revolution*.

The February revolution actually *abolished* the constitutional monarchy and nominally *abolished* the rule of the bourgeoisie. The Prussian March revolution was intended to *establish* nominally a

---

[a] In the *Neue Rheinische Zeitung*: "the revolution".— *Ed.*

constitutional monarchy and to *establish* actually the rule of the bourgeoisie. Far from being a *European revolution* it was merely a stunted after-effect of a European revolution in a backward country. Instead of being ahead of its century, it was over half a century behind its time. From the very outset it was a *secondary* phenomenon, and it is well known that secondary diseases are harder to cure and at the same time cause more harm than the primary diseases do. It was not a question of establishing a new society, but of resurrecting in Berlin a society that had expired in Paris. The Prussian March revolution was not even a *national, German* revolution; from the outset it was a *provincial Prussian* revolution. All sorts of provincial uprisings—in Vienna, Cassel, Munich etc.—took place alongside it and contested its lead.

Whereas 1648 and 1789 gained boundless self-confidence from being at the apex of creation, it was the ambition of the Berlin revolution of 1848 to constitute an anachronism. Its light was like that of the stars which reaches us, the inhabitants of the Earth, only after the bodies from which it emanated have been extinct for a hundred thousand years. The March revolution in Prussia was, on a small scale — just as it was on a small scale in everything — such a star for Europe. Its light was that of the corpse of a society which had long ago decayed.

The German bourgeoisie developed so sluggishly, timidly and slowly that at the moment when it menacingly confronted feudalism and absolutism, it saw menacingly confronting it the proletariat and all sections of the middle class whose interests and ideas were related to those of the proletariat. The German bourgeoisie found not just one class *behind* it, but all Europe hostilely *facing* it. Unlike the French bourgeoisie of 1789, the Prussian bourgeoisie, when it confronted the monarchy and aristocracy, the representatives of the old society, was not a class speaking for the *whole* of modern society. It had sunk to the level of a kind of *social estate* as clearly distinct from the Crown as it was from the people, with a strong bent to oppose both adversaries and irresolute towards each of them individually because it always saw both of them either in front of it or behind it. From the first it was inclined to betray the people and to compromise with the crowned representative of the old society, for it itself already belonged to the old society; it did not represent the interests of a new society against an old one, but renewed interests within an obsolete society. It stood at the helm of the revolution not because it had the people behind it but because the people drove it before them; it stood at the head not because it represented the initiative of a new social era but only because it represented the rancour of an old one. A stratum of the old state that had failed to break through and was thrown up on the surface of the new state by the force of an earthquake; without faith in itself, without faith in the people, grumbling at those above, trembling before those below, egoistic towards both sides and aware of its egoism; revolutionary in relation to the conservatives and conservative in relation to the revolutionaries. It did not trust its own slogans, used phrases instead of ideas, it was intimidated by the world storm and exploited it for its own ends; it displayed no energy in any respect, but resorted to plagiarism in every respect, it was vulgar because unoriginal, and original in its vulgarity; haggling over its own desires, without initiative, without faith in itself, without faith in the people, without a world-historic mission, an abominable dotard finding himself condemned to lead and to mislead the first youthful impulses of a virile people so as to make them serve his own senile interests—sans eyes, sans ears, sans teeth, sans everything[a]—such was the *Prussian bourgeoisie* which found itself at the helm of the Prussian state after the March revolution.

[*Neue Rheinische Zeitung* No. 170, December 16, 1848]

Cologne, December 15. The *theory of agreement,* which the bourgeoisie, on attaining governmental power in the shape of the *Camphausen* Ministry, immediately declared the "broadest" basis of the Prussian *contrat social,* was by no means an empty theory; on the contrary, it grew on the tree of "*golden*" life.

The sovereign by the grace of God was by no means subjected to the sovereignty of the people as a result of the March revolution. The Crown, the absolutist state, was merely compelled to come to an understanding with the bourgeoisie, to *come to an agreement* with its old rival.

The Crown is ready to sacrifice the aristocracy to the bourgeoisie, the bourgeoisie is ready to sacrifice the people to the Crown. Under these circumstances the monarchy becomes bourgeois and the bourgeoisie monarchical.

Only these two powers still exist since the March revolution. They use each other as a sort of lightning-conductor against the revolution. Always, of course, on the "*broadest democratic basis*".

Therein lay the *secret of the theory of agreement.*

The oil and wool merchants [155] who formed the first Ministry after the March revolution took pleasure in their role of protecting the

---

[a] Cf. Shakespeare. *As You Like It,* Act II, Scene 7.—*Ed.*

exposed Crown with their plebeian wings. They were highly delighted at having gained access to the Court and reluctantly driven by pure magnanimity to abandon their austere Roman pose, i.e. the Roman pose of the United Diet, to use the corpse of their former popularity to fill the chasm that threatened to engulf the throne. Minister *Camphausen* plumed himself on being the *midwife* of the constitutional throne. The worthy man was evidently deeply moved by himself, his own magnanimity. The Crown and its hangers-on reluctantly suffered this humiliating protection and made *bonne mine à mauvais jeu*,[a] hoping for better days to come.

The *bourgeois gentilhomme*[b] was easily taken in by a few honeyed words and curtsies from the partly disintegrated army, the bureaucracy that trembled for its positions and salaries, and the humiliated feudals, whose leader[c] was engaged in a constitutional educational journey.

The Prussian bourgeoisie was *nominally* the ruler and did not for a moment doubt that the powers of the old state had placed themselves unreservedly at its disposal and had become devoted adjuncts of its own omnipotence.

Not only in the Ministry but throughout the monarchy the bourgeoisie was intoxicated with this delusion.

Did not the army, the bureaucracy and even the feudal lords act as willing and obedient accomplices in the only heroic deeds the Prussian bourgeoisie performed after the March revolution, namely, the often sanguinary machinations of the civic militia against the unarmed proletariat? Did not the subdued *Regierungspräsidenten* and penitent divisional generals listen with admiration to the stern patriarchal admonitions which the *local councillors* addressed to the people — the only efforts, the only heroic deeds of which these local councillors, the local representatives of the bourgeoisie (whose obtrusive servile vulgarity the Windischgrätzes, Jellachiches and Weldens afterwards repaid with kicks), were capable after the March revolution? Could the Prussian bourgeoisie have doubted after this that the former ill will of the army, bureaucracy and feudal aristocracy had been transformed into respectful loyalty to the bourgeoisie, the magnanimous victor who had put a curb both upon itself and upon anarchy?

---

[a] A good face on a bad game.—*Ed.*

[b] An ironical allusion to the German liberal leaders whom Marx compares with Jourdain, hero of Molière's comedy *Le bourgeois gentilhomme*.—*Ed.*

[c] The reference is to the Prince of Prussia.—*Ed.*

Clearly the Prussian bourgeoisie now had only one task — to settle itself comfortably in the saddle, get rid of the troublesome anarchists, restore "law and order" and retrieve the profit lost during the March storm. It was now merely a question of reducing to a minimum the *costs* of its rule and of the March revolution which had brought it about. The weapons which, in its struggle against the feudal society and the Crown, the Prussian bourgeoisie had been compelled to demand in the name of the people, such as the right of association and freedom of the press, were they not bound to be broken in the hands of a deluded people who no longer needed to use them to fight *for* the bourgeoisie and who revealed an alarming inclination to use them *against* the bourgeoisie?

The *bourgeoisie was convinced* that evidently only one obstacle stood in the way of its *agreement* with the Crown, in the way of a deal with the old state, which was resigned to its fate, and that obstacle was the people — *puer robustus sed malitiosus*,[a] as Hobbes says. The *people* and the *revolution*!

The *revolution* was the *legal title of the people*; the vehement claims of the people were based on the revolution. The revolution was the bill of exchange drawn by the people on the bourgeoisie. The bourgeoisie came to power through the revolution. The day it came to power was also the day this bill became due. The bourgeoisie had to *protest* the bill.

Revolution on the lips of the people meant: you, the bourgeois, are the *Comité du salut public*, the Committee of Public Safety, to whom we have entrusted the government not in order that you should *come to an agreement* with the Crown regarding your own interests but in order that you should implement our interests, the interests of the people, *in face of* the Crown.

Revolution was the people's protest against the agreement between the bourgeoisie and the Crown. The bourgeoisie that was making an agreement with the Crown *had therefore to protest* against the *revolution*.

And that was done under the great *Camphausen*. *The March revolution was not recognised.* The representative National Assembly at Berlin set itself up as the *representative of the Prussian bourgeoisie*, as the *Agreement Assembly*, by *rejecting* the motion recognising the March revolution.[156]

The Assembly sought to undo what had been done. It vociferously declared to the Prussian people that the people did not come to an agreement with the bourgeoisie in order to make a revolution against

---

[a] A robust but malicious fellow (Thomas Hobbes, *De cive*, Preface).—*Ed.*

the Crown, but that it was making a revolution in order that the Crown would come to an agreement with the bourgeoisie against the people! Thus was the *legal title* of the revolutionary people annulled and the *legal basis* secured for the conservative bourgeoisie.

The legal basis!

Brüggemann, and through him the *Kölnische Zeitung,* have prated, fabled and moaned so much about the "legal basis", have so often lost and recovered, punctured and mended that "legal basis", tossed it from Berlin to Frankfurt and from Frankfurt to Berlin, narrowed and widened it, turned the simple basis into an inlaid floor and the inlaid floor into a false bottom (which, as we know, is a principal device of performing conjurors), and the false bottom into a bottomless trapdoor, so that in the end the legal basis has rightly turned for our readers into the basis of the *Kölnische Zeitung;* thus, they could confuse the shibboleth of the Prussian bourgeoisie with the private shibboleth of Herr Joseph Dumont, a necessary invention of *Prussian* world history with the arbitrary hobby-horse of the *Kölnische Zeitung,* and regard the legal basis simply as the basis on which the *Kölnische Zeitung* thrives.

The *legal basis,* namely, the *Prussian legal basis!*

The *legal basis* on which Camphausen, the knight of the great debate, the resurrected phantom of the United Diet and the Agreement Assembly, acted *after* the March revolution—is it the constitutional law of 1815 or the law of 1820 regarding the Provincial Diet, or the edict of 1847, or the electoral and agreement law of April 8, 1848 [157]?

It is none of these.

"Legal basis" simply meant that the revolution had gained no ground and the old society had not lost its ground; that the March revolution was only an "occurrence" that gave the "impulse" for an "agreement" between the throne and the bourgeoisie, preparations for which had long been made within the old Prussian state, and the need for which the Crown itself had already announced in earlier royal decrees, but had not, prior to March, considered as "*urgent*". In short, the "*legal basis*" meant that *after* the March revolution the bourgeoisie wanted to negotiate with the Crown on the same footing as *before* the March events, as though no revolution had taken place and the United Diet had achieved its goal without a revolution. The "legal basis" meant that the legal title of the people, *revolution,* did not exist in the *contrat social* between the Government and the bourgeoisie. *The bourgeoisie deduced its claims from the old Prussian legislation, in order that the people should not deduce any claims from the new Prussian revolution.*

Naturally, the *ideological cretins* of the bourgeoisie, its journalists, and suchlike, had to pass off this embellishment of the bourgeois interests as the real interests of the bourgeoisie, and persuade themselves and others to believe this. The phrase about the legal basis acquired real substance in the mind of a *Brüggemann*.

The *Camphausen* Government fulfilled its task, the task of being an *intermediate link* and a *transitional stage*. It was the *intermediate link* between the bourgeoisie which had risen on the shoulders of the people and the bourgeoisie which no longer required the shoulders of the people; between the bourgeoisie which apparently represented the people in face of the Crown and the bourgeoisie which really represented the Crown in face of the people; between the bourgeoisie coming away from the revolution and the bourgeoisie which had come out as the core of the revolution.[a]

In keeping with its role, the Camphausen Government coyly and bashfully confined itself to *passive resistance* against the revolution.

Although it rejected the revolution in theory, in practice it *resisted* only its claims and *tolerated* only the re-establishment of the old political authorities.

The bourgeoisie in the meantime believed that it had reached the point where *passive resistance* had to turn into *active offensive*. The *Camphausen* Ministry resigned not because it had committed some blunder or other, but simply because it was the *first* Ministry following the March revolution, because it was the *Ministry of the March revolution* and by virtue of its origin it had to conceal that it represented the bourgeoisie under the guise of a dictatorship of the people. Its dubious origin and its ambiguous character still imposed on it certain conventions, restraints and considerations with regard to the sovereign people which were irksome to the bourgeoisie, and which a second Ministry originating directly from the Agreement Assembly would no longer have to reckon with.

Its resignation therefore puzzled the saloon-bar politicians. It was followed by the *Hansemann* Government, the *Government of Action,* as the bourgeoisie intended to proceed from the period when it *passively* betrayed the people to the Crown to the period of *active* subjugation of the people to its own rule exercised in agreement with the Crown. The *Government of Action* was the *second* Government *after* the March revolution; that was its whole secret.

---

[a] This is evidently a misprint: is should read "the core of the counter-revolution".— *Ed.*

[*Neue Rheinische Zeitung* No. 183, December 31, 1848]

Cologne, December 29.

"Gentlemen, business is business!"[a]

In these few words Hansemann epitomised the whole liberalism of the United Diet. This man was the required head of a government based on the Agreement Assembly, a government which was to turn *passive resistance* to the people into an *active offensive* on the people, the *Government of Action*.

No Prussian Government contained so many *bourgeois* names! Hansemann, Milde, Märker, Kühlwetter, Gierke! Even *von Auerswald*, the sort of label acceptable at Court, belonged to the liberal aristocracy of the Königsberg opposition which paid homage to the bourgeoisie. *Roth von Schreckenstein* alone represented the old bureaucratic Prussian feudal nobility among this rabble. *Roth von Schreckenstein!* The surviving title of a vanished novel about robbers and knights by the late *Hildebrandt*.[b] But *Roth von Schreckenstein* was merely the feudal setting for the bourgeois jewel. *Roth von Schreckenstein* in a bourgeois government meant this, spelled out in capital letters: the Prussian feudalists, the army and bureaucracy are guided by the newly arisen star, the Prussian bourgeoisie. These powerful figures have placed themselves at its disposal, and the bourgeoisie has set them up in front of its throne, just as bears were placed in front of the rulers of the people on old heraldic emblems. Roth von Schreckenstein is merely intended to be the bear of the bourgeois Government.

On *June 26* the Hansemann Government presented itself to the National Assembly. Its effective existence began only in *July*. The *June revolution* was the background of the Government of Action, just as the *February revolution* formed the background of the Government of Mediation.

The bloody victory of the Paris bourgeoisie over the proletarians of Paris was exploited against the people by the Prussian bourgeoisie, just as the bloody victory of the Croats at Vienna was exploited against the bourgeoisie by the Prussian Crown. The suffering of the Prussian bourgeoisie after the Austrian November was *retribution* for the suffering of the Prussian people after the French June. In their short-sighted narrow-mindedness the German philistines mistook

---

[a] A quotation from Hansemann's speech in the first United Diet on June 8, 1847.—*Ed.*

[b] The reference is to Hildebrandt's novel *Kuno von Schreckenstein oder die weissagende Traumgestalt.—Ed.*

themselves for the French bourgeoisie. They had overturned no throne, they had not abolished feudal society, still less its last vestiges, they did not have to uphold a society they themselves had created. After June, as after February, they believed, as they had since the beginning of the sixteenth century and during the eighteenth century, that they would be able in their traditional crafty money-making manner to pocket three-quarters of the profit produced by someone else's labour. They had no inkling that behind the French June lurked the Austrian November and behind the Austrian November, the Prussian December. They did not suspect that whereas in France the throne-shattering bourgeoisie was confronted by only one enemy, the proletariat, the Prussian bourgeoisie, grappling with the Crown, possessed only one ally — the people. Not as if these two groups had no hostile and contradictory interests, but because they were still welded together by *the same* interests in face of a third power which oppressed them both equally.

The Hansemann Government regarded itself as a *government of the June revolution*. In contrast to the "red robbers", the philistines in every Prussian town turned into "respectable republicans", without ceasing to be worthy royalists, and occasionally overlooking the fact that their "reds" wore *white-and-black*[a] cockades.

In his speech from the throne on June 26, Hansemann gave short shrift to Camphausen's mysteriously nebulous "monarchy on *the broadest democratic basis*".

"*Constitutional monarchy based on the two-chamber system* and the joint exercise of legislative power by the two Chambers and the Crown"—that was the dry formula to which he reduced the portentous motto of his enthusiastic predecessor.

"Modification of the most essential relationships that are incompatible with the new constitution, liberation of property from the fetters that hamper its most *advantageous utilisation* in a large part of the monarchy, reorganisation of the administration of justice, reform of fiscal legislation and particularly *annulment of tax exemptions* etc." and above all "*strengthening of the power of the state* which is necessary for safeguarding the *freedom* which has been won" (by the citizens) "against reaction" (i.e. using the freedom in the interests of the feudal aristocracy) "and anarchy" (i.e. using the freedom in the interests of the people) "and for *restoring the shaken trust*"

—such was the Government's programme, the programme of the Prussian bourgeoisie in office, whose classical representative is *Hansemann*.

In the United Diet Hansemann was the most bitter and the most cynical adversary of trust, for—"*Gentlemen, business is business!*" Hansemann in office proclaimed the "*restoration of the shaken trust*" a

---

[a] Black and white were the Prussian colours.—*Ed.*

foremost necessity, for—this time he addressed the *people* as previously he had addressed the *throne*—for

"*Gentlemen, business is business!*"

Previously it was a question of the trust that *gives* money, this time of the trust that *makes* money; then it was a matter of *feudal* trust, the sincere trust in God, King and Fatherland, now it was *bourgeois* trust, trust in trade and commerce, in interest-bearing capital, in the solvency of one's commercial friends, that is, commercial trust; it is not a matter of faith, charity or hope, but of *credit.*

Hansemann's words, "*restoration of the shaken trust*", expressed the fixed idea of the Prussian bourgeoisie.

Credit depends on the confidence that the exploitation of wage labour by capital, of the proletariat by the bourgeoisie, of the petty bourgeois by the big bourgeois, will continue in the traditional manner. Hence any political stirring in the proletariat, whatever its nature, even if it takes place under the direct command of the bourgeoisie, shakes this trust, impairs credit. "Restoration of the shaken trust" when uttered by Hansemann signifies:

Suppression of every political stirring in the proletariat and in all social strata whose interests do not completely coincide with the interests of the class which believes itself to be standing at the helm of state.

Hansemann accordingly placed the "*strengthening of the power of the state*" side by side with the "restoration of the shaken trust". But he was mistaken as to the character of this "power of the state". He sought to strengthen the state power which served credit and bourgeois trust, but he strengthened the state power which demands trust and if necessary extorts this trust with the help of grape-shot, because it has no credit. He wanted to economise on the costs of bourgeois rule but instead burdened the bourgeoisie with the exorbitant millions which the restoration of Prussian feudal rule cost.

He told the workers very curtly that he had an excellent remedy for them. But before he could produce it the "shaken trust" must first of all be restored. To restore this trust the working class had to give up all political activity and interference in matters of state and revert to its former habits. If it followed his advice and trust were restored, this mysterious potent remedy would prove effective, if only because it would no longer be required or applicable, since in this case the malady itself—the subversion of the bourgeois law and order—would have been eliminated. And what need is there of medicine when there is no malady? But if the people obstinately stuck to their purpose, very well, then he would "*strengthen* the power of the state", the police, the army, the courts, the bureaucracy, and would set his bears on them, for "trust" had become a "money matter", and:

"Gentlemen, business is business!"

Hansemann's programme, even though he may smile at this, was an *honest* programme, a well-intentioned programme.

He wanted to strengthen the power of the state not only against anarchy, that is against the people, he wanted to strengthen it also against reaction, that is against the Crown and feudal interests insofar as they attempted to assert themselves against the purse and the *"most essential"*, that is the most modest, political claims of the bourgeoisie.

The very composition of the Government of Action was a protest against this "reaction".

It differed from all previous Prussian Ministries in that its real *Prime Minister* was the *Minister of Finance*. For centuries the Prussian state had carefully concealed the fact that the departments of war, internal and foreign affairs, church and school matters and even the royal household as well as faith, charity and hope depended on profane *financial* matters. The Government of Action placed this tiresome bourgeois truth uppermost by placing Herr Hansemann at its head, a man whose ministerial programme like his opposition programme was summarised in the words:

"Gentlemen, business is business!"

The monarchy in Prussia became a "money matter".

Now let us pass from the programme of the Government of Action to its actions.

It really carried out its threat of *"strengthening the power of the state"* against *"anarchy"*, that is against the working class and all sections of the middle class who did not stick to the programme of Herr Hansemann. It can even be said that, apart from increasing the tax on beet-sugar and spirits, this *reaction* against so-called *anarchy,* i.e. against the revolutionary movement, was the only serious action of this Government of Action.

Numerous lawsuits against the press based on Prussian Law or, where it did not exist, on the *Code pénal*, numerous arrests on the same "sufficient grounds" (Auerswald's formula), introduction of a system of constables in Berlin [158] at the rate of one constable per every two houses, police interference with the freedom of association, the use of soldiers against unruly citizens and of the civic militia against unruly proletarians, and the introduction, by way of deterrent, of a state of siege—all these events of Hansemann's

Olympiad are still vividly remembered. There is no need to give details.

This aspect of the efforts of the Government of Action was summarised by *Kühlwetter* in the following words:

"A state that wants to be really free must have a really large police force as its executive arm",

to which Hansemann himself muttered one of his usual remarks:

"This will also greatly help to *restore trust* and *revive the rather slack commercial activity.*" [a]

The Government of Action accordingly "*strengthened*" the old Prussian police force, the judiciary, the bureaucracy and the army, who, since they receive their *pay* from the bourgeoisie, also *serve* the bourgeoisie, as Hansemann thought. At any rate, they were "*strengthened*".

On the other hand, the mood of the proletariat and bourgeois democrats was expressed by *one* event. Because a few reactionaries maltreated some democrats in Charlottenburg, the people stormed the residence of the Prime Minister in Berlin.[159] This shows how popular the Government of Action had become. The next day Hansemann tabled a law against riotous gatherings and public meetings. This shows how cunningly he intrigued against reaction.

Thus the actual, tangible, popular activity of the Government of Action was of a purely *police* character. In the eyes of the proletariat and the *urban* democrats this Ministry and the Agreement Assembly, whose majority was represented in the Ministry, and the Prussian bourgeoisie, the majority of whom constituted the majority in the Agreement Assembly, represented the *old,* refurbished *police and bureaucratic state.* To this was added resentment against the bourgeoisie, because it governed and in the *civic militia* had become an integral part of the police.

The "achievement of the March events", as the people saw it, was that the liberal gentlemen of the bourgeoisie, too, took *police* duties upon themselves. There was thus a double police force.

Not the actions of the Government of Action, but the drafts of its organic laws show clearly that it "*strengthened*" the "*police*"—the ultimate expression of the old state—and spurred it into action only in the interest of the bourgeoisie.

In the Bills relating to *local government, juries,* and the *civic militia,* introduced by the Hansemann Ministry, *property* in one form or

---

[a] Quotations from the speeches made by Kühlwetter and Hansemann in the Prussian National Assembly on August 9, 1848.—*Ed.*

another always forms the demarcation line between the *lawful* and the *unlawful*. All these Bills contain the most servile concessions to royal power, for the bourgeois Ministry believed that royalty had become harmless to it and was its ally; but to compensate for that the ascendancy of capital over labour is all the more ruthlessly emphasised.

The civic militia law approved by the Agreement Assembly was directed against the bourgeoisie itself and had to provide a legal pretext for disarming it. According to the fancy of the bourgeoisie, however, it was to become valid only after the enactment of the local government regulation and the promulgation of the Constitution, that is after the consolidation of the rule of the bourgeoisie. The experience which the Prussian bourgeoisie has gained in connection with the civic militia law may contribute to its enlightenment and show it that for the time being all its actions that are meant to be directed against the people are only directed against itself.

As far as the people are concerned, the Hansemann Ministry is in *practice* epitomised by the old-Prussian police and in *theory* by the offensive *Belgian* differentiation between bourgeois and non-bourgeois.[160]

Now let us pass on to another section of the ministerial programme, to *anarchy against reaction.*

In this respect the Ministry has more pious wishes to show than real deeds.

Among the pious *bourgeois* wishes are the partition and sale of domains to private owners, the abandonment of banking to free competition, the conversion of the *Seehandlung*[161] into a private institution etc.

It was unfortunate for the Government of Action that all its economic attacks against the feudal party took place under the aegis of a *compulsory loan,* and that in general its attempts at reformation were seen by the people merely as financial expedients devised to replenish the treasury of the strengthened "power of the state". Hansemann thus won the hatred of one party without winning the approval of the other. And it has to be admitted that he only ventured to attack feudal privileges in earnest when "*money matters*" closest to the Minister of Finance, when *money matters as understood by the Ministry of Finance,* became pressing. In this narrow sense he told the feudal lords:

"Gentlemen, business is business!"

Thus even his positively bourgeois efforts directed against the feudalists reveal the same police taint as his negative measures designed to *"revive commercial activity"*. For in the language of political economy the *police* is called *exchequer*. The increase in the beet-sugar and liquor duties which Hansemann passed through the National Assembly roused the indignation of the money-bags, standing with God for King and Fatherland, in Silesia, the Marches, Saxony, East and West Prussia etc. But while this measure angered the industrial landowners in the old Prussian provinces, it caused no less displeasure among the bourgeois distillers in the Rhine Province, who perceived that their conditions of competition compared with those of the old Prussian provinces had been made even more unfavourable. And to crown all, it angered the working class in the old provinces, for whom it only meant, and could only mean, a *rise in the price of a prime necessity*. This measure therefore merely amounted to replenishing the treasury of the "strengthened power of the state". This example suffices, since it is the only action against the feudalists *actually* taken by the Government of Action, the only Bill of this nature which really became law.

Hansemann's "Bills" abrogating all *exemptions* from graduated and land taxes,[162] and his projected income tax caused the landowning votaries of "God, King and Fatherland" to respond as if bitten by a tarantula. They denounced him as a *communist* and even today the Prussian Dame of the Cross[a] crosses herself three times at the mention of Hansemann's name. That name sounds to it like Fra Diavolo.[b] The repeal of all exemptions from the land tax, the only important measure to be introduced by a Prussian Minister during the glorious reign of the Agreement Assembly, failed because of the *narrow-mindedness of the Left concerning principles.* Hansemann himself had justified this narrow-mindedness. Was the Left to provide new financial resources for the Ministry of the *"strengthened power of the state"* before the Constitution had been completed and sworn to?

The bourgeois Ministry *par excellence* was so unlucky that its most radical measure had to be frustrated by the radical members of the Agreement Assembly. It was so barren that its whole crusade against feudalism merely resulted in a *tax increase,* which was equally odious to all classes, and the abortive outcome of its entire financial acumen was a *compulsory loan:* two measures, which ultimately only provided *subsidies for the campaign of the counter-revolution against the bourgeoisie.* But the *feudal lords* were convinced of the "nefarious" intentions of

---

[a] An allusion to the *Neue Preussische Zeitung* also known as the *Kreuz-Zeitung.—Ed.*

[b] *Fra Diavolo*—a sobriquet of Michele Pezza, an Italian bandit; the title character of an opera by Auber.—*Ed.*

the *bourgeois* Ministry. Thus even the financial struggle of the Prussian bourgeoisie against feudalism merely proved that owing to its unpopularity and impotence it was only able to collect *money against itself* and— *Gentlemen, business is business!*

Just as the bourgeois Ministry succeeded in equally offending the urban proletariat, the bourgeois democrats and the feudal lords, so did it manage to alienate and antagonise even the *peasantry* oppressed by feudalism, and in this it was eagerly supported by the *Agreement Assembly.* It should not be forgotten that during half of its existence this Assembly was appropriately represented by the Hansemann Ministry and that the bourgeois martyrs of today were yesterday the train-bearers of Hansemann.

During Hansemann's rule Patow introduced a Bill abolishing feudal obligations (see the criticism of it we published earlier[a]). It was a most wretched botchwork, the product of the helpless bourgeois desire to abolish feudal privileges, those "conditions that are incompatible with the new constitution", and of bourgeois fear of revolutionarily attacking any kind of property whatever. Wretched, timid and narrow-minded egoism blinded the Prussian bourgeoisie to such an extent that it repulsed the *peasantry*, its *essential ally.*

On *June 3* deputy *Hanow* moved

"that all pending proceedings which concern the settlement of landowner-peasant relations and the commutation of services be immediately discontinued at the request of one of the sides until the promulgation of a new law based on just principles".

Not until the *end of September*, that is four months later, under the Pfuel Government, did the Agreement Assembly pass a Bill designed to discontinue pending proceedings between landowners and peasants, after rejecting all liberal amendments and retaining the "reservation about the provisional establishment of current obligations" and the "collection of disputed dues and arrears".[163]

In *August*, if we are not mistaken, the Agreement Assembly declared that *Nenstiel's* motion that "*labour services be abolished immediately*" was *not urgent.*[164] Could the peasants be expected to consider it an urgent matter for them to take up the cudgels for this Agreement Assembly which had thrown them back into conditions inferior to those they had actually won after the March events?

The French bourgeoisie began by emancipating the peasants. Together with the peasants it conquered Europe. The Prussian bourgeoisie was so preoccupied with its *most narrow*, immediate

---

[a] See present edition, Vol. 7, pp. 117-18, 290-95 and 327-32.—*Ed.*

interests that it foolishly threw away even this ally and turned it into a tool of the feudal counter-revolutionaries.

The *official* history of the dissolution of the bourgeois Ministry is well known.

Under its aegis, the "power of the state" was "strengthened" to such an extent and the popular energy so weakened that already on July 15 the Dioscuri Kühlwetter and Hansemann were obliged to issue a warning against reactionary machinations of civil servants, and especially *Landräte*, to all *Regierungspräsidenten* in the monarchy; that later an "*assembly of the nobility and big landowners for the protection*" of their privileges[165] met in Berlin alongside the Agreement Assembly; and that finally, in opposition to the so-called Berlin National Assembly, a "diet of local communities for the protection of the threatened property rights of landowners", a body originating in the Middle Ages, was convoked in Upper Lusatia on September 4.

The energy expended by the Government and the so-called National Assembly against these increasingly menacing counter-revolutionary symptoms found adequate expression in paper admonitions. The bourgeois Ministry reserved bayonets, bullets, prisons and constables exclusively for the people "*so as to restore the shaken trust and revive commercial activity*".

The incidents at *Schweidnitz*, where the soldiery in fact murdered the bourgeoisie in the person of the civic militia, finally roused the National Assembly·from its apathy. On August 9 it braced itself for a heroic deed, that of the Stein-Schultze army order, whose most drastic measure of coercion was an appeal to the *tact* of the Prussian officers.[166] A measure of coercion indeed! Did not royalist honour forbid the officers to follow the dictates of bourgeois honour?

On *September 7*, a month after the Agreement Assembly had passed the Stein-Schultze army order, it once more decided that its decision was a real decision and should be carried out by the Ministers. Hansemann refused to do this and resigned on September 11, after appointing himself a bank director at a yearly salary of 6,000 talers, for—*Gentlemen, business is business!*

Finally, on *September 25*, the Agreement Assembly gratefully agreed to *Pfuel's* thoroughly watered-down formula of acceptance of the Stein-Schultze army order, which by that time Wrangel's parallel army order and the large number of troops concentrated around Berlin had turned into a *bad joke*.

A mere glance at these dates and the history of the Stein-Schultze army order suffices to show that the army order was not the *real* reason for Hansemann's resignation. Is it likely that Hansemann, who did not shy at recognising the revolution, should have shied at this paper proclamation? Are we to believe that Hansemann, who, whenever the portfolio slipped from his fingers, always picked it up again, has this time, in a fit of virtuous exasperation, left it on the ministerial benches to be hawked about? No, our Hansemann is no fanatic. Hansemann was simply duped, just as in general he was the representative of the duped bourgeoisie. He was allowed to believe that on no account would he be dropped by the Crown. He was made to lose his last semblance of popularity in order that the Crown should at last be able to sacrifice him to the rancour of the country junkers and get rid of this bourgeois tutelage. Moreover, the plan of campaign agreed upon with Russia and Austria required that the Ministry should be headed by a general appointed by the camarilla from outside the Agreement Assembly. The old "power of the state" had been sufficiently "strengthened" under the bourgeois Ministry to venture on this coup.

Pfuel was a disappointment. The victory of the Croats at Vienna made even a Brandenburg a useful tool.

Under the Brandenburg Ministry the Agreement Assembly was ignominiously dispersed, fooled, derided, humiliated and persecuted, and the *people*, at the decisive moment, remained *indifferent*. The *defeat* of the Assembly was the *defeat of the Prussian bourgeoisie*, of the *constitutionalists*, hence a *victory for the democratic party*, however dear it had to pay for that victory.

And the *imposed* Constitution?

It had once been said that never would a "scrap of paper" be allowed to come between the King and *his* people.[167] Now it is said: there shall be *only a scrap of paper* between the King and *his* people. The *real* Constitution of Prussia is the *state of siege*. The imposed French Constitution had only one article—the 14th, which invalidated it.[168] Every article of the imposed Prussian Constitution is an Article 14.

By means of this Constitution the Crown grants new privileges—that is upon *itself*.

It permits itself to dissolve the Chambers indefinitely. It permits Ministers in the interim to issue any desired law (even those affecting property and so forth). It permits deputies to impeach Ministers for such actions, but at the risk, under the state of siege, of being classed as "internal enemies". Finally, it permits itself, should the stock of the counter-revolution go up in the spring, to replace this nebulous "scrap of paper" by a Christian-Germanic Magna Charta[169] *organically* growing out of the distinctions of the medieval social estates, or to drop the constitutional game altogether. Even in the latter case the conservative bourgeois would fold their hands and pray:

"*The Lord gave, and the Lord hath taken away; blessed be the name of the Lord!*"[a]

The history of the Prussian bourgeois class, like that of the German bourgeois class in general between March and December, shows that a purely *bourgeois revolution* and the establishment of *bourgeois rule* in the form of a *constitutional monarchy* is impossible in Germany, and that only a feudal absolutist counter-revolution or a *social republican revolution* is possible.

But that the viable section of the bourgeoisie is bound to awake again from its apathy is guaranteed above all by the *staggering bill* which the counter-revolution will present it with in the spring and, as our Hansemann so sensibly says:

"*Gentlemen, business is business!*"

Written by Marx on December 9, 11, 15 and 29, 1848

Printed according to the newspaper

First published in the *Neue Rheinische Zeitung* Nos. 165, 169, 170 and 183, December 10, 15, 16 and 31, 1848

---

[a] Job 1:21.—*Ed.*

A NEW ALLY OF THE COUNTER-REVOLUTION

Cologne, December 11. The counter-revolution has acquired a new ally: the Swiss Federal Government.

Already five days ago we learned from a thoroughly trustworthy source that the recent rumours of an intended incursion of the German refugees into Baden, of arming at the frontier, and of a mythical battle near Lörrach between volunteer insurgents and imperial troops—that all these peculiar rumours were "agreed upon" between the ruling party of Furrer-Ochsenbein-Munzinger in the Swiss Federal Council and the German imperial authority in order to give the said party an excuse for taking measures against the refugees and thereby helping to establish a good agreement with the imperial power.[a]

We did not immediately communicate this news to our readers, because we could not unreservedly believe in such an intrigue. We waited for confirmation, and confirmation was not long in coming.

It was already noticeable that these rumours were not published by Baden newspapers which, being on the spot, should be the best and earliest informed, but by Frankfurt newspapers.

It was furthermore noticeable that the *Frankfurter Journal* was already informed from Berne on December 1 that the Federal Council had issued a circular on the question of the refugees and sent a commissioner, whereas the Berne newspapers, several of which (*Verfassungs-Freund* and *Suisse*) are in direct contact with members of the Federal Council, did not publish the news until December 3.

---

[a] See this volume, pp. 116-17 and 141-42.— *Ed.*

Now at last we have the circular to the cantonal authorities before us in the *Suisse*,[a] and if previously we could still doubt the adhesion of Switzerland to the new Holy Alliance,[170] now all doubts have been removed.

The circular begins with *rumours* of new armings of the political refugees and of an intended new incursion into the Baden area. These rumours, which all Switzerland and all Baden know to be false, serve as the *grounds* for the new extraordinary measures against the refugees. The decisions of the Federal Assembly about Tessin are mentioned only to justify the competence of the Federal Council to adopt these measures but not its obligation to do so; on the contrary the essential difference between the situation in Tessin and in the northern cantons is *expressly recognised.*

Then come the following instructions:

1) All refugees who took part in Struve's expedition,[171] or who otherwise offer no personal guarantees of tranquil behaviour, are to be removed from the frontier cantons;

2) all refugees without distinction are to be kept under close supervision;

3) a list of all refugees coming under 1) is to be sent to the Federal Council and to all frontier cantons, and

4) possible exceptions to internment are to be left to the decision of the representative of the Confederation, Dr. Steiger, whose instructions in general are to be followed.

Then follows the demand for the "*strict*" fulfilment of these instructions, since otherwise, if it becomes necessary to call out troops, the costs will have to be borne by the frontier canton concerned.

The whole circular is drafted in harsh language, highly insulting to the refugees, and concludes with the words:

"Switzerland must not become an assembly area for foreign parties which so greatly misconceive their situation on neutral soil and so often trample under foot the interests of the country that hospitably receives them."

Now compare this bitter language with that of the Note of November 4[b]; bear in mind that the rumours on which the circular is based are *notoriously false*; that, as we have been informed from the frontier today, the representative of the Confederation, Dr. Steiger, has *already completed* his inspection in the Aargau canton, against which the imperial authority put forward most complaints, and has

---

[a] *La Suisse* No. 291, December 6, 1848.—*Ed.*

[b] Note of the *Vorort* Berne to the Imperial Government (see this volume, pp. 67-68 and 136).—*Ed.*

found that the refugees concerned were interned long ago and that he has no more to do there (he is already in Liestal); that the Note of November 4 already asserts and the Swiss press (e.g. *Schweizer Bote, Basellandschaftliches Volksblatt, National-Zeitung* etc.) long ago proved that all the frontier cantons fulfilled their duties long ago; bear in mind, finally, that after long uncertainty, after the most contradictory reports about the closing of the frontier, now for the last two or three days all our Swiss newspapers and letters have been unanimous in saying that *absolutely no* measures of coercion are being applied against Switzerland, and indeed that the order given to certain frontier posts for stricter supervision of the movement of people was revoked already 24 hours later; bear all this in mind and say whether the circumstances do not confirm in the minutest detail the report given by us above.

At any rate, it is well known that Herren Furrer, Ochsenbein, Munzinger etc. have long cherished a burning desire to put an end once for all to the "excesses of the refugees".

We congratulate Herr Schmerling on his new friends. We only wish that, if *he* too were to enter Switzerland as a refugee—which could very well happen before the three years' official duration of the present Federal Council expires—these friends of his will not consider him as one of those refugees who "offer no personal guarantees".

Written on December 11, 1848

First published in the *Neue Rheinische Zeitung* No. 166, December 12, 1848

Printed according to the newspaper

Published in English for the first time

THE CALUMNIES
OF THE *NEUE RHEINISCHE ZEITUNG*

Cologne, December 13. The article of the *Neue Rheinische Zeitung* of July 4,[a] on account of which the responsible publisher, *Korff*, the editor-in-chief, *Marx*, and the editor of the *Neue Rheinische Zeitung*, *Engels*, are to appear before the assizes on the 20th inst., concludes with the following words:

"Those are the actions of the *Government of Action*, the Government of the Left Centre, the *Government of transition to an old aristocratic, old bureaucratic and old Prussian Government*. As soon as Herr Hansemann has fulfilled his *transitory function*, he will be dismissed.

"The Berlin Left, however, must realise that the old regime is willing to let it keep its small parliamentary victories and large constitutional designs as long as the old regime in the meantime is able to seize all the really important positions. *It can confidently recognise the revolution of March 19 inside the Chamber provided the revolution can be disarmed outside of it.*

"*Some fine day the Left may find that its parliamentary victory coincides with its real defeat. Perhaps German development needs such contrasts. The Government of Action recognises the revolution in principle in order to carry out the counter-revolution in practice.*"

Facts have proved to what extent the *Neue Rheinische Zeitung* has **calumniated** the Prussian Government and its henchmen.

Written by Marx on December 13, 1848

First published in the *Neue Rheinische Zeitung* No. 168, December 14, 1848

Printed according to the newspaper

Published in English for the first time

---

[a] "Arrests" (see present edition, Vol. 7, pp. 177-79) quoted below.—*Ed.*

URSULINE CONVENT.—
RECRUITING FOR THE GRAPE-SHOT KING.—
THE "BURGHERS' COMMUNE".—
COMMISSION ON A GENERAL CUSTOMS TARIFF

Berne, December 9. The last convent in the Berne canton, that of the Ursulines in Pruntrut in the Jura, is approaching its end. The Government Council [*Regierungsrat*][a] has decided to propose to the Great Council the dissolution of this convent in fulfilment of the Diet's decision banning from Switzerland all orders affiliated to the Jesuits (to which the Ursulines belong).

After Radetzky had again allowed the Neapolitan-Swiss recruits through Lombardy, King Ferdinand likewise immediately suggested that recruiting should again be allowed in Switzerland. Lucerne and the *Ur*-cantons naturally hastened to permit recruitment; the Berne Government, for whom the enlistment agreements[172] are anyway a thorn in the flesh, luckily found an excuse to continue prohibiting recruitment for the present. It states in particular that according to the enlistment agreement (which is a relic inherited from the revered regime of Herr Neuhaus), the recruits would be obliged to go via Genoa, a route which is still barred to them; and further, the Neapolitan Government would first have to indemnify the Swiss in Naples for the damage by looting etc., done on May 15.[173] The god-fearing *Beobachter*[b] is of course fearfully shocked by this violation of inviolable Swiss loyalty, which moreover prevents a great number of fine young canton citizens from making a glorious career (!), jeopardises the future of the Berne soldiers in Naples, causes recruiting sergeants present in Berne to starve, and reduces the income of the publicans on whose premises the military bounty would be drunk away. These are the kind of arguments with which the reactionary Swiss press wages its war.

---

[a] i.e. the Government of the canton.— *Ed.*
[b] *Schweizerischer Beobachter.—Ed.*

The local conservative patricians have suffered a hard blow. For there is a so-called burghers' commune within the commune itself. This commune, the core of which is the patriciate, made sure, in spite of all the revolutions, that the former monastery estates and other state and town domains to which it is entitled as the former holder of sovereignty, should not be transferred with sovereignty to the state or the town respectively, but be kept by it in collective ownership. Only a small part of these highly valuable estates, on which the patricians still wax fat today, is to go to the town, but the "burghers" always refused to give it up. Now at last, through the choice of Berne as the federal capital and the consequent heavy city expenses, the burghers' commune has been forced to surrender its share to the town commune, the so-called residents' commune,[174] and moreover to pledge a "substantial" contribution to the costs of the federal capital. The patricians declare Zion to be in danger, and they have good reason, for the federal capital threatens their purses very seriously.

The Federal Council has formed under the presidency of the head of the Trade and Customs Department, Herr Näff, a commission which is to prepare the abolition of canton duty and the creation of a Swiss customs tariff, and propose the necessary measures. Switzerland will also get protective tariffs now, which will not, it is true, be high but will completely achieve their purpose owing to the advanced development of most branches of Swiss industry and to the low wages. England, Paris, Mühlhausen and Lyons will suffer most from these measures.

Written by Engels on December 9, 1848

First published in the *Neue Rheinische Zeitung* No. 168, December 14, 1848

Printed according to the newspaper

Published in English for the first time

ADDRESS OF THE CENTRAL COMMISSION OF THE WORKERS' ASSOCIATIONS OF SWITZERLAND TO THE EXECUTIVE OF THE MARCH ASSOCIATION IN FRANKFURT AM MAIN[175]

*To the Executive of the March Association
in Frankfurt am Main*

Citizens,

The German associations of Switzerland held a Congress here in Berne on the 9th, 10th and 11th of this month; they have joined together in a permanent union and appointed the Berne Association as the District Union.[176]

The undersigned Central Commission herewith informs you of the founding of the Union.

It also informs you that the Congress has decided to enter into correspondence with the March Association. A closer union with the latter is excluded by Article 1 of our common Rules, in which the Swiss associations explicitly declare themselves for a democratic social republic.[177]

The Congress has also instructed us to make known to you its decided disapproval of the measures taken by the German imperial authority against Switzerland. These measures, as unjust as they are ridiculous, not only serve to compromise Germany in the eyes of all Europe; for us German workers in Switzerland they have the particular disadvantage that they jeopardise our position materially and put us German democrats in a false position in relation to our friends, the democrats of Switzerland.

We hope that one of the delegates of the March Association will take the earliest opportunity to inform the so-called National Assembly[a] of this official expression of opinion of the German workers in Switzerland.

---

[a] The German National Assembly in Frankfurt.—*Ed.*

In the meantime we look forward to your communications and letters.

Greetings and fraternal good wishes.

The Central Commission
of the German Workers' Associations
of Switzerland

Berne, December 1848[a]

Written by Engels in mid-December 1848

Printed according to the manuscript

First published in *Beiträge zur Geschichte der deutschen Arbeiterbewegung*, Heft 4, 1960

Published in English for the first time

---

[a] The back of the document bears the address: "To Herr Trützschler, deputy at Frankfurt am Main."—*Ed.*

[DISMISSAL OF DRIGALSKI]

Cologne, December 17. The "citizen and communist" Drigalski,[a] who introduced the censorship, abolished it again, and then threatened to **suspend** the local newspaper,[b] has, we have just heard, been **suspended** himself. A pity, a great pity!

Postscript. Misfortune travels fast! Herr Spiegel, *Regierungspräsident*, also bids us farewell. According to reports current all over the town, he has been **dismissed**.

Written by Marx on December 17, 1848

First published in the supplement to the *Neue Rheinische Zeitung* No. 172, December 19, 1848

Printed according to the newspaper

Published in English for the first time

---

[a] See this volume, pp. 75-80.—*Ed.*
[b] The *Neue Rheinische Zeitung.*—*Ed.*

THE TRIAL OF GOTTSCHALK AND HIS COMRADES

[*Neue Rheinische Zeitung* No. 175, December 22, 1848]

Cologne, December 21. This morning the trial of *Gottschalk, Anneke* and *Esser* began at the extraordinary assizes here.

The accused were escorted like the lowest criminals *in fetters* from the new remand prison to the court building, where a not inconsiderable armed force was present.

Our readers are aware that we regard the jury system as at present organised as anything but a guarantee. The register qualification gives a definite class the privilege of choosing the jury from its midst. The method of compiling the lists of jury members gives the Government the monopoly of selecting from the privileged class those individuals who suit it. For the Herr *Regierungspräsident* draws up a list of a certain number of individuals which he selects from the lists of jury members of the entire administrative area; the *judicial* representatives of the Government prune this list down to 36, if our memory does not deceive us. Finally, at the time of the actual formation of the jury, the Public Prosecutor's office has the right to prune for a third time the last list, the outcome of class privilege and a double governmental distillation, and to reduce it to the final requisite dozen.

It would be a real miracle if such a constitution of the jury did not place accused persons who have openly opposed the privileged class and the existing state authority directly in the absolute power of their most ruthless enemies.

But the *conscience* of the jurymen, we shall be told in reply, their *conscience*; could one demand a greater guarantee than that? But, *mon Dieu*, a man's conscience depends on his knowledge[a] and his way of life.

The conscience of a republican is different from that of a royalist, that of a property owner is different from that of one who owns no property, that of a thinking person is different from that of one incapable of thought. One who has no vocation for being a juryman other than that of the register qualification has the conscience of the register qualification.

The "conscience" of the privileged is precisely a privileged conscience.

Although, therefore, the jury as at present constituted appears to us to be an institution for asserting the privileges of a few and by no means an institution for safeguarding the rights of all; although, in the present case especially, the Public Prosecutor's office has made the most extensive use of its powers in order to eradicate from the last list the last dozen names displeasing to it — nevertheless we have not a moment's doubt of the *acquittal* of the accused. Our guarantee is the *bill of indictment*. Reading it, one could believe it an ironically phrased defence document of Gottschalk and his comrades.

Let us summarise this *indictment*, the only analogy to which is the indictment against Mellinet and Co. (the Risquons-Tout trial in Antwerp [178]).

In Cologne there is a Workers' Association.[179] Gottschalk was president of it, and Anneke and Esser members of its Executive Committee. The Workers' Association, the indictment informs us,

"had a special organ, the *Arbeiter-Zeitung*, edited by Gottschalk, and anyone who did not have the opportunity of attending in person the meetings of the Association could learn from this newspaper the dangerous *tendencies* of the Association to flatter the proletariat and work for communism and the overthrow of the existing order".[b]

Therefore, one could acquaint oneself with *tendencies* but not with *illegal acts*. *The proof is*: Until the arrest of Gottschalk and the others, the prosecuting magistrates did not bring forward any charge against the *Arbeiter-Zeitung*, and *after* Gottschalk's arrest it was only once condemned—in the monster trial instituted by the prosecuting magistrates here, on the charge of insulting these magistrates.[180]

"But the *Arbeiter-Zeitung* itself," the indictment admits, "does not seem to have taken the trouble to conceal anything in its reports on the subject" (the proceedings of

---

[a] In the original there is a pun on the words *Gewissen* (conscience) and *Wissen* (knowledge).—*Ed.*

[b] Here and below the indictment is quoted from M. F. Anneke's book *Der Politische Tendenz-Prozess gegen Gottschalk, Anneke und Esser*, which is named later in this article.—*Ed.*

the Workers' Association, of the meetings of its Executive Committee and of its branches).

If, therefore, the *Arbeiter-Zeitung* could not be prosecuted on account of its "reports" of the proceedings of the Workers' Association, then this Association itself could not be prosecuted on account of its proceedings.

The only accusation levelled against the Workers' Association is the same as that against the *Arbeiter-Zeitung*, viz the *objectionable tendency of this Association*. Do the March achievements include also *trials based on tendency*, trials against tendencies that have remained mere tendencies? Up to now our *September Laws*[181] have not yet been promulgated. Gottschalk and his comrades were by no means arrested and accused because of illegal reports of the *Arbeiter-Zeitung* or illegal proceedings of the Workers' Association. The indictment makes no secret of this. It was not the previous activity of the Workers' Association that set the wheels of justice in motion, but—listen to this:

"From June 14 to 17 of this year a Congress was held in Frankfurt of delegates from a multitude of democratic associations that have arisen in Germany. Gottschalk and Anneke were delegates representing the Cologne Workers' Association. As is known, this Congress expressed itself *openly in favour of a democratic republic*, and the *authorities here expected a repercussion of the movement there*, when on Sunday, June 25, once more a general meeting of the Workers' Association was announced to be held in the Gürzenich Hall."

The authorities here expected a repercussion of the Frankfurt movement. But what movement had taken place in Frankfurt? The *Democratic Congress* had expressed itself *openly* in favour of the *objectionable* tendency of a *democratic republic*. A *"repercussion"*, therefore, of this *"tendency"* was expected and it was intended to engage in a struggle against this *echo*.

As is known, the *Democratic Congress* in Frankfurt and the *Central Committee* in Berlin, appointed to carry out its decisions, held their sessions without any opposition from the authorities.[182]

The German governments therefore, in spite of the *objectionable tendency*, had to recognise the lawfulness of the Frankfurt Congress and of the organisation of the democratic party decided upon by the Congress.

But the Cologne authorities *"expected nevertheless"* a *repercussion* of the Frankfurt movement. They expected to have an opportunity of catching Gottschalk and his comrades on illegal ground. In order to create this opportunity, on June 25 the police authorities sent "police inspectors *Lutter* and *Hünnemann*" to attend the general meeting of the Workers' Association in the Gürzenich Hall and "specially instructed them to observe what took place there". At the same general meeting there happened to be present "the book-binder Johann *Maltheser*", who, as the indictment states regretfully, "*would be a chief witness, if he were not in the pay of the police authorities*", that is to say, in other words, if he were not a *paid police spy*. Finally, there was present there, probably out of pure patriotic fanaticism, the "**candidate assessor von Groote**", who gives Anneke's speech at the general meeting "in more detail than anyone else, *since he wrote it down during the sitting itself*".

It is clear that the Cologne authorities *were expecting a crime to be committed* on June 25 by *Gottschalk* and his comrades. All arrangements were made by the police to confirm the occurrence of this possible crime. And once the authorities "*expect*", they do not want to *expect* in vain.

"The reports" of the police inspectors and other minor assistants officially sent to confirm an *expected* crime

> "gave occasion for the state authorities on July 2 to demand a judicial investigation against Gottschalk and Anneke on account of their inflammatory speeches delivered" (it should say *expected*) "at that public meeting. Their arrest and the seizure of their papers took place on July 3.
> "On July 5, after a number of witnesses had been heard and more detailed information had become available, the investigation was extended to the whole previous activity of the leaders of the Workers' Association and thereby to several members of the latter, especially to the cooper *Esser* etc. The results of the investigation of the accused relate in part to their speeches in the Workers' Association, in part to their papers and the printed material spread by them".

The *real result of the investigation—we shall prove it tomorrow from the text of the indictment itself*—is that the movement expected on June 25 was confined to a movement of the authorities—this echo of the Frankfurt movement; that *Gottschalk and his comrades have had to atone for the deceived expectation of the authorities on June 25 by undergoing six months' close confinement during examination. Nothing is more dangerous than to deceive the state authority's expectations of earning a medal for saving the fatherland.* No one likes to be disappointed in his expectations, least of all the *state authority*.

If the whole way in which the crime of June 25 was *staged* shows us the state authority as the sole creator of this crime drama, the text of the indictment enables us to admire the astute versatility by which it spun out the prologue over six months.

We quote word for word from *Der Politische Tendenzprozess gegen Gottschalk und Konsorten*, published by M. F. Anneke, Publishing House of the *Neue Kölnische Zeitung*.

"After the investigation had gone on for about five to six weeks, it was declared closed by the Examining Magistrate Leuthaus, who had replaced Herr Geiger, the latter having been promoted to the post of Police Superintendent. Public Prosecutor Hecker, however, after looking through the dossiers, put forward new *demands* to which the examining magistrate agreed. After about 14 days, the preliminary investigation was closed for the second time. After Herr Hecker had made a fresh study of the dossiers at his leisure, *he once more put forward a number of new demands.* The examining magistrate did not want to accept them, nor did the Council Chamber. Herr Hecker appealed to the board of prosecuting magistrates and this instance laid down that some of the demands should be allowed, but others rejected. Among the latter, for example, was the demand that *on the basis merely of a list of names of persons from all parts of Germany* which was found in Anneke's portfolio, all these persons, some 30 or 40 in number, *should be subjected to judicial investigation.*

"After the investigation had been successfully spun out so far, and could not reasonably be still further extended, the Council Chamber on September 28 ordered the dossiers to be handed over to the board of prosecuting magistrates. The latter confirmed the indictment on October 10, and on October 28 the Prosecutor-General signed the bill of indictment.

"*It was therefore luckily too late for this trial to come before the regular quarterly assizes, which had begun on October 9.*

"After November 27 an extraordinary session of the assizes was fixed. *It was intended that if possible this session also should be missed.* The dossiers of the preliminary examination were sent to the Ministry of Justice with the request that the trial should be referred to another court of assizes. However, the Ministry of Justice found no sufficient grounds for this and towards the end of November the accused *Gottschalk, Anneke* and *Esser* were finally referred to the extraordinary assizes here on December 21."

During this long prologue, the *first examining magistrate, Geiger, was promoted to acting Police Superintendent,* and *Public Prosecutor Hecker to Chief Public Prosecutor.* Since Herr *Hecker* in this last capacity was moved from *Cologne* to *Elberfeld shortly before the beginning* of the extraordinary assizes, he will not appear before the jury at the same time as the accused.

[*Neue Rheinische Zeitung* No. 176, December 23, 1848]

Cologne, December 22. On what day did the Gürzenich general meeting, which was convened to confirm an *"expected"* crime, take place? It was on *June 25.* This was the day of the definitive defeat of the *June insurgents* in Paris. On what day did the state authorities begin proceedings against Gottschalk and his comrades? It was on July 2, i.e. at the moment when the Prussian bourgeoisie and the Government allied with it at that time, carried away by their thirst for revenge, believed that the time had come to finish off their political opponents. On *July 3,* Gottschalk and his associates were arrested. On *July 4,* the *present counter-revolutionary* Ministry in the person of *Ladenberg* joined the *Hansemann* Ministry. On the same day, the *Right wing* in the Berlin Agreement Assembly ventured on a *coup d'état* by unceremoniously rejecting in *the same sitting*, after part of the Left wing had dispersed,[183] a decision regarding *Poland* which had been adopted by a majority.

These facts are eloquent. We could prove by the testimony of witnesses that on July 3 a "certain" person declared: "The arrest of Gottschalk and his associates has made a favourable impression on the public." It suffices, however, to point to the issues of the *Kölnische*, the *Deutsche*, and the *Karlsruher Zeitung* of the dates mentioned to convince oneself that during those days it was not the "echo" of the imaginary *"Frankfurt movement"*, but rather the "echo" of *"Cavaignac's movement"* which resounded a thousandfold in Germany and, among other places, also in *Cologne*.

Our readers will recall: On June 25 the Cologne authorities "expected" a repercussion of the "Frankfurt movement" on the occasion of the general meeting of the Workers' Association in the Gürzenich Hall. They will recall further that the starting point for the judicial investigation against Gottschalk and his comrades was not any actual crime committed by Gottschalk etc. *prior to* June 25, but solely the *expectation* of the authorities that on June 25 at last some palpable crime *would be* committed.

The expectation in regard to June 25 was disappointed and suddenly June 25, 1848, is transformed into the year 1848. The accused are made *responsible for the movement of the year 1848.* Gottschalk, Anneke and Esser are charged with

"having *in the course of the year 1848"* (note the elasticity of this expression) "made a *conspiracy* in Cologne with the aim of changing and overthrowing the Government concerned and of fomenting a civil war by misleading the citizens into taking up arms against one another, *or at any rate*" (take note!), *"or at any rate* by speeches at public meetings, by printed material and posters, having incited to attempts at assassination and *suchlike aims".*

That is to say, therefore, they are charged with having made a *conspiracy,* "*or at any rate*" with not having "made" **any** conspiracy. But then at any rate "to attempts at assassination and *suchlike* aims". That is to say, to attempts at assassination or something of the sort! How magnificent the juridical style is!

So it is stated in the board of prosecuting magistrates' decision for committal to trial.

In the conclusion of the indictment itself, mention of *conspiracy* is *dropped* and "in *accordance* with it" Gottschalk, Anneke and Esser are charged with

"having in the *course of the year 1848,* by speeches at public meetings as well as by printed material, *directly* incited their fellow citizens to alteration of the Constitution *by force,* to armed rebellion against the royal power and to the arming of one part of the citizens against another, without, however, these incitements having been successful—a crime envisaged in Article 102, in combination with Articles 87 and 91 of the Penal Code".

And why did the authorities *in the course of the year 1848* not intervene before July 2?

Incidentally, for the gentlemen to be able to speak of an *"alteration of the Constitution by force"*, they would *in the first place* have had to furnish proof that a *Constitution existed*. The Crown has *proved* the contrary by sending to the devil the Agreement Assembly. If the agreers had been more powerful than the Crown, they would perhaps have conducted the proof in the *reverse direction*.

As regards the incitement "to *armed* rebellion against the royal power and to the *arming* of one part of the citizens against another", the indictment tries to prove it:

1. by speeches of the accused in the course of the year 1848;
2. by unprinted;
3. by printed documents.

Ad. 1. The *speeches* provide the indictment with the following *corpus delicti*[a]:

At the sitting of May 29, *Esser* finds that a *"republic"* is the *"remedy for the suffering of the workers"*. *An incitement to armed rebellion against the royal power!* Gottschalk declares that *"the reactionaries* will *bring about* the republic". Some workers complain that they do not have enough "to keep body and soul together". Gottschalk replies to them: "You should learn to *unite*, to distinguish your friends from your disguised enemies, to make yourselves capable of *looking after your own affairs*."

An obvious *incitement to armed rebellion against the royal power* and *to the arming of one part of the citizens against another!*

The indictment sums up its proofs in the following words:

"The witnesses who have been examined concerning these earlier meetings, both members and non-members, on the whole speak only in praise of Gottschalk and Anneke, especially the former. He is said to have always warned against excesses, and to have tried to calm rather than incite the masses. In doing so he indeed indicated the republic as the final goal of his efforts, which, however, was to be achieved not by a street riot but only by the majority of the people being won over to the view that there was no salvation except in a republic. *As is clearly seen, by thus setting out to undermine gradually the foundations of the existing order, he was understandably often hard put to it to restrain the impatience of the vulgar crowd."*

It is precisely because the accused *calmed* the masses instead of *inciting* them that they showed *clearly* their nefarious tendency

---

[a] Body of the crime.—*Ed.*

gradually to undermine the foundations of the existing order, that is, in a *legal* way to make a *use, objectionable* to the authorities, of freedom of the press and the right of association. And that is what the indictment calls: "*Incitement to armed rebellion against the royal power and to the arming of one part of the citizens against another*"*!!!*

Finally comes the general meeting of *June 25*, which was "*expected*" by the authorities. In regard to it, the indictment says: "*detailed testimonies are available*". And what results from these detailed testimonies?—That Gottschalk made a report on the Frankfurt events; that the union of the three democratic associations in Cologne was discussed,[184] and that Gottschalk delivered a "concluding speech", which especially attracted the attention of **Maltheser** and the **candidate assessor von Groote**, and ended with the "*point*": "To go on waiting requires more courage than to strike at random. One must wait until the reaction takes a step which results in pressure for the proclamation of a republic." *Obvious incitement to armed rebellion against the royal power and to the arming of one part of the citizens against another!!!*

As far as *Anneke* is concerned, according to the indictment

"*there is nothing more against him* than that, in the debate *on the union of the three associations*" (the three democratic associations of Cologne), "he spoke very vigorously for this union, addressing the meeting also as *republican citizens*".

A speech in favour of the "*union*" of the three democratic associations of Cologne is obviously "*incitement to the arming of one part of the citizens against another*"!

And the mode of address as "*republican citizens*"! Herren **Maltheser** and **von Groote** might have felt themselves insulted by this mode of address. But does not General *von Drigalski* address himself and the citizens of Düsseldorf as "*communist citizens*"?

Looking at this net product of the "*expected*" general meeting of June 25, one can understand that the state authority had to take refuge in the *course of the year 1848*, and that is what it did by acquiring information about the movement in this year through the seizure of letters and printed documents; for example, it confiscated three issues of the *Arbeiter-Zeitung* which could be bought for four pfennigs a copy in any street.

From the letters, however, it became convinced of the "*political fanaticism*" prevailing in Germany in the year 1848. A letter of Professor *Karl Henkel* from Marburg to Gottschalk seemed to it particularly "fanatical". To punish him it denounced this letter to the Hesse Government and had the satisfaction that a judicial investigation would be instituted against him.

But the final result derived from the letters and printed documents is that in 1848 fanaticism of all kinds was at work in people's minds and on paper, and in general events took place which resembled as closely as one egg does another "*armed rebellion against the royal power and the arming of one part of the citizens against another*".

Gottschalk and his comrades, however, were busily occupied with all this, whereas the state authority only became aware of the "*repercussion*" of this astonishing movement through confiscating the printed documents and letters of the accused![185]

Written by Marx on December 21 and 22, 1848

Printed according to the newspaper

First published in the *Neue Rheinische Zeitung* Nos. 175 and 176, December 22 and 23, 1848

Published in English for the first time

THE PRUSSIAN COUNTER-REVOLUTION AND THE PRUSSIAN JUDICIARY[186]

Cologne. The chief result of the revolutionary movement of 1848 is not what the peoples won, but what they lost—the *loss of their illusions.*

June, November and *December* of 1848 are gigantic milestones on the path to the disenchantment and disintoxication of the minds of the European peoples.

High in the list of the last illusions which keep the German people in chains is its *superstitious faith* in the *judiciary.*

The prosaic north wind of the Prussian counter-revolution has blighted also this flower of the people's imagination, whose true Motherland is Italy—eternal Rome.

The actions and statements of the *Rhenish Court of Appeal,* of the *Supreme Court of Berlin,* and of the *Courts of Appeal* of *Münster, Bromberg* and *Ratibor,* against *Esser, Waldeck, Temme, Kirchmann* and *Gierke* prove once again that the French *Convention* is and remains the beacon for all revolutionary epochs. It inaugurated the revolution by means of a decree *dismissing all officials.* Judges, too, are nothing but officials, as the above-mentioned courts have testified before the whole of Europe. Turkish *kadis* and Chinese collegiums of mandarins can countersign without qualms the most recent decrees of those "*high*" courts against their colleagues.

Our readers already know the decrees of the Berlin Supreme Court and of the Ratibor Court of Appeal. Today we are concerned with the *Münster Court of Appeal.*[187]

First of all, however, a few words more about the *Rhenish Court of Appeal*, the *summus pontifex*[a] of Rhenish jurisprudence, which has its seat in Berlin.

As is well known, the Rhenish jurists (with a few honourable exceptions) found nothing more urgent to do in the Prussian Agreement Assembly than to cure the Prussian Government of its old prejudice and old resentment. They proved to that Government in fact that their previous opposition merely signified as much as the opposition of the French parliament before 1789[188]—the obstinate and would-be liberal assertion of *guild interests*. Like the liberal members of the French National Assembly of 1789, so the liberal Rhenish jurists in the Prussian National Assembly of 1848 were the *worthiest of the worthy* in the army of servility. The Rhenish-Prussian prosecuting magistrates outdid the old-Prussian inquisitorial judges in "political fanaticism". The Rhenish jurists had, of course, to maintain their reputation also *after* the dissolution of the Agreement Assembly. Thought of the laurels of the old-Prussian Supreme Court prevented the Rhenish-Prussian Court of Appeal from sleeping. Its chief presiding judge *Sethe* sent to judge of the Supreme Court of Appeal *Esser* (not to be confused with the "well-meaning" Cologne "Essers"[b]) a letter similar to that of the presiding judge of the Supreme Court *Mühler* to judge of the Secret Supreme Court *Waldeck*[189] But the Rhenish-Prussian court was able to go one better than the old-Prussian court. The presiding judge of the Rhenish Court of Appeal[c] played a trump card against his competitors by committing the treacherous *rudeness* of informing the Berlin public of the letter to Herr Esser in the *Deutsche Reform*,[d] before he had communicated it to Herr Esser himself. We are convinced that the *entire Rhine Province* will reply to Herr Sethe's letter *by a monster address to our worthy veteran countryman, Herr Esser*.

Not something is rotten in the "state of Denmark",[e] but *everything*. Now for *Münster*!

Our readers have already heard of the protest of the Court of Appeal in Münster against the reappointment of its director *Temme*.

The matter can be summarised as follows:

The Ministry of the counter-revolution had, directly or indirectly, insinuated to the Secret Supreme Court, the Rhenish Court of

---

[a] The supreme pontiff.—*Ed.*
[b] Esser I and Esser II.—*Ed.*
[c] Sethe.—*Ed.*
[d] No. 56, December 21, 1848 (morning edition).—*Ed.*
[e] Shakespeare, *Hamlet*, Act I, Scene 4.—*Ed.*

Appeal, and the Courts of Appeal in Bromberg, Ratibor and Münster, that the *King[a] would view with extreme disfavour the return of Waldeck, Esser, Gierke, Kirchmann and Temme to their high judicial posts, because they had continued to attend the Assembly in Berlin and had participated in the decision to refuse to pay taxes. So would those courts protest against it.*

All the high courts (at the outset the Rhenish Court of Appeal vacillated; great artists achieve their successes not by being the first but by being the last to perform) accepted this suggestion and sent protests from and to Berlin. The *Münster Court of Appeal* was stupid enough to address *directly to the King* (the so-called *constitutional* King) a protest against *Temme,* which states word for word

"that by participation in the illegal sittings of a faction of the adjourned National Assembly he had put himself in open rebellion against His Majesty's Government and by taking part in voting in favour of the motion on refusing to pay taxes he had taken the path of revolution and tried to hurl the fire-brand of anarchy into the fatherland",

and which then continues:

"It is contrary to our sense of justice, to the demands of the public for integrity on the part of the director of a provincial collegium of magistrates, and to the responsibilities of the latter concerning the training of young law officers and his position in relation to the junior officials of courts, that after such events the aforesaid *Temme* should retain his official position in the collegium here. Therefore, Your Majesty, we feel compelled by our consciences most humbly to express the urgent desire to see ourselves freed from official relation to director Temme."[b]

The address is signed by the whole collegium except for one member, a brother-in-law of *Minister of Justice Rintelen.*

On December 18, this Minister of Justice sent Herr Temme in Münster a copy of this address "*for his decision*", after Temme had already resumed his post here *without opposition from the cowards.*

During the morning of December 19, as the *Düsseldorfer Zeitung* reports, Temme appeared for the first time in a plenary sitting of the provincial Court of Appeal and took his seat as director beside deputy chief presiding judge von Olfers. As soon as the sitting began, he asked to speak and in brief said approximately the following:

"He had received a rescript from the Minister of Justice with a copied enclosure. This enclosure contained a petition of the 'high collegium', to which he now had the honour to belong, protesting against his reinstatement in his post. The Minister of Justice had sent him this petition for his information and 'for him to take a

---

[a] Frederick William IV.—*Ed.*

[b] Quoted from the *Preussischer Staats-Anzeiger* No. 229, December 19, 1848,—*Ed.*

decision accordingly'. The protest of the 'high collegium' was obviously based on his political activity; but of this as in general of his political views, he did not intend to speak here, for he did not have to defend them before the 'high collegium'. Further, as far as his 'decision' was concerned, he had already given effect to it by taking his seat here as director, and he could assure the 'high collegium' that he would not vacate it until judgment and law compelled him to do so. Moreover, he was not of the opinion that the collegial relationship should be upset by the diversity of political views; for his part at least that would be avoided as far as possible."[a]

The worthiest of the worthy were thunderstruck. They sat there dumb, motionless, like stone figures, as if a Medusa's head had been hurled into the collegium of mandarins.

The worthy Court of Appeal in Münster! In its professional zeal it has caused numerous people to be questioned and arrested because they wanted the decision of the National Assembly on the refusal to pay taxes to be carried out. By its statement about Herr Temme, which had even been addressed directly to the throne, the worthy provincial Court of Appeal has formed itself into—a party and pronounced a *prejudiced opinion,* and therefore it is impossible for it any longer to play the role of judge in relation to another party.

It will be recalled that the alleged coercion of the Prussian National Assembly by the Berlin mob was used as the pretext for the first coup d'état of the Brandenburg Ministry.[190] In order not to exercise any coercion against the deputies, the Ministry continued the "*wild chase*"[191] begun against them in Berlin, even *after* the deputies had returned to their homes!

Minister of Justice Rintelen states in his decree, which we reprint further below:

"The illusion deliberately fostered by many persons, that the hitherto existing criminal laws, particularly those concerned with crimes against the state, are no longer valid since March of this year, has greatly contributed to increase anarchy and has perhaps also had a dangerous influence on individual courts."

Most of the actions of Herr Rintelen and of the courts *under his jurisdiction* provide further proof that since the forcible dissolution of the National Assembly only *one* law continues to be valid in Prussia, *the arbitrary will of the Berlin camarilla.*

On March 29, 1844, the Prussian Government promulgated the notorious disciplinary law against the judges,[b] by which, through a mere decision of the Ministry, they could be deprived of their posts,

---

[a] Quoted from the report "Münster, vom 20. Dez." published in the *Düsseldorfer Zeitung* No. 336, December 23, 1848.—*Ed.*

[b] "Gesetz, betreffend das gerichtliche und Disziplinar-Strafverfahren gegen Beamten."—*Ed.*

moved or pensioned off. The last *United Diet*[192] abolished this law and restored the validity of the fundamental principle that judges could be dismissed, moved or pensioned off only by a lawfully delivered judgment.[a] The imposed Constitution confirms this principle. Are not these laws being trampled under foot by the courts which, in accordance with the prescription of the Minister of Justice, Rintelen, want by *moral compulsion* to drive their politically compromised colleagues into giving up their posts? Are not these courts turning themselves into an officer corps which casts out any member whose political views do not suit its royal Prussian "*honour*"?

And is there not also a law on the *non-liability* and *inviolability* of the *people's representatives*?

Hot air and empty sound!

If the *Prussian Constitution* had not annulled itself already by its own articles and the manner of its origin, it would be annulled owing to the simple fact that its ultimate guarantor is the *Supreme Court of Berlin*. The Constitution is guaranteed by the *responsibility of the Ministers*, and the *non-liability of the Ministers* is guaranteed by the court that has been granted to them, which is no other than the *Supreme Court in Berlin*, the classical representative of which is Herr *Mühler*.

The most recent rescripts of the Supreme Court, therefore, are neither more nor less than the obvious *cassation of the imposed Constitution.*

In *Austria*, owing to the Government's direct *threats to plunder* the bank,[193] which the Viennese people left *untouched* at the time of its greatest and most justified resentment against financial feudalism, the *bourgeoisie* realises that its betrayal of the proletariat surrendered precisely what this betrayal was intended to safeguard—*bourgeois property*. In *Prussia*, the *bourgeoisie* sees that, owing to its cowardly trust in the Government and its treacherous distrust of the people, the indispensable *guarantee of bourgeois property—bourgeois administration of justice*—is threatened.

With the dependent state of the judiciary, the bourgeois administration of justice itself becomes dependent on the Government; that is to say, bourgeois law itself is replaced by the arbitrary action of officials. *La bourgeoisie sera punie, par où elle a péché*—the bourgeoisie will be punished by that in which it has sinned—by the *Government.* That the servile statements of the highest Prussian courts are only the first symptoms of the approaching absolutist

---

[a] The reference is to the "Verordnung über einige Grundlagen der künftigen Preussischen Verfassung".—*Ed.*

transformation of the courts, is borne out by the following recent decree of the Ministry of Justice:

"By the general ordinance of October 8 of this year, my predecessor in office has already called attention to the fact that it is the prime task of the judicial authorities to maintain respect for the law and its effective action, that they can best serve their country by fulfilling this task, because true freedom can flourish only on the basis of law. Since then, unfortunately, in many places there have occurred very serious outbreaks of an anarchist activity which mocks at law and order; in some parts of the country even violent revolts against the authorities have taken place and have not everywhere been energetically countered. In view of such a regrettable state of affairs, I now, after His Majesty's Government has taken a decisive step to save the state, which has been brought to the brink of the abyss, I now address myself anew to the judicial authorities and the Public Prosecutors of the whole country, to request them to do their duty everywhere and without regard for persons. Whoever the guilty person may be, he must not escape the legal punishment that has to be brought to bear in the speediest possible way.

"With especially deep regret I have been compelled to note, both from individual reports of the provincial authorities and from official newspapers, that some judicial officials also, unmindful of their special professional duties, have in part let themselves be carried away into committing obviously illegal actions, and in part have not shown the courage and fearlessness through which alone terrorism could be successfully countered. I expect steps to be taken in regard to them also, with establishment of the facts and if necessary the institution of a judicial investigation, without lenience and with the utmost expedition, for officials responsible for the administration of justice, who are entrusted with preserving the prestige of the laws, have by their own violation of the law been doubly at fault; and it is especially necessary to expedite the proceedings against them because the operation of the law must not be allowed to remain in the hands of such officials. If among those guilty there are officials in respect of whom, on the basis of existing regulations, a formal investigation cannot be made, or on whom suspension from office, which must always be considered as a duty in cases of this kind, cannot be imposed without higher authorisation, then steps must be taken to establish the facts in order to justify the investigation without a special instruction, and after that the requisite permission obtained as speedily as possible. With regard to candidate assessors and junior lawyers attending the courts, it must be borne in mind that there are special rules governing their dismissal from state service.

"The illusion deliberately fostered by many persons: that the hitherto existing criminal laws, particularly those concerned with crimes against the state, are no longer valid since March of this year,

has greatly contributed to increase anarchy and has perhaps also had a dangerous influence on individual courts. In view of the excellent state of mind of the Prussian judicial officials, which on the whole they still display, it suffices to point to the well-known juridical principle that laws remain in force until annulled or modified through legislation, as well as to the express provision of Article 108 of the constitutional document of the 5th of this month, in order to be assured that the honourable Prussian judicial officials, in their whole-hearted interest for true moral and political freedom, will put above everything the prestige of law and order.

"Guided by these principles and scorning all personal dangers, we shall go forward confident of victory over crime, over anarchy. Precisely thereby we shall most essentially contribute to ensure that the Prussian state, previously so brilliant, will once again display its moral strength and will no longer tolerate—to use the words of a brave Frankfurt deputy—that wickedness and gross violence should continue to exist among us.

"The presiding judges of the courts, and also the Prosecutor-General in Cologne, should accordingly instruct the officials of their departments to do what is necessary, and keep me informed in respect of which officials, and for what offences, suspensions are being pronounced and judicial investigations instituted.

Berlin, December 8, 1848

Minister of Justice *Rintelen*"

If one day the revolution in Prussia is victorious, it will not find it necessary, like the February revolution, to abolish the irremovability of the older class of judges by a special decree. It will find this caste has given documentary evidence of the renunciation of its privilege in the authentic declarations of the *Rhenish Court of Appeal, the Supreme Court in Berlin,* and the *Courts of Appeal in Bromberg, Ratibor and Münster.*

Written by Marx about December 23, 1848

First published in the *Neue Rheinische Zeitung* No. 177, December 24, 1848

Printed according to the newspaper

Published in English for the first time

MEASURES AGAINST GERMAN REFUGEES.—
RETURN OF TROOPS FROM TESSIN.—
THE PATRICIANS' COMMUNE

Berne, December 24. The new measures of the Federal Council, which are so gratefully recognised by the Empire, do not merely consist of the circular and Steiger's journey of inspection[a]; they consist in particular of the expulsion from Switzerland of three absolutely non-dangerous refugees who published an absolutely blameless, merely informative pamphlet about the latest rising in Baden,[b] and furthermore of the steps taken against the newspaper *Die Revolution* and against the so-called *Hilf Dir* military association.[194]

The volunteer commander, J. Ph. Becker of Biel, who has been a citizen of the Berne canton for the past year, was the head of a military organisation of the above name, which is said to have had the aim of organising all the German volunteers living in Switzerland into a German Legion. It seems a dangerous business but was not really so at all. The Legion only existed on paper; there was no question of weapons, still less of drilling; its only object was to hinder more over-hasty and unplanned volunteer campaigns, and since *all* these are necessarily over-hasty and unplanned—as is proved by the two of Lucerne, the two of Baden, and the one of Val d'Intelvi [195]—the military association would inevitably have led to the prevention of such volunteer campaigns *altogether*. For that reason neither the Baden nor the Swiss Government had anything to do with it, and as the leaders of the organisation owing to all sorts of beloved memories of all secret societies as well as to more or less

---

[a] See this volume, pp. 180-81.—*Ed.*

[b] T. W. Löwenfels, F. Neff und G. Thielemann, *Die zweite republikanische Aufstand in Baden*, Basel, 1848.—*Ed.*

bragging behaviour gave the Government a pretext for intervening; and as, moreover, the whole plan came under the Berne law on volunteer insurgents, there was the best possible opportunity to see here a far-reaching conspiracy and preparations for a new attack on Baden in the near future. Added to this was Becker's indiscretion in announcing, on the title page, his weekly *Revolution* as the "organ of the democratic military association '*Hilf Dir*'". That was enough: Herr Ochsenbein, who by chance or intentionally came to Biel, brought about the intervention of the public authorities. The specimen issue of the *Revolution* was seized, one of the editors, Michel, banished from the canton, and Becker's house searched. After that there were second thoughts. The attack on the freedom of the press was too provocative. The distraint was again lifted, and the *Revolution* will continue to appear[a]; but a judicial investigation against Becker has begun, and it will probably be the end of the military association "*Hilf Dir*". The German imperial philistine can once more sleep in peace.

In Tessin, all the troops have been discharged. The extent to which the Tessiners were slandered by the East Swiss is shown by the excellent understanding between the Bernese battalion sent there and the population. It is true, of course, that this battalion began by behaving quite differently from the men of Zurich and Appenzell. At one of the banquets given to the officer corps, Colonel Seiler of Berne declared that neutrality was a necessary evil, and that he looked forward to the time when the Swiss, free from these fetters, would fight for liberty in the ranks of the other peoples. The battalion collected a day's pay as a contribution for the refugees from Italy. If the gentlemen from Zurich and Appenzell had acted in the same way instead of taking pleasure in fulfilling odious gendarme functions and fraternising with Austrian officers, the Tessiners would have given them a very different reception.

Some days ago there was a highly amusing meeting of philistines in Berne. The residents' commune met to decide whether they wanted to take over the burden of being the seat of the Federal Government. The patricians, beaten in the last burghers' commune meeting,[b] and seeing with their own eyes that the property dispute between the burghers and the residents was really beginning, wanted to have their revenge here. With the actual handing over of the property of the residents' commune the town was made independent of the patriciate, they lost a large number of lucrative posts and the main

---

[a] Subsequently it appeared as *Die Evolution.—Ed.*

[b] See this volume, pp. 183-84.—*Ed.*

props of their overwhelming influence in the Commune Council, not to mention the direct heavy financial loss. So they launched into all their intrigues in order—to remove again the seat of the Federal Government from Berne! They declared that the costs of the seat of the Federal Government had been stated so uncertainly that there was a risk of being shamefully cheated by the Federal Council. Further, the state and not the town should bear the bulk of the costs; and under these pretexts they proposed to grant a miserable 300,000 francs, but no more. The law concerning the seat of the Federal Government demands however unreserved acceptance of the conditions within a month, and the month expires on December 28. The acceptance of the proposals made by the patricians was thus equivalent to a refusal to make Berne the seat of the Federal Government. The patricians' plausible proposals for economy and safeguards met with tremendous approval from the Berne philistines, so that the radicals who wanted *à tout prix* to keep the federal capital there almost despaired of succeeding in their object. It was debated all day, and not till evening did the radicals collect 419 votes against 314 for the unconditional acceptance of the obligations proposed by the Federal Assembly. There you have an example of the petty parochialism which dares to try to lay down the law, even in the capital city of Switzerland!

Written by Engels on December 24, 1848

First published in the supplement to the *Neue Rheinische Zeitung* No. 180, December 28, 1848

Printed according to the newspaper

Published in English for the first time

LETTER OF THE CENTRAL COMMISSION
OF THE WORKERS' ASSOCIATIONS IN SWITZERLAND
TO THE ASSOCIATION IN VIVIS

TO THE ASSOCIATION IN VIVIS

Friends, Brothers,

We, the Central Commission set up by the Congress, have before us for reply your letter of December 7.[196] Since the Congress has now established the foundations for the unification of the various associations, we shall not deal with your reproaches to the Zurich Association[197] but go straight on to answer the different points of your letter which concern the proposed centralisation.

You demand, first, that at the Congress the votes of associations given only by letter should be included in the count, justifying this by reference to the democratic principle. The Congress discussed this matter and also the reasons you give, but it believed that it could not accept them. It took the view that in that case no congress would be necessary and the associations would only need to send letters to the Central Commission, which could then add up the votes and proclaim the result. This is more or less the manner in which the associations have been in communication up to now and which yielded no results, while the Congress was easily able to put matters to rights in a few days. And this was because more can be achieved, and understanding can more easily be reached, in a few hours of oral consultation than by years of correspondence. Associations which send no delegates cannot, of course, take part in the *debates* of the Congress, they cannot hear what reasons for and against are being put forward, and since in the end these reasons decide the voting, they cannot, of course, vote either. Otherwise it would not be possible ever to reach a majority decision. If you think this is not democratic, we take the view that no democratic state in the world has ever accepted your opinion in this respect, but invariably taken ours: in America, in Switzerland, in France, as in all former democracies, the principle has always held good that those who send no delegates cannot vote either. Incidentally, the Congress has seen to it that in future every association can be represented by the Congress taking over the entire costs of the delegates. At this Congress, too, you could perhaps have been represented; Lausanne, which lacked the means to send a delegate, arranged for a citizen in Berne[a] to represent them and sent him his instructions.[198]

It is certainly to be regretted that up to now there has been so little unity among the associations in Switzerland, and also that so many contradictory proposals for the Central Association were put forward. For this very reason it was an excellent idea of the Zurich Association to suggest a Congress. The provisional regulations which it drafted were, of course, only a suggestion on which the Congress had to vote, and which it altered considerably, as you will see from the enclosed printed copy of the minutes. But now, when a beginning at least has been made through the debates of the delegates of ten different associations, it is most desirable that the unrepresented associations should adhere to the centralisation which has at last been started and that they should yield in the same way that almost every other represented association has yielded on one point or another of its opinion and submitted to the decisions of the majority. Without mutual concessions we can never achieve anything.

Your suggestion that the Executive of the "*Hilf Dir*" military association be proclaimed the Central Association was very seriously considered, but was rejected. The *Hilf Dir* military association is a banned association under the local laws (the law on volunteers) and thus all *associations* joining it as *associations* would likewise be in danger of being dissolved and deprived of their funds. Moreover, the military association will only take over the military organisation, but does not see it as its task to represent the associations also with respect to social-democratic propaganda and correspondence with Germany. The Berlin Central Committee and the Workers' Committee in Leipzig[199] would not be able to risk entering into correspondence with the military association, even on innocent matters, without exposing themselves to dissolution and arrest; and the other way round, the military association would likewise not be able to conduct a regular correspondence with these committees without exposing itself to the most persistent persecution by the Swiss authorities. Above all, however, we want a centralisation which does not give the governments any pretext for new persecutions of

---

[a] Frederick Engels.—*Ed.*

refugees, a centralisation which cannot be harmed and which is therefore in a position to perform its functions. The deputy from Biel[a] himself was of this opinion and spoke against transferring the duties of the Central Association to the Executive of the military association. But all are, of course, free to join the military association; they are only asked not to join it *as associations,* so that the association can never be harmed as such, but only individual persons, if perchance new persecutions should take place.

Having thus replied to each of the points mentioned in your letter, we refer you to the enclosed minutes for the further decisions of the Congress and ask you on behalf of the Congress to join the Union of German Associations founded hereby and to advise us as soon as possible of your having done so.

We appeal to you again: give way in secondary matters as others have given way and will give way in future, so as to save the main object; join the nucleus of the Union which has already been founded by several associations with much sacrifice in money and time, and which can only succeed if we all stand together, forget the past and no longer allow ourselves to be divided by minor differences of opinion!

Greetings and fraternal good wishes.

On behalf of the Congress,
The Central Commission

Berne, about December 25, 1848
Address: Herr   N.   Berger,
Käfichgässlein No. 109, Bern

Written by Engels

First published in *Beiträge zur Geschichte der deutschen Arbeiterbewegung,* Heft 4, 1960

Printed according to the manuscript

Published in English for the first time

---

[a] Julius Standau.—*Ed.*

REFUTATION

The *literary lumpenproletariat* of Herr Dumont, which accepts with the most touching passive resistance all the kicks bestowed on it by the *Neue Rheinische Zeitung,* is trying to revenge itself by denouncing the editors of the *Neue Rheinische Zeitung* to the police on account of articles which they have *not* written. Thus, according to the *Kölnische Zeitung* of December 25, *Freiligrath* is alleged to be the author of a report from Cologne in the *Deutsche Schnellpost,* published in New York, and *for that reason* is said to have participated in the cat's concert dedicated to the patrons of the *Kölnische Zeitung* on November 3. It seems that the laurels won by "*Maltheser*"[a] prevent the editors of the *Kölnische Zeitung* from sleeping.

Written on December 26, 1848

First published in the *Neue Rheinische Zeitung* No. 179, December 27, 1848

Printed according to the newspaper

Published in English for the first time

---

[a] See this volume, p. 191.—*Ed.*

THE NEW "HOLY ALLIANCE"

Cologne, December 30. It is already generally known that some months ago a new "Holy Alliance" was concluded between Prussia, Austria and Russia.[200] The treaty itself will very shortly be brought into the light of day and it will be possible for it to be made public. The soul of this alliance of the rulers "by the grace of God and the knout" is Russia. On the other hand, the whole of Russian policy and diplomacy, with few exceptions, is borne on the shoulders of Germans or German Russians. Indeed, wherever absolutism and counter-revolution are actively at work, Germans are always to be found, but nowhere more so than at the focal point of the permanent counter-revolution, Russian diplomacy. There, in the first place, is Count Nesselrode, a German Jew; then come Baron von Meyendorf, ambassador in Berlin, from Estonia, and his assistant, adjutant of the Tsar, Colonel Count Benkendorff, also from Estonia. Working in Austria is Count Medem, a Courlander, with several assistants, including a Herr von Fonton, all of them Germans. Baron von Brunnow, Russian ambassador in London, also a Courlander, acts as an intermediate and mediating link between—Metternich and Palmerston. Finally, in Frankfurt, Baron von Budberg, a Livonian, acts as Russian chargé d'affaires. These are a few examples. We could cite several dozen more, without mentioning the creatures of the Petersburg Tsar[a] who occupy high and highest posts in Germany and at the same time are in high Russian pay.

The role played by the Austrian Archduchess Sophia, now the Dowager Empress, in the cause of the Holy Alliance and the enemies of the people, is so notorious as to need no description. Sophia

---

[a] Nicholas I.—*Ed.*

herself, however, is in turn powerfully influenced by Grand Duchess Helena, wife of Grand Duke Michael and daughter of Prince Paul von Württemberg. Helena serves as the most intimate link between Nicholas and Sophia and the notorious Archduke Ludwig.

Moreover, already some months ago these persons agreed on the plan according to which the Austrian martial-law Emperor[a] will marry the surviving daughter[b] of the Grand-ducal married couple in order that the new "Holy Alliance" will be indissolubly welded together and Russia brought ever closer to its goal, the establishment in Germany of the most complete rule of the knout.

Written on December 30, 1848

First published in the *Neue Rheinische Zeitung* No. 183, December 31, 1848

Printed according to the newspaper

Published in English for the first time

---

[a] Franz Joseph.—*Ed.*
[b] Catherine.—*Ed.*

THE REVOLUTIONARY MOVEMENT[201]

Cologne, December 31. Never was a revolutionary movement opened with such an edifying overture as the revolutionary movement of 1848. The Pope gave it the blessing of the Church,[202] and Lamartine's aeolian harp vibrated with tender philanthropic tunes to the text of *fraternité*, the brotherhood of members of society and nations.

> Welcome all ye myriad creatures!
> Brethren, take the kiss of love![a]

Driven out of Rome, the Pope is at present staying at Gaeta under the protection of the tigerish idiot Ferdinand; Italy's "*iniciatore*"[203] conspires against Italy with Austria, Italy's traditional mortal enemy, whom in happier days he threatened to excommunicate. The recent French presidential elections have given statistical proof of the unpopularity of Lamartine, the traitor. There has been no event more philanthropic, humane, and weak than the February and March revolutions, nothing more brutal than the inevitable consequences of this *humanity of weakness*. The proofs are Italy, Poland, Germany, and, above all, those who were defeated in June.

But the defeat of the French workers in June was the defeat of the June victors themselves. Ledru-Rollin and the other men of the Mountain were ousted by the party of the *National*, the party of the bourgeois republicans; the party of the *National* was ousted by Thiers-Barrot, the dynastic opposition; these in turn would have had to make way for the legitimists[204] if the cycle of the three restorations had not come to an end, and if Louis Napoleon were something

---

[a] Schiller, "An die Freude".—*Ed.*

more than an empty ballot-box by means of which the French peasants announced their entry into the revolutionary social movement, and the French workers their condemnation of all leaders of the preceding periods—Thiers-Barrot, Lamartine and Cavaignac-Marrast. But let us note the fact that the inevitable consequence of the defeat of the revolutionary French working class was the defeat of the republican French bourgeoisie, to which it had just succumbed.

The defeat of the working class in France, the victory of the French bourgeoisie was at the same time the renewed fettering of the nationalities who had responded to the crowing of the Gallic cock with heroic attempts to liberate themselves. Prussian, Austrian and English *Sbirri*[a] once more plundered, ravished and murdered in Poland, Italy and Ireland. The defeat of the working class in France, the victory of the French bourgeoisie was at the same time the defeat of the middle classes in all European countries where the middle classes, united for the moment with the people, had responded to the crowing of the Gallic cock with sanguinary insurrections against feudalism. Naples, Vienna, Berlin! The defeat of the working class in France, the victory of the French bourgeoisie was at the same time a victory of East over West, the defeat of civilisation by barbarism. The suppression of the Rumanians by the Russians and their tools, the Turks, began in Wallachia[205]; Croats, Pandours, Czechs, Serezhans[206] and similar rabble throttled German liberty in Vienna, and the Tsar is now omnipresent in Europe. The overthrow of the bourgeoisie in France, the triumph of the French working class, the emancipation of the working class in general, is therefore the rallying-cry of European liberation.

But *England*, the country that turns whole nations into its proletarians, that takes the whole world within its immense embrace, that has already once defrayed the cost of a European Restoration, the country in which class contradictions have reached their most acute and shameless form—*England* seems to be the rock against which the revolutionary waves break, the country where the new society is stifled even in the womb. England dominates the world market. A revolution of the economic relations in any country of the European continent, in the whole European continent without England, is a storm in a teacup. Industrial and commercial relations within each nation are governed by its intercourse with other nations, and depend on its relations with the world market. But the

---

[a] Policemen.—*Ed.*

world market is dominated by England, and England is dominated by the bourgeoisie.

The liberation of Europe, whether brought about by the struggle of the oppressed nationalities for their independence or by overthrowing feudal absolutism, depends therefore on the successful uprising of the French working class. Every social upheaval in France, however, is bound to be thwarted by the English bourgeoisie, by Great Britain's industrial and commercial domination of the world. Every partial social reform in France or on the European continent as a whole, if designed to be lasting, is merely a pious wish. And only a *world war* can overthrow the old England, as only this can provide the Chartists, the party of the organised English workers, with the conditions for a successful rising against their gigantic oppressors. Only when the Chartists head the English Government will the social revolution pass from the sphere of utopia to that of reality. But any *European war* in which England is involved is a world war, waged in Canada as in Italy, in East Indies as in Prussia, in Africa as on the Danube. A European war will be the first result of a successful workers' revolution in France. England will head the counter-revolutionary armies, just as it did during the Napoleonic period, but through the war itself it will be thrown to the head of the revolutionary movement and it will repay the debt it owes in regard to the revolution of the eighteenth century.

The table of contents for 1849 reads: **Revolutionary rising of the French working class, world war.**

Written by Marx on December 31, 1848   Printed according to the newspaper

First published in the *Neue Rheinische Zeitung* No. 184, January 1, 1849

SWISS-ITALIAN AFFAIRS

Berne, December 28. The Swiss troops have hardly been withdrawn from the Lombardy border and Radetzky's chicaneries are already beginning again. He has written to the federal representatives in Tessin saying there is a disturbing trade in weapons on the frontier, and the federal representatives have talked the Tessin Government into authorising several house searches in Mendrisio. A few muskets have been found and confiscated. It cannot be foreseen on what grounds this violation of the privacy of the home and seizure of foreign property will be justified. It is only surprising that the Tessin Government has lent itself to such practices.

The Neapolitan recruiting in Lucerne and the *Ur*-cantons[a] appears however to be leading nowhere. It is not as if they had not found a sufficient number of stalwart Alpine lads who would give their skins for ready money and be happy to do Croat services in Ferdinand's army; on the contrary! But the whole business is foundering on the impossibility of getting from Switzerland to Naples.

According to the enlistment agreements,[207] the recruits must be transported via Genoa, and the Turin Government refuses transit. It is now said that the recruits are to be brought to Trieste and embarked there. This news has caused great alarm among the recruits. They do not want to go to Austria. They are afraid of being put among real Croats and led against the Magyars, and they are now petitioning the Lucerne Government Council to insist on the Genoese route. Strange. As if it were not a matter of indifference to these henchmen of the counter-revolution whether they massacre Magyars or Messinese! But of course there is a big difference between Austrian paper money and Neapolitan full-weight gold ducats!

---

[a] See this volume, p. 183.—*Ed.*

Incidentally, the Lucerne Government seems to imitate the Bernese Government in wanting to suspend the enlistment agreements till the Swiss merchants in Naples and Messina are indemnified.[208] At least, it has inquired of the Federal Council about the arrangements for compensation. So that leaves only the *Ur*-cantons, and these will not suffer any encroachment upon the right of every citizen to sell himself as long as the Federal Constitution allows it, i.e. as long as the present enlistment agreements have still to run. This right of self-sale is one of the finest and oldest privileges of the free *Ur*-Swiss, and if these brave "first-born sons of freedom" tried to defend their "five-hundred-year-old rights" against the new Federal Constitution, it was above all on account of this special right which the new Constitution has annulled. The military enlistment agreements are really a vital matter for the *Ur*-cantons. For five hundred years they have been the drainage channel for the superfluous population, and hence the best guarantee for the existing barbarous state of things. Annul the enlistment agreements, and you will unleash a real revolution in these so-called *clean,* i.e. in fact extremely unclean, democracies.

The younger sons of peasants, now setting off for Naples and Rome, will have to stay at home; they will find no occupation either in their own cantons or in the rest of Switzerland, which is already suffering enough from "over-population"; they will form a new class of peasant proletarians, who by their very existence must bring all the old relations of property, property acquirement and law of these pastoral races, established for a thousand years, into the utmost confusion. Where would these sterile mountain lands get the means to feed the paupers deposited there from all sides on the frontier by expulsion orders? The core of such a class of paupers already exists and threatens in an exceedingly disagreeable way this traditional patriarchalism. And even if—which is not to be expected—in the next few years the European revolution observes the same respect as hitherto towards Swiss neutrality, the article of the new Federal Constitution forbidding enlistments is preparing a revolutionary ferment which will eventually completely uproot the oldest and most firmly entrenched seat of reactionary barbarism in Europe. Like the monarchies, the reactionary republics are going under, dying of pecuniary consumption, of the "pale melancholy of financial need".

Written by Engels on December 28, 1848

First published in the supplement to the *Neue Rheinische Zeitung* No. 185, January 3, 1849

Printed according to the newspaper

Published in English for the first time

A BOURGEOIS DOCUMENT [209]

Cologne, January 4. In England, where the rule of the bourgeoisie has reached the greatest development, public charity too, as we know, has assumed the most noble and magnanimous forms. In English workhouses [a]—public institutions in which the surplus labour population is allowed to vegetate at the expense of bourgeois society—charity is cunningly combined with the *revenge* which the bourgeoisie wreaks on the wretches who are compelled to appeal to its charity. Not only do the poor devils receive the most wretched and meagre means of subsistence, hardly sufficient for the propagation of the species, their activity, too, is restricted to revolting, unproductive, meaningless drudgery, such as work at the treadmill, which deadens both mind and body. These unfortunate people have committed the crime of having ceased to be an object of exploitation yielding a profit to the bourgeoisie—as is the case in ordinary life—and having become instead an object of expenditure for those born to derive benefit from them; like so many barrels of liquor which, left unsold in the warehouse, become an object of expenditure to the wine merchant. To bring home to them the full magnitude of their crime, they are deprived of everything that is granted to the lowest criminal—association with their wives and children, recreation, talk—everything. Even this "*cruel charity*" of the English bourgeoisie is due not to sentimental but to thoroughly practical and rational reasons. On the one hand, if all the paupers in Great Britain were suddenly thrown into the street, bourgeois order and commercial activity would suffer to an alarming extent. On the

---

[a] Here and below this word is given in English in the original.—*Ed.*

other hand, British industry has alternate periods of feverish over-production, when the demand for hands can hardly be satisfied, and the hands are nevertheless to be obtained as cheaply as possible, followed by periods of slack business, when production is far larger than consumption and it is difficult to find useful employment even at half pay for half the labour army. Is there a more ingenious device than the workhouse for maintaining a reserve army in readiness for favourable periods while converting them in these pious institutions during unfavourable commercial periods into machines devoid of will, resistance, claims and requirements?

The Prussian bourgeoisie differs favourably from the English bourgeoisie, since in contrast to British political arrogance reminiscent of pagan Rome it displays Christian humility and meekness in the most servile reverence before throne, altar, army, bureaucracy and feudalism; instead of displaying the commercial energy which conquers whole continents, it engages in domestic retail trade of a Chinese type, and tries to confound the impetuous titanic spirit of inventiveness in industry by clinging staunchly and virtuously to the traditional semi-guild routine. But the Prussian bourgeoisie approaches its British ideal in one respect—in its *shameless maltreatment of the working class.* That, as a body, it in general lags behind the British bourgeoisie, is due simply to the fact that, on the whole, as a *national class,* it has never achieved anything of importance and never will, because of its lack of courage, intelligence and energy. It does not exist on a national scale, it exists only in *provincial, municipal, local, private* forms, and in *these* forms it confronts the working class even more ruthlessly than the English bourgeoisie. Why is it that since the Restoration the peoples longed for Napoleon, whom they had just before chained to a lonely rock in the Mediterranean[a]? Because it is easier to endure the tyranny of a genius than that of an idiot. Thus the English worker can feel a certain national pride in face of the German worker, because the master who enslaves him enslaves the whole world, whereas the master of the German worker, the German bourgeois, is himself *everybody's servant,* and nothing is more galling and humiliating than to be the *servant of a servant.*

We publish here without any alterations the "*Worker's Card*", which proletarians engaged on municipal works have to sign in the good city of Cologne; this historical document shows the cynical attitude of our bourgeoisie towards the working class.

---

[a] An allusion to Elba, the island to which Napoleon I was exiled during the Bourbon restoration in 1814.—*Ed.*

WORKER'S CARD

§1. Every worker must *strictly obey* the instructions and orders of *all municipal supervisors*, who have been sworn in as *police officers*. *Disobedience and insubordination will entail immediate dismissal.*

§2. No worker is allowed to move from one section to another or to leave the building-site *without the special permission of the supervisor*.

§3. Workers purloining wheelbarrows, carts or other equipment from another section in order to use them in their work will be dismissed.

§4. Drunkenness, disturbance of the peace, and starting up squabbles, quarrels and fights entail immediate dismissal.—In *appropriate cases* moreover legal proceedings will be taken against the culprits.

§5. A worker arriving *ten minutes late* at his place of work will be given no work on that *particular half day*; if this should occur three times he *may* be dismissed altogether.

§6. If workers are dismissed at their own request or by way of punishment, they will receive their wages at the next regular pay-day in accordance with the work done.

§7. A worker's dismissal is noted in the Worker's Card.—Should the dismissal be by way of punishment, the worker, *according to the circumstances*, is barred from re-employment either at the same place of work or at all municipal works.

§8. The *police* are always to be informed when workers are dismissed by way of punishment and of the reasons for their dismissal.

§9. Should workers have any *complaints* to make *against the building-site supervisor*, these are to be lodged with the *town clerk of works* through an elected delegation of three workers. This officer will examine the cause of the complaint on the spot and *give his decision*.

§10. The working hours are from six thirty in the morning to twelve noon and from one o'clock in the afternoon till evening darkness sets in. (Wonderful style!)

§11. The worker is employed on these conditions.

§12. Payment is made on the building-site on Saturday afternoon.

The sworn building-site supervisor, for the present [...] whose instructions have to be obeyed.

Cologne			Assigned to section of ... and has etc.
Signature ⎫	of the worker	⎰	Signature of the building-site supervisor
or sign ⎭			

Could the *Russian* edicts of the Autocrat of All the Russias to his subjects be couched in more Asiatic terms?

The municipal, and even "*all municipal* supervisors, who have been sworn in as *police officers*", must be "strictly obeyed". "*Disobedience* and *insubordination* will entail *immediate* dismissal." First of all, therefore, *passive obedience*. Then, according to §9, the workers have the right to complain to "the *town clerk of works*". The decisions of this pasha are irrevocable and directed, of course, *against the workers*, if only in the interests of the hierarchy. And once this decision has been taken and the municipal interdict laid upon the workers, woe to them, for they will then be placed under *police surveillance*. The last semblance of their civic freedom disappears, for, according to §8, "the *police* are always to be informed when workers are dismissed by way of punishment and of the reasons for their dismissal".

But gentlemen, if you dismiss a worker, if you terminate a contract by which he gives *his labour* for *your wages*, what on earth has the *police* to do with this termination of a *civil agreement*? Is the municipal worker a convict? Have you *denounced* him to the *police* because he did not pay due deference to you, his hereditary, most wise and noble-minded masters? Would you not deride the citizen who *denounced* you to the *police* for having broken some delivery contract, or failed to pay a bill when it was due, or drunk too much on New Year's eve? Of course you would! But as regards the worker you are bound by no civil agreement, you lord it over him with the caprice of the *lords by the grace of God*! The police must, on your behalf, keep a record of his conduct.

Under §5, a worker arriving *ten minutes* late is punished with the loss of *half a day's labour*. What a punishment in comparison with the offence! You are *centuries* late, but the worker is not allowed to arrive *ten minutes* after half past six without losing *half a working day*.

Finally, in order that this patriarchal arbitrariness should not be in any way restricted and the worker be entirely dependent on your whim, you have left the mode of punishment, as far as possible, to the discretion of your uniformed servants. Dismissal and denunciation to the police is, according to §4, to be followed in "*appropriate* cases", that is in cases which you will be pleased to regard as appropriate, by "legal proceedings against the culprits". Under §5, the worker who arrives late for the third time, i.e. ten minutes after half past six, "*may*" be dismissed altogether. In case of dismissal by way of punishment, §7 states, "the worker, *according to the circumstances*, is barred from re-employment either at the *same* place of work or at *all* municipal works", and so on and so forth.

What scope for the whims of the annoyed bourgeois is given in this criminal code of our municipal Catos, these great men who grovel before Berlin!

This model law shows *what sort of Charter our bourgeoisie*, if it stood at the helm of state, *would impose on the people*.

Written by Marx on January 4, 1849   Printed according to the newspaper

First published in the *Neue Rheinische Zeitung* No. 187, January 5, 1849

A NEW-YEAR GREETING

Cologne, January 8. That priests and precentors, vergers and organ-blowers, barbers and night-watchmen, field guards, gravediggers etc. send us New-Year greetings, is a custom that is as old as it is ever recurrent, and one which leaves us cold.

The year 1849, however, is not content with the traditional. Its arrival has been marked by something unprecedented, a New-Year greeting from the King of Prussia.[a]

It is a New-Year wish addressed not to the Prussian people, nor "To my dear Berliners", but "To my army".[210]

This royal New-Year message looks on the army "with pride" because it remained loyal

"when" (in March) *"revolt disturbed the peaceful development of liberal institutions towards which I wished cautiously to lead My people".*

Previously people spoke of the March events, of "misunderstandings", and so forth. Now there is no longer need for disguise: the March "misunderstandings" are cast in our face as *"revolt"*.

The royal New-Year greeting breathes on us the same spirit as that which emanates from the columns of the "Dame of the Cross".[b] Just as the former speaks of "revolt", so the latter speaks of inglorious "March criminals", of the criminal rabble which upset the tranquillity of Court life in Berlin.

If we ask why the March "revolt" should be so particularly revolting, we are told in reply: "because it disturbed the peaceful development of liberal (!!) institutions etc."

---

[a] Frederick William IV.—*Ed.*

[b] That is *Kreuz-Zeitung (Neue Preussische Zeitung).—Ed.*

If you were not peacefully at rest in Friedrichshain,[211] you March rebels, you would now have to be rewarded with "powder and shot" or penal servitude for life. By your wickedness did you not indeed disturb "the peaceful development of liberal institutions"? Does one need to be reminded of that royal Prussian development of "liberal institutions", of the most liberal development in the squandering of money, of the "peaceful" expansion of bigotry and royal Prussian jesuitry, of the peaceful development of police and barrack rule, of spying, deception, hypocrisy, arrogance, and finally the most disgusting brutalisation of the people alongside of the most shameful corruption among the so-called upper classes? There is all the less need for such a reminder because we have only to look around, to stretch out our hands, in order to see that "disturbed development" again in full bloom and to refresh ourselves with a double edition of the above-mentioned "liberal institutions".

"My army," the royal message of greetings goes on to say, "has kept its old glory and won new glory."

Indeed it has! It has won so much glory that at most the Croats could lay claim to greater.

But where and how has it won it? In the first place:

"It adorned its banners with new laurels when Germany required our weapons in Schleswig."

The Prussian Note sent by Major Wildenbruch to the Danish Government[212] is the basis on which the new Prussian glory has been erected. The entire conduct of the war conformed excellently to that Note, which assured the Danish Herr cousin[a] that the Prussian Government was not at all in earnest, it was merely throwing out a bait to the republicans and throwing sand in the eyes of other people in order to gain time. And to gain time is to gain everything. Later agreement would be reached in the jolliest of ways.

Herr Wrangel, about whom public opinion was led astray for rather a long time, Herr Wrangel left Schleswig-Holstein secretly like a thief in the night. He travelled in civilian clothes in order not to be recognised. In Hamburg all the innkeepers declared that they could not give him shelter. They considered their houses, and the windows and doors in them, to be dearer to them than the laurels of the Prussian army, which were despised by the people although embodied in this illustrious gentleman. We should not forget either that the only success in this campaign of useless and senseless

---

[a] Frederick VII.—Ed.

movements hither and thither, which was wholly reminiscent of the procedure of the old imperial courts of justice (see our issues at the time[a]), was a strategic mistake.

The only surprising thing about this campaign is the inexpressible cheek of the *Danes,* who mischievously hoaxed the Prussian army and completely cut off Prussia from the world market.

To complete the Prussian glory in this connection, one must include also the peace negotiations with Denmark and the Malmö armistice which resulted from them.[213]

If the Roman Emperor,[b] on sniffing a coin in the receipts from the public conveniences, could say: "*Non olet*" (it does not smell), the Prussian laurels won in Schleswig-Holstein, on the other hand, are marked in ineradicable characters: "*Olet!*" (it stinks!).

Secondly, "My army victoriously overcame hardships and dangers when it was necessary to combat insurrection in the Grand Duchy of Posen".

As far as the "victoriously overcome hardships" are concerned, they are as follows: Prussia, firstly, exploited the magnanimous illusion, fostered by smooth words from Berlin, of the Poles, who regarded the "*Pomeranians*" as German comrades-in-arms against *Russia,* and therefore calmly disbanded their army, let the Pomeranians march in, and only reassembled their scattered military cadres when the Prussians most vilely maltreated them when they were defenceless. And as for the Prussian feats of heroism! The heroic deeds of the "glorious" Prussian army were accomplished not *during* the war, but *after* the war. When Mieroslawski was presented to the June victor, Cavaignac's first question was how the Prussians had managed to be defeated at *Miloslaw.* (We can prove this by eyewitnesses.) 3,000 Poles, hardly armed with scythes and pikes, struck twice and twice forced 20,000 Prussians to retreat, although the latter were well organised and liberally equipped with weapons.[214] In its wild flight the Prussian cavalry itself threw the Prussian infantry into confusion. The Polish insurrection kept its hold on Miloslaw, after twice driving the counter-revolutionaries out of the city. Still more shameful than the Prussians' *defeat at Miloslaw* was their final *victory at Wreschen,* prepared for by a defeat.[215] If an unarmed but Herculean opponent confronts a coward armed with pistols, the coward flees and fires his pistols from a respectable distance. That is how the Prussians behaved at *Wreschen.* They fled to

---

[a] A reference to Engels' articles "The War Comedy" and "The Armistice with Denmark" (see present edition, Vol. 7, pp. 42-44 and 266-69).—*Ed.*

[b] Vespasian.—*Ed.*

a distance at which they could fire grape-shot, grenades containing 150 bullets, and shrapnel against pikes and scythes which, as is well known, cannot be effective at a distance. Previously shrapnel had only been fired by Englishmen against semi-savages in the East Indies. Only the stalwart Prussians, in fanatical fear of Polish courage and conscious of their own weakness, used shrapnel against their so-called fellow citizens. They had, of course, to look for a method of killing masses of Poles at a distance. Close to, the Poles were too terrible. Such was the *glorious victory at Wreschen.* But, as already stated, the heroic deeds of the Prussian army begin only *after* the war, just as the heroic deeds of the prison warder begin *after* sentence has been pronounced.

That *this* glory of the Prussian army will go down in history is guaranteed by the thousands of Poles killed with shrapnel, pointed bullets etc. as a result of Prussian treachery and black-and-white trickery, and by those later branded with lunar caustic.[216]

Adequate testimony to this second laurel wreath of the counter-revolutionary army has been provided by the villages and towns burnt by the Prussian heroes, by the Polish inhabitants beaten up and massacred in their homes with rifle-butts and bayonets, and by the acts of plunder and violence of all kinds committed by the Prussians.

Immortal glory for these Prussian warriors in Posen, who paved the way trodden shortly afterwards by the Neapolitan executioner,[a] who battered with shot and shell his loyal capital city and allowed the soldiery to plunder it for 24 hours.[217] Honour and glory to the Prussian army for the Posen campaign! For it served as a shining example for the Croats, Serezhans, Ottochans[218] and other hordes of Windischgrätz and Co., who, as Prague (in June), Vienna, Pressburg etc. have proved, were inspired to be its most worthy imitators.

And, lastly, even *this* courage of the Prussians against the Poles occurred only owing to fear of the Russians.

"All good things come in threes."[b] Hence "My army" also had to win a triple glory. The occasion for it was not lacking. For "its participation in the maintenance of order (!) in South Germany won fresh recognition for the name of Prussia".

Only malice or an attempt at belittlement could make one deny that "My army" performed the most effective services as jailor and policeman for the Federal Diet, which modernised itself on being rebaptised and had itself called the Central Authority.[219] It is equally undeniable that the Prussian name gained full recognition in

---

[a] Ferdinand II.—*Ed.*
[b] Lessing, *Minna von Barnhelm,* Act I, Scene 2.—*Ed.*

guzzling South-German wine, meat, cider etc. The starving Brandenburgers, Pomeranians etc. grew patriotic paunches, the thirsty ones refreshed themselves, and in general succeeded in polishing off everything that the South Germans who provided them with billets set before them with such heroic courage that the Prussian name has gained the most noisy recognition there. It is a pity that the billet money has not yet been paid; the recognition would be still noisier.

The glory of "My army" is really inexhaustible; nevertheless, one must not omit to mention that

"whenever I called, it stood ready, in complete loyalty and in *complete discipline*",

nor omit to communicate to posterity the equally remarkable statement that

"My army countered abominable calumnies by its excellent spirit and *noble self-control*."

How flattering for "My army" is this greeting, evoking as it does the pleasant recollection of its "complete discipline" and "noble self-control", and at the same time once more its heroic deeds in the Grand Duchy,[a] and furthermore the laurels it won in Mainz, Schweidnitz, Trier, Erfurt, Berlin, Cologne, Düsseldorf, Aachen, Coblenz, Münster, Minden etc. We others, however, who do not belong to "My army", can in this way widen our limited conceptions as humble subjects. To shoot down old men and pregnant women, to rob (officially documented in the neighbourhood of *Ostrowo*), to maltreat peaceful citizens with rifle-butts and sabres, to destroy houses, to make attacks in the night on unarmed people with weapons hidden under cloaks, waylaying (recall what happened at Neuwied)—these and similar heroic deeds are termed in Christian-German language "*complete discipline*" and "*noble self-control*"! Long live self-control and discipline, since those murdered under this watchword are in fact dead.

The few passages of this royal Prussian New-Year greeting which we have touched upon here show us that this document in its significance and spirit is on the same level as the manifesto of the Duke of Brunswick[b] about 1792.[220]

Written by Marx on January 8, 1849

First published in the *Neue Rheinische Zeitung* No. 190, January 9, 1849

Printed according to the newspaper

Published in English for the first time

---

[a] Posen.—*Ed.*
[b] Karl Wilhelm Ferdinand.—*Ed.*

THE MAGYAR STRUGGLE[221]

Cologne, January. While in Italy the first counterblow is already being struck against the counter-revolution of last summer and autumn, in the plains of Hungary the last stage of the struggle to suppress the movement which arose directly out of the February revolution is being completed. The new Italian movement is the prologue of the movement of 1849, the war against the Magyars is the epilogue to the movement of 1848. Probably this epilogue will yet pass into the new drama that is being prepared in secret.

Like the first scenes of the revolutionary tragedy of 1848, which rapidly succeeded one another, and like the fall of Paris and Vienna, this epilogue too is heroic, and pleasantly heroic after the partly colourless and partly petty episodes of the period between June and October. The last act of 1848 passes through *terrorism* into the first act of 1849.

For the first time in the revolutionary movement of 1848, for the first time since 1793, a nation surrounded by superior counter-revolutionary forces dares to counter the cowardly counter-revolutionary fury by revolutionary passion, the *terreur blanche* by the *terreur rouge*.[a] For the first time after a long period we meet with a truly revolutionary figure, a man who in the name of his people dares to accept the challenge of a desperate struggle, who for his nation is Danton and Carnot in one person—*Lajos Kossuth.*

The superiority of forces is frightful. The whole of Austria, 16 million fanaticised Slavs in the forefront, against 4 million Magyars.

Mass uprising, national manufacture of arms, issue of banknotes, short shrift for anyone hindering the revolutionary movement, revolution in permanence—in short, all the main features of the

---

[a] The white terror by the red terror.—*Ed.*

glorious year 1793 are found again in the Hungary which Kossuth has armed, organised and inspired with enthusiasm. This revolutionary organisation, which on pain of utter ruin had to be completed, so to speak, in 24 hours, was lacking in Vienna, otherwise Windischgrätz would never have been able to enter it. We shall see whether he will succeed in entering Hungary in spite of this revolutionary organisation.

Let us take a closer look at the struggle and the combatant parties.

The Austrian monarchy arose out of the attempt to unite Germany in a single monarchy just as the French kings up to Louis XI did in France. The attempt failed because of the pitiful provincial narrow-mindedness of both the Germans and the Austrians, and because of the corresponding petty commercial spirit of the Habsburg dynasty. Instead of the whole of Germany, the Habsburgs obtained only those South-German lands which were in direct conflict with the isolated Slav tribes, or in which a German feudal nobility and German burghers ruled jointly over enslaved Slav tribes. In both cases the Germans of each province required support from outside. This support they received through the association against the Slavs, and this association came into being through the union of the provinces in question under the sceptre of the Habsburgs.

That is how German Austria originated. It suffices to read in any textbook how the Austrian monarchy came into being, how it split up and arose again, all in the course of struggle against the Slavs, to see how correct this description is.

Adjacent to German Austria is Hungary. In Hungary the Magyars waged the same struggle as the Germans in German Austria. A German wedge driven between the Slav barbarians in the Archduchy of Austria and Styria went hand in hand with the Magyar wedge driven in the same way between the Slav barbarians on the Leitha. Just as in the south and north, in Bohemia, Moravia, Carinthia and Kraina the German nobility ruled over Slav tribes, Germanised them and so drew them into the European movement, the Magyar nobility likewise ruled over Slav tribes in the south and north, in Croatia, Slavonia and the Carpathian territories. The interests of both were the same; opponents of both were natural allies. The alliance of the Magyars and the Austrian Germans was a necessity. All that was still lacking was some great event, a heavy attack on both of them, in order to make this alliance indissoluble. Such an event came with the Turks' conquest of the Byzantine Empire. The Turks threatened Hungary and, secondly, Vienna, and for centuries Hungary came indissolubly under the Habsburg dynasty.

But the common opponents of both became gradually weak. The Turkish Empire became powerless, and the Slavs lost the strength to revolt against the Magyars and Germans. Indeed, a part of the German and Magyar nobility ruling in Slav lands adopted Slav nationality and thereby the Slav nationalities themselves became interested in preserving the monarchy, which had more and more to defend the nobility against the developing German and Magyar bourgeoisie. The national contradictions were disappearing and the Habsburg dynasty adopted a different policy. The same Habsburg dynasty which had climbed to the German imperial throne on the shoulders of the German burghers became more decisively than any other dynasty the champion of the feudal nobility against the burghers.

In the same spirit Austria participated in the partition of Poland.[222] The important Galician elders and army commanders, the Potockis, Lubomirskis and Czartoryskis, betrayed Poland to Austria and became the most loyal supports of the Habsburg dynasty, which in return guaranteed them their possessions against attacks from the lower nobility and burghers.

But the burghers in the towns continually grew in wealth and influence and the progress of agriculture alongside that of industry changed the position of the peasants in relation to the landowners. The movement of the burghers and peasants against the nobility became more and more menacing. And since the movement of the peasants, who everywhere are the embodiment of national and local narrow-mindedness, necessarily assumes a local and national character, it was accompanied by a resurgence of the old national struggles.

In this state of affairs, Metternich achieved his master stroke. With the exception of the most powerful feudal barons, he deprived the nobility of all influence on state administration. He sapped the strength of the bourgeoisie by winning to his side the most powerful financial barons—he had to do this, the state of the finances made it compulsory for him. Supported in this way by the top feudal and financial aristocracy, as well as by the bureaucracy and the army, he far more than all his rivals attained the ideal of an absolute monarchy. He kept the burghers and the peasantry of each nation under control by means of the aristocracy of that nation and the peasantry of every other nation, and he kept the aristocracy of each nation under control by its fear of that nation's burghers and peasantry. The different class interests, the national features of narrow-mindedness, and local prejudices, despite their complexity, were completely held in check by their mutual counteraction and allowed the old scoundrel Metternich the utmost freedom to manoeuvre. How far he succeeded in this setting of one nation against another is proved by the Galician scenes of slaughter when the democratic Polish movement which began in the interests of the peasantry was crushed by Metternich by means of the Ruthenian peasants themselves who were animated by religious and national fanaticism.[223]

The year 1848 first of all brought with it the most terrible chaos for Austria by setting free for a short time all these different nationalities which, owing to Metternich, had hitherto been enslaving one another. The Germans, Magyars, Czechs, Poles, Moravians, Slovaks, Croats, Ruthenians, Rumanians, Illyrians and Serbs came into conflict with one another, while within each of these nationalities a struggle went on also between the different classes. But soon order came out of this chaos. The combatants divided into two large camps: the Germans, Poles and Magyars took the side of revolution; the remainder, all the Slavs, except for the Poles, the Rumanians and Transylvanian Saxons, took the side of counter-revolution.

How did this division of the nations come about, what was its basis?

The division is in accordance with all the previous history of the nationalities in question. It is the beginning of the decision on the life or death of all these nations, large and small.

All the earlier history of Austria up to the present day is proof of this and 1848 confirmed it. Among all the large and small nations of Austria, only three standard-bearers of progress took an active part in history, and still retain their vitality—the *Germans*, the *Poles* and the *Magyars*. Hence they are now revolutionary.

All the other large and small nationalities and peoples are destined to perish before long in the revolutionary world storm. For that reason they are now counter-revolutionary.

As for the *Poles*, we refer the reader to our article about the debates on the Polish question in Frankfurt.[a] In order to curb their revolutionary spirit, Metternich had appealed to the Ruthenians, a nationality differing from the Poles by its somewhat different dialect and especially by its Greek orthodox religion. The Ruthenians had belonged to Poland for a long time and learned only from Metternich that the Poles were their oppressors. As though in the old Poland the Poles themselves were not oppressed just as much as the Ruthenians, as though under Austrian domination Metternich was not their common oppressor!

---

[a] See present edition, Vol. 7, pp. 337-81.— *Ed.*

So much for the Poles and Ruthenians who, moreover, because of their history and geographical position, are so sharply separated from Austria proper that we have had to get them out of the way first of all in order to reach clarity in regard to the chaos of the other peoples.

Let us, however, also remark at the outset that the Poles have revealed great political understanding and a true revolutionary spirit by now entering into an alliance with their old enemies, the Germans and Magyars, against the pan-Slav counter-revolution. A Slav people for whom freedom is dearer than Slavism proves its vitality by this fact alone, and thereby already assures a future for itself.

We pass now to Austria proper.

Situated to the south of the Sudetic and Carpathian mountains, in the upper valley of the Elbe and in the region of the Middle Danube, Austria in the early Middle Ages was a country populated exclusively by Slavs. By language and customs these Slavs belong to the same stock as the Slavs of Turkey, the Serbs, Bosnians, Bulgarians, and the Slavs of Thrace and Macedonia; these, in contrast to the Poles and Russians, are called Southern Slavs. Apart from these related Slav nationalities, the vast region from the Black Sea to the Bohemian forests and Tyrolean Alps was inhabited only by a few Greeks in the south of the Balkans, and in the Lower Danube region by scattered Rumanian-speaking Wallachians.

Into this compact Slav mass a wedge was driven by Germans from the west and the Magyars from the east. The German element conquered the western part of Bohemia and pushed forward on both sides of the Danube as far as the other side of the Leitha. The Archduchy of Austria, part of Moravia, and the greater part of Styria were Germanised and thus separated the Czechs and Moravians from the inhabitants of Carinthia and Kraina. In the same way Transylvania and Central Hungary up to the German frontier was completely cleared of Slavs and occupied by Magyars, who here separated the Slovaks and a few Ruthenian localities (in the north) from the Serbs, Croats and Slovenes, and subjected all these peoples to their rule. Finally, the Turks, following the example of the Byzantines, subjugated the Slavs south of the Danube and the Sava, and the historical role of the Southern Slavs was ended for ever.[224]

The last attempt of the Southern Slavs to play an independent part in history was the Hussite war,[225] a national peasant war of the Czechs under the flag of religion against the German nobility and the supremacy of the German Emperor. The attempt failed, and ever since then the Czechs have remained fettered under the yoke of the German Empire.

On the other hand, their conquerors—the Germans and Magyars—took over the historical initiative in the Danube regions. Without the aid of the Germans and particularly of the Magyars, the Southern Slavs would have become Turkish, as actually happened to part of them, indeed Mohammedan, as the Slavs of Bosnia still are today. And for the Southern Slavs of Austria this is a service which is not too dear even at the price of exchanging their nationality for German or Magyar.

The Turkish invasion of the fifteenth and sixteenth centuries was a second edition of the Arab invasion of the eighth century. Charles Martel's victory was repeatedly rewon at the walls of Vienna and on the Hungarian plain. As then at Poitiers, and later at Wahlstatt, during the invasion of the Mongols,[226] there was here once more a threat to the whole of European development. And where it was a matter of saving this, how could it be achieved by a few nationalities, like the Austrian Slavs, which had long ago disintegrated and become impotent and which, moreover, themselves needed to be saved?

The situation internally was like that externally. The class that was the driving force and standard-bearer of the movement, the bourgeoisie, was everywhere German or Magyar. The Slavs could only with difficulty give rise to a national bourgeoisie, and the Southern Slavs only in quite isolated cases. And with the bourgeoisie, industrial power and capital were in the hands of Germans or Magyars, German culture developed, and intellectually too the Slavs became subordinate to the Germans, even as far as Croatia. The same thing happened—only later and therefore to a lesser extent—in Hungary, where the Magyars together with the Germans took the lead in intellectual and commercial affairs. But the Hungarian Germans, although they retained the German language, became genuine Hungarians in disposition, character and customs. Only the newly introduced peasant colonists, the Jews and the Saxons in Transylvania, are an exception and stubbornly retain an absurd nationality in the midst of a foreign land.

And if the Magyars were a little behind the German Austrians in civilisation, they have recently brilliantly overtaken them by their political activity. Between 1830 and 1848 there was more political life in Hungary alone than in the whole of Germany, and the feudal forms of the old Hungarian Constitution were better exploited in the interests of democracy than the modern forms of South-German constitutions. And who was at the head of the movement here? The

Magyars. Who supported Austrian reaction? The Croats and Slovenes.

Against the Magyar movement, as also against the reawakening political movement in Germany, the Austrian Slavs founded a Sonderbund[227]—*pan-Slavism.*

Pan-Slavism did not originate in Russia or Poland, but in Prague and in Agram.[228] Pan-Slavism means the union of all the small Slav nations and nationalities of Austria, and secondarily of Turkey, for struggle against the Austrian Germans, the Magyars and, eventually, against the Turks. The Turks are only incidentally included here and, as a nation which is also in a state of complete decline, can be entirely disregarded. In its basic tendency, pan-Slavism is aimed against the revolutionary elements of Austria and is therefore reactionary from the outset.

Pan-Slavism immediately gave proof of this reactionary tendency by a double betrayal: it sacrificed to its petty national narrow-mindedness the only Slav nation which up to then had acted in a revolutionary manner, the *Poles;* it *sold* both itself and Poland to the *Russian Tsar.*

The direct aim of pan-Slavism is the creation of a Slav state under Russian domination, extending from the Erzgebirge and the Carpathians to the Black, Aegean and Adriatic seas—a state which would include, besides the German, Italian, Magyar, Wallachian, Turkish, Greek and Albanian languages, also approximately a dozen Slav languages and basic dialects. All this would be held together not by the elements which have hitherto held Austria together and ensured its development, but by the abstract quality of Slavism and the so-called Slav language, which is at any rate common to the majority of the inhabitants. But where does this Slavism exist except in the minds of a few ideologists, where is the "Slav language" except in the imagination of Herren Palacký, Gaj and Co., and, to some extent, in the old Slav litany of the Russian church, which no Slav any longer understands? In reality, all these peoples are at the most diverse stages of civilisation, ranging from the fairly highly developed (thanks to the *Germans*) modern industry and culture of Bohemia down to the almost nomadic barbarism of the Croats and Bulgarians; in reality, therefore, all these nations have most antagonistic interests. In reality, the Slav language of these ten or twelve nations consists of an equal number of dialects, mostly incomprehensible to one another, which can be reduced to different main stems (Czech, Illyrian, Serbian, Bulgarian) and which, owing to the total neglect of all literature and the lack of culture of the majority of these peoples, have become a sheer patois, and with few exceptions have always had above them an *alien*, non-Slav language as the written language. Thus, pan-Slav unity is either pure fantasy or—*the Russian knout.*

And what nations are supposed to head this great Slav state? Precisely those nations which for a thousand years have been scattered and split up, those nations whose elements capable of life and development were *forcibly* imposed on them by other, non-Slav peoples, those nations which were saved from downfall in Turkish barbarism by the victorious arms of non-Slav peoples, small, powerless nationalities, everywhere separated from one another and deprived of their national strength, numbering from a few thousand up to less than two million people! They have become so weak that, for example, the race which in the Middle Ages was the strongest and most terrible, the Bulgarians, are now in Turkey known only for their mildness and soft-heartedness and set great store on being called *dobre chrisztian*, good Christians! Is there a single one of these races, not excluding the Czechs and Serbs, that possesses a national historical tradition which is kept alive among the people and stands above the pettiest local struggles?

Pan-Slavism was at its height in the eighth and ninth centuries, when the Southern Slavs still held the whole of Hungary and Austria and were threatening Byzantium. If at that time they were unable to resist the German and Magyar invasion, if they were unable to achieve independence and form a stable state even when both their enemies, the Magyars and Germans, were tearing each other to pieces, how will they be able to achieve it today, after a thousand years of subjection and loss of their national character?

There is no country in Europe which does not have in some corner or other one or several ruined fragments of peoples, the remnant of a former population that was suppressed and held in bondage by the nation which later became the main vehicle of historical development. These relics of a nation mercilessly trampled under foot in the course of history, as Hegel says,[a] these *residual fragments of peoples* always become fanatical standard-bearers of counter-revolution and remain so until their complete extirpation or loss of their national character, just as their whole existence in general is itself a protest against a great historical revolution.

Such, in Scotland, are the Gaels, the supporters of the Stuarts from 1640 to 1745.

Such, in France, are the Bretons, the supporters of the Bourbons from 1792 to 1800.

---

[a] See G. W. F. Hegel, *Vorlesungen über die Philosophie der Geschichte. Einleitung.—Ed.*

Such, in Spain, are the Basques, the supporters of Don Carlos.

Such, in Austria, are the pan-Slavist *Southern Slavs,* who are nothing but the *residual fragment of peoples,* resulting from an extremely confused *thousand years of development.* That this residual fragment, which is likewise extremely confused, sees its salvation only in a reversal of the whole European movement, which in its view ought to go not from west to east, but from east to west, and that for it the instrument of liberation and the bond of unity is the *Russian knout*—that is the most natural thing in the world.

Already before 1848, therefore, the Southern Slavs had clearly shown their reactionary character. The year 1848 brought it fully into the light of day.

When the February storm broke, who made the Austrian revolution? Vienna or Prague? Budapest or Agram? The Germans and Magyars, or the Slavs?

It is true that among the more educated Southern Slavs there was a small democratic party which, although not wanting to renounce its nationality, nevertheless desired to put it at the disposal of the struggle for freedom. This illusion, which succeeded in arousing sympathy also among West-European democrats, sympathy that was fully justified as long as the Slav democrats took part in the struggle against the common enemy—this illusion was shattered by the bombardment of Prague. After that event all the South-Slav races, following the example of the Croats, put themselves at the disposal of Austrian reaction. Those leaders of the South-Slav movement who continue to talk drivel about the equality of nations, about democratic Austria, and so on, are either stupid dreamers, such as, for example, many journalists, or they are scoundrels like Jellachich. Their democratic assurances have no more significance than the democratic assurances of official Austrian counter-revolution. It suffices to say that in practice the restoration of the South-Slav nationality begins with the most savage outbursts of fury against the Austrian and Magyar revolution, with a first great good turn rendered to the Russian Tsar.

Apart from the higher nobility, the bureaucracy and the military, the Austrian camarilla found support only among the Slavs. The Slavs played the decisive part in the fall of Italy, the Slavs stormed Vienna, and it is the Slavs who are now attacking the Magyars from all sides. At their head as spokesmen are the Czechs under Palacký, as leaders of armed forces the Croats under Jellachich.

That is the gratitude shown for the fact that the German democratic press in June everywhere sympathised with the Czech democrats when they were shot down by Windischgrätz, the same Windischgrätz who is now their hero.

To sum up:

In Austria, apart from Poland and Italy, it is the Germans and Magyars in 1848, as during the past thousand years already, who have assumed the historical initiative. They represent the *revolution*.

The Southern Slavs, who for a thousand years have been taken in tow by the Germans and the Magyars, only rose up in 1848 to achieve their national independence in order thereby at the same time to suppress the German-Magyar revolution. They represent the *counter-revolution*. They were joined by two nations, which had likewise long ago degenerated and were devoid of all historical power of action: the Saxons and the Rumanians of Transylvania.

The Habsburg dynasty, whose power was based on the union of Germans and Magyars in the struggle against the Southern Slavs, is now prolonging the last moments of its existence through the union of the Southern Slavs in the struggle against the Germans and Magyars.

That is the political aspect of the question. Now for the military aspect.

The region inhabited exclusively by Magyars does not form even one-third of the whole of Hungary and Transylvania. In the area from Pressburg, northwards from the Danube and Theiss up to the rear of the Carpathians there live several million Slovaks and a few Ruthenians. In the south, between the Sava, Danube and Drava, there live Croats and Slovenes; farther to the east, along the Danube is a Serb colony of more than half a million people. These two Slav stretches are linked by the Wallachians and the Saxons of Transylvania.

On three sides, therefore, the Magyars are surrounded by natural enemies. If the Slovaks, occupying the mountain passes, were of a less lukewarm disposition, they would be dangerous opponents, in view of their region being excellently adapted for guerilla warfare.

As things are, however, the Magyars have only to withstand from the north attacks of invading armies from Galicia and Moravia. In the east, on the other hand, the Rumanians and Saxons rose up in a mass and joined the Austrian army corps there. Their situation is an excellent one, partly because of the mountainous nature of the country and partly because they occupy most of the towns and fortresses.

Finally, in the south are the Banat Serbs, supported by the German colonists, the Wallachians and also an Austrian corps, protected by the vast Alibunar morass and almost impregnable.

The Croats are protected by the Drava and the Danube, and since they have at their disposal a strong Austrian army with all its auxiliary resources, they advanced into the Magyar region already before October and now have little difficulty in holding their line of defence on the Lower Drava.

Finally, from the fourth side, from Austria, the serried columns of Windischgrätz and Jellachich are now advancing. The Magyars are encircled on all sides, and encircled by an enemy of vastly superior power.

The fighting is reminiscent of that against France in 1793, but with the difference that the sparsely populated and only half-civilised country of the Magyars is far from having at its disposal the resources which the French Republic then had.

The weapons and munitions manufactured in Hungary are bound to be of very poor quality; in particular, it is impossible for the manufacture of artillery to go ahead rapidly. The country is far smaller than France and every inch of territory lost is therefore a much greater loss. All that is left to the Magyars is their revolutionary enthusiasm, their courage and the energetic, speedy organisation that Kossuth was able to give them.

But for all that, Austria has not yet won.

> "If we fail to beat the imperial troops on the Leitha, we shall beat them on the Rabnitz; if not on the Rabnitz, we shall beat them at Pest; if not at Pest, then on the Theiss, but in any case we shall beat them."[a]

So said Kossuth, and he is doing his utmost to keep his word.

Even with the fall of Budapest, the Magyars still have the great Lower Hungarian steppe, a terrain as it were specially created for cavalry guerilla warfare and offering numerous almost unassailable points between the swamps where the Magyars can dig themselves in. And the Magyars, who are almost all horsemen, possess all the qualities needed to wage such a war. If the imperial army dares to enter this desert region, where it will have to obtain all its provisions from Galicia or Austria, for it will find nothing, absolutely nothing on the spot, it is impossible to see how it will be able to hold out. It will achieve nothing in a closed formation; and if it splits up into flying detachments it is lost. Its clumsiness would deliver it irretrievably into the hands of the swift Magyar cavalry detachments, without any possibility of pursuit even if it should be victorious, and every isolated soldier of the imperial army would find a mortal

---

[a] From Kossuth's speech in the Hungarian parliament on November 9, 1848 (*Közlöny*, November 11, 1848).—*Ed.*

enemy in every peasant, in every herdsman. War in these steppes is like war in Algeria, and the clumsy Austrian army would require years to end it. And the Magyars will be saved if they hold out for only a few months.

The Magyar cause is not in such a bad way as mercenary black-and-yellow[a] enthusiasm would have us believe. The Magyars are not yet defeated. But if they fall, they will fall gloriously, as the last heroes of the 1848 revolution, and only for a short time. Then for a time the Slav counter-revolution will sweep down on the Austrian monarchy with all its barbarity, and the camarilla will see what sort of allies it has. But at the first victorious uprising of the French proletariat, which Louis Napoleon is striving with all his might to conjure up, the Austrian Germans and Magyars will be set free and wreak a bloody revenge on the Slav barbarians. The general war which will then break out will smash this Slav Sonderbund and wipe out all these petty hidebound nations, down to their very names.

The next world war will result in the disappearance from the face of the earth not only of reactionary classes and dynasties, but also of entire reactionary peoples. And that, too, is a step forward.

Written by Engels about January 8, 1849   Printed according to the newspaper

First published in the *Neue Rheinische Zeitung* No. 194, January 13, 1849

---

[a] The colours of the Austrian flag.—*Ed.*

HERR MÜLLER.—
RADETZKY'S CHICANERY TOWARDS TESSIN.—
THE FEDERAL COUNCIL.—LOHBAUER

Berne, January 8. The Neapolitan Government, which is getting more and more worried about the non-arrival of Swiss recruits, has now sent one of its Swiss staff officers, Herr Tobias Müller, here to confer with the Federal Council about the change of the route of the recruits, as the stipulated port of embarkation, Genoa, is closed to them. This Herr Müller is eminently suitable for such a mission. Not only has he fought in Italy against freedom for many years; he had already in 1831 taken up arms in his home town (Freiburg) against the revolution. Radetzky, who knows his men, received him with distinction, embraced him in front of his General Staff, and praised him and the Swiss in Naples in general in glowing terms for their "loyalty to their *King*" (!) and their bravery in the service of their "King". However, Herr Müller will very likely come up against difficulties: even the liberalism which prevails in the Federal Council is no friend to the enlistment agreements,[229] any more than are the liberal governments of Berne and Lucerne.

While Radetzky fraternises with the Swiss in Naples, his chicaneries against Tessin are beginning all over again. He has informed the Government there that Mazzini is still hiding in the canton and has even revealed to it his hiding-place. He further complains that weapons are continuing to be smuggled into Lombardy. The Government has decided to investigate the first point and, if Mazzini is really again in the canton, to expel him; as to the second point, the Government let it lie on the table, since it was not its business to serve the Austrians as frontier guard. Radetzky has incidentally threatened to enforce the closing of the frontier again if smuggling of arms does not cease.

The Federal Council is busy with the draft laws to be put before the next Federal Assembly. Among these are the Customs Law, organisation of postal services, proposals for military organisation, and so on. It must be admitted that while the highly esteemed Frankfurt Assembly in its extravagant helplessness and helpless extravagance has not up to now produced anything but its own *misère*, the Swiss federal authorities are quietly carrying through one bourgeois centralisation step after another. A number of centralising laws will be put before the Councils in March, will be debated and adopted in May and June, and will come into force in June. For such small, detailed reforms the present ruling liberal generation of Swiss politicians (one cannot say statesmen) have an incontestable talent. In a few years the centralisation of Switzerland will be completed as far as the Constitution allows, and then the Constitution itself will become a fetter on the further development of the country, and the one and indivisible republic will become a necessity. All this on the—impossible—supposition that the European storm which is building up will leave Switzerland as neutral as did the year 1848.

But really, what kind of a nation is this, which in a time of revolution like the present is striving for no more than the abolition of cantonal customs, cantonal posts and other cantonal institutions which for many many years past have been heavily oppressive! Which in the midst of the birthpangs of a new historical epoch sees as its highest goal an improved edition of the historically outdated Federal Republic and the *first beginnings*, already necessitated by the Sonderbund war,[230] of bourgeois centralisation! What small beer in the ferment of the glorious European movement!

The Federal Council has moreover taken an extremely strange step. It has again appointed the well-known Herr *Lohbauer* of Berlin as Professor of Military Science. Herr Lohbauer, refugee of 1830, radical, later renegade, was, as is well known, summoned through the Eichhorn clique in the forties to Berlin, where he worked on the *Staats-Zeitung*,[a] on the *Janus* and on other ultra-reactionary and pietist organs of the press. Herr Lohbauer is, if we are not much mistaken, the author of that lackey's kick in the shape of an article in the *Staats-Zeitung* with which Herwegh was thrown out of the royal states after his letter to His Majesty. Herr Lohbauer was never a soldier, and yet he is to lecture here on military science.[231] Only Herr Ochsenbein, who appointed him, can know the meaning of that.

---

[a] *Allgemeine Preussische Staats-Zeitung.—Ed.*

In most of the cantons the Great Councils are now in agreement, and fighting against the pettiest local interests. The Zurich Great Council has elected our friend Dr. Alcibiades Escher as Burgomaster (*id est* chief of the Executive). The Berne Great Council will meet on the 15th.

Written by Engels on January 8, 1849

First published in the *Neue Rheinische Zeitung* No. 194, January 13, 1849

Printed according to the newspaper

Published in English for the first time

THE LAST VOLUNTEER INSURGENTS

Berne, January 8. The second instance of the Court of Appeal here has sentenced Herr J. Ph. Becker and Herr H. Hattemer in Biel, the first to one year, the second to six months' exile from the canton, for founding the military association *"Hilf Dir"*.[232] The other accused were acquitted. This brings to an end the famous story of the much-talked-of third volunteer insurgents' campaign, and the Central Authority can now once more devote its entire valuable time to the question of the German monarch and the German fleet. God bless their sour efforts for the well-being of the "whole fatherland".

Written by Engels on January 8, 1849

First published in the *Neue Rheinische Zeitung* No. 195, January 14, 1849

Printed according to the newspaper

Published in English for the first time

BUDGET

Berne, January 9. The Cantonal Budget has now been so far discussed in the Government Council that it can be presented to the Great Council which is to assemble shortly. It conforms with other European budgets in also having a deficit, of 43,000 francs out of a total of about 5 million francs. Of these 5 million, about 800,000 francs are covered by revenue from state property, 1,800,000 by indirect taxes, the rest by tolls. Thus the population pays per head almost exactly 4 Swiss francs (1 taler 18 sgr.) in direct taxes, and about $3^1/_2$ francs in indirect taxes. If all the reductions proposed by Finance Director Stämpfli (leader of the local radicals) had gone through, the result would have been a surplus of 80,000 francs instead of a deficit. But this did not suit the liberal majority of the Government Council, who calmly leave it to the aristocrats to make the eternal complaint of the "disastrous financial situation" in order to lay the blame for this on the radical Stämpfli. In reality, the canton's finances were brought into complete disorder and squandered by the notorious Neuhaus Government, and if order has been restored now, we have only Herr Stämpfli to thank for this.

Written by Engels on January 9, 1849

First published in the *Neue Rheinische Zeitung* No. 195, January 14, 1849

Printed according to the newspaper

Published in English for the first time

PRIESTS' REBELLION

Neuchâtel, January 9. We now have a priests' rebellion here. The *vénérable compagnie des pasteurs,*[a] who had led a splendid life among the pious regiment of God's grace—every pastor was the Eichhorn of his parish—have suffered a hard blow through the Republic. That is, the reverend gentlemen must be elected in future by the parishes themselves, and only for a *limited period.* Imagine the alarm! God's word no longer granted by one of God's ordained authorities, but hired out by the hour for ready cash just like a donkey or a day-labourer! The decision is taken, not by God-given will of the Royal Government, but by profane free competition, the pastor sinks to the position of an ordinary hired worker, the flock becomes a profane "employer" and can dismiss its worker if he does not carry out his task to its satisfaction. The indignation of the venerable company exceeds all bounds. They immediately issued a proclamation in which, in the most pitiful and lamentable way, they bleated against the desecration of the most holy. Naturally this only aroused universal derision. But in secret, these gentlemen, the old friends of the Jesuits and the Sonderbund, are intriguing against the Republic and conspiring to restore Frederick William, by the grace of God. The Government is magnanimous enough to allow these impotent machinations to go on for the time being. The patriotic associations will be adequate to counterbalance the ambitions of the priests. These patriotic associations are now forming everywhere. Starting from the mountains, from La Chaux-de-Fonds, Locle and the Traverstal, the home of our revolution,[233] they are spreading all over

---

[a] The venerable company of pastors.—*Ed.*

the canton. Even the royalist village of Les Ponts has got its own association. This organisation of democracy through the people itself will be the best means of thwarting the plots of all the *bédouins*[a] and priests.

Written by Engels on January 9, 1849

First published in the *Neue Rheinische Zeitung* No. 195, January 14, 1849

Printed according to the newspaper

Published in English for the first time

---

[a] The local nickname of royalist candidates for election to the Swiss National Council (see this volume, p. 7).— *Ed.*

THE SWISS PRESS

Berne, January 11. Year by year the political press in Switzerland becomes increasingly active. Besides some twenty literary magazines, there are now 98 political newspapers in the 22 cantons. But one should not imagine that among them there are any large-size newspapers like the German or even the French. Except for a few newspapers in the Waadt canton, they are all only half a printed sheet and in quarto, and scarcely a dozen of them are published daily; a small number appear five times, most of them three times and some only once a week. With few exceptions they are all wretchedly managed and written. And, of course, on the restricted basis of cantonal conditions in this country, and in the extremely petty polemics which is the only possible kind here, how can any considerable journalistic talent develop and what really talented journalist would consent to be restricted to these meagre conditions and to the space of a quarto sheet that appears three times a week!

The best quality of the Swiss press is its brazenness. People say such things to one another publicly in the newspapers, make unblushingly such insolent personal attacks, that a Rhenish Public Prosecutor for whom Article 370[a] of the *Code pénal*[234] is sacrosanct would not be able to stand it for three days in such a country.

But that is all. If one leaves out of account this recklessness which, incidentally, is quite without wit or humour, almost nothing is left but the most servile bowing and scraping to the repellent narrow-mindedness of a small nation, which in addition to its smallness is split and immeasurably puffed up—a nation of antediluvian Alpine

---

[a] See this volume, p. 317.—*Ed.*

herdsmen, hidebound peasants and disgusting philistines. That in large countries a newspaper takes the lead from its party and never undertakes anything against the interests of the party is quite understandable, and does little harm to freedom of discussion, because every trend, even the most progressive, has its press organs. But in the parochial conditions of Switzerland, the parties themselves are parochial, and the press is just as parochial as the parties. Hence the narrow-minded viewpoints from which everything is looked at; hence the absence of any press organs for trends which are indeed progressive, but which even in Germany have long been current. Hence the fear of even the most radical newspapers to diverge one iota from the narrow-minded programme of their party calculated only on the most immediate future, their fear to attack even the most extreme features of Swiss national narrow-mindedness. Anyone who violated sacred national feeling would immediately be punished by patriarchal lynch justice. What else does the honest Swiss need his fists for?

Such is the average level of the Swiss press. Above this level are the best newspapers of Romance Switzerland and Berne; below this level is the great mass of newspapers of East Switzerland.

Let us begin with the press of the Swiss capital. In Berne a certain centralisation of the Swiss press is already taking place. The press of the canton is already concentrated there and is beginning to a certain extent to gain the influence befitting a capital city.

The chief organ of the reactionary, or as it is called here the aristocratic, party is the *Schweizerischer Beobachter*, which the *Berner-Zeitung* rightly calls the *Moniteur* of Swiss officers in the service of foreign states. This prim little newspaper (issued three times a week) praises the heroic deeds of the Swiss Croats in Italy, attacks the radicals with the dirtiest weapons, defends the enlistment agreements,[235] fulsomely praises the aristocrats, extols Radetzky and Windischgrätz, defends the murder of Robert Blum, slanders the revolution in all countries and denounces refugees to the Government. This noble sheet has really no editor; it is compiled from all kinds of dispatches and items from idle sons of patricians, and from place-seekers of the Municipal Council. A worthy companion to it is the *Intelligenzblatt*, an organ which has on the front page only announcements, while the back page is filled with articles praising the pietism and profit-making of the patrician landowners. *Die Biene* is intended to act as the *Charivari* of this party. But since nowadays the patrician gentlemen on the whole have more to weep over than to laugh at, the humour of this *Biene* is of a terribly dull and lame variety.

The moderate or liberal party, the party of Ochsenbein, has the *Berner Verfassungs-Freund* as its main organ. This newspaper, the editor of which is Dr., formerly Professor, Karl Herzog, is regarded as the semi-official organ of Ochsenbein. Edited by a fairly experienced hand, but without a trace of talent, the newspaper limits itself to defending the actions of the Government and Federal Council, insofar as these actions emanate from the Ochsenbein party. In regard to the eastern cantons, especially the *Ur*-cantons,[236] it is of course fearfully liberal, and even in matters of foreign policy it sometimes issues a resounding trumpet-call in order, behind the warlike tone, to smuggle in the most non-committal neutrality. A more or less obscure newspaper, the *Bundeszeitung*, steers approximately the same course, as does also the French newspaper, *La Suisse*, edited in bad French by the Piedmontese Bassi. While not so directly linked with the Government as the *Verfassungs-Freund*, it is no less zealous in flattering the ruling liberal majority, and with great persistence but little success it attacks the revolutionary press of French Switzerland, in particular the *Nouvelliste Vaudois*. It behaves more decently in regard to the Italian question in which its editor takes a direct part.—These three newspapers appear daily.

The radical party has the largest number of newspapers. At their head is the *Berner-Zeitung*, of which the editor-in-chief is the barrister Niggeler, Vice-President of the Great Council and member of the Council of States. This newspaper is the organ of the markedly radical party of the German part of the canton, represented in the Government Council by Finance Director Stämpfli. Implementation of democracy in the legislation and administration of the canton, from which much ancient rubbish has still to be removed, the greatest possible centralisation throughout Switzerland, abandonment of the policy of neutrality at the first opportunity—these are the main principles in the editing of this newspaper.

The most eminent representatives of Berne radicalism participate in this work, and it is therefore not surprising that the *Berner-Zeitung* is the best edited newspaper not only in the canton, but in the whole of German Switzerland. If the editors and contributors could write quite freely the newspaper would be much better still, the one and indivisible Helvetian republic[237] would come into prominence, with a very red coloration at that; but that cannot be done just now; the party would not yet tolerate it. Appearing alongside the *Berner-Zeitung* from January 1, and also daily, is *L'Helvétie fédérale*, the successor of the newspaper *Helvétie*, formerly published in Pruntrut[a]

---

[a] The French name is Porrentruy.— *Ed.*

in the Jura, organ of the Jura radicals and their leader, Colonel Stockmar, a member of the Government Council. The old *Helvétie* was definitely red; the new one is equally so, indeed in an even more marked degree.

The *Schweizer Zeitung* (previously *Der Freie Schweizer*) is likewise a representative of radicalism, but exclusively of the bourgeois variety, and therefore restricts itself wholly to demanding economic reforms which are advantageous to the ruling, propertied class. For the rest, however, this newspaper too goes beyond the usual Swiss cantonal narrow-mindedness (neutrality, sovereignty of the cantons etc.). Besides these three dailies, the Berne radicals have also a humorous newspaper, and in fact the only good one in Switzerland—the *Gukkasten* of Jenni. The *Gukkasten* (a weekly) restricts itself purely to Swiss and, particularly, Berne canton interests, but precisely for this reason it has succeeded in becoming a power in the land, so that it played an important part in the fall of the Neuhaus Government and is now trying to ensure that the Ochsenbein party does not remain at the helm too long. The merciless wit by which Jenni seeks to strip the halo of popularity from every one of the governing personalities, including Ochsenbein himself, has brought him innumerable court cases and vexations under the Neuhaus Government, and subsequently threatening letters and savage attacks. But all in vain, and the highly placed gentlemen of Berne still await the appearance of each fresh Saturday issue of the *Gukkasten* with considerable trepidation. When Blum was shot, the *Gukkasten*'s weekly cartoon depicted an executioner's block and axe, surrounded by a mass of broken crowns, with the caption: "The only remedy." When the sedate bourgeois of Berne waxed indignant over this, it was followed by a cartoon in the next issue showing a lamp-post with a crown dangling from it, and with the caption: "*Suaviter in modo, fortiter in re*[a]—in memory of Messenhauser!"

Until the New Year, the *Seeländer Anzeiger*, published by J. A. Weingart, a member of the National Council and the Great Council, was the sole representative of socialism. The *Seeländer Anzeiger* preaches a curious mixture of tearfully sentimental and philanthropic socialism with red revolution. It keeps the former for the Berne canton, but speaks of the latter as soon as it deals with foreign countries. As regards literary form, this weekly is one of the worst edited periodicals of the canton. For the rest, in spite of the Christian soft-hearted outpourings of his soul, Herr Weingart in politics supports the most outspoken radicalism. Since the New Year, the

---

[a] Mild in manner, radical in substance.—*Ed.*

Seeländer Anzeiger has had a rival in the shape of another weekly, *Der Unabhängige*, which it is true has set itself a rather thankless task: in the conditions of the Berne canton and Switzerland in general to find starting points for propaganda of the fundamentals of socialism and to propose measures for getting rid of at least the most blatant evils. At any rate, this little newspaper is the only one in the whole of Switzerland which has adopted the right course to gain support for its ideas in this country, and if its chances of success are in proportion to the fury it has already aroused among the high and highest authorities, then its prospects are by no means bad.

Of the newspapers published outside the city, I shall mention only one: the *Evolution*, as Becker, the leader of the volunteer insurgents, has now renamed his *Revolution*.[a] This most outspoken of all the newspapers published in Switzerland alone calls for a new European revolution, for which it tries to win supporters among its entourage. By way of thanks, the peaceful burghers detest it, and it finds few readers, apart from the German refugees in Switzerland, Besançon and Alsace.

In a forthcoming article I shall examine in more detail the newspapers published outside Berne.[238]

Written by Engels on January 11, 1849

First published in the *Neue Rheinische Zeitung* No. 197, January 17, 1849

Printed according to the newspaper

Published in English for the first time

---

[a] See this volume, p. 205.—*Ed.*

PROTECTIONIST AGITATION.—
RECRUITING INTO THE NEAPOLITAN ARMY

Berne, January 12. The protective tariff agitation in Switzerland is growing more and more lively, and so, in the same proportion, is the movement in the interest of preserving the free trade system which has existed up to now. The arguments of both sides are equally excellent and it is very hard to see how Switzerland will extricate itself from the dilemma. The protectionist party points to the yearly increasing pressure of foreign competition on home industry and the proportionately vanishing prospects for providing work for the growing unemployed population. As against this the free traders stress the price increases of industrial products, affecting the agricultural majority of the people, and the impossibility for a nation of two million people to protect a border as extended, and as suitable for smuggling, as the Swiss border, without ruinous expense. Both parties are perfectly right; without protective tariffs one branch of Swiss industry after another is ruined; with protective tariffs the federal finances are ruined. To unite both, the *Berner Verfassungs-Freund* proposes a *juste-milieu* tariff which would ruin both together. In March the Federal Councils will have to break their teeth on the impossible solution of this problem.

In Geneva for some time past, Neapolitan recruiting officers were seen going around trying to raise recruits for the service of His Bombarding Majesty.[239] Ferdinand must need the sturdy Swiss very badly if he even allows recruiting in cantons with which he has no enlistment agreement. But the Geneva Government soon put an end to these activities. It declared all engagements already entered into as null and void, forbade all recruiting, and threatened the recruiting officers with harsh punishment. The mercenaries of the Neapolitan hyena thereupon withdrew in all haste from the Geneva area.

Written by Engels on January 12, 1849

First published in the *Neue Rheinische Zeitung* No. 197, January 17, 1849

Printed according to the newspaper

Published in English for the first time

MÜLLER.—THE FREIBURG GOVERNMENT.— OCHSENBEIN

Berne, January 13. The great Herr Tobias Müller has at last arrived in the canton of Uri and is demanding from the Government that the depot of Neapolitan recruits, which was previously in Genoa, now be moved to Altorf, from whence he will send them by one route or another to Naples. It is not known whether the Government will agree to his demands; even if it does, it is still questionable whether the other governments bound by the enlistment agreement will be satisfied with the proposed move.—A troop of Lucerne recruits are, it is said, to be forwarded via Trieste to Naples, to the scandal of the whole civilised world.

The Freiburg Government, which in general is guilty of strangely arbitrary actions, has again, despite the new Federal Constitution, had a Schwyz canton citizen deported. Already earlier it had just as unceremoniously thrown out Herr Sieber of Zurich, editor of the *Wächter* of Murten, and present co-editor of the *Berner-Zeitung.* Both cases will come before the Federal Assembly, and it is hoped it will see that the Constitution is respected.

A wonder has come to pass: the press organ of the neutral Herr Ochsenbein, the *Verfassungs-Freund*, recognises repentantly that the Tessiners were not so much in the wrong in their quarrels with Radetzky and the East-Swiss troops.[a] He stammers his *pater, peccavi*[b] and tries to cover the matter up with an *Iliacos intra peccatur muros et extra.*[c] And yet the Tessin government councillors are the most confirmed anti-neutralists among the supporters of what Ochsen-

---

[a] See this volume, p. 136.—*Ed.*

[b] Father, I have sinned.—*Ed.*

[c] Sins are committed inside and outside the walls of Ilion.—*Ed.*

bein, in a malicious appeal to Swiss narrow-mindedness, calls "foreign policy". But the Tessiners have become very popular in Berne as a result of the reports of the Berne soldiers, and Herr Ochsenbein has got to remain popular in Berne; and finally, this is the bottom of the business, the Federal Council, without any cause, has just *made* the canton of Tessin again *responsible* for all further complications with Radetzky. But whenever Herr Ochsenbein perpetrates in the Federal Council a practical dirty trick, the *Verfassungs-Freund* must, in theory, clothe it in magnanimous and noble language. That's how they rule the stupid peasants in this country. Oh, democracy!

Written by Engels on January 13, 1849

First published in the *Neue Rheinische Zeitung* No. 197, January 17, 1849

Printed according to the newspaper

Published in English for the first time

MONTESQUIEU LVI[240]

[*Neue Rheinische Zeitung* No. 201, January 21, 1849]

Cologne, January 20. The "honourable" *Joseph Dumont* allows an anonymous writer, who is not paid by him but pays him and who in the feature section seeks to influence the *primary electors*, to address the *Neue Rheinische Zeitung* in the following way[a]:

> "The *Neue Rheinische Zeitung*, the *Organ of Democracy*, has been pleased to take notice of the articles published in this paper under the title 'To the Primary Electors', and to state that they were taken from the *Neue Preussische Zeitung*.[241]
>
> "In face of this *lie*, we simply declare that these articles are paid for *as advertisements*, and that, with the exception of the first one, taken from the *Parlaments-Korrespondenz*, they were written in Cologne and their author has up to now not even seen, let alone read, the *Neue Preussische Zeitung*."

We understand how important it is for Montesquieu LVI to authenticate his *property*. We also understand how important for Herr Dumont is the statement that he is "*paid*" even for the leaflets and advertisements which he sets up, prints and distributes in the interest of his class, the *bourgeoisie*.

As for the anonymous writer, he is aware of the French saying: "Les beaux esprits se rencontrent."[b] It is not his fault that his own intellectual products and those of the *Neue Preussische Zeitung* and of the "Prussian associations"[242] are as alike as two peas.

We *have never read* his advertisements in the *Kölnische Zeitung*, but the leaflets produced by Dumont's printing-house and sent to us from various quarters, we deemed worthy of a casual glance. Now,

---

[a] Here follows the statement by the *Kölnische Zeitung* editors published in their paper on January 20, 1849 (issue No. 17), following the address "To the Primary Electors".— *Ed.*

[b] Great minds think alike.— *Ed.*

however, comparison has shown us that the same stuff plays the simultaneous role of advertisement and leaflet.

In order to atone for the injustice we have done to the anonymous Montesquieu LVI we have imposed upon ourselves the harsh penance of reading all his advertisements in the *Kölnische Zeitung* and making his intellectual private property available to the German public as "common property".[243]

Here is wisdom!

Montesquieu LVI is chiefly concerned with the *social question*. He has found the "easiest and simplest way" to *solve* it, and he extols his Morison pill[244] with the most unctuous, naively shameless pathos of a quack.

"The easiest and simplest way, however, to achieve this" (that is the solution of the social question) "is to accept the Constitution imposed on December 5 last year, revise it, then make everyone swear allegiance to it, and thus to establish it. *This is our only way to salvation. Consequently,* any man who has a sympathetic heart for the misery of his poor brothers, who wants to feed the hungry and clothe the naked ... anyone, in short, who *wants to solve the social question*[a] ... *should not vote for anyone who is opposed to the Constitution*" (Montesquieu LVI).

Vote for Brandenburg-Manteuffel-Ladenberg, and the *social question* will be solved in the "simplest" and "easiest way"! Vote for Dumont, Camphausen, Wittgenstein or else for *dii minorum gentium*[b] such as Compes and Mevissen—and the *social question* will be solved! The "social question" for *a vote*! He who "wants to feed the hungry and clothe the naked" should vote for Hansemann and Stupp! One social question less for each vote! Acceptance of the imposed Constitution—*voilà la solution du problème social!*[c]

We do not for a moment doubt that neither Montesquieu LVI nor his patrons in the citizens' associations will wait for the imposed Constitution to be accepted, revised, sworn, and promulgated before "feeding the hungry and clothing the naked".[245] Measures have already been taken to this end.

During the last few weeks circulars have been distributed here in which capitalists inform craftsmen, shopkeepers etc. that, in view of the present state of affairs and the revival of credit, the rate of interest, for philanthropical reasons, has been raised from 4 to 5 per cent. First solution of the social question!

The Municipal Council here has in the same spirit drawn up a "*Worker's Card*" for the unfortunate people who must either starve

---

[a] In the *Kölnische Zeitung*: "social questions".—*Ed.*
[b] The gods of minor nations.—*Ed.*
[c] There is the solution of the social problem!—*Ed.*

or sell their hands to the city (cf. No. 187 of the *Neue Rheinische Zeitung*[a]). It will be remembered that under this Charter imposed on the workers, the worker who has lost his job is bound by contract to place himself under *police surveillance*. Second solution of the social question!

Shortly after the March events, the Municipal Council established an eating-house in Cologne at cost prices, beautifully furnished, with fine rooms that could be heated etc. *After* the granting of the Constitution other premises were substituted for this, premises managed by the poor-law administration, where there is no heating, no crockery, where food may not be consumed on the spot and where a quart of indescribable gruel costs eight pfennigs. Third solution of the social question!

While they ruled Vienna the workers guarded the Bank, the houses and the wealth of the bourgeois who had fled. These same bourgeois, on their return, denounced these workers to Windischgrätz as "robbers" who ought to be *hanged*. The unemployed who applied to the Municipal Council were put into the army to fight Hungary. Fourth solution of the social question!

In Breslau the wretched people who were obliged to seek refuge in the poor-house were calmly exposed to cholera by the Municipal Council and the Government, which deprived them of the most essential physical necessaries of life, and took notice of the victims of their cruel charity only when they themselves were attacked by the disease. Fifth solution of the social question!

In the Berlin Association "with God for King and Fatherland",[246] a supporter of the imposed Constitution declared that it was distressing that in order to further one's interests and plans one still had to pay compliments to the "*proletariat*".

That is the solution of the "solution of the social question"!

"The Prussian spies are so dangerous because they are never paid but are always hoping to be paid," says our friend Heine. And the Prussian bourgeois are so dangerous because they never pay but always promise to pay.

During an election the English and French bourgeois spend quite a lot of money. Their corrupt practices are well known. The Prussian bourgeois "are the most shrewd"! They are much too virtuous and upright to dip into their pocket; they pay with the "*solution of the social question*". And that costs nothing. Montesquieu LVI, however, as Dumont officially assures us, pays at least for the advertisements

---

[a] See this volume, pp. 218-21.—*Ed.*

in the *Kölnische Zeitung* and adds—gratis—the solution of the "*social questions*".

The practical part of our Montesquieu's *petites œuvres* thus boils down to the following: Vote for Brandenburg-Manteuffel-Ladenberg! Elect Camphausen-Hansemann! Send us to Berlin, just let our people establish themselves there. That is the *solution of the social question!*

The immortal *Hansemann* has solved these questions. First, the establishment of law and order to revive credit. Then, the solution of the "social question" with powder and shot, as in 1844, when "my dear Silesian weavers ought to be helped"![247]

Vote therefore for the friends of the imposed Constitution!

But Montesquieu LVI accepts the imposed Constitution only to be able afterwards to "revise" and "swear allegiance to it"!

My dear Montesquieu! Once you have accepted the Constitution you can revise it only on its own basis, that is insofar as it suits the King and the Second Chamber consisting of country squires, financial magnates, high-ranking officials and clerics. This only possible revision has been judiciously indicated already in the imposed Constitution itself. It consists in abandoning the constitutional system and restoring the former Christian-Germanic *system of estates.*

After the acceptance of the imposed Constitution this is the only possible and only permitted revision, which cannot have escaped the shrewd Montesquieu.

Thus the *petites œuvres* of Montesquieu LVI, in their practical part, amount to this: Vote for Hansemann-Camphausen! Vote for Dumont-Stupp! Vote for Brandenburg-Manteuffel! Accept the imposed Constitution! Elect delegates who accept the imposed Constitution—and all this under the pretext of solving "the social question".

What the hell does the pretext matter to us, when it is a question of the imposed Constitution.

But our Montesquieu of course prefaces his practical instructions for the solution of "the social question", the quintessence of his monumental work, with a theoretical part. Let us examine this theoretical part.

The profound thinker explains first *what the "social questions" are.*

"What then, in effect, is the social question?

"Man must and wants to live.

"To live he needs dwellings, clothes and food.

"Dwellings and clothes are not produced by nature at all, and only a scanty and by no means sufficient amount of food grows naturally.

"Hence man himself must procure everything to satisfy these needs.

"This he does by labour.

"*Labour, therefore, is the first condition of our life; without labour we cannot live.*

"Among primitive peoples everybody built his own hut, made his own clothes from animal skins and gathered fruit for his meals. That was the primitive state.

"But if man needs nothing beyond shelter, clothes and food, if he satisfies merely his *physical* wants, then he remains at the same level as the animals, for animals can do this too.

"But man is a higher being than an animal, he needs more, he needs joy, he must raise himself to moral values. But he can do that only if he lives in society.

"But once men began to live in societies entirely new conditions arose. They soon perceived that work was much easier when each individual performed only one particular job. Thus, one made clothes, another built houses, a third provided food, and the first gave the second what he lacked. The various social estates of men thus developed automatically, one becoming a hunter, another a craftsman, and a third a cultivator. But men did not stop at this, for humanity must go forward. People began to invent. They invented spinning and weaving, they learned to forge iron and tan hides. The more inventions were made the more diverse did the crafts become, and the easier did farming become with the aid of the plough and spade which the handicrafts gave it. One thing helped another and everything was interconnected. Then intercourse started with neighbouring peoples; one people had what the other needed, and the latter possessed things the former lacked. These were exchanged. Thus *trading* arose, that is a new branch of human activity. Thus culture advanced step by step; from the first clumsy inventions through the centuries down to the inventions of our day.

"Thus, the sciences and the arts arose among men and life became ever richer and more varied. The physician treated the sick, the clergyman preached, the merchant traded, the farmer tilled the land, the gardener grew flowers, the mason built houses, for which the carpenter made the furniture, the miller ground flour from which the baker baked bread. Everything was interconnected, no one could live in isolation, nobody could satisfy all his needs himself.

"These are the social relations.

"They have arisen quite naturally of their own accord. And if today you make a revolution which destroys the very foundations of these relations, and if tomorrow you start life anew, *then relations exactly the same as the present ones will arise again.* This has been so for thousands of years among all the nations on earth. And if anyone draws a distinction between the workers and the bourgeoisie this is a *big lie. We all work,* each in his own way, each according to his strength and abilities. The physician works when he visits the sick, the musician when he plays a dance tune, the merchant when he writes his letters. Everyone works, each at his job."

> *Here is wisdom! He that hath ears to hear, let him hear.*[a]
>
> *What, then, in effect is the situation with the physiological question?*

Every corporeal being presupposes a certain weight, density etc. Every organic body consists of various component parts, each of which performs its own special function, and reciprocal interaction takes place between the organs.

"These are physiological relations."

---

[a] Matthew 11 : 15.— *Ed.*

Montesquieu LVI cannot be denied an original talent for simplifying science. He ought to be granted a patent (without government guarantee).

The products of labour cannot be produced without labour. One cannot reap without sowing, one cannot have yarn without weaving etc.

Europe will bend in admiration before the great genius who here, in Cologne, without any aid from the *Neue Preussische Zeitung* has himself brought these truths to light.

In their work men enter into certain relations with one another. There takes place a *division of labour* which may be more or less diversified. One person bakes, another forges iron, one person agitates [*wühlt*], another wails [*heult*],[248] Montesquieu LVI writes and Dumont prints. *Adam Smith,* acknowledge thy master!

These discoveries, that *labour* and the *division of labour* are essential conditions of life of every human society, enable Montesquieu LVI to draw the conclusion that the existence of the "*various social estates*" is quite natural, that the distinction between "bourgeoisie and proletariat" is a "*big lie*", that even if a "*revolution*" were completely to destroy the existing "social relations" today, "*relations exactly the same as the present ones will arise again*", and finally that for anyone who has "a sympathetic heart for the misery of his poor brothers" and who wishes to gain the respect of Montesquieu LVI, it is absolutely necessary to elect delegates in keeping with the ideas of Manteuffel and the imposed Constitution.

"*This has been so for thousands of years among all the nations on earth*"*!!!* In Egypt there was labour and division of labour—and *castes*; in Greece and Rome labour and division of labour—and *free men and slaves*; in the Middle Ages labour and division of labour—and *feudal lords* and *serfs, guilds, social estates* etc. In our day there is labour and division of labour—and *classes*, one of which owns all means of production and all means of subsistence, while the other lives only so long as it sells its labour,[249] and it sells its labour only so long as the employing class enriches itself by purchasing this labour.

Is it not obvious, therefore, that "*for thousands of years it has been the same among all the nations on earth*" as it is in *Prussia* today, since *labour and division of labour* have always existed in one form or another? Or is it, on the contrary, evident that the social relations, the property relations, were always overthrown by the constantly changing method of labour and division of labour?

In 1789 the bourgeois did not tell feudal society that an aristocrat should remain an aristocrat, a serf a serf and a guildsman a guildsman—because there is no society without labour and division of labour. There is no life without breathing of air. Hence, argues Montesquieu LVI, breathe the stuffy air and do not open any window.

One must possess the naively clumsy insolence of a German imperial philistine grown grey in crass ignorance to contribute oracular pronouncements upon problems on which our century is breaking its teeth, after having rammed the first elements of political economy—labour and division of labour—in a superficial and distorted manner into his inert head.

"There is no society without labour and division of labour.

Therefore

"Elect friends of the imposed Prussian Constitution, and only friends of the imposed Constitution, as delegates."

This epitaph some day will be inscribed in large letters on the walls of the magnificent marble mausoleum which a grateful posterity will feel obliged to erect for Montesquieu LVI (not to be confused with Henry CCLXXXIV of Reuss-Schleiz-Greiz-Lobenstein-Eberswalde[a]) who solved the social question.

Montesquieu LVI does not conceal from us "*where the difficulty lies*" and what he intends to do as soon as he is proclaimed a lawgiver.

"*The state*," he teaches us, "*must see to it that everybody receives sufficient education to be able to learn something useful in this world.*"

Montesquieu LVI has never heard that under existing conditions the division of labour replaces complex labour by simple labour, the labour of adults by that of children, the labour of men by that of women, the labour of the independent workers by automatons; that, in proportion as modern industry develops, the education of workers becomes unnecessary and impossible. We refer the Montesquieu of Cologne neither to *Saint-Simon* nor to *Fourier* but to *Malthus* and *Ricardo*. This worthy should first acquaint himself with the rudiments of present-day conditions before trying to improve them and making oracular utterances.

"*The community must take care of people who have been reduced to poverty as a result of illness or old age.*"

And if the community itself is reduced to poverty which will be the inevitable result of the 100-million tax imposed simultaneously with the new Constitution and the epidemically recurring states of siege—what then, Montesquieu?

---

[a] An allusion to Henry LXXII, Prince of Reuss-Lobenstein-Ebersdorf.—*Ed.*

"When new inventions or commercial crises destroy entire industries the state must come to their assistance and find remedies."

Little versed as he may be in the things of this world, it can hardly have escaped the Montesquieu of Cologne that "new inventions" and commercial crises are features just as permanent as the Prussian ministerial decrees and legal basis. New inventions, especially in Germany, are only introduced when competition with other nations makes it vital to introduce them; and should the newly arising branches of industry be expected to ruin themselves in order to render assistance to the declining ones? The new industries that come into being as a result of inventions come into being precisely because they can produce more cheaply than the declining industries. What the deuce would be the advantage if they had to feed the declining industries? But it is well known that the state, the Government, only seems to give. It has to be given something first in order to give. But who should give to it, Montesquieu LVI? The declining industry, so that it declines even faster? Or the rising industry, so that it withers even as it rises? Or those industries that have not been affected by the new inventions, so that they go bankrupt because of the invention of a new tax? Think it over carefully, Montesquieu LVI!

And what about the commercial crises, my dear man? When a European commercial crisis occurs the Prussian state is above all anxious to extract the last drops, by means of distraint etc., from the usual sources of revenue. Poor Prussian state! In order to neutralise the effect of commercial crises, the Prussian state would have to possess, in addition to national labour, a third source of income in Cloud-Cuckoo-Land. If royal New-Year greetings,[a] Wrangel's army orders or Manteuffel's ministerial decrees could indeed conjure up money, then the *"refusal to pay taxes"* would not have caused such panic among the Prussian "well-beloved loyal subjects", and the social question, too, would have been solved without an imposed Constitution.

It will be remembered that the *Neue Preussische Zeitung* called our *Hansemann a communist* because he intended to do away with exemption from taxation. In Cologne our Montesquieu, who has never read the *Neue Preussische Zeitung*, has *all by himself* conceived the idea of calling everyone a "communist" and "red republican" who endangers the imposed Constitution. Therefore, vote for Manteuffel, or you are not only personal enemies of labour and the division of labour, but also communists and red republicans.

---

[a] See this volume, pp. 222-26.—*Ed.*

Acknowledge Brüggemann's latest "legal basis" or renounce the *Code civil.*[250]

Figaro, tu n'aurais pas trouvé ça![a]

More about Montesquieu LVI tomorrow.

[*Neue Rheinische Zeitung* No. 202, January 22, 1849]

Cologne, January 21. With the sly petty cunning of an experienced *horse-dealer, Montesquieu LVI* seeks to sell the "gift horse", the imposed Constitution, to the primary electors. He is the Montesquieu of the horse-fair.

Anyone not wanting the imposed Constitution wants a republic, and not just a republic, but a red republic! Unfortunately, the issue in our elections is least of all a republic, or a red republic; it is simply this:

Do you want the old *absolutism* together with a refurbished *system of social estates,* or do you want a bourgeois *system of representation*? Do you want a political constitution in keeping with the "existing social relations" of past centuries, or do you want a political constitution in keeping with the "existing social relations" of your century?

In this case, therefore, it is least of all a question of fighting against bourgeois property relations similar to the struggle that is taking place in France and is being prepared in England; rather it is a question of a struggle against a political constitution which endangers "*bourgeois* property relations" by surrendering the helm of state to the representatives of "*feudal* property relations", to the King by the grace of God, the army, the bureaucracy, the country squires, and a few financial magnates and philistines who are allied with them.

Beyond a doubt, the imposed Constitution has solved the social question in keeping with the views of these gentlemen.

What is the "*social question*" as understood by the *government official*? It is the maintenance of his salary and his present position, which is superior to the people.

What is the "*social question*" as understood by the nobility and its big landowners? It is the maintenance of the hitherto existing feudal rights of the landowners, seizure of the most lucrative posts in the army and civil service by the families of the landed nobility, and

---

[a] Figaro, you would not have found that out! An allusion to "*Ah, Figaro, pends-toi; tu n'as pas deviné celui-là!*" (Figaro, hang yourself; you didn't find that one!) from Beaumarchais' comedy *La folle journée, ou le mariage de Figaro,* Act V, Scene 8.— *Ed.*

finally direct alms from the public purse. Apart from these palpable *material* and therefore "*most sacred*" interests of the gentlemen "with God for King and Fatherland"[a] it is for them, of course, also a question of preserving those social privileges which distinguish their race from the inferior race of the bourgeois, peasants and plebeians. The old National Assembly was dispersed precisely because it dared to lay hands on these "most sacred interests". As we have already indicated, these gentlemen, by "revision" of the imposed Constitution, understand simply the introduction of a *system of social estates*, that is to say, a form of political constitution representing the "social" interests of the feudal aristocracy, the bureaucracy and the monarchy by the grace of God.

We repeat, there is not the slightest doubt that the imposed Constitution solves the "social question" in keeping with the views of the aristocracy and the bureaucracy, in other words, it presents these gentlemen with a form of government which ensures the exploitation of the people by these demigods.

But has the imposed Constitution solved the "social question" from the standpoint of the *bourgeoisie?* In other words, does the bourgeoisie receive a political system enabling if freely to administer the affairs of its class as a whole, i.e. the interests of commerce, industry and agriculture, to make the most productive use of public funds, to manage the state budget as cheaply as possible, to protect national labour effectively from without, and within the country to open up all sources of national wealth silted by feudal mud?

Does history provide a single example showing that under a king imposed by the grace of God, the bourgeoisie ever succeeded in achieving a political system in keeping with its material interests?

In order to establish a constitutional monarchy it was twice compelled to get rid of the Stuarts in Britain, and the hereditary Bourbons in France, and to expel William of Orange from Belgium.[251]

What is the reason for this?

A hereditary king by the grace of God is not a particular individual but the physical representative of the old society within the new society. State power in the hands of a king by the grace of God is state power in the hands of the old society existing now merely as a ruin; it is state power in the hands of the feudal social estates, whose interests are profoundly antagonistic to those of the bourgeoisie.

---

[a] A quotation from Frederick William III's decree of March 17, 1813, on organising the army reserve.—*Ed.*

But it is precisely the "*King by the grace of God*" who forms the basis of the imposed Constitution.

Just as the feudal strata of society regard the monarchy by the grace of God as their *political apex*, so does the monarchy by the grace of God regard the feudal estates as its *social foundation*, the well-known "*monarchical wall*".[252]

Therefore, whenever the interests of the feudal lords and of the army and bureaucracy controlled by them clash with the interests of the bourgeoisie, the monarchy by the grace of God will invariably be impelled to a coup d'état and a revolutionary or counter-revolutionary crisis will arise.

Why was the National Assembly dispersed? Only because it upheld the interests of the bourgeoisie against the interests of feudalism; because it wanted to abolish the feudal relations hampering agriculture, to subordinate the army and bureaucracy to trade and industry, to stop the squandering of public funds and abolish aristocratic and bureaucratic titles.

All these were questions *chiefly* and *directly* affecting the *interests of the bourgeoisie*.

Thus, *coups d'état* and *counter-revolutionary crises* are vital conditions for the monarchy by the grace of God, which the March and similar events compelled to humiliate itself and reluctantly to accept the semblance of a bourgeois monarchy.

Can *credit* ever revive again under a political system which inevitably culminates in coups d'état, counter-revolutionary crises and states of siege?

What a delusion!

Bourgeois industry *must* burst the fetters of absolutism and feudalism. A revolution against both only demonstrates that bourgeois industry has reached a level when it must either win an appropriate political system or perish.

The system of bureaucratic tutelage guaranteed by the imposed Constitution spells *death* for industry. It is sufficient to look at the Prussian administration of mines, the factory regulations etc. When an English manufacturer compares his costs of production with those of a Prussian manufacturer, he will always first of all note the time losses which the Prussian manufacturer incurs because he has to observe bureaucratic rules.

What sugar-refiner does not remember the Prussian trade agreement with the Netherlands in 1839?[253] What Prussian factory owner does not blush at the memory of 1846, when the Prussian Government in deference to the Austrian Government banned exports to *Galicia* for a whole province, and when one bankruptcy after another occurred in Breslau the Prussian Government declared with astonishment that it had had no idea that there were such important exports to Galicia etc.!

Men of the same race are placed at the helm of state by the imposed Constitution, and this "gift" itself comes from the same men. Consequently, examine it twice.

The Galicia adventure draws our attention to another point.

At that time the counter-revolutionary Prussian Government in league with Austria and Russia sacrificed Silesian industry and Silesian trade.[254] This manoeuvre will be constantly repeated. The banker of the Prussian-Austrian-Russian counter-revolution, from which the monarchy by the grace of God with its monarchical walls will always have to seek *outside* support, is *England*. The same *England* is German industry's most dangerous opponent. These two facts, we believe, speak for themselves.

At home, an industry fettered by bureaucracy and an agriculture fettered by feudal privileges; abroad, a trade sold by the counter-revolution to England—such is the fate of Prussia's national wealth under the aegis of the imposed Constitution.

The report of the "Financial Commission" of the dispersed National Assembly has thrown sufficient light on the management of national wealth by the grace of God.

The report however mentions only by way of example the sums taken from the treasury to support the tottering monarchical walls and gild foreign pretenders to the absolute monarchy (Don Carlos). But these monies, purloined from the pockets of the rest of the citizens to enable the aristocracy to live in appropriate style and to keep the "buttresses" of the feudal monarchy in good condition, are only of secondary importance compared with the state budget imposed simultaneously with Manteuffel's Constitution. The main features of the imposed state budget are, first of all, a *strong army* to enable the minority to rule the majority; as large an army as possible of officials so that as many of them as possible, by virtue of their private interests, are alienated from the common interest; unproductive employment of public monies in order that wealth, as the *Neue Preussische Zeitung* says, should not make the *subjects* overbold; immobilisation wherever possible of public monies instead of employing them in industry in order that at easily predictable moments of crisis the Government by the grace of God should independently confront the people. The basic principle of the imposed Prussian Constitution is to use the taxes for maintaining the state power as an oppressive, independent and sacred force contraposed to industry, commerce and agriculture, instead of *degrading* it into a profane *tool* of bourgeois society.

The gift is worthy of the donor. The Constitution is of a piece with the present Prussian Government that presented it. To characterise *this Government's hostility towards the bourgeoisie* it is sufficient to point to its proposed *trade regulations*. On the pretext of *advancing towards association* the Government attempts to *return to the guild system*. Competition compels the manufacturer to produce more and more cheaply and therefore on a constantly increasing scale, i.e. with *more capital*, with a continuously *expanding division of labour* and constantly *increasing use of machinery*. Every new division of labour depreciates the traditional skill of the craftsmen, every new machine ousts hundreds of workers, production on a larger scale, that is with more capital, ruins small trade and petty-bourgeois enterprise. The Government promises to protect the handicrafts against the factories, acquired skills against division of labour, and small capital against big capital, by means of *feudal guild institutions*. Thus, the German nation, particularly the Prussian, which only with the utmost difficulty and effort resists complete defeat by English competition, is to become its defenceless prey, forced to accept a form of trade organisation that is incompatible with modern means of production and is already burst wide open by modern industry.

We are certainly the last people to desire the rule of the bourgeoisie. We were the first in Germany to raise our voice against the bourgeoisie when today's "men of action" were spending their time complacently in petty squabbles.

But we say to the workers and the petty bourgeois: it is better to suffer in modern bourgeois society, which by its industry creates the material means for the foundation of a new society that will liberate you all, than to revert to a bygone form of society, which, on the pretext of saving your classes, thrusts the entire nation back into medieval barbarism.

But medieval social estates and conditions are, as we have seen, the *social foundation* of the Government by the grace of God. This Government is unsuitable for modern bourgeois society. It necessarily tries to create a society in its own image. It is *entirely consistent* when it attempts to replace free competition by the guild system, mechanical spinning by the spinning-wheel and the steam plough by the hoe.

Why is it then that, under these circumstances, the Prussian bourgeoisie, in complete contrast to its French, English and Belgian predecessors, proclaims as its shibboleth the imposed Constitution (and with it the monarchy by the grace of God, the bureaucracy and the junkers)?

The commercial and industrial sections of the bourgeoisie throw themselves into the arms of the counter-revolution for fear of the revolution. As though counter-revolution were not the overture to revolution.

There is moreover a section of the *bourgeoisie* that, quite indifferent to the interests of its class as a whole, pursues its own particular interests, which may even be inimical to those of its class.

These are financial magnates, big creditors of the state, bankers, and rentiers, whose wealth increases proportionately to the poverty of the people, and finally men whose business depends on the old political structure, e.g. *Dumont* and his literary lumpenproletariat. These are ambitious professors, lawyers and similar persons, who can only hope to obtain respectable posts in a state where betrayal of the people's interests to the Government is a lucrative business.

These are individual manufacturers who do well out of their transactions with the Government; contractors whose considerable profits depend on the general exploitation of the people; philistines who lose their importance in political life on a large scale; local councillors who under cover of the old institutions arrange their private shady affairs at the expense of the public; oil merchants who by betrayal of the revolution have become Excellencies and Knights of the Eagle[a]; bankrupt cloth merchants and speculators in railway shares who have become royal bank directors[b] etc., etc.

"It is they who are the friends of the imposed Constitution." If the bourgeoisie has a *sympathetic heart for these poor brothers* and if it wants to be worthy of the respect of Montesquieu LVI, then it should elect *delegates in keeping with the imposed Constitution.*

Written by Marx on January 20-21, 1849   Printed according to the newspaper

First published in the *Neue Rheinische Zeitung* Nos. 201 and 202, January 21 and 22, 1849

---

[a] Probably an allusion to the supporters of the Prussian royal house, whose coat of arms featured an eagle.—*Ed.*

[b] An allusion to Camphausen and Hansemann.—*Ed.*

[ANSWER FROM COLONEL ENGELS]²⁵⁵

Cologne. We have received from Colonel Engels the following answer to our question of two days ago.

"To the insertion in No. 203 of the *Neue Rheinische Zeitung* the answer is No.

"Only private persons have permitted themselves to express the opinion, unlawful in my view, that not enough by a long chalk has been done to these houses by the soldiers.

"*Cologne*, January 24, 1849

Engels, Colonel,
2nd Commandant

"To the esteemed editors of the *Neue Rheinische Zeitung*."

We will very likely have new questions to put to Herr Engels in the next few days, and particularly about the elections.

Written by Engels on January 25, 1849

First published in the supplement to the *Neue Rheinische Zeitung* No. 205, January 26, 1849

Printed according to the newspaper

Published in English for the first time

THE PRUSSIAN WARRANT FOR THE ARREST
OF KOSSUTH

Cologne, January 21. We have just received the following edifying document published in the *Oppelner Kreisblatt*:

"*Warrant of Arrest.* According to a statement of the royal imperial Austrian governmental commission in Cracow, measures have been taken in Hungary to enable Kossuth under a false name to reach Hamburg via Breslau. It is supposed that he will take the route through Myslowitz, Gleiwitz and Kosel.

"On the basis of instructions from the Herr *Oberpräsident* of the province of Silesia, I order all police authorities, local courts and gendarmerie to keep a sharp look-out for Kossuth, whose description is given below, and in the event of his appearance on their territory to arrest him and to deliver him to me safely for further steps."

(Here follows, as already stated, Kossuth's description.) This edifying document is signed:

"Oppeln, January 17, 1849

Royal *Landrat Hoffmann*"

What have our readers to say to that? The Manteuffels of Upper Silesia by the grace of God would be quite pleased to arrest the great agitator Kossuth if he were defeated and succeeded in crossing the frontier, and to deliver him to his executioners for the speediest pardon with gunpowder and shot. If Kossuth is in actual fact handed over, this will be *the most foul betrayal, the most infamous violation of international law* that history has ever known.

Under the old legislation of the German Confederation,[256] of course, Prussia was obliged to hand over to German Austria, on the demand of the latter, political refugees charged with actions carried out on the *territory of the German Confederation*. The revolution overthrew the old legislation of the German Confederation, and *even under the Pfuel Government refugees from Vienna* were safe in Berlin.

But Prussia has no such obligations in relation to *Hungary*. Hungary is an independent state and if Prussia hands over Hungarian refugees who can be charged only with actions carried out on Hungarian territory, it commits the same *disgraceful and infamous* deed as if it handed over Russian or Polish refugees to Russia.

Even under the Bodelschwingh regime the authorities did not dare to hand over to Austria the refugees from Galicia and Cracow who had crossed the border into Prussia.[257] But, on the other hand, of course, at that time we were under an absolute monarchy, and today we are a constitutional state!

Moreover, if Kossuth crosses into Prussian territory he will not be a political refugee but a *belligerent party that has crossed into neutral territory*.

German Austria, an independent union of states, is waging war against Hungary, an independent state; the reason for it is no concern of Prussia's. Even in 1831 the authorities did not dare to hand over to Russia the Poles who had crossed the border into Prussia[258]; but at that time, too, we were under an absolute monarchy, and today we are a constitutional state!

We draw the attention of public opinion to the benevolent intentions of the Prussian Government in regard to Kossuth. We are convinced that this will suffice to arouse such a storm of sympathy for the greatest man of the year 1848, and such a storm of indignation against the Government, that even a Manteuffel will not dare to oppose it.

But, of course, for the time being Kossuth still rules in Debreczin, with the enthusiastic support of the entire Magyar people; his valiant hussars still gallop over the Hungarian plains,[259] Windischgrätz still stands in perplexity facing the swamps of the Theiss, and your warrants of arrest are ridiculous rather than frightening!

Written by Engels on January 21, 1849

First published in the *Neue Rheinische Zeitung* No. 207, January 28, 1849

Printed according to the newspaper

Published in English for the first time

THE BERLIN *NATIONAL-ZEITUNG*
TO THE PRIMARY ELECTORS

[*Neue Rheinische Zeitung* No. 205, January 26, 1849]

Cologne, January 25. Although rarely, it does happen from time to time that one has the pleasure of seeing a signpost of the good old pre-March times rising out of the alluvial deposit which the double deluge of revolution and counter-revolution has left behind. Mountains have been shifted, valleys have been filled up, and forests levelled to the ground, but the signpost still stands in its old place, painted in the old colours, and still bearing the old inscription: "To Schilda!"[260]

Just such a signpost stretches its wooden arm towards us from No. 21 of the *Berlin National-Zeitung* with the inscription: "*To the primary electors.* To Schilda!"

The well-meant advice of the *National-Zeitung* to the primary electors states first of all:

"The hour has come when the Prussian people is about to exercise for the second time its hard-won universal suffrage" (as if the so-called universal suffrage, granted from above, with its different interpretation in each village, were the same suffrage as that of April 8![261]), "from which are to come the men who for the second time have to declare what is the spirit (!), the opinion (!!) and the will (!!!) not of separate social estates and classes, but of the whole people."

We shall not speak of the turgidly clumsy style of this sentence which advances slowly and long-windedly from one word to the next. Universal suffrage, it says, should reveal to us the will not of separate social estates and classes, but of the whole people.

Fine! But what does "the whole people" consist of?

Of "separate social estates and classes".

And what does "the will of the whole people" consist of?

Of the separate contradictory "wills" of the "separate social estates and classes", hence precisely of the will which the *National-*

Zeitung describes as the direct opposite of the "will of the whole people".

What a great logician the *National-Zeitung* is!

For the *National-Zeitung*, however, there exists a *single* will of the whole people, which is not the sum of contradictory wills, but a united, definite will. How can that be?

It is—the will of the majority.

And what is the will of the majority?

It is the will which derives from the interests, the situation in life, and the living conditions of the majority.

Consequently, in order to have one and the same will, the members of the majority must have the same interests, the same situation in life, and the same living conditions, or for the time being they must be linked with one another by their interests, their situation in life, and their living conditions.

In plain language: the will of the people, the will of the majority, is the will not of separate social estates and classes, but of *a single class* and of those other classes and sections of classes which are subordinated to this one ruling class socially, i.e. industrially and commercially.

"But what are we to say to that?" That the will of the whole people is the will of a ruling class?

Of course, and it is precisely universal suffrage that acts as the compass needle which, even if only after various fluctuations, nevertheless finally points to this class which is called upon to rule.

And this good *National-Zeitung* still continues, as in 1847, to chatter about an imaginary "will of the whole people"!

Let us proceed. After this elevating exordium the *National-Zeitung* astounds us with the following significant remark:

"In January 1849 the state of affairs is different from the May days of 1848 so rich in hope and elation" (why not also in piety?).

> All was then adorned with blossom,
> And the sun's rays shone with laughter,
> And the birds sang so full of hope,
> And the people hoped and thought—
> They were deep in thought.[a]

"At that time there seemed to be complete unanimity that the great reforms, which should have been undertaken in Prussia already long ago if on the foundations laid in 1807-14 there had been further construction in the spirit of that time and in accord with the higher level of culture and understanding since achieved, would now have to be carried out completely and without delay."

---

[a] Heinrich Heine, *Deutschland. Ein Wintermärchen*, Caput VIII.—*Ed.*

"At that time there seemed to be complete unanimity"! Grand, delightful naivety of the *National-Zeitung*! At that time, when the Guards, gnashing their teeth in fury, were retreating from Berlin, when the Prince of Prussia had to flee in haste from Berlin in a postilion's jacket, when the upper ranks of the nobility and bourgeoisie had to suppress their anger at the ignominy which the King was made to suffer in the palace-yard when the people forced him to remove his hat before the dead bodies of those killed during the March days—"at that time there seemed to be complete unanimity"!

Heaven knows, it is already overdoing it to have imagined anything of the sort. But now, after one has had to admit to having been cheated, to proclaim one's cheated gullibility from the house-tops—truly, *c'est par trop bonhomme!*[a]

And on what did there "seem to be complete unanimity"?

On "that the great reforms, which *should have been* undertaken ... if ... *there had been* further construction ... would now *have* to be carried out".

On that there was—no, there *seemed* to be—complete unanimity.

The great March achievement, expressed in worthy language!

And what "reforms" were these?

Development of the "foundations laid in 1807-14 in the spirit of that time and in accord with the higher level of culture and understanding since achieved".

That is to say in the spirit of 1807-14, and at the same time in quite a different spirit.

The "*spirit* of that time" consisted quite simply in the extremely *material* pressure of the French of that time on the Prussian junker monarchy of that time, as well as in the likewise unfavourable financial deficit of the Prussian kingdom at that time. In order to make the bourgeois and the peasant capable of paying taxes, in order to introduce at least in appearance among the royal Prussian subjects some of the reforms which the French had lavished on the conquered parts of Germany—in short, in order in some degree to patch up the decayed monarchy of the Hohenzollerns that was splitting at every seam, *for the sake of that* a few niggardly so-called urban by-laws, redemption orders, army institutions etc. were introduced. The only distinction of these reforms was that they were a whole century behind the French revolution of 1789, and indeed even behind the English revolution of 1640. And that is supposed to be the foundations for Prussia that has been revolutionised?

---

[a] That is too simple-minded!—*Ed.*

But old-Prussian conceit always sees Prussia in the centre of world history, whereas in reality world history has always dragged the "state of reason"[a] after it, through the mire. This old-Prussian conceit has, of course, to ignore the fact that as long as Prussia was not kicked by the French, it calmly remained on the undeveloped foundations of 1807-14 and never stirred at all. It has to ignore the fact that these foundations were long ago forgotten when the glorious bureaucratic-junker royal Prussian monarchy in February last year received a new and so powerful push from the French that it most gloriously toppled over from its "foundations of 1807-14". It has to ignore the fact that for the royal Prussian monarchy it was in no way a question of these foundations, but merely one of warding off the further consequences of the push received from France. But Prussian conceit ignores all that, and when it suddenly receives the push, it cries out, like a child crying for its nurse, for the decayed foundations of 1807-14.

As if the Prussia of 1848, as regards territory, industry, trade, means of communication, culture and class relations, were not a totally different country from the Prussia of the "foundations of 1807-14"!

As if since that time two quite new classes — the industrial proletariat and the class of free peasants — had not intervened in its history; as if the Prussian bourgeoisie of 1848 were not quite different from the timid, docile and grateful petty bourgeoisie of the time of the "foundations"!

But all that is of no avail. A loyal Prussian must not know anything but his "foundations of 1807-14". Those are the foundations on which further construction will take place — and that is the end of the matter.

The beginning of one of the most colossal historical revolutions is shrunken into nothing more than the ending of one of the pettiest pseudo-reform swindles — that is how revolution is understood in old Prussia!

And in this self-complacent narrow-minded fantasy from the country's history "there seemed to be complete unanimity" — of course, only in Berlin, thank God!

Let us proceed.

"Those social estates and classes which had to renounce privileges and special rights ... which were destined in the future to stand only on an equal footing with all

---

[a] Marx uses ironically the expression *Staat der Intelligenz* by which Hegel designates the Prussian state (see G. W. F. Hegel, *Vorlesungen über die Geschichte der Philosophie. Vorrede, gesprächen zu Heidelberg den 29-sten Oktober 1816* (Note).—*Ed.*

their fellow citizens ... seemed prepared for that renunciation—inspired by the conviction that the old state of things had become untenable, that it was in their own well-understood interest...."

Look at this meek and mild, sincerely humble bourgeois—how once again he conjures away the revolution! The nobility, the priests, the bureaucrats, the officers, "seemed prepared" to renounce their privileges, not because the armed people forced them to do so, not because in the first moments of terror at the European revolution, the demoralisation and disorganisation irresistibly spreading in their own ranks made them incapable of resistance—no! The peaceful, benevolent "agreements" (to use Herr Camphausen's language) of February 24 and March 18,[a] which were advantageous to both sides, "inspired" them with the "conviction" that this "was in their own well-understood interest"!

That the March revolution, and above all February 24, was in the well-understood interest of the Herren cabbage-junkers, members of church councils, *Regierungsräte*, and Guards lieutenants—that is indeed a truly monumental idea!

But, unfortunately!

"Today it is no longer like that. The beneficiaries and adherents of the old state of affairs, far from themselves helping, *as is their duty* (!), to see that the old rubbish is cleared away and the new house built, want only to prop up the old ruins beneath which the ground shook so dangerously and to embellish them with some forms in appearance appropriate to the new period."

"Today it is no longer like that"—as it *appeared* to be in May, i.e. it is no longer what it was not in May, or it is precisely the same as it was in May.

That is the sort of language in which the Berlin *National-Zeitung* is written and, what is more, its writers are proud of it.

In a word: May 1848 and January 1849 differ from one another only *in appearance*. Previously the counter-revolutionaries *seemed* to understand their duty—today they actually and openly do not, and the peaceful bourgeois moans about it. After all, it is the *duty* of the counter-revolutionaries to renounce their interests for the sake of their own well-understood interest! It is their *duty* themselves to cut their vital arteries—yet, they do not do so—thus moans the exponent of well-understood interest!

And why do your enemies not do now what, as you say, is nevertheless their duty?

---

[a] On February 24, 1848, Louis Philippe was overthrown in France; March 18, 1848—the beginning of the revolution in Prussia.—*Ed.*

Because in the spring you yourselves did not do *your* "duty", because at that time, when you were strong, you behaved like cowards and quaked before the revolution that was to make you great and powerful; because you yourselves let the old rubbish remain and complacently admired yourselves in the mirror wearing the aureole of a half success! And now, when the counter-revolution has become strong overnight and sets its foot on your neck, when under *your* feet the ground shakes dangerously—now you demand that the counter-revolution should become your servant, should clear away the rubbish that you were too weak and cowardly to clear away, that it, grown mighty, should sacrifice itself for you who are weak?

What childish fools you are! But wait a little and the people will rise up and with a single mighty push will throw you to the ground together with the counter-revolution against which you are now so impotently yapping!

[*Neue Rheinische Zeitung* No. 207, January 28, 1849, second edition]

Cologne, January 27. In our first article we did not take into account one circumstance which could, at any rate apparently, serve to excuse the *National-Zeitung*; the *National-Zeitung* is not free in what it writes—it is under *martial law*. And under martial law it has, of course, to sing:

> Bid me not speak, bid me be silent,
> To keep my secret is for me a duty;
> I would for you my inmost soul lay bare,
> 'Tis only fate that will not let me do so!!! [a]

Even under martial law, however, newspapers are not published in order to say the opposite of what they think; moreover, martial law has nothing to do with the first half, which we considered previously, of the article in question.

Martial law is not to blame for the inflated, nebulous style of the *National-Zeitung*.

Martial law is not to blame for the fact that after March the *National-Zeitung* created for itself all sorts of naive illusions.

Martial law does not at all compel the *National-Zeitung* to make the 1848 revolution the train-bearer of the reforms of 1807-14.

---

[a] Goethe, "Mignon". From the novel *Wilhelm Meisters Lehrjahre*, Book V, Chapter 16.—*Ed.*

In short, martial law in no way compels the *National-Zeitung* to entertain such absurd notions about the course of development of the revolution and counter-revolution in 1848 as we proved it to hold two days ago. Martial law affects not the past but the present.

Therefore, in our criticism of the *first* half of the article in question, we did not take martial law into account, and precisely for this reason we shall take it into account today.

After ending its historical introduction, the *National-Zeitung* addresses the primary electors in the following way:

"It is a matter of safeguarding the progress initiated, of consolidating the achievements."

What "progress"? What "achievements"? The "progress" expressed in the fact that "today it is no longer like that", as it "appeared" to be in May? The "achievement" that "the beneficiaries of the old state of affairs are far from themselves helping, as is their duty, to see that the old rubbish is cleared away"? Or the granted "achievements" which "prop up the old ruins and embellish them with some forms in appearance appropriate to the new period"?

Martial law, gentlemen of the *National-Zeitung*, is no excuse for absence of thought and confusion.

The "progress" which just now has been most successfully "initiated" is regression to the old system, and we are daily advancing farther along this path of progress.

The sole "achievement" left to us—and it is not a specifically Prussian, not a "March" achievement, but the result of the 1848 European revolution—is the most general, most determined, most blood-thirsty and most violent counter-revolution, which is itself only a phase of the European revolution, and hence only the generator of a new, universal and victorious revolutionary counterblow.

But perhaps the *National-Zeitung* knows that just as well as we do, and only dare not say it because of martial law? Listen to this:

"We do not want a *continuance of the revolution*; we are enemies of all *anarchy*, all *acts of violence* and *arbitrariness*; we want *law, tranquillity* and *order*."

Martial law, gentlemen, compels you at most to be *silent*, never to *speak*. Therefore we put on record the sentence just quoted: if it is *you* who are speaking through its words, so much the better; if it is martial law that is speaking, there is no need for you to make yourselves its organ. Either you are revolutionary, or you are not. If you are not, then we are opponents from the outset; if you are, you should have been *silent*.

But you speak with such conviction, you have such an honest past, that we can safely assume that martial law has absolutely nothing to do with this asseveration.

"We do not want a continuance of the revolution." That means: we want the continuance of the counter-revolution. For it is a historical fact that either one does not put an end to violent counter-revolution at all, or one does so only through revolution.

"We do not want a continuance of the revolution", that means: we recognise that the revolution is ended, that it has reached its goal. And the goal which the revolution had reached on January 21, 1849, when the above-mentioned article was written, this goal was precisely—counter-revolution.

"We are enemies of all anarchy, all acts of violence and arbitrariness."

That means enemies also of the "anarchy" which occurs after every revolution until the new conditions have been consolidated, enemies of the "acts of violence" of February 24 and March 18, enemies of the "arbitrariness" which ruthlessly shatters a decayed system and its decrepit legal supports!

"We want law, tranquillity and order"!

Indeed, the time has been well chosen to bow down before "law, tranquillity and order", to protest against the revolution, and to concur in the cheap outcry against anarchy, acts of violence and arbitrariness! It has been well chosen, at the very moment when under the protection of bayonets and cannons the revolution is officially branded as a *crime*, when "anarchy, acts of violence and arbitrariness" are openly put into practice through ordinances countersigned by the King, when the "law", imposed on us by the camarilla, is always used *against* us and never *for* us, when "tranquillity and order" consist in leaving the counter-revolution in "peace", so that it can re-establish *its* old-Prussian "order" of things.

No, gentlemen, it is not martial law that speaks through you — it is most unadulterated *Odilon Barrot*, translated into Berlin language, with all his narrow-mindedness, all his impotence, all his pious wishes.

There is no revolutionary who is so tactless, so childish, so cowardly, as to deny the revolution at the very moment when counter-revolution is celebrating its most glittering triumphs. If he cannot speak, he acts, and if he cannot act, he prefers to remain perfectly silent.

But is it not possible, perhaps, that the gentlemen of the *National-Zeitung* are pursuing a cunning policy? Are they perhaps speaking so tamely in order on the eve of the elections to win over to the opposition yet another section of the so-called moderates?

From the very first day that the counter-revolution swooped down on us, we said that from now on there are only two parties: "revolutionaries" and "counter-revolutionaries"; only two slogans: "the democratic republic" or "the absolute monarchy".[a] Everything in between is no longer a party but only a faction. The counter-revolution has done everything to make our statement come true. The elections are the most brilliant confirmation of that.

And at such a time, when the parties confront one another so sharply, when the struggle is being conducted with the greatest ferocity, when only the overwhelming superiority of organised soldiery prevents the struggle from being fought out arms in hand—at such a time all conciliation policy ceases. One needs to be Odilon Barrot himself to play the role of Odilon Barrot at such a time.

But our Berlin Barrots have their reservations, their conditions, their interpretations. They are wailers, but by no means simply wailers; they are wailers with a reservation: "that is to say", wailers from the quiet opposition:

"We, *however*, want *new* laws, such as are required by the awakened free spirit of the people and the principle of equality; we want a *genuinely democratic-constitutional order*" (i.e. a genuine absurdity); "we want tranquillity which rests on *more* than bayonets and martial laws, which is a politically and morally (!) based pacification of mind arising from the conviction, guaranteed by deeds and institutions, that every class of the people has its rights etc., etc."

We can spare ourselves the labour of completing this sentence, written in conformity with martial law. It suffices to say that these gentlemen "want" not revolution, but only a small nosegay from the *results* of revolution; a little democracy, but also a little constitutionalism; a few new laws, abolition of feudal institutions, bourgeois equality etc., etc.

In other words, the gentlemen of the *National-Zeitung* and those from the Berlin ex-Lefts, whose organ it is, want to obtain from the counter-revolution precisely that for which the counter-revolution dispersed them.

Nothing learnt and nothing forgotten![262]

These gentlemen "want" the very things they will never obtain except by a new revolution. But they do not want a new revolution.

A new revolution would bring them also quite other things than are contained in the above-quoted modest bourgeois demands. And

---

[a] See this volume, p. 178.—*Ed.*

for that reason these gentlemen are quite right in not wanting any revolution.

Fortunately, however, historical development is little concerned about what the Barrots "want" or "do not want". The Parisian prototype Barrot also "wanted" on February 24 only to achieve quite modest reforms, in particular a ministerial portfolio for himself; and he had hardly laid hands on both of these when the waves broke over him and he disappeared with all his virtuous petty-bourgeois retinue in the revolutionary deluge. Now, too, when at last he has once more obtained a ministerial post, he again "wants" various things; but nothing of what he wants is coming about. Such has ever been the fate of the Barrots. And the same thing will happen to the Berlin Barrots as well.

Under martial law or without it, they will continue to bore the public with their pious wishes. At most they will secure the adoption on paper of a few of these wishes, and finally they will be put on the shelf either by the Crown or by the people. In any case they will be put on the shelf.

Written by Marx between January 25 and 27, 1849

First published in the *Neue Rheinische Zeitung* No. 205 and No. 207 (second edition), January 26 and 28, 1849

Printed according to the newspaper

Published in English for the first time

THE SITUATION IN PARIS

Paris, January 28. The danger of a popular uprising has been removed for the time being by the vote of the Chamber *against* dealing with the prohibition of the clubs as a matter of urgency, i.e. against prohibition of the clubs in general.[263] But a new danger is emerging: *the danger of a coup d'état.*

Read today's issue of the *National* and say whether fear of a coup d'état is not visible in *every line*.

"Today's vote is a fatal blow for the Cabinet, and we now challenge Messrs. Odilon Barrot, Faucher and *tutti quanti* to hold their portfolios any longer...."

So far the *National* seems to be of good cheer. But listen to the end of the sentence:

"...without entering into open revolt against the spirit and letter of the Constitution!"

And what would Messrs. Odilon Barrot, Faucher and *tutti quanti* care about entering into open revolt against the Constitution? Since when have Barrot and Faucher been enthusiastic about the Constitution of 1848!

The *National* no longer *threatens* the Ministers; it shows them that they must resign, it shows the President[a] that he must dismiss them. And that in a country where for the last thirty years the resignation of the Ministers after such a vote has been a matter of course!

It is to be hoped, says the *National,* that the President of the Republic will realise that the majority and the Cabinet are in

---

[a] Louis Bonaparte.—*Ed.*

complete disagreement, that by dismissing the Cabinet, he will strengthen the ties between him and the majority, and that there is only one obstacle to a good understanding between him and the majority: the Cabinet.

Yes, the *National* is trying to ensure the Ministry an honourable retreat: it would like the charge against the Ministers to be dropped. The vote is punishment enough. This extreme measure could be avoided until the Ministers have really violated the Constitution by an accomplished act.

Yes, the newspaper finally exclaims, *everything* makes it the *duty* of the Cabinet to resign; its own words are binding upon it to such an extent that we hesitate to believe it will dare to remain in power. Monsieur Barrot stated this evening that if the urgency motion is rejected, the *Assembly itself* will bear the responsibility for events. Very well, when responsibility ceases, power too must cease. If the Cabinet does not want to be responsible for events, then it must not direct them. By rejecting responsibility, Monsieur Barrot has tendered his resignation.

In short, the *National* does not believe in the voluntary retirement of the Ministry any more than in its dismissal by the President.

But if the Ministry wants to defy the vote of the Assembly, then there is nothing left for it except—a *coup d'état.*

Dissolution of the National Assembly and preparation for the restoration of the monarchy by military force, that is what lurks behind the fear of the *National* of the Ministry continuing in office.

Therefore the *National* and the red newspapers ask the people only to remain calm and to give no pretext for intervention, since any revolt can only support the Cabinet which is falling, can only be of service to the royalist counter-revolution.

That a coup d'état is becoming ever more imminent, is proved by the incidents involving Changarnier and the officers of the mobile guard.[264] The *bouchers de Cavaignac*[a] have no desire to let themselves be used for a royalist coup; that is why they are to be dissolved; they murmur and Changarnier threatens to have them cut to pieces, and he puts their officers under arrest.

The situation seems to become more complicated; in fact, however, it is becoming very simple, as simple as it always is on the eve of a revolution.

The conflict between the Assembly and the President together with his Ministers has reached breaking point. France can no longer exist in the state of impotence which has reigned in it for the last ten

---

[a] Cavaignac's butchers.—*Ed.*

months; the deficit, the depressed state of industry and commerce, the pressure of taxation, which ruins agriculture, become daily more intolerable; large-scale, trenchant measures become more and more urgent, and each new Government is more impotent and inactive than the one before; until finally Odilon Barrot has carried inactivity to the extreme and for six weeks has done absolutely nothing at all.

In that way, however, he has greatly simplified the situation. After him, there can no longer be any Ministry of the decent republic. The mixed governments (the Provisional Government and the Executive Commission [265]), the Government of the *National*, the Government of the old Lefts—that has all been gone through, it is all worn out, used up. Now it is the turn of Thiers, and Thiers is the undisguised restoration of the monarchy.

Restoration of the monarchy or — a *red republic*, this is now the only alternative in France. The crisis may still be delayed for a few weeks, but it is bound to break out. Changarnier-Monk[266] with his three hundred thousand, who are entirely at his disposal for 24 hours, seems reluctant to wait any longer.

Hence the anxiety of the *National*. It recognises its inability to master the situation; it knows that any forcible change of government will bring its strongest enemies into power, that it is equally lost with a monarchy and a red republic. Hence its sighing for a peaceful deal, its politeness to the Ministers.

We shall very soon see whether it is necessary for the final victory of the red republic that France should go through the monarchical phase for a while. It is possible, but not probable.

But one thing is certain: the decent republic is falling to pieces, and after it—even if there are first of all some small intermezzi—the only possibility is the *red republic*.

Written on January 28, 1849

First published in the *Neue Rheinische Zeitung* No. 209, January 31, 1849

Printed according to the newspaper

Published in English for the first time

[THE SITUATION IN PARIS]

Cologne, January 30. When yesterday morning we announced in a special edition the imminent outbreak of a storm in Paris, wailers[267] among the primary electors to the First Chamber wrote under our fly-sheet: *It's a lie! It's no use intimidating us!* and other such philistine strong expressions.

These miserable people regarded our special edition as a mere electoral manoeuvre, as if the First Chamber and the Second Chamber too, and the entire Prussian movement into the bargain, could induce us to falsify the history of the European revolution!

Stupp is an elector to the First Chamber! The rentier von *Wittgenstein* is an elector to the First Chamber! Chancellor von *Groote* is an elector to the First Chamber! And yet the revolutionary monster in Paris is capable of roaring afresh! *Quelle horreur!*

In our issue today, we said, *inter alia,* on the Paris situation:

"The danger of a popular uprising has been removed for the time being by the vote of the Chamber *against* dealing with the prohibition of the clubs as a matter of urgency, i.e. against prohibition of the clubs in general. But a new danger is emerging: *the danger of a coup d'état....* If the Ministry wants to defy the vote of the Assembly, then there is nothing left for it except—a *coup d'état.* Dissolution of the National Assembly and preparation for the restoration of the monarchy by military force, that is what lurks behind the fear of the *National* of the Ministry continuing in office.... That a coup d'état is becoming ever more imminent, is proved by the incidents involving Changarnier and the officers of the mobile guard.... The situation seems to become more complicated; in fact, however, it is becoming very simple, as simple as it always is on the eve of a revolution. The conflict between the Assembly and the President together with his Ministers has reached breaking point.... *Restoration of the monarchy* or — a *red republic*, this is now the only alternative in France.... The decent republic is falling to pieces, and after it — even if there are first of all some small intermezzi—the only possibility is the *red republic*." [a]

In the special edition we announced the crisis for the 29th.

The reports of the 29th from Paris printed below will show our readers how accurate our reports were and the striking correctness of our description today of the French situation.[268]

Written on January 30, 1849

First published in the special supplement to the *Neue Rheinische Zeitung* No. 209, January 31, 1849

Printed according to the newspaper

Published in English for the first time

---

[a] See this volume, pp. 281-83.— *Ed.*

THE *KÖLNISCHE ZEITUNG* ON THE ELECTIONS[269]

Cologne, January 30. The *Kölnische Zeitung* has at last also obtained reports on the elections, and they are indeed reports which to some extent pour oil on its wounds.

"The democratic reports on the elections," exclaims the worthy Brüggemann, intoxicated with joy, "the democratic reports on the elections" (i.e. the *Neue Rheinische Zeitung*) "have *grossly exaggerated*. Protests are now reaching us *from all sides*." [a]

From all sides! The *Kölnische Zeitung* intends to crush us with the weight of its "protests". Will two pages of compressed election bulletins, each one a "gross exaggeration" of the *Neue Rheinische Zeitung*, each one proving a victory of the constitutionalists, produce a deep-red blush of shame on our cheeks?

On the contrary.

"Protests are now reaching us from all sides."

The worthy Brüggemann does not "exaggerate". He actually got *summa summarum four* whole protests: from the west (Trier), north (Hamm), south (Siegburg) and east (Arnsberg)! Are those not "protests from all sides" against the "gross exaggeration of the democratic reports on the elections"?

For the time being, let us leave to the *Kölnische Zeitung* the pleasure of believing that the constitutionalists were victorious in these four decisive localities. At any rate this pleasure is soured by pain because all the same in many places the constitutionalists were defeated owing to the "masses' susceptibility to being seduced".

---

[a] Quoted from the article "Die Wahlen", *Kölnische Zeitung* No. 25, January 30, 1849.—*Ed.*

Naive confession of the constitutionalists that *for them* the "masses" are not "susceptible to being seduced"!

One consolation, however, remains for the *Kölnische Zeitung*. And what is this consolation? It is that the Coblenz correspondent of the *Deutsche Zeitung* is a comrade in misfortune, that in this unfortunate state of affairs he uttered appropriate words, worthy of figuring in the first columns of the *Kölnische Zeitung*:

> "Note that the *political question* in this point also, as everywhere, becomes a small one compared with the social question, that it *becomes entirely merged in the latter*."

Until a few days ago the *Kölnische Zeitung* did not want to hear about the social question. On this subject belonging to the other world it never had occasion to speak, or at most it did so with a certain frivolity (insofar as it is possible for the *Kölnische Zeitung* to be frivolous). It adopted an atheistic, disbelieving, free-thinking attitude towards it. Then suddenly it underwent the same experience as the fisherman in *A Thousand and One Nights*. Just as, before the fisherman, the genie arose gigantically out of the bottle he had fished up from the sea-bed and unsealed, so before the trembling *Kölnische Zeitung* there suddenly arises out of the election urn the menacing gigantic spectre of the "social question". Terrified, the worthy Brüggemann sinks to his knees; his last hope vanishes, the spectre at a gulp swallows his entire "political question", which for years he had tenderly cherished, together with its legal basis and accessories.

Clever policy of the *Kölnische Zeitung*. It tries to put a good face on its *political* defeat by means of its *social* defeat.

This discovery that it has been defeated not only in the political field, but in the social field as well, is the greatest experience it has gained from the primary elections!

Or was perhaps the *Kölnische Zeitung* enthusiastic even earlier over the "social question"?

In point of fact, Montesquieu LVI had stated in the *Kölnische Zeitung* that the social question was infinitely important and that recognition of the imposed Constitution was the solution of the social question.[a]

But recognition of the imposed Constitution—that is pre-eminently what the *Kölnische Zeitung* calls the "*political* question".

Prior to the elections, therefore, the social question became merged in the *political* question, *after* the elections the political question becomes merged in the *social* question. That, therefore, is

---

[a] See this volume, p. 255.—*Ed.*

the difference, that is the experience from the primary elections, namely, that what is correct *after* the elections is exactly the opposite of what was gospel truth *prior* to the elections.

"The political question becomes merged in the social question"!

Let us leave out of account that already before the elections we explained as clearly as possible that there could be no talk of a "social question" as such, that each class has its *own* social question, and that this social question of a definite class involves at the same time a definite political question for this class.[a] Let us leave out of account all these light-hearted marginal notes when confronting the serious, solid *Kölnerin*, and let us analyse as far as possible the line of thought and mode of speech of this strong-charactered and profound newspaper.

By the social question, the *Kölnische Zeitung* understands the question: how are the petty bourgeoisie, the peasants and the proletariat to be helped?

And now, since at the primary elections the petty bourgeoisie, peasants and proletarians emancipated themselves from the big bourgeoisie, the upper nobility and the higher bureaucracy, now the *Kölnische Zeitung* exclaims: "The political question becomes merged in the social question"!

A fine consolation for the *Kölnische Zeitung*! Therefore the fact that the workers, peasants and petty bourgeoisie routed by striking majorities the big bourgeois and other highly respected constitutional candidates of the *Kölnische Zeitung* is no defeat of the "constitutionalists", but merely a victory of the "social question"! The fact that the constitutionalists were defeated does not prove that the democrats were victorious, but that politics has no part to play in the face of material questions.

Profound thoroughness on the part of our neighbouring journalist[b]! These petty bourgeois, hovering on the brink of ruin, are they enthusiastic about the imposed Constitution? These peasants, oppressed by mortgages and usurers, and crushed under feudal burdens, are they enthusiastic about the finance and feudal barons who are their exploiters, and for whose direct benefit the imposed Constitution was invented? And, finally, these proletarians, who suffer simultaneously from the administrative passion of our bureaucrats and from the lust for profit of our bourgeoisie, have they any reason to rejoice that the imposed Constitution provides a new tie linking these two classes that suck the blood of the people?

---

[a] See this volume, pp. 262-63.—*Ed.*

[b] That is of Brüggemann.—*Ed.*

Are not all these three classes interested above all in the abolition of the First Chamber, which represents not them, but their direct opponents and oppressors?

In point of fact, the *Kölnische Zeitung* is right: the social question swallows up the political question. In the interest of the "social question" the classes that have newly joined the political movement will vote against their own political interests and for the imposed Constitution!

Can the petty bourgeois and peasants, and, the more so, the proletarians, find a better political form for representing their interests than the democratic republic? Are not precisely these classes the most radical, the most democratic, of society as a whole? Is it not precisely the proletariat that is the specifically *red* class?—That does not matter, exclaims the *Kölnische Zeitung*, the social question swallows up the political question.

According to the *Kölnische Zeitung*, the victory of the social question is at the same time the victory of the imposed Constitution.

But the "social question" of the *Kölnische Zeitung* has also a very special feature. Read the report of the *Kölnische Zeitung* on the elections to the First Chamber[270] and their "fortunate outcome", which consists in the fact that Herr Joseph Dumont has become an elector. That at any rate solves the real social question for the *Kölnische Zeitung*, and compared with it all the subordinate "social questions" which could perhaps crop up in connection with elections to a plebeian Second Chamber disappear.

May the storm of the world-historic "political question", which at the present time is menacingly rising in Paris, not mercilessly break to pieces the *Kölnische Zeitung*'s delicate "social question"!

Written by Marx on January 30, 1849

First published in the *Neue Rheinische Zeitung* No. 210, February 1, 1849

Printed according to the newspaper

Published in English for the first time

THE STRUGGLE IN HUNGARY[271]

Cologne, February 2. The war in Hungary is nearing its end. "*Parturiunt montes, nascetur ridiculus mus.*" [a]

Thus spoke the *Kölnische Zeitung* a few days ago.[b] It had been fooled by Welden into thinking that the Assembly in Debreczin had dissolved both itself and the army, and that Kossuth was about to flee to Grosswardein with the rest of his following.

The mountain in labour this time was none other than the *Kölnische Zeitung* itself.

The 17th Army Bulletin,[c] to which Welden imputed the above lie, reports two new operations of the imperial troops: firstly, the departure of a corps from Pest via Gyöngyös to Miskolcz, and secondly, Schlick's plan to operate in two columns against Tokaj, one via Kaschau, the other via Janosfalva and Baranya. Both are concentric movements against the Theiss, behind which the Magyars have taken up positions.

From the border of Transylvania to Szegedin the Theiss describes a semicircle the centre of which is Grosswardein: this semicircle forms the Magyar defence line. On the Upper Theiss it is covered by the fortresses of Sziget and Munkács; on the Middle Theiss by impassable swamps which begin a few miles from Munkács, accompany the Theiss on both sides to its mouth and render an

---

[a] "The mountains are in labour and a ridiculous mouse will be born" (Horace, *De Arte Poetica*, 139).—*Ed.*

[b] "Ungarn (Vom Kriegs-Schauplatz)", *Kölnische Zeitung* No. 25 (supplement), January 30, 1849.—*Ed.*

[c] "17. Armee-Bulletin", *Wiener Zeitung* No. 19, January 23, 1849.—*Ed.*

attack from north and west very difficult. In the south the Körös and its tributaries offer a line of defence which is likewise covered by uninterrupted swamps and moreover by the advanced fortress of Temesvár. So, defended on three sides by swamps and rivers, the Debreczin Heath stretches away to the Transylvanian hills and offers the Magyars an excellent point for concentrating their armies, all the better since Bem has freed their rear by the conquest of Transylvania.

So long as the Magyars hold their ground on the Drava and in the Banat, Debreczin, the centre of their operations, can only be attacked from the north (Schlick) and west (Windischgrätz), and both the above movements are said to be preludes to this attack.

Miskolcz and Tokaj, the two towns to which the imperial troops are now marching, are barely six miles[a] from each other. Tokaj is one of the most advantageous crossing points over the Theiss; Miskolcz lies close enough to enable the troops sent there, depending on circumstances, to join Schlick's corps at Tokaj or to cross the Theiss by themselves a little lower down and if successful to advance on Debreczin.

This plan of the imperial army, which the 17th Bulletin trumpets around the world with such pomp, is, however, not so easy to carry out. From Pest to Miskolcz is more than 30 miles, across desolate heath land, inhabited either by hardly anybody or else by enemies. From Eperies to Tokaj it is also 30 miles, also through decidedly hostile and poor country. The provisioning alone of the two advancing corps would greatly delay their march; the bad roads, which with the present thaw are becoming completely impassable, make it quite impossible for them to reach their destination in less than a fortnight. And once arrived they will find themselves facing the Magyar army, at the crossings of the Theiss, entrenched between swamps, in positions with covered flanks, where the imperial troops cannot deploy their superior strength, where, on the contrary, a few regiments can hold up a whole army. Nay, even were they to succeed in forcing the crossings over the Theiss, the Austrian artillery and heavy cavalry would be utterly lost between the swamps, in marshy ground, in which they will constantly be bogged.

What grandiose successes these two columns have had so far can already be seen from the fact that the 18th Army Bulletin, which we reported yesterday,[b] is completely *silent* about them. Where they are,

---

[a] One German mile is equal to 4.7 English miles.—*Ed.*

[b] *Neue Rheinische Zeitung* No. 211, February 2, 1849 (a report from Vienna with a reprint of the 18th Army Bulletin from the *Wiener Zeitung* No. 24, published on January 28, 1849).—*Ed.*

how far they have advanced, what successes they have had—of that Welden tells us *not one syllable*, and for good reasons.

But, says Welden,

"according to the news received from Hungary, our troops enjoy *brilliant success* everywhere"

—and the *Kölnische Zeitung* believes Herr Welden.

Let us look a little more closely at these "brilliant successes".

Four "successes" are reported. Of these three are in areas where there is no decisive fighting, but where the Magyars are merely striving to keep the imperial troops busy at points of secondary importance and thus to divide them. Only the fourth "success" has been won on the Theiss, where Hungary's fate is being decided.

In the north-west, between the Waag and the Gran, in the south-west, between the Drava and the Danube, and in the south, in the Banat, three Hungarian corps are so far keeping a considerable part of the imperial forces busy, thereby preventing Windischgrätz from pushing forward to the Theiss with any considerable numbers. Against these three corps the imperial forces, so they say, have had "brilliant successes". *Voyons!*[a]

First success. In the north-east, where "Slovakia"[272] is now placed, Baron Csorich has beaten General Görgey at Schemnitz and has taken Schemnitz. When one considers that Görgey's corps is simply a lost outpost which has to stand its ground in the rear of the imperial army as long as possible; and when one considers that Görgey is operating not on Magyar but on purely Slovak ground, one sees that this success is not very "brilliant".

Moreover, Csorich was to be supported by Götz and Sossay's columns. But Sossay was urgently called to Neutra "there to assist in the pacification of the part of the country *already occupied*" (a *purely Slav* comitat[b]), and Götz had his hands full "maintaining his position at Mossocz and *protecting* the Turócz comitat from the insurgents whom Lieutenant-Field Marshal Csorich had *beaten* and *scattered*(!!)".

"The *at-last-to-be-hoped-for*" (hence still a long way off) "capture of Leopoldstadt and the occupation of Neuhäusel ... *should* suffice to strengthen the good spirit which is *beginning* (!) to develop everywhere in the Trentschin comitat and to *contribute* to the restoration of law and order."

What brilliant successes! The at-last-to-be-hoped-for capture of a not-yet-captured fortress offers the hope that the much-hoped-for

---

[a] Let us see!—*Ed.*
[b] A comitat is a Hungarian county.—*Ed.*

good spirit of a long since occupied region will not, one hopes, always remain a pious wish, and the hope that law and order may at least partially approach realisation!

An uncaptured fortress, a beaten army which nevertheless threatens an entire comitat and keeps several army corps in check, a much-hoped-for good spirit here, an only too real bad spirit there, risings threatened everywhere, and all this on Slovak, not Magyar territory—that is the first "brilliant success"!

Second "brilliant success". A second doomed outpost of the Magyars is in the south-west, between the Danube and the Drava, under the partisan leader Damjanich. Here the brilliant success consists in Count Nugent having ordered the occupation of Kaposvár so as to reach the enemy's flank. What brilliant success there is in that is not yet clear. The occupation of Eszék by imperial troops is, it is true, reported by several papers, but the 18th Bulletin does not yet know of it and does not even expect it.

Third "brilliant success". General Todorovich has captured Werschetz in the Banat and is "energetically pursuing" the Magyars to Moravicza.

From Werschetz to Moravicza is exactly *three miles* and the position at Moravicza between the Alibunar swamp and the mountains is far more favourable than that at Werschetz.

At any rate it is well known that the Banat is so far from the centre of operations and that the attacks against the Magyars have been so sporadic that even the most brilliant successes of the imperials would here be of no importance whatsoever.

Fourth "brilliant success". Hitherto we have seen the imperial troops, it is true, operating on not very decisive terrain, but at least we saw them operating with some semblance of success. Now at last we come to a decisive terrain, and here the success consists in a *defeat* of the imperial troops.

General Ottinger had advanced from Pest as far as the Theiss, to Szolnok. The road was fairly good; from Pest to Szolnok there is a railway, and all that was needed was to follow the rails. The imperial advanced guard had already occupied the bridge at Szolnok. The crossing of the Theiss appeared to be secured for the right wing of the imperial troops. The left wing under Schlick, operating from Tokaj, the centre from Miskolcz, the right wing under Ottinger from Szolnok, were to force the Theiss crossings and march concentrically on Debreczin. But the imperial gentlemen had reckoned without their host. The Magyars crossed the frozen river, drove Ottinger back four miles all the way to Czegléd, and only gave up the pursuit when Ottinger had received reinforcements near Czegléd and taken up a strong position. According to the Bulletin, it is true, the Magyars are supposed to have gone back across the Theiss, but at all events they now control the crossing and Herr Ottinger, having so hastily retreated, will hardly force it so soon.

These are the "brilliant successes" of the imperial troops against the disbanded, demoralised, scattered army of Kossuth's rebels. A glance at the map shows that the Magyars have lost nothing since they decided to retreat behind the Theiss. As the latest Austrian *unofficial* reports announce, they are at Miskolcz and await the attacks of Schlick and Windischgrätz. They will not accept battle there either, but will withdraw behind the Theiss. The decisive battle will be fought at the crossings of this river, or, if these are forced, in the Debreczin Heath. And even if the Magyars are routed here, guerilla warfare will begin in the heaths and swamps of Lower Hungary and in the Transylvanian mountains in the same way as it has already begun in the "parts of the country already occupied", to the great regret of the 18th Bulletin. What such warfare can achieve in a sparsely populated country and on a suitable terrain has been proved by the Carlist bands in Spain, and is now being proved again by Cabrera.[273]

But Kossuth has not come to that yet. Although the *Kölnische Zeitung* in its childlike naivety had him taken prisoner yesterday, he is still free and has a considerable army at his disposal. For him it is no longer a question of standing his ground for months on end; he only needs to offer resistance for three or four more weeks. In three to four weeks at most the tables will be turned in Paris: either the Restoration wins there for the moment, and then Hungary may fall, too, so that the counter-revolution may be altogether triumphant; or the revolution will win, and then the Austrian gentlemen will march in haste to the Rhine and to Italy, to be chased back to Hungary by the Red Pantaloons.[a]

In conclusion, let us note the most brilliant of all the imperial troops' successes: Herr Welden's bulletins have at last found a believer who swears by them — and this One is the *Kölnische Zeitung*.

Written by Engels on February 2, 1849	Printed according to the newspaper
First published in the *Neue Rheinische Zeitung* No. 212, February 3, 1849	Published in English for the first time

---

[a] The French army.—*Ed.*

CAMPHAUSEN

Cologne, February 3. We learn from an entirely reliable source that the Brandenburg Ministry will resign before the Chambers open, and that Herr Camphausen will be presented to the Chambers at their opening as the new Prime Minister.

We were sure that something of the kind was being prepared when, a few days ago, the shrewd statesman's friends here spread a rumour that he was tired of political activity:

> Oh! the bustle makes me weary;
> What use all the joy and pain?
> Sweet peace come, and
> In my heart begin your reign! [a]

and for that reason wanted to withdraw into peaceful domestic life and restrict his reflections to the less agitating field of speculation in dairy produce.

It should be clear to every intelligent person: Herr Camphausen felt the need to get himself invited once again to save the Crown and, "touched by his own magnanimity", to play a second time the role of "midwife of the constitutional throne" with his well-known aplomb.

The bourgeois opposition in the Chamber will rejoice at this parliamentary "victory". The Germans are forgetful and easily forgive. Those same Lefts who last year opposed Herr Camphausen will gratefully welcome his new accession to office as a great concession on the part of the Crown.

---

[a] Goethe, "Wandrers Nachtlied".—*Ed.*

But in order that the people should not allow itself to be deceived a second time, we shall briefly recall the most outstanding deeds of this thinking statesman.

Herr Camphausen resurrected the *United Diet* that was buried on March 18 and reached agreement with it on some of the basic principles of the future Constitution.[274]

Herr Camphausen thereby reached agreement on the *legal basis*, i.e. indirect denial of the revolution.

Herr Camphausen furthermore conferred on us the blessing of *indirect elections*.[275]

Herr Camphausen once again denied the revolution as regards one of its chief results, by transforming the Prince of Prussia's flight into a study trip and recalling him from London.[276]

Herr Camphausen organised the civic militia in such a way that from the outset it was transformed from being the arming of the people into the arming of a class, so that the people and the militia confronted each other as enemies.

At the same time Herr Camphausen allowed the old-Prussian bureaucracy and army to be reconstituted and to become daily more capable of preparing counter-revolutionary coups d'état.

Herr Camphausen was responsible for the memorable shrapnel slaughter of practically unarmed Polish peasants.[277]

Herr Camphausen began the war against Denmark to provide an outlet for superabundant patriotism and to restore the popularity of the Prussian Guards. Having achieved this aim, he made every effort to help secure the adoption in Frankfurt of the disgraceful Malmö armistice,[278] which was essential for Wrangel's march on Berlin.

Herr Camphausen confined himself to abolishing a few reactionary old-Prussian laws in the Rhine Province, but left the whole police-state civil-code legislation in existence in all the old provinces.

Herr Camphausen was the first to intrigue against the unity—at that time still definitely revolutionary—of Germany, first of all by convening alongside the Frankfurt National Assembly his Berlin agreement parliament and subsequently by acting in every way against the decisions and influence of the Frankfurt Assembly.

Herr Camphausen demanded of his Assembly that it should restrict its constitutional mandate merely to "reaching agreement".

Herr Camphausen further demanded of it that it should issue an address to the Crown in which it acknowledged this—as if it were a constitutional chamber which could be adjourned or dissolved at will.

Herr Camphausen further demanded of it that it should deny the revolution and even made this a question of confidence in the Cabinet.

Herr Camphausen laid before his Assembly a draft Constitution, which is on much the same lines as the imposed Constitution[a] and aroused a universal storm of indignation at the time.

Herr Camphausen boasted of having been the Minister of mediation, but this mediation was nothing but mediation between the Crown and the bourgeoisie for joint betrayal of the people.

Herr Camphausen at last resigned when this betrayal had been fully negotiated and was sufficiently mature to be put into practice by the Government of Action and its constables.[279]

Herr Camphausen became the ambassador to the so-called Central Authority and continued to be so under all the Ministries. He remained ambassador at the time when in Vienna the Croatian, Ruthenian and Wallachian troops violated German territory, fired on Germany's leading city and set it ablaze and treated it more outrageously than any Tilly treated Magdeburg.[280] He remained ambassador and did not lift a finger.

Herr Camphausen remained ambassador under Brandenburg, thereby taking his share in the Prussian counter-revolution, and subscribed his name to the recent Prussian Circular Note which openly and without disguise demanded the restoration of the old Federal Diet.[281]

Herr Camphausen now at last takes over the Ministry in order to cover the retreat of the counter-revolutionaries and to safeguard the November and December achievements for us for a long time to come.

These are some of the great deeds of Herr Camphausen. If he now becomes Minister he will hasten to add to the list. For our part, we shall keep the most precise possible account of them.

Written by Marx on February 3, 1849

First published in the *Neue Rheinische Zeitung* No. 213, February 4, 1849

Printed according to the newspaper

Published in English for the first time

---

[a] "Entwurf eines Verfassungs-Gesetzes für den preussischen Staat", May 20, 1848.—*Ed.*

FROM THE BANAT

From the Banat. Hardly have the Serbs, Austrians, Banat Germans, Croats, Gipsies and Turkish Serbs succeeded in pushing the Magyars back a little when the bitterest quarrels are breaking out in the newly-manufactured Banat-Serbian nation. Stratimirovich stood on his own initiative as candidate for the dignity of voivode and thereby incurred such enmity from Patriarch Rajachich that the latter issued an order to arrest and deliver the most popular Serbian leader wherever he might be found.

Up to now the Turkish Serbs have supplied 20,000 auxiliary troops to the Banat Serbs. How many Russians are among them it is difficult to say. As recently as on January 19, 700 Serbs and 400 armed Gipsies crossed the Danube at Boljevcze and Pancsova to help the Banatians. That is how the Austrian united monarchy [*Gesamt-monarchie*] is keeping alive!

The power of the Hungarian insurrection is by no means destroyed, but at present is still very considerable, for numerous volunteers flock to the Magyar detachments from all parts of the country. The Magyars still have four strong army corps in the field: in Upper Hungary under Görgey, on the Theiss under Kossuth, in the Banat against the Serbs and in Transylvania under Bem; these can still fight for several months if they carefully avoid any major blow. The fighting has already lasted six whole weeks, and yet the number of Hungarian fighters has increased rather than decreased.

If they succeed, as is their intention, in prolonging hostilities until war breaks out in Upper Italy, the cause is by no means lost. Even in the Ödenburg comitat right on the Austrian border, one finds the liveliest sympathy for Kossuth among the country people; quite recently in a village, after a black-and-yellow[a] sermon, the peasants cheered the dictator,[282] whereupon a detachment of troops came, arrested the seven most respected persons in the place and marched them off; to this hour nobody knows what has become of them.

Written by Engels on February 3, 1849

First published in the second supplement to the *Neue Rheinische Zeitung* No. 213, February 4, 1849

Printed according to the newspaper

Published in English for the first time

---

[a] Colours of the Austrian flag.—*Ed.*

THE 19th ARMY BULLETIN
AND COMMENTARIES ON IT

The 19th Army Bulletin has been published.[a] Even assuming we give credence to this document, the recent advantages gained by the imperial troops are hardly worthy of mention.

We are told nothing of the army corps in the Slovak (north-west) comitats. Obviously, therefore, this corps still has its hands full with "pacifying the parts of the country already occupied".

We are also told nothing of the troops sent from Pest to Miskolcz, who were to establish contact between Windischgrätz and Schlick, and who, as will no doubt be remembered, we prophesied would have rather a long journey.[b] Of these troops, whose advanced posts, according to supposed letters from Schlick's camp, are said to be already at Miskolcz, we also hear nothing. Proof that they have not got very far.

We likewise hear nothing of the Banat Gipsy bands.

And, lastly, we are told nothing whatsoever of the troops sent out against Bem. In general, for some time now not only the official bulletins but also the otherwise so boastful unofficial fabrications have maintained a total silence with respect to Bem. Sufficient proof that the imperial troops have not won any laurels fighting against him either. Thus, with no news whatsoever of Bem, we ought not to be at all surprised if very soon he suddenly appears at Schlick's rear, or on his flanks, and manages to upset the whole imperial plan.

---

[a] "19. Armee-Bulletin", *Wiener Zeitung* No. 27, February 1, 1849.—*Ed.*

[b] See this volume, p. 291.— *Ed.*

We hardly need mention that the Bulletin does not say a word either about the storming of Leopoldstadt, a lie which has been spread six times by the martial-law newspapers, and six times believed by Mama Dumont.[a] We must assume therefore that there is still "hope" that this fortress will be captured.

All this, then, is *not* said in the Bulletin. What does it actually say?

It has knowledge of the situation in three places: on the Slavonian border, at Szolnok, and on the Upper Theiss. Of course, from these three places it once more reports "brilliant successes".

First:

"Master of the Ordnance Count Nugent, who set out on January 25 from Kanizsa to march to Fünfkirchen in order to disperse the rebels who had banded together there, transferred his headquarters to Fünfkirchen on January 29. The rebels, numbering 4,000 men with 10 cannon, left that town on January 26 and may have taken the direction of Esseg to assemble there, sheltered by the fortress which is occupied by the rebels. They will not, however, succeed in doing this as that fortress is encircled by the brigade of Colonel van der Null of the Gradiskan border regiment, and Master of the Ordnance Count Nugent also will follow them in that direction. The appearance of the royal imperial army in the Baranya and Tolna comitats has completely annihilated the elements hostile to the Government."

Let us first note that according to this the Esseg fortress on the Drava has not been taken, as the rumours circulating since the establishment of martial law maintained, but has so far only been "encircled", an encirclement which is all the more likely to be broken by the "4,000 men with 10 cannon" as it is *absolutely impossible* to maintain an encirclement on the left bank of the Drava because of the extensive swamps.

The further success is that Nugent has advanced as far as Fünfkirchen. As, according to the 18th Bulletin, Kaposvár had been occupied by the imperial troops, all that has been gained is that the army has advanced its position by some ten miles parallel to the Drava. The result of this is nothing but more difficulty in provisioning, which will grow worse in the same measure as the army approaches the heart of Hungary. Incidentally the Magyars appear to be pursuing the same tactics here as Görgey did in the Slovak region: they hold the towns as long as possible and then begin to fight a guerilla war in the countryside. What is said about the pacification of the Baranya and Tolna comitats reminds one entirely of the way Slovakia was pacified. We shall soon be hearing that the army has been unable to advance here either because it has first to restore peace and order in the comitats that have already been conquered.

---

[a] i.e. the *Kölnische Zeitung.—Ed.*

Second:

"As was already reported in the 18th Bulletin, the Ottinger cavalry brigade, reinforced by three battalions of infantry and two batteries of foot-artillery, has taken up position at Czegléd. On receiving the news that the rebels intended to attack that position, Field Marshal Prince Windischgrätz felt decided to march against them with all available troops, hoping that the rebels would accept battle. However, they did not dare to risk a decisive engagement this time either, and seeing the reinforcements approaching, they hastily withdrew across the Theiss, with the Grammont brigade in pursuit."

Well then! The fact that Windischgrätz himself went to Czegléd "with all available troops" proves that Herr Ottinger must have suffered a severe set-back there. Even the "three battalions and two batteries" received as reinforcements were of no avail! All the gains amount to is that the Austrians are at Szolnok, that is once more on the Theiss.

It is odd that Windischgrätz should be annoyed that the rebels have yet again refused to accept *battle*. As though it had not been the plan from the very outset where possible for the time being to avoid all decisive battles, to lure the imperial troops as far into Hungary as possible and to organise peasant war and guerillas in their rear! When the time is ripe they will "risk a decisive engagement".

Third:

"Having already successfully cleaned up the Zips, Lieutenant-Field Marshal Count Schlick has by now achieved the same with respect to the rebels in the Zemplin comitat, and has then set out for Tokaj where Kossuth's supporters have gathered from various points. On January 19 the advanced guard of Lieutenant-Field Marshal Schlick, under the command of Major Piattoli, encountered the enemy at Szanto and drove him back towards Tokaj. On January 21 reconnaissance showed that the enemy had retreated and taken up a rather favourable position at Tokaj, Tarczal and Keresztúr. On January 22 Lieutenant-Field Marshal Count Schlick opened the general assault on that position. Major Herczmanovsky led his gallant Stephan battalion along with a squadron of imperial light cavalry and four cannon in the attack on Keresztúr, while Lieutenant-Field Marshal Count Schlick advanced on Tarczal via Tallya and Mad with the main column. The battle ended in victory for the imperial troops. The enemy suffered considerable losses, particularly in dead among the Polish legion.[a]"

This advantage comes as a complete surprise. Schlick drove the Hungarians' advanced posts back a few miles and met them in battle at Tallya and Keresztúr. "The battle ended in victory for the royal imperial troops," says the laconic report of success. Not a word about whether Tallya and Keresztúr have been taken, or whether the Magyars have withdrawn across the Theiss. The same will probably

---

[a] This legion was nearly 3,000 men strong and fought against the imperial troops from December 1848.—*Ed.*

happen with this battle, which was such a great victory and so singularly lacking in success, as happened with Ottinger's last victory, which in the end turned out to be a defeat. No skill is required to "clean up the Zips" since the Zips is inhabited mainly by Germans. The Zemplin comitat is inhabited by Ruthenians,[283] who for the time being are still friendly towards the imperial troops, and here, too, it sounds odd to hear talk of "cleaning up".

The main conclusion to be drawn from the Bulletin is that the imperial troops are occupying two positions on the Theiss at a great distance from each other. The two corps have no contact with each other. Kossuth will probably quite soon attempt the decisive blow: he will either throw all his forces into separate attacks on the two corps, or break through between them, march on Pest, and attack the Austrians from the rear.

And while this state of affairs persists, while the imperial troops, despite their superior strength, advance only with extreme hesitation and caution, all their columns operating individually without thinking of concentrating their forces, while the Magyars stand armed on the other side of the Theiss, the martial-law press reports that Kossuth has been taken prisoner near Stry in Galicia. And German newspapers reprint that.

Written by Engels on February 5, 1849

First published in the *Neue Rheinische Zeitung* No. 214, February 6, 1849

Printed according to the newspaper

Published in English for the first time

THE FIRST TRIAL
OF THE *NEUE RHEINISCHE ZEITUNG*[284]

[SPEECH BY KARL MARX]

Gentlemen of the jury! The proceedings today have a certain importance because Articles 222 and 367 of the *Code pénal*[285] invoked in the indictment against the *Neue Rheinische Zeitung* are the only ones from Rhenish legislation available to the state authorities, unless there is direct incitement to revolt.

You are all aware of the very special predilection of the prosecuting magistrates for taking legal action against the *Neue Rheinische Zeitung*. In spite of all their diligence, however, up to now they have not succeeded in accusing us of any other offences than those envisaged in Articles 222 and 367. In the interests of the press, therefore, I consider it necessary to make a closer examination of these articles.

But before I enter into a legal analysis, allow me to make a personal observation. The Public Prosecutor has described as a *vilification* the passage in the incriminated article which states: "Is Herr Zweiffel perhaps combining the executive with the legislative power? Are the laurels of Chief Public Prosecutor supposed to cover the weak points of the people's representative?"[a] Gentlemen, it is quite possible for someone to be a very good Chief Public Prosecutor and at the same time a bad people's representative. He is perhaps a good Chief Public Prosecutor only because he is a bad people's representative. The prosecution seems to be little versed in parliamentary history. What underlies the question of incompatibility, which takes up so much space in the proceedings of the constitutional Chambers? The distrust of executive officials, the

---

[a] See present edition, Vol. 7, p. 179.—*Ed.*

Zwei

politische Prozesse.

Verhandelt vor den Februar-Assisen in Köln.

I.

Der erste Preßprozeß der Neuen Rheinischen Zeitung.

II.

Prozeß des Kreis-Ausschusses der rheinischen Demokraten.

Köln, 1849.
Verlag der Expedition der Neuen Rheinischen Zeitung.

Title-page of the pamphlet *Two Political Trials* containing Marx's and Engels' speeches at the Cologne trials

suspicion that an executive official will readily sacrifice the interests of society to the interests of the existing Government and is therefore fitted to be anything rather than a people's representative. And now consider in particular the situation of a Public Prosecutor. In what country would it not be considered incompatible with the high post of people's representative? I remind you of the attacks on Hébert, Plougoulm and Bavay in the French and Belgian press, and in the French and Belgian Chambers, attacks aimed precisely against the contradictory combination of the qualities of a Prosecutor-General and a parliamentary deputy in the same person. These attacks never resulted in the institution of court proceedings, not even under Guizot, and the France of Louis Philippe and the Belgium of Leopold ranked as model constitutional states. In England, it is true, matters are different with the Attorney-General and Solicitor-General. [a] But their position is also essentially different from that of a *procureur du roi*. They are indeed more or less judicial officials. We, gentlemen, are not constitutionalists, but we take up the standpoint of the gentlemen who are accusing us in order to beat them on their own ground with their own weapons. Hence we appeal to constitutional usage.

The Public Prosecutor would like to wipe out a large period of parliamentary history—by means of a moral platitude. I decisively reject his charge of vilification, and I explain it as due to his ignorance.

I pass now to a discussion of the juridical question.

My defence counsel[b] has already proved to you that without the Prussian law of July 5, 1819, [286] the indictment on the charge of insulting Chief Public Prosecutor Zweiffel would have been invalid from the outset. Article 222 of the *Code pénal* speaks only of "*outrages par paroles*", of *oral* insults, not of written or printed ones. The Prussian law of 1819, however, was intended to supplement Article 222, not to abolish it. The Prussian law can extend to written insults the punishment prescribed in Article 222 only where the *Code* would impose it if the insults were in oral form. Written insults must occur under the same circumstances and conditions as envisaged by Article 222 for oral insults. It is therefore necessary to define exactly the meaning of Article 222.*

---

* Article 222 reads textually as follows: "Lorsqu'un ou plusieurs magistrats de l'ordre administratif ou judiciaire auront reçu dans *l'exercice de leurs fonctions ou à l'occasion de cet exercice* quelque outrage par paroles tendant à inculper leur honneur ou

---

[a] These titles are in English in the German original.—*Ed.*
[b] Schneider II.—*Ed.*

In the motives given for Article 222 (Exposé par M. le conseiller d'état Berlier, séance de février 1810 [a]) it is stated:

> "Il ne sera donc ici question que des *seuls outrages* qui compromettent la *paix publique* c.àd. de ceux dirigés contre les fonctionnaires ou agents publics dans l'exercice ou à l'occasion de l'exercice de leurs fonctions; dans ce cas ce n'est plus un particulier, c'est l'ordre public qui est blessé... La hiérarchie politique sera dans ce cas prise en considération: celui qui se permet des *outrages ou violences* envers un officier ministériel est coupable sans doute, mais il commet un moindre *scandale* que lorsqu'il outrage un magistrat."

That is to say, in translation:

> "It will therefore be a question here *only* of insults which violate *public order*, public peace, that is to say, therefore, insults directed against officials or public agents during the exercise of or in connection with the exercise of their functions; in this case it is no longer a private person, it is public order which is harmed.... In this case the political hierarchy will be taken into consideration: one who indulges in insults or acts of violence directed against a ministerial official is undoubtedly guilty, but he causes a lesser scandal than when he insults a judge."

From these motives, gentlemen, you see what the legislator intended by Article 222. Article 222 is "*only*" applicable to insults directed against officials which violate, put at risk, public order, public peace. When is public order, *la paix publique*, violated? Only when a revolt for the purpose of overthrowing the laws is attempted or when the implementation of the existing laws is prevented, i.e. when resistance is exercised against the official who is executing the law, when the *performance of his office* by a functioning official is interrupted or impaired. The resistance can be confined to mere grumbling, to insulting language; it can go as far as acts of violence, forcible insubordination. *Outrage*, insult, is merely the lowest degree of *violence*, of insubordination, of violent resistance. Hence in the motivation there is mention of "*outrages ou violences*", "insults *or* acts of violence". The concept is the same in both; *violence*, act of violence, is only an aggravation of *outrage*, of insult against the functioning official.

In these motives, therefore, it is presumed: 1) that the official was insulted during the exercise of his office; 2) that he was *present in*

leur délicatesse, celui qui les aura ainsi outragés sera puni d'un emprisonnement d'un mois à deux ans." ["If one or more officials of the administrative or judicial system during *the exercise of their functions or on the occasion of such exercise* have been subjected to insult by words tending to impugn their honour or delicacy, the person who has insulted them in this way will be punished by imprisonment from one month to two years."]—*Note by Marx.*

---

[a] Expositions by Counsellor of State Berlier, sitting of February 1810.—*Ed.*

person when he was insulted. In no other case does a real disturbance of public order take place.

The same presumption is to be found in the whole section concerning "*outrages et violences envers les dépositaires de l'autorité et de la force publique*", i.e. "insults and acts of violence against those who are entrusted with public power and public authority". The various articles of this section present the following gradations of acts of resistance: facial expressions, words, threats, acts of violence; the last-named in their turn are graded according to their gravity. Finally, in all these articles provision is made for more severe punishment in cases where these various forms of insubordination occur in a court of law. Here the greatest "*scandal*" is caused and there is the most blatant hindrance to the execution of the laws and violation of the *paix publique*.

Article 222, therefore, is applicable to *written* insults against officials only when they occur 1) in the presence in person of the official, 2) during the performance of his office. My defence counsel, gentlemen, has cited such an example for you. He himself would have come under Article 222 if, for example, now during the assizes proceedings he had insulted the presiding judge in a written proposal or something of that sort. On the other hand, under no circumstances can this article of the *Code pénal* be applied to a newspaper article which "insults" in the absence of the functioning official and long after the performance of his official duty.

This interpretation of Article 222 gives you the explanation for what appears to be a defect, an inconsistency, of the *Code pénal*. Why am I permitted to insult the King, whereas I am not permitted to insult the Chief Public Prosecutor? Why does the *Code* not prescribe any punishment for *lèse-majesté* as Prussian Law[287] does?

Because the King himself never performs the functions of an official, but always causes them to be performed by someone else, because the King never acts towards me in a personal way, but always only through his representatives. The despotism of the *Code pénal* deriving from the French Revolution is immensely different from the patriarchal-schoolmasterly despotism of Prussian Law. The Napoleonic despotism strikes me down as soon as I actually obstruct state power, even if it is only by insulting an official who, during the performance of his office, exercises state power in relation to me. On the other hand, outside the performance of his office, the official becomes an ordinary member of civil society, without privileges, without special protection. Prussian despotism, on the other hand, confronts me in the shape of an official with a superior, sacrosanct being. His official character is as integral part of his personality as consecration is of a Catholic priest. For Prussian laymen, i.e. those who are not officials, the Prussian official always remains a priest. To insult such a priest, even one who is not functioning, who is not present, and who is back in private life, remains a profanation of religion, a desecration. The higher the official the more serious the profanation of religion. The highest degree of insult to a state priest is therefore an insult offered to the King, *lèse-majesté*, which according to the *Code pénal* is a criminal impossibility.

But it will be said that if Article 222 of the *Code pénal* speaks only of *outrages* against officials "*dans l'exercice de leurs fonctions*", of insults against officials during the exercise of their functions, then there would be no need to prove that the *presence in person* of the official is presumed by the legislator and is the necessary condition for any insult coming under Article 222. But to the words "*dans l'exercice de leurs fonctions*", Article 222 adds "*à l'occasion de cet exercice*".

The public prosecution translates this: "with relation to their office". I shall prove to you, gentlemen, that this translation is incorrect and is directly contrary to the intention of the legislator. Take a look at Article 228 of the same section. It states: Anyone who *strikes* an official "*dans l'exercice de ses fonctions ou à l'occasion de cet exercice*" will be punished by imprisonment for two to five years. Can this be translated: "with relation to his office"? Can one deal *relative* blows? Is the presumption of the presence in person of the official abandoned here? Can I thrash one who is not present? It is obvious that this must be translated: "Anyone who strikes an official on the *occasion* of the performance of his official duty". The phrase in Article 228 is word for word the same as in Article 222. The words "*à l'occasion de cet exercice*" have obviously the same meaning in both. Far from excluding the condition of the *presence in person* of the official, therefore, this addition on the contrary presupposes it.

The history of French legislation offers you a further striking proof. You will recall that in France in the first period of the Restoration, the parties were inexorably opposed to one another — in parliament, in the courts of justice; in Southern France they were literally at daggers drawn. The assize courts at that time were nothing but martial-law tribunals of the victorious party against the defeated party. The opposition press lashed out mercilessly at the verdicts of the juries. Article 222 was no weapon against this hateful polemic because this article could only be applied to insults against jurymen while they were in session and present in person. Hence in 1819 a new law was concocted which punishes any attack on the *chose jugée*, on a verdict which has been pronounced. The *Code pénal* knows nothing of this inviolability of a judicial verdict. Would it have been supplemented by a new law if Article 222 dealt with insults "*with relation to*" the performance of an office?

What then is the meaning of the phrase: "*à l'occasion de cet exercice*"? It is intended to do no more than safeguard an official from attacks shortly *before* or *after* the performance of his office. If Article 222 spoke only of "insults and acts of violence" against an official during the actual duration of the performance of his office, I could throw a court bailiff down the stairs after the execution of his warrant and maintain that I had not insulted him until he had ceased to confront me in the official capacity of a court bailiff. I could attack and thrash a justice of the peace while he was on the way to my home to carry out his judicial police function and could avoid the punishment envisaged in Article 228 by maintaining that I had maltreated him not during but prior to his performance of his office.

The phrase "*à l'occasion de cet exercice*", *on the occasion* of the performance of an office, is intended therefore to ensure the safety of an official performing his official function. It concerns insults or acts of violence which take place, it is true, not directly during the performance of an official duty, but shortly *before* or *after* it, and—what is the essential thing—are *vitally* connected with the performance of the office, and therefore under all circumstances presuppose the *presence in person* of the maltreated official.

Is any further proof needed that Article 222 is not applicable to our newspaper article, even if by it we insulted Herr Zweiffel? When that article was written, Herr Zweiffel was *absent*; at that time he was living not in Cologne, but in Berlin. When that article was written, Herr Zweiffel was not functioning as Chief Public Prosecutor, but as an agreer.[a] Hence he could not be insulted or abused as functioning Chief Public Prosecutor.

Apart from all that I have said so far, there is another way in which it can be shown that Article 222 is not applicable to the incriminated *Neue Rheinische Zeitung* article.

This follows from the distinction which the *Code pénal* draws between *insult* and *calumny*. You will find this distinction precisely defined in Article 375. After speaking of "calumny", it states here:

"Quant aux injures ou aux expressions outrageantes qui ne renfermeraient l'imputation d'aucun fait précis" (in Article 367 on calumny this is called: "des faits, qui s'ils existaient", facts which "if they were real *facts*"), "mais celle d'un vice déterminé, ... la peine sera une amende de seize à cinq cent francs".—"Defamations or

---

[a] i.e. a deputy of the Prussian National Assembly, called upon to work out a Constitution by agreement with the Crown.—*Ed.*

insulting expressions which do not contain the imputation of a definite fact, but certainly the imputation of a definite vice, will ... be punished by a fine of sixteen to five hundred francs."

Article 376 states further:

"All other defamations or insulting expressions ... entail a simple police punishment."

What, therefore, does calumny involve? Defamations which charge the one defamed with a *definite fact.* And what does insult involve? The imputation of a definite vice and insulting expressions in general terms. If I say: you have stolen a silver spoon, that is a calumny against you in the sense of the *Code pénal.* If, on the other hand, I say: you are a thief, you have thievish desires, then I am *insulting* you.

But the article in the *Neue Rheinische Zeitung* by no means reproaches Herr Zweiffel by saying: Herr Zweiffel is a traitor to the people, Herr Zweiffel has made infamous statements. On the contrary, the article states explicitly: "Herr Zweiffel, moreover, is said to have declared that he would within a week put an end to March 19, the clubs, freedom of the press and other outrages of the evil year 1848 at Cologne on the Rhine."[a]

Herr Zweiffel, therefore, is charged with having made a quite definite statement. Hence if one of the two Articles 222 and 367 were applicable in this case, it would not be Article 222, which deals with insults, but only Article 367, which is concerned with calumny.

Why has the public prosecution applied Article 222 to us instead of Article 367?

Because Article 222 is much more indefinite and makes it much easier to smuggle in a conviction once it is intended that there shall be a conviction. Violation of "*délicatesse et honneur*", of delicacy and honour, admits of no exact measurement. What is honour, what is delicacy? What is the violation of them? It depends purely on the individual with whom I am dealing, on his degree of education, on his prejudices, on his imagination. There is no other measuring rod for it than the *noli me tangere*[b] of the pretentious vanity of an official who imagines himself to be incomparable.

But Article 367, too, which concerns calumny, is inapplicable to the article in the *Neue Rheinische Zeitung.*

Article 367 demands a "*fait précis*", a definite fact, "*un fait qui peut exister*", a fact which can be a *real* fact. But Herr Zweiffel is not charged with having abolished freedom of the press, with having

---

[a] See present edition, Vol. 7, p. 179.— *Ed.*

[b] Not to be touched.— *Ed.*

closed down the clubs and destroyed the March gains in some place or other. It is a mere statement that is laid to his charge. Article 367, however, calls for the imputation of definite facts,

"which, if they were real facts, would expose the one to blame for them to criminal or police court proceedings or even merely to the contempt or hatred of the citizens".

The mere *statement* about doing something or other does not expose me to either criminal or police court proceedings. It cannot even be said that it necessarily exposes me to the hatred or contempt of the citizens. A statement can, it is true, be the expression of a very base, hateful and contemptible frame of mind. Nevertheless, is it not possible that in my excitement I may utter a statement which threatens actions that I am incapable of carrying out? Only an act proves whether my statement is *seriously* meant.

Moreover, the *Neue Rheinische Zeitung* says: "Herr Zweiffel *is said* to have declared." In order to calumniate someone I must not cast doubt on my own assertion as occurs here with the use of the "*is said*"; I must express myself categorically.

Finally, gentlemen of the jury, the "*citoyens*", the citizens, whose hatred or contempt, according to Article 367, must be evoked by my imputation of a fact for it to be a *calumny*, these *citoyens*, these citizens no longer exist at all in political matters. There are only party adherents. What earns me hatred and contempt among the members of one party earns me love and honour among the members of the other party. The organ of the present Ministry, the *Neue Preussische Zeitung*, has accused Herr Zweiffel of being a kind of *Robespierre*.[a] In its eyes, in the eyes of its party, our article did not expose Herr Zweiffel to hatred and contempt, but freed him from the burden of hatred and contempt which he had been made to bear.

It is of very great interest to attach weight to this remark, not so much for the pending case as for all cases where an attempt may be made by the public prosecution to apply Article 367 to political polemics.

In general, gentlemen of the jury, if you want to apply to the press Article 367 on calumny as interpreted by the public prosecution, then you abolish freedom of the press by means of the Penal Code, whereas you have recognised this freedom by a Constitution and won it by a revolution. You sanction every arbitrary action of the officials, you permit every official villainous action, you punish only the denunciation of villainy. What then is the use of the hypocrisy of a free press? If existing laws enter into open contradiction to a newly achieved stage of social development, then it is up to you, gentlemen

---

[a] See this volume, p. 30.—*Ed.*

of the jury, to come between the dead behests of the law and the living demands of society. It is up to you then to anticipate legislation until it knows how to comply with social needs. This is the noblest attribute of the assize court. In the present case, gentlemen, this task is facilitated for you by the letter of the law itself. You have only to interpret it in the sense of our time, our political rights, and our social needs.

Article 367 concludes with the following words:

"La présente disposition n'est point applicable aux faits dont la loi autorise la publicité, ni à ceux que l'auteur de l'imputation était, *par la nature de ses fonctions ou de ses devoirs, obligé de révéler ou de réprimer.*"—"The present provision is not applicable to facts which the law permits to be made public, nor to those which, *owing to the nature of his office or his duty*, the author of the imputation *was bound* to reveal or prevent."

There is no doubt, gentlemen, that the legislator was not thinking of the free press when he spoke of the *duty* of denunciation. But neither did he think that this article would ever be applied to the free press. It is well known that under Napoleon there was no freedom of the press. Hence if you want to apply the law to a stage of political and social development for which it was not intended, then apply it *fully*, expound it in the spirit of our time, let the press have the benefit also of this concluding sentence of Article 367.

Article 367, taken in the narrow sense of the public prosecution, excludes proof of truth and only permits denunciation when it is supported by public documents or already available judicial verdicts. Why should the press *post festum*, after a judgment has been pronounced, still make its denunciation? It is by profession the public watchdog, the tireless denouncer of those in power, the omnipresent eye, the omnipresent mouthpiece of the people's spirit that jealously guards its freedom. If you interpret Article 367 in this sense, and that is how you must interpret it if you do not want to take away the freedom of the press in the interests of governmental power, the Code offers you at the same time a means of dealing with encroachments of the press. According to Article 372, in a case of denunciation, the proceedings and decision regarding the offence of calumny should be suspended during the investigation of the facts. According to Article 373, a denunciation which proves to be a calumny is punishable.

Gentlemen, you need only to glance at the incriminated article to convince yourselves that the *Neue Rheinische Zeitung* far from having any *intention* of insult or calumny, merely fulfilled its duty of denunciation when it attacked the local prosecuting magistrates and police. The hearing of the witnesses has proved to you that in regard to the police we have reported only the real facts.

The point of the whole article, however, lies in the prophecy of the subsequently carried out counter-revolution; it is an attack on the Hansemann Ministry, which marked its entry by the peculiar assertion that the greater the police force, the freer the state. This Ministry imagined that the aristocracy had been defeated and that only one task remained for it to accomplish: to rob the people of their revolutionary achievements in the interests of a particular class, the bourgeoisie. Thus it paved the way for the feudal counter-revolution. What we denounced in the incriminated article was nothing more and nothing less than the obvious phenomenon, from the evidence of our most immediate surroundings, of systematic counter-revolutionary activity on the part of the Hansemann Ministry and the German governments in general.

It is impossible to regard the arrests in Cologne as an isolated occurrence. To be convinced of the contrary, one has only to cast a fleeting glance at the history of the period. Shortly before there was the prosecution of the press in Berlin, based on the provisions of the old Prussian Law. A few days later, on July 8, J. Wulff, President of the Düsseldorf People's Club, was arrested, and house searches were carried out among many committee members of this club. Wulff was subsequently acquitted by the jury, as indeed at that time no political trial received the sanction of the jury. On the same date, July 8, in Munich, officers, officials and supernumerary officials were forbidden to take part in public meetings. On July 9, Falkenheim, President of the "Germania" Association in Breslau, was arrested. On July 15, in the Citizens' Association [288] in Düsseldorf, Chief Public Prosecutor Schnaase delivered a speech containing a formal indictment of the People's Club, the President of which had been arrested on July 8 by his order. There you have an example of the lofty impartiality of the prosecuting magistrates, an example of how the Chief Public Prosecutor acts at the same time as adherent of a party, and the party adherent as Chief Public Prosecutor. Undeterred by the legal proceedings taken against us because of our attack on Zweiffel, we then denounced Schnaase. [a] He took care not to reply to us. On the same day that Chief Public Prosecutor Schnaase delivered his philippic against the Düsseldorf People's Club, the Democratic District Association in Stuttgart was closed down by a royal ordinance. On July 19, the Democratic Students' Association in Heidelberg was dissolved, as also on July 27 all democratic associations in Baden and shortly afterwards all those in Württem-

---

[a] Reference to the report "Bürgerverein" (Düsseldorf), published in the *Neue Rheinische Zeitung* No. 48, July 18, 1848.—*Ed.*

berg and Bavaria. And ought we to have remained silent about this obvious conspiracy of treason against the people on the part of all the German governments? The Prussian Government at that time did not dare to do what the governments of Baden, Württemberg and Bavaria did. It did not dare because the Prussian National Assembly had just begun to get an inkling of the counter-revolutionary conspiracy and to show fight against the Hansemann Ministry. But, gentlemen of the jury, I tell you frankly, with the utmost conviction: if the Prussian counter-revolution is not smashed soon by a Prussian people's revolution, freedom of association and freedom of the press will be completely destroyed in Prussia as well. They have already been partially done away with by the states of siege. In Düsseldorf and in some Silesian regions the authorities have even dared to re-introduce *censorship.*

However, it is not merely the general state of affairs in Germany, but the general Prussian state of affairs that obliged us to view with extreme distrust every action of the Government and to denounce to the people the slightest symptoms of its system. The prosecuting magistrates here in Cologne have given us quite special grounds for exposing them before public opinion as a counter-revolutionary tool. In July alone, we had to denounce three illegal arrests. On the first two occasions Public Prosecutor Hecker remained silent, on the third occasion he tried to justify himself, but after our reply he kept silent for the simple reason that there was nothing he could say.[289]

And under these circumstances the public prosecution dares to assert that it is not a question of a denunciation, but of a petty malicious calumny? This view is based on a peculiar misunderstanding. As far as I am concerned, I assure you, gentlemen, that I prefer to follow the great events of the world, to analyse the course of history, than to occupy myself with local bosses, with the police and prosecuting magistrates. However great these gentlemen may imagine themselves in their own fancy, they are *nothing,* absolutely *nothing,* in the gigantic battles of the present time. I consider we are making a real sacrifice when we decide to break a lance with *these* opponents. But, firstly, it is the duty of the press to come forward on behalf of the oppressed in its immediate neighbourhood. And furthermore, gentlemen, the edifice of servitude has its most specific support in the subordinate political and social powers which directly confront the private life of an individual, of a living person. It is not sufficient to fight against general relationships and the highest authorities. The press must decide to enter the lists against a *specific* police officer, a *specific* Public Prosecutor, a *specific Landrat.* What caused the defeat of the *March revolution?* It reformed only the highest political summit, it left all the groundwork of this summit intact—the old bureaucracy, the old army, the old boards of prosecuting magistrates, the old judiciary which had been created, had developed and grown grey in the service of absolutism. The first duty of the press now is *to undermine all the foundations of the existing political state of affairs.* (Applause in the hall.)

[SPEECH BY FREDERICK ENGELS]

Gentlemen of the jury, the previous speaker has been concerned mainly with the charge of insulting the Chief Public Prosecutor, Herr Zweiffel. Permit me now to draw your attention to the accusation of calumniating the police. It is primarily a matter of the legal provisions on which the indictment is based.

Article 367 of the Penal Code states:

"A person is guilty of the offence of calumny who in public places or in public meetings, or in an authentic and public document or in a *printed* or unprinted *writing* which has been exhibited, *sold* or distributed, accuses anyone of such facts which, if they were true, would expose the one to blame for them to criminal or police court proceedings or even merely to the *contempt* or *hatred of the citizens.*"

Article 370 adds:

"If through process of law the fact constituting the object of the accusation is *proved to be true,* the author of the accusation is free from all punishment.... *Only* proof which arises from a *judicial verdict* or some other *authentic document* is regarded as *legal proof.*"

Gentlemen, the public prosecution has given you *its* interpretation of these provisions of the law and on that basis has asked you to pronounce us guilty. Your attention has already been drawn to the fact that these laws were promulgated at a time when the press was under censorship and political relationships were quite different from what they are now, and on these grounds my defence counsel[a] has expressed the opinion that you should no longer consider these obsolete laws as binding upon you. The public prosecution has concurred with this view, at least as regards Article 370. It made a statement to the following effect: "For you, gentlemen of the jury, it will be mainly a question of whether the truth of the facts in question has been *proved*"—and I thank the prosecution for this admission.

But even if you should not be of the opinion that at least Article 370 in its limitation of the proof of truth is obsolete, you will certainly think that the articles cited must have a different interpretation from

---

[a] Schneider II.—*Ed.*

that which the public prosecution tries to give them. It is precisely the privilege of the jury to interpret the laws, independently of all traditional judicial practice, as their common sense and conscience dictate. We are indicted under Article 367 for having accused the police officers in question of actions which, if they were true, would expose them to the contempt and hatred of the citizens. If you interpret these words "hatred and contempt" in the sense that the prosecution would like to give them, then, so long as the provisions of Article 370 remain in force, all freedom of the press ceases to exist. In that case, how can the press fulfil its primary duty, the duty of protecting the citizens against excesses committed by officials? As soon as it denounces such an excess to public opinion, it will be brought before the assize court and—if things turn out as the prosecution would like—will be sentenced to imprisonment, a fine and loss of civil rights; unless it is able to adduce a judicial verdict, i.e. unless it publishes its denunciation only when it no longer serves any purpose!

How little appropriate to present-day conditions are the passages of the laws that have been cited, at least in the interpretation that the prosecution would like to give them, is proved by a comparison with Article 369. This states:

> "With regard to calumnies which have been given currency by means of *foreign newspapers*, legal proceedings can be taken against those who sent the articles to the newspapers ... or who helped towards the *import and circulation* of these newspapers within the country."

According to this article, gentlemen, it would be the duty of the public prosecution daily and hourly to institute proceedings against the royal Prussian postal officials. For is there even a single one of the three hundred and sixty-five days of the year on which the Prussian postal service by the conveyance and delivery of some foreign newspaper or other does not help towards "the import and circulation" of calumnies in the sense of the prosecution? Nevertheless, it does not occur to the public prosecutors to institute proceedings against the postal service.

Furthermore, bear in mind, gentlemen, that these articles of the law were written at a time when the censorship made it *impossible* to calumniate *officials* through the press. According to the legislator's intention, therefore, those articles could only serve the purpose of protecting *private persons*, but not *officials*, from calumny, and in that way only have they any meaning. But owing to the fact that since the winning of freedom of the press the actions of officials also can be placed before the forum of public opinion, the point of view is essentially altered. And it is precisely here, where there are such contradictions between old legislation and new political and social conditions, it is precisely here that the jury has to intervene and by a new interpretation adapt the old law to the new conditions.

But, as already stated: the prosecution itself has recognised that, despite Article 370, for you, gentlemen, it is mainly a question of whether the truth has been proved. The prosecution has therefore attempted to invalidate the proof of truth as we placed it before you by the evidence of witnesses. Let us therefore look at the newspaper article in question to test whether the accusations have in fact been proved and whether, at the same time, they really constitute a calumny. At the beginning of the article, it is stated:

"Six to seven policemen entered Anneke's residence between 6 and 7 in the morning, immediately maltreated the maid in the hall" [a] etc.

Gentlemen, you have heard Anneke's evidence on this point. You will recall that I wanted to question the witness Anneke again about the maltreatment of the servant girl and that the presiding judge declared this interrogation superfluous since the matter had been sufficiently established. I ask you now: have we calumniated the police in this matter?

Further: "Once they found themselves in the anteroom, the urging turned into assault during which one of the policemen smashed a glass door. Anneke was pushed down the stairs." Gentlemen, you heard the evidence of the witness Anneke; you will recall that the witness Esser told how the policemen came out of the house with Anneke "at full speed" and *bundled* him into the van. I ask you again, gentlemen, have we committed any calumny here?

Finally, there is a passage in the article the correctness of which has not been proved with *literal exactitude*. It is as follows: "One of these four pillars of justice was already at this early hour somewhat unsteady, being filled with 'spirit', the true fluid of life: firewater."

I admit, gentlemen, that all that has been established here by what Anneke expressly stated is as follows: "Judging by their behaviour, the policemen could very well have been drunk", that it has only been established that the policemen *behaved* as if they were drunk. But, gentlemen, compare what we said two days later in reply to the rejoinder of Public Prosecutor *Hecker*: "The insult could only refer to one of the policemen of whom it was said that he was *unsteady* at an early hour for more or less spiritual or spirituous reasons. If the investigation, however, as we do not doubt for one moment, should

---

[a] See present edition, Vol. 7, p. 177.—*Ed.*

prove the correctness of the evidence, namely the brutalities committed by the agents of the public authority, then we believe that we shall have only acted in the interests of the gentlemen accused by us by carefully emphasising, with the complete impartiality becoming the press, the *only extenuating circumstance*. And this affable statement of the only extenuating circumstance is transformed into an insult by the Public Prosecutor."[a]

You see from this, gentlemen, that we ourselves called for an investigation of the facts in question. It is not our fault that the investigation did not take place. Moreover, as far as the reproach of drunkenness is concerned, I ask you of what importance can it be for a royal Prussian policeman if it is said that he has drunk a glass too much? As to whether that can be regarded as a calumny, I appeal to public opinion throughout the Rhine Province.

And how can the prosecution speak of calumny when the alleged victims of calumny are not named, not even precisely indicated? There is the mention of "six to seven policemen". Who are they? Where are they? Have you heard, gentlemen, of any *particular* policeman who has been exposed to "the hatred and contempt of the citizens" as a result of this article? The law expressly demands that the calumniated individual must be precisely indicated. In the passage of the article in question no particular policeman but at most the royal Prussian police as a whole can find that it has been defamed. It can feel insulted by newspapers making public the fact that illegal and brutal acts are committed by members of this corps with impunity. But, gentlemen, it is no crime to accuse the royal Prussian police in general of brutal behaviour. I challenge the public prosecution to show me the passage in the law which makes it punishable to insult, defame or calumniate the royal Prussian corps of policemen, if indeed there can be any talk of calumny here.

In general, the public prosecution has regarded the article in question as merely proof of an unbridled passion for calumniation. Gentlemen, the article has been read to you. Did you find in it that we considered in isolation the more or less unimportant illegalities which occurred at the time in Cologne, that we exploited them and exaggerated them in order to satisfy our alleged rancour against the lower officials? Did we not, on the contrary, put these facts in their place as a link in the great chain of attempts on the part of reaction which were taking place at the time throughout Germany? Did we confine ourselves to the police and the prosecuting magistrates in

---

[a] "Legal Proceedings against the *Neue Rheinische Zeitung*" (see present edition, Vol. 7, p. 187).— *Ed.*

Cologne, or did we go into the matter more thoroughly and trace its causes as far back as the secret Ministry of State in Berlin?[290] But, of course, it is less dangerous to attack the great secret Ministry of State in Berlin than the little Public Prosecutor's office in Cologne—and as a proof of this we stand here before you today.

Look at the end of the article.[a] It states: "Those are the actions of the Government of Action, the Government of the Left Centre, the Government of transition to an old aristocratic, old bureaucratic and old Prussian Government. As soon as Herr Hansemann has fulfilled his transitory function, he will be dismissed."

You will remember, gentlemen, what happened in August of last year: how Hansemann was "dismissed" as superfluous, of course under the more decent form of voluntary resignation, and how the Pfuel-Eichmann-Kisker-Ladenberg Ministry, literally an "old aristocratic, old bureaucratic, old Prussian Ministry", immediately succeeded him.

The article says further: "The Berlin Left, however, must realise that the old regime is willing to let it keep its small parliamentary victories and large constitutional designs as long as the old regime in the meantime is able to seize all the really important positions. It can confidently recognise the revolution of March 19 inside the Chamber provided the revolution can be disarmed *outside* of it."

I certainly need waste no words in proving how correct this view of the situation was. You yourselves know that in proportion as the power of the Left in the Chamber increased, the power of the people's party *outside* the Chamber was destroyed. Do I need to enumerate for you the unpunished brutal actions of the Prussian soldiery in innumerable cities, the increasing imposition of states of siege, the many cases of disarming the civic militia, and finally Wrangel's heroic expedition against Berlin, in order to show how the revolution was actually disarmed and how in actual fact the old power seized all decisive positions.

And then at the end is the remarkable prophecy: "Some fine day the Left may find *that its parliamentary victory coincides with its real defeat*."

How literally this came to pass! The very day on which the Left at last achieved a majority in the Chamber was the day of their real defeat. It was precisely the parliamentary victories of the Left that led to the coup d'état of November 9, to the removal and adjournment of the National Assembly, and finally to its dissolution

---

[a] The reference is to the article "Arrests" quoted at the beginning of this speech.—*Ed.*

and the imposing of a Constitution. The parliamentary victory of the Left directly coincided with its complete defeat outside parliament.[291]

This political forecast which has so literally come true, gentlemen, is therefore the result, the summing up, the conclusion that we drew from the acts of violence which had taken place throughout Germany, including Cologne. And yet there has been talk of a blind passion for calumniation. In actual fact, does it not look as if we have been brought before you today, gentlemen, in order to answer for the crime that we correctly reported correct facts and drew the correct conclusions from them?

To sum up: You, gentlemen of the jury, have at the present moment to decide about freedom of the press in the Rhine Province. If the press is to be forbidden to report what occurs before its very eyes; if in every complicated case it has to wait until a judicial verdict has been passed on it; if it must first ask every official, from the Minister down to the policeman, whether he would feel his honour or delicacy impugned by the facts of the case being mentioned, irrespective of whether these facts are true or not; if the press is faced with the alternative of either falsifying events or remaining completely silent—then, gentlemen, freedom of the press is at an end, and if that is what you want, then pronounce us "*guilty*"!

Delivered on February 7, 1849

First published in the *Neue Rheinische Zeitung* No. 221, February 14, 1849, and also in the pamphlet *Zwei politische Prozesse*, Köln, 1849, Verlag der Expedition der *Neuen Rheinischen Zeitung*

Printed according to the newspaper

Published in English for the first time

THE TRIAL OF THE RHENISH
DISTRICT COMMITTEE OF DEMOCRATS[292]

[SPEECH BY KARL MARX]

[*Neue Rheinische Zeitung* No. 231, February 25, 1849]

Gentlemen of the jury, if this action had been brought *before* December 5, I could have understood the charge made by the Public Prosecutor. Now, *after* December 5, I do not understand how he dares to invoke against us laws which the Crown itself has trampled under foot.

On what does the public prosecution base its criticism of the National Assembly and of the decision on the refusal to pay taxes? On the laws of April 6 and 8, 1848.[293] And what did the Government do on December 5, when it on its own authority granted a Constitution and imposed a new electoral law on the country? It tore up the laws of April 6 and 8, 1848. These laws are no longer valid for the supporters of the Government, so why should they still be valid for the opponents of the Government? On December 5 the Government took its stand on a *revolutionary* basis, namely, on a *counter-revolutionary* basis. In relation to it there are now only revolutionaries or accomplices. Even the mass of citizens who act on the basis of the existing laws, who uphold the existing law in face of infringements of that law, have been turned into rebels by this Government itself. *Before* December 5 opinion concerning the removal of the National Assembly, its dispersal and the introduction of a state of siege in Berlin could have been divided. *After* December 5 it is a well-established fact that these measures were intended to usher in the counter-revolution and that therefore every means was permissible against a group that itself no longer recognised the conditions under which it was a *government* and consequently could no longer be acknowledged by the country as a government.

Gentlemen, the Crown could have preserved at least the semblance of legality, but it has not deigned to do so. It could have dispersed the National Assembly and then let the Ministry come forward and tell the country: "We have dared to carry out a coup d'état—circumstances have forced us to do it. Formally, we have exceeded the bounds of the law, but there are moments of crisis when the very existence of the state is at stake. At such moments there is only *one* inviolable law — the existence of the state. There was no Constitution when we dispersed the Assembly. Therefore no Constitution could be infringed. But there exist two organic laws—those of April 6 and 8, 1848. Actually there is only *one* organic law, the *electoral law*. We call on the country to carry through new elections in accordance with *this* law. We, the *responsible Ministry*, will then appear before the Assembly that has emerged from these primary elections. This Assembly, we trust, will recognise that the coup d'état was a *saving action* necessitated by circumstances. It will subsequently sanction the coup d'état. It will declare that we infringed a legal formula in order to save the country. Let it pass judgment on us."

If the Ministry had acted in this way, it could have had some *semblance* of right to arraign us. The Crown would have saved the semblance of legality, but it could not, it *would* not do it.

The March revolution, as seen by the Crown, was a savage fact. One savage fact can be erased only by another savage fact. By rejecting new elections on the basis of the law of April 1848, the Ministry *denied* its own *responsibilities and rejected the very court to which it was responsible.* At the very outset it turned the appeal from the National Assembly to the people into a mere pretence, a fiction, a deception. By inventing a First Chamber based on the property qualification as an integral part of the Legislative Assembly, the Ministry tore up the organic laws, departed from the legal basis, falsified the people's elections and prevented the people from passing any verdict on the "saving action" of the Crown.

And so, gentlemen, the fact cannot be denied, and no future historian will deny it: the Crown has made a revolution, it has overthrown the existing legal system, it cannot appeal to the laws it has itself so scandalously annulled. After successfully carrying out a revolution one can hang one's opponents, but one cannot convict them. They can be put out of the way as defeated enemies, but they cannot be arraigned as criminals. After a revolution or counter-revolution has been consummated the annulled laws cannot be used against the *defenders* of these laws. That would be a cowardly pretence of legality which you, gentlemen, will not sanction by your verdict.

I have already told you, gentlemen, that the Government has falsified the verdict which the people passed on the "saving action of the Crown". The people nevertheless has already decided *against* the

Crown and *for* the National Assembly. The elections to the Second Chamber are the only lawful elections because they alone were based on the law of April 8, 1848. Practically all the deputies who were for the refusal to pay taxes were re-elected to the Second Chamber, many of them even two or three times. Schneider II, my co-defendant, is himself a deputy for Cologne. Thus, the question of the National Assembly's right to vote for the refusal to pay taxes has in fact been decided already by the people.

But irrespective of this highest pronouncement, you will all agree with me, gentlemen, that in the present case no crime in the ordinary sense of the word has been committed, that no infringement of the law falling within your. jurisdiction has occurred. Under ordinary conditions the existing laws are enforced by the public authorities; whoever breaks these laws or prevents the public authorities from enforcing them is a criminal. In the present case one public authority has broken the law, another public authority, it makes no difference which, has upheld it. The struggle between two political powers lies neither within the sphere of civil law, nor within the sphere of criminal law. The question of who was in the right, the Crown or the National Assembly, is a matter for history. All the juries, all the courts of Prussia together cannot decide it. Only one power can supply the answer — history. I do not understand, therefore, how, on the basis of the *Code pénal*, we could be placed in the dock.

That this was a struggle between two powers, and only power can decide between two powers—that, gentlemen, has been declared by both the revolutionary and the counter-revolutionary press. This was proclaimed even by an organ of the Government a short time before the struggle was decided. The *Neue Preussische Zeitung*, the organ of the present Ministry, clearly realised this. A few days before the crisis it said approximately the following: It is no longer a question of right but of power, and the old monarchy by the grace of God will show that it still has this power. The *Neue Preussische Zeitung* correctly understood the situation. Power against power. Victory would decide between them. The counter-revolution carried the day but we have seen only the first act of the drama. The struggle in England lasted over twenty years. Charles I came out on top several times and ended up on the scaffold. Who, gentlemen, can guarantee to you that the present Ministry and the officials who acted and continue to act as its tools will not be convicted of high treason by this Chamber or its successors?

Gentlemen, the Public Prosecutor has tried to base his accusation on the laws of April 6 and 8. I have been compelled here to demonstrate to you that it is these laws which acquit us. But I make no secret of the fact that I have never recognised these laws and never will. They never had any validity for the deputies elected by the people, still less could they prescribe the course of the March revolution.

How did the laws of April 6 and 8 come into being? By agreement between the Government and the *United Diet*. It was an attempt to maintain continuity with the old legal system and to play down the revolution which had done away with that system. Men like Camphausen thought it important to preserve a semblance of legal continuity. And how did they preserve this semblance? By a series of obvious and absurd contradictions. Let us for a moment adopt the old legal point of view. Was not the very existence of Minister Camphausen, a *responsible Minister*, a Minister who had not climbed the ladder of officialdom, unlawful? The position of Camphausen, the *responsible Prime Minister*, was unlawful. This official, who has no *legal* existence, convenes the United Diet to have it pass laws it was not *legally* competent to pass. This inconsistent and self-contradictory playing with formalities was called legal progress, maintenance of the legal basis!

But let us leave aside the formal aspect, gentlemen. What was the United Diet? It represented old, decayed social relations. It was against these relations that the revolution was directed. And the representatives of the vanquished society are asked to endorse organic laws designed to recognise, guide and organise the revolution against this old society! What an absurd contradiction! The Diet was overthrown together with the old monarchy.

On this occasion we are directly confronted by the so-called *legal basis*. It is the more necessary for me to deal with this point since we are justly regarded as opponents of the legal basis, and since the laws of April 6 and 8 owe their existence merely to the formal recognition of the legal basis.

The Diet represented primarily big landed property. Big landed property was indeed the foundation of medieval, *feudal society*. *Modern bourgeois society, our* own society, on the other hand, is based on industry and commerce. Landed property itself has lost all its former conditions of existence, it has become dependent on commerce and industry. Agriculture, therefore, is carried on nowadays on industrial lines, and the old feudal lords have now sunk to the level of producers of cattle, wool, corn, beetroots, spirits etc., i.e. people who trade in industrial products just as any other merchant. However much they may cling to their old prejudices, they are in fact being turned into bourgeois, who manufacture as much as possible and as cheaply as possible, who buy where they can get goods at the lowest price and sell where they can obtain the highest price. The mode of living, production and income of these gentlemen therefore gives the lie to their traditional pompous notions. Landed property, as the predominant social factor, presupposes a *medieval mode of production and commerce*. The United Diet represented this medieval mode of production and commerce which had long since ceased to exist, and whose representatives, though they clung to the old privileges, likewise enjoyed and exploited the advantages of the new society. The new bourgeois society, grounded on an entirely different foundation, on a changed mode of production, was bound to seize also political power, which had to be wrenched from the hands of those who represented the interests of a declining society, a political power, whose whole structure has arisen out of entirely different material conditions of society. *Hence the revolution.* The revolution was consequently directed as much against the *absolute monarchy*, the supreme political expression of the old society, as against the *representation by estates*, which represented a social system that had been long ago destroyed by modern industry or, at most, the still presumptuous ruins of the dissolved *estates* which bourgeois society was overtaking and pushing into the background more and more every day. How then was the idea conceived to allow the United Diet, the representative of the old society, to dictate laws to the new society which asserted its rights through the revolution?

Allegedly in order to maintain the *legal basis*. But, gentlemen, what do you understand by maintaining the legal basis? The maintenance of laws belonging to a bygone social era and framed by representatives of vanished or vanishing social interests, who consequently give the force of law only to those interests which run counter to the public needs. But society is not founded upon the law; that is a legal fiction. On the contrary, the law must be founded upon society, it must express the common interests and needs of society — as distinct from the caprice of the individuals — which arise from the material mode of production prevailing at the given time. This *Code Napoléon*, which I am holding in my hand, has not created modern bourgeois society. On the contrary, bourgeois society, which emerged in the eighteenth century and developed further in the nineteenth, merely finds its legal expression in this Code. As soon as it ceases to fit the social relations, it becomes simply a bundle of paper. You cannot make the old laws the foundation of the new social development, any more than these old laws created the old social conditions.

They were engendered by the old conditions of society and must perish with them. They are bound to change with the changing conditions of life. To maintain the old laws in face of the new needs and demands of social development is essentially the same as hypocritically upholding out-of-date particular interests in face of the up-to-date general interests. *This maintenance of the legal basis* aims at asserting such particular interests as if they were the *predominant* interests when they are *no longer dominant*; it aims at imposing on society laws which have been condemned by the conditions of life in this society, by the way the members of this society earn their living, by their commerce and their material production; it aims at retaining in function legislators who are concerned only with particular interests; it seeks to misuse political power in order forcibly to place the interests of a minority above the interests of the majority. The maintenance of the legal basis is therefore in constant conflict with the existing needs, it hampers commerce and industry, it prepares the way for *social crises,* which erupt in *political revolutions.*

That is what adherence to the legal basis and the maintenance of the legal basis really mean. Relying on these phrases about the legal basis, which arise either from conscious deceit or unconscious self-deception, the United Diet was convoked, and this Diet was made to frame organic laws for the National Assembly the need for which was created by the revolution and which owed its existence to the revolution. And on the strength of these laws the National Assembly is to be judged!

The National Assembly represented modern bourgeois society as against the feudal society represented in the United Diet. It was elected by the people for the purpose of independently enacting a Constitution appropriate to the conditions of life which had come into conflict with the old political organisation and laws. It was therefore from the very beginning a sovereign, constituent assembly. The fact that it all the same stooped to entertain the point of view of the agreement was mere formal courtesy towards the Crown, mere ceremony. I need not here go into the question whether the Assembly—in opposition to the people—had the right to adopt the standpoint of agreement. It considered that a collision with the Crown should be averted by a display of goodwill on both sides.

One thing is certain, however: the laws of April 6 and 8, which were agreed with the United Diet, were formally invalid. The only material significance they have is that they state and lay down the conditions under which the National Assembly could really express the sovereign will of the people. The laws passed by the United Diet were merely a formula by which the Crown was saved the humiliation of having to proclaim: *I have been defeated!*

[*Neue Rheinische Zeitung* No. 232, February 27, 1849]

Now, gentlemen of the jury, I shall proceed to examine more closely the speech of the Public Prosecutor.[a]

He said:

"The Crown ceded part of the power which had been wholly in its hands. Even in the ordinary course of things a deed of renunciation does not go beyond what is clearly stated in the words of renunciation. But the law of April 8, 1848, neither grants the National Assembly the right to refuse to vote taxes, nor stipulates that Berlin must necessarily be the seat of the National Assembly."

Gentlemen, power lay *broken* in the hands of the Crown, and the Crown ceded power in order to save the fragments. You will remember that immediately after his accession to the throne, the King[b] formally pledged his word of honour at Königsberg and Berlin not to concede constitutional government. You will remember that when opening the United Diet in 1847 the King solemnly swore that he would not allow a scrap of paper to come between him and *his* people.[294] After the March events of 1848, in the imposed Constitution, the King proclaimed himself a *constitutional* monarch. He put this abstract, outlandish flummery, that scrap of paper, between himself and his people. Will the Public Prosecutor dare to assert that the King voluntarily contradicted in so manifest a way his own solemn declarations, that in the eyes of the whole of Europe he voluntarily committed the glaring inconsistency of permitting the agreement or the Constitution! The King made the concessions which the revolution *compelled* him to make. Neither more nor less.

The popular analogy which the Public Prosecutor has made unfortunately proves nothing. It is true that if I renounce anything, I renounce only what I have *expressly* renounced. If I made you a gift, it would indeed be impudent if, on the basis of the deed of gift, you tried to compel me to undertake further obligations. But after the March events it was the people that made the gift and the Crown which received it. Obviously, the nature of the gift must be interpreted in accordance with the intentions of the giver and not those of the receiver, i.e. in accordance with the intentions of the people and not those of the Crown.

The absolute power of the Crown was broken. The people had won the day. The two sides concluded a truce and the people was cheated. The Public Prosecutor himself has taken pains to demonstrate at some length that the people was deceived. To

---

[a] Bölling.—*Ed.*
[b] Frederick William IV.—*Ed.*

challenge the right of the National Assembly to refuse to vote taxes, the Public Prosecutor has explained to you in detail that if there was something of this kind in the law of April 6, 1848, it was certainly no longer to be found in the law of April 8, 1848. The interval of two days was thus used to deprive the representatives of the people of the rights which had been conceded to them two days earlier. Could the Public Prosecutor have more strikingly compromised the *honesty* of the Crown, could he have more irrefutably proved the *intention to deceive* the people?

The Public Prosecutor says further:

"The right to *transfer* and *prorogue* the National Assembly is a consequence of the executive power and is recognised in all constitutional countries."

As to the right of the *executive* to *transfer* the meeting place of the legislative Chambers, I challenge the Public Prosecutor to cite even a single law or example in support of his assertion. In England, for instance, according to an old historical prerogative, the King could convene Parliament wherever he pleased. There is no law stating that London is the legal seat of Parliament. As you know, gentlemen, in England the most important political freedoms are in general sanctioned not by Statute Law but by Common Law; such, for instance, is the case with freedom of the press. But should an English Ministry take it into its head to transfer Parliament from London to Windsor or Richmond, it is sufficient to put the idea into words to realise how impossible it is.

True, in countries that have a constitutional government, the Crown has the right to *prorogue* the Chambers. But it must not be forgotten that on the other hand all constitutions specify *for how long* the Chambers can be prorogued and when they have to be summoned again. Prussia had no Constitution, it was only going to be created; no legal time-limit for summoning a prorogued Chamber existed, consequently no prorogation right of the Crown existed. Otherwise the Crown could have prorogued the Chamber for ten days, for ten years, or for ever. How could one be sure that the Chambers would ever be summoned or allowed to meet for any length of time? The existence of the Chambers alongside the Crown was left to the discretion of the Crown, the legislative power—if one could speak of legislative power in this context—had become a fiction.

Gentlemen, this example shows where any attempt to compare the conflict between the Prussian Crown and the Prussian National Assembly with the conditions obtaining in constitutional countries leads to. It leads to the *maintenance of absolute monarchy*. On the one hand, the rights of a constitutional executive power are conferred upon the Crown, on the other, there is no law, no tradition, no organic institution able to impose on it the restrictions proper to a constitutional executive power. The representatives of the people are expected to play the role of a *constitutional* Chamber confronting an *absolute* monarchy!

Is there any need to explain that in the case under consideration no *executive power* confronted a *legislative power,* that the constitutional division of powers cannot be applied to the *Prussian National Assembly* and the Prussian Crown? Let us disregard the revolution and consider only the official *theory of agreement.* Even according to this theory two sovereign powers confronted each other. That is beyond any doubt. One of these two powers was bound to break the other. Two sovereign powers cannot function simultaneously, side by side, *in one state.* This is an absurdity, like the squaring of the circle. Material force had to decide the issue between the two sovereign powers. But it is not our task here to go into the question of whether agreement was possible or impossible. It is sufficient that two powers entered into relations with each other in order to conclude an agreement. Camphausen himself admitted that agreement might not be achieved. From the rostrum he pointed out to the agreers the danger that faced the country if the agreement did not come into being. The danger lay in the initial relationship of the Agreement Assembly to the Crown, and after the event an attempt is made to hold the National Assembly responsible for this danger by denying this initial relationship, by turning the Assembly into a *constitutional Chamber*! It is an attempt to overcome a difficulty by leaving it out of account.

Gentlemen, I think I have shown you that the Crown had no right either to transfer or to prorogue the Assembly of agreers.

But the Public Prosecutor did not confine himself to examining whether the Crown had the *right* to transfer the National Assembly; he has tried to prove that this transfer was *expedient.* "Would it not have been expedient," he exclaims, "if the National Assembly had obeyed the Crown and moved to Brandenburg?" According to the Public Prosecutor, the expediency of such an act was due to the position of the Chamber itself. The Chamber was not free in Berlin, and so forth.

But is it not obvious what purpose the Crown pursued in ordering this transfer? Had not the Crown itself divested all officially advanced reasons for the transfer of any semblance of veracity? It was not a question of freedom of deliberation, but of whether the Assembly should be sent home and a Constitution imposed, or whether a spurious Assembly should be created by summoning more docile representatives. When, unexpectedly, a sufficient number of deputies arrived in Brandenburg to form a quorum, the pretence was abandoned and the National Assembly was declared to be dissolved.

Incidentally, it goes without saying that the Crown had no right to declare the National Assembly either free or unfree. No one but the Assembly itself could decide whether it had the necessary freedom of deliberation or not. Nothing would be more convenient for the Crown than, whenever the National Assembly passed resolutions the Crown disliked, to declare that it was not free, that it was irresponsible, and to ban it!

The Public Prosecutor has also spoken about the Government's duty to protect the dignity of the National Assembly against the terrorism of the Berlin population.

This argument sounds like a satire on the Government. I will not speak here of its treatment of individuals, of men who, after all, were the elected representatives of the people. It sought to humiliate them in every possible way, they were persecuted in the most infamous way and a sort of wild chase[295] was organised against them. But let us leave aside individuals. How was the dignity of the National Assembly and of its *work* maintained? Its archives were given over to the soldiery who used the documents of the various departments, the royal messages, draft laws and preliminary studies, as spills to light pipes with, burned them in stoves, and trampled on them.

Not even the formalities of a legal warrant were observed; the archives were seized without even an inventory being drawn up.

It was part of the plan to destroy all this work which had cost the people so much, in order to make it easier to vilify the National Assembly and to quash the planned reforms which were abhorrent to the Government and the aristocracy. Is it not simply ridiculous to assert after all this that the Government transferred the National Assembly from Berlin to Brandenburg out of tender concern for its dignity?

Now I come to the statement of the Public Prosecutor regarding the *formal validity* of the decision to refuse payment of taxes.

The Public Prosecutor says that in order to make the decision on the refusal to pay taxes formally valid, the Assembly should have submitted it to the *Crown for sanctioning.*

But, gentlemen, the Crown in its own person did not face the Assembly, it was represented by the Brandenburg Ministry. Consequently, according to the absurd claim of the Public Prosecutor, the Assembly should have reached an agreement with the Brandenburg Ministry to proclaim that Ministry guilty of high treason and to prevent it from collecting taxes. What meaning can this demand have other than that the National Assembly should submit unconditionally to every request of the Brandenburg Ministry?

Another reason why the tax refusal decision was formally invalid, says the Public Prosecutor, was that a motion can become law only after the *second reading*.

On the one hand, when dealing with the National Assembly *essential* forms of procedure are ignored which ought to have been binding and, on the other, the National Assembly is expected to observe even the most unessential *formalities*. As simple as that! A Bill objectionable to the Crown is passed in the first reading, after which the second reading is prevented by force of arms, and the Bill remains invalid because there was no second reading. The Public Prosecutor does not take into consideration the exceptional state of affairs that obtained when, threatened with bayonets in their meeting hall, the people's representatives adopted this decision. The Government commits one arbitrary act after another. It has flagrantly violated the principal laws, the Habeas Corpus Act, and the Civic Militia Law.[296] It arbitrarily establishes an unlimited military despotism under the guise of the state of siege. It sends the people's representatives to the devil, and while on the one hand impudently infringing *all laws*, it, on the other hand, demands the most punctilious observation of even the *rules of procedure*.

Gentlemen, I do not know whether it is deliberate misrepresentation—I am far from assuming this on the part of the Public Prosecutor—or ignorance when he says:

"The National Assembly did not want any *negotiations*" and it "did not seek any negotiations".

If the people blame the Berlin National Assembly for anything, it is for its desire for negotiations. If the members of the Assembly themselves regret anything, it is their desire for an agreement. It was this desire for an agreement which gradually alienated the Assembly from the people, caused it to lose all its positions, and finally, when it was not backed by the nation, exposed it to the attacks of the Crown. When at last it wanted to assert its will it found itself alone and powerless, precisely because it had no will and had not been able to assert it at the right time. It first manifested this desire for an agreement when it renounced the revolution and sanctioned the *theory of agreement*, when it degraded itself by turning from a revolutionary National Assembly into a dubious society of agreers. It carried the weakness for negotiation to extremes when it accepted Pfuel's pseudo-recognition of Stein's army order as valid. The publication of this army order was itself a farce, since it could only be regarded as a comical echo of Wrangel's army order.[297] Nevertheless, instead of going beyond it, the Assembly snatched at the attenuated interpretation of the Pfuel Ministry, which made the order meaningless. To avoid any serious conflict with the Crown, the Assembly accepted the feeble semblance of a demonstration against the old reactionary army as a real demonstration. It hypocritically pretended seriously to regard what was no longer even a pseudo-solution of the conflict as the real solution of the conflict. As little as the Assembly wanted to fight, so eager was it for negotiations—and the Public Prosecutor describes it as pugnacious and quarrelsome.

Need I mention another symptom showing the conciliatory nature of this Chamber? You will remember, gentlemen, the agreement between the National Assembly and Pfuel about the law suspending commutations.[a] If the Assembly was unable to destroy the enemy in the army, then it was above all necessary to win a friend in the peasantry. But it refrained from attempting even this. To negotiate, to avoid a conflict with the Crown, to avoid it at any cost—that was the Assembly's chief concern, which it placed above even its own self-preservation. And this Assembly is blamed for not wanting to negotiate, not attempting to negotiate!

It still tried to negotiate when the conflict had already broken out. You know, gentlemen, the pamphlet by *Unruh*,[b] a man of the Centre. You will have seen from it that every attempt was made to avoid a clash; that deputations were sent to the Crown and were turned away; that some deputies tried to argue with the Ministers and were superciliously and arrogantly rebuffed; that the Assembly offered to make concessions and that these were derided. Even at the time when it could only be a matter of preparing for war, the Assembly still wanted to make peace. And the Public Prosecutor accuses this Assembly of not wanting to negotiate and not attempting to negotiate!

The Berlin National Assembly was obviously abandoning itself to a very great illusion and did not understand its own position and its own conditions of existence, when *before* the conflict and even *during* the conflict it believed that an amicable arrangement and negotiation with the Crown was still possible and worked towards it.

---

[a] See this volume, p. 175.—*Ed.*
[b] H. V. Unruh, *Skizzen aus Preussens neuester Geschichte*, Magdeburg, 1849.—*Ed.*

The Crown did not want and could not want any negotiation. Gentlemen of the jury, let us not deceive ourselves concerning the nature of the struggle which began in March and was later waged between the National Assembly and the Crown. It was not an ordinary conflict between a Ministry and a parliamentary opposition, it was not a conflict between men who were Ministers and men who wanted to become Ministers, it was not a struggle between two political parties in a legislative Chamber. It is quite possible that members of the National Assembly belonging to the minority or the majority believed that this was so. The decisive factor, however, is not the opinion of the agreers, but the real historical position of the National Assembly as it emerged both from the European revolution and the March revolution engendered by the latter. What took place here was not a political conflict between two parties within the framework of *one* society, but a *conflict between two societies*, a social conflict, which had assumed a political form; *it was the struggle of the old feudal bureaucratic society with modern bourgeois society*, a struggle between the society of *free competition* and the *society of the guild system*, between the society of landownership and the industrial society, between the society of faith and the society of knowledge. The *political* expression corresponding to the old society was the Crown by the grace of God, the bullying bureaucracy and the independent army. The *social* foundation corresponding to this old political power consisted of privileged aristocratic landownership with its enthralled or partially enthralled peasants, the small patriarchal or guild industries, the strictly separated social estates, the sharp contradiction between town and country and, above all, the domination of the countryside over the town. The old political power—the Crown by the grace of God, the bullying bureaucracy, the independent army—realised that its essential material basis would disappear from under its feet, as soon as any encroachment was made on the basis of the old society, privileged aristocratic landownership, the aristocracy itself, the domination of the countryside over the town, the dependent position of the rural population and the laws corresponding to these conditions of life, such as the local government regulations, the criminal law and so forth. The National Assembly made such an attempt. On the other hand, that old society realised that political power would be wrenched from its hands, as soon as the Crown, the bureaucracy and the army lost their feudal privileges. The National Assembly wanted to abolish these privileges. It is not surprising, therefore, that the army, the bureaucracy and the nobility joined forces in urging the Crown to effect a coup de main, and it is not surprising that the Crown, knowing that its own interests were closely linked with those of the old feudal bureaucratic society, allowed itself to be impelled to a coup d'état. For the *Crown represented* feudal aristocratic society, just as the *National Assembly represented* modern bourgeois society. The conditions of existence in modern bourgeois society require that the bureaucracy and the army should be reduced from being rulers of commerce and industry to their tools, and *turned* into mere organs of bourgeois intercourse. This society cannot tolerate that restrictions are placed on agriculture by feudal privileges and on industry by bureaucratic tutelage. This is contrary to free competition, the vital principle of this society. It cannot tolerate that foreign trade relations should be determined by considerations of the Court's international policies instead of by the interests of national production. It must subordinate fiscal policy to the needs of production, whereas the old state has to subordinate production to the needs of the Crown by the grace of God and the patching up of the monarchical walls, the social pillars of this Crown. Just as modern industry is indeed a leveller, so modern society must break down all legal and political barriers between town and country. Modern society still has *classes*, but no longer *social estates*. Its development lies in the struggle between these classes, but the latter stand united against the estates and their monarchy by the grace of God.

The monarchy by the grace of God, the supreme political expression, the supreme political representative of the old feudal bureaucratic society, is consequently unable to make any *sincere* concessions to modern bourgeois society. Its own instinct of self-preservation, and the society which backs it and on which it leans will constantly impel it to retract the concessions it has made, to maintain its feudal character and to risk a counter-revolution. Counter-revolution is a constantly recurrent condition of existence for the Crown after a revolution.

On the other hand, modern society, too, cannot rest until it has shattered and abolished the political power, the traditional official power, by which the old society still forcibly maintains itself. For the rule of the Crown by the grace of God is the rule of antiquated social strata.

Hence no peace is possible between these two societies. Their material interests and needs bring them into mortal combat. One side must win, the other must lose. That is the only possible negotiation between them. Hence, too, there can be no peace between the supreme political representatives of these two societies, between the Crown and the representatives of the people. Thus, the National Assembly had only the choice of either yielding to the old society or confronting the Crown as an independent power.

Gentlemen, the Public Prosecutor has described the *refusal to pay taxes* as a measure "which shakes the *foundations of society*". The refusal to pay taxes has nothing to do with the foundations of society.

Generally speaking, gentlemen, why do taxes, the granting or the refusal of taxes, play such an important role in the history of constitutionalism? The reason is very simple. Just as serfs purchased privileges from the feudal lords with ready money, so do entire nations purchase privileges from feudal monarchs. Monarchs needed money for their wars with foreign nations and especially for their struggle against the feudal lords. The more commerce and industry developed the greater grew their need for money. But the third estate, the middle classes, grew to the same extent and disposed of increasing financial resources; and in the same degree they purchased liberties from the monarchs by means of taxes. To make sure of these liberties they retained the right at definite intervals to renew the monetary obligations, i.e. the right to vote or to refuse to vote taxes. You can trace the details of this development especially well in English history.

In medieval society, therefore, taxes were the only bond between the emerging bourgeois society and the ruling feudal state, a bond which compelled the state to make concessions to bourgeois society, to allow its development and to meet its needs. In modern states this right to grant and refuse taxes has been turned by bourgeois society into a means of controlling the Government, the committee administering its general interests.

You will find therefore that *partial tax refusal* is an integral part of every constitutional mechanism. This type of tax refusal operates whenever a *budget* is rejected. The current budget is voted only for a definite period; moreover, after being prorogued the Chambers must be reconvened after a very short interval. Hence it is impossible for the Crown to make itself independent. Rejection of a budget means a definite tax *refusal* if the Ministry does not win a majority in the new Chamber or if the Crown does not nominate a Ministry in accordance with the wishes of the new Chamber. The rejection of a budget is therefore the *parliamentary form of a refusal to pay taxes*. This form could not be employed in the conflict under consideration because a Constitution did not yet exist, but had first to be created.

But a refusal to pay taxes as it has occurred here, a refusal which not only rejects a new budget but prohibits even the payment of current taxes, is by no means unprecedented. It happened very frequently in the Middle Ages. Even the old German Imperial Diet and the old feudal Diets of Brandenburg adopted decisions on refusing to pay taxes. Nor is there any lack of examples in modern constitutional states. In England in 1832 the refusal to pay taxes led to the downfall of Wellington's Ministry. And bear in mind, gentlemen, that in England it was not Parliament which decided to refuse taxes, but the people which proclaimed and carried out this decision on its own authority.[298] England, however, is the historic land of constitutionalism. Far be it from me to deny that the English revolution, which brought Charles I to the scaffold, began with refusal to pay taxes. The North American revolution, which ended with the Declaration of Independence of North America from England, started with refusal to pay taxes. The refusal to pay taxes can be the harbinger of very unpleasant events in Prussia too. It was not John Hampden, however, who brought Charles I to the scaffold, but only the latter's own obstinacy, his dependence on the feudal estates, and his presumptuous attempt to use force to suppress the urgent demands of the emerging society. The refusal to pay taxes is merely a sign of the split between the Crown and the people, merely evidence that the conflict between the Government and the people has already reached a menacing degree of tensity. It is not the cause of the split or the conflict, it is merely an expression of this fact. At the worst, it leads to the overthrow of the existing Government, the existing political system. The foundations of society are not affected by this. In the present case, moreover, the refusal to pay taxes was a means of society's self-defence against the Government, which threatened its foundations.

Finally, the Public Prosecutor accuses us of having gone further in the incriminated appeal than the National Assembly itself. He says:

"For one thing, the National Assembly did not publish its decision."

Gentlemen, am I to give a serious reply to the accusation that the decision not to pay taxes was not even published in the *Statute Book*?

Furthermore, he says that, unlike us, the National Assembly did not incite to the use of *force* and in general did not take a revolutionary stand, but wanted to remain on a legal basis.

The Public Prosecutor previously described the National Assembly as unlawful, now he considers it lawful—in each case to present us as criminals. But if the collection of taxes is declared unlawful, am I not obliged to resist by force the forcible practice of this illegality? Even from this standpoint, therefore, we were entitled to repel force by force. Incidentally, it is quite correct that the National Assembly wanted to keep to a purely legal basis, that of passive resistance. Two roads were open to it, the revolutionary road—it did not take it, those gentlemen did not want to risk their necks—or the refusal to pay taxes which did not go beyond passive resistance. It took the second road. But to give effect to the refusal to pay taxes the people had to take a revolutionary stand. The conduct of the National Assembly was by no means a criterion for the people. The National Assembly, as such, has no rights; the people has merely entrusted it with the defence of the people's rights. If the Assembly does not act in accordance with the mandate it has received, then this mandate lapses. The people then takes the stage itself and acts on its own authority. If, for example, a national assembly were to sell itself to a treacherous government, the people would have to kick them out, both the Government and the Assembly. If the Crown makes a counter-revolution, the people has the right to reply with a revolution. It does not require the sanction of a national assembly to do this. The fact that the Prussian Government is attempting to commit a treasonable act has been stated by the National Assembly itself.

Gentlemen of the jury, to sum up briefly, the Public Prosecutor cannot charge us under the laws of April 6 and 8, 1848, after these laws have been torn up by the Crown itself. These laws by themselves are not decisive, as they were arbitrarily concocted by the United Diet. The decision of the National Assembly regarding the refusal to pay taxes had the force of law both formally and materially. We went further than the National Assembly in our appeal. This was our right and our duty.

In conclusion, I repeat that only the first act of the drama is over. The struggle between the two societies, the medieval and the bourgeois society, will again be waged in political forms. As soon as the Assembly meets, the same conflicts will arise again. The *Neue Preussische Zeitung*, the organ of the Government, already prophesies—the same people have elected again, that means the Assembly will have to be dispersed a second time.

Whatever new path the new National Assembly may choose, the inevitable result will be—either *complete victory of the counter-revolution* or a *new victorious revolution.* It may be that the victory of the revolution is possible only after the counter-revolution has been completed.

Delivered on February 8, 1849   Printed according to the newspaper

First published in the *Neue Rheinische Zeitung* Nos. 231 and 232, February 25 and 27, 1849, and also in the pamphlet *Zwei politische Prozesse*, Köln, 1849, Verlag der Expedition der *Neuen Rheinischen Zeitung*

THE TAX-REFUSAL TRIAL

Cologne, February 9. If the verdict of the jury the day before yesterday in the case against our newspaper was of great importance for the press, the acquittal yesterday of Marx, Schneider and Schapper is decisive for all tax-refusal cases brought for trial in the Rhenish courts. The fact itself was quite simple and admitted of no doubt. The incriminated document states:

"The Rhenish District Committee of Democrats calls upon all democratic associations in the Rhine Province to have the following measures decided upon and carried out:

"1. Since the Prussian National Assembly itself has ruled that taxes are not to be paid, their forcible collection must be *resisted everywhere and in every way.*

"2. *In order to repulse the enemy a people's militia* must be organised everywhere....

"3. The authorities are to be asked everywhere to state publicly whether they recognise the decisions of the National Assembly and intend to carry them out. In case of refusal *committees of public safety* are to be set up.... Municipal councils opposed to the Legislative Assembly should be elected afresh by a *universal vote.*"[a]

This document is intelligible enough. Quite apart from the question whether the decision on the refusal to pay taxes is legally valid or not the document obviously presented an example of incitement to revolt and to civil war. The accused also did not conceal that the word "enemy" (see Paragraph 2) should be understood as the *internal* enemy, the armed might of the Government. Neverthe-

---

[a] See this volume, p. 41 (Marx's italics here).—*Ed.*

less the state authorities, despairing of a conviction under this article of the Code, have selected a milder indictment: the call for rebellion and resistance to the agents of state power (Article 209 et seq.).

Hence the case turned only on the political question: whether the accused were authorised by the decision of the National Assembly on the refusal to pay taxes to call in this way for resistance to the state power, to organise an armed force against that of the state, and to have government authorities removed and appointed at their discretion.

After a very brief consultation, the jury answered this question in the *affirmative*.

After this verdict, most likely *Lassalle* and *Cantador* will soon also be set free. There is no reason to expect that the Cologne board of indicting magistrates will be of a different opinion from that of the jury in the case of Marx, Schneider and Schapper.

Incidentally, tomorrow we shall return in particular to the question of Lassalle.[299] There seems to be a benevolent intention to drag out his case beyond the next assizes (in March) and thus to impose on him three more months of detention under examination. It is to be hoped, however, that the verdict of the Cologne jury will frustrate such philanthropic plans. Tomorrow we shall give some pleasant details as to how Lassalle is being treated in Düsseldorf prison.[a]

Written by Marx on February 9, 1849

First published in the *Neue Rheinische Zeitung* No. 218, February 10, 1849

Printed according to the newspaper

Published in English for the first time

---

[a] See this volume, p. 344.—*Ed.*

POLITICAl TRIAL

From Weimar Region, February 3. Under this date-line the *Frankfurter Journal* writes:

"Now at last the days are approaching when our first assize court will deliver its verdict here on the results of the impending political examinations. After the commencement of the proceedings had been continually postponed from one week to the next, now at last, according to what is being said, it is definitely fixed for the 15th of this month. The court sittings will open with the trial of the leaders of the democratic party who were arrested here and in Jena in October last year, Dr. Lafaurie, candidate Rothe, the student Amelung, Dr. Otto and the writer Jäde. These are almost the only ones of the mass of people arrested during those days against whom the Public Prosecutor could find material at all for an indictment. The examination conducted against the writer Deinhard, resident here, who was also arrested at that time, yielded so little result that after Deinhard had spent two months in the unhealthy prison cells of our criminal court, the Public Prosecutor was unable even to frame an indictment against him. Candidate Lange from Jena, who was also arrested at that time, suffered four attacks of haemorrhage in Weimar prison, and was only then taken in a half-dead state to his parents in Jena, where he died soon afterwards, on January 7 of this year, after again being interrogated for three consecutive days by the criminal court. Our jurymen, however, will be very surprised when, instead of the alleged plans for high treason, rumours of which have been so much spread and discussed, they will be presented with the simple, trifling facts on which the indictment against the above-mentioned persons is based."

(It is to be hoped that at its next victory the people will not, as in March, be so simple-minded or forgetful as to allow all their executioners to remain in their lucrative posts. On the contrary, it is fairly safe to assume that it will hasten to subject the whole gang of reactionary officials, and among them first and foremost the blood-thirsty legal hypocrites also called "judges", to six months of detention under examination in Pennsylvanian prisons,[300] and then for further reform will use them in railway and road construction.)

Written about February 9, 1849

Printed according to the newspaper

First published in the *Neue Rheinische Zeitung* No. 218, February 10, 1849

Published in English for the first time

LASSALLE

Cologne, February 10. We promised yesterday[a] to return to the question of *Lassalle*. Already for eleven weeks Lassalle has been confined in Düsseldorf prison, and only now has the investigation of simple facts which no one denies come to an end, only now is the Council Chamber reaching a decision. The case has been successfully prolonged to a point where the Council Chamber and board of indicting magistrates, by merely keeping to the maximum legal term, can drag out the case beyond the forthcoming Düsseldorf assizes and so favour the prisoner with a further three months of detention under investigation!

And what a detention under investigation that is!

It is well known that recently a deputation of various democratic associations of Cologne handed Prosecutor-General Nicolovius an address signed by several thousand citizens which requested: 1) speedier examination of the case against the Düsseldorf political prisoners, 2) decent treatment of them during their detention under investigation. Herr Nicolovius promised to take these just demands into consideration as far as possible.

From the following example, however, it can be seen how much concern is shown in Düsseldorf prison for the Prosecutor-General, the laws and the most ordinary requirements of decency.

On January 5 a prison warder went so far as to indulge in brutal treatment of Lassalle, and to cap it all he went to the prison governor and complained that Lassalle had assaulted him.

An hour later the prison governor accompanied by the examining magistrate[b] entered Lassalle's cell and, without greeting him, took

---

[a] See this volume, p. 341.—*Ed.*

[b] Ebermeier.—*Ed.*

him to task for what had occurred. Lassalle interrupted him by remarking that among educated people it was customary to offer a greeting when entering anyone's room, and that he considered himself entitled to demand this politeness from the prison governor.

This was too much for the prison governor. In a fury he advanced on Lassalle, pushed him back against the window and, gesticulating furiously, shouted at the top of his voice:

"Listen you, here you are *my* prisoner and nothing more: you have to comply with the prison rules, and if you don't like it, I shall have you thrown into a *dark cell*, and *something even worse* could happen to you!"

At this, Lassalle also lost his temper and told the prison governor that the latter had no right to punish him on the basis of the prison rules since he was in detention under investigation; that loud shouting was no use and proved nothing; and although the building was a prison, *this* was nevertheless *his* room, and if the prison governor (pointing his finger at him) came *here to him*, he had to greet him.

Now the governor completely lost his head. He rushed at Lassalle, brandished his fists at him and shouted:

"Don't point your finger at me or I shall slap you in the face with my own hand so that...."

Lassalle immediately requested the examining magistrate to bear witness to this scandalous treatment and placed himself under his protection. The examining magistrate tried to calm the prison governor, but succeeded only after the latter had several times repeated his threat to strike Lassalle.

After this edifying scene Lassalle addressed a proposal to the Public Prosecutor, von Ammon, that proceedings should be instituted against the prison governor, Herr Morret. Indeed, the violent actions of the governor constitute not only maltreatment and serious insult, but also an act exceeding his official powers.

Herr von Ammon replied that an investigation into prison officials exceeding their official powers could not be instituted without previous permission from the administrative authorities, and told Lassalle to apply to the Government. In so doing he referred to an old Cabinet Order of 1844.[301]

Article 95 of the granted so-called Constitution states:

"No previous permission from the authorities is required for instituting proceedings against public civil or military officials for violating the law by exceeding their official powers."

Article 108 of the same Charter expressly abrogates all laws that contradict this Charter. But it was in vain that Lassalle referred the Public Prosecutor to Article 95. Herr von Ammon insisted on his conflicting view regarding competence and dismissed Lassalle with the pleasant remark: "You seem to forget that you are a prisoner under investigation!"

Were we not right in saying that the so-called Constitution has been granted only against us, and not against the officials?

Thus, threats of slaps in the face, the dark cell and *corporal punishment*—for that is the "something worse" which Herr Morret was keeping in reserve—that was the "decent treatment" of political prisoners that the deputation was promised!

Incidentally, let us point out that, according to the law, prisons for investigation should be *quite separate* from penal prisons and that prisoners in the former should be under a totally different regime from that of prisoners serving a sentence. In Düsseldorf, however, there is no special prison for preliminary investigation, and prisoners under investigation, after being illegally confined in a penal prison, must in addition obey the *rules for sentenced prisoners*, can be put in a dark cell and can be subjected to corporal punishment! In order to achieve this praiseworthy aim in regard to Lassalle, the aforesaid Morret summoned a disciplinary commission which is to see that Herr Lassalle gets a share of the above-mentioned pleasant things. And the Herren examining magistrates and public prosecutors apparently accept all this quite calmly or else they hide behind conflicting views on competence!

Lassalle addressed himself to the Prosecutor-General. We, for our part, are giving publicity to the whole case in order that public opinion will support the prisoner's complaint.

We hear, incidentally, that Lassalle has at last been released from solitary confinement and is at least sharing the same prison as Cantador.

Written by Marx on February 10, 1849

First published in the *Neue Rheinische Zeitung* No. 219, February 11, 1849

Printed according to the newspaper

Published in English for the first time

WAR.— DISCORD BETWEEN THE GOVERNMENT AND THE SOUTHERN SLAVS

The *Kölnische Zeitung*, which is known to support Windischgrätz against the Magyars, today describes the reports of Magyar victories appearing in the reactionary *Breslauer Zeitung*, which is hostile to the Magyars, as "utterly ridiculous exaggerations".[a] We have printed those reports and shall, of course, await further information before going into them in greater detail. This much is certain—that the imperial troops have met unexpected obstacles on the Theiss, otherwise they would have crossed the river long ago; according to "reliable" Austrian reports, Schlick has already marched on Debreczin a dozen times, whereas he has not even crossed the Theiss!

Meanwhile, for the edification of that reliable source, Schwanbeck, we should like to present a few short news items taken from the royal imperial Augsburg newspaper,[b] on whose reliability one can surely depend. It will be remembered that for some time now we have been drawing attention to the so-called democratic group of the Austrian Slavs,[c] and also to the conflict which these fanatics were bound to become involved in with the Olmütz Government. We described Jellachich as the first and Stratimirovich as the second representative of this trend.[302] That this particular group, whose mouthpiece is the *Südslavische Zeitung* at Agram, is also gaining ground in *Croatia itself*

---

[a] *Kölnische Zeitung* No. 35 (first supplement), February 10, 1849.—*Ed.*
[b] *Allgemeine Zeitung.*—*Ed.*
[c] See this volume, pp. 235-36.—*Ed.*

is borne out by the following article taken from the Augsburg *Allgemeine Zeitung*[a]:

"As I have already reported, the machinations of the Serbian General Stratimirovich are gaining in importance as he has many followers among the Serbs and seems to exert a particular influence on the Tchaikists.[303] We do not doubt the general claim that his attempts to stir up opposition to Patriarch Rajachich do not stem from any kind of agreement with the Magyars but simply from his own ambitious aims; only how sad it is to see the Slav element, which Austria should and must cling to in the storm, being itself abandoned to the storms of egoistical factionalism! Stratimirovich is offended as he felt he had been thwarted in his hopes of succeeding to the position of voivode on the death of General Šuplikac, and he now broods on vengeance. Whether this is at the expense of the union which is so necessary amongst the people and at the expense of the well-being of his own country, does not worry him. Stratimirovich was fortunate enough to distinguish himself at the very beginning of the struggle against the Magyars with a small troop of victorious Serbs[304]; he was also fortunate enough to make himself indispensable, as it were, and in particular to achieve more at St. Thomas and the Roman ramparts[305] than did many other generals one could name with regular troops. He quickly rose from the rank of *Oberleutnant* to that of general. Assigned to the deputation which his country sent to Olmütz, he succeeded in helping to fulfil the Serbs' most cherished wishes as far as their nationality and independence were concerned, and when this was followed shortly afterwards by the sudden death of Šuplikac, who had only just recently been appointed voivode, the wish of the troops and of the country designated him as the probable successor. That is how things stand from this point of view. But in *Croatia, too,* things *do not seem as bright* as they tend to appear in the usual superficial reports. Reliable persons coming from that country assert that people are not happy about the Ban's[b] absence being prolonged and that his popularity is endangered, since the Croats see in him their Ban and *not simply the Austrian Lieutenant-Field Marshal.* Nor, apparently, is the appointment of Baron Kulmer as Minister meeting with the kind of approval in the country that had been initially expected, as he is generally considered to be a tool in the hands of the Court. The news of his appointment is said even to have given rise to a hostile demonstration during which part of the forest-land he owns in Croatia *was set on fire.* From all this, and also from the daily increasing irritation revealed in the language of the Agram newspapers, it becomes clear that one will not be able to deal with the Slavs so easily."

On the other hand, the same newspaper confirms Dembiński's arrival at Debreczin. It reports from Pest:

"General Dembiński really is in Debreczin. Members of the Hungarian House of Representatives are there also in large numbers, and by contrast the insurgents can only count 11 magnates among their number. Fortune appears to have turned its back on the rebel leader Bem in Transylvania; at least, despite his boastful reports, refugees seeking help keep arriving at the rump parliament. A decree issued by *Közlöny* of Debreczin, the Magyar *Moniteur,* states that Meszaros, the Minister of War, has resigned because of illness, and has been replaced by General Vetter."

---

[a] Here and elsewhere reports from Pest of February 1 and from Vienna of February 2 and 3, 1849, are quoted. They were published in the *Allgemeine Zeitung* No. 38, February 7, 1849.—*Ed.*

[b] The Governor or Regent, i. e. Jellachich.—*Ed.*

It contains the following on Dembiński himself:

"*Vienna*, February 3. The fanatic Magyars expect the talents of that famous Polish general, Dembiński, who is said to have been placed in supreme command of all Magyar troops, to bring them great success. Born in 1791, Dembiński came to Vienna in 1807 to attend the Engineering Academy, fled from the town secretly in 1809 and, at the age of eighteen, joined the ranks of the Fifth Polish Mounted Rifle Regiment. He fought against the Russians and so distinguished himself in the 1812 campaign at the battle of Smolensk that Napoleon promoted him to captain on the very battlefield. Too proud to enter the service of the Russians, he thereupon lived in quiet seclusion for many years, until the Polish revolution of 1830 gave him the opportunity to distinguish himself as a colonel with his cavalry brigade of 4,000 men. He managed to delay the whole Russian force of 60,000 men under Marshal Diebitsch for a whole day during the battle of Grokhov.[306]"

Written by Engels on February 10, 1849

First published in the *Neue Rheinische Zeitung* No. 219, February 11, 1849

Printed according to the newspaper

Published in English for the first time

[THE WAR IN HUNGARY]

At last official Austrian reports have again arrived from Transylvania. They confirm Bem's rapid advance to the vicinity of Hermannstadt, which was seriously threatened by him, and inform of a battle which occurred on January 21 somewhere between Hermannstadt and Mediasch (Medgyes), in which the Magyars are said to have been beaten. They are said to have been pursued as far as Stolzenburg, some of them having already taken the road to Torda (Torenburg) in the direction of Klausenburg. Five cannon and four ammunition wagons are said to have fallen into the hands of the Austrians under Puchner. The resistance put up by the Magyars is described as having been very stubborn. We shall await further reports to ascertain whether this "victory" was really so "brilliant". The Austrians give their own losses as 60-70 dead and 98 wounded.

Just how credible the Austrian reports are can be seen from the Transylvanian documents published on this occasion in the *Wiener Zeitung*.[a]

In an address to the Hermannstadt civic militia on January 19 Bem's army is described as "the Hungarian troops who have been repulsed by the victorious army in Hungary, and have had to flee to Transylvania". Puchner too, in his order of the day, boasts about huge victories in Hungary, which of course for us were long ago reduced to their true value by the news which came later.

---

[a] *Wiener Zeitung* No. 32, February 7, 1849.—*Ed.*

The Rumanians are said to have marched 25,000 men of the *Landsturm* to Hermannstadt. On the other hand, the Szeklers[307] and the Hungarians in Transylvania can hardly be relied on; Puchner, in his order of the day, and the Transylvanian papers agree that the royal imperial black-and-yellow[a] spirit cannot make any headway amongst them at all, and that they are joining the movement wherever Bem shows himself.

In Hungary itself the peasant risings in the rear of the imperial troops are beginning to assume a serious character. On January 15 the imperial troops occupied and subjugated *Gran* on the Danube, above Pest, but on January 26 they left the town again. They marched towards Ofen[b] because Windischgrätz needed them urgently after the battle at Szolnok. Immediately the royal imperial standards and eagles were torn down, Madarasz's posters[308] calling for revolt were put up, and people were heard to shout "*Eljen*[c] Kossuth". The peasants from the left bank of the Danube who had not surrendered their arms came into the town, fired on chief justice Koller, took juror Biro off to Komorn,[309] abolished the jurisdiction of the comitats, and appointed chief notary Palkovicz as president. The imperial troops sent orders for the pontoon bridge to be brought up; Simunich intended to cross the Danube at this point in order to carry out Wrbna's order to march immediately to Pest. Since, however, at the same time a letter arrived from the National Defence Committee[310] at Debreczin with the order that the *Landsturm* was to be organised, and the enemy's supplies cut off or destroyed, it was decided that the bridge should not be brought up and that the orders from Debreczin would be carried out. The comitat moved to Batorkesz, where it is protected from Komorn. Furthermore troops are said to have been sent from Ofen to Gran. This news is taken from the official *Wiener Zeitung*.

For the rest, the very fact that the Austrians have no fresh news whatsoever from the Theiss to a certain extent provides confirmation—by way of omission—of the Magyars' reports that they have been victorious. On the other hand, the *Magyar* correspondent of the *Breslauer Zeitung* again reports a number of interesting and highly probable facts. Colonel Montecuccoli of the royal imperial army is reported taken prisoner by the Magyars at Gyöngyös. Kövesd (five miles this side of Miskolcz) and Keresztúr (north of Tokaj) are said to be in the hands of the Magyars. The imperial troops sallying forth from Temesvár are said to have been almost completely annihilated

---

[a] Colours of the Austrian imperial flag.—*Ed.*
[b] The Hungarian name is Buda.—*Ed.*
[c] Long live.—*Ed.*

by the Hungarians hurriedly approaching from Szegedin. The newspaper then adds:

"Very bad blood has been caused in Ofen by the fact that the lovable poet and Catholic priest *Czuczar* has been led away in heavy irons to six years' confinement in a fortress because of an inspiring war-song he had composed. In general one notices that the military rule is becoming *much stricter* here since the most recent defeats suffered by the Austrian troops. Arrests for the most innocuous remarks are the order of the day. Any strangers coming here from Debreczin and the surrounding area are immediately taken off to police headquarters, subjected to strict interrogation, and then released with the prohibition to say a word about events. Curiosity, however, knows no restraint and people here are fairly well informed. It is believed that the Hungarian Theiss army will renew its attack on the imperial troops at Szolnok in the next few days.— The news has come from Debreczin that the Hungarian General Mór Perczel has been appointed commander in Transylvania. Bem will head the Banat army in Hungary.

"The Hungarian *regular* forces are given at 160,000, and if one considers that these forces are being led by two world-famous generals, Dembiński and Bem, and that in addition to the natural defences afforded by Transylvania and the great Theiss area, the Hungarians also have the majority of the fortresses and the most important of them under their control, then it seems more than ridiculous that warrants of arrest should be made out for Kossuth in Vienna. They must think the public is totally blind to be fooled by manoeuvres of that kind."

Meanwhile new quarrels are breaking out daily among the little nations which have been liberated from what is described as the oppression of the Mágyars—they are quarrelling either among themselves or with the Austrian Government. The *Constitutionelles Blatt aus Böhmen* says:

"A deputation of Rumanians was due to arrive at Olmütz to lodge a complaint about the encroachments of the Serbs from the Banat.— In Istria, where language and customs are pre-eminently Italian, people are most strenuously resisting the plan to incorporate this province in Croatia, and protests against it have been made and published."

In the Voivodina the Karlowitz Government has voiced support for Stratimirovich and annulled the warrant for his arrest issued by Patriarch Rajachich. The Patriarch will not have anything to do with a voivode; before the Voivodina is constituted, he says, the districts of Kikinda and Becse, of Bács and Baranya must be united with it. He says this should be aimed at and, on the other hand, the machinations and intrigues of ambitious people should be restrained, "so that the imperial army *does not treat the Serbs as it did the Magyar rebels*"![a] The *Südslavische Zeitung* is already beginning to make serious complaints, but these dreamers will, of course, only

---

[a] A quotation from Rajachich's proclamation published in the *Südslavische Zeitung* and cited by the *Constitutionelles Blatt aus Böhmen* No. 31, February 6, 1849.— *Ed.*

open their eyes when it is too late and military rule has been established in their province. Incidentally anyone can see that these differences of opinion can only be most helpful to the Magyar cause.

Here is just a sample of the way in which these Serbs wage war, and it is confirmed by two South-Slav newspapers, *Vestnik* and *Napredak,* dated January 27. Weisskirchen in the Banat wanted to surrender and sent a deputation to General Todorovich to this end. Todorovich had already heard earlier that the people of Weisskirchen had killed all the Serbs in their town, and he asked the deputation: "Who among you delegates is a Serb?" The Germans shrugged their shoulders. "Go then," said Todorovich, "I'm not going to negotiate with you." Thereupon the Serbian army stormed Weisskirchen and captured it. Only two Serbs were found in the town, and both of them had had their eyes put out. Travellers say that Todorovich then had fifty main culprits sought out and all fifty hanged. He stood the rest in a line and had every fifth person shot. Reports have it that 400 were shot in this way.

Those are the valiant heroes with whom the *Kölnische Zeitung* sympathises!

Written by Engels on February 10, 1849

First published in the *Neue Rheinische Zeitung* No. 219 (second edition), February 11, 1849

Printed according to the newspaper

Published in English for the first time

[THE DIVISION OF LABOUR
IN THE *KÖLNISCHE ZEITUNG*]

Cologne, February 10. With the best will in the world, we were unable last week to pay attention even to our best friends, our nearest neighbours. Other matters — everyone knows which — kept us busy.[311] Let us hasten now to make up for the omission and turn our gaze first of all to our neighbouring journalists.

The division of labour is carried out in the *Kölnische Zeitung* with rare team work. We shall disregard the more remote part of the newspaper, pages 3 and 4, where the noble Wolfers praises Belgium and does his best to ensure that Henry V regains the throne of his forefathers and grants a Constitution "on the Belgian model". We shall keep only to the newspaper's frontispiece, its first page. Here our friend Schücking has his own little nook in the basement where he displays for his votaries the latest products of his doctrinaire fantasy and fantastic doctrinairism in prose and verse. Who does not know the interesting "Political Conversations", in which the talented author endeavoured — as he himself says — to extricate a Mephistopheles from the pigskin of a German professor, but succeeded only in producing a Wagner?[312] Above this basement nook, on the first floor, Herr Dumont has opened his spacious political salons, in which these great men Brüggemann and Schwanbeck (not to be confused with Weissbrodt) do the honours of the house. Brüggemann is responsible for the *thinking* part, for saving principle in all catastrophes, for preserving the legal basis despite all earthquakes, for the elegiac genre, for swan-songs and requiems. Schwanbeck is responsible for the *declamatory* part, for the exalted lyricism, for moral indignation, for dithyrambs and storms. Intoxicated with enthusiasm, Schwanbeck's phraseology reaches the highest peaks of Olympus, and if its course is not always steady, it never ceases to be rhythmical and, in fact, it accounts for almost all the involuntary hexameters in which the *Kölnische Zeitung* abounds.

The first one whom we come across today is precisely this same sublime Schwanbeck. In an article, *de dato* "Cologne, February 7",[a] he enlightens us about the after-pains of absolutism and the after-pains of revolution.

The great Schwanbeck pours out all the vials of his wrath on the Prussian people because it either did not vote at all or voted in the wrong way.

"This National Assembly *should* put the finishing touch to the construction of a constitutional-monarchical state, and yet, who still doubts that some in this Assembly will undermine this construction work because they are no longer monarchists, and others because they are still absolutists and have not yet become constitutionalists, and both of them because they are just not supporters of a constitutional monarchy? From the two opposite poles storms will blow, a dead past will fight against a distant, perhaps never attainable future, and who knows whether the present will not be lost as a result!"

Note the mighty strength of the style resulting from these classic lines. Every phrase is a rugged, compressed entity, every word has the stamp of moral indignation. Picture in your mind as tangibly as possible the struggle between the "dead past" and the "distant, perhaps never attainable future". There cannot be anyone who does not seem to see how the "perhaps never attainable future" will nevertheless be attained by the "dead past", how like furies the two of them come to blows, and how, precisely because of the unattainability of the one and the dead state of the other, the present is being increasingly lost while storms blow from the opposite poles!

Do not regard this as a trifle. For if we are allowed to pronounce an opinion about such great men, we must say: if in Brüggemann the thought usually runs away with the style, in Schwanbeck, on the other hand, the style runs away with the thought.

And, in fact, who would not in virtuous indignation lose sight of the style when one finds that an Assembly to whom not only the King of Prussia but also the *Kölnische Zeitung* itself has given the mission of putting the finishing touch to the construction of a constitutional-monarchical state, that such an Assembly consists of people either too far to the Left or too far to the Right to achieve the aforesaid benevolent aim? Especially when "storms blow from the opposite poles" and "the present will be lost" for the *Kölnische Zeitung*!

---

[a] *Kölnische Zeitung* No. 33, February 8, 1849.—*Ed.*

It is bad enough for the *Kölnische Zeitung* when the people elect deputies who do not want *what* they *"should"* want according to the *Kölnische Zeitung*; but it is even worse for the people when it scoffs at the Cassandra voice of a Schwanbeck and, instead of a man of a constitutional-monarchical pattern from "the great centre of the nation", it elects people who have either ceased to be monarchists or have not yet become constitutionalists. *Tu l'as voulu, George Dandin!*[a] Schwanbeck will exclaim sadly when the terrible conflict between the dead past and the perhaps never attainable future swallows up the present!

"In other words, the signs of *reaction* and the signs of a *new* or, rather, a *permanent revolution* have not failed to appear."

After this notable discovery, Cassandra-Schwanbeck takes a look at Austria. Schwanbeck's look at Austria is always watchful. Austria is his second fatherland; here earlier, he waxed indignant at the tyranny of Viennese demagogy, here he now devours the Magyars, here the author of lofty dithyrambs is finally moved also by a tender feeling, a slight pang of conscience over those on whom martial law bestowed the mercy of gunpowder and shot! Hence the tender glance which the prophet full of foreboding casts on Austria in each of his leading articles.

"What then has changed?" (namely, in Austria). "Unrestricted bureaucracy has been replaced by unrestricted democracy, and then by unrestricted military power, and in the end everything has remained as it was!"

Sad result of the revolutions, melancholy consequence of peoples never having been willing to heed the voice of misunderstood Cassandras! "In the end everything has remained as it was!" True, Metternich's traditional government differs in many respects from the present counter-revolutionary military rule; and, in particular, the good-natured Austrian people of Metternich's time is quite different from the present revolutionary people which grinds its teeth in fury; moreover, in history the counter-revolution has always led merely to a more thoroughgoing, bloodier revolution. But what does that matter? "In the end everything has remained as it was", and despotism remains despotism.

The philistine pot-house politicians who constitute "the great centre of the German nation", to use one of Schwanbeck's expressions, these worthies who at every temporary counterblow exclaim: "What was the use of rebellion, we are again precisely

---

[a] You asked for it, George Dandin! (Molière, *George Dandin*, Act I, Scene 9).—*Ed.*

where we were before", these profound experts on history who can never see more than two paces in front of them—they will be delighted to find that the great Schwanbeck has precisely the same point of view as they have.

After this inevitable glance at Austria, Cassandra once more turns to Prussia and prepares to cast a glance into the future. The elements of reaction and the elements of revolution are duly weighed against each other. The Crown and its servants, Wrangel, martial law (with pious wishes for its abolition), and the "Prussian associations"[313] are each in turn subjected to a thorough scrutiny. Then he goes on to say:

"However, in spite of all that we must nevertheless admit that the number of our reactionaries is not a very heavy item in the balance of forces. Worse is the fact that the *great centre of the nation* has become so accustomed to absolutism that it is still quite unable to understand self-government, out of sheer *laziness*. You, who were absent from those elections in such large numbers ... you are the true supporters of absolutism! ... There is no more disgusting phenomenon in the whole world than a nation which is *too lazy for free political life*."

"Great centre of the German nation", you are unworthy of your Schwanbeck!

This "centre of the nation" which "is too lazy for free political life" is, as it later turns out, no other than the *bourgeoisie*. A painful admission, hardly made less bitter by the self-satisfaction of moral indignation about this disgraceful "indolence" of the great centre of the nation!

"But matters are still worse with the after-pains of the *revolution*. Our nation is richer than one would imagine in persons of a romantic and fantastic character, in clever demagogues" (a naive admission!) "and in thoughtless masses devoid of any trace of political education. The year 1848 had to show us for the first time what a *mass of anarchical elements* was concealed in this calm, justice-loving, sensible people, how a vague yearning for revolution took possession of it, and how the *convenient* means" (at any rate far more "convenient" than profound leading articles full of dithyrambs in the *Kölnische Zeitung*) "of revolution came to be regarded ... as a panacea."

Whereas the "centre" is too *lazy*, the periphery, the "mob", the "thoughtless masses" are too industrious. The "clever demagogues" linked with the "mass of anarchical elements", in contrast to the "laziness" and "indolence" of the bourgeoisie, are bound, of course, to evoke gloomy forebodings in the soul of a Schwanbeck!

"Such is the natural course of things: the blow gives rise to the counterblow."

With this further great achievement of thought, which is bound to serve later on as the theme for some eloquent variations, Cassandra comes to an end and draws the following conclusion:

"The right path to a truly free political life will be available only when *the great centre of the nation, the strong and intelligent bourgeoisie,* has become sufficiently united and powerful to make these deviations to the Left and the Right an impossibility. We have before us a North-German newspaper in which ... the following is written: '... the bourgeoisie has already gained the upper hand over both extremes — the Left and the Right — and the future belongs to it alone!' We fear this rejoicing is still premature; if proof of this is desired 'the elections in Prussia will provide it'."

Such is the great song of lamentation expressing the moral indignation of the newest Cassandra at the wrongness of this wicked world, which is unwilling to advance along the lines advocated by the *Kölnische Zeitung*. Such is the result of Schwanbeck's researches into the "dead past", the "distant, perhaps never attainable future", and the doubtful "present": The real, decisive struggle is being waged not between the feudal bureaucratic monarchy and the bourgeoisie, nor between the bourgeoisie and the people, it is being waged between the monarchy and the people, between the *absolutists* and the *republicans;* and the *bourgeoisie,* the *constitutionalists* are withdrawing from the field of battle.

We shall not indulge here in any further comments on whether the bourgeoisie has really withdrawn from the struggle, whether it has done this from laziness or from weakness, and what the elections in Prussia prove. It is sufficient, the *Kölnische Zeitung* admits, that in the present struggle the bourgeoisie is no longer in the forefront, that it is no longer its interests which are at stake, and that the struggle is being waged for an absolute monarchy or a republic.

And now compare that with the *Neue Rheinische Zeitung* since November of last year, and say whether we did not give an analysis in every issue and at every opportunity — on the occasion of the counter-revolution in Vienna, the counter-revolution in Berlin, and the imposed Constitution — and whether in the long article "The Bourgeoisie and the Counter-Revolution"[a], and in several articles before the primary elections, we did not explain in detail how the weakness and cowardice of the German bourgeoisie made counter-revolution possible, and how the counter-revolution, for its part, pushed the bourgeoisie aside and made inevitable a direct struggle between the relics of feudal society and the extreme pole of modern society, between the monarchy and the republic! What we, three months ago, described as historically inevitable due to the whole course of the German revolution, the *Kölnische Zeitung* presents in the form of a weak and confused conjecture, as the result of charlatan attempts to guess the contents of the ballot-box in the forthcoming elections on March 5. And this weak and confused

---

[a] See this volume, pp. 154-78.—*Ed.*

conjecture is held to be such a discovery that it is at once put forward piping hot for the indulgent public to enjoy in the shape of a turgid, pompous leading article prefaced with the sign △. Naive *Kölnerin*!

Written by Marx on February 10, 1849

First published in the *Neue Rheinische Zeitung* No. 219 (second edition), February 11, 1849

Printed according to the newspaper

Published in English for the first time

FROM THE THEATRE OF WAR

We print below the fifth report of the Galician army corps,[a] which *confirms* in part the *Magyars' reports of victory.* It is clear that Schlick suffered defeat at Tarczal and Tokaj before the Theiss, otherwise he would not have retreated as far as Boldogkőváralya, five miles from the battlefield. The description of the battle is also significantly uncertain. What is certain, however, is that Schlick *retreated* from the Theiss after being involved in heavy fighting there. The report that he later drove the Hungarians back across the Theiss is no more than a martial-law rumour.

News coming in from Transylvania is quite different from what Puchner's latest reports of victory would lead one to expect. Instead of fleeing to Thorenburg after the battle at Hermannstadt, Bem *threatened* that town *once more* on January 26. Although he had received reinforcements, Puchner was forced to withdraw all his troops and concentrate them before the town of Hermannstadt. This makes it appear as if the battle of Hermannstadt and all the later encounters were no more than a prelude and as if the really decisive battle was still to be fought. In the Bukovina also there is already fear of another invasion by Bem, who, even according to Austrian reports, has 40,000 men with him.

In the South, according to letters from Agram which have appeared in the *Constitutionelles Blatt aus Böhmen,* which is hostile to the Magyars, the town of Esseg has been stormed by the imperial

---

[a] See "Fünfter Armeebericht des F. M. Z. Schlick", *Wiener Zeitung* No. 33, February 8, 1849.—*Ed.*

troops. The Magyar garrison is meanwhile still holding out inside the fortress. The differences of opinion between Stratimirovich and Rajachich still persist.

Written by Engels on February 12, 1849

First published in the *Neue Rheinische Zeitung* No. 220, February 13, 1849

Printed according to the newspaper

Published in English for the first time

DEMOCRATIC PAN-SLAVISM[314]

[*Neue Rheinische Zeitung* No. 222, February 15, 1849]

Cologne, February 14. We have often enough pointed out that the romantic dreams which came into being after the revolutions of February and March, such as ardent fantasies about the universal fraternal union of peoples, a European federative republic, and eternal world peace, were basically nothing but screens hiding the immeasurable perplexity and inactivity of the leading spokesmen of that time. People did not see, or did not want to see, what had to be done to safeguard the revolution; they were unable or unwilling to carry out any really revolutionary measures; the narrow-mindedness of some and the counter-revolutionary intrigues of others resulted in the people getting only sentimental phrases instead of revolutionary deeds. The scoundrel Lamartine with his high-flown declarations was the classical hero of this epoch of betrayal of the people disguised by poetic floridity and rhetorical tinsel.

The peoples who have been through the revolution know how dearly they have had to pay because in their simplicity at the time they believed the loud talk and bombastic assurances. Instead of safeguards for the revolution—everywhere reactionary Chambers which undermined the revolution; instead of fulfilment of the promises given at the barricades—counter-revolution in Naples, Paris, Vienna, Berlin, the fall of Milan, and the war against Hungary; instead of the fraternal union of peoples—renewal of the Holy Alliance on the broadest basis under the patronage of England and Russia. And the very same persons who in April and May responded jubilantly to the high-flown phrases of the epoch, now only blush with shame at the thought of how at that time they allowed themselves to be deceived by idiots and rogues.

People have learned by bitter experience that the "European fraternal union of peoples" cannot be achieved by mere phrases and pious wishes, but only by profound revolutions and bloody struggles; they have learned that the question is not that of a fraternal union of all European peoples under a single republican flag, but of an alliance of the revolutionary peoples against the counter-revolutionary peoples, an alliance which comes into being not on *paper*, but only on the *battlefield*.

Throughout Western Europe these bitter but necessary experiences have completely discredited Lamartine's phrase-mongering. In the east, on the other hand, there are still sections, ostensibly democratic, revolutionary sections, which are not tired of echoing these phrases and sentimental ideas and preaching the gospel of the European fraternal union of peoples.

These sections—we leave out of account some ignorant German-speaking dreamers such as Herr A. Ruge etc.—are the *democratic pan-Slavists* of the various Slav peoples.

The programme of democratic pan-Slavism lies before us in the shape of a pamphlet: *Aufruf an die Slaven*. Von einem russischen Patrioten, Michael *Bakunin*, Mitglied des Slavencongresses [315] in Prag. Koethen, 1848.[a]

Bakunin is our friend. That will not deter us from criticising his pamphlet.

Hear how Bakunin at the very beginning of his Appeal adheres to the illusions of last March and April:

"The very first sign of life of the revolution was a cry of hate against the old oppression,[b] a cry of sympathy and love for all oppressed nationalities. The peoples ... felt at last the disgrace with which the old diplomacy had burdened mankind, and they realised that the well-being of the nations will never be ensured as long as there is a single nation anywhere in Europe living under oppression.... Away with the oppressors! was the unanimous cry; all hail to the oppressed, the Poles, the Italians and all the others! No more wars of conquest, but only the one last war fought out to the end, the good fight of the revolution for the final liberation of all peoples! Down with the artificial barriers which have been forcibly erected by congresses of despots[c] in accordance with so-called historical, geographical, commercial and strategical necessities! There should be no other frontiers[d] than those natural boundaries drawn in accordance with justice and democracy and established by the sovereign will of the peoples themselves on the basis of their national characteristics. Such is the call issued by all the peoples." Pp. 6, 7.

---

[a] *Appeal to the Slavs.* By a Russian patriot Mikhail Bakunin, member of the Slav Congress in Prague. Koethen, 1848.— *Ed.*

[b] In Bakunin's pamphlet: "gegen die alte Unterdrückungspolitik"—"against the old policy of oppression".—*Ed.*

[c] A reference to the Vienna Congress of 1814-15.—*Ed.*

[d] In Bakunin's pamphlet: "zwischen den Nationen"—"among the nations".—*Ed.*

In this passage we already find reproduced all the rapturous enthusiasm of the first months after the revolution. There is not a word about the actually existing obstacles to such a universal liberation, or about the very diverse degrees of civilisation and the consequent equally diverse political needs of the individual peoples. The word "freedom" replaces all that. There is not a word about the actual state of things, or, insofar as it does receive attention, it is described as absolutely reprehensible, arbitrarily established by "congresses of despots" and "diplomats". To this bad reality is counterposed the alleged will of the people with its categorical imperative, with the absolute demand simply for "freedom".

We have seen who proved to be the stronger. The alleged will of the people was so disgracefully deceived precisely because it trusted in such fantastic abstraction from the conditions actually prevailing.

"By its plenipotentiary power the revolution declared the despotic states dissolved; dissolved the Prussian state ... Austria ... the Turkish Empire ... and, finally, the last hope of the despots ... the Russian Empire ... and as the final goal of all—the universal federation of the European republics." P. 8.

As a matter of fact, here in the west it must strike us as peculiar that after all of these beautiful plans have come to grief at the *first* attempt to fulfil them they can still be regarded as something meritorious and great. Certainly, the unfortunate thing was precisely that although the revolution "by its own plenipotentiary power declared the despotic states dissolved", at the same time "by its own plenipotentiary power" it did not lift a finger to carry out its decree.

At that time the Slav Congress was convened. The Slav Congress adopted completely the standpoint of these illusions. Listen to this:

"With a lively sense of the common ties of history (?) and blood, we swore not to allow our fates to separate us again from one another. Pronouncing a curse on the policy of which we have so long been the victims, *we ourselves asserted* our right to complete *independence* and *vowed* that henceforth this should be *common to all the Slav peoples*. We recognised the independence of Bohemia and Moravia ... we held out our fraternal hand to the German people, to democratic Germany. In the name of those of us who live in Hungary, we offered the Magyars, the furious enemies of our race ... a fraternal alliance. Nor did we forget in our alliance for liberation those of our brothers who groan under the Turkish yoke. We solemnly condemned the treacherous policy which three times cut Poland into pieces.... All that we proclaimed, and together with the democrats of all peoples (?) we demanded freedom, equality and the brotherhood of all nations". P. 10.

Democratic pan-Slavism today still puts forward these demands:

"At that time we felt confident of our cause ... *justice* and *humanity* were wholly on our side, and nothing but illegality and barbarity on the side of our enemies. The ideas to which we devoted ourselves were *no empty figments of a dream*, they were the ideas of the *sole true and necessary policy*, the policy of *revolution*."

"Justice", "humanity", "freedom", "equality", "fraternity", "independence"—so far we have found nothing in the pan-Slavist manifesto but these more or less ethical categories, which sound very fine, it is true, but *prove absolutely nothing* in historical and political questions. "Justice", "humanity", "freedom" etc. may demand this or that a thousand times over; but if the thing is impossible it does not take place and in spite of everything remains an "empty figment of a dream". The pan-Slavists' illusions ought to have become clear to them from the role played by the mass of the Slavs after the Prague Congress. They ought to have understood that all pious wishes and beautiful dreams are of no avail against iron reality, and that their policy at any time was no more the "policy of revolution" than was that of the French Republic. Nevertheless, today, in January 1849, they still come to us with the same old phrases, in the content of which Western Europe has been disillusioned by the bloodiest counter-revolution!

Just a word about "universal fraternal union of peoples" and the drawing of "boundaries established by the sovereign will of the peoples themselves on the basis of their national characteristics". The United States and Mexico are two republics, in both of which the people is sovereign.

How did it happen that over Texas[316] a war broke out between these two republics, which, according to the *moral theory*, ought to have been "fraternally united" and "federated", and that, owing to "geographical, commercial and strategical necessities", the "sovereign will" of the American people, supported by the bravery of the American volunteers, shifted the boundaries drawn by nature some hundreds of miles further south? And will Bakunin accuse the Americans of a "war of conquest", which, although it deals a severe blow to his theory based on "justice and humanity", was nevertheless waged wholly and solely in the interest of civilisation? Or is it perhaps unfortunate that splendid California has been taken away from the lazy Mexicans, who could not do anything with it? That the energetic Yankees by rapid exploitation of the Californian gold mines will increase the means of circulation, in a few years will concentrate a dense population and extensive trade at the most suitable places on the coast of the Pacific Ocean, create large cities, open up communications by steamship, construct a railway from New York to San Francisco, for the first time really open the Pacific Ocean to civilisation, and for the third time in history give world trade a new direction? The "independence" of a few Spanish Californians and Texans may suffer because of it, in some places "justice" and other moral principles may be violated; but what does that matter compared to such facts of world-historic significance?

We would point out, incidentally, that this theory of universal fraternal union of peoples, which calls indiscriminately for fraternal union regardless of the historical situation and the stage of social development of the individual peoples, was combated by the editors of the *Neue Rheinische Zeitung* already long before the revolution, and in fact in opposition to their best friends, the English and French democrats. Proof of this is to be found in the English, French and Belgian democratic newspapers of that period.[317]

As far as pan-Slavism in particular is concerned, in the *Neue Rheinische Zeitung* No. 194[a] we showed that, apart from the well-meaning self-deceptions of the democratic pan-Slavists, it has in reality no other aim than to give the Austrian Slavs, who are split up and historically, literarily, politically, commercially and industrially dependent on the Germans and Magyars, a basis of support, in Russia on the one hand, and on the other hand in the Austrian united monarchy, which is dominated by the Slav majority and dependent on Russia. We have shown how such little nations, which for centuries have been taken in tow by history against their will, must necessarily be counter-revolutionary, and that their whole position in the revolution of 1848 was actually counter-revolutionary. In view of the democratic pan-Slavist manifesto, which demands the independence of all Slavs without distinction, we must return to this matter.

Let us note first of all that there is much excuse for the political romanticism and sentimentality of the democrats at the Slav Congress. With the exception of the Poles—the Poles are not pan-Slavists for very obvious reasons—they all belong to peoples which are either, like the Southern Slavs, necessarily counter-revolutionary owing to the whole of their historical position, or, like the Russians, are still a long way from revolution and therefore, at least for the time being, are still counter-revolutionary. These sections, democratic owing to their education acquired abroad, seek to bring their democratic views into harmony with their national feeling, which is known to be very pronounced among the Slavs; and since the real world, the actual state of things in their country, affords no basis, or only a fictitious basis for such reconciliation, there remains for them nothing but the other-worldly "airy kingdom of dreams",[b] the realm of pious wishes, the policy of fantasy. How

---

[a] See this volume, pp. 233-36.— *Ed.*
[b] Heinrich Heine, *Deutschland. Ein Wintermärchen*, Caput VII.— *Ed.*

splendid it would be if the Croats, Pandours[318] and Cossacks formed the vanguard of European democracy, if the ambassador of a republic of Siberia were to present his credentials in Paris! Certainly, such prospects would be very delightful; but, after all, even the most enthusiastic pan-Slavist will not demand that European democracy should wait for their realisation—and at present it is precisely those nations for whom the manifesto specially demands independence that are the special enemies of democracy.

We repeat: apart from the Poles, the Russians, and at most the Turkish Slavs, no Slav people has a future, for the simple reason that all the other Slavs lack the primary historical, geographical, political and industrial conditions for independence and viability.

Peoples which have never had a history of their own, which from the time when they achieved the first, most elementary stage of civilisation already came under foreign sway, or which were *forced* to attain the first stage of civilisation only by means of a foreign yoke, are not viable and will never be able to achieve any kind of independence.

And that has been the fate of the Austrian Slavs. The Czechs, among whom we would include the Moravians and Slovaks, although they differ in respect of language and history, have never had a history of their own. Bohemia has been chained to Germany since the time of Charles the Great. The Czech nation freed itself momentarily and formed the Great-Moravian state, only immediately to come under subjection again and for five hundred years to be a ball thrown from one to another by Germany, Hungary and Poland. Following that, Bohemia and Moravia passed definitely to Germany and the Slovak regions remained with Hungary. And this historically absolutely non-existent "nation" puts forward claims to independence?

The same thing holds for the Southern Slavs proper. Where is the history of the Illyrian Slovenes, the Dalmatians, Croats and Shokazians[319]? Since the eleventh century they have lost the last semblance of political independence and have been partly under German, partly under Venetian, and partly under Magyar rule. And it is desired to put together a vigorous, independent, viable nation out of these tattered remnants?

More than that. If the Austrian Slavs were a compact mass like the Poles, the Magyars and the Italians, if they were in a position to come together to form a state of 12-20 million people, then their claims would surely be more serious. But the position is just the opposite. The Germans and Magyars have pushed themselves in between them like a broad wedge to the farthest extremities of the

Carpathians, almost to the Black Sea, and have separated the Czechs, Moravians and Slovaks from the Southern Slavs by a broad band 60-80 miles[a] wide. To the north of this band are $5\,^1/_2$ million Slavs, to the south $5\,^1/_2$ million Slavs, separated by a compact mass of 10-11 million Germans and Magyars, made allies by history and necessity.

But why should not the $5\,^1/_2$ million Czechs, Moravians and Slovaks form one state, and the $5\,^1/_2$ million Southern Slavs together with the Turkish Slavs form another state?

Take a look at any good linguistic map at the distribution of the Czechs and their neighbours akin to them in language. They have thrust themselves into Germany like a wedge but on both sides they have been eaten into and pressed back by the German element. One-third of Bohemia speaks German; for every 34 Czechs in Bohemia there are 17 Germans. Yet it is precisely the Czechs who are supposed to form the core of the intended Slav state; for the Moravians, too, are considerably interspersed with Germans, and the Slovaks with Germans and Magyars and furthermore completely demoralised in a national respect. And what a Slav state that would be, in which in the final analysis the *German urban bourgeoisie would hold sway*!

The same thing applies to the Southern Slavs. The Slovenes and Croats cut off Germany and Hungary from the Adriatic Sea; but Germany and Hungary *cannot* allow themselves to be cut off from the Adriatic Sea on account of "geographical and commercial necessities", which, it is true, are no obstacle to Bakunin's fantasy, but which nevertheless do exist and are just as much vital questions for Germany and Hungary as, for example, the Baltic Sea coast from Danzig to Riga is for Poland. And where it is a question of the existence, of the free development of all the resources of big nations, such sentimental considerations as concern for a few scattered Germans or Slavs will not decide anything! This apart from the fact that these Southern Slavs are likewise everywhere mingled with German, Magyar, and Italian elements, that here too a mere glance at a linguistic map shows the planned South-Slav state torn into disconnected tatters, and that at best the whole state would be delivered into the hands of the *Italian* bourgeois of Trieste, Fiume and Zara, and the *German* bourgeois of Agram, Laibach, Karlstadt, Semlin, Pancsova and Weisskirchen!

But could not the Austrian Southern Slavs unite with the Serbs, Bosnians, Morlaks[320] and Bulgarians? Certainly they could if, besides the difficulties mentioned above, there did not exist also the age-old

---

[a] German mile equals 4.7 English miles.—*Ed.*

hatred of the Austrian frontier dwellers for the Turkish Slavs on the other side of the Sava and Unna; but these people, who for centuries have considered one another as rascals and bandits, despite all their racial kinship hate one another infinitely more than do the Slavs and Magyars.

In point of fact, the position of the Germans and Magyars would be extremely pleasant if the Austrian Slavs were assisted to get their so-called rights! An independent Bohemian-Moravian state would be wedged between Silesia and Austria; Austria and Styria would be cut off by the "South-Slav republic" from their natural *débou-ché*[a] — the Adriatic Sea and the Mediterranean; and the eastern part of Germany would be torn to pieces like a loaf of bread that has been gnawed by rats! And all that by way of thanks for the Germans having given themselves the trouble of civilising the stubborn Czechs and Slovenes, and introducing among them trade, industry, a tolerable degree of agriculture, and culture!

But it is precisely this yoke imposed on the Slavs under the pretext of civilisation that is said to constitute one of the greatest crimes of the Germans and Magyars! Just listen to this:

"Rightly do you rage, rightly do you breathe vengeance against that *damnable German policy*, which has thought of nothing but your ruin, which *has enslaved you for centuries....*" P. 5.

"...The *Magyars*, the *bitter enemies* of our race, who number hardly four millions, have presumed to seek to impose their yoke on eight million Slavs...." P. 9

"I know all that the Magyars have done to our Slav brothers, what crimes they have committed against our nationality, and how they have trampled underfoot our language and independence." P. 30.

What then are the great, dreadful crimes committed by the Germans and Magyars against the Slav nationality? We are not speaking here of the partition of Poland,[321] which is not at issue here, we are speaking of the "centuries of injustice" supposed to have been inflicted on the Slavs.

In the north, the Germans have reconquered from the Slavs the formerly German and subsequently Slav region from the Elbe to the Warthe; a conquest which was determined by the "geographical and strategical necessities" resulting from the partition of the Carolingian kingdom. These Slav areas have been fully Germanised; the thing has been done and cannot be undone, unless the pan-Slavists were to resurrect the lost Sorbian, Wendish and Obodritian languages[322] and impose them on the inhabitants of Leipzig, Berlin and Stettin. But up to now it has never been disputed that this conquest was to the advantage of civilisation.

---

[a] Outlet.—*Ed.*

In the south, the Germans found the Slav races already split up. That had been seen to by the non-Slav Avars,[323] who occupied the region later inhabited by the Magyars. The Germans exacted tribute from these Slavs and waged many wars against them. They fought also against the Avars and Magyars, from whom they took the whole territory from the Ems to the Leitha. Whereas they carried out Germanisation here by force, the Germanisation of the Slav territories proceeded much more on a peaceful basis, by immigration and by the influence of the more developed nation on the undeveloped. German industry, German trade and German culture by themselves served to introduce the German language into the country. As far as "oppression" is concerned, the Slavs were not more oppressed by the Germans than the mass of the German population itself.

As regards the Magyars, there are certainly also a large number of Germans in Hungary, but the Magyars, although numbering "hardly four millions", have never had the occasion to complain of the "damnable German policy"! And if during *eight centuries* the "eight million Slavs" have had to suffer the yoke imposed on them by the four million Magyars, that alone sufficiently proves which was the more viable and vigorous, the many Slavs or the few Magyars!

But, of course, the greatest "crime" of the Germans and Magyars is that they prevented these twelve million Slavs from becoming *Turkish*! What would have become of these scattered small nationalities, which have played such a pitiful role in history, if the Magyars and Germans had not kept them together and led them against the armies of Mohammed and Suleiman, and if their so-called oppressors had not decided the outcome of the battles which were fought for the defence of these weak nationalities! The fate of the "twelve million Slavs, Wallachians and Greeks" who have been "trampled underfoot by seven hundred thousand Osmans" (p. 8), right up to the present day, does not that speak eloquently enough?

And finally, what a "crime" it is, what a "damnable policy" that at a time when, in Europe in general, big monarchies had become a "historical necessity", the Germans and Magyars united all these small, stunted and impotent little nations into a single big state and thereby enabled them to take part in a historical development from which, left to themselves, they would have remained completely aloof! Of course, matters of this kind cannot be accomplished without many a tender national blossom being forcibly broken. But in history nothing is achieved without violence and implacable ruthlessness, and if Alexander, Caesar and Napoleon had been capable of being moved by the same sort of appeal as that which pan-Slavism now makes on behalf of its ruined clients, what would have become of history! And are the Persians, Celts and Christian Germans of less value than the Czechs, Ogulians and Serezhans [324]?

Now, however, as a result of the powerful progress of industry, trade and communications, political centralisation has become a much more urgent need than it was then, in the fifteenth and sixteenth centuries. What still has to be centralised is being centralised. And *now* the pan-Slavists come forward and demand that we should "set free" these half-Germanised Slavs, and that we should abolish a centralisation which is being forced on these Slavs by all their material interests!

In short, it turns out these "crimes" of the Germans and Magyars against the said Slavs are among the best and most praiseworthy deeds which our and the Magyar people can boast of in their history.

Moreover, as far as the Magyars are concerned, it should be specially pointed out here that, particularly since the revolution, they have acted much too submissively and weakly against the puffed-up Croats. It is notorious that Kossuth made all possible concessions to them, excepting only that their deputies were not allowed to speak the Croatian in the Diet. And this submissiveness to a nation that is counter-revolutionary by nature is the only thing with which the Magyars can be reproached.

[*Neue Rheinische Zeitung* No. 223, February 16, 1849]

Cologne, February 15. We concluded yesterday with the proof that the Austrian Slavs have never had a history of their own, that from the historical, literary, political, commercial and industrial points of view they are dependent on the Germans and Magyars, that they are already partly Germanised, Magyarised and Italianised, that if they were to establish independent states, not they, but the German and Italian bourgeoisie of their towns would rule these states, and finally, that neither Hungary nor Germany can tolerate the detachment and independent constitution of such unviable, small intercalated states.

All that, however, would still not be decisive. If at any epoch while they were oppressed the Slavs had begun a *new revolutionary history*, that by itself would have proved their viability. From that moment the revolution would have had an interest in their liberation, and the special interest of the Germans and Magyars would have given way to the greater interest of the European revolution.

Precisely that, however, never happened. The Slavs—once again we remind our readers that here we always exclude the Poles—were always the *main instruments of the counter-revolutionaries*. Oppressed at home, outside their country, wherever Slav influence extended to, they were the *oppressors of all revolutionary nations*.

Let no one object that we speak here on behalf of German national prejudices. In German, French, Belgian and English periodicals, the proofs are to be found that it was precisely the editors of the *Neue Rheinische Zeitung* who already long *before* the revolution most decisively opposed all manifestations of German national narrow-mindedness.[325] Unlike many other people, they did not castigate the Germans at random or on the basis of mere hearsay; on the contrary, they proved from history and mercilessly exposed the despicable role that Germany has certainly played in history, thanks to its nobles and burghers and thanks to its crippled industrial development; they have always recognised the superiority of the great historical nations of the west, the English and the French, compared with the backward Germans. But precisely for that reason we should be permitted not to share the fantastic illusions of the Slavs and allowed to judge other peoples as severely as we have judged our own nation.

Up to now it has always been said that the *Germans* have been the *Lanzknechte*[a] of despotism throughout Europe. We are far from denying the shameful part played by the Germans in the shameful wars against the French revolution from 1792 to 1815, and in the oppression of Italy since 1815 and of Poland since 1772; but who stood behind the Germans, who used them as their mercenaries or their vanguard? England and *Russia*. After all, up to the present day the Russians boast of having brought about the fall of Napoleon through their innumerable armies, which is at any rate largely correct. This much, at least, is certain, that of the armies which by their superior power drove back Napoleon from the Oder as far as Paris, three-quarters consisted of Slavs, Russians or Austrian Slavs.

And then, too, the Germans' oppression of the Italians and Poles! A wholly Slav power and a semi-Slav power competed in the partition of Poland; the armies which crushed Kosciuszko consisted for the most part of *Slavs*; the armies of Dibich and Paskevich were exclusively *Slav* armies. And in Italy for many years the *Tedeschi*[b] alone had the ignominy of being regarded as oppressors. But, once again, what was the composition of the armies which best let themselves be used for oppression and for whose savage acts the

---

[a] Spear-bearers.— *Ed.*
[b] Germans.—*Ed.*

Germans were blamed? Once again, they consisted of *Slavs*. Go to Italy and ask who suppressed the Milan revolution; people will no longer say: the *Tedeschi*—since the *Tedeschi* made a revolution in Vienna they are no longer hated—but: the *Croati*. That is the word which the Italians now apply to the whole Austrian army, i.e. to all that is most deeply hated by them: *i Croati!*

Nevertheless, these reproaches would be superfluous and unjustified if the Slavs had anywhere seriously participated in the movement of 1848, if they had hastened to join the ranks of the revolutionary peoples. A single courageous attempt at a democratic revolution, even if it were crushed, extinguishes in the memory of the peoples whole centuries of infamy and cowardice, and at once rehabilitates a nation, however deeply it had been despised. That was the experience of the Germans last year. But whereas the French, Germans, Italians, Poles and Magyars raised high the banner of the revolution, the *Slavs one and all* put themselves under the banner of the *counter-revolution*. In the forefront were the Southern Slavs, who had already for many years upheld their counter-revolutionary separatist aims against the Magyars; then came the Czechs, and behind them—the *Russians*, armed for battle and ready to appear on the battlefield at the decisive moment.

It is well known that in Italy the Magyar hussars went over to the Italians *en masse*, that in Hungary whole Italian battalions put themselves at the disposal of the Magyar revolutionary Government and are still fighting under the Magyar flag; it is well known that in Vienna the German regiments sided with the people and even in Galicia were by no means reliable; it is well known that masses of Austrian and non-Austrian Poles fought against the Austrian armies in Italy, in Vienna and in Hungary, and are still fighting in the Carpathians; but where has anyone ever heard of Czech or South-Slav troops revolting against the black-and-yellow flag[a]?

On the contrary, up to now it is known only that Austria, which was shaken to its foundations, has been kept alive and for the time being is once again in safety owing to the enthusiasm of the Slavs for the black-and-yellow flag; that it was precisely the Croats, Slovenes, Dalmatians, Czechs, Moravians and Ruthenians who put their contingents at the disposal of Windischgrätz and Jellachich for suppressing the revolution in Vienna, Cracow, Lemberg and Hungary; and what furthermore we have now learned from Bakunin is that the Prague *Slav Congress was dispersed* not by Germans, but by Galician, Czech and Slovak *Slavs*, and "*nothing but Slavs*"! P. 33.

---

[a] The colours of the Austrian flag.—*Ed.*

The revolution of 1848 compelled all European peoples to declare themselves for or against it. In the course of a month all the peoples ripe for revolution had made their revolution, and all those which were not ripe had allied themselves against the revolution. At that time it was a matter of disentangling the confused tangle of peoples of Eastern Europe. The question was which nation would seize the revolutionary initiative here, and which nation would develop the greatest revolutionary energy and thereby safeguard its future. The Slavs remained silent, the Germans and Magyars, faithful to their previous historical position, took the lead. As a result, the Slavs were thrown completely into the arms of the counter-revolution.

But what about the Slav Congress in Prague?

We repeat: the so-called democrats among the Austrian Slavs are either scoundrels or fantasts, and the latter, who do not find any fertile soil among their people for the ideas imported from abroad, have been continually led by the nose by the scoundrels. At the Prague Slav Congress the fantasts had the upper hand. When the fantasy seemed dangerous to the *aristocratic* pan-Slavists, Count Thun, Palacký & Co., they betrayed the fantasts to Windischgrätz and the black-and-yellow counter-revolution. What bitter, striking irony is contained in the fact that this Congress of dreamers, defended by the dreamy Prague youth, was dispersed by soldiers of their own nation, and that, as it were, a military Slav Congress was set up in opposition to the day-dreaming Slav Congress! The Austrian army which captured Prague, Vienna, Lemberg, Cracow, Milan and Budapest—that is the real, active Slav Congress!

How unfounded and vague was the fantasy at the Slav Congress is proved by its results. The bombardment of a town like Prague would have filled any other nation with inextinguishable hatred of its oppressors. But what did the Czechs do? They kissed the rod which had bloodily chastised them, they eagerly swore obedience to the flag under which their brothers had been slaughtered and their wives ravished. The street-fighting in Prague was the turning-point for the Austrian democratic pan-Slavists.[326] In return for the prospect of obtaining their pitiful "national independence", they bartered away democracy and the revolution to the Austrian united monarchy, to the "centre", "the systematic enforcement of despotism in the heart of Europe", as Bakunin himself says on p. 29. And for this cowardly, base betrayal of the revolution we shall at some time take a bloody revenge against the Slavs.

It has at last become clear to these traitors that they have nevertheless been cheated by the counter-revolution and that for the Austrian Slavs there can be no thought of either a "Slav Austria" or a "federative state of nations with equal rights", and least of all of democratic institutions. Jellachich, who is no bigger a scoundrel than most of the other democrats among the Austrian Slavs, bitterly regrets the way in which he has been exploited, and Stratimirovich, in order not to allow himself to be exploited any longer, has proclaimed an open revolt against Austria. The Slovanská-Lípa associations[327] once more everywhere oppose the Government and every day gain fresh painful experience of the trap into which they let themselves be enticed. But it is now too late; powerless in their own homeland against the Austrian soldiery, which they themselves re-organised, rejected by the Germans and Magyars whom they have betrayed, rejected by revolutionary Europe, they will have to suffer the same military despotism which they helped to impose on the Viennese and Magyars. "Submit to the Emperor so that the imperial troops do not treat you as if you were rebellious Magyars" — these words of the Patriarch Rajachich express what they have to expect in the immediate future.

How very differently have the *Poles* behaved! For the last eighty years oppressed, enslaved, plundered, they have always been on the side of the revolution and proclaimed that the revolutionisation of Poland is inseparable from the independence of Poland. In Paris, Vienna, Berlin, Italy, Hungary, the Poles shared the fighting in all the revolutions and revolutionary wars, regardless whether they were fighting against Germans, against Slavs, against Magyars, or even against *Poles*. The Poles are the only Slav nation that is free from all pan-Slavist aspirations. They have, however, very good reasons for that: they have been oppressed mainly by *their own* so-called *Slav brothers*, and among the Poles hatred of Russians takes precedence over hatred of Germans, and with full justification. But because the liberation of Poland is inseparable from the revolution, because Pole and revolutionary have become synonymous, for Poles the sympathy of all Europe and the restoration of their nation are as certain as are for the Czechs, Croats and Russians the hatred of all Europeans and a most bloody revolutionary war of the entire west against them.

The Austrian pan-Slavists ought to understand that all their desires, insofar as they can be fulfilled, have been realised in the restoration of the "Austrian united monarchy" under Russian protection. If Austria collapses, what is in store for them is the revolutionary terrorism of the Germans and Magyars, but by no means, as they imagine, the liberation of all the nations enslaved under the sceptre of Austria. They must therefore wish that Austria continues to hold together, and indeed that Galicia remains with

Austria, so that the Slavs retain a majority in the state. Here, therefore, *pan-Slavist* interests are already *directly opposed* to the restoration of *Poland*, for a Poland without Galicia, a Poland that does not extend from the Baltic to the Carpathians, is no Poland. But equally for that reason a "Slav Austria" is still a mere dream; for without the supremacy of the Germans and Magyars, without the two centres of Vienna and Budapest, Austria will once again fall apart, as its whole history up to recent months has proved. Accordingly, the realisation of pan-Slavism would have to be restricted to Russian patronage over Austria. The openly reactionary pan-Slavists were therefore quite right in holding fast to the preservation of the united monarchy; it was the only means of saving anything. The so-called democratic pan-Slavists, however, were in an acute dilemma: either renunciation of the revolution and at least a partial salvation of nationality through the united monarchy, or abandonment of nationality and salvation of the revolution by the collapse of the united monarchy. At that time the fate of the revolution in Eastern Europe depended on the position of the Czechs and Southern Slavs; we shall not forget that at the decisive moment they betrayed the revolution to Petersburg and Olmütz for the sake of their petty national hopes.

What would be said if the democratic party in Germany commenced its programme with the demand for the return of Alsace, Lorraine, and Belgium, which in every respect belongs to France, on the pretext that the majority there is Germanic? How ridiculous the German democrats would make themselves if they wanted to found a pan-Germanic German-Danish-Swedish-English-Dutch alliance for the "liberation" of all German-speaking countries! German democracy, fortunately, is above such fantasies. German students in 1817 and 1830 were peddling that kind of reactionary fantasies and today throughout Germany are being given their deserts. The German revolution only came into being, and the German nation only began to become something, when people had freed themselves completely from these futilities.

But pan-Slavism, too, is just as childish and reactionary as pan-Germanism. When one reads the history of the pan-Slavist movement of last spring in Prague, one could imagine oneself back in the period of thirty years ago: tricolour sashes, ancient costumes, ancient Slav Masses, complete restoration of the time and customs of the primeval forests; the Svornost—a complete replica of the German *Burschenschaft*, the Slav Congress—a new edition of the Wartburg Festival,[328] the same phrases, the same fantasies, the same subsequent lamentation: "We had built a stately house",[a] etc. Anyone who would like to read this famous song translated into Slav prose has only to read Bakunin's pamphlet.

Just as in the long run the most pronounced counter-revolutionary frame of mind, the most ferocious hatred of Frenchmen, and the most narrow-minded national feeling, were to be found among the members of the German *Burschenschaften*, and just as later they all became traitors to the cause for which they had pretended to be enthusiastic — in exactly the same way, only more speedily, because 1848 was a year of revolution, the democratic semblance among the democratic pan-Slavists turned into fanatical hatred of Germans and Magyars, into indirect opposition to the restoration of Poland (Lubomirski), and into direct adherence to the counter-revolution.

And if some sincere Slav democrats now call on the Austrian Slavs to join the revolution, to regard the Austrian united monarchy as their chief enemy, and indeed to be on the side of the Magyars in the interests of the revolution, they remind one of a hen which despairingly circles the edge of a pond where the young ducklings which she has hatched out now suddenly escape from her into a totally foreign element into which she cannot follow them.

But let us not harbour any illusions. Among all the pan-Slavists, nationality, i. e. imaginary common Slav nationality, *takes precedence over the revolution.* The pan-Slavists want to join the revolution on condition that they will be allowed to constitute all Slavs without exception, regardless of material necessities, into independent Slav states. If we Germans had wanted to lay down the same fantastic conditions, we would have got a long way in March! But the revolution does not allow of any conditions being imposed on it. Either one is a revolutionary and accepts the consequences of the revolution, whatever they are, or one is driven into the arms of the counter-revolution and one day finds oneself, perhaps without knowing or desiring it, arm in arm with Nicholas and Windischgrätz.

We and the Magyars should guarantee the Austrian Slavs their independence—that is what Bakunin demands, and people of the calibre of Ruge are capable of having actually made such promises to him in secret. The demand is put to us and the other revolutionary nations of Europe that the hotbeds of counter-revolution at our very door should be guaranteed an unhindered existence and the free right to conspire and take up arms against the revolution; it is demanded that we should establish a counter-revolutionary Czech

---

[a] A song by August Binzer written in 1819 on the dissolution of a student association in Jena.—*Ed.*

state in the very heart of Germany, and break the strength of the German, Polish and Magyar revolutions by interposing between them Russian outposts at the Elbe, the Carpathians and the Danube!

We have no intention of doing that. To the sentimental phrases about brotherhood which we are being offered here on behalf of the most counter-revolutionary nations of Europe, we reply that hatred of Russians was and still is the *primary revolutionary passion* among Germans; that since the revolution hatred of Czechs and Croats has been added, and that only by the most determined use of terror against these Slav peoples can we, jointly with the Poles and Magyars, safeguard the revolution. We know where the enemies of the revolution are concentrated, viz. in Russia and the Slav regions of Austria, and no fine phrases, no allusions to an undefined democratic future for these countries can deter us from treating our enemies as enemies.

And if Bakunin finally exclaims:

> "Truly, the Slav should not *lose* anything, he should *win*! Truly, he should live! And we shall live. As long as the *smallest part* of our rights is contested, as long as a *single member is cut off from our whole body*, so long will we fight *to the end*, inexorably wage a *life-and-death struggle*, until the Slavs have their place in the world, great and free and independent—

if revolutionary pan-Slavism means this passage to be taken seriously, and in its concern for the imaginary Slav nationality leaves the revolution entirely out of account, then we too know what we have to do.

Then there will be a struggle, an "inexorable life-and-death struggle", against those Slavs who betray the revolution; an annihilating fight and ruthless terror—not in the interests of Germany, but in the interests of the revolution!

Written by Engels on February 14-15, 1849   Printed according to the newspaper

First published in the *Neue Rheinische Zeitung* Nos. 222 and 223, February 15 and 16, 1849

PRUSSIAN FINANCIAL ADMINISTRATION
UNDER BODELSCHWINGH AND CO.

Cologne, February 16. Herr von Bodelschwingh, the Minister who was "dismissed" in March, is in a hurry to step back into the light from the concealment where he has meantime been: von Bodelschwingh has been elected deputy to the Second Chamber. A worthy choice by the Teltow Peasants' Association.

If the democratic press has hitherto concerned itself little with the ex-Ministers and other ex-individuals, it is now time to illuminate the former doings of this species of persons. We now refresh the memories of our readers and of the Public Prosecutor as to Herr von Bodelschwingh's conduct in office as Finance Minister.

Herr von Bodelschwingh became Finance Minister in the spring of 1842 and occupied this post until May 3, 1844.

He used to enjoy talking of his conduct in office. He had a predilection for "revelations". For instance he revealed to the commissions of the estates[329] on October 24, 1842, that "the finances in Prussia are subject to a *limited* publicity, namely, that resulting from the triennial publication of the state budget estimates in the Collected Statutes". He went on to explain the manner in which a Prussian state budget is drawn up. It is based "principally on averages calculated from the final accounts of the administration in the three years preceding the drawing up of the budget estimates".

On October 26 the same Herr von Bodelschwingh revealed further that revenue in the last seven years had risen by more than $5^1/_2$ million talers and that a further increase was to be expected (*Staats-Zeitung* Nos. 306 and 307[a]). At that time one *had no choice* but

---

[a] Here and further quotations are from the report on the sittings of the united estates committees on October 25 and 26 presided by Bodelschwingh published in the *Allgemeine Preussische Zeitung* Nos. 306 and 307, November 4 and 5, 1842.— *Ed.*

to believe the Finance Minister because the "limited publicity" surrounded Prussia's finances with an impenetrable obscurity. Now, however, one must at least doubt the truth of the assurances the Finance Minister then gave, because a number of things have recently become public about the way the finances were formerly administered.

The financial estimates published in the Collected Statutes are supposed to be based on the calculation of the average special budget estimates of the individual departments of the administration, which are produced on the basis of the *actual* revenue of the previous 3 years. If this is correct, each budget estimate in the Collected Statutes must contain the approximate average of actual revenue and expenditure over the previous years. If this is not the case, the budget estimate, according to Herr von Bodelschwingh's own statement, is *fraudulent, a fraudulent public document.*

In 1844 a budget estimate was published in the Collected Statutes (p. 96)[a] which was countersigned by Herr von Bodelschwingh. In this estimate, the sum of 57,677,194 talers concludes both the income and expenditure columns. That then must have been the amount of the average revenue and expenditure of the previous years. In fact, however, both revenue and expenditure in the years before were far higher. The Government later informed the members of the First United Diet of the final accounts of the Exchequer for 1840-46.[330] According to these the amounts are

	for revenue	for expenditure
1843	73,822,589 talers	79,102,787 talers
1842	73,876,338 "	75,269,431 "
1841	71,987,880 "	74,185,443 "
	219,686,807 talers	228,557,661 talers

So the correct average total revenue was 73,228,935 talers, and expenditure 76,185,887 talers. Herr von Bodelschwingh therefore understated both revenue and expenditure, to be specific, he failed to mention 15,551,741 talers of revenue and 18,508,693 talers of expenditure *for each year.* These sums, it is true, might have to be adjusted to some extent when precisely accounted for, insofar as the triennial averages of the special budget estimates for the individual departments of administration are not drawn up entirely anew when each budget is drawn up and may stretch back beyond 1841, indeed

---

[a] *Gesetz-Sammlung für die Königlichen Preussischen Staaten 1844*, Berlin.—*Ed.*

as far back as 1838. A significant reduction in the sums not accounted for will however not be produced as a result; for in 1840, annual revenue again amounted to 71,059,475 talers and expenditure to as much as 77,165,022 talers. We have no official figures for the years 1839 and 1838. However, since with the same financial legislation the state income in peacetime does not alter suddenly but only gradually, one can safely assume that the state revenue in 1838 and 1839 totalled at least 70 million talers.

Herr von Bodelschwingh's budget estimate is, therefore, *fraudulent* like many, probably, of those of his predecessors and of his two successors up to 1848. Herr von Bodelschwingh must have known that he was publishing something incorrect. The real condition of the state finances was not unknown to him. The divergences from the truth were so conspicuous that Bergius, a *Regierungsrat* in Breslau, and following him even Bülow-Cummerow, without being acquainted with the accounts, publicly pointed out these inaccuracies in advance. Of course, if Herr von Bodelschwingh had come out with the truth, his revelations and speeches before the commissions of the Provincial Diets would have met with a different reception. With the "limited publicity" given to Prussian finances, he was able to cut a fine figure, whereas with full publicity only disgrace and censure would have awaited him. He spoke with satisfaction of the increase of $5^1/_2$ million talers in revenue, but failed to mention that from 1840 to 1843 *expenditure* had exceeded revenue by 14,976,401 talers. Although the country had had to provide 290,746,282 talers in those 4 years, these large sums still could not cover the inordinate expenditure of 305,722,683 talers. Such an expenditure without war, without adequate representation of industrial and commercial interests abroad, without a navy, without significant financial assistance for agriculture and trades at home! Magnificent buildings for the King, favouritism in the civil service, presents to junkers and bureaucrats, and the army with its parades and reviews had cost the country enormous sums. Well, of course, Herr von Bodelschwingh was not the man to confess that. So he drew up a fraudulent budget to persuade the people that less was being taken in revenue and less spent.

The drawing-up of fraudulent budgets is and will always be a dubious undertaking. The laws of Prussia prescribe severe penalties for such misconduct by officials. The budget estimates published in the Collected Statutes are after all public documents. No one will question that. It is true Prussian Law has laid down no special penalties for civil servants drawing up fraudulent public documents. However, a decree of June 3, 1831 (von Kamptz's *Jahrbücher*, Vol. 37,

p. 407[a]) stipulates that in the case of such acts the penalties for fraud or misconduct by officials are applicable. And the findings of the Prussian courts have since then been in accordance with this. Concerning misconduct by officials, Prussian Law, Part II, Section 20, § 333[b], lays down the following:

> "Whoever wilfully contravenes the regulations of his office shall be *immediately dismissed* and furthermore sentenced, according to the nature of the misconduct and the injury caused, to an appropriate fine or imprisonment or confinement in a fortress and declared ineligible for all public offices."

Dismissal and a declaration of ineligibility for all public offices along with fine or imprisonment are then what *according to the law* awaits persons who draw up fraudulent budgets. Should Herr von Bodelschwingh not be able to clear himself of the strongest suspicion of having published a fraudulent budget, it is the *duty* of the judge to pass these sentences on him. We demand that he and the Public Prosecutor should elucidate the affair.

The fine, imprisonment or confinement in a fortress are to be decided according to the nature of the injury caused. The injury which Herr von Bodelschwingh in company with his predecessors and his successors in office has inflicted on the country is so great, is of such magnitude, as can only be inflicted on a whole people by Ministers and other persons in the highest positions. It is our intention here to establish the amount involved; at the same time we observe that we immediately encounter in this connection a further ministerial abuse of office.

The Cabinet Order of January 17, 1820 fixes the necessary *expenditure* for the Prussian state budget at 50,863,150 talers. It then goes on to say verbatim:

> "The aforementioned sum, which We have accepted as the requirement for current administration, may *in no circumstances* be increased. The heads of the individual administrative departments are personally responsible in this to Us, and the whole Ministry of State the more so, particularly as the total sum approved by Us is sufficient for the purposes indicated in the budget instructions to date."

What is meant by the "requirement of current administration" emerges quite unambiguously from the further context, in which the administration of the government debt is contrasted with "current administration". Expenditure for current administration means all

---

[a] K. A. Kamptz, *Jahrbücher für die Preussische Gesetzgebung, Rechtswissenschaft und Rechtsverwaltung*, Bd. 37, Berlin, 1831.— *Ed.*

[b] *Allgemeines Landrecht für die Preussischen Staaten*, 2. Theil, 20-sten Titel, § 333.— *Ed.*

those payments from the treasury which are not used for paying the interest on or paying off the national debt. These, as we have seen, according to the Cabinet Order of January 17, 1820, which has not been rescinded to this day, must never exceed the sum of 50,863,150 talers. The Cabinet Order is published in the Collected Statutes of 1820, and there has never been any doubt that such orders published before the declaration of constitutional monarchy had legal force in Prussia. Any excess over the legally prescribed sum therefore contravenes the law and is abuse of office by the Ministers.

The accounts for the state financial administration for 1840-46 which were conveyed to the First United Diet and the digests of the final accounts of the financial administration for 1847[a] which were submitted to the now dissolved National Assembly, provide proof that every Minister from 1840 to 1847 failed each year to comply with his obligations. Each year they spent more, substantially more, on current administration than they were legally entitled to. To put matters in a more balanced perspective, we shall now stop referring to Herr von Bodelschwingh alone, and refer instead to all the Ministers of Finance from 1840 to 1847. To be specific, they were: Count Alvensleben from 1835 to 1842, von Bodelschwingh from 1842 to 1844, Flottwell from May 3, 1844, to August 16, 1846, and von Duesberg from that time until the overthrow of the Ministry by the March revolution. All these Ministers are equally involved. A simple presentation of the facts will make it clear how the nascent prosperity of a country is ruined by a succession of corrupt senior officials.

Current expenditure, that is expenditure for the year, after deduction of the part used for the national debt, could not, as we have seen, legally amount to more than ... 50,863,150 talers.

In 1840 however expenditure was 77,165,022 talers.
From this subtract:
    for the paying off of debts . . . . . 8,579,345 ”
    allegedly transferred to the
       treasury reserves . . . . 613,457 ”

                 Total 9,192,802 talers

What is left is therefore the expendi-
    ture on current administration . . 67,972,220 talers

---

[a] "Uebersicht von der Resultaten den Finanzverwaltung im Jahre 1847" in *Vorlagen an die National-Versammlung,* [Berlin] 1848.— *Ed.*

Accordingly in that year were illegally disbursed	. . . .	17,109,070 talers
In 1841 expenditure was	74,185,443 talers	
Of which the national debt and the treasury reserves took	14,419,563 "	
Therefore for current administration .	59,765,880 talers	
Thus in excess of the legal	50,863,150 "	
		8,902,730 talers
In 1842 expenditure was	75,269,431 talers	
Of this, nothing was transferred to the treasury reserves, and the national debt took	8,684,865 "	
Current expenditure therefore remains	66,584,566 talers	
Thus in excess of the legal sum		15,721,416 talers
In 1843 expenditure was	79,102,787 talers	
The treasury reserves and the national debt took	8,261, 981 "	
Expenditure on current administration according to this amounted to .	70,840,806 talers	
Above the legal	50,863,150 "	
was spent	. . . .	19,977,656 talers
In 1844 expenditure amounted to . . .	78,243,308 talers	
Of this, deduct for the treasury reserves and for paying the interest on and paying off the debts	9,252,605 "	
So that current expenditure remained	68,990,703 talers	
In other words, in excess of the	50,863,150 "	
		18,127,553 talers
In 1845 expenditure amounted to . . .	77,903,361 talers	
Nothing is transferred to the treasury reserves, and the national debt took	7,267,082 "	
Current expenditure was therefore . .	70,636,279 talers	
That is, in excess of the legal	50,863,150 "	
		19,773,129 talers

In 1846 expenditure was	78,562,335	talers
Nothing is passed to the treasury reserves, and the national debt took	7,423,831	"

Expenditure for current administration remained	71,138,504	talers
Therefore in excess of the legal . .	50,863,150	"

20,275,354 talers

In 1847 expenditure amounted to . . .	80,392,730	talers
From this deduct	6,207,650	"
expended on social relief and	7,209,192	"
for the national debt, a total of . . .	13,416,842	"

There remains therefore expenditure on current administration	66,975,888	talers
Thus in excess of the legal . .	50,863,150	"

16,112,738 talers

Total	135,999,646	talers

Almost **one hundred and thirty-six million talers** have been **illegally** squandered in the last 8 years under the administration of Ministers Alvensleben, Bodelschwingh, Flottwell and Duesberg out of the state coffers, that is out of the people's purse, the earnings of the poor! And these people are walking about with their stars and their medals, and, as in the case of Flottwell, still hold high offices of state! The daily press recently aired the case of an official in the judiciary — thought to be a democrat — who was imprisoned because he was accused of having parted improperly with 50 talers. 50 talers and 136 million!

It may be that the sum fixed in 1820 no longer corresponded to the needs of the state in more recent times. But then the Government ought to have come forward openly and *legally* announce new budget estimates. But it did not wish, it did not dare to do so. It did not wish to because of its absolutist hankerings, it did not dare to because it was afraid to lay bare the administration of finances. Reviews with Queen Victoria, christenings, weddings, churches, the Bishopric of Jerusalem, the old, half-forgotten papers of Frederick II,[331] knights' castles, helmets, Guards lieutenants, junkers, priests and bureaucrats etc., etc., what role these plagues of the people have played and still play in the finances of Prussia is not for the people to know. So the *Prussian* management was continued in secret, and Ministers became criminals even in the eyes of the law in force. They have not, of course, found a judge yet.

The manner in which the management of the Prussian finances under Frederick William IV is exhausting the state coffers emerges from the following analysis.

1840.	Carried over from previous years	16,949,157 talers
	Revenue for current year	71,059,475 "
		Total 88,008,632 talers
	From this deduct expenditure for current year	77,165,022 "
	Balance in hand	10,843,610 talers
1841.	Carried over from previous years	10,843,610 talers
	Revenue for current year	71,987,880 "
		Total 82,831,490 talers
	From this deduct expenditure for current year at	74,185,443 "
	Balance in hand	8,646,047 talers

(The budget drawn up by Alvensleben in the Collected Statutes is balanced with 55,867,000 talers for revenue and expenditure!)

1842.	Carried over from previous years	8,646,047 talers
	Revenue for current year	73,876,338 "
		Total 82,522,385 talers
	Expenditure for current year	.75,269,431 "
	Balance in hand	7,252,954 talers
1843.	Carried over from previous years	7,252,954 talers
	Revenue for current year	73,822,589 "
		Total 81,075,543 talers
	Expenditure for current year	79,102,787 "
	Balance in hand	1,972,756 talers

1844. Carried over from previous years . . . .   1,972,756 talers
Revenue for current year   75,976,613   "

                                                    Total   77,949,369 talers

Expenditure for current year   78,243,308   "

Deficit . . . .   293,939 talers

1845. Revenue for current year . . . .   77,025,034 talers
Deduct from this deficit from 1844   293,939   "

Leaving . . . .   76,731,095 talers
Expenditure for current year . . . . , .   77,903,361   "

Thus deficit . . . .   1,172,266 talers

1846. Revenue for current year . . . .   75,721,698 talers
Deduct from this deficit from 1845   1,172,266   "

                                                    Leaves   74,549,432 talers
Expenditure for current year   78,562,335   "

Thus deficit . . . .   4,012,903 talers
(The First United Diet is convened by the Royal Decree
of February 3. It does not however vote any credits.)

1847. Revenue for current year . . . . · . . .   79,518,543 talers
Deduct from this deficit from 1846   4,012,903   "

                                                    Leaves   75,505,640 talers
Expenditure for current year amounts to   80,392,730   "

Thus deficit . . . .   4,887,090 talers

In order to meet the most necessary expenditure, 4,000,000 talers are *drawn from the treasury reserves,* by which means revenue is raised to 83,518,543 talers. So *the old administration began the year 1848 with a deficit in the treasury,* and *with the depletion of the treasury reserves.* The balance in the current account was reduced over the 8 years 1840-47 from 16,949,157 talers to a deficit of 4,887,090, that is by 21,836,247 talers.

Revenue in the 8 years amounted to . . .   598,988,170 talers
Expenditure   620,824,417   "

A deficit therefore of exactly the
    sum just calculated . . . .   21,836,247 talers

No denials can undo this reduction in the reserves, even though the Government seeks to conceal it by carrying over balances of revenue and expenditure from one year to another, in fact in such a way that an apparent credit balance is still shown in the accounts when there is already a deficit. Thus in "peacetime", when "calm" and "order" prevailed, the Prussian finances were ruined by the Prussian Government. When the movements of 1848 came and the money-market suffered, the state was not able to support the private sector but at this time of depression was forced to demand new sacrifices to ensure its survival. The Herren bourgeois have the Prussian ex-Ministers and their aiders and abettors to thank for that. If the latter had not violated the law when in office, there would have been 136 million talers ready cash available instead of the deficit, and credit could then have been maintained. That is the injury caused, to which § 333 of the Prussian criminal law refers.

Deficit in the treasury—and just look at the revenue! Every year we have noted a revenue from over 71 to approximately 80 million. But that is only the *net* revenue, that is the surplus from the various administrative departments after *deduction of administrative costs*. In taxation, customs, the post-office, forestry etc., all the salaries, office expenses etc. concerning these departments of the administration have been subtracted in advance, and only the remaining balance is entered as revenue. And yet the country has had to pay for the salaries and office expenses for tax, forestry, postal officials etc., as well as the gratuities and presents to the *Oberpräsidenten* and commanding generals. These administrative expenses deducted in advance are estimated at 20,887,541 talers in the budget estimates for 1847. If we add this, annual revenue amounted to between 90 and 100 million and annual expenditure was actually over 100 million talers. The people produced sums of this order—and an empty treasury is the result!

The Cabinet Order of January 17, 1820, contained, as we have seen, an instruction concerning how Ministers should conduct their official business. Herr von Bodelschwingh has acted, we cannot assume otherwise, knowingly and wilfully in defiance of this instruction. He therefore again incurs the penalty of the above-mentioned § 333, Section 20, Part II of Prussian Law. The law passes sentence upon him of *dismissal, a fine or confinement in a fortress* and *ineligibility for all public offices*. Since the injury he has inflicted upon the country is of the greatest magnitude, the severest sentence of imprisonment permitted by the law must be applied to him.

The ex-Ministers von Alvensleben, Flottwell and von Duesberg find themselves in exactly the same situation.

The civil laws themselves stipulate that these ex-ministerial gentlemen are obliged to compensate the country for the injury inflicted on it, in other words the illegally disbursed 136 million talers. In this case Prussian Law, § 341, Section 20, Part II, decrees:

"Whenever an official cannot make good the injury done to the state or to any third person by deliberate dereliction of duty, he shall, *after serving his sentence, be detained for labour in a public institution* until such time as the injury has by one means or another been made good."

And one more trifle! As administrative surpluses the following sums were transferred to the treasury reserves:

From	the	administration	of	1840	. . . . .	613,457	talers
"	"	"	"	1841	. . . . .	2,837,000	"
"	"	"	"	1843	. . . . .	1,000,000	"
"	"	"	"	1844	. . . . .	2,000,002	"

Together   6,450,459 talers

According to accounts relating to the treasury reserves, however, since July 1, 1840, only 6,423,332 talers[a] from administrative savings were transferred to the treasury. In the Government's current account, therefore, 27,127 talers[b] more were entered as *transferred to the treasury* than *the latter received*. Herr von Alvensleben, Herr von Bodelschwingh, Herr Flottwell and Herr von Duesberg, what has become of the 27,127 talers? They were surely not embezzled, by any chance, were they?

Will a Public Prosecutor and a bench of judges be found for these ex-ministerial gentlemen? Meanwhile Herr von Bodelschwingh is a member of the Second Chamber!

Written by Marx on February 16, 1849

Printed according to the newspaper

First published in the *Neue Rheinische Zeitung* No. 224, February 17, 1849

Published in English for the first time

---

[a] "Denkschrift über die Verwaltung des Staatsschatzes für die Zeit von 1840 bis 1846" in *Der Erste Vereinigte Landtag in Berlin 1847*, 1. Theil.— *Ed.*

[b] In the *Neue Rheinische Zeitung:* "17, 127 talers"; in the article "Further Contribution on the Old-Prussian Financial Administration" it was corrected as a misprint (see this volume, p. 418).— *Ed.*

STEIN

Cologne, February 16. The Breslau *"Association for Law and Order"* (an association "with God for King and Fatherland"[332]) has addressed an open letter to Dr. Julius Stein which states, *inter alia*, that the *Neue Rheinische Zeitung* let itself be deceived just as much as the worthy philistines of Breslau by the conservative speeches of Herr Stein and "considered him lost for the cause of democracy".

We like definite positions. We have never flirted with a parliamentary party. The party *we* represent, the party of the people, exists in Germany as yet only in an elementary form. But where it is a matter of a struggle against the *existing Government*, we ally ourselves even with our enemies. We accept as a fact the official Prussian opposition as it has arisen out of the hitherto pitiful conditions of German culture, and therefore, during the electoral struggle, we put *our* own views into the background.[a] Now, *after* the elections, we are again asserting our old ruthless point of view in relation not only to the Government, but also to the official opposition.

The "Association for Law and Order" is mistaken. We do not consider Herren Stein, Waldeck and Co. as "lost for the cause of democracy". We have always congratulated democracy on not being represented by people like Stein, Waldeck and Co.

In one of our first issues we stated that the extreme Left of the Berlin Agreement Assembly, with the exception of three or four persons, would form the extreme Right in a Convention.[b] We never included Stein and Waldeck among these three or four persons.

---

[a] See this volume, p. 514.— *Ed.*

[b] "Die Sitzung der Nationalversammlung vom 7. und 8. August", published in the *Neue Rheinische Zeitung* No. 74, August 13, 1848.— *Ed.*

As for Herr Stein himself, we recall the time when he attacked the republicans on fanatically constitutional grounds, when in the *Schlesische Zeitung* he roundly *denounced* the representatives of the working class and *had them denounced* by a schoolteacher whose ideas were akin to his own and who is now a member of the "Association for Law and Order".

Just as pitiful as the Agreement Assembly itself was the so-called democratic group of this Assembly. It could be foreseen that these gentlemen, in order to be re-elected, would now recognise the imposed Constitution. It is characteristic of the standpoint of these gentlemen that *after* the elections they are disavowing in the democratic clubs what *before* the elections they assented to at meetings of the electors. This petty, crafty liberal slyness was never the diplomacy of revolutionaries.

Written on February 16, 1849

First published in the *Neue Rheinische Zeitung* No. 225, February 18, 1849

Printed according to the newspaper

Published in English for the first time

THREE STARS VERSUS TRIANGLE

Cologne, February 16. A few days ago we offered condolences to the leading article of the *Kölnische Zeitung* signed Δ which saw in the elections to the Second Chamber (see No. 33 of the *Kölnische Zeitung*) the defeat of the *"great Centre"* of the German nation and discerned two Chambers, one of which would not yet be constitutional, the other not yet monarchical.[a]

"Storms will blow from opposite poles, a dead past will fight against a distant, perhaps never attainable future."

And what will become of the "*Centre* of the German nation"? Thus wailed *Schwanbeck*.

Brüggemann, of the three stars, is storming from the "opposite pole" against his friend in today's issue of the same *Kölnische Zeitung*.[b]

No Centre, says the man of the "legal basis", the merry gentleman who, with solemn pedantry, invariably raises the *status quo* to an immortal *principle*; *no Centre*, that is the joke of it. No Centre, that is *no cowardice, no indecision, no hollow ambition!* No Centre, that is the doctrine of it! The Centre will in future dissolve into a "*true*" Left and a "*true*" Right! That is the true meaning of it.

Thus Brüggemann, the "true" man of "*true*" decision.

In other words: Brüggemann shifts from *the Centre* to *the Right*: the "parliamentary correspondence" has brought him to parleying. We tremble for the Right.

---

[a] See this volume, pp. 354-59.— *Ed.*

[b] Reference is to the leading article "Kein Zentrum" signed *** in the *Kölnische Zeitung* No. 40, February 16, 1849.— *Ed.*

But let the melancholy $\triangle$, dying of too much thinking in the night, argue with the merry three stars. *Ça ne nous regarde pas!*[a]

Written by Marx on February 16, 1849

First published in the *Neue Rheinische Zeitung* No. 225, February 18, 1849

Printed according to the newspaper

Published in English for the first time

---

[a] That does not concern us.—*Ed.*

THE VIENNA CORRESPONDENT
OF THE *KÖLNISCHE ZEITUNG*

Cologne, February 17. One riddle less in world history! Herr Schwanbeck, editor of the *Kölnische Zeitung* who writes under the sign△, and at the same time writes reports for that paper from *Vienna* under the sign♀♀, has, as is well known, continued as long as possible under both trade marks to slander the Magyars, accusing them of cowardice and villainy, and has not merely defeated but repeatedly annihilated them, and acclaimed in dithyrambs the entry of the combined army with its courts martial into the various towns and comitats of Hungary.

Herr Schwanbeck himself now solves the riddle; like Achilles, only our Schwanbeck himself can heal the wounds he has caused.

And what is the solution of the riddle?—It is *fear of Welden.* Hence the vilification of the Viennese and Magyars, the miserable lies about the military successes of the Austrians, the crawling and ogling in relation to the Croats and Pandours.[333]

For, says the famous Schwanbeck, for, he says:

"Up to now, in fact, anyone who dared to doubt the victorious advance of the imperial army at *all* points of the monarchy was formally belied by Governor Baron Welden and awarded the honorary title of *malicious scoundrel*" (*Kölnische Zeitung* No. 40).[a]

Out of respect for Welden, readers of the *Kölnische Zeitung* have for two months had to be lied to and deceived by the Vienna reports about the war in Hungary under the sign of♀♀.

---

[a] Published on February 16, 1849.—*Ed.*

Goethe said of *Pustkuchen*:

"If even whales have lice, then I must have mine too." [a]

Kossuth can say the same of *Schwanbeck*.

Written by Engels on February 17, 1849

First published in the *Neue Rheinische Zeitung* No. 225, February 18, 1849

Printed according to the newspaper

Published in English for the first time

---

[a] Goethe, "Zahme Xenien" V.— *Ed.*

SAEDT

Cologne, February 17. Every little market town has its *esprit fort*[a]; the Cologne prosecuting magistrates have theirs too. The *esprit fort* of the Cologne prosecuting magistrates is a certain *Saedt, homo novus atque ignotus*[b] (which being translated means profound thinker).

There are two kinds of audacity: the audacity of superiority and the audacity of intellectual poverty which derives its strength from its official position, from being conscious of fighting with privileged weapons etc. Which of the two kinds the *esprit fort* of the Cologne prosecuting magistrates showed yesterday afternoon in expounding his case against Kinkel,[334] the public themselves will decide when the minutes of the court proceedings are available to them. At the same time they will take into consideration that Herr Saedt is still young.

However, it would not be in accordance with our journalistic function if we were any longer to withhold from the European public *one* utterance of our *esprit fort*. We know that the Demosthenes of the Cologne prosecuting magistrates tried by means of a subsequent interpretation to make amends for the passage we shall cite. But we have too much respect for the original inspiration of the ebullient genius to allow us to depreciate it by the enfeebling commentary arising from subsequent reflection.

Herr *Saedt*, deputy Public Prosecutor, said:

In German: "Sie dürfen alles, was ich sage, widerlegen, aber Sie dürfen meinen Vortrag nicht kritisieren."

---

[a] Wit.—*Ed.*
[b] A man new and unknown.—*Ed.*

In French: M. *Saedt*, substitut du procureur du roi, s'adressant à l'accusé:

"Libre à vous de réfuter tout ce que je viens de dire, mais il ne vous appartient pas de critiquer le réquisitoire d'un substitut du procureur du roi." (Avis[a] à la *Réforme*, à la *République* et à la *Révolution*.)

In English: The Queen's Counsel, Mr. *Saedt*, to the defendant:

"You may refute all I say, but you have no right to criticise my speech" (N. B. Our English contemporaries, principally the *Northern Star*, are requested to publish the above).

In Italian: Sig. *Saedt*, accusatore publico, replicò:

"Dite quanto volete in rifutazione di questo che ho detto, ma vi è difeso di criticare il mio requisitorio." (Avviso[a] all' *Alba*, al *Contemporaneo* ed alla *Concordia*.)

In Spanish: El fiscal, Sennor *Saedt*, dijo, hablando al acusado:

"Sennor, Vmd puede refutar todo que ho dicho; pero el que vengo de decir por requisitorio, es defendido de tocarlo." (Pregamos los jornales radicales de Madrid de publicar esas lineas.[b])

In Danish: "De kunne gjensige alt hvad jeg siger, men De have intet Ret at kritisere mit Requisitoire (Angreb)." (De danske demokratiske Tidender ville vaere meget glaedt at meddele det danske Publikum den foregaaende Bewiis af de preussiske Magistraters Sandhed.[c])

Let Herr Saedt decide for himself in which language his utterance sounds most amusing.

Written by Engels on February 17, 1849

First published in the *Neue Rheinische Zeitung* No. 225, February 18, 1849

Printed according to the newspaper

Published in English for the first time

---

[a] For consideration.—*Ed.*

[b] We request the radical newspapers in Madrid to reprint these lines.—*Ed.*

[c] The Danish democratic newspapers will gladly inform the Danish public of the above statement which testifies to the truthfulness of the Prussian judiciary officials.—*Ed.*

THE *KÖLNISCHE ZEITUNG*
ON THE MAGYAR STRUGGLE

Cologne, February 17.

> "I have now the basis found
> Wherein my anchor holds for ever"

—sings the brave Schwanbeck from the Protestant hymn-book. The indignant champion of virtue, despite the "Austrian Note" and the "feeling of deepest indignation",[a] finally comes forward in support of Windischgrätz on the *front page* of the *Kölnische Zeitung*.[b] Listen to this:

> "The so-called democratic press in Germany has sided with the Magyars in the Austro-Hungarian conflict.... Certainly strange enough! The German democrats siding with that aristocratic caste, for which, in spite of the nineteenth century, its own nation has never ceased to be *misera contribuens plebs*[c]; the German democrats siding with the most arrogant oppressors of the people!"

We do not quite remember whether we have already drawn the attention of the public to one peculiar characteristic of the brave Schwanbeck, namely, that he is accustomed to give only conclusions without any premises. The passage quoted above is just such a conclusion, the premise of which has never seen the light of day.

But even if the Magyars were an "aristocratic caste" of the "most arrogant oppressors of the people", what does that prove? Does it make Windischgrätz, the murderer of Robert Blum, the slightest bit

---

[a] Quoted from the leading article "Die österreichische Note vom 4. Februar" published in the *Kölnische Zeitung* No. 37, February 13, 1849.—*Ed.*

[b] In the leading article "Der ungarische Krieg" published in the *Kölnische Zeitung* No. 41, February 17, 1849.— *Ed.*

[c] Poor tax-paying plebeians.— *Ed.*

better? Do the knights of the "united monarchy", the special enemies of Germany and friends of Schwanbeck—Windischgrätz, Jellachich, Schlick and their like—want perhaps to *suppress* the "aristocratic caste" and introduce freedom of peasant landowner-ship? Are the Croats and Czechs perhaps fighting for Rhenish par-cellation of the land and the *Code Napoléon?*

In 1830, when the Poles rose against Russia, was it then a question whether merely an "aristocratic caste" was at their head?[335] At that time it was in the first place a question of driving out the foreigners. The whole of Europe sympathised with the "aristocratic caste", which certainly started the movement; for the Polish republic of the nobility was at any rate a huge advance compared with Russian despotism. And was not the French suffrage of 1830, which was the monopoly of 250,000 voters, in point of fact just as great a political enslavement of the *misera contribuens plebs* as the rule of the Polish nobility?

Let us suppose that the March revolution in Hungary was purely a revolution of the nobility. Does that give the Austrian "united" monarchy the right to oppress the Hungarian nobility, and thereby also the Hungarian peasants, in the way it oppressed the Galician nobility and, *through the latter*, the Galician peasants as well (cf. the Proceedings of the Lemberg Provincial Diet of 1818)? But the great Schwanbeck, of course, is not obliged to know that the greater part of the Hungarian nobility, just like the greater part of the Polish nobility, consists of mere proletarians, whose aristocratic privileges are confined to the fact that they cannot be subjected to corporal punishment.

The great Schwanbeck, of course, is even less obliged to know that Hungary is the only country in which since the March revolution feudal burdens on the peasants have legally and in fact totally ceased to exist. The great Schwanbeck declares the Magyars to be an "aristocratic caste", "most arrogant oppressors of the people", "aristocrats"—and this same great Schwanbeck does not know, or does not want to know, that the Magyar *magnates*, the Esterházys etc., deserted at the very beginning of the war and came to Olmütz to pay homage, and that it is precisely the "aristocratic" officers of the Magyar army who from the beginning of the struggle until now have every day carried out a fresh betrayal of their national cause! Otherwise, how is it that today the majority of the Chamber of Deputies is still with Kossuth in Debreczin, whereas only eleven magnates are to be found there?[336]

This is the Schwanbeck of the *front* page, the Schwanbeck of the dithyrambs in the leading article. But the Schwanbeck of the third page, the man who stormed Leopoldstadt[a] six times, captured Eszék four times, and several times crossed the Theiss, Schwanbeck the strategist had after all to have his revenge.

"But then the war took a lamentable, truly pitiable course. Continually, almost without a struggle, the Magyars abandoned all their positions; without any resistance they evacuated even their fortified royal city, and faced with Jellachich's Croats retreated beyond the Theiss."

"Almost without a struggle"—i.e. after they *had held back* the Austrians for *two whole months* between the Leitha and the Theiss— they retreated "almost without a struggle". Gallant Schwanbeck, who judges the greatness of a general not by the *material* results he achieves but by how many men he has allowed to be killed!

"Without any resistance, they evacuated their fortified royal city"! But one should know that *Ofen* is indeed fortified on the western side, but not on the eastern side. The Danube was ice-bound, so the Austrians could march across it with cavalry and carts, occupy Pest and from there bombard defenceless Ofen.

If Deutz had not been fortified and the Rhine had been frozen over and if, in view of that, a French army had marched across the Rhine in the neighbourhood of Wesseling and Worringen, and at Deutz had trained 100 cannon on Cologne, then gallant Schwanbeck would surely have advised Colonel Engels to defend Cologne to the last man. Brave Schwanbeck!

The Magyars, "faced with Jellachich's Croats retreated beyond the Theiss". And will the great Schwanbeck deny that these "Croats" totalled 250,000-300,000 men, including the corps of Windischgrätz, Jellachich, Götz, Csorich, Simunich, Nugent, Todorovich, Puchner etc., etc., and the irregular troops at the River Drava and in the Banat? And all those are "Jellachich's Croats"? Incidentally, that a Schwanbeck, himself a kinsman of the Croats and not much in his element in history and geography, should be enthusiastic about the Croats is easy to understand.

But of course: "... we, too, are far from regarding the official reports from the Austrian army headquarters as *gospel truth*." On the contrary, Schwanbeck at times finds in reports, for example Schlick's,

"*a gap* which the reader has to fill in with *all kinds of suppositions* and *in the end it is not surprising* (!!) that these suppositions *turn out to be more doubtful than they ought to*

---

[a] A district in Vienna.—*Ed.*

be (!!!). We suspect that Puchner, too, is accustomed to draw up his bulletins in *somewhat too rosy colours.* According to them, he is having a most splendid triumphal march against the 'rebel general'.[a] Then suddenly *to our very great astonishment* (!) we read an appeal from him in which he implores the Saxons and Wallachians at all costs not to lose heart, and then we suddenly learn that the defeated Bem is in front of Hermannstadt in the middle of Saxony, and the poor Germans (!!) finally can think of no better resort than to look to the Russians for protection. *There is a slight contradiction here between the official reports and the events,* a contradiction for which only the *inaccuracy* (!!) of the former can be blamed."

Citizen Schwanbeck confesses that the Austrian bulletins, and following them the *Kölnische Zeitung,* lied most shamelessly about the alleged progress .of the Austrians; when later on it is no longer possible to deny that it was a lie, truth-loving Schwanbeck calls it "a slight contradiction between the official reports and the events"!

"But if we by no means regard the Austrian army reports as oracles, that still does not mean the Magyar victory bulletins have gained the least bit in our eyes" (which have been busy with the above "slight contradiction"). "They are the products of *fantasy,* and would be quite pleasant reading if only they were not so *dreadfully ludicrous.*"

These "bulletins" are so "dreadfully ludicrous" that up to now they have asserted nothing but what the great Schwanbeck himself has to admit is in accordance with the facts. Or is Tokaj in the hands of Schlick? Has a single Austrian crossed the Theiss at Szolnok? Have the imperial troops advanced a single step in the last 14 days?

The 22nd Austrian Bulletin, which we have just received (see below[b]) saves Citizen Schwanbeck the trouble of replying. It makes it clear to us that the Austrians are not yet even as far as was asserted in the 20th and 21st bulletins.

"After all there is no change: the war in Hungary is approaching its end by giant strides."

That is clear. Schwanbeck already said so 14 days ago: "The war in Hungary is coming to an end. *Parturiunt montes, nascetur ridiculus mus.*"[c] That was on the very day when Schwanbeck announced for the first time that the Austrians had victoriously entered Debreczin. Since then 14 days have elapsed and in spite of the Magyars having "terribly exaggerated", the Austrians have still not crossed the Theiss, much less entered Debreczin.

---

[a] The *Kölnische Zeitung* has "rebel generals".—*Ed.*

[b] See this volume, pp. 404-08.—*Ed.*

[c] The mountains are in labour and a ridiculous mouse will be born (Horace, *De Arte Poetica,* 139).— *Ed.*

"It cannot surprise anyone that Bem's crowd which is being joined from all sides by fleeing bands of Hungarians, has swollen into an army for which the numerically small imperial forces in Transylvania are no match."

It certainly does not! But what can surprise us is how it is possible to speak about "being joined from all sides by fleeing bands of Hungarians" so long as the Hungarians occupy the line of the Theiss and Maros and Citizen Schwanbeck, despite his most ardent prayers, is unable to smuggle a single imperial soldier across it; further, it surprises us that the "fleeing bands" suddenly form an army, without the armies which are pursuing them being at once at hand to drive them from each of their new positions. But, of course, the great Schwanbeck believes that the Hungarians, having been beaten in his nebulous fantasy, would immediately flee from the Danube as far as the Aluta, without looking back to see whether they were being pursued or not.

Citizen Schwanbeck has made himself the Carnot of the nineteenth century by discovering the new manoeuvre by which *fleeing bands* coming from all sides can suddenly form a *victorious army*.

This new victorious army could, of course, cause serious complications. However, says Schwanbeck:

"We shall see *in what way Russia here will pronounce its veto.*"

The brave Schwanbeck, who here calls on Russia for help against the Magyars, is the same Schwanbeck who on March 22 of last year published an article full of moral indignation against the Russian Tsar[a] and declared that if Russia interfered in our affairs (and after all the Magyar affair is certainly our affair), then he, Schwanbeck, would issue a call that *would make the Tsar's throne tremble*. This is the same Schwanbeck who from the beginning has had the duty in the *Kölnische Zeitung* of salvaging the liberal reputation of the newspaper in the safe countries of Eastern Europe by timely manifestations of hatred against the Russians and obligatory shrewd expression of free-thinking. But the East-European complications seem to annoy him and in order to be able to devote himself wholly to his "feeling of deepest indignation" at the Austrian Note,[337] he calls on the Russians to come to Transylvania to end the struggle.

The best reply to the whole of this moralising and Windischgratz-like blustering article is the 22nd Austrian Army Bulletin,

---

[a] Nicholas I.—*Ed.*

which the readers will find below. In order to explain to Schwanbeck, who right up to the last sentence of his article reveals partly boundless ignorance of geography and strategy, and partly
dependence on the *Neue Rheinische Zeitung*, where he stands with
this Bulletin, we are simultaneously giving our own comments on it.

Written by Engels on February 17, 1849

First published in the *Neue Rheinische Zeitung* No. 225, February 18, 1849

Printed according to the newspaper

Published in English for the first time

BULLETIN No. 22

No. 22, the "Victory Bulletin" of the imperial army, has been published.[a] It is the funniest that has yet appeared.

"Owing to the greater distance of the theatre of war, which, with the retreat of the rebels across the Theiss has been pushed back as far as Transylvania, we have not until now been able to supply news of the successes gained by the army of His Highness Field Marshal Prince zu Windischgrätz."

From the Theiss to Transylvania is after all a distance of forty miles and more. As yet not a single Austrian has crossed the Theiss. Yet when Schlick is on the Hernath and Windischgrätz at Szolnok, with neither of them able to advance one step further, this is described in the swaggering language of royal imperial reports as follows: the theatre of war has been pushed back as far as Transylvania.

And what is the nature of the "successes gained by the army of His Highness Prince Windischgrätz"?

First "success":

"After the retreat from Pest one section of the rebels headed in the direction of Grosswardein and Debreczin, the other under Görgey made their way to Schemnitz and, after plundering the mountain towns, at first set off via Neusohl for Rosenberg. There, however, finding that the St. Marton and Turany passes had already been occupied by Major-General von Götz's troops, they headed for the Zips, where they met with a battalion of Nugent's infantry led by Major von Keisewetter, with whom battle took place at Kirchdorf and Hertnek on February 3 and 4.

"In the meantime reinforcements sent from Eperies by Lieutenant-Field Marshal Count Schlick immediately strengthened the occupation of the Braniszka Pass, and as

---

[a] In the *Wiener Zeitung* No. 38, February 14, 1849, and in other Austrian newspapers.— *Ed.*

another column of Deym's brigade advanced from Kaschau via Margitfalva, and the always active Major-General von Götz with Prince Jablonowsky's brigade, which had reached Telgarth via Brisen on the 8th inst., was also immediately detached against Leutschau, it looks as if the rebels, threatened on all sides in the Zips, are even more encircled than ever, all the roads along the Galician border from Neumarkt, Krosci-enko, Piwniczna, Tylicz as far as Dukla having at the same time been occupied in greater numbers under the command of Lieutenant-Field Marshal Vogel operating from Tarnów, and the *Landsturm* having been mustered all the way along that section."

The "direction of Grosswardein and Debreczin" is no more than an exaggerated euphemism used by Herr Welden to describe the fact that the Hungarians have reached the *Theiss*. He might just as well have claimed that they had withdrawn "in the direction" of the Black Sea.

Welden then goes on to tell us that Görgey "made for Schemnitz after the retreat from Pest". We have known this for a long time and what Herr Welden should have informed us of outright is how Görgey was *driven out* of the town. Earlier there had been a great deal of boasting that Görgey had been thrown back towards the Theiss, and almost annihilated in fact. Now the victory report sud-denly admits that he has occupied the *Zips*, which has already been "cleaned up" by Schlick several times, and is now *operating in Schlick's rear*. The extent to which Görgey is threatening the imperial troops in this position can be seen from the way in which reinforce-ments are hurriedly sent against him. *Götz's* corps was never suc-cessful against him (Csorich's corps has disappeared from the battlefield, and one concludes that the "ridiculous exaggerations" of the Magyars must have been right after all when they reported that Windischgrätz recalled it post-haste to Pest); Schlick had sent a column to the Braniszka Pass against Görgey "from Eperies" (i. e. four weeks ago); in addition, a second column was detached against him "from Kaschau", in other words also from Schlick's corps; and yet in spite of all these reinforcements, Görgey, in his position in the Carpathian Mountains, represents such a threat to the Austrians that Vogel in *Galicia*, operating from Tarnów, has reinforced all the positions on a sector of some twenty miles and *has mustered the Landsturm*.

In other words: instead of "being threatened on all sides in the Zips" Görgey is in fact *himself threatening* not only *Schlick's* posi-tion on the Hernath but also *Galicia*. And that is the worst thing that could happen to the imperial forces. An invasion of this purely Polish part of Galicia could have very unpleasant consequences for the Austrians at a time when the peasants have been disappointed in the royal imperial promises.

Second "success":

"Up to now heavy drifting ice on the Theiss has made the crossing of the river difficult both at Tokaj and Szolnok for that column of the First Army Corps which has advanced as far as the right bank. This has given the enemy time to turn more towards Transylvania, after an unsuccessful attempt on Arad, in order to link up with the column led by Bem, the rebel chief, who, as we have already reported earlier, on being pushed back from the Bukovina, marched via Bistritz and Maros-Vásárhely to Hermannstadt, where he was so powerfully repulsed by the general-in-command, Baron Puchner.

"The column of rebels which left Grosswardein for Klausenburg headed towards Karlsburg where they attempted to take Mühlenbach on the 5th. In this area, between Deva, Hatzeg and Szászváros, there is a formation of 3,000 Rumanians under the command of Captain Czernovich, which is guarding this section against the rebels—there is also a good garrison at the fortified castle at Deva.

"Meanwhile the general in command in the Banat, Lieutenant-Field Marshal Baron Rukavina, has formed a division under Lieutenant-Field Marshal von Gläser and Major-General Baron Mengen out of units of the Todorovich corps, and it is to operate in the Maros valley against Transylvania and simultaneously to threaten Grosswardein."

So the Austrians have *still not crossed the Theiss*; their successes consist in having for three weeks been unable, here in the decisive sector of the war, to advance *one single step*.

"Drifting ice" has apparently allowed the Magyars to turn "more" towards Transylvania. What a delightful use of the word "more"! If the Magyars were able to detach a column from Debreczin in the direction of Arad and Klausenburg that is proof that they have *more troops* than are required to defend the Theiss line. Or would Welden have us believe that the Magyars would take advantage of drifting ice, which can be over within a week, to expose their most important position and send the troops so urgently needed on the Theiss off on a stroll to Transylvania, which takes at least four to five weeks there and back?

The Hungarian column which fired on Arad came from the Banat according to an earlier bulletin. In addition a second column "from Grosswardein" has therefore gone to Transylvania. After these reinforcements we shall soon be hearing from Bem.

And how do things look in Transylvania? The Magyar reinforcements have advanced as far as Karlsburg and Mühlenbach. But no one need fear that things are going badly for the imperial forces! For there are after all 3,000 Rumanians at Hatzeg, Deva and Szászváros "who are guarding this section against the rebels".

Which "section"? Well, the section from Hatzeg etc., namely a "section" which is *completely off* the Magyars' route, and where it would not occur to them to march! The Magyar column is marching from Karlsburg to Hermannstadt in order to link up with Bem, i. e. in an easterly direction; the 3,000 Rumanians are to the south-west, in the furthermost corner of Transylvania, and will most probably stay there until the second Magyar column moves up the Maros from Arad and disperses them.

In addition, however, the newly formed Banat division led by Gläser is said "to be operating in the Maros valley against Transylvania and *simultaneously* threatening Grosswardein".

"Simultaneously"!!

In order "to threaten Grosswardein" this division—assuming it had already reached the Maros, whereas it is in fact no further than the Temes—would have to cover a distance of 20 miles to the *north* (in a straight line) crossing the Maros, the White, the Black and the Rapid Körös and three lines of swamps. In order to be able to operate in the Maros valley against Transylvania, the same division would have to march about 30 miles to the *east*. These two movements, one northwards and the other eastwards, it is supposed to execute *"simultaneously"*!

Third success:

"The two brigades of Major-General Dietrich and Count Pallfy, which were part of the corps of Master of the Ordnance Count Nugent, have both advanced, the one heading left via Boly to Mohács, the other via Siklos-Baranyavar towards Esseg, where the fortress is surrounded by royal imperial troops right up to the foot of the glacis, and has already made surrender proposals."

An important success already credited to Nugent himself two weeks ago, which now turns out not to have been achieved yet, for the "two brigades" have still not reached Esseg!

Fourth success:

"The rebels led by Nemegey crossed the Danube at Mohács, and in the defile between Bezdán and Zombor fell into the hands of the Serbs who were in that area having advanced along the left bank of the Danube from the Roman rampart, and on this occasion the greater part of the rebel army was massacred and dispersed by the Serbs."

Assuming this to be correct, it could have been no more than a small-scale guerilla skirmish. Long ago the Austrians trumpeted the news that the Magyars who had been driven back from the Drava were supposed to have retreated as far as Szegedin, i. e. as far as the Theiss!

Fifth and final "success":

"After the surrender of Leopoldstadt the division under Lieutenant-Field Marshal von Simunich received orders from the Herr Field Marshal[a] to advance along the Waag towards Komorn to tighten the blockade of this fortress.—During this advance

---

[a] Windischgrätz.—*Ed.*

fighting broke out on the 8th inst. not far from Neuhäusel between the division and a detachment of rebels which had set out from Komorn and crossed the Neutra above Naszvad to plunder the area, and above all to take salt into the fortress, where it is scarce and where diseases are already very much on the increase.—In this battle four companies of the Archduke Wilhelm's infantry and a squadron of Banderial hussars attacked an enemy unit of 1,200 men so courageously that the commander, one officer and 90 Honveds[a] were taken prisoner and a considerable number of dead and wounded were left behind on the battlefield."

Here the "success" amounts to Simunich managing, over a period of more than two weeks, to push forward *exactly seven miles* in an area which had already been three or four times "pacified", "cleaned up" and "purged", where a "good spirit" has begun to germinate once more — and that comes to half a mile a day; add to that the constant battles and you will understand why Simunich the hero has still not covered the ten miles from Leopoldstadt to Komorn.

These then are the "successes of His Highness Prince Windischgrätz": pompous reiteration of earlier bulletins, boastful statements about what is to happen, and the result of it all is that in reality *nothing has happened.* The case with the bulletins is exactly the same as that of the great Schwanbeck with the Prussian Chamber: "the present is being lost" for them through a "dead past" and a "distant, perhaps never attainable future".[b]

Written by Engels about February 17, 1849

First published in the supplement to the *Neue Rheinische Zeitung* No. 225, February 18, 1849

Printed according to the newspaper

Published in English for the first time

---

[a] Soldiers of the Magyar Defence Committee.—*Ed.*

[b] Engels refers to the leading article in the *Kölnische Zeitung* No. 33, February 8, 1849, quoted by Marx in his article "The Division of Labour in the *Kölnische Zeitung*" (see this volume, pp. 354-59).— *Ed.*

CROATS AND SLOVAKS IN HUNGARY

Cologne, February 18. Whilst for some days now the Austrian papers have been spinning yarns about Ottinger having been victorious over Dembiński—at Debreczin!!—the storm clouds are gathering with increasing density in the Slav provinces of Hungary, threatening the royal imperial united monarchy. For some time now—since the storming of Vienna, in fact[a]—we have been drawing people's attention to the inevitability of a split between the Austrian Government and the Slavs.[b] That split is now an open one.

Let us begin with the *Serbs*. The *Grazer Zeitung* received from Temesvár the following report supporting the Austrian view:

"Serbian encroachments are beginning in the Banat, and, if the signs are not deceptive, this will eventually require *armed intervention*, especially since some of the Serbs are being more presumptuous than even the Magyarisers[338] in their attempts totally to suppress the other nationalities in the voivodeship, and the Rumanians and the Germans there are therefore arming for open resistance. The split between the senior military authorities and the voivodeship is *already almost an open one*, and I can assure you that we must prepare ourselves for a *struggle with the Serbs*. At any event we have now come to see that the sympathy that was supposed to exist for the Austrian cause is not of the same purity as that of the Croats. Matters will shortly come to a *head*."

It is well known that Karlowitz, the seat of the Banat Government, i. e. of the Serbian chief committee, the vice-president of which is the "rebel" Stratimirovich,[339] has been declared in a state of siege.

---

[a] After November 1, 1848.—*Ed.*

[b] See this volume, pp. 347-49.— *Ed.*

But just what is one to make of the "purity" of the Croats' "sympathy"? This is what we hear:

> "*Prague*, February 13. The events in Croatia are causing a great stir in Czech circles. Now, they say, the question of whether Jellachich will stick by his country or by the dynasty will have to be resolved. *The officers are already saying quite openly that, when we have finished with Hungary, it will be a case of marching to Croatia.*"

This is what the *Deutsche Allgemeine Zeitung*[a] says, and the Slav *Constitutionelles Blatt aus Böhmen* is just as clear:

It has received information dated February 11 from Kremsier to the effect that written reports of dissatisfaction among the Slovaks and Croats were becoming daily more numerous. There were none but Magyars among the newly appointed commissioners of the Austrian Government in the Slovak comitats, their decrees were issued in Magyar, and they "threatened people with death" if they refused to accept their official communications. It is further reported that Jellachich was highly dissatisfied that his troops were to be split up and some of them employed on garrison-duty, whilst other troops were to be placed under his command. The ruse is a good one. Jellachich, who has been under suspicion for six to eight weeks anyway, and has been kept under surveillance by Windischgrätz's agents, is being thus rendered harmless. And at this point the *Constitutionelles Blatt aus Böhmen* adds:

> "What is Jellachich likely to say about the state of siege at *Karlowitz*? Might his reaction not be to think: It could be your turn next — ? For now there is only Agram, the Croats, who have not had the principle of equality amongst the various nationalities applied to them — for the Germans, the Hungarians, the Poles, the Italians and the Czechs in particular have already become familiar with that equality of status that a state of siege creates."

Furthermore, it is already known that Windischgrätz has appointed a new Hungarian government commission in Pest, which, to the great consternation of the Croats, is laying claim to all the rights which the old Hungarian Government possessed, thus reducing to naught the intended kingdom of the Southern Slavs. The Croats were already dreaming of being independent of Hungary and suddenly a decree arrives from Pest addressed to the Croatian authorities demanding submission—and on top of it all the decree is written in *Magyar*, without a Croat translation!! The *Slavenski jug* immediately publishes it in the original and cannot contain its indignation.[340] The Croats are foaming; they are being treated just as

---

[a] *Deutsche Allgemeine Zeitung* No. 48, February 17, 1849.—*Ed.*

they were under Kossuth! And that is the reward they get for their faithful efforts to save the united monarchy!

Anyone wanting to know how all this fits together should read the Vienna *Presse*. In that paper there is an article in which Prince Windischgrätz is openly reproached for having allowed himself already to become too closely involved with the *Hungarian aristocracy*. He is accused of allowing a great number of Magyar magnates, some of whom had been captured, others having changed their allegiance, to walk about Pest as they please; he is even said to have conferred distinctions on them and so on.

It is obvious that the aristocrat Windischgrätz knows full well that he can only achieve his goal of maintaining the power of the nobility in Hungary by maintaining the *Magyar* nobility in power. That is why he is granting the Magyar magnates protection and giving them preferential treatment. He is indifferent to any suffering this may cause to the Croats and the Slovaks: having finished the business of subduing Hungary and restoring the rule of the aristocracy there, he will manage to deal with the Slavs, who are in disarray and powerless without Austrian leadership — just think of Prague![341]

And the great Schwanbeck seeks the nobility not in *Windischgrätz's* camp but in *Kossuth's*! *Voilà ce que c'est que d'être un savant sérieux!*[a]

Written by Engels on February 18, 1849

First published in the *Neue Rheinische Zeitung* No. 226, February 19, 1849

Printed according to the newspaper

Published in English for the first time

---

[a] That is what it means to be a serious savant.—*Ed.*

MILITARY ART OF THE ROYAL
IMPERIAL ARMY

Cologne, February 18. Windischgrätz is exceptionally unlucky. He could have become one of the greatest generals of the century if he did not always have the most unpredictable accidents. Schwanbeck has already proved that he would have done incomparable heroic deeds if the Hungarians had only stood their ground against him. But the worst thing that has happened to the great Windischgrätz is now revealed by the royal imperial semi-official correspondence in the Augsburg *Allgemeine Zeitung*. For in its supplement of February 15 of this year, that newspaper says word for word the following:

"Concerning the operations of Prince Windischgrätz in the month of January, I must recall that eight army columns were intended to march into the interior of Hungary in the middle of December and at that time were ten to twelve days from Buda-Pest. This disposition of the Field Marshal had been made *in anticipation of a rational form of warfare*. The Magyars *thwarted* this anticipation by putting up a fabulously superior force *everywhere except where* it could have produced the most favourable outcome, if such were at all possible. Of the columns to which Windischgrätz had given dates at the Hungarian capitals, *only* those of the Ban,[a] of Lieutenant-Field Marshal Wrbna and the reserve corps led by the Field Marshal were able to carry out their orders; the superiority of the Magyar forces prevented the other formations from doing so."

Windischgrätz had counted on the Magyars pursuing a "*rational form of warfare*". If they had conducted this rational warfare, Windischgrätz would have signally defeated them. But what they did was to put up a "*fabulously superior force everywhere except where*" it could have been at all effective. And in consequence of this

---

[a] Jellachich.—*Ed.*

boundless irrationality all the dispositions of the great Windischgrätz came to nothing.

Just because the Magyars made one blunder after another, and because even the gods themselves fight in vain against stupidity, Windischgrätz's most learned combinations foundered on the Magyars' ignorance of strategy!

> Did ever a fellow have luck as bad
> As Burgomaster Tschech has had — [a]

and Field Marshal Windischgrätz, who could not beat his enemies simply because they were *too stupid* for him?!

Written by Engels on February 18, 1849	Printed according to the newspaper
First published in the *Neue Rheinische Zeitung* No. 226, February 19, 1849	Published in English for the first time

---

[a] From a popular song about Burgomaster Tschech's attempt on Frederick William IV on July 26, 1844:

> Hätte je ein Mann so'n Pech
> Wie der Bürgermeister Tschech etc.—*Ed.*

PROCLAMATION OF A REPUBLIC IN ROME [342]

The Italian Constituent Assembly is quite unlike the Frankfurt National Assembly. The Italians know that the unity of a country split into feudal principalities can only be established by abolishing dynastic rule. The Italians led the dance in 1848, and they are leading again in 1849. But what progress! Italy no longer has Pius IX, nor France her Lamartine. The fantastic period of the European revolution, the period of enthusiasm, goodwill and flowery speeches, was fittingly concluded with fire-balls, massacres on a grand scale and deportations. Austrian Notes, Prussian Notes and Russian Notes were the most appropriate replies to Lamartine's proclamations.

From their Pythian tripod of thoroughness and perseverance the Germans are in the habit of looking down with haughty disdain on the superficiality of the Italians. A comparison between the Italian 1848 and the German 1848 would provide the most striking answer. In drawing this comparison one would above all have to take into account that revolutionary Italy was kept in check by Germany and France, whereas revolutionary Germany was not restricted in her movements.

The *republic in Rome* is the beginning of the revolutionary drama of 1849.

Written about February 21, 1849

First published in the *Neue Rheinische Zeitung* No. 228, February 22, 1849

Printed according to the newspaper

Published in English for the first time

WINDISCHGRÄTZ.—JEWS AND SOUTHERN SLAVS

Jews are known to be cheated cheats everywhere, but especially in Austria. They exploited the revolution and are now being punished for it by Windischgrätz. Incidentally, anybody who knows how powerful the Jews are in Austria will appreciate what an enemy Windischgrätz has taken on by issuing the following proclamation:

Pest, February 13 (official Wiener Zeitung, evening supplement). "Proclamation. In my proclamations of November 13 and December 13 of last year and of January 7 of this year I acquainted all inhabitants of Hungary with the task I have to solve, namely, the restoration of peace, order and legality. I have also had the satisfaction of seeing the effect, evident everywhere, of these proclamations. Only individual localities, duped by infamous agitators, are still attempting to disturb the so necessary calm and order by spreading Kossuth's appeals, orders and decisions. Inhabitants of Hungary! You have seen what leniency I have exercised, on the assumption that the majority are misled and seduced rather than truly rebellious people; but whoever still tries to make common cause with the Debreczin party of rebellion, to accept or spread its orders, or to maintain any kind of connection with it and to stir up the communities, can no longer count on any leniency, he must receive the punishment for high treason.

"I am sending out in various directions troops, whose commanders will be authorised to use the jus gladii[a]; anyone found carrying on him a proclamation by Kossuth, or any writing, letter, newspaper etc., issued by his party, will inexorably be treated under martial law, in the same way as anyone concealing arms or inciting people to disobedience.—Any postmaster or postal employee who accepts such writings, letters or proclamations from the area of Debreczin, or worse, forwards them, will be hanged.—Finally, I would like to warn the Jews of Ofen and Pest, but particularly those of Old Ofen, to refrain from entering into any understanding under any name whatever with the traitor Kossuth, the so-called honvédmi bizotmány,[b] and the rebel Assembly, for it has come to my knowledge that it is in fact mainly Israelites who allow themselves to be used as spies and suppliers of the rebels, and that they also make it their business to spread false and bad news about the alleged victories

---

[a] The right of the sword.— Ed.
[b] Defence Committee.— Ed.

of the rebels so as thereby to arouse fear and mistrust; hence, for every Israelite who is sentenced under military or martial law for the above-mentioned offences, the Jewish community to which he belongs will pay a fine of 20,000 guldens C. M.[343] Ofen Headquarters, February 11, 1849.

Alfred Prince zu Windischgrätz m. p.,[a] Royal Imperial Field Marshal"

It is clear from this proclamation that things are going very badly for "citizen and communist" Windischgrätz.[b]

And, incidentally, to come back to the Jews: Windischgrätz's attempt to filch money from them has already "begun to be put into effect" as the *Code Napoléon* says. For the *Constitutionelles Blatt aus Böhmen* reports the following:

"The Jews are to pay a lump sum of 1,200,000 florins in redemption of the abolished toleration tax, and that in five years, but they have not paid the quotas due either last year or this. The amount in arrears has now been called in.— The printer *Eisenfels* was arrested yesterday."

It seems to us priceless that the Jews must still pay for their emancipation. In Prussian this is called "redemption of feudal dues".

Otherwise there is nothing to report from Hungary except that in *Pest* the forwarding agent Franz *Förster* was shot under martial law on February 8 for taking part in a revolt by attempting to confiscate the steamboat *Hermine* in Gran.

The *Leipziger Zeitung* reports as follows on the increasingly comical complications among the Slavs (the *Neue Rheinische Zeitung* has, of course, known this for a long time):

"*Vienna*, February 14. From several provinces of the monarchy we hear of stubborn refusals to supply the demanded recruits. In the Praschin district of Bohemia the peasants refuse under the pretext that the Imperial Diet has not sanctioned the latest recruiting ordered on such a lavish scale. Quite a noticeable ferment is observed in the countryside even more than in the capital, Prague. If, as we are assured, the Government shortly proposes compensation for the abolished *Urbar* duties,[344] a new and more serious shock will be added to the innumerable and seemingly endless shocks of our public life. Confusion is growing in the South-Slav areas; but evidently a most dangerous storm is brewing, the aim and end of which cannot yet be discerned. General Todorovich has had a state of siege declared in Karlowitz, the seat of the Serbian National Committee.[c] The chaos in Serbian affairs is further increased by the specifically Austrian efforts of Consul Mayerhofer. With barely concealed fury the Southern Slavs cry: Betrayal! They claim that *all the measures taken lately by the Government in Hungary are directed towards restoring ultra-Magyarism, insofar as it is disguised in old aristocratic garb.* In Agram, the agitation has reached a

***

[a] Sign-manual.— *Ed.*

[b] Engels draws a parallel here with the "citizen and communist" Drigalski (see this volume, pp. 75-80).— *Ed.*

[c] Chief Otbor.— *Ed.*

most disturbing degree.—Jellachich is in Szolnok. The following is a reliable fact: He has protested against the separation and dismemberment of his corps. He had to do this in order not to jeopardise his exceptional popularity in the Slav world. In Croatia there is energetic pressure for the convocation of the Provincial Diet.[a] With this the dictatorship with which Jellachich was vested in the summer will come to an end." [345]

Written by Engels on February 21, 1849

First published in the *Neue Rheinische Zeitung* No. 228, February 22, 1849

Printed according to the newspaper

Published in English for the first time

---

[a] Sabor.— *Ed.*

FURTHER CONTRIBUTION ON THE OLD-PRUSSIAN FINANCIAL ADMINISTRATION

Cologne, February 21. We must supplement our article in No. 224 of the newspaper on von Bodelschwingh and Co. and the Prussian financial administration.[a] At the end of that article we pointed out that the books of the treasury show 27,127 Reichstalers (17,127 is a misprint) less than were transferred to it according to the accounts of the exchequer. Since then we have found in the accounts published by the Government[346] a note which solves the riddle as to the whereabouts of this money.

The fact is that the so-called savings on the cost of administration in 1844, amounting to 2,000,002 Reichstalers, were not paid in cash to the treasury but were used to buy Prussian state bonds to this amount. Because of the market rate at the time, a loss of 27,127 Reichstalers was incurred on their purchase. The Prussian Ministers are, or were, brilliant financiers! The present case makes this obvious again. So we no longer need to ask the Herren ex-Ministers what has become of these 27,127 Reichstalers, we can tell them that, owing to their cleverness in this one business deal, not merely 27,000 but more than 400,000 Reichstalers have been lost. This reproach is incurred in the first place by Herr Flottwell, for he was Finance Minister at the time. It may be that he is an honest man. But it makes no difference to the country whether its Ministers harm it owing to incapacity or to ill will. An investigation of this matter can be of interest at most to the Minister's family.

In his memo on the treasury dated April 6, 1847, the then Finance Minister von Thile says quite frankly that in regard to the treasury the following two principles hold good:

---

[a] See this volume, pp. 379-89.— *Ed.*

1. that the balance in hand must always be in *cash, in coin of the realm*;

2. that no payments of any kind may be made from the treasury except for the purpose of armaments.

As far as the first principle is concerned, it is correct that, if there is to be a treasury at all, it has a rational meaning only if it consists of *cash or precious metal*. A government which is unable to rely on the strength of the people may, of course, need a reserve for so-called difficult times. If its credit, too, is impaired on the Stock Exchange, it must have some means in reserve to help it escape from this embarrassment, but that can only be done by means of cash or precious metal. Gold and silver are at all times the means to open the hearts of the bourgeois. But depreciated paper of little worth is the most certain way to lose also the "respect" of the Stock Exchange. When the credit of the state has fallen so low that the aid of the treasury is essential, there is nothing more humiliating on the Stock Exchange than to have to offer state bonds for sale and look for buyers. Anyone who has ever observed the activity of one of the larger stock exchanges will know what contempt is to be seen in the features and gestures of the money speculators when at such times they are offered government securities. For the rest, the speculator may be a Commerce Counsellor and very "well-intentioned".

The purchase of state bonds, therefore, was the most incompetent operation that the Prussian Government could undertake.

Herr von Thile states in the above-mentioned memo that he was *compelled* to accept state bonds to the value of 1,972,875 Reichstalers instead of 2,000,002 Reichstalers in *cash*. We do not attach any importance to this excuse of being "compelled". But if the accounts are correct, the purchase of the government securities was carried out by the exchequer. Otherwise the whole amount would have had to be supplied to the state treasury in cash. Hence Herr Flottwell seems to have been closely connected with the successful financial operation.

How petty-bourgeois parsimony, which is eager to save a small sum in interest but is not capable of dealing with the greater financial enterprises of a state, ends most ignominiously by doubling the loss, is evident from the figures given below.

To the loss on purchase compared with the nominal value .... 27,127 Rt.
must be added the far greater loss on sale. From March to the beginning of July 1848 the market

rate of the state bonds fluctuated between 66% G.
(April 4) and 83½% Br.[a] (March 21). Since the market rate falls at once when a large amount of scrip is
put on sale, one must assume that the Government
did not receive more than 70% in getting rid of its
state bonds. The loss incurred on the sale, therefore, was probably not less than 30% of the nominal
value of 1,972,875 Rt., i.e. .... 591,840 Rt.

                                      a total of   618,967 Rt.

From this loss must be subtracted the interest for 3
years at 69,048 Rt. .... 207,144 Rt.

Hence the net loss probably amounts to .... 411,823 Rt.

Almost a quarter of the total amount has been lost and furthermore
the state's credit has become still weaker owing to the depreciated
market rate of the state bonds.

We cite this small sample of the wisdom of Prussian Ministers of
Finance and Exchequers *à la* Flottwell-Thile only because it forms a
necessary supplement to our article mentioned above. Otherwise we
would not concern ourselves with minor matters when great ones
provide us with such rich material.

Written by Marx on February 21, 1849   Printed according to the newspaper

First published in the *Neue Rheinische*   Published in English for the first
Zeitung No. 229, February 23, 1849   time

---

[a] G. (*Geld*—money)—market rate at which the scrip is in demand; Br.
(*Brief*—letter)—market rate at which the scrip is offered for sale.— *Ed.*

A DENUNCIATION

Cologne, February 22. In the *Oberpostamts-Zeitung*, the former editor[a] of which was a paid agent of Guizot (cf. Taschereau's *Revue rétrospective*[347]) and an unpaid agent of Metternich, as is notoriously also the entire Thurn und Taxis postal service—that crab-sidling system of national carriers, which is a burden to German industry and is in conflict with the railways; whose continued existence after the March revolution is almost incomprehensible and whose immediate abolition will be one of the first acts of the German Constituent Assembly shortly to be opened (the assembly in St. Paul's Church[b] was notoriously never a Constituent Assembly) for since Joseph II it has never been anything but a refuge for Austrian spies—in this imperial organ for denunciation belonging to the ex-Prince of Thurn und Taxis, the responsible editor H. Malten (already recognisably described by the old *Rheinische Zeitung*) states the following, asserting that it is a reprint of a Paris report from a newspaper which we do not read[c]:

"To the shame of the German name, we have to admit that there are Germans who engage in agitation among us on the most extensive, not to say most shameless scale. There exists here a special Bureau of Reds, by which all inflammatory articles that in any way incite against order in human society are dispatched to the provinces as speedily as possible. It is not enough that Germans participate in this unseemly business on behalf of France; we owe it to them also that a nefarious propaganda is continually spreading its network throughout Germany. From the witches' cauldron of this same revolutionary kitchen the German part of the Rhine valley throughout its entire length is inundated with revolutionary literature about which the *Neue*

---

[a] K. P. Berly.—*Ed.*
[b] The Frankfurt National Assembly.—*Ed.*
[c] Below is cited the reprint in the *Frankfurter Oberpostamts-Zeitung* No. 44, February 20, 1849, of the Paris correspondence published in *Die Deutsche Reform.*—*Ed.*

Rheinische Zeitung could have a lot to say, if it did not find it fitting to maintain a careful silence on this subject. In Upper Baden, for several months already the lower strata of the people have been subjected to agitation from Paris. That there are connections between the democrats here and the refugees in Switzerland is also a fact."

In reply to this foul denunciation we declare: 1) that we *have never concealed our* connections with the French, English, Italian, Swiss, Belgian, Polish, American and other democrats, and 2) that we ourselves produce here in Cologne the "revolutionary literature" with which *we* actually do "inundate the German part of the Rhine valley" (and not it alone!). For that we need no assistance from Paris; for several years we have been accustomed to our Parisian friends receiving more from us than we get from them.

Written on February 22, 1849

First published in the *Neue Rheinische Zeitung* No. 229, February 23, 1849

Printed according to the newspaper

Published in English for the first time

BULLETIN No. 23.—
FROM THE THEATRE OF WAR

Army Bulletin No. 23[a] has appeared. It says:

"Simultaneously with the already announced successes achieved against the insurgents by our gallant army under Colonel Urban in Northern Transylvania despite the cold and the heavy snowfall, we were gratified to hear of a similar and no less brilliant success at Arad achieved by the troops of Lieutenant-Field Marshal Gläser, who according to his orders is instructed to operate in the Maros valley against Transylvania with his division composed of units from the Todorovich corps.

"The insurgents attempted to cross at Szadorlak in a strong column, and thus threatened our left flank. Thereupon Lieutenant-Field Marshal Gläser ordered two battalions of Peterwardein border guards[348] to capture the first houses of Old Arad and brought up one battalion of Leiningen and then one battalion of Illyrian Banaters for the assault.

"After a drawn-out, bloody engagement the enemy was thrown back, all the batteries set up by the insurgents on the right bank of the Maros facing the fortress were destroyed, and all the cannon mounted in them, 23 in number, were captured; of these, 11 heavy guns were removed to the fortress, 3 were sunk in the Maros, 3 were spiked, 2 were placed at the disposal of the royal imperial Austro-Serbian army corps and 4 dismantled by the valiant Temesvár artillery; 3 enemy ammunition wagons were captured, and in addition enemy ammunition dumps were blown up in several places.

"Because of the hostility displayed by its inhabitants Old Arad was subjected to a grenade attack from the fortress and in many places fires were started which continued to burn all night.— Forty prisoners were also taken in the fighting.

"According to a dispatch of February 13 just received from Master of the Ordnance Count Nugent in Esseg, the fortress of Esseg surrendered on the same day without waiting to be attacked.

"Three of the gates were immediately occupied by the besieging troops, and on the morning of the 14th the garrison laid down its arms on the glacis.

---

[a] Published in the *Wiener Zeitung* No. 42, February 18, 1849, and in other newspapers.—*Ed.*

"On the 13th news came from Berthodfalva, a few hours from Eperies, about the column of General Götz, who—as we have already related—had joined up with the brigade of General Prince Jablonowsky at Tyrnau and pursued the fleeing rebel corps under Görgey towards Leutschau.

"This news said that the enemy column, which is indeed a strong one and is accompanied by a strong train of artillery and wagons, after forcing the Zips where it destroyed all bridges and roads, had taken the road from Eperies to Kaschau in order to seek contact with the other rebel hordes in the area of the Theiss.

"Lieutenant-Field Marshal Count Schlick with his three brigades has taken up a position at Torna on the flank of this laboriously moving and all-devastating enemy column, so as to be best able to attack it as soon as he has linked up with the column under General Götz, which has indeed now been done via Margitfalva, Einsiedl and Schmöllnitz.

"General Götz engaged in a skirmish with a rebel raiding-party at Margitfalva, in which several hussars were captured, who supplied detailed information about the position and intentions of the enemy.

"As a large unit under Lieutenant-Field Marshal Schulzig has taken up positions at Miskolcz, we shall shortly be able to give a detailed report of events in these areas.

"Vienna, February 17, 1849."

From this victory report it emerges, then, that Esseg really has capitulated and that Arad has been relieved by the imperial forces; whether their success on the Maros is of the importance that the bulletin would attribute to it, remains to be seen.

On the other hand, the situation of the imperial forces on the Upper Theiss is very poor. According to the last bulletin, Schlick was at Tokaj firing across the Theiss at the Hungarians drawn up on the other side, and today we find him beating a hasty retreat in a north-westerly direction, to avoid the danger of being attacked in the rear by Görgey and being caught between two fires.

Görgey's manoeuvre is really brilliant. By forcing the Zips into the Sáros comitat, occupying Eperies and continuing from there down the River Hernath, following exactly the same path that Schlick had taken, he fell on him full in the rear and forced him to withdraw from Tokaj *more than twelve miles deep* into the Torna comitat, and so to take up a position between Götz (in the Zips) and Schulzig (at Miskolcz). Thus Görgey is now able to advance directly to the Theiss and *reinforce the main Magyar army* with his entire column which is "*indeed a strong one*", and, as the bulletin itself says, is well equipped with artillery. Perhaps he still has a few words to say to Schlick in passing.

Further unofficial news about Hungary circulating in Vienna is as follows:

Vienna, February 18. According to the latest reports of the 18th from Pest, we may shortly expect decisive news from the Theiss area. After the arrival of the news that Szegedin has surrendered and sent a deputation to meet the advancing Serbs, the Ban of Croatia[a] has set up his headquarters at Szolnok, and everyone is preparing for a major battle. The inhabitants of Szegedin, who had offered to deliver cattle and supplies to the imperial army, have had a levy of half a million guldens imposed on them. The people of Szegedin are known to have hitherto been the keenest supporters of Kossuth. They supplied his army with everything. From Debreczin reports up to the 12th have been reaching Pest through refugees. Mészáros is still in charge of the Ministry of War, and Kossuth is more fanatical than ever. The former has written to Prince Windischgrätz that he and his forces will defend themselves to the last man, and would rather perish than surrender. In view of the very gloomy news from Transylvania, where Bem appears to be the master, this sort of language is quite explicable. According to the war reports of the Kossuth faction in Debreczin, Kronstadt has been captured by the Szeklers[349] after a street-battle etc. Other rumours, however, would have it that the Russians have come to the rescue and saved the situation.

The *Breslauer Zeitung* has a dispatch from the Hungarian border which is on the whole favourable to the Austrians, but is nevertheless forced to admit that the Austrian war bulletins only give a highly incomplete picture of the battles in Transylvania and beyond the Theiss because they always stress only the gains of the royal imperial troops, and make no mention whatsoever of the thorny way in which they have been achieved, for all reports direct from the theatre of war agree that the Magyars have been defending themselves with the utmost desperation for the last few weeks, and have inflicted severe damage on the royal imperial army. The regiments under Schlick, Ottinger and Götz have already suffered significant losses, and the Croats, who are already longing to be back home and still feel a deep-seated respect for the Hungarian cavalry, are showing signs of a mood that is giving their Ban cause for misgivings.

It is even said that odd units of the Croat battalions have gone over to the Magyars, which I cannot vouch for however. What is causing Prince Windischgrätz most trouble is the condition of the roads, which is quite appalling in the present thaw, especially between the Danube and the Theiss, rendering the transportation of heavy artillery downright impossible; only with the greatest effort and on wagons with wheel-rims a foot across is it possible to move the 3- and 6-pound cannon. Twelve-pound batteries, in which the superiority

---

[a] Jellachich.—*Ed.*

of Austrian artillery really lies, are totally untransportable, thus creating an equalisation of the armaments of the two sides that must necessarily prolong the fighting. Even if its outcome is not in doubt (!), many a day may well elapse before Windischgrätz can report to Olmütz: "The country is quiet!" In the end the Magyar forces, which still have a strength of 60,000-70,000 men, could concentrate in Transylvania, where *Bem reigns supreme,* and the nature of the terrain is particularly favourable to a stubborn defence.

The Vienna *Lloyd*[a] also says that Pest is arming strongly:

"Since yesterday (the 14th) reinforcements for the Theiss army have been leaving continuously. A decisive battle is expected to take place there in the next few days. These new forces being sent to the Theiss could number at least 11,000 men."

The *Österreichischer Correspondent* mentions a victory of the Serbs over a greatly superior force of Magyars at Szento. Unfortunately, the otherwise so omniscient bulletin knows nothing about this.

This much is certain: for the present "the war in Hungary" is not yet "coming to an end".

Written by Engels on February 23, 1849

First published in the *Neue Rheinische Zeitung* No. 230, February 24, 1849

Printed according to the newspaper

Published in English for the first time

---

[a] *Lloyd* No. 84, February 18, 1849.—*Ed.*

LATEST NEWS OF THE MAGYARS.— VICTORY ON THE THEISS.— BRUTALITY OF THE AUSTRIANS.—STATE OF THE WAR IN GENERAL

The *Allgemeine Oder-Zeitung* cites the following, among other things, from the reports of a Hungarian who left Pest on the 17th:

When the Magyar army withdrew from Pest to the other side of the Theiss, the dismay of the inhabitants of the two cities[a] was extreme, especially on the part of the Magyars, who saw their last hope of freedom dashed and lamented that in abandoning the capital the army was disgracing itself before all Europe. Nevertheless, the policy of the Hungarian Government was a shrewd one, *fully realising* as it did that *in their eagerness to save their property* the inhabitants of the two cities would have helped the enemy. Later on, of course, when it turned out that the Austrian Government was not sparing any of those involved, these people realised that they were up against an implacable enemy. The atrocities committed by the Austrian troops in the area of Buda-Pest exceeded all bounds. In this, the Croats outdid all the others. What they could not use they destroyed. Two days after the retreat of the Hungarians across the Theiss an army corps of 20,000 men under *Ottinger* occupied Szolnok, with its rearguard in *Abony*. In this position the Austrians were attacked by a Hungarian corps about 12,000 strong under Perczel, and would have been completely annihilated had not an advancing Hungarian army unit under Brigadier *Kasinsky* been delayed. In any case, the Austrians saw themselves forced to flee, which they did under cover of night, and were unable to rally their forces until they reached *Czegléd*. It was remarkable to watch the terror that seized them — that is the cavalry and the officers — and how they were forever shouting, "Onward! Onward! The butchering dogs" (as they call the Hungarian hussars) "are hard on our heels!"

On the 21st the Hungarians arrived at Abony, and this time they were 22,000 strong. General *Dembiński* was with them, though not in command at that stage. The day after the battle at Szolnok a division of Austrian cuirassiers[350] advanced as far as St. Marton, where the Hungarian outposts were positioned, and what occurred there was incredible: they were attacked by six Hungarian hussars who killed twenty of them and took some of them prisoner.

---

[a] Buda (Ofen) and Pest, which were then two independent cities.—*Ed.*

At dawn on the 23rd the Hungarians reached Czegléd, where the Austrians had taken up a very favourable position. The Hungarians attacked, beat the Austrians and pursued them through the town right out into the vineyards of Alberty. There they heard that an Austrian corps of considerable size was marching via Alau towards *Debreczin*, and this news compelled them to give up the pursuit. General Dembiński, however, expressed his dissatisfaction with the entire execution of this attack, which in his opinion should have led to the complete annihilation of the Austrian corps.

The news of the defeat of Ottinger's corps reached Pest straightaway, and the townspeople once again sought out their red feathers, but their hopes were soon disappointed. The Hungarians crossed the Theiss and burned the bridge at Szolnok. This was used by the Austrians as a pretext to boast of victories, and fear of their brutality safeguarded them against contradiction. It was a sorry state of affairs for the local populace, who had hoped that they had already been freed from the Austrian yoke. The Austrians came in greater numbers and with demands even harsher than before.

Some houses were forced to billet 30 to 40 soldiers, and the officers were callous enough to throw old men out of their beds and lie down in them themselves, saying, "You Hungarians can sleep on the ground. That's good enough for you dogs."

These reports will be continued.[a]

The *Schlesische Zeitung*, a reactionary paper every bit as good as the *Breslauer Zeitung*, gives for its part the following account of the state of affairs in Hungary:

Pest, February 12. The war is dragging on longer than one would have expected, which is primarily due to the fact that the Magyars have found a staunch ally in the mild winter. The overflowing of the rivers as well as the almost completely impassable roads are confronting the Austrian army with well-nigh insuperable obstacles. The Theiss is now the demarcation line between the opposing armies. There is fighting now at one point, now at another, from Tokaj to Szegedin, a distance of more than 40 miles. The halfway point on this line is Szolnok. There has already been fierce fighting at this point, but *it still remains under the control of the Magyars*. It is of importance because it is situated in the centre of fighting.

On the Upper Theiss, i.e. in the area of Tokaj, *the Magyars are rising up in large numbers*, the population having been driven to desperation by the cruelties of the war. The population in and around Miskolcz is extremely agitated, as in the whole of Borsod comitat. The gains made here by the Austrians are always quickly snatched away from them again. Downstream from Szolnok, and indeed a long way upstream too, the land on both sides of the Theiss is so badly flooded that *it is under water for a mile on either side in many places, which usually lasts well on into April*. Only the local inhabitants are familiar with this terrain. Any foreign military force entering it can easily be driven by them into the swamps and floods.

Further downstream around Csongrad and Szantó the roads are at present quite impassable for an army corps, for the artillery would sink in the marshy roads. This is the road to Szegedin and Arad. The Austrian army, particularly the Croats, attempted to push forward here but became convinced that it was impossible. Rumour has it that for this reason Prince Windischgrätz has fallen out with Jellachich. The latter got as far as the steppes of Keczkemet, but was pushed back again. This region is inhabited by the Cumans and the Jazyges,[351] an extremely powerful race of men who are

---

[a] See this volume, pp. 443-44.—*Ed.*

noblemen every one and recognise only the imperial palatine as their supreme authority. They are impassioned Magyars.

Between the Theiss and the border of Transylvania the towns are considerable distances apart, it is true, but are unusually populous. Thus, for example, the market-town of Csoba has a population of 24,000, and Gozula nearly 18,000. All are enthusiastic Magyars.

Further down in the Banat the Serbs are certainly pressing forward, but the Hungarians, nevertheless, still hold a good deal of country.

If General Bem succeeds in the plan which he now seems to have of setting out from Hermannstadt (in Transylvania) by way of the Szászváros and Deva through the mountain passes to Hungary and joining the Magyars there, their cause will take a favourable turn. And there are no particularly great obstacles in his path. For *Transylvania is almost completely conquered*, and the Wallachians were already defeated when Bem turned on the Saxons. Many of these are said to have joined up with him in the area of Kronstadt, doubtless only because there was no other course open to them. Only the fortress of Karlsburg (between Klausenburg and Mühlenbach) might have offered some resistance, but it is said to be in the hands of the Hungarians already.

On the right bank of the Danube, as in the Carpathians, the fighting is mostly confined to skirmishes. All along the stretch from the borders of Styria to the Danube patrol-corps have been formed which keep the Austrian army under General Nugent on the move. Several of these have respected Hungarians at their head. The occasional sorties made from Komorn serve to protect these guerillas. Even this virginal fortress would have fallen had the winter lasted another month, for it would then have been possible to approach it across the frozen rivers. On one side flow two arms of the Danube; on the other, the Waag and the Neutra. The fortress itself rises scarcely 50 feet above the plains, but from there it is quite inaccessible. Cannon-ball can hardly reach it, whereas the besieged are, on the other hand, able to inflict great damage on the besiegers. When Napoleon sent out Marshal Duroc to Komorn to reconnoitre during the war with the Austrians, not long before the Treaty of Pressburg,[352] the Marshal returned with the laconic verdict: "*Sire! imprenable.*"[a]

In the Carpathians, too, the Magyars still have support, and neither is there any lack of patrol-corps, particularly in the comitats of Trentschin, Honth and Abaujvár.

From all this it is evident that the war is *still far from being at an end*, and that Austria will still have to raise large fighting forces before it **conquers an enemy** *whose morale is improving with every day that passes*, and which is now better led, partly by French and Polish officers, than it was in the beginning.

Written by Engels on February 24, 1849

Printed according to the newspaper

First published in the *Neue Rheinische Zeitung* No. 231, February 25, 1849

Published in English for the first time

---

[a] Your Majesty, impregnable!—*Ed.*

[MORE NEWS OF THE MAGYARS]

No fresh news direct from the theatre of war. The *Allgemeine Oder-Zeitung* continues the "Reports of a Hungarian"; owing to lack of space we must hold it over until our next issue. How Görgey is proceeding in Kaschau and what fear he inspires in the Austrians is proved by a letter from *Pest* dated February 10:

"The news is now spreading that General *Görgey* has occupied the town of *Kaschau*. His first measure was to depose the entire Town Council, all the imperial customs officials and salt-office officials, and an enormous levy was imposed on the burghers. Early this morning a fully equipped brigade left the town, consisting of one battalion of fusiliers, two divisions of light cavalry, four battalions of infantry and two cavalry batteries, with all the necessary wagons of ammunition, powder and field-requisites, marching in the direction of Waitzen."

Further we hear again from Transylvania from various sources of the Russians' entry, while the official reports still remain silent about it. Thus reports of the 9th have arrived from Bucharest giving an account of the entry of the Russians at the request of the citizens of Hermannstadt and Kronstadt, adding that the advancing Russians had immediately encountered a unit of Szeklers and given them a sound beating. Yet the newly arrived courier sent by Lieutenant-Field Marshal Puchner from Hermannstadt on the 8th, who reports the destruction of Bem's army at Salzburg, says nothing about the entry of the Russians, and even Puchner's official report is silent on this point.

In Pressburg, J. Csenkly of Hetye in Hungary has been sentenced to four years prison for illegal possession of arms.

In Croatia the conflict between the nationalist Southern Slavs and the royal imperial authorities is becoming increasingly more violent.

Thus the *Constitutionelles Blatt aus Böhmen* is informed from Agram, February 15:

"Bitterness against the Ministry is growing here from day to day. News comes in almost hourly showing all too clearly that the Government is not in earnest with its pledges to the Croats, indeed indicating on the contrary that it is eager to effect the restoration of the old system of Magyar oppression. The agitation caused by the recently mentioned Magyar official letter from Count Almásy[a] had still not subsided when another Magyar order from the Ofen Board of Works arrived, enjoining the chief engineer in Croatia to apply henceforth to the Hungarian central authorities, as all the obstacles which had hitherto disrupted the old" (pre-March) "conduct of official business had been completely eliminated. This Magyar official order, which aroused irritation in all quarters, was followed by another, German, decree from the Vienna Ministry of Trade, whereby the chief engineer, Vauthier-Rauchefort, one of the keenest supporters of the Magyars, about whom there had been frequent complaints that he was in secret communication with Kossuth, was called to the office of the Ministry of Public Works and appointed ministerial adviser."

In consequence of this, the Ban's Council in Agram[b] has now issued an official edict prohibiting all authorities from carrying out orders originating from "Magyar insolence" and instructing them instead to send such unlawful communications to the Ban's Council, who will see to it that these are used as proof of the usurpation of its authority. At the same time this edict announces that not only is there no Magyar administration in the three united kingdoms[c] but that no interference from it in official business would ever be tolerated.

At the same time, refusal to be conscripted is on the increase in Bohemia. Today we hear:

The majority of the communities in the Prachin district of Bohemia are refusing to enforce conscription, since they have been informed that the decree in question originated from the Ministry and not from the Imperial Diet. It is to be feared that the peasant disturbances in this region may shortly spread to the whole country.

In short, despite all efforts, old Austria is disintegrating more and more every day. A revolutionary push from Italy or France, and it will belong to the past.

Written by Engels about February 24, 1849

First published in the second supplement to the *Neue Rheinische Zeitung* No. 231, February 25, 1849

Printed according to the newspaper

Published in English for the first time

---

[a] See this volume, p. 410.— *Ed.*
[b] i. e. the government of Croatia during the 1848-49 revolution.— *Ed.*
[c] i.e. Croatia, Slavonia and Dalmatia.— *Ed.*

THE RUSSIANS IN TRANSYLVANIA[353]

Cologne, February 26. *Ten thousand Russians are in Transylvania.*

It can no longer be denied, all concealment and obfuscation has become impossible, the facts are there, the *official Wiener Zeitung*[a] *itself* has admitted it.

So these were the tremendous victories of the imperial hired soldiery, this is the result of all the pompous bulletins of Welden, Windischgrätz, Schlick and Puchner: the great-power Austria *had to call in Russian help* to get the better of four and a half million Magyars.

At this new turning-point in Hungarian affairs let us survey once more the course of the war as the most recent news reflects it.

The territory which at this moment is occupied by the Magyars under Kossuth forms a large rectangle, 70-90 miles long and 30-40 miles wide, bounded in the north and the west by the Theiss, in the east by the Carpathians and in the south by the Maros. It embraces in an area of 2,500 square miles the central Hungarian plain and the mountainous regions of Transylvania. In addition Komorn on the Upper Danube is also in the hands of the Hungarians.

In the *south*, where the Magyars were always weakest, the Austrians, Slovenes and Austrian Serbs succeeded with the help of Turkish Serbs and disguised Russians[b] to push the Magyars beyond the Maros. There fighting took place near Arad, in which the Austrians advanced to the northern (right) bank of the Maros.

---

[a] An apparent reference to the report published in the *Wiener Zeitung* No. 44, February 21, 1849, and given on pp. 435-36 of this volume.— *Ed.*

[b] A mistake by Engels: Russians did not take part in the battle at Arad.— *Ed.*

According to their own assertion they gained a victory and captured fifteen pieces of siege artillery trained on Arad, but, equally according to their own statement, withdrew again across the Maros. As far as we know, up to now they have not yet succeeded in breaking through the line of the Maros and as long as that does not happen there can be no question of the great expedition which Rukavina is supposed to undertake against Grosswardein and Transylvania.

In the *west* and the *north-west* the Theiss with its extensive floods and boundless marshes provides the Magyars with an almost impregnable line of cover. As long as the Russians did not take part in the fighting this was the decisive centre of the theatre of war. Once Windischgrätz was in Debreczin the war would have dissolved into mere guerilla fighting. The Magyars knew this and therefore their main army did not offer serious resistance anywhere up to the Theiss. They were only concerned to hold out until the end of the cold weather which enabled the imperial forces to pass all rivers and marshes like firm ground, and which delivered Pest and Ofen into their hands with hardly a chance of resistance. While the main army thus withdrew slowly, the two wings remained in advanced positions, in the north in the Slovak comitats and in the south between the Drava and the Danube, held out as long as they could, forced the enemy army to divide and in the end withdrew, the one through the Carpathians towards the Theiss, the other across the Danube back to the Banat army.

Only the inane ignorance of German hack journalists who had sold themselves to Austria and had never had a map in their hands or followed a strategic operation, could see in this masterly plan, based on detailed knowledge and survey of the terrain, nothing else than cowardice, sheer cowardice, on the part of the Magyars. People of any sense and knowledge would at least have lied and boasted less absurdly than the mass of the German common liars, who had gone grey under censorship, corruption and gross ignorance.

Success has demonstrated the operational skill of the Magyars. It took six weeks for the first imperial soldier of the main army to see the Theiss, and while the river was then still frozen over, the battles of Szolnok, Czegléd, Tarczal and Tokaj showed the Austrians how Hungarians fight when offering serious resistance. Ottinger thrown back beyond Czegléd, Schlick to Boldogkőváralya and a general lament over the Magyars' sudden and unexpected resistance from all the martial-law papers, hitherto delirious with victory — those were the first results of the "victorious" advance of the Austrians to the Theiss. Then followed the thaw, the Magyars withdrew over the Theiss and the ice-drift prevented the imperial troops from following them. The ice-drift ceased, but not the inundations and swamping of both banks to a breadth of several miles. The imperial troops stood helpless facing the swamps and the torrential river and no one dared to cross although Windischgrätz sent reinforcement after reinforcement from Pest. But *the Magyars dared to cross*, because a short time ago we suddenly heard that Miskolcz, four miles this side of the Theiss, was again in their hands and, as we shall see later, the official royal imperial reports have done more than confirm this.

While Windischgrätz, Jellachich and Schlick were thus glad to be able to hang on to their positions, Nugent in the south gave battle to Damjanich, and in the north Götz, Simunich and Csorich to Görgey. In the south, where the Hungarian Banat army had already been pushed back, the Austrians succeeded in breaking up Damjanich's cut-off corps into guerilla forces, which still keep in check a sizable body of troops in the area between the Drava, the Danube and the forest of Bakony. In the north on the other hand, Görgey, one of the swiftest and most daring insurgent leaders, managed to defend the Slovak comitats for two whole months against three entire army corps by bold large-scale guerilla warfare and a series of brilliant individual actions. Although the royal imperial bulletins annihilated him countless times, he always reappeared on the field of battle, repulsed one Austrian general after another, and prevented their unification through rapid marches and constantly repeated attacks. Only the fall of Leopoldstadt decided his retreat before a three- or fourfold superiority. He retreated into the Upper Carpathians and by that gave the imperial troops such a fright that the whole of Galicia was armed, then thrust forward into the Zips and from there into Eperies and Kaschau. There he stood in the rear of Schlick. The latter, cut off from Windischgrätz by the Magyar corps which had advanced to Miskolcz, and now in danger of being surrounded on three sides, retreated hastily in a north-westerly direction, intending to unite with Götz and his associates in Leutschau. Then suddenly "powerful hostile forces" thrust at Polgár and Tiszafüred across the Theiss, unite with the column from Miskolcz and advance towards Rimaszombat, i.e. between Windischgrätz and Schlick. This forces Schlick to change his entire plan, leave Götz in the Carpathians to his fate and get ahead of the main column of the Magyars through a hasty south-westerly march in the direction of Rimaszombat.

By this masterly devised manoeuvre of the Magyars Schlick is thrown back into Slovakia, Götz is isolated in the Upper Carpathians, the unification of Görgey with the main Magyar army is assured and the whole of North-East Hungary liberated from the imperial troops.

All these events, which occurred between February 10 and 14, are admitted even in the official *Wiener Zeitung*. Among the rest of the howling Austrian and German press too, a curious lowering of the tone could recently be observed. Not to mention the mourning of our nearest neighbours, the Augsburg *Allgemeine Zeitung* is forced today to admit:

"The struggle may be yet a little prolonged. The country is too big and the insurgents have good leaders in the Poles." [a]

And now even the *Constitutionelles Blatt aus Böhmen*:

"The reports from Hungary which have arrived here to date vary widely in character. Those from the south are clearly favourable to our forces, those from the north *clearly unfavourable*."

And in another article:

"If we glance over the newest facts from Hungary in the various journals of decidedly conservative colour there seems to be a *slight up-and-down movement* in the successes of the imperial army.

"The occupation of Kaschau by Görgey too is not conducive to a belief in the dissolution of the Hungarian army, its destruction and dispersal and the ending of the war, which was regarded as imminent at the beginning of the year."

It is "still difficult to explain how, with the well-ordered troop combinations and with geographically correct manoeuvres which we have a right to expect from such an excellently organised and led army, isolated bodies of Magyar troops are in a position to move about with not insignificant forces in the line of operations, or behind it, or to converge again in places from which we believed them to have been dislodged for the whole duration of the campaign".

That is how things are in the north-west. It is no longer a case of defending the line of the Theiss against the Austrians; it is the Austrians who must not let themselves be thrown back into Slovakia and behind the Danube. For the last week the *Hungarians*, not the Austrians, *have been the attackers*.

And finally in the *south-east*, in Transylvania? Here the bulletins reported Bem as being defeated again and again by Puchner, here the "rebels" seemed to be completely defeated. Then suddenly the *Wiener Zeitung*[b] brings the following official lamentation:

"Since the bloody victory which the commanding general, Baron von Puchner, secured on January 21 against the three times stronger enemy at Hermannstadt, the troops retained for the defence of the town *could unfortunately not prevent* their communication with *the Banat and Karlsburg being severed by the enemy*, who had settled in the surrounding area like vandals, confiscating all stores of food and animals ready

---

[a] *Allgemeine Zeitung* No. 54, February 23, 1849.—*Ed.*
[b] No. 44, February 21, 1849.—*Ed.*

for slaughter and having them carried away together with other pillaged property to the depot at Klausenburg.

"With the shortages which in consequence had arisen on our side, the complaints and petitions of the flourishing chief cities of the loyal Saxon region, Kronstadt and Hermannstadt, became ever louder and more urgent. Even earlier, when these towns *were threatened by the marauding and perfidious Szekler hordes,* they appealed in their distress to the Russian commanding general in Wallachia, von Lüders, for possible assistance. When, through the *severing of the lines of communication with the main imperial army operating in Hungary, all prospects of an early arrival* of reinforcements vanished, when the enemy *attracted daily new rebel groups* and succeeded through deceitful pretences in *inciting all the Szeklers anew to disloyalty and armed insurrections,* Lieutenant-Field Marshal von Puchner was stormed on all sides with requests to call for Russian support so that the most prosperous part of the loyal Saxon region should not be abandoned to ruin and the blind destructive fury of blood-thirsty marauders.

"Moved by the imperative need to attack Bem, the chief of the rebels, *before the rebel mobs who were converging to his assistance from several sides made him overwhelmingly strong, but at the same time unable* with *his small forces to face the enemy resolutely* and protect the Saxon region from the devastation of the Szeklers, Lieutenant-Field Marshal von Puchner felt impelled to listen to the voice of humanity and to take into consideration the requests for Russian assistance made jointly by the Rumanian and Saxon nations, although he had received no authority for this from the Imperial Government. To this end he assembled a Council of War on February 1 in Hermannstadt. Just at the closure of this assembly a courier brought the official news from Kronstadt that *the armed Szekler hordes, 15,000 strong,* had crossed the frontiers of their region and that as a result, with the rich trading centre of *Kronstadt* now *threatened* with inevitable destruction *by these bands,* delay created the greatest danger.

A lot could be said about this royal imperial *Miserere,* but it is not necessary. Every line breathes consciousness of defeat, shame at being unable to tell any more lies and at having to abjure all past boastings.

So that was at the bottom of all the official bulletins and of the Magyar "exaggerations"! The Magyars attacking and advancing on the Theiss, the Austrians halted on the Maros, Transylvania irretrievably lost to the imperial cause unless the *Russians* intervene!

There is in Germany a literary lumpenproletariat, cowardly and lying stay-at-homes, who dare to revile as cowards these Magyars, this heroic nation of a few millions which so ran to earth the whole great Austria, the entire proud "united monarchy", that Austria is lost without the Russians.

"This fact," the official report continues ashamedly,

"this fact conclusively influenced the decision of the Council of War, which eventually *called in the help of the Russians for the protection of Hermannstadt and Kronstadt.* Consequent on the request made by Lieutenant-Field Marshal von Puchner, 6,000 imperial Russian troops entered Kronstadt on February 1 and 4,000 entered Hermannstadt on February 4 for the period of the threatening danger."

To know how many Russians are taking part in the fighting against the Magyars we shall have to await the next "Magyar exaggerations".

The further reported successes of Puchner, however insignificant, would never have come about without the Russian auxiliary troops, to judge from all that has happened hitherto.

Let it be known and not forgotten that Bulletin No. 24,[a] which appeared on the previous evening, ascribes the advantages secured from February 4 to 7 solely to the fighting abilities of the imperial troops and is completely silent about the entry of the Russians.

As we know, Bem stood before Stolzenburg. From there Puchner drove him on the 4th to Mühlenbach (where he claims to have captured 16 guns), then on the 6th to Szászváros, and on the 7th to Deva. There Bem still is.

Supposing this is true, Puchner would never have succeeded in pushing back 12 miles in 4 days a commander like Bem, who had crossed Transylvania with the greatest speed several times from one end to the other and who had always proved himself far superior to the constantly defeated Austrian, had it not been due to the most crushing superiority in numbers, due to the Russian auxiliary troops and Russian staff officers who are in any case better soldiers than these old-fashioned Austrians.

If Bem stands indeed near Deva his plan is obvious. He has withdrawn from Mühlenbach to the Maros and proposes to leave Transylvania for a time to the Austrians, who have their hands full with the Szekler guerilla bands, and to move down the Maros towards Arad, to push the Serbs back into the Banat and to advance on Kossuth's left wing. That Puchner should pursue him is out of the question for the present. But Gläser at Arad and Rukavina at Temesvár will soon get to hear of Bem and before a week has passed we shall probably hear how the indefatigable Pole operates against Szegedin and against the right wing of Windischgrätz. At least it is impossible to draw any other conclusions from the direction in which he is moving.

Without the Russians Puchner would have been annihilated and Transylvania subjugated in a few days. The Szeklers and the Magyars of the territory were themselves enough to keep the Saxons and the Wallachians in check. Bem could have followed as the victor the route which he now takes in his retreat, could have joined up with Kossuth and Dembiński and by that means have decided the outcome of the campaign. Victory was assured for their combined forces. Pest would have been taken in a few days and — *on March 15 Dembiński was of course in Vienna.*

---

[a] *Wiener Zeitung* No. 45, February 22, 1849.—*Ed.*

Then the Russians join the fray and throw the weight of the Tsar's Empire into the scales on Austria's side. And that, of course, is decisive.

Such indeed are the heroic deeds of these brave knights of martial law, Windischgrätzes, Jellachiches, Nugents and Schlicks. To set upon a small nation of four and a half million from eight sides with all Austria's might, to call for help from Turkish Croats, Bosnians and Serbs and in the end, as soon as the small nation has gathered its strength and driven out the traitors from its midst, to be soundly and roundly beaten!

These were indeed glorious laurels which the invincible Windischgrätz gained with the help of Russian reinforcements! Wonderful victories won by the alliance of the united European barbarians against the most advanceed outpost of European civilisation.

No one could have guessed, however, that the most subtle point in the grandiose campaign plan of Windischgrätz, the last strategic trump of the great general, was to be the appeal to the Russians. And yet, one might have known it: Has Austria ever been victorious by other means?

The Magyars, the last indomitable fighters of the revolution of 1848, may well succumb like the heroes of June in Paris or the fighters of October in Vienna, overwhelmed by the superior forces which again surround them on all sides. It will depend on the degree of the Russian participation whether the war against them will come to an end speedily or otherwise. If we West Europeans in the meantime persist in our silent apathy, if we offer only passive resistance and sighs of impotence to the infamous and traitorous attack of the Russians on our Magyar brothers, then the Magyars are lost — *and it will be our turn next.*

Indeed, the invasion of Transylvania by the Russians is the most infamous betrayal, the most villainous breach of international law in history. What is the open coalition of the despots in 1792, what is the silent connivance of the German powers at Russia in the Polish war, what is the partition of Poland itself [354] in comparison with this cowardly, treacherous strangling of a small heroic nation, carried out underhand and with typical Russian perfidy. What are all the infamies of past British, Russian and Austrian policies compared with this unmentionable villainy.

Austria wages a war of oppression against the Magyars, *Russia* attacks them from behind, and *Prussia* stands at the border, warrant in hand, to arrest the refugees and hand them over to their executioners. One year after the European revolution, on February

21, 1849, the Holy Alliance [355] stands before us resurrected in all its martial-law banditry and police blackguardism.

Thus far have we come. They dare to do such things in front of the whole of Europe and all Europe does not dare to move a finger. The official French Republic quietly rejoices and wishes that it too bordered on Russia so as to exterminate the anarchists the more easily. Why after the revolution in France and in Germany did we show so much generosity, magnanimity, consideration and kind-heartedness, if we did not wish the bourgeoisie again to raise its head and betray us, and the calculating counter-revolution to plant its foot on our neck?

But be patient. The "hydra of revolution" is not yet stilled. Look to Italy—the power of hired bayonets is not the last decisive power of history. Be patient. The day will come, and come soon, when a new revolution will make its bloody round through Europe, a revolution which, instead of bending its knee before mere phrases about the republic or haggling over the paltry "gains of March", will not sheathe its sword until it has avenged all the betrayal and all the infamy of the last nine months. Then we shall call to account all those who have permitted and supported this disgraceful betrayal of our Magyar fellow fighters. And then, despite the Russians, we shall strike off the shackles of Hungary and Poland!

Written by Engels on February 26, 1849

First published in the *Neue Rheinische Zeitung* No. 232, February 27, 1849

Printed according to the newspaper

Published in English for the first time

RUSSIAN INVASION.— SERBS.—
PROSPECTS FOR THE AUSTRIANS.—
FROM THE THEATRE OF WAR

There is absolutely no fresh news from the war theatre. But from all quarters reports are arriving which confirm our report of yesterday about the bad situation in which the imperial troops find themselves everywhere, except in Transylvania freed with the help of the Russians.[a] As proof we are reproducing below a dispatch from the Pressburg correspondent of the *Breslauer Zeitung* and the concluding paragraphs of the "Reports of a Hungarian" from the *Allgemeine Oder-Zeitung*.

The Austrians have without any doubt only reluctantly decided to appeal to the Russians. It is crystal-clear that the Russian invasion is bound to give a new impetus to the pan-Slavist movements of the Czechs and the Southern Slavs. These nationalities who have for a long time been used to look to the Tsar as their natural patron and ultimate liberator, are now receiving striking proof that Austria has neither the power nor the will to ensure their national development. And now for the first time the Russian Tsar[b] enters upon the stage, acts for them at the decisive moment and confirms with deeds the hopes which they place in him. Thus the Tsar now appears before the Austrian Serbs, Croats, Czechs etc. as the supreme protector of the Slav nationality as he did previously before the Turkish Serbs. And that the Slav national aspirations can be as menacing for the Austrian "united monarchy" as the armed resistance of the Magyars we have seen repeatedly.

With the Russian invasion of Transylvania the Tsar has taken a new step towards the realisation of pan-Slavism. He has proclaimed

---

[a] See this volume, pp. 432 and 453-55.— *Ed.*
[b] Nicholas I.— *Ed.*

the alliance of the Russians and the Austrian Slavs and made himself the *de facto* sovereign of the Austrian Slavs. The others are of course already under his sway. The Poles are his servants, the Turkish Slavs his vassals, and now he poses as the protector of the Austrian Slavs too. Only one more step and Austria falls completely under his suzerainty just like Turkey. At this price the "united monarchy" saves itself for a few months from destruction at the hands of the revolution!

At a people's assembly at Mitrowitz in the Banat the Serbs proclaimed the Patriarch[a] supreme ruler of their nation and Stratimirovich a rebel, declaring martial law against all enemies of the Emperor. The Patriarch who in Temesvár directs the affairs of the Voivodina, together with Todorovich and the Serbian deputies, is said to confirm these resolutions. At the battle of Arad the very popular Serbian Major Jovanovich fell into the hands of the Magyars. The following shows that the Magyars were in any case not defeated as decisively in this battle as the bulletins alleged. The Patriarch offered to the Magyar General Damjanich (who thus, as we incidentally learn, was fortunate enough to reach the Banat army across the Danube and the Theiss) to exchange Jovanovich against 200 Magyars. Damjanich replied that as far as he knew the Serbs did not have 200 Magyar prisoners in their hands! The Serbs, by the way, are arming on some scale in Serbia as within the Banat. In the Serbian principality a national convention[b] has been summoned and is discussing the mobilisation of 1,000 auxiliary troops in each of the country's 18 districts.

So that one should see what a small and nationally mixed country the new Serbian Voivodina is and how absurd the pretensions of the pan-Slavists are to create small Slav states in all corners of Hungary, we give the following statistical notes from the Belgrade *Serbske Noviny*:

"The Voivodina comprises territorially the following: 1. the Sirmische comitat[c], 2. the Peterwardein regiment, 3. the comitat of Bács, 4. the battalion of the Tchaikists,[356] 5. the comitat of Torontal, 6. the former German Banat regiment (now named Pancsova regiment), 7. the former Illyrian Banat regiment (now called Weisskirchen regiment) and the comitat of Temesvár. The area totals 719 square miles, with 75 towns and market centres, 706 villages, 221,182 houses and 1,605,808 inhabitants. The inhabitants can be divided according to their national origin into 917,916 Serbs, 26,200 Slovaks, 13,000 Bulgarians, 283,000 Wallachians, 278,400 Germans, 6,160 French and 81,132 Magyars. Of the inhabitants 877,620 are Greek Orthodox, 627,994

---

[a] Rajachich.—*Ed.*

[b] Skupština.— *Ed.*

[c] This comitat, like the Peterwardein regimental district, was part of the Military Border Area.—*Ed.*

Roman Catholics, 12,494 United Catholics, 46,311 Lutherans, 30,642 Calvinists, 17 Arians [357] and 10,730 Jews. The Catholic Southern Slavs are included among the 917,916 Serbs. The former border regiment of the Wallachian Banat remains outside the territory of the Voivodina, and will be incorporated into Transylvanian Rumania (Wallachia)."

This small so-called national Serbian country thus contains 700,000 Germans, Wallachians, Magyars etc. compared with 900,000 Serbs. And the 900,000 Serbs are not even all Serbs but include also the "Catholic Southern Slavs", that is the Shokazians [358] of Syrmien and of the comitat of Bács, who are not Serbs at all. And this is supposed to be a nation with national needs and above all the need to be separate from Hungary!

We now give the report of the *Breslauer Zeitung*:

"*Pressburg*, February 18. The wet and stormy weather has made the notorious roads of our country so bottomless that the large army corps can move forward only with untold difficulties, and the heavy artillery and other heavy vehicles are indeed getting stuck. Under these circumstances the numerous Hungarian patrol-corps are gaining one advantage after the other and the Austrian army is being fooled in a variety of ways. The commander-in-chief of the latter[a] seems indeed to have become impatient and would very much like to lead a major attack, for which purpose he has dispatched large forces in the direction of Szolnok. As a result the rumour circulates that a serious encounter has taken place there and that the Magyars have been thrown back beyond the Theiss.— One can, however, entertain a certain suspicion concerning these reports because the Hungarians are at present *too well led* not to make use of the golden opportunity to draw the enemy into the marshes of the Theiss and to destroy him there without any great difficulty. The many patrol-corps which *spring up everywhere* in Lower Hungary will not fail to harass him on all sides if he should advance too far, cut off his supplies and capture and destroy any troops which move away from the main army. In a certain sense the war in lower Hungary can be *compared with Napoleon's campaign in Russia,* and if the Austrian army should advance too far it could meet with fate similar to that of the French at the time.— Under these circumstances Windischgrätz will be in a *difficult position.* To act quickly and secure with one decisive blow a change of fortune for his cause is virtually impossible, but if he hesitates the strength of the Magyars will continue to grow. Capitulation is said to have been offered but the Magyars have declined with disdain.— If we cast a glance at the map we shall see that the Austrian army, despite its advances and its reported victories, *is surrounded by large and small formations of the Magyar army as if by a net.* From the borders of Styria via the Plattensee[b] to Esseg in Croatia the country appears to have been conquered but *everywhere there are patrol-corps* which seriously molest the Austrians.

"On the other side, that is from the Danube to the Carpathians, things are no better. One becomes convinced of this when one reads the reports of the Austrians being driven hither and thither through constant engagements. Here the Hungarian patrol-corps have a particularly suitable terrain, and most of the inhabitants, *even the majority of the Slovaks,* secretly side with them. Only this explains how the Magyars can continue to make their sallies far into Galicia almost with impunity. In the east the

---

[a] Windischgrätz.—*Ed.*
[b] Lake Balaton.— *Ed.*

Theiss is the great barrier which protects the Magyars, and wherever the Austrians have attempted to push across they have always been thrown back with losses.

"If it should come to a major battle, and if the Austrians should lose it, as they possibly might, then their retreat would be a very dangerous one. For they could well fear that the people would rise up everywhere. The commander-in-chief does not seem to conceal the precariousness of his situation."

The following is the end of the "Reports of a Hungarian" from the *Allgemeine Oder-Zeitung*.[a] This could also serve as proof how little "exaggerated" the Magyar reports are.

"Thanks to Kossuth's clever measures all the youth of Pest has gone off to Debreczin. People with detailed knowledge of events on the other side of the Theiss say that the Hungarian army is 120,000-150,000 strong, commanded by three capable Polish generals[b] and supported by a considerable contingent of artillery and that in case of need it could be augmented by the 100,000-strong Hungarian *Landsturm*. The well-known Rosa with his troops occupies the forest of Bakony.

"The Austrians put three bridges across the Theiss, one near Szolnok, one near Tiszafüred and the third near Zibok, which the Hungarians used to cross the river and to defeat the enemy on the 11th inst.

"Order and the strictest discipline rule throughout the Hungarian army, especially since the Polish generals have assumed supreme command. The comitats on the other side of the Theiss are resolved to defend themselves to the last man and the majority of the young men who fled to Debreczin on the entry of the Austrians into Pest have joined the Hungarian army, whose soldiers range from 17 to 40, and even 60 years of age, all inspired with love for their country.

"Kossuth, I hear from reliable sources, recently made in Debreczin a speech, such as has never been heard before.

"The hall was filled with deputies and other persons, the gallery with ladies; he made the deputies and all present swear to stand by him in the struggle against Austria. All hands rose to take the oath. A long silence followed this taking of the oath, then he pronounced in a strong voice just these words: **'Now the fatherland is saved.'**

"The majority of royal imperial troops who were stationed in Pest and Buda were withdrawn in the direction of Erlau and Czegléd and only about 4,000 men remained. There was talk of the headquarters of Prince Windischgrätz being moved to Erlau. In spite of the great victories which the Austrians claimed to have won but which in fact the Hungarians won, they did not fail to train the cannon of the fortress of Buda on the town of Pest. An order was given to the inhabitants of the fortress to lay in provisions for themselves for three months. Those who were unable to do so were to leave their homes.

"Why all these fearful preparations, in absolute contradiction to the absurd news according to which the Austrian army operates now near Debreczin, now in Transylvania! Even the soldiers are demoralised. Officers and soldiers complain loudly that they have been forced to take up arms against the Hungarians, who have not done them any harm. *The most stupid and at the same time the most cruel are the Bohemians.*

"The former Prime Minister, Count Louis Batthyány, was interrogated fourteen times and refused fourteen times to answer, saying: 'I was a Minister and I shall

---

[a] See this volume, pp. 427-28.—*Ed.*

[b] Henryk Dembiński, Józef Bem and Józef Wysocki.—*Ed.*

only answer when summoned before a tribunal of Hungarian magnates.' Generals Moga and Hrabovsky, two old men whose life was without blemish, were sentenced to twenty years confinement in a fortress; Count Lasar, son-in-law of General Moga and colonel of the Honvéd,[359] was to be executed but the magnanimous Prince Windischgrätz commuted his sentence to *10 years imprisonment in chains,* loss of his title of nobility and dismissal in disgrace from the army!!"

Written by Engels on February 27, 1849

First published in the *Neue Rheinische Zeitung* No. 233, February 28, 1849

Printed according to the newspaper

Published in English for the first time

SPEECH FROM THE THRONE

[*Neue Rheinische Zeitung* No. 234, March 1, 1849]

Cologne, February 28. The speech from the throne which to the great indignation and annoyance of the *Kölnische Zeitung* was reported *prematurely* yesterday evening to the readers of the *Neue Rheinische Zeitung*, proved to be *authentic*. Only a single passage, the one relating to the *state of siege* in Berlin, was altered overnight. In so doing the Brandenburg Ministry destroyed the whole point of its speech.

This passage, as reported by us yesterday evening in its original form, reads:

"To restore the rule of law, a state of siege had to be proclaimed in the capital and its immediate environs. This cannot be lifted until such time as public safety, which is still threatened and for which this measure was essential, is durably safeguarded by firm laws. The drafts of these laws will be presented to you without delay." [360]

This passage, even though it was hushed up, gives away the whole secret of the speech from the throne. In plain language it means: the *exceptional* states of siege will be lifted as soon as the *general* state of siege has been imposed on the entire kingdom by laws and has become part of our constitutional customs. The series of these "firm" laws will begin with September legislation [361] on associations and the press. [a]

[*Neue Rheinische Zeitung* No. 235, March 2, 1849]

Cologne, March 1. Let us first of all note that the speech from the throne has the full approval of the *Kölnische Zeitung*. The paper

---

[a] The *Neue Rheinische Zeitung* then gave the text of the speech from the throne.—*Ed.*

raises a few objections about the actions of the Government mentioned in the speech from the throne, but none at all about the speech itself.

"The King's speech from the throne is truly a *constitutional speech from the throne*"—

thus the sagacious newspaper begins its reprint of the speech from the throne in a paraphrasing leading-article form.[a]

"*A constitutional* speech from the throne"! Of course, to anyone who had expected a "speech directly from the King's heart", an importunate moralising outpouring of the heart such as used to occur in the United Diet, or a Brandenburg-Wrangel type of rodomontade with clinking of spurs and twirling of moustaches, this document must seem extremely "constitutional".

One thing is certain: Manteuffel coped with his task far better than Camphausen by completely leaving out the "talented declamation" of 1847.[362] The bourgeois Minister presented a document of bourgeois-like dullness, limping and boring in language and content. With the greatest *bonhomie*, the Minister from the nobility submits to using the boring constitutional form in order by its means in fluent, easy language to scoff at the Chambers and all constitutionalism.

As for the serious content of the speech from the throne, this is reduced to practically nothing owing to the hushing up of the passage about the retention of the state of siege, which we mentioned yesterday. This was the only passage in which the Ministry spoke to the Chambers honestly and frankly.

One would have to be the *Kölnische Zeitung* or the Berlin *National-Zeitung* to take the rest of the speech from the throne seriously. One who only with respectful awe and solemn mien ventures to observe such constitutional supreme state functions as were performed the day before yesterday in Berlin, will, of course, in his innocence never be able to understand how something so holy can be misused in frivolous wit. But anyone who attaches as little importance to the whole constitutional comedy as Herr Manteuffel does will not be so lacking in taste as to take *au sérieux* the document which the Minister caused to be delivered the day before yesterday to the reverential public of the White Hall[363] through the lips of the King by the grace of God.

We believe we shall be doing Herr Manteuffel a service if we point out the correct meaning of his speech from the throne to the

---

[a] *Kölnische Zeitung* No. 51, March 1, 1849.—*Ed.*

German public, which unfortunately is not accustomed to witty sallies.

You expect Manteuffel to boast of his successfully accomplished counter-revolution, to threaten the Chambers with loaded rifles, razor-sharp swords etc., in the manner of a clumsy sergeant-major *à la* Wrangel. Nothing of the kind! Manteuffel passes over all this with only a few lightly uttered phrases, as if it were something quite self-evident.

"The events that are fresh in the memory of all of you, gentlemen deputies of the First and Second Chambers, compelled me in December of last year to dissolve the Assembly which had been convened to reach agreement on the Constitution. At the same time — being convinced of the absolute necessity of finally restoring a firmly based state of public law — I gave the country a Constitution, the content of which faithfully fulfils the promises I made in March of last year."[364]

Herr Manteuffel speaks as if it were a question of some most insignificant trifle — the replacement of an old frock-coat by a new one, the appointment of a supernumerary official or the arrest of an agitator. Forcible transference, adjournment and dissolution of a sovereign assembly, state of siege, a sabre-rule — in short, the whole coup d'état — is reduced to "events that are fresh in the memory of all of you". In exactly the same way as the knightly Ban Jellachich would relate with the most elegant insouciance how his red-coats had burned alive the inhabitants of some village or other.

And now you have the "*faithful fulfilment* of the promises I made in March of last year" in the form of the imposed so-called Constitution. And do you consider cunning Manteuffel to be so limited in intelligence as to have said that in all seriousness? *Allons donc!*[a]

Such a beginning is striking. But one must be able to make use of this initial astonishment in order to pass on to still more astonishing things. Herr Manteuffel can do that:

"Since then the tension under which a great part of the country was living a few months ago has given way to a calmer mood; confidence, which previously had been so deeply shaken, is gradually being restored, trade and industry are beginning to recover from the stagnation to which they threatened to succumb."

What glances the worthy deputies have exchanged when they heard those words! Trade and industry are recovering! And why not? Why should not this same Manteuffel who can impose a Constitution be able to impose also an upswing in "trade and industry"? The aplomb with which Manteuffel utters this colossal

---

[a] Oh, nonsense!—*Ed.*

assertion is truly remarkable. *Mais nous marchons de surprise en surprise*[a]:

> "You know, gentlemen, that I have reserved for you the right to revise the Constitution. It is for you now to come to an agreement on this among yourselves and with my Government."

Of course, gentlemen, "come to an agreement"! But the humour of the situation lies precisely in the fact that two such Chambers as Manteuffel imposed on "My people" *can* never "come to an agreement among themselves"! Otherwise why was the First Chamber invented? And if, gentlemen, you were even to come to an agreement *among yourselves*, which is by no means to be expected, you would then have to come to an agreement with "My Government"— and that you will never arrive at, Manteuffel can guarantee!

And so, gentlemen deputies of the First and Second Chambers, you are already sufficiently busy revising the Constitution. Since "I" have learnt from experience that an *agreement* between *two* agents is already impossible, "I" considered it expedient on this occasion to try to achieve an agreement between *three factors which admit of no agreement*. And if you do not go on trying to come to an agreement until doomsday without getting one inch farther forward, Manteuffel will pledge himself to become a contributor to the *National-Zeitung*.

Therefore, gentlemen, "come to an agreement"!

If, however, contrary to all human expectation, you after all succeed in solving what for decency's sake can only be called your task, you will still not be a single step farther forward. To meet such a case "My Government" has issued a dozen laws "for implementing the Constitution", which strip this Constitution of the last semblance of liberalism. Among other things, they include two decrees on trade corporations[365] which are worthy of the year 1500, and which can give such an advantageously combined representative institution as you are work that will make your head ache for ten years.

> "All these decrees will be presented to you without delay for your approval."

Therefore, gentlemen, "approve" them!

But then "My Government" will without delay put before you proposals concerning the state of siege—September laws, gagging laws,[366] laws for suppression of clubs etc. And until you "have approved" them—and it is to be hoped that this will never happen—the state of siege will, of course, continue.

---

[a] But we go from surprise to surprise.—*Ed.*

And do you think that with that your work will have been accomplished? On the contrary, the most important thing only comes now:

> "In addition you will have to undertake a discussion of various laws, which are in part essential for implementing the Constitution and the drafts of which will gradually be put before you. I particularly recommend for your most careful consideration the drafts for the new local government system and for the new district, regional and provincial systems, the law on education, the law on church administration, the law on income tax, the law on land taxation, the law on redemption from corvée obligations, and on the abolition without compensation of some of them, and also on the establishment of annuity offices."

With these different occupations, gentlemen, which altogether amount to about three dozen organic laws containing several thousand paragraphs, you will have, God willing, so much to do that the revision of the Constitution as well as the approval of the preliminary laws, and the discussion of drafts laid before you will be at most half fulfilled. If you manage to do even that much you will have accomplished a superhuman labour. In the meantime the state of siege will continue everywhere and will also be introduced where it does not yet exist (who is to prevent us from putting the whole of Prussia in a state of siege "district by district"?); in the meantime the imposed so-called Constitution with the imposed additional laws will continue in force. Consequently there will remain the hitherto existing botched local government system, the existing district, regional and provincial system of representation, the existing absence of freedom of education, the exemption of the higher nobility from land taxation, and the corvée obligations of the peasants.

In order, however, that you will not be able to complain, there will be laid before you, in addition to all these unfulfillable tasks, *two budgets*— for 1849 and for 1850. Will you rise from your seats in indignation at so much work? So much the better, gentlemen deputies of the First and Second Chambers. In that case, on the basis of the imposed so-called Constitution "My Government" will continue to levy the hitherto existing taxes for all eternity. In addition, there is still some money left of the 25 million voted by the United Diet, and if "My Government" should need more, it will know what it has to do.

But should you wish to follow in the footsteps of the dissolved National Assembly, then, gentlemen, I will remind you that the "organisation, fighting capacity and loyalty" of the Prussian army "have withstood the severest tests"—especially in the great drive against the agreers in November of last year.

And now, gentlemen deputies of the First and Second Chambers, after steps have been taken to ensure that, because of the composition of the two Chambers, you will not be able to reach agreement *among yourselves*, and because of the composition of "My Government" you will not be able to reach agreement *with this Government*, after such a disorderly mass of materials has been laid before you that, apart from anything else, you will never be able to complete even the tiniest part of it, and after in this way the preservation of the bureaucratic-feudal-military despotism has been guaranteed—now take note of what the fatherland expects of you:

"Gentlemen deputies of the First and Second Chambers! The fatherland now confidently expects from the co-operation of its representatives with My Government the consolidation of the re-established legal order so as to be able to enjoy constitutional liberties and their peaceful development. The protection of these liberties and of legal order—these two fundamental conditions of public welfare—will always be the object of My conscientious care. In this work I count on your assistance. May your activity, with God's help, serve to exalt the honour and glory of Prussia, whose people, in close union with their princes, have already successfully overcome many hard times, and may it prepare for the fatherland in both the narrower and the broader sense a peaceful and blessed future!"

That is the speech from the throne of Citizen Manteuffel. And there are people who are so greatly lacking in taste that they call such a skilful comedy a *"constitutional speech from the throne"*!

Truly, if anything could prompt Herr Manteuffel to surrender his portfolio, it would be such a misinterpretation of his best intentions!

Written on February 28-March 1, 1849

First published in the *Neue Rheinische Zeitung* Nos. 234 and 235, March 1 and 2, 1849

Printed according to the newspaper

Published in English for the first time

FROM THE THEATRE OF WAR IN TRANSYLVANIA AND HUNGARY

There is still no up-to-date news from the theatre of war. What we learn consists almost entirely of further details about events which are already known.

On the upper reaches of the Theiss the Magyars occupy both sides of the river. Through Görgey's daring manoeuvre—"carried out with a degree of dexterity not expected of him" (*Constitutionelles Blatt aus Böhmen*)—the entire country to the east of the Theiss and Hernath has been cleared of the enemy. Through the simultaneous advance of Dembiński across the Theiss the imperial troops have been thrown back along their whole left wing and centre and only below Szolnok they are still at the Theiss. So when the Austrian newspapers report that Schlick "has joined the main army" or that he "has reached the head of the main army" that means no more than that the remains of the 4 brigades he commands *have been thrown back* onto Windischgrätz's troops instead of securing the left wing.

Profiting by this opportunity, as the Magyar correspondent of the *Breslauer Zeitung* reports,

"the major part of the Polish regiment of Rothkirch has gone over to the Hungarians and entered Debreczin in triumph. Among the prisoners there are also two generals. *The comitats of Zips, Sáros, Abaujvár, Zemplin, Unghvar and Heves are thus, due to the complete defeat and expulsion of the imperial troops, again under the control of the Hungarians*".

The *Constitutionelles Blatt aus Böhmen* confirms in two reports of the 20th from Pest that Görgey has joined up with the main Magyar army and that this army "has again taken up a threatening position" and "seems to be decided to give battle".

The above-mentioned Magyar correspondent goes on to report:

"From Kaschau many refugees have arrived in Pest. Count Szirmay, one of the richest Hungarian magnates, has been killed by the enraged people in the most gruesome manner. He had caused himself to be hated because it was due to his betrayal that Schlick entered Kaschau. He had also attempted to raise a volunteer battalion for the imperial army. He was a major in the imperial army."

How precarious the situation on the left wing is for the Austrians is demonstrated by the regular dispatches of reinforcements there. Nearly every day Ban Jellachich inspects in Pest new troops leaving for there. The Magyar correspondent in a report on the 22nd says:

"On the 20th a brigade with a large quantity of artillery left Pest in the direction of Hatvan. It consisted mostly of Croats. Ban Lieutenant-Field Marshal Jellachich held a review of the brigade and delivered an address to it. The public which attended looked on unmoved. Then a general came rushing up and shouted, 'Off with your hats when the Emperor is acclaimed!' The public turned about as one man and left. From that too you can judge of the mood, which is getting more bitter every day."

The reinforcements which Görgey brought to the main Magyar army consist according to the *Constitutionelles Blatt aus Böhmen* of 9,000 men, including 1 battalion of grenadiers, 1 battalion of Este infantry, 2 battalions of Wasa, 8 divisions (16 squadrons) of hussars, 30 cannon and 12 howitzers. That these figures underestimate rather than overestimate the truth may be concluded from the sentiments of the paper from which they were taken.

At Windischgrätz's centre and right wing little has changed. Szolnok on the Theiss is still in the hands of the Austrians while the Magyars hold the opposite bank. While the former build entrenchments at Szolnok, both sides shoot at each other with cannon across the Danube.

Szegedin, lower down on the Theiss, which has been reported three or four times as captured by the Austrians, has according to today's reports been taken yet again. This time however by troops dispatched from Pest, which had joined up near Szegedin with the Serbs approaching from the south to seize this important point dominating the confluence of the Maros with the Theiss. *Se non è vero, è ben trovato.*[a]

On the other hand the Austrian correspondent reports from a private letter that

"shortly after its capture *Arad* was wrested from the imperial troops, some of the latter having dispersed too quickly into the houses of the town to look for food, and

---

[a] It's well devised even if it is not true.— *Ed.*

the insurgents availed themselves of this circumstance to assemble rapidly and drive back our troops. The commanders are said not to have been to blame, as they could not prevent the totally exhausted troops, allegedly Serbs and men from Peterwardein,[367] from seeking food".

The heroic deeds of the Serbian army stationed here consist mainly in destroying and burning, looting, torturing with fire, killing and raping. The places around Szegedin, as well as Maria-Theresienstadt, Zombor and other places have been treated most disgustingly by these Turkish barbarians and have been almost destroyed. One need only hear what the pro-Czech *Constitutionelles Blatt aus Böhmen* says:

"In the Banat the Serbs are advancing victoriously, but robbery and arson mark their passage and many Hungarian and German localities have had to pay a terrible price for daring to show sympathy for the cause of the Hungarians. Zombor, an important trading city, has been partly consumed by flames, as the Serbs set fire to all houses whose owners had earlier taken part in enforcing the martial law applied against the Serbs by the Hungarians.

"Yesterday and today there is general talk here that the Serbs have finally succeeded in taking Szegedin, and in that case we can only commiserate with the many Hungarians who live there, for the Serbs will hardly treat them with lenience."

Further back, on the Drava and Danube, the army of Nugent is concentrated around *Peterwardein*, the surrender of which is "to be hoped for", to use the language of an earlier bulletin. His army too is distinguishing itself by the most shameful barbarities. The inhabitants of Siklosz are said to have shot at the Imperials after they had previously welcomed them with open arms. What does Nugent do? He immediately surrounds the town, trains cannon loaded with shrapnel on all the gates and sets the place on fire. Whoever escaped from the flames fell victim to the shrapnel. The *Kölnische Zeitung* finds this "strange".

To sum up all these operations we must agree with the following judgment borrowed from the *Leipziger Zeitung*:

"Military experts assure us that in the operations in Hungary significant mistakes have been committed and that Prince Windischgrätz *failed to reveal himself as an outstanding army commander.*"

A conclusion to which we had already been led almost every day for a long time.

Finally we have now from *Transylvania* the reports of the local papers on the entry of the Russians. In *Kronstadt* this event was preceded by a declaration of martial law. From this town the *Satellit* of February 2 reports:

"In order to prevent the threatened attack on Kronstadt by the Szeklers, yesterday and today strong contingents of Cossacks, Russian riflemen, grenadiers and a whole artillery park with the necessary personnel under the command of the imperial Russian General von Engelhardt have entered Kronstadt and been quartered on the population. Tomorrow a further battalion of Russian infantry is expected. The cannon have been installed between the Promenade and the Schlossberg and adequately supplied for immediate action. Day and night they are guarded by a strong contingent of Cossacks and grenadiers, while Russian riflemen guard the fortifications."

Further, dated February 6, a report on the fighting between Engelhardt and the Szeklers:

"February 4 was a hot day for our district. Early in the morning the Russian Major-General Engelhardt went on reconnaissance towards Honigberg with a battalion of Russian infantry, 170 Cossacks, two pieces of field artillery and three companies from the 1st Rumanian Border Regiment. Halfway there he noticed numerous Szekler groups moving through the mist towards Petersberg, probably in order to attack Kronstadt from there. The Russians advanced against them and the Szeklers opened cannon-fire. As the enemy was numerically superior the Russian general sent immediately into the town for his remaining troops. They arrived with 84 Austrian dragoons and 45 hussars after more than two hours during which Engelhardt engaged the Szeklers with attacks by the Cossacks, skirmishes and cannon-fire. Then General Engelhardt attacked the four times (!) stronger (!) enemy in earnest, drove him from the heights between Petersberg and Honigberg and after five and a half hours of fighting forced him to retreat. On the Russian side 1 officer and 2 privates were killed, on the Austrian side 1 officer and 3 privates (2,400 Russians and about 500 Austrians were involved in the fighting). The enemy suffered 150 casualties in killed and wounded and fled leaving cannon, weapons, munitions etc. behind."

Kronstadt (Siebenbürger Wochenblatt).[a] The following proclamation to the citizens of Kronstadt was made by the Russian general.

"To the citizens of Kronstadt. Some evil-minded Kronstadt citizens have spread the false rumour that I had quarrelled with the royal imperial Austrian General von Schurter and that I had intended to leave the town with my troops! I have on the contrary found a good comrade in Herr General von Schurter and shall continue to esteem and honour him as such. If I have sent back my baggage-carts to Wallachia that has been done simply and solely in the interest of the local inhabitants as it would have been difficult for them to find forage for the 700 uhlans who are arriving today as well as for the teams of horses of the baggage-carts. The entire contents of the baggage-carts, consisting of biscuits, remain in the town and only the empty carts were dispatched. This false rumour is therefore an infamous and stupid lie; even if I myself were not in accord with General von Schurter I would nevertheless remain here for the protection of this city, for that is the All-highest will of my Emperor and Lord.[b]

"Kronstadt, January 29 (February 10), 1849

Major-General *von Engelhardt*"

---

[a] The reports from this newspaper cited here and below were also published in the *Grazer Zeitung* No. 56, February 25, 1849.—*Ed.*

[b] Nicholas I.— *Ed.*

Kronstadt, February 10. The expected Russian uhlans arrived here yesterday afternoon. The Szeklers, whom the imperial Russian General von Engelhardt taught a lesson (!) on the 4th inst., have nevertheless again crossed the River Alt near Hidveg and have entered Marienburg. From there they yesterday again molested the community of Heldsdorf and requisitioned a quantity of bread, hay and oats (*Siebenbürger Wochenblatt*).

Written by Engels on March 1, 1849

First published in the *Neue Rheinische Zeitung* No. 235, March 2, 1849

Printed according to the newspaper

Published in English for the first time

[EUROPEAN WAR INEVITABLE]

Cologne, March 2. The second sitting of the Second Chamber has produced two not uninteresting results: firstly, that the Right has so far been **21** votes stronger than the Left, not ten as we were informed yesterday; and secondly, the *official announcement of the termination of the armistice of Malmö*.[368] The latter event naturally leads to a thousand-and-one diplomatic speculations. Thus, the Russian Cabinet is said to have concluded conditionally a mutual defensive and offensive alliance with Denmark; a Russian courier is said to have brought to Berlin the order to resist all possible demands of the Chamber absolutely etc. We shall report tomorrow what is substantiated of these rumours.

We learn from *Italy*: in *Turin* Gioberti is *definitely dismissed* and *Chiodo* definitely Prime Minister. The Chamber has sanctioned the change of ministry and in agreement with the Ministers has decided on the **immediate resumption of the war against Austria**.[369] The Austrian expedition to Ferrara gives ample cause for this.

In *Tuscany* it seems that Laugier's attempt at reaction is failing completely.[370] The Grand Duke,[a] despairing of his luck, is said to have set sail to his Holy Father[b] in Gaeta.

Apart from the alleged retreat of the Austrians from Ferrara (already reported yesterday by the *Wiener Zeitung*) there is nothing new from the *Roman Republic*.

According to the *Moniteur du soir*, Sicily **has proclaimed a republic**.[371]

---

[a] Leopold II.—*Ed.*
[b] Pius IX.—*Ed.*

Favourable news beyond all expectation has reached us from Hungary. According to *imperial* as well as Magyar reports the **Magyars have reached Hatvan, three stages from Pest.** This victorious advance is the first result of Görgey's collaboration with the main Magyar army. The Austrians are sending all their troops post-haste towards Hatvan. In a few days a *decisive battle* will be fought there.[372]

This is the condensed content of the news which arrived this evening. War in Denmark, war in Italy, and more war than ever in Hungary—involvements every one of which would suffice in these times, calamitous for all the existing powers, to engender a *European war.* That war will come, it must come. It will divide Europe into two armed camps, not according to nations or national sympathies, but according to the level of civilisation. On the one side the revolution, on the other the coalition of all outmoded estate-classes and interests; on the one side civilisation, on the other barbarism. The victory may be tardy but it cannot be in doubt.

Written by Engels on March 2, 1849

First published in the special supplement to the *Neue Rheinische Zeitung* No. 235, March 2, 1849

Printed according to the newspaper

Published in English for the first time

FROM THE THEATRE OF WAR

How things stand with the imperial cause emerges from the silence of the official reports better than from any other circumstance. Tonight, it is true, we have not received our Vienna letters and newspapers, but the Berlin evening papers, which customarily bring the news from Vienna at the same time as the *Wiener Zeitung*, do not contain anything either. Profound silence from the otherwise so talkative Vienna commandant's office on the operations on the Theiss, the Maros and in Transylvania.

Unofficial reports make up for this. The pro-Austrian reports from Vienna and the Magyar report in the *Breslauer Zeitung* from Hungary agree on one fact: *the Magyar army stands at Hatvan, six miles from Pest,* where a decisive battle is in preparation.

Some say: the insurgents have been *driven back* into this area by Schlick, Schulzig and Götz; others maintain: the victorious Magyars have *advanced* into this area.

Who is right?

A glance at the map decides the question. According to the latest news, Görgey marched from Kaschau down along the Hernath so as to join up with Dembiński. Dembiński on his part crossed the Theiss below the Hernath estuary and advanced in a north-westerly direction through Miskolcz. As a result the left wing (Schlick, Schulzig and Götz, who has been driven into the Upper Carpathians) was threatened at its communications with the main army and attacked simultaneously by Dembiński on the right and by Görgey on the left flank. The Schlick-Schulzig corps therefore withdrew at once from Torna to Rimaszombat. According to the latest (royal imperial official) news, the two armies confronted each other at Rimaszombat.

Now we suddenly find the whole position completely changed. The Magyars have gone from Rimaszombat, over twenty miles from Pest, to Hatvan, six miles from Pest, and a *decisive battle* is expected there.

If Schlick had beaten the Magyars their line of retreat would not have been to the Danube, where they would have encountered the centre of the enemy army, but to the Theiss and Hernath, where the entire region is in Magyar hands. But if the Magyars retained the upper hand they could not advance from their positions on the Upper Theiss and Hernath in order to reach Pest *in any other direction* than that of *Hatvan.* For the way from Kaschau to Pest leads in a straight line through Rimaszombat and Hatvan! The roads from Miskolcz to Pest and from Polgár and Tiszafüred (the two crossing points of the main Magyar army over the Theiss) to Pest also lead through Hatvan!

If then, as the Vienna reports say,

"the insurgents under Görgey and Dembiński, pursued by Generals Schlick, Schulzig and Götz, have been driven into the area of Hatvan",

they have been pressed to the very point *to which they would anyway have had to get as victors,* the point on which all the various Magyar corps marching upon Pest would converge.

Hence: either the Austrian generals are such dolts that their victories lead the enemy to exactly *the same result* as their defeats, that they render a better service to their enemies when they defeat them than when they let themselves be defeated by them, or the imperial reports have once again lied brazenly.

That the latter is the case—although we do not wish thereby in the least to diminish the clumsiness of the royal imperial generals—that yet another attempt has been made to cover up a shameful defeat by pompous assertions of victory, is proved by the concluding sentence:

"It is to be expected, therefore, that in the next few days a major blow will be struck against them [the insurgents]." [a]

There is at Hatvan either only one Magyar corps or a whole army. In the first case one cannot speak of a "major blow"; in the second case it will hardly be credited that the three corps of the royal imperial left wing, which could not even cope with Görgey alone, have defeated and "pursued" an entire army of which Görgey's troops form only a small part.

And even if the main Hungarian army had been "driven" to

---

[a] Here and above we are quoting from Bulletin No. 24 of the Austrian army published in the *Wiener Zeitung* No. 45, February 22, 1849.—*Ed.*

Hatvan, would it wait there until the entire army of Windischgrätz had come to the aid of the "pressing" Austrian corps so as to strike a "major blow", or would it march back as fast as possible to the Theiss, hindered by nobody since its rear is completely free?

It is as clear as daylight: since Görgey joined the main Magyar army the Austrians have been driven back at all points of their left wing and centre. Where Schlick and his associates are roaming, nobody tells us.

The present position of the Magyars, north-east of Pest, speaks, however, more clearly than all reports. For the Magyars to be able to march from Rimaszombat to Hatvan, Schlick had first to be rendered harmless, that is chased ten miles further back to the Slovak mountain towns, where, separated from the main army by the Danube bend, he stands quite isolated and powerless. Then, the vanguard of the main royal imperial army, even the main army itself, had to be thrown back five to seven miles further; for it is not long since Windischgrätz occupied all the country as far as Erlau, in which town he actually wanted to set up his headquarters! And both these events must have taken place, otherwise how did a Magyar army get within six miles of Pest?

Until more accurate reports come in we shall hardly have any alternative but to give credence to the Magyar "exaggeration" of the *Breslauer Zeitung*, evidently written in Pest, the more so because this "exaggeration" bears all the internal and external marks of the greatest truthfulness. It reports that the Magyars standing at Hatvan belong to the Hungarian *northern army*. (Görgey, who, moreover, has evidently been reinforced by a corps of the Theiss army.) It says:

"As on January 27, when the Hungarian *Theiss army* twice beat the imperial army at Szolnok and at Czegléd, so also now in Pest everything is being evacuated and prepared for a retreat, following the repeated victories of the *northern army* over the imperial Lieutenant-Field Marshal Count *Schlick*. All military offices, regimental stores etc. have been forwarded to Raab since the day before yesterday. The *victorious Hungarian northern army*, which can shake hands with the Hungarian Theiss army, according to the unanimous statements of travellers, yesterday *set up its outposts* three stages from Pest, that is in *Hatvan.* It is commanded by the Polish General *Klapka* and the excellent Hungarian General *Görgey*, both of whom are, however, under the *supreme command of Dembiński.* As on January 27, a proclamation was also issued yesterday, signed by Commander Count Wrbna, informing the inhabitants of both towns[a] that the rebels were threatening to advance on Pest, and so part of the garrison had gone to meet the enemy. The inhabitants were therefore particularly warned to keep calm, since at any attempt at an insurrection the Ofen fortress would at once begin a bombardment. *In Pest a great battle is expected in the next few days.*

"*Postscript.* A courier just arrived from Pest has brought news that *much artillery has left Ofen under grenadier escort, and that between today and tomorrow one must be prepared for*

---

[a] Buda and Pest.—*Ed.*

a battle in the neighbourhood of Pest. The Komorn garrison has driven out the imperial forces from Old Szony."

Moreover, Kossuth has recently given very palpable proof that he is in no mind to tolerate the Austrians behaving like veritable barbarians in that part of the country which for strategic reasons he must abandon. He has used the only means which helps in such cases: to retaliate measure for measure. The Magyar correspondent (*Breslauer Zeitung*) writes:

"In *Debreczin, the imperial Colonel Fligely* is said *likewise to have been shot in reprisal for the shooting* in *Ofen,* contrary to all international law, *of the Hungarian Major Spöll.*—From an Austrian officer we learnt at the same time that Windischgrätz has received a letter of the Hungarian Government, according to which *reprisals will immediately follow any repetition of the execution* of Hungarian prisoners. *The 73 imperial staff officers* who are held prisoners in Debreczin have also *sent a letter to Windischgrätz* in which they implore him to refrain from further action against Hungarian prisoners of war so as to spare their own lives. On this occasion we were given the names of five *imperial generals* who are *prisoners* in Debreczin. These two letters have had more effect on Windischgrätz than all the German addresses and interpellations in connection with the execution of Blum, and *since then no executions at all have taken place in Ofen*; however, it must be noted that the sentences have also been postponed, probably to a more favourable time. Yesterday a number of ladies of high rank were arrested in Pest. The Hungarian women yield nothing to the Polish women in patriotic enthusiasm and sacrifice."

From the other sectors of the theatre of war we have only very scanty Austrian news. In the south-west the royal imperial General Dietrich entered Sexard (Tolna comitat) on the 14th, drove out Kossuth's hussars and arrived in Pest on the 19th. So, here too, on the right bank of the Danube, there are still Kossuth's hussars and they are even holding towns!

A correspondent of the *Allgemeine Oder-Zeitung* reports from Transylvania that *Bem*, whom the imperial bulletins have already reported to be either dead or a prisoner, has repulsed Herr Puchner in the Banat, whither the latter had pursued him, has marched to Klausenburg, where he won over a large number of Hungarian and Szekler groups, and has again *taken the offensive* against the united Austrians and Russians in the Saxon region.[373] We shall leave open for the time being the question of how much truth there is in this report. In part it is, however, confirmed by the report of the *Grazer Zeitung* from Temesvár that the insurgent troops, pressed into Transylvania, have again tried to enter the Banat at Facset-Lugos and that the imperial troops were thereby forced to leave Arad in great haste so as not to be cut off.[a]

---

[a] *Grazer Zeitung* No. 54, February 23, 1849.—*Ed.*

These reports _prove how correctly we have understood the position of the warring parties. A decisive victory over the imperial army before Pest, the outbreak of war in Italy, and Austria will fall to pieces in spite of all Russian interventions!

Written by Engels on March 2, 1849

First published in the *Neue Rheinische Zeitung* No. 236, March 3, 1849

Printed according to the newspaper

Published in English for the first time

LASSALLE

Cologne, March 3. People still remember the notorious case where an unfortunate girl was brought before the *assize court* on a charge of *infanticide*. The jury acquitted her. Later on, she was brought before a police court for *concealment of pregnancy*. Amid the general laughter of the public, the Court's decision to prosecute was quashed.

The Düsseldorf Court is following in the footsteps of its illustrious predecessor.

By a decision of the Düsseldorf Court dated February 22, *Lassalle, Cantador* and *Weyers* were committed to the *assize court, charged with making inflammatory speeches*. We have no objection to that. But by a decision of the same Court, *Lassalle* is a *second time* being brought before a *police court* on the grounds that in a *speech at Neuss*[347] he is alleged to have called for "*violent resistance to officials*" (a crime under Articles 209, 217).[375]

Let us, first of all, establish the facts.

Among the circumstances adduced as motives for Lassalle's committal to the assize court is *this same speech at Neuss*. The Court alleges that in this speech he "*called for arming against the state power*" (a crime under Articles 87, 91, 102).

On the *basis of one and the same speech*, therefore, Lassalle is brought on one occasion before the assize court, and on a second occasion before the police court. If the jury acquits him, he will be convicted by the police court. And if the police court does not convict him, in any case he will remain in custody on remand until the police court acquits him. Whatever the verdict of the jury, Lassalle will continue to be deprived of his freedom, and the Prussian state is saved.

We repeat: it is on the basis of *one and the same speech* that Lassalle is committed by the Düsseldorf Court first to the assize court and secondly to the police court. It is the *same* fact in each case.

Furthermore, apart from that.

If in a speech I "call for arming against the state power", is it not self-evident that I am calling for "violent resistance to officials"? The *existence* of the state power is embodied precisely in its *officials*, the army, the administration and the courts. Apart from this, its physical embodiment, it is but a shadow, an idea, a name. The overthrow of the Government is impossible without violent resistance to its officials. If in a speech I call for *revolution*, it is superfluous to add: "*offer violent resistance to the officials*". According to the procedure of the Düsseldorf Court, *everyone* without exception who is committed to the assizes under Articles 87 and 102 on a charge of incitement to overthrow the Government can subsequently be brought before the police court under Articles 209 and 217.

And is there not in the *Code d'instruction criminelle*[376] an article which states:

"Toute personne acquittée légalement ne pourra plus être reprise ni accusée à raison du même délit"?

In *translation*:

"No one who is legally acquitted can again be taken in charge or accused on the basis of the same offence."

But it makes no difference to the actual state of affairs whether *after* I have been acquitted by the jury I am *subsequently* brought before the police court for the same offence, or whether the verdict of the jury is annulled *in advance* by my being first of all 1) committed for trial before the assize court and 2) brought before the police court for the same offence.

We ask the Düsseldorf Court whether its patriotic zeal has not clouded its legal acumen. We ask Examining Magistrate *Ebermeier* whether he is entirely free from *personal enmity* towards Lassalle. We ask, finally, a certain official of the Düsseldorf Public Prosecutor's office whether he did not declare: "The acquittal of Cantador and Weyers is of no great concern to us, but we must in any case hold Lassalle."

We doubt whether Lassalle has the same desire to be listed for an incredibly long period in the inventory of "*subjects of the state*" *par excellence*.

The Lassalle case is important for us not only because it concerns the liberty and rights of a fellow-citizen, one of our party friends. It is above all important because the issue is whether the exclusive competence of the *assize court for political offences* will or will not suffer the same fate as all the so-called *March gains*, whether the salaried lawyers will be able at their discretion to degrade the assize court with its unpaid jury to the mere semblance of a court of justice, in the event of some fact not being recognised by the jury as a political crime or offence, by immediately referring the same fact to the judgment of a police court as an ordinary offence. Why in general have these crimes and offences been withdrawn from the competence of ordinary courts and referred to the assize court? Obviously it has been presumed that, in spite of the honour and sensitivity of the salaried judges, in political trials they represent anything but the interests of the accused.

We shall take up this subject again.[a]

Written by Marx on March 3, 1849

First published in the *Neue Rheinische Zeitung* No. 237, March 4, 1849

Printed according to the newspaper

Published in English for the first time

---

[a] See this volume, pp. 474-76.—*Ed.*

THE WAR IN HUNGARY

Cologne, March 3. Today's news from the Hungarian theatre of war is limited to a confirmation and partial elaboration of yesterday's. It is said, indeed, to be Dembiński himself who stands at Hatvan, while *two French generals* stand a few miles further back at Gyöngyös with a Magyar corps. The magnitude of the danger is shown by the continuing dispatches of troops from Pest to the Theiss.

According to other, also imperial, reports of the 25th from Pest, *Windischgrätz* has set up his headquarters in Gödöllö, almost halfway between Pest and Hatvan, and his vanguard under General *Zeisberg* is already back in *Gyöngyös*.

"The rebels," it is said, "are retreating as before at Szolnok, but this time they will hardly escape without bloodshed, since General *Götz* is operating from the mountain towns, and Lieutenant-Field Marshal Schlick has *again* taken the offensive, so there is joint action from all sides."

Here we learn various new things. First, the great military commander *Götz*, whom we had lost sight of on the Galician border after his defeat by Görgey high up in the Carpathian Mountains, reappears. He reappears—in the mountain towns, fifteen to twenty miles south-west of his last position. So, during the week he was lost, Görgey's alleged "pursuer" has effected quite a considerable *retreat*.

We also hear that Schlick has *again taken* the offensive. So he had given it up for a time. Instead of "driving back" the Magyars to Hatvan, as we were told yesterday, he was the one to be "driven back". Today, then, it is indirectly admitted that Schlick has suffered a setback. Where, we are not told. Neither are we told where he is now. Presumably, Görgey has driven him back from Rimaszombat through Lasoncz in the direction of Ipolyság, and now he is trying to push forward again over the mountains.

Finally, it is said that the Magyars are again retreating and that Gyöngyös has again been taken from them. How far this news is correct we leave open. But even if it is correct, the question still arises whether only the Magyar advance guard has gone back to the main army, whether the movement backwards is a movement of *concentration*, or whether it is a retreat. In the first case it would merely be the precursor of a decisive battle. In the other case, if the Magyars should again cross the Theiss without accepting a decisive battle, neither would that prove anything at all in favour of the imperial army. One could only conclude in that case that the Magyars had thought it necessary to make their demonstration at the gates of Pest so as to encourage their followers, to train their young soldiers who are not yet much used to open battle, and perhaps also to make some recruits in the districts Jazyg and Kuman, while at the same time being not sufficiently advanced in their military organisation to venture a decisive blow with safety.

We hear from all sides that the Magyars do not confine themselves to defending their position with the forces they have already gathered, but that, on the contrary, they are using their unassailable position behind the Theiss for preparation on the grandest scale. The Austrian reports themselves admit:

"The Hungarian forces have gained time to organise and have now *become impressive*."

And the Magyar correspondent of the *Breslauer Zeitung* reports from Debreczin:

"The *Magyar troops* have of late had *frequent military exercises*, in particular *great battle manoeuvres under fire*, at which *Frau Kossuth* always appeared in a carriage-and-six and sought to encourage the soldiers by friendliness and praise. Kossuth's spouse is certainly a remarkable woman, full of ambition and patriotism, who willingly shares all dangers with her husband, and one of the clumsiest slanders which the Austrian party sought to spread from the beginning so as to discourage the Hungarian patriots and make them distrustful, was its announcement that Kossuth had already sent his wife and family to Hamburg to hasten to North America ahead of him."

That the Royal Imperial Government is becoming less and less confident in a rapid and happy outcome of the Hungarian war is proved by the negotiations with Debreczin, which are constantly resumed in spite of the hostilities. They founder, however, on two Austrian demands: *compensation* to Austria *for the costs of war,* and the *handing over of all the principal leaders*.

While the main Magyar army occupied Hatvan, the Magyar left wing attacked Szolnok, where the Austrians had dug entrenchments and, according to one report, had even put up a bridge across the Theiss. The Honvéds crossed, attacked the Austrians, and are said to have driven them out of Szolnok.

In the *south* the capture of Szegedin by the Austrians is still questionable. Today the *Constitutionelles Blatt aus Böhmen* declares again that Szegedin is still in the hands of the Magyars, who have beaten off two assaults by the Serbs. Knićanin, on the other hand, is said to have destroyed part of the garrison during a sortie.

From a report by Rukavina taken from the *Grazer Zeitung* it is clear that the fortress of Arad was certainly not relieved by the entry of the Serbs and Austrians, but that, on the contrary, the Austrians have retreated again without having achieved anything and have again abandoned Old and New Arad to the Magyars (Bulletin No. 23 is accordingly to be corrected).[a] This report says, after describing the course of the fighting similarly to the Bulletin [b]:

> "*Since it was neither timely* nor intended to occupy Old Arad for further operations, our brave troops, having fully carried out their intentions (!), withdrew again the very same day to New Arad and on the 9th, under quite minor vanguard skirmishes, *to their previously determined positions.* Enemy losses are considerable. Our losses were, besides 80 men, three officers killed and five wounded. Temesvár, February 10, 1849. Baron *Rukavina,* Lieutenant-Field Marshal."

The Magyar correspondent of the *Breslauer Zeitung* reports from Transylvania that not 10,000 but 20,000 Russians are in Transylvania and unashamedly take part in the fighting against the Magyars and Szeklers. Nevertheless, the *Szeklers* are said to have *resumed the offensive,* crossed the Aluta at Marienburg and occupied Heldsdorf near Kronstadt. Incidentally, the Transylvanian mail has again failed to arrive in Vienna for several days. Concerning the Russian intervention the *Breslauer Zeitung* writes "from Hungary".

> "The entry of the Russians into Transylvania has immensely embittered not only Hungarians but Austrians as well, since for several weeks it has been no secret that the Russians had offered their aid on condition that *Austria* gave its *consent* to the *incorporation of the Danubian principalities into Russia,* which has for long been the Russians' intention. This *consent has been fully granted.*"

Subsequently we have learnt from the *Constitutionelles Blatt aus Böhmen* that part of Görgey's corps has indeed *advanced* through the Carpathians *to Sandec in Galicia.* Unit after unit was sent there from Zymiec, and the Magyars eventually retreated again, probably motivated by Görgey's changed plan.

---

[a] See this volume, pp. 423-24.— *Ed.*

[b] *Grazer Zeitung* No. 54, February 23, 1849.— *Ed.*

The Austrian Government has at last realised that in the present state of the war in Hungary it is utterly lost unless it concedes the demands of the Southern Slavs. It has further seen that it cannot put a better curb on militant and freedom-proud Hungary, once it has been subjugated, than a series of small Slav states separated from Hungary, which will restrain the Magyar element on all sides. It has therefore prevailed upon Windischgrätz to "reorganise" Hungary. Croatia, Slavonia, the Serbian Voivodina and Transylvania will be separated from Hungary, constituted into three independent provinces and, along with Galicia and Dalmatia, chained to the "German hereditary dominions". The Ban's Council commission sent from Agram to the Hungarian Royal Chancellory [a] in Pest has obtained from Windischgrätz the order for the Royal Chancellory to pay out the Croat finances which it has hitherto administered. The Hungarian central authorities in Ofen have been instructed in future to regard Croatia, Slavonia, the Voivodina and Transylvania as not belonging to their sphere. For the time being the Slovaks are apparently to be fobbed off with an order to the royal imperial commissioners to conduct their correspondence in the Slovak language. The Slovaks, incidentally, are not inclined to be driven in the slightest degree to national fanaticism, in spite of all the royal imperial efforts. They alone of all the Slav peoples of Hungary have decided Magyar sympathies.

Nevertheless, the sympathies of the Croats for the Austrian Government are not yet too certain. The royal imperial troops rule the country; a priest at Agram, who declared the Slavs to be the saviours of the Emperor and the entire monarchy, landed his village in a temporary state of siege and won himself the title of "traitor to the Emperor". In Agram there are constant complaints about the "machinations" of the *Magyar party*, and as a result the Committee of Public Safety has threatened all disseminators of malicious rumours with court martial.

In Agram there has been a comical affair, with which we will end today's report on Hungary: Bishop Haulik deposed the Vice Archpriest Stoos, one of the "most respected Croat patriots", on account of a pamphlet against the celibacy of priests. Moreover, he refused to celebrate a requiem mass for Voivode Šuplikac because the latter was allegedly a heretic and did not believe that the Holy Ghost proceeds equally from the Son and from the Father. The man moreover issues all his writings in Latin. Now the whole storm of

---

[a] The supreme financial body of Hungary subordinate to the Austrian Emperor and the state treasury in Vienna.— *Ed.*

Croat pan-Slavist patriotism is rising against Bishop Haulik, and the poor bishop must feel that his Croats believe even more in Ban Jellachich than in the Holy Ghost.

Written by Engels on March 3, 1849

First published in the *Neue Rheinische Zeitung* No. 237, March 4, 1849

Printed according to the newspaper

Published in English for the first time

[FROM THE HUNGARIAN THEATRE OF WAR]

Direct news from the theatre of war is today again very scanty. From Pest we hear that the Magyars, after giving the Austrians a wholesome fright by their sudden advance, are again withdrawing to the Theiss. According to the *Lloyd*[a] the imperial troops are said to be occupying the line from Waitzen to Consencz (?) and from Hatvan to Szolnok. Windischgrätz has really departed from Pest into the area of Gyöngyös.

On the other hand, it is confirmed today that Bem in Transylvania has once again *decisively beaten* the hero Puchner. Bem had assembled his troops at Deva, in that narrow defile where the martial-law papers were already hoping that Puchner and Rukavina would block him and force him to capitulate. For according to an earlier bulletin, 3,000 Rumanians were standing there, barring every exit. To the great astonishment of all believers in the bulletins, instead of 3,000 Rumanians, there are suddenly no fewer than 4,000 Magyars with 8 cannon standing there, with whom Bem has joined. On February 9 he attacks the pursuing Austrians, defeats them after fourteen hours' fighting, wipes out several whole regiments and drives the fleeing royal imperial army *back to Hermannstadt,* where it re-formed only on the 12th. The Austrian right wing tried to make a stand at Alvinz on the Maros, but was thrown back to Karlsburg.

So *Bem is again master of the western half of Transylvania.* In the *eastern half* the Szeklers stand behind the Aluta, two hours from

---

[a] *Lloyd* No. 99, February 27, 1849, evening edition.— *Ed.*

Kronstadt. The following is the official report on the fighting at the latter place:

"The hostile advance into Burzenland of the Szeklers, who have repeatedly perjured themselves (!), induced the Russian General Engelhardt to make a reconnaissance in strength in the direction of Petersberg at 7 a.m. on the 4th of this month with one Russian battalion, 150 Cossacks and two cannon, supported by one battalion of the 1st Regiment of Rumanians.

"Barely an hour from Kronstadt the reconnaissance already encountered the enemy who was moving in strong columns from Honigberg in the direction of Petersberg and who, noticing the weakness of our troops, attacked them with tenfold superior strength, without, however, making them yield.

"During the engagement the Kronstadt garrison was alerted, the entire military force followed the reconnaissance and two Russian battalions with six cannon, then a squadron of Savoy dragoons entered the line of battle in two columns.

"Although under heavy, well-maintained fire from covered positions, the Russian artillery forced the enemy's centre to yield, while a second detachment of Russian troops took the heights near Petersberg, well occupied by the enemy, and thereby made the enemy's retreat general.— He withdrew through Honigberg across the Alt bridge, which he destroyed behind him, and took up positions on the other side, but here also was forced by well-aimed artillery fire to retreat further, and with that the engagement, which had begun at 8 a.m., ended at 2 p.m.

"The enemy's retreat across the Alt was so rapid that only three prisoners could be taken. His strength was 8,000 to 9,000 infantrymen, 500 cavalrymen, all well armed, and six cannon. An enemy column approximately 1,200 men strong, which was moving from Marienburg to Szunyogszeg, returned to Heldsdorf at the beginning of the bombardment." [a]

According to this, the Szeklers are masters of the eastern half of the country, and in spite of the 20,000 Russian soldiers, who have marched to the chief Saxon cities, *all Transylvania*, with the exception of Kronstadt and Hermannstadt, is *in the hands of the Magyars*.—What credit the brutish Flemings of Transylvania, our kith and kin, do to us Germans, emerges from the following fact:

"*Kronstadt*, February 5. The local Town Council has *sent a message of thanks* to General von *Lüders*, who is in command of the Russian troops in the Danubian principalities." [b]

On the Bukovina border the imperial gentlemen are not advancing either. They claim to have got as far as Bistritz, but the matter is still in doubt. Listen to the *Constitutionelles Blatt aus Böhmen*:

"Colonel Urban has already advanced from the Bukovina side as far as Bistritz in Transylvania, and Lieutenant-Field Marshal von Malkowsky was already by then two miles from Bistritz in Maroszeny, where he reconnoitred, and on the second day withdrew to his headquarters in Dorna to obtain reinforcements and thereupon to advance at once."

---

[a] *Grazer Zeitung* No. 59, February 28, 1849.—*Ed.*
[b] *Die Presse* No. 50, February 28, 1849.—*Ed.*

"Two hours from" a town which one occupies, one no longer "reconnoitres". So Bistritz is still Magyar, and Malkowsky has retreated to Watra Dorna, in Bukovina territory.

In conclusion we add the following correspondence of the *Constitutionelles Blatt aus Böhmen* of February 23 from Pest:

"In the near future there is likely to be a decisive blow struck in the theatre of war in our neighbourhood. Two days ago there was already that brisk activity at headquarters which usually precedes important actions. Today, as I learnt from a fairly reliable source, the Prince himself[a] is to start and move his headquarters further forward to Gödöllö, Grassalkovich's one-time country-seat, four hours' journey from here. According to the statements of some officers, the Hungarian fighting force is surrounded (!) so that it must expect complete defeat unless (!) it again finds a little back door open (!!). The day before yesterday a convoy of more than 300 prisoners was brought in, and all from the above areas.

"The convoy consisted of Honveds of various battalions, deserted troops of the line, hussars and two carts of civilian prisoners. The greatest sensation was caused by a lady who rode at the front in a cart and was wrapped up to her nose in a cloak and shawl. The gullible crowd took her for the wife of General Görgey; later they made her a mistress of the latter. She had been arrested because her short, curly hair and her strong, somewhat unfeminine features aroused the suspicion that she was a man disguised as a woman. On examination her right to wear petticoats was indeed established, but important letters of highly treasonable content and 2,000 florins in Hungarian banknotes were found in her bustle."

Written by Engels on March 4, 1849

Printed according to the newspaper

First published in the *Neue Rheinische Zeitung* No. 237 (second edition), March 4, 1849

Published in English for the first time

---

[a] Windischgrätz.—*Ed.*

THE PROCEEDINGS AGAINST LASSALLE

Cologne, March 3. Our readers will remember the deputation which at the beginning of this year appeared before Prosecutor-General Herr Nicolovius to intercede for *Lassalle, Cantador* and *Weyers*, who were arrested in Düsseldorf in November.[377] At the time the Prosecutor-General promised that those arrested should be granted every facility consistent with the purpose of detention before trial; he promised to have the inquiry conducted as speedily as possible and gave the solemn assurance that it was not remotely thinkable that the inquiry would be as long drawn out as was the case in the trial of Gottschalk and comrades.[a]

Since then two months have gone by, our readers have in the meantime had occasion to obtain evidence of the "facilities" which Lassalle in particular has enjoyed during this period [b]; they know the civility with which Herr Morret, the prison governor, behaved, how the prisoner on remand was threatened with penitentiary discipline, how an extraordinary court was set up for him whose sentence is still awaited, and which may possibly be confinement in a cell.

The second promise, of the speediest possible conduct of the inquiry, was to be kept as brilliantly as the first.

The inquiry has now been in progress for almost three and a half months; Lassalle was, as we know, arrested on November 22. This lengthy period has not sufficed to bring the accused before the quarterly assizes due to start in Düsseldorf on the 5th inst. Without extraordinary assizes three more months of detention will be required before the case can be brought before a jury, although the

---

[a] See this volume, pp. 191-92.— *Ed.*
[b] See this volume, pp. 344-46.—*Ed.*

examining magistrate had already declared the inquiry closed more than three weeks ago.

After the obvious, undeniable procrastination of which the Rhenish prosecution was guilty in the Gottschalk trial, after the general disapproval which the proceedings evoked at the time, after the specific warning not to fall into the same error again, the Prosecutor-General stated today to a deputation consisting of Herren K. Schapper, K. Marx, F. Engels, M. Rittinghausen, P. Hatzfeldt and H. Bürgers, that the work necessary to prepare the proceedings could not be completed in time for the next quarter session!

Herr Nicolovius maintained, it is true, that this was purely due to the course of the inquiry itself, which had assumed an unexpectedly wide scope, and he could not admit that the trial's postponement, which had now become necessary, had been caused by the *way* the inquiry was conducted.

We will not reproach the Prosecutor-General for shielding his officials; this is entirely in keeping with the hierarchical order; but we are not obliged to be so considerate.

We have remarked above that the examining magistrate had already declared the inquiry closed more than three weeks ago. Two days after the accused had gone through the final hearing, Lassalle was suddenly called before the examining magistrate again. A letter was placed before him in which, during the November days, he had called for armed reinforcement for Düsseldorf. He did not deny having written the letter, and following this statement the inquiry was again resumed. The accused are now said to owe it to this additional inquiry that their trial will not come before the next assizes. For that is the revelation which Herr Nicolovius made to the deputation today.

It is clear. If the fatal letter, which entailed new hearings of witnesses, in consequence of which the examining judges' findings are too late for the preparations necessary for the public hearing to be completed within the next three weeks, if this document had only been received by the public prosecution in office during the inquiry, when the inquiry was nearing completion, or if Public Prosecutor von Ammon I had at once passed it on to the examining magistrate for use during the inquiry, then nobody could be taken to task and the accused could only blame their cruel fate for putting new material in the way of an already voluminous investigation at such a late hour. But this is not the case.

That letter which is said to have caused the whole delay *has been in the hands of Herr von Ammon for almost three weeks* without his bothering to pass it on to the examining magistrate. So exactly the time which would have sufficed entirely to prepare the proceedings for the next assizes, exactly that time was allowed by the Public Prosecutor to elapse, so as to instigate a new investigation afterwards, when the inquiry was closed. The Public Prosecutor will not deny the accuracy of this fact; he has himself already admitted that the letter had been quietly lying in his cabinet for that length of time.

We therefore ask: was it not obviously the intention of Herr von Ammon to protract the trial in this way? Is he not guilty of deliberately causing an evident intentional delay? We at least cannot find any motive which could entitle the representative of the public prosecution to withhold from the inquiry for weeks on end a document on which he himself places the greatest value. We hear, it is true, that the Public Prosecutor has used the three weeks to make provisional inquiries. But to us it appears irresponsible to wish to make inquiries only when the investigation in progress is alone called upon to provide the necessary information on the facts of the case.

To us it appears that the true motive for this procedure is nothing but fear of the public proceedings of a trial which has already been decided in favour of the accused by the recent trials in Cologne, and secret hopes of an early amnesty, which would, of course, be preferable to acquittal by jury.

Written by Marx on March 3, 1849

First published in the *Neue Rheinische Zeitung* No. 238, March 6, 1849

Printed according to the newspaper

Published in English for the first time

MAGYAR VICTORY

Cologne, March 5. The Magyar reports on the war in Hungary, according to the *Kölnische Zeitung*, are nothing but "fantasies" and "ridiculous exaggerations". It is the more remarkable that up to now the brave *Kölnerin* has *not yet proved a single case of exaggeration*. But how could it, indeed? Up to now confirmation of the Magyar news has invariably arrived three days later!

We did not proceed as the *Kölnische Zeitung* did. From the beginning we decidedly took the side of the Magyars. But we have never allowed our bias to influence our judgment of the Magyar reports. We have not declared these reports to be either exaggeration or gospel; we have compared them with the rest of the news and *established* their trustworthiness *critically*. And thus we found, indeed, that in the main they contained correct news, that a few days later they were invariably confirmed, directly or indirectly, by the Austrian bulletins.

After this preamble, we open our Hungarian report for today with the news that according to the Magyar correspondence (*Breslauer Zeitung*) **Bem won a brilliant victory over Puchner and on February 15 took Hermannstadt by storm.** This news is taken from the *official Hungarian Moniteur* (*Közlöny*) of February 21. In Debreczin this victory was celebrated on the 20th with a gun salute and *Te Deum*. During the battle, Bem received two shots in the left hand, as a result of which he had to have three fingers amputated. "*There is no longer any trace of the Russians in Transylvania.*" Puchner is said to have fled to Temesvár.

We see that this news bears the stamp of complete trustworthiness. Yesterday, the news from Transylvania about Bem covered events up to the 12th, on which day Puchner tried to reassemble his troops that had been driven back in wild flight from Deva to Szászváros, from Szászváros to Mühlenbach, from Mühlenbach to Hermannstadt, in position before Hermannstadt. In Hermannstadt itself, as we know, he found only 4,000 Russians for his reinforcement, who, however, were evidently insufficient, with the rest of his army, to hold the ground against Bem's army. It is therefore absolutely credible that Bem—"*unfortunately* a good soldier", as the Augsburg *Allgemeine Zeitung* says—delivered there the last decisive blow to the admittedly incapable Puchner and stormed the town itself.

With this victory Bem is again *master of all Transylvania*. Only Kronstadt, situated in the extreme south-eastern corner, and the environs of Bistritz in the extreme north-east are still in imperial hands. Malkowsky has made an incursion into the Bistritz area from Bukovina. We know that this noble hero evacuates the whole of Bukovina and retreats close to the Russian border whenever Bem merely shows up in the distance. Now, when Bem is 30 to 40 miles away, the brave Malkowsky has again taken the offensive and has been operating for three weeks in the Carpathians. The result of this daring enterprise is that Malkowsky has occupied Bistritz, a *Saxon* town, and thereby has in *three weeks* occupied precisely *five miles* of Transylvanian territory. The 25th *Army Bulletin*, just arrived (see below), reports that his troops have "once again fought a very lucky battle", so lucky that after the battle "they returned to their positions in Bistritz", that is, they did *not even retain the battlefield*. Very lucky, indeed!

In the *south* the Hungarians, according to the same Magyar report, have also won at *Arad* a *significant victory*, at which 300 men of the Leiningen regiment went over to them.

From the *Theiss* the news is as follows. According to the Bulletin, Windischgrätz transferred his headquarters to Hatvan on the 24th, and to Gyöngyös on the 25th, which does not mean, however, that he was in Gyöngyös on the 25th. On this the Magyar correspondent, again a day in advance of the Austrian news, reports:

"From Pest we learn from a reliable source that *Windischgrätz was beaten at Zibakhaza on the 26th*, and that, therefore, in Ofen everything is held in readiness for retreat. The pontoon equipment has already left for Raab. The artillery park, however, was taken from the General Meadow at Ofen into the fortress itself. Two thousand men are said to have gone over to the Hungarians from the Croats. A great sensation has been caused in Pest by the arrest of Mr. A. Wodjaner, the son of the richest banker in Hungary."

On this arrest, which has caused the greatest scandal in Pest and which shows the Hungarian bourgeoisie what it has to expect from the imperial army, another report says the following:

"Kossuth had founded a cloth factory on shares, without himself being a shareholder. Wodjaner was appointed its director. The factory was endowed with a working capital of 60,000 florins. When Pest was occupied by imperial troops, 20,000 florins of this were requisitioned without regard to the representations that the enterprise was one of private industry. In spite of this objection, and although the 20,000 florins had already been paid, on February 25 the demand was made that now the entire 60,000 florins should be paid over. When the partner, Albert Wodjaner, opposed this demand, he was publicly arrested on February 26, which created much stir. Thereupon the 60,000 florins were paid, and on the next day he was released."

The division of Hungary in the interest of the Southern Slavs is confirmed. The *Pesther Courier* reports the following:

"*Pest*, February 22. Yesterday a manifesto of His Majesty the Emperor was published in the Pest comitat, according to which in future the *Kameralgüter*[378] of Croatia,[378] the Serbian Voivodina, of the Bács, Torontal, Temes and Csanád comitats and of Transylvania are to be administered separately from the other estates belonging to the Hungarian Crown. According to the same manifesto, passports must in future be issued in German and the work of the Hungarian customs offices which formerly existed at the frontiers, will have to cease."[a]

To complete the above news we now give, first, the remaining reports of the Magyar correspondence, from which one can see how little Debreczin dreams of defeat:

"From a reliable source I can report to you that Count Erbach, the second aide of Prince Windischgrätz, has been taken prisoner and brought to Debreczin. In the Debreczin *Moniteur* (*Közlöny*), of February 13, Ernst Kiss is named as Field Marshal and resident in Debreczin. The *Wiener Zeitung* made out long ago that this Hungarian hero had gone over to the imperial side. General L. Mészáros is again Minister of War. The same issue also contains the proceedings of the House of Representatives[b] of February 12, in which an excerpt from Kossuth's speech is very remarkable for its indication that the Court in Olmütz appears to have condescended, behind the back of Windischgrätz, to take part in peace negotiations. In the night of February 25-26 many wagons of wounded men were taken to Pest from Szolnok. Windischgrätz is now in Gödöllö near Pest, but Jellachich is still in Pest. In the place of General Ottinger, Lieutenant-Field Marshal Count Schlick, whose previous army corps was almost wiped out at Tokaj and in the Zips, has taken over command of the imperial army at Szolnok."

Furthermore, we give a report of the *Constitutionelles Blatt aus Böhmen* on the conduct of the war in the south, which is the more trustworthy as it appears in a paper written in the Slav interest:

"According to authentic reports, Szegedin is in the hands of Serbs, who have imposed on this poor town a contribution of 500,000 florins C. M.; but it is

---

[a] Reprinted in *Die Presse* No. 51, March 1, 1849.—*Ed.*
[b] State Assembly.—*Ed.*

to be feared that the payment of this sum, a considerable one for Szegedin, will not be the only blow to strike the inhabitants. The Serbs have much to avenge, and we have no reason to believe that they will be generous in revenge. Many refugees have already arrived here from the Banat area and their accounts amply confirm these sad conjectures. The streets are everywhere crowded with their poor comrades in misfortune, who, not knowing where to turn, roam about hungry, desperate and without shelter; for their huts, where they slept calm and carefree only yesterday, have now become heaps of rubble! I spoke to one of these refugees, who vividly described the sufferings he had undergone during the flight; while he barely escaped death in one place, in another he nearly lost his hand, since some Serbs, who assaulted him in rapacious fury, wanted to hack off his hand because they could not pull the signet ring from his finger quickly enough. But I will not trouble you further with accounts of similar cruelties and atrocities."

Finally, the official Bulletin No. 25 itself, which tells us further only that Götz and Jablonowsky have again occupied the towns of Eperies and Kaschau abandoned by General Görgey as he moved on:

"His Excellency Field Marshal Prince Windischgrätz started out on the 24th inst. from Ofen and on that day transferred his headquarters to Hatvan and, on the 25th, to Gyöngyös. Thereby communications with the corps of Lieutenant-Field Marshal Count Schlick were restored. According to reports received from Transylvania, the most active and careful Colonel Urban has again survived a very happy skirmish with the insurgents in Baiersdorf, in the neighbourhood of Bistritz. To obtain precise information on the position of the insurgents, Colonel Urban started from Jád on the 18th inst., marched through Bistritz via Heidendorf to the junction of the roads to Baiersdorf and Szeretfalva, where he sent off an outflanking column under Major Wieser against Szeretfalva. With the main force he advanced against Baiersdorf, there encountered the Polish Legion and stormed the place with bayonets. After this heated and victorious battle the enemy was driven back towards Magyaros. In this battle the seriously wounded insurgent Colonel Riczko, two officers and 200 men were taken prisoner; three guns, a cart, an imperial and an insurgent standard, ammunition and baggage were captured. Unfortunately, we on our side lost Senior Lieutenant Count Baudissin of the Savoy dragoons, who there met a hero's death for Emperor and fatherland. After the purpose of this enterprise had been achieved, Colonel Urban returned to his position in Bistritz. Colonel Urban speaks with high praise of the courage and endurance of all his troops, of the Rumanian auxiliaries as well as of the Galician cordon battalion, the regiments of the Karl Ferdinand infantry and the Savoy dragoons. In Upper Hungary, the division of Baron Ramberg, consisting of Götz's and Jablonowsky's brigades, occupied Eperies and Kaschau on the 21st inst."

Written by Engels on March 5, 1849

First published in the *Neue Rheinische Zeitung* No. 238, March 6, 1849

Printed according to the newspaper

Published in English for the first time

FROM THE PREPARATORY
MATERIALS

Karl Marx

[PROHIBITION OF A TORCHLIGHT PROCESSION FOR GOTTSCHALK]

NOTE[379]

At 10 o'clock on Friday (December 23) a deputation from the Workers' Association went to see Geiger, the Police Superintendent, to get permission to hold a torchlight procession for Gottschalk. Geiger stated that he could not permit this as "it was not allowed". A second deputation then went to see Commandant Engels.

He asked for the names of those who wished to see him. Beckhausen and another man came in and explained that they had come from police headquarters and that permission to hold the torchlight procession had been refused there. They now wished to request him.

Engels was already prepared. No names had yet been mentioned, nothing had yet been said about for whom and for what purpose the torchlight procession was to be held; he interrupted:

"The authorities had the men arrested and so on; it is true that they have been acquitted by the jury; but because they once had them arrested the authorities cannot now allow the torchlight procession to take place."

He also refused *"under any circumstances"* to allow a song with accompaniment.

Written by Marx in December 1848

First published in the book: W. Kühn, *Der junge Hermann Becker*, Bd. I, Dortmund, 1934

Printed according to the manuscript

Published in English for the first time

Karl Marx

FRAGMENT OF THE DRAFT OF "THE BOURGEOISIE AND THE COUNTER-REVOLUTION"[380]

5) ... in a word *low* ... thus even these unseemly things already made him into a type characteristic of the class which he represented, and thus lent him a charm of his own for the impartial observer of Prussian bourgeois natural history.

Let us pass on from the programme to its execution, and let us not forget that the Hansemann Ministry characterises the epoch in which the upstart German philistine is at pains to play the role of the English or French bourgeois.

Hansemann, characteristic of his Ministry....

Written by Marx at the end of December 1848

First published in: Marx/Engels, *Gesamtausgabe*, Abt. 1, Bd. 7, 1935

Printed according to the manuscript

Published in English for the first time

Karl Marx

DRAFT OF A SPEECH AT THE TRIAL OF THE *NEUE RHEINISCHE ZEITUNG*[381]

II. JURIDICAL

Ad Article 222.

"Lorsqu'un ou plusieurs magistrats de l'ordre administratif ou judiciaire auront reçu *dans l'exercice de leurs fonctions ou à l'occasion de cet exercice* quelque outrage par paroles tendant: inculper leur honneur ou leur délicatesse, celui qui les aura ainsi outragés, sera puni d'un emprisonnement d'un mois à deux ans.—Si l'outrage a eu lieu à l'audience d'une cour ou d'un tribunal, l'emprisonnement sera de deux à cinq ans."[a]

What is *honneur*? What is *délicatesse*?

The distinction between "insult" and "calumny" is contained in *Article 375*, which reads as follows:

"Quant aux injures ou aux expressions outrageantes qui ne renfermeraient l'imputation *d'aucun fait précis*, mais *celle d'un vice* déterminé, si elles ont été proférées dans des lieux ou réunions publics ou insérées dans des écrits imprimés ou non, qui auraient été répandus et distribués, la peine sera une amende de seize francs à cinq cents francs." *§ 376.* "Toutes autres injures ou expressions outrageantes qui n'auront pas eu ce double caractère de gravité et de publicité, ne donneront lieu qu'à des peines de simple police."[b]

---

[a] "If one or more officials of the administrative or judiciary system *during the performance of their official functions or on the occasion of this performance* have been subjected to insult by words tending to impugn their honour or delicacy, the person who has insulted them in this way will be punished by imprisonment from one month to two years.— If the insult took place at the sitting of a court or tribunal, the imprisonment will be from two to five years."—*Ed.*

[b] "As regards insults or insulting expressions which do not contain the imputation of *any precise act,* but *that of a definite vice,* if they have been put forward in public places or meetings or inserted in writings, whether printed or not, which have been disseminated and distributed, the punishment will be a fine of from sixteen to five hundred francs." *§ 376.* "All other insults or insulting expressions which do not have this double character of seriousness and publicity will entail only a simple police punishment."—*Ed.*

Calumny, therefore, is present only where I impute to someone a *fait précis,* a definite act, which he himself is supposed to have committed. If I call someone a thief, then only Article 375 is applicable. The term "thief" is not a "*fait précis*", it is not at all the imputation of an "act", but only an "*expression outrageante*", the imputation of a "definite vice". Yesterday at such and such a place you stole a couple of silver spoons, is on the other hand calumny. Instead of the fine under § 375 it incurs the much heavier punishment of imprisonment and loss of civil rights. The reason is: in the latter case the thing is more probable, greater damage to honour, and so on. Just as Article 375 concerns a private person, Article 222 concerns an official when the *délit*[a] is committed against him in the performance of his duties. In accordance with the hierarchical spirit of the Code, an insult to a functioning official is punished more severely than an insult to an ordinary person. In content and concept, Article 222 is entirely identical with Article 375. Article 222 is simply an intensification of the punishment, as of the crime. Article 375 is applied in respect of officials engaged in performing their function.

Article 222 does not take the place of Article 367, where the crime of calumny against functioning officials is committed, but of Article 375. Otherwise crimes against private persons would be more severely punished than crimes against functioning officials, which is contrary to the spirit of the Code.

Therefore 1) Article 222 is identical with Article 375.

2) Article 222 differs from Article 367, just as 367 does from 375.

As regards Zweiffel, the *only* incriminating statement can be: "Furthermore, Herr Chief Public Prosecutor Zweiffel is said to have stated that within eight days etc. he would put an end to it."[b] Hence Article 222 (375) is not applicable, for which it would have to be said: "Zweiffel is said to have made base and dishonourable statements"...[c] and the particular statement is a "*fait précis*", a definite and precisely adduced utterance.

But Article 222 is not applicable for other reasons, too:

2) Zweiffel was not functioning at all.

---

[a] Offence.—*Ed.*

[b] The reference is to the following passage in the incriminated article "Arrests" printed in the *Neue Rheinische Zeitung*: "Chief Public Prosecutor Zweiffel, moreover, is said to have declared that he would within a week put an end to March 19, the clubs, freedom of the press and other outrages of the evil year 1848 at Cologne on the Rhine" (see present edition, Vol. 7, p. 179).— *Ed.*

[c] The manuscript is indecipherable here.— *Ed.*

A page from Marx's draft of a speech at the trial of the *Neue Rheinische Zeitung*

The words in Article 222 *"dans l'exercice de leurs fonctions ou à l'occasion de cet exercice"* and the words *"outrage par paroles"* express the same thought, and demonstrate in an equally convincing way that in this article the legislator had in view only insults which occur *immediately* on the occasion of an official function, hence must be made *orally*, and that Article 222 does not cover insults which are made in written form *long* after *the completion of the official function.*

If the insult must have taken place *"par paroles"*, orally, then that already implies that it is made during the performance of the official function. If we prove that in Article 222 the legislator had in view only insults uttered in the *presence in person* of the official, it is thereby shown that no insult comes under Article 222 which is made long afterwards and in the absence of the official *in written form.* (A written insult in itself presupposes the absence of the person insulted, the presence of the person insulted presupposes an *oral* insult.)

In the motives given for Article 222 (exposé par M. le conseiller d'état Berlier, séance du 6 février 1810), it is stated:

"Il ne sera donc ici question que des seuls outrages qui compromettent la *paix publique* c.à d. de ceux dirigés contre les fonctionnaires ou agents publics dans l'exercice ou à l'occasion de l'exercice de leurs fonctions; dans ce cas ce n'est plus seulement un particulier, c'est l'ordre public qui est blessé... La hiérarchie politique sera dans ce cas prise en considération: celui qui se permet des *outrages ou violences* envers un officier ministériel est coupable, sans doute, mais il commet un moindre scandale que lorsqu'il outrage un magistrat."[a]

It follows from this:

The legislator regards *the* insult against which he invokes Article 222 as the lowest degree of *resistance* to a functioning official, as a revolt and *résistance* against the functioning official which is confined to grumbling without going as far as acts of violence. How otherwise could such an *"outrage"* violate *"la paix publique"*? *La paix publique* is violated only when a revolt for overthrowing the laws is undertaken in one way or another, or when any official performing the duties of his office testifies to resistance to the law, whether by deed or only by insulting utterances. If today I insult the Chief Public

---

[a] "It will therefore be a question here only of insults which violate *public peace*, that is to say, insults directed against officials or public agents during the performance or on the occasion of the performance of their functions; in this case it is no longer a private person, it is public order which is harmed.... In this case the political hierarchy will be taken into consideration: one who indulges in *insults or acts of violence* directed against a government agent is undoubtedly guilty, but he causes a lesser scandal than when he insults a judge."—*Ed.*

Prosecutor in a newspaper, I do not thereby disturb *la paix publique*, and it is expressly stated in the motives quoted above:

"Il ne sera donc ici question que des *seuls* outrages qui compromettent la paix publique."

In the same passage it is stated:

"Ainsi qui se permet des *outrages ou violences* envers un officier."[a]

Outrage and *violence* are here regarded as identical in concept and are treated as crimes differing only in the degree of their gravity. But just as *violence* can only be committed in the presence in person of the functioning official, so *outrage*, the lowest degree of the same offence, requires the personal presence of the official. Otherwise the insult does not cause any *disturbance to the performance of an official function*, and therefore also no disturbance of *la paix publique*.

If, however, this presence in person of the official (the insulted person) is necessary, the insult can only be committed orally, *par parole*, and cannot be extended to include insults in writing, or at any rate only in those cases where written insults are possible during the performance of an official function. (For example, the examining magistrate.) Hence, too, there is no provision for *lèse-majesté* in the Code. If the Code understands insults to officials only in such a way that the official is insulted during the performance of his office and in fact in his own *presence in person*, crimes of *lèse-majesté* in this sense would be impossible, because the King does not perform any function *personally*, but only causes it to be performed by others, and consequently can never be insulted in the sense of Article 222, during *appearance in person* and *immediate functioning*.

By the addition of "*à l'occasion de cet exercice*", it seems that the matter assumes a different character and that the requirement of presence in person ceases to exist. This interpretation is best refuted by § 228, which states:

"Tout individu qui, même sans armes, et sans qu'il en soit résulté de blessures, aura frappé un magistrat dans l'exercice de ses fonctions, ou à l'occasion de cet exercice, sera puni d'un emprisonnement de deux à cinq ans. —Si cette voie de fait a eu lieu à l'audience d'une cour ou d'un tribunal, le coupable sera puni du carcan."[b]

---

[a] "Thus anyone who indulges in *insults or violence* against an official."—*Ed.*

[b] "Any person who, even unarmed and without any wounds resulting, strikes an official during the performance of his functions, or on the occasion of this performance, will be punished by imprisonment from two to five years.—If such an act has taken place during the sitting of a court or tribunal, the guilty person will be punished by the pillory."—*Ed.*

Presence in person, therefore, continues to be essential through the words "*à l'occasion*", for I cannot strike anyone in his absence. Moreover, "*à l'occasion*" does not mean "in relation to ", but "on the occasion of". I cannot deal any "relative" blows.

The legislator has added here the words "*à l'occasion*" only so that the case envisaged by Articles 222 and 228 is not restricted merely to the *duration* of the official action, so that the insult can take place also *immediately before* or *immediately afterwards*, but always *immediately* linked with the official function, and must take place in the presence in person of the official.

As I can strike an official only in his presence, so, too, the case envisaged by Article 222, since it contains the same phrase "*à l'occasion de cet exercice*" as is required also by Article 228 concerning *coups*[a] and *blessures*,[b] can take place only in the presence of the official and therefore by means of words.

There is no calumny in respect of the police:

a) Proof of the truth.

b) Because they are not *named*. The word "policeman" does not denote a particular individual, but is a collective concept.

There is no calumny in respect of Zweiffel:

a) Zweiffel not accused of any "*faits, qui s'ils existaient*"[c] etc., but merely of "*mots*".[d] This distinction justified. An "utterance"[e] not only does not make one punishable by law, but equally does not make "the citizen hated and despised".

b) Zweiffel "is said". An assertion which is to be believed must not cast doubt on itself....[f]

Article 367 concludes with the words:

"La présente disposition n'est point applicable aux faits dont la loi autorise la publicité, ni à ceux que l'auteur de l'imputation était, par la nature de ses fonctions ou de ses devoirs, obligé de révéler ou de réprimer."[g]

---

[a] Blows.—*Ed.*

[b] Wounds.—*Ed.*

[c] "Facts, which if they were real facts."—*Ed.*

[d] Words.—*Ed.*

[e] This, evidently, refers to Zweiffel's utterance cited in the incriminated article "Arrests" (see p. 486).—*Ed.*

[f] Here the manuscript is illegible.—*Ed.*

[g] "The present provision is not applicable to facts which the law permits to be made public, nor to those which the author of the imputation, owing to the nature of his functions or duties, was bound to reveal or repress."—*Ed.*

There is, in addition:

§ 372. "Lorsque les faits imputés seront punissables suivant la loi, et que l'auteur de l'imputation les aura dénoncés, il sera, durant l'instruction sur ces faits, sursis à la poursuite et au jugement du délit de calomnie." [a]

§ 309.

Written by Marx on February 7, 1849

Printed according to the manuscript

First published in Russian in: Marx and Engels, *Collected Works*, Vol. 43, 1976

Published in English for the first time

---

[a] "When the acts imputed are punishable in accordance with the law and they have been denounced by the author of the imputation, he shall be remanded for proceedings and decision in regard to the offence of calumny during the investigation of these acts."—*Ed.*

APPENDICES

SUMMONS FOR KARL MARX[382]

Cologne, November 13. The *"redacteur en chef"* of the *Neue Rheinische Zeitung* has just received a fresh *summons*, for November 14, from the examining magistrate's court here.

First published in the *Neue Rheinische Zeitung* No. 142, November 14, 1848

Printed according to the newspaper

Published in English for the first time

KARL MARX

Cologne, November 14. Upon the news that **Karl Marx**, the *redacteur en chef* of the *Neue Rheinische Zeitung*, had received a summons to appear this morning before the examining magistrate's court, a considerable crowd of people gathered at the Court of Appeal to demonstrate their sympathy and await the outcome. When Karl Marx reappeared he was greeted with loud applause and accompanied to the Eiser Hall, where he said a few words of thanks for the people's sympathy and stated that he had merely been questioned in the *final hearing* of the *Hecker* case, for Herr Hecker, former Public Prosecutor, now Chief Public Prosecutor, believed he had been denounced as a republican by Karl Marx through the publication in the *Neue Rheinische Zeitung* of a document signed "*Hecker*".[a]

First published in the *Neue Rheinische Zeitung* No. 143, November 15, 1848

Printed according to the newspaper

Published in English for the first time

---

[a] See the article "Public Prosecutor 'Hecker' and the *Neue Rheinische Zeitung*" (present edition, Vol. 7, pp. 485-89).— *Ed.*

FREDERICK ENGELS' PETITION
FOR PERMISSION TO RESIDE IN BERNE[383]

DRAFT

To the Directorate of Justice and Police of the Canton of Berne, in Berne.

On the instruction of the passport office, I take the liberty of submitting a petition for permission to reside in Berne.

I was living in Cologne (Rhenish Prussia) as a writer, when I became involved in the court investigation[a] instituted following the unrest which broke out in that city on September 25 and 26 of this year and was threatened with arrest. I evaded this arrest by flight, and a few days later a warrant was issued against me (*Kölnische Zeitung* of October 1, 2 and 3),[b] through which my status as political refugee is established. I offer if necessary to produce a copy of this warrant for the Directorate.

On arrival in Switzerland I preferred to claim the hospitality of the canton and city of Berne rather than that of any other place

1. because Berne is sufficiently far from the German border to deprive the German authorities of any pretext for importuning the Swiss Government with claims and assertions that I am abusing the right of asylum by subversive activities etc.[c];

2. because just now Berne affords me the opportunity to study in the work of the Swiss Federal Assembly the practical effect of a Constitution from which Germany in any case can learn much,

---

[a] The following phrase: "instituted against me on a charge of instigating to revolt etc., etc.", is crossed out in the manuscript.— *Ed.*

[b] See present edition, Vol. 7, p. 593.— *Ed.*

[c] The following phrase: "calling for an uprising against the German Government etc.", is crossed out in the manuscript.— *Ed.*

particularly at a time when the German people may be in a position to give itself a Constitution similar to this in one or another respect.

I presume that my exile will not be of too long a duration, for apart from the slight prospect of stability of the present order of things in Prussia, I have every reason to expect a verdict of acquittal from the Cologne jury, and by my flight I mainly intended only to escape a lengthy detention on remand. I believe, therefore, that by next spring I shall be able to return to my country.

As far as my means of subsistence are concerned, they are perfectly secured, as I can prove if necessary.

Also on the instruction of the passport office, I enclose the passport which the French Provisional Government issued on request when in the month of April of this year I returned from Paris to my homeland, and which was forwarded to me from Cologne.

I take this opportunity to assure the Directorate of my highest esteem.

Frederick Engels

Berne, Postgasse No. 43 B,
c/o Herr Haeberli, November 15, 1848

First published in Russian in: Marx and Engels, *Works* (first edition), Vol. XXV, 1934, and in German in: Marx/Engels, *Gesamtausgabe*, Abt. 1, Bd. 7, 1935

Printed according to the manuscript

Published in English for the first time

DECISION OF THE LOCAL COURT CHAMBER

Cologne, November 21. The Chamber of the provincial court of justice in Cologne this morning committed Dr. jur. *Becker* to the Court of Assizes. On the other hand, it decided with respect to the co-defendants *Wachter, Bürgers, Engels* and associates that the records should be laid aside until these persons had given themselves up in custody.

First published in the *Neue Rheinische Zeitung* No. 149, November 22, 1848

Printed according to the newspaper

Published in English for the first time

500

[DECISION OF THE COURT CHAMBER CONCERNING ENGELS AND OTHER CO-DEFENDANTS]

Cologne, November 22. On November 21 the Chamber of the provincial court of justice in Cologne committed Dr. jur. *Becker* to the Court of Assizes. On the other hand, it decided with respect to the co-defendants *Wachter, Bürgers, Engels* and associates that the records should be laid aside until these gentlemen had given themselves up in custody.

Herr *Bürgers* followed this hint, stepped up to the bar and was acquitted.

First published in the *Neue Kölnische Zeitung* No. 58, November 23, 1848

Printed according to the newspaper

Published in English for the first time

A DEPUTATION TO CHIEF PUBLIC PROSECUTOR ZWEIFFEL

Cologne, November 22. Yesterday Herren Karl Marx, Karl Schapper and Schneider II were to appear before the examining magistrate on account of the appeal in the name of the Rhenish District Committee of Democrats (No. 147 of the *Neue Rheinische Zeitung*).[a] It was generally said that there was to be an immediate arrest of those summonsed. However unlikely this appeared to many well versed in the law, the People's Committee[384] nevertheless took the occasion to obtain assurance on this point by sending a deputation to Chief Public Prosecutor Zweiffel. The latter stated as expected that no warrant for the arrest of the summonsed had been applied for and that such a warrant could only possibly be issued if the appeal were to lead to rebellion; because in that case the *offence* of the summonsed under Articles 209 and 217[385] (which at present could only be tried in a police court) would become a *crime.*

Incidentally, contrary to the view of the Chief Public Prosecutor that according to the point of law mentioned the summons *should have been* issued, the deputation expressed the view that at this time, when the National Assembly exists in Berlin as the only legitimate authority in Prussia, steps must immediately be taken above all against those officials and authorities who violently oppose the

---

[a] See this volume, p. 41.— *Ed.*

decisions of the National Assembly or invite such opposition, as happened recently in the case of *Oberpräsident* Eichmann in Coblenz.[a]

First published in the *Neue Rheinische Zeitung* No. 150, November 23, 1848

Printed according to the newspaper

Published in English for the first time

---

[a] See this volume, p. 37.— *Ed.*

[COMMUNICATION ON THE HEARING OF MARX, SCHAPPER AND SCHNEIDER II BY THE EXAMINING MAGISTRATE]

Cologne, November 25. In the questioning of Marx, Schapper and Schneider II before the examining magistrate's court on account of the second appeal issued in the name of the Rhenish District Committee of Democrats,[a] the statement of the accused, to the effect that they had drawn up and signed that appeal, was recorded, and thereupon the questioning was closed. None of the accused persons was arrested. This in reply to various letters received by the District Committee.

First published in the *Neue Rheinische Zeitung* No. 153 (second edition), November 26, 1848

Printed according to the newspaper

Published in English for the first time

---

[a] See this volume, p. 46.— *Ed.*

504

TRIALS OF THE *NEUE RHEINISCHE ZEITUNG*

Cologne, December 5. A few days ago the *redacteur en chef* of the *Neue Rheinische Zeitung, Karl Marx,* was once more summoned to the examining magistrate's court. Four articles induced the Central Authority to sue for libel: 1. Schnapphahnski; 2. an article from Breslau on Lichnowski; 3. an article in which there is talk about a *"falsifying"* report by a certain "comical Stedtmann"; 4. the publication of the "declaration of treason against the people", adopted in the Eiser Hall, against the Frankfurt majority on the Schleswig-Holstein question.[386]

The *Neue Rheinische Zeitung* is now most eagerly awaiting further libel charges from Berlin, Petersburg, Vienna, Brussels and Naples.

The first case of the *Neue Rheinische Zeitung* versus the prosecuting magistrates and the police will be heard on December 20.[387]

We have so far not heard that any Rhenish prosecuting magistrate has found any article of the *Code pénal* applicable to the crude, obvious violations of the law by all the Rhenish authorities.

"Distinguendum est!" "Il faut distinguer" [a] is the motto of the brave Rhenish prosecuting magistrates.

First published in the *Neue Rheinische Zeitung* No. 161, December 6, 1848

Printed according to the newspaper

Published in English for the first time

---

[a] One must distinguish.—*Ed.*

[MANDATE OF THE LAUSANNE WORKERS' ASSOCIATION FOR FREDERICK ENGELS]

Brother,

Because of the impossibility of sending a delegate we have elected you to represent us at the Workers' Congress in Berne[388]; as an old fighter for the proletariat you will certainly not fail in your task here either, although you will have to deal in this case not with bourgeois and other sordid souls, for it is only proletarians whom you will have to act with and for; accordingly, we tell you briefly our wishes regarding a central association.

1) The purpose of the united associations must be:
   a. Foundation of a central association and a central treasury.
   b. *Social* and political education of the workers.
   c. To establish contact with the German Workers' Committee in Leipzig,[389] in order chiefly to strengthen the links between the workers.
2) The duty of the elected central association must be:
   a. To establish contact with the Workers' Committee in Leipzig.
   b. To facilitate correspondence, mainly to distribute the paper (*Verbrüderung*) issued by the Central Committee.
   c. To administer the central treasury and to render its accounts every six months.
   d. Immediately to inform the fraternal associations of all important events.
3) Duties of the fraternal associations to each other and to the central association:
   a. Every member pays a contribution of at most 1 batz[a] per month, while the exchange of letters is always conducted not pre-paid by either side.

---

[a] A Swiss coin, equal to 30-32 pfennigs.— *Ed.*

b. Every branch association must issue cards to its members.

c. Every member holding a card has free entry into every association, but the card must be signed by the president of the last association of which he was a member.

Concerning our choice: As before we think that the Berne Association is the most suitable one. In case our last circular should be discussed: it was purely the consequence of the fact that already this summer we had nominated the Berne Association to be the Central Association, but since we had no information at all on the state of affairs, we called a meeting here which decided on the above circular. We have rejected the contribution of $^1/_2$ batz per week because it would lead to a reduction in the number of members and thus the income would not be much higher.

In the name of the forty-one members of the Association

Greetings and handshake
G. Schneeberger
Bangert
Chr. Haaf

Lausanne, 8.12.1848

First published in: Marx/Engels, *Gesamt-ausgabe*, Abt. 1, Bd. 7, 1935

Printed according to the manuscript

Published in English for the first time

A page of the minutes of the Congress of German Workers' Associations in Switzerland, at which Engels was the secretary

[COMMUNICATION CONCERNING ORDERS
FOR THE *NEUE RHEINISCHE ZEITUNG*
FOR THE FIRST QUARTER OF 1849]

Orders for the *Neue Rheinische Zeitung* for the next quarter, January to March 1849, should be placed as soon as possible, namely in **Cologne** at the Dispatch Department of the paper (at 17 Hutmacher); **outside** Cologne, at any post-office in Germany.

For France, subscriptions will be accepted by M. *G. A. Alexandre,* 28 Brandgasse, *Strassburg,* and at 23 rue Notre Dame de Nazareth, *Paris,* and by the Royal Chief Post-Office in *Aachen;* for England by Messrs. *J. J. Ewer* & Co., 72 Newgate Street, *London;* for Belgium and Holland by the respective royal post-offices and the post-office in *Liége.*[a]

By the abolition of the stamp duty the price of the subscription is reduced and from now on this is for *Cologne* **only 1** *taler* **7** *silver groschen* **6** *pfennigs;* at all Prussian post-offices, postage included, **only 1** *taler* **17** *silver groschen* per quarter; for subscribers in other parts of Germany a proportional amount for postage is added.

The editorial board remains unchanged.

The previous months' issues of the *Neue Rheinische Zeitung* are its programme. Through its personal connections with the heads of the democratic party in England, France, Italy, Belgium and North America the editorial board is able to reflect the political and social movement abroad more correctly and clearly for its readers than any other paper. In this respect the *Neue Rheinische Zeitung* is the organ not only of German, but of European democracy.

---

[a] In issues Nos. 176-95 of the *Neue Rheinische Zeitung* this passage reads as follows: "For France, subscriptions will be accepted by the Royal Chief Post-Office in Aachen; for Holland by the royal post-offices and for Great Britain by the Belgian royal post-office in Ostend."— *Ed.*

Advertisements: A brevier line of column width (4 columns per page) or the equivalent space: 1 silver groschen 6 pfennigs.

Advertisements of all kinds obtain very wide circulation through the many connections of our paper.

The Responsible Publishers of the *Neue Rheinische Zeitung*

Published in the *Neue Rheinische Zeitung* Nos. 172-95, December 19, 1848-January 14, 1849

Printed according to the newspaper

Published in English for the first time

PRESS LAW PROCEEDINGS
AGAINST THE *NEUE RHEINISCHE ZEITUNG* ADJOURNED

Cologne, December 20. The proceedings instituted against the *Neue Rheinische Zeitung* came before the assizes today. Dr. *Marx*, the *redacteur en chef*, Herr *Korff*, the responsible publisher of the *Neue Rheinische Zeitung*, and Herr *Engels* were the defendants. The latter was absent. The charge was that of insulting Chief Public Prosecutor Zweiffel and libelling the police. The proceedings were adjourned on grounds of nullity.[390]

First published in the *Neue Rheinische Zeitung* No. 174, December 21, 1848

Printed according to the newspaper

Published in English for the first time

DRIGALSKI'S LAWSUIT
AGAINST THE *NEUE RHEINISCHE ZEITUNG*

Cologne, December 21. Today Dr. *Marx* was again summoned before the examining magistrate for alleged libel against the "citizen and communist" Herr *Drigalski*.[a] How many proceedings against the *Neue Rheinische Zeitung* this new one makes, it is difficult to say, there being so many of them.

We regret, incidentally, that Herr Drigalski misjudges us so badly. He has only our articles about him to thank if he gets a little bit of European fame. What black ingratitude, Herr "citizen and communist" *Drigalski*!! A sign that the times are becoming more and more corrupt when appreciation for services rendered has disappeared even from a royal Prussian communist heart.

First published in the *Neue Rheinische Zeitung* No. 175, December 22, 1848

Printed according to the newspaper

Published in English for the first time

---

[a] See this volume, pp. 75-80.— *Ed.*

FROM THE MINUTES OF THE COMMITTEE MEETING
OF THE COLOGNE WORKERS' ASSOCIATION
JANUARY 15, 1849

After the minutes of the previous meeting have been read and adopted, Röser, the Chairman, asks whether Citizen Prinz, the editor, is present and, on being told that he has already left, says that as an official of the Association Prinz should be taken to task for his recent conduct and for the changes he has made in the paper[a] without notifying the Association....

Citizens Marx and Schapper, seconded by many others, move that in addition to Citizen Prinz as editor of the official organ of the Association an editorial commission should be appointed which should see that this organ truly represents the interests of the Association and is directed in the spirit of our party.[391]

The motion is adopted and Citizens Schapper, Röser and Reiff are appointed to this editorial commission.

Citizen Westermann reads out the "statement" issued from Brussels by Dr. Gottschalk and cannot declare himself in agreement with his course.[392]

However, Citizen Marx, seconded by Schapper, moves that the matter should be left aside for the time being, since the statement issued was too doubtful and vague for any definite conclusions to be drawn from it; but that, to clear up the matter, a commission be appointed which should sum up the parts that appear vague, and send a letter to Dr. Gottschalk asking him for clarification and explanation.

This motion meets with general approval, and Citizens Dr. Marx, Anneke, Schapper, Röser and Esser are nominated and appointed to the commission....

---

[a] *Freiheit, Brüderlichkeit, Arbeit.—Ed.*

Citizen Anneke proposes that the forthcoming elections[393] be discussed at future meetings.

Citizen Schapper thinks that, if this had been done about four weeks ago, we could perhaps have achieved something good as a party of our own, but it is now too late, since we are not at all organised yet; it would not be possible for the Workers' Association to get its own candidates elected.

Citizen Marx is also of the opinion that the Workers' Association as such would not be able to get candidates elected now; nor is it for the moment a question of doing anything with regard to principle, but of opposing the Government, absolutism, and the rule of feudalism, and for that, simple democrats, so-called liberals, who are also far from satisfied with the present Government, are sufficient. Things have to be taken as they are. Since it is now important to offer the strongest possible opposition to the absolutist system, plain common sense demands that if we realise that we cannot get our own view of principle accepted in the elections, we should unite with another party, also in opposition, so as not to allow our common enemy, the absolute monarchy, to win.

It is hereupon resolved to take part in the general electoral committees which are to be set up in this town after its division into electoral districts, and to represent the general democratic principle there.

Citizens Schapper and Röser are appointed to effect a closer liaison between workers and democrats; they are to take part in the committee meetings of the Democratic Association[394] and report here on them.

First published in the *Freiheit, Arbeit* No. 3, January 21, 1849

Printed according to the newspaper

Published in English for the first time

RECORD OF ENGELS' RESIDENCE PERMIT
FOR THE CANTON OF BERNE
AND HIS DEPARTURE FOR GERMANY

Alien's surname and Christian name	—	Engels, Friedrich
Place of birth or home	—	Barmen (Prussia)
Profession	—	Writer
Wife and children	—	—
Nature of deposit	—	Passport issued by the Government of France dated March 30, 1848, for one year[395]
Place of residence for which permit is issued:		
Community	—	Berne
District	—	Berne
Residence permit:		
Date	—	December 23, 1848
Valid until	—	December 31, 1849
Fee	—	40 guldens
Remarks	—	Based on the decision of the *Regierungsrat* of December 9, 1848. This permit was issued moreover with the proviso that the applicant would conduct himself in a peaceable and absolutely irreproachable manner. Left for Germany. Documents extracted January 18, 1849.[a]

First published in Russian in the magazine *Voprosy Istorii* No. 11, 1970

Printed according to the manuscript

Published in English for the first time

---

[a] The last two sentences are in a different handwriting.—*Ed.*

[ENGELS BEFORE THE EXAMINING MAGISTRATE]

Cologne, January 27. Yesterday one of the September refugees, Frederick *Engels*, editor of the *Neue Rheinische Zeitung*, again appeared before the examining magistrate. After a brief hearing it was stated that there was no case against him. This announcement serves to correct a brief notice in the *Düsseldorfer Zeitung*.

First published in the *Neue Rheinische Zeitung* No. 207 (second edition), January 28, 1849

Printed according to the newspaper

Published in English for the first time

JURY ACQUITS
MARX, ENGELS AND KORFF

Cologne, February 7, 2 p. m. *Marx, Engels* and the *responsible publisher* of the *Neue Rheinische Zeitung*, who had been accused of libelling the police and offending the delicacy of Herr *Zweiffel* and Herr *Hecker*, have just been acquitted by the jury.

First published in the *Neue Rheinische Zeitung* No. 216, February 8, 1849

Printed according to the newspaper

Published in English for the first time

ACQUITTAL OF THE *NEUE RHEINISCHE ZEITUNG*

Cologne, February 8. As we have already reported in some copies of yesterday's issue, at the assizes session yesterday the case was heard against the *redacteur en chef, Marx,* the editor, *Engels,* and the responsible publisher of the *Neue Rheinische Zeitung,* concerning the article dated *Cologne,* July 4 (in the issue of July 5, 1848[a]). The article concerned the arrest of Herr Anneke and led to a charge of libelling the police who made the arrest (Art. 367 of the *Code pénal*) and of insult to Chief Public Prosecutor Zweiffel (Art. 222 of the *Code pénal*). The defendants were *acquitted* by the jury after brief deliberations.

This trial, the first of the many proceedings instituted against the *Neue Rheinische Zeitung,* is important because this time the above-cited Articles 222 and 367 (in connection with Art. 370) were interpreted and applied in the decisions of the jury quite differently from the way done earlier by the Rhenish police courts. Except for those relating to direct instigation to civil war and rebellion, these articles are the only ones which the acumen of the Rhenish prosecution has so far succeeded in applying to the press. The jury's verdict of acquittal is therefore a new guarantee of the freedom of the press in Rhenish Prussia.

We shall report the proceedings as soon as possible in excerpt.[b]

---

[a] See the article "Arrests" (present edition, Vol. 7, pp. 177-79).— *Ed.*
[b] See the *Neue Rheinische Zeitung* No. 221, February 14, 1849. For the speeches by Marx and Engels at this trial see this volume, pp. 304-22.— *Ed.*

Today *Marx* again stands before the jury along with *Schneider*, the deputy for Cologne, and *Schapper*, for an appeal to **refuse to pay taxes**, which they issued as members of the District Committee of Democrats.[a]

First published in the *Neue Rheinische Zeitung* No. 217, February 9, 1849

Printed according to the newspaper

Published in English for the first time

---

[a] See this volume, p. 41.— *Ed.*

[JURY ACQUITS MARX, SCHNEIDER II AND SCHAPPER]

Cologne, February 8, 1 p. m. *Marx, Schneider II* and *Schapper* have just been *acquitted* by the jury.[a]

First published in the *Neue Rheinische Zeitung* No. 217, February 9, 1849

Printed according to the newspaper

Published in English for the first time

---

[a] For Marx's speech at the trial see this volume, pp. 304-17.— *Ed.*

TWO TRIALS
OF THE *NEUE RHEINISCHE ZEITUNG*

Cologne, February 8. Yesterday and today two press cases were again heard in the assizes against Marx, editor-in-chief of the *Neue Rheinische Zeitung*, Engels and Schapper, members of the paper's staff, and today against Marx, Schapper and the lawyer Schneider II, who are charged with having incited the people against the Government in connection with refusal to pay taxes. The crowd of people was extraordinary. In both cases the accused undertook their own defence and sought to prove that the charges were groundless, in which they succeeded insofar as the jury in both cases pronounced a verdict of *not guilty*.

In political trials the Government nowadays really has no luck at all with the juries. A few officers of the local garrison [a] who took part in the popular movements in September of last year may fare worse; they fled over the border to Belgium when things went awry, but have now presented themselves again and are awaiting the decision in the proceedings which have already been instituted against them.[396]

First published in the *Deutsche Londoner Zeitung* No. 203, February 16, 1849

Printed according to the newspaper
Published in English for the first time

---

[a] Adamski and Niethake.—*Ed.*

522

DEMOCRATIC BANQUET[397]

Mülheim on the Rhine, February 11 (received late). Today a democratic banquet took place here, arranged by the Workers' Association. Members of the Cologne Workers' and Democratic Associations were invited. Instrumental music and songs alternated with toasts supported by lengthy speeches.

Bengel, President of the local Workers' Association, developed the connection of the present with the past in a long report. *Lucas* gave a toast to the guests, especially the men who, like the *redacteur en chef* of the *Neue Rheinische Zeitung Karl Marx,* who was present, had in words and deeds upheld the rights of the working class long before the February revolution. *Schapper* toasted the "democratic republic". *Karl Marx* spoke of the participation of the German workers in the struggles in France, England, Belgium and Switzerland. He raised a toast to *Gladbach,* one of the few agreers[a] who truly represented the interests of the people. *Frederick Engels* toasted the Hungarians and Kossuth. *Ott* of Worringen spoke about constitutional liberalism, aristocracy and democracy, *Fischbach* about the misery of the people and means of redress. *Gladbach* cast a retrospective glance at the dissolved National Assembly and in a lively report criticised its weakness, its indecision, and its lack of revolutionary understanding. *Krahe,* finally, spoke on the slogan of the February revolution: "Liberty, Equality, Fraternity."

The first democratic banquet in the Rhine Province was so successful that it will surely be imitated.

First published in the *Neue Rheinische Zeitung* No. 225, February 18, 1849

Printed according to the newspaper

Published in English for the first time

---

[a] Deputies of the Prussian National Assembly.— *Ed.*

REPORT ON THE GENERAL MEETING
OF THE WORKERS' ASSOCIATION
FEBRUARY 1849

Röser, the President, opened the meeting and, after a brief introduction concerning the reason for calling a general meeting, called upon Citizen Schapper to speak on the effectiveness of the Association since the last general meeting.

Citizen Schapper gave a detailed account of the work done at the committee meetings which have taken place so far and by the branch associations, and outlined the main issues which had been dealt with.

He then expounded the plan for reorganising the Association, which consists in the following:

To increase the present total of three branch associations until there are eight or nine of them in the most convenient parts of the city; to make enrolment in one of these branches a condition of membership of the Association; to fix a monthly contribution of one silver groschen, nine pfennigs of which to be retained in the branch associations to provide for a library, and three pfennigs to be paid into the general treasury of the Workers' Association; and to hold a general meeting every fortnight in the Eiser Hall, which all members of the branch associations may attend without having to pay a special contribution, a condition which is not, however, applicable to non-members. In addition he announced that Herr Marx and Herr Engels had also offered to deliver fortnightly social lectures, alternating with the President of the Association, these also to be free of charge to members.

Citizen Schapper proposed that a vote be taken to ascertain whether the Association approved of this plan, and also that a commission be appointed to draw up the Statute for the Association in which the plan should be set forth exactly.

A vote was taken. The proposed plan was approved and passed on to a commission, which had already been nominated for this purpose at a committee meeting, to draw up the Statute of the Association in accordance with the plan and present it for approval at the next general meeting.[398]

Citizen Bedorf reported on the income and expenditure of the Association and on the state of the treasury.

The meeting confirmed the decisions taken by the committee to resume publication of the former newspaper *Freiheit, Brüderlichkeit, Arbeit,* and to appoint Chr. Jos. Esser to the post of editor.

It was decided to hold a general meeting on the Sunday after Shrove Tuesday, and on that occasion to lay down the Statute of the Association.

The meeting was then closed.

First published in the *Freiheit, Brüderlich-keit, Arbeit* No. 3, February 15, 1849

Printed according to the newspaper

Published in English for the first time

MINUTES OF THE COMMITTEE MEETING OF THE COLOGNE WORKERS' ASSOCIATION FEBRUARY 15, 1849

COMMITTEE MEETING, FEBRUARY 15, 1849

The minutes of the previous meeting are read and adopted. Citizen Carstens[a] then proposes that the red flag, previously confiscated, should be recovered from the police authorities along with the 250 copies of Freiligrath poems which are rightful property of the Workers' Association. The proposal is adopted. At the same time Citizen Schapper proposes that the money transmitted by the Workers' Association to Citizen Esser, which at his arrest was unlawfully extorted from him to pay transport costs, should be recovered from the person concerned. This proposal too was adopted. Thereupon Citizen Schapper spoke on the current political issues and said, among other things, the following:

Although the elections are now over it is quite impossible to give an exact overall assessment of the strength of the various parties. It is true that the Second Chamber has hardly come up to our expectations but nevertheless it has still turned out fairly well in view of the bribery and threats of the wailers' party.[399] As for the First Chamber, the whole verminous band of ultra-reactionaries and wailers is represented there, and it is therefore only of use to us insofar as, should it one day come to a clash, we then shall have the most splendid opportunity of removing the most active of the wailers.

The Chamber elected in Saxony has turned out to be very democratic. Already divided, Germany will be split up even further by the intended secession of Schleswig from Holstein,[400] and that through Germany's impotent narrow-minded Central Authority, which has suffered further disgrace and humiliation over the

---

[a] Friedrich Lessner.— Ed.

Austrian question owing to the fathers of the Confederation at Frankfurt, intimidated by Austria's threats, having declared the separation of Austria from Germany, against which the Austrian Cabinet has now protested.

In Hungary the Magyars have so far done well and would continue to do so were the French Government, quite inconsistently with its own principle, not to look calmly on as the Russians entered Transylvania to suppress Hungarian freedom. The same applies to Italy where, despite counter-revolutionary activity, the revolution is once more in the ascendant, and where Tuscany, regardless of its pietist Grand Duke,[a] will unite with Rome to form a closer-knit republic.[401]

Citizen Schapper then spoke in detail about Hungary, Italy and also France where Bugeaud, the general of the army in the Alps, has stated that they are called upon to purge France of all its socialist elements, and so on. Then he spoke about Odilon-Barrot and the Chamber, and then about California, the land of gold, where despite the great quantities of gold there is nevertheless a shortage of all essential provisions. After that he spoke about the notorious petition initiated by a group of pietists from the Wupper valley, who demand that an ardent prayer be addressed to heaven each time a session of the Chambers is opened!

After that, on a motion by Engels, the Association decided to appoint a commission which is to contact one of the democratic associations to make the necessary arrangements for a banquet to be held here to celebrate the anniversary of the February revolution in France,[b] and that the commission be composed of Citizens Schapper, Röser and Reiff.

The meeting was then closed.

First published in the *Freiheit, Brüderlich-keit, Arbeit* No. 6, February 24, 1849

Printed according to the newspaper

Published in English for the first time

---

[a] Leopold II.—*Ed.*
[b] See this volume, pp. 529-30.— *Ed.*

LETTER OF THE COLOGNE COMMANDANT
COLONEL ENGELS
TO THE *OBERPRÄSIDENT*
OF THE RHINE PROVINCE

To Your Excellency the *Oberpräsident* of the Rhine Province Herr *Eichmann*

The editor of the *Rheinische Zeitung,* Herr Marx (!), is becoming increasingly more audacious now that he has been acquitted by the jury, and it seems to me high time that this man was deported, as one certainly does not have to put up with an alien who is no more than tolerated in our midst, befouling everything with his poisonous tongue, especially as our own home-grown vermin are doing that quite adequately.

This morning I again demanded his deportation from Police Superintendent *Geiger.* He asked me to submit my request in writing, which I did, and it ran as follows:

"About nine months ago (!) the Commandant's Department was obliged to refuse *Marx,* the editor of the *Neue Rheinische Zeitung,* permission to be accepted as a citizen of *Cologne* and to become a naturalised Prussian [402] on weighty and adequate grounds. This man's behaviour has since then been such that it seems to me highly dangerous to continue to tolerate him here any longer. He takes the liberty to insult in any way he thinks fit our Constitution, our King[a] and the highest government officials in his increasingly popular paper, constantly seeking to promote even greater feelings of discontent and indirectly calling upon the people to revolt. The Commandant's Department therefore demands, in the interest of the security of the fortress of Cologne, that the Police Department order the deportation of *Marx,* whose presence has been tolerated hitherto."

---

[a] Frederick William IV.—*Ed.*

I have the honour of informing Your Excellency immediately of this matter, as in the final instance an appeal might be addressed to you regarding this case. The deportation of this man would strengthen the position of the police and restore to them greater respect, and I request Your Excellency's support in this matter and beg you to confer with the General Headquarters should you deem it necessary.

I remain, with the deepest respect,

Your Excellency's most obedient servant

Engels, Colonel

Cologne, February 17, 1849

First published in the *Zeitschrift für Geschichtswissenschaft* No. 5, 1969

Printed according to the journal

Published in English for the first time

BANQUET OF FEBRUARY 24

Cologne, February 27. The day before yesterday a banquet was given in the Eiser Hall to celebrate the anniversary of the French February revolution. The great hall, which holds between 2,000 and 3,000 people, was filled to capacity.

Karl Marx, elected President by acclamation, had to decline since he was otherwise engaged. At general request, *Karl Schapper* took the chair and opened the meeting with a toast to the memory of the victims fallen in February and June in Paris and in all other revolutionary struggles of 1848.

Schneider, the lawyer and Cologne deputy, then took leave of his electors. Deputy *Gladbach* soon afterwards also said a few words on the causes of success of the recent counter-revolution and invited the people of Cologne to rise for the protection of their representatives in the event of new acts of violence against the Chamber. (This in reply to the denunciation in today's *Kölnische Zeitung*.[403])

The following toasts were also proposed: Dr. *Rittinghausen* to the democratic social republic. *F. Engels*, editor of the *Neue Rheinische Zeitung*: to the fighting Italians, above all the Rome republic. *C. Cramer*: to the memory of Robert Blum. Deputy *Wöhler* of the Frankfurt National Assembly: to German democracy. *Guffanti*, merchant: to Ledru-Rollin and the French democrats. Ex-bombardier *Funk*: damnation to tyrants. Dr. *Weyll*: to the women present. Dr. *Becker*: to the democrats of all nations. *Kurth*, carpenter: to Kossuth and the Magyars. *Schapper*: to the political prisoners and refugees, in particular the Germans in Besançon.[404] *Carstens*,[a] worker: to the future social revolution. Ferd. *Wolff*, editor

---

[a] Friedrich Lessner.— *Ed.*

of the *Neue Rheinische Zeitung*: to the right to work. *Hausmann,* worker: to unity. *C. Cramer*: to Mieroslawski and the Polish fighters of 1848. *Kamp,* publican of Bonn: to the fraternity of all nations. *Blum,* student: to the Wuppertal democrats. *Müller,* worker: to Mellinet, Tedesco and the other 15 Risquons-Tout defendants in Antwerp.[405] *Röser,* worker: to the memory of Robespierre, Saint-Just, Marat and the other heroes of 1793.

The celebration, which was from time to time enlivened by music, the singing of the *Marseillaise,* the song of the Girondists[a] etc. and performances of the Workers' Choral Society under the direction of Herr Herx, concluded with a cheer for the "general democratic social republic".

A collection for the German refugees in Besançon was taken during the meeting and yielded a not inconsiderable sum.

During the whole evening troops were in the district and strong patrols passed through the streets; this was, however, occasioned rather by the repeated scuffles of the soldiers among themselves than by the banquet.

First published in the *Neue Rheinische Zeitung* No. 233, February 28, 1849

Printed according to the newspaper

Published in English for the first time

---

[a] The patriotic song *Les Girondins* popular in 1848, which was known more by its refrain "Mourir pour la patrie" ("To die for the fatherland").— *Ed.*

NOTES
AND
INDEXES

NOTES

[1] Marx's article "The Crisis in Berlin" and his series of articles "Counter-Revolution in Berlin" were written in response to the first moves in the counter-revolutionary coup d'état in Prussia. On November 1, 1848, Frederick William IV dismissed the moderate liberal Pfuel Ministry, and an openly counter-revolutionary Ministry headed by Brandenburg and Manteuffel was formed. On November 9 a royal decree transferred the Prussian National Assembly from Berlin to Brandenburg, a small provincial town. This was the beginning of the coup d'état which ended with the dissolution of the Assembly on December 5, 1848. The *Neue Rheinische Zeitung*, under Marx's editorship, started a campaign to mobilise the people against the counter-revolution.

In English this article was first published in the collection: Karl Marx and Frederick Engels, *Articles from the "Neue Rheinische Zeitung". 1848-49*, Progress Publishers, Moscow, 1972.

The *Neue Rheinische Zeitung* was founded by Marx as a militant organ intended to reach and to influence the masses and, by their ideological and political education and consolidation, to prepare the ground for a mass party of the German proletariat. At the same time, it served to direct the activities of the Communist League which Marx and Engels founded in 1847 and regarded as the embryo of the future proletarian party. At the peak of the 1848 revolution, the League itself was too weak and numerically small to immediately rally the workers. There was no point in secret activity during the revolution, and Marx and Engels instructed League members throughout Germany to use the legal opportunities afforded by joining the workers' associations and democratic societies which were being formed. In the situation that had arisen only a proletarian revolutionary newspaper could direct and co-ordinate the activities of Communist League members and mobilise the masses to carry through the tasks of the bourgeois-democratic revolution.

It was decided to publish the newspaper in Cologne, the capital of the Rhine Province, one of the most economically and politically advanced regions in Germany (here there were considerable cadres of the proletariat, and the *Code Napoléon* which was in force provided for greater freedom of the press than Prussian Law). The newspaper was given the name of *Neue Rheinische Zeitung* to emphasise that it was to continue the revolutionary-democratic traditions of the *Rheinische Zeitung* edited by Marx in 1842 and 1843. Taking account of the specific circumstances, with no independent mass workers' party in Germany, Marx,

Engels and their followers entered the political scene as the Left, actually proletarian, wing of the democratic movement. This determined the stand of the *Neue Rheinische Zeitung*, which began to appear under the subtitle *Organ der Demokratie* (Organ of Democracy).

The first issue of the newspaper appeared in the evening of May 31, 1848, and was dated June 1. The editorial board consisted of Karl Marx (editor-in-chief), Heinrich Bürgers, Ernst Dronke, Georg Weerth, Ferdinand and Wilhelm Wolff and Frederick Engels, joined in October 1848 by the poet Ferdinand Freiligrath. All the editors were members of the Communist League. The editorial board was known for its unanimity of views, smooth working and precise division of functions. Besides reading and answering letters and helping the editor-in-chief, each member had to deal with a definite range of questions. The editorial board had its correspondents in different parts of Germany and abroad. It established regular contacts with a number of democratic periodicals in other countries.

As a rule, Marx and Engels wrote the editorials formulating the newspaper's stand on the most important questions of the revolution. These were marked "* Köln" or "** Köln". Sometimes editorial articles marked with one asterisk were printed in other sections under the heading of News from Italy, France, Hungary, Switzerland and other countries. In addition to editorials, Engels wrote articles on other subjects, including the course of the revolutionary liberation movement in Italy, the revolutionary war in Hungary, the political life of Switzerland, and so on. Wilhelm Wolff contributed articles on the agrarian question, on the condition of the peasants and the peasant movement, particularly in Silesia. He was also responsible for the current events section. Georg Weerth wrote feuilletons and Ernst Dronke contributed various reports (including reports from Paris). The only article which Heinrich Bürgers wrote for the *Neue Rheinische Zeitung* was practically rewritten by Marx. He was more successful as the newspaper's representative at workers' meetings. Freiligrath published his revolutionary poems in the newspaper.

The *Neue Rheinische Zeitung* was a daily (from September 1848 it appeared every day except Monday). On some days a second edition was put out in order to supply the readers with prompt information on all the most important revolutionary developments in Germany and Europe; supplements were printed when there was too much material for the four pages of the issue, and special supplements and special editions in the form of leaflets carried the latest and most important news.

Even in the first months of the newspaper's existence the bourgeois shareholders started to complain of the consistent revolutionary line of the *Neue Rheinische Zeitung*, its militant internationalism and political denunciations of the Government. Its editors were persecuted by the Government and attacked in the feudal monarchist and liberal bourgeois press. Shareholders were especially scared off by articles in defence of the June 1848 uprising of the Paris proletariat.

To make Marx's stay in the Rhine Province more difficult, the Cologne authorities, on instructions from Berlin, refused to reinstate him in his rights as a Prussian citizen (which Marx had renounced in 1845), and on several occasions instituted legal proceedings against him and other editors of the *Neue Rheinische Zeitung*. On September 26, 1848, when a state of siege was declared in Cologne, several democratic newspapers, including the *Neue Rheinische Zeitung*, were suspended. To avoid arrest, Engels, Dronke and Ferdinand Wolff had to leave Germany for a time. Wilhelm Wolff stayed in Cologne but for several months lived in hiding. When the state of siege was lifted the paper resumed publication on October 12, thanks to the great efforts of Marx who contributed all his ready money to the paper. Until January 1849, the main burden of the work, including editorial articles, lay on Marx's shoulders since Engels had to stay out of Germany (in France and Switzerland).

Persecution of the *Neue Rheinische Zeitung* editors by the legal authorities and the police was particularly intensified after the counter-revolutionary coup in Prussia in November-December 1848. On February 7, 1849, Marx, Engels and Hermann Korff, the responsible publisher, were summoned to appear before a jury in Cologne, and the next day Marx, together with Schapper and lawyer Schneider, was brought to trial as the leader of the Rhenish District Committee of Democrats. But in both cases Marx and his associates were acquitted thanks to skilful defence.

The failure of these prosecutions compelled the authorities to resort to other means for the prohibition of the revolutionary periodical. In May 1849, when the counter-revolution went into the offensive all over Germany, the Prussian Government issued an order for Marx's expulsion from Prussia on the grounds that he had not been granted Prussian citizenship. Marx's expulsion and new repressions against other editors of the *Neue Rheinische Zeitung* put an end to the publication of the newspaper. Its last issue (No. 301), printed in red ink, came out on May 19, 1849. In their farewell address to the workers, the editors of the *Neue Rheinische Zeitung* said, "Their last word everywhere and always will be: *emancipation of the working class!*" p. 3

² By the "*theory of agreement*" (*Vereinbarungstheorie*) the Prussian liberal bourgeoisie sought to justify its policy of compromise in the revolution. The "agreement theory" meant that the Prussian National Assembly convened in May 1848 was to draft a Constitution and introduce a constitutional system, not on the basis of its sovereign and constitutive rights, but "by agreement with the Crown". By accepting this formula, which was advanced by the Camphausen-Hansemann Government, the Assembly's liberal majority in fact abandoned the principle of popular sovereignty and gave freedom of action to the counter-revolutionaries who wanted to restore the absolute power of the King. Beginning with the early issues of the *Neue Rheinische Zeitung* Marx and Engels sharply criticised the "theory of agreement" calling its supporters "agreers" and the Berlin Assembly—the "Agreement Assembly". They warned that this theory would only serve the King as a screen for preparing a counter-revolutionary coup d'état and the forcible dissolution of the Assembly. p. 3

³ This article, as well as a number of other reports below, was written by Engels during his forced stay in Switzerland. On September 26, 1848, a state of siege was declared in Cologne and an order was issued for the arrest of some of the editors of the *Neue Rheinische Zeitung,* including Engels. Engels emigrated from Prussia to Belgium, where he was arrested by the Brussels police and on October 4 deported to France. After a short stay in Paris Engels went on foot to Switzerland (see his travel notes "From Paris to Berne" in Vol. 7 of the present edition, pp. 507-29). About November 9 Engels arrived in Berne via Geneva and Lausanne and remained there until January 1849. While in emigration he regularly sent to the *Neue Rheinische Zeitung* articles and various items of information. p. 7

⁴ In 1707-1806 the *principality of Neuenburg and Vallendis* (the German names for Neuchâtel and Valangin) was a dwarf state under the rule of Prussia. In 1806, during the Napoleonic wars, Neuchâtel was ceded to France. In 1815, by decision of the Vienna Congress, it was incorporated into the Swiss Confederation as its 21st canton but at the same time retained its vassal dependence on Prussia. On February 29, 1848, a bourgeois revolution in Neuchâtel put an end to Prussian

rule and a republic was proclaimed. However, up to 1857 Prussia constantly laid claim to Neuchâtel and was forced to renounce it officially only under pressure from France.   p. 7

5 An allusion to General Pfuel's participation in the suppression of the national liberation uprising in Posen, a duchy under Prussia's rule, which took place in the spring of 1848. On his orders the insurgents who had been taken prisoner had their heads shaved and their hands and ears branded with lunar caustic (in German *Höllenstein*, i.e. stone of hell); hence his nickname "von Höllenstein".

p. 7

6 The *Holy Hermandad* (Holy Brotherhood)—a league of Spanish towns set up at the end of the fifteenth century with the approbation of the King to fight against the powerful feudal lords. From the middle of the sixteenth century the armed detachments of the Holy Hermandad performed police duties. Thus the police in general was often ironically labelled the "Holy Hermandad".   p. 7

7 In accordance with the Constitution of the Swiss Confederation adopted on September 12, 1848, the *National Council* (*Nationalrat*) consisted of deputies elected every three years by universal suffrage. The Constitution also provided for the existence of the *Council of States* (*Ständerat*) made up of two deputies from each canton. The two Councils constituted the Federal Assembly (*Bundesversammlung*), the supreme legislative body in Switzerland.

Great Councils (*Gross Räte*)—legislatures of urban cantons set up under the Swiss Constitution of 1803.   p. 7

8 In English this article was first published in the collection: Karl Marx and Frederick Engels, *Articles from the "Neue Rheinische Zeitung". 1848-49*, Progress Publishers, Moscow, 1972.   p. 9

9 *Demi-cantons*—out of the 22 Swiss cantons three—Appenzell, Basle and Unterwalden—were for various reasons (geographical, religious etc.) divided into demi-cantons: Appenzell into Innerrhoden and Ausserrhoden, Basle into Basle and Baselland, and Unterwalden into Obwalden and Nidwalden.

Diet (*Tagsatzung*)—supreme organ of the Swiss Confederation which existed until the latter was reorganised and transformed from a union of states into a federal state in 1848. The Diet consisted of representatives of the separate cantons. In 1848 it adopted a new Constitution and yielded place to the Federal Assembly consisting of two Chambers (the National Council and the Council of States).   p. 9

10 The *Ur-cantons* (*Urkantönli*) are the mountain cantons of Uri, Schwyz and Unterwalden which in the thirteenth and fourteenth centuries formed the nucleus of the Swiss Confederation. During the civil war of 1847 these cantons, as members of the Sonderbund, opposed the progressive forces of Switzerland.

Separatists—members of the Sonderbund, a separatist union formed by the seven economically backward Catholic cantons of Switzerland in 1843 to resist progressive bourgeois reforms and defend the privileges of the Church and the Jesuits. The decree of the Swiss Diet of July 1847 on the dissolution of the Sonderbund served as a pretext for the latter to start hostilities against the other cantons early in November. On November 23, 1847, the Sonderbund army was defeated by the federal forces.   p. 9

11 During the bourgeois revolution of 1820-23 in Spain, the liberal party split into a Right wing, the *Moderados*, and a Left wing, the *Exaltados*.   p. 10

[12] On May 21, 1847, the canton of Geneva adopted a new bourgeois-democratic Constitution. Among other things, it legalised freedom of faith and the election of the State Council (the cantonal Government) directly by the people, granted suffrage to persons living on allowances, introduced free primary instruction etc. The canton's previous Constitution was abolished by its Great Council as a result of a popular uprising in October 1846 in which a decisive role was played by the workers of Saint-Gervais.   p. 12

[13] For the proletarian uprising in Paris on June 23-26, 1848, see present edition, Vol. 7, pp. 124-28 and 130-64.

The popular uprising in Vienna on October 6-7, 1848, flared up in response to the Austrian Government's order to dissolve the Hungarian Sejm and to dispatch Austrian troops to aid the Croatian Ban Jellachich who, supported by the Emperor's court, had started a counter-revolutionary campaign against Hungary and been defeated by the Hungarian revolutionary forces on September 29. Headed by the petty-bourgeois democrats, the masses prevented the Vienna garrison from marching to Hungary and seized control of the city after a fierce struggle. However, the insurgents did not receive the necessary support from other revolutionary forces in Austria and Germany and revolutionary measures were sabotaged by the Vienna bourgeoisie. The Hungarian troops were not energetic enough in their march to the aid of the insurgents and were halted by Jellachich on October 29 while the counter-revolutionary army of Windischgrätz had already been fighting in the city itself from October 26. On November 1 the resistance of the insurgents was broken. The restoration of the Habsburgs to power was accompanied by savage counter-revolutionary terror.   p. 12

[14] In the spring of 1798, after the troops of the French Directory entered Switzerland, the one and indivisible Helvetian Republic was proclaimed there and a Constitution adopted on the pattern of the French Constitution of 1795. For the first time in the history of the country a central government was created, the equality of the cantons declared, the privileges of the estates and feudal dependence of the peasants abolished, the medieval guilds liquidated etc. Swiss participation in France's wars against the forces of the anti-French coalition was accompanied by a struggle between the progressive and reactionary forces within the country for preserving or abolishing the Helvetian Republic. The latter was abolished in 1803 by Napoleon, who restored, with certain modifications, the previous decentralised state system of the Swiss Confederation. In 1815 the Vienna Congress acknowledged Switzerland's permanent neutrality and approved the Federal Act adopted by the Swiss Diet in 1814, which limited the powers of the central Government still more. Though particularism was restored, on the whole the anti-feudal measures of the Helvetian Republic remained in force.   p. 12

[15] The riot which took place on October 24, 1848, in Freiburg (Fribourg) was organised by the Catholic priests led by Bishop Marilley, and aimed at overthrowing the democratic Government of the canton. It was quickly suppressed.   p. 12

[16] In English this article was first published in full in the collection: Karl Marx and Frederick Engels, Articles from the "Neue Rheinische Zeitung". 1848-49, Progress Publishers, Moscow, 1972. Prior to this, an excerpt from the article published in the Neue Rheinische Zeitung on November 12, 1848, appeared under the title "We Refuse to Pay Taxes" in the book: Karl Marx, On Revolution, ed. by S. K. Padover, New York, 1971 ("The Karl Marx Library" series).   p. 14

[17] Speaking of the Brandenburg Ministry, Frederick William IV said: "Either Brandenburg in the Assembly or the Assembly in Brandenburg." In its issue of November 9, 1848, the *Neue Preussische Zeitung* changed this to: "Brandenburg in the Assembly and the Assembly in Brandenburg."   p. 14

[18] The Emperor Charles V is said to have ordered his own funeral to be performed and to have taken part in the burial service shortly before his death.   p. 14

[19] The criminal code of Charles V (*Constitutio criminalis carolina*), adopted by the Imperial Diet in Regensburg in 1532, was notorious for its extremely cruel penalties.   p. 14

[20] During the uprising of August 10, 1792, which overthrew the French monarchy, Louis XVI (of the Bourbon dynasty originating from the Capet dynasty) sought protection in the National Assembly. The next day he was arrested. The Convention which tried him found him guilty of conspiring against the freedom of the nation and the state security and sentenced him to death. On January 21, 1793, Louis XVI was guillotined. In its issues Nos. 19, 21, 22, 26 and 98 for June 19, 21, 22, 26 and September 9, 1848, the *Neue Rheinische Zeitung* published a series of articles under the title "Die Verhandlungen des National-Konvents über Louis Capet, Ex-König von Frankreich" describing the trial of Louis XVI.

p. 14

[21] Marx is speaking here about the Austrian Imperial Diet which was in session in Vienna from July 1848. The majority of its Slav deputies were associated with the bourgeoisie or the landowners and sought to set up a Slav federal constitutional-monarchic state under the supremacy of Austria and its Emperor. During the Vienna uprising of October 6-7, 1848, the deputies belonging to the Czech national-liberal party urgently left Vienna for Prague, where they continued to provide assistance to the fugitive Emperor in Olmütz (Olomouc) in his struggle against the Vienna insurgents.   p. 15

[22] When on November 9, 1848, the Prussian National Assembly was informed of the royal decree transferring it from Berlin to Brandenburg the majority of the Right-wing deputies obediently left the building.   p. 15

[23] On June 28, 1848, the Frankfurt National Assembly decided to set up a provisional Central Authority (*Zentralgewalt*) consisting of the Imperial Regent (Archduke John of Austria) and an Imperial Ministry. This provisional Central Authority had neither a budget nor an army of its own, possessed no real power, and was an instrument of the counter-revolutionary policy of the German princes.

p. 16

[24] In the preface to his book *Kahldorf über den Adel in Briefen an den Grafen M. von Moltke*, which Heine published in March 1831, he says with reference to the French revolution of 1830: "The Gallic cock has now crowed a second time, and in Germany, too, day is breaking."   p. 17

[25] *Lazzaroni*—a contemptuous nickname for declassed proletarians, primarily in the Kingdom of Naples. They were repeatedly used by the Government in the struggle against liberal and democratic movements.   p. 17

[26] The *Academic Legion*—a student militarised organisation founded in Vienna in March 1848. Each faculty of the University formed a detachment divided into companies. The Legion consisted mostly of radical democrats. It also included University lecturers and professors as well as writers, poets, journalists and physicians. The Academic Legion played a significant role in the Austrian

revolutionary movement in 1848. It was dissolved after the suppression of the October uprising in Vienna.

The *civic militia* (*Bürgerwehr*)—the Vienna national guard formed after the March events; it was in its social composition a motley organisation: besides artisans and small shopkeepers, it included representatives of the bourgeoisie. Its bourgeois units took part in firing on the workers' demonstration already in August 1848. During the October uprising in Vienna the bourgeois elements of the national guard were pushed into the background and the artisans and small shopkeepers had the upper hand.   p. 17

27 This refers to the speech made by Brandenburg in the Prussian National Assembly on November 9, 1848. In this and other articles that follow, when speaking of events and debates in the Prussian National Assembly, use has been made as a rule of the shorthand reports subsequently published as a separate book: *Verhandlungen der constituirenden Versammlung für Preussen*, Berlin, 1848.
     p. 18

28 In its issue of November 3, 1848, the *Kölnische Zeitung* carried an article about an imaginary African tribe, the Hyghlans, an intermediate form between man and ape. "Many of them," it said, "learn Arabic." On November 5, the *Neue Rheinische Zeitung* ridiculed the report, adding: "This discovery is at any rate of the greatest importance for the party of the wailers for whom the Hyghlans will provide a fitting reinforcement."

For the *wailers* see Note 127.   p. 18

29 According to the French Constitution adopted on November 4, 1848, the presidential elections had to take place in December 1848. The President, as head of the executive, was given wide powers by the Constitution, which reflected the growing counter-revolutionary trend among the ruling bourgeoisie, which had been frightened by the June uprising of the workers in Paris. As a result of the December 10 elections Louis Bonaparte became President of the Republic. Three years later he carried out a coup d'état.   p. 18

30 Marx draws an analogy between the events in Versailles on June 20, 1789 (when the delegates of the States General, which on June 17 declared themselves to be the National Assembly, took an oath in the tennis-court not to disperse until a Constitution had been drawn up), and the events in Berlin on November 11, 1848. On November 9, 1848, a royal decree was read to the delegates transferring the sittings of the Prussian National Assembly from Berlin to Brandenburg but the majority decided to continue their deliberations in Berlin. The next day they were expelled from the building (the playhouse) where their sittings had been held hitherto; from November 11 to 13 the delegates met in the Berlin shooting-gallery, which was occupied by soldiers in the evening of November 13.   p. 18

31 This decision was adopted by the Prussian National Assembly on November 11, 1848, at a sitting in the Berlin shooting-gallery (see *Verhandlungen der constituirenden Versammlung für Preussen. 1848*, Bd. 9, Suppl.-Bd.).   p. 19

32 The *Neue Rheinische Zeitung* No. 142 (second edition) and No. 143, for November 14 and 15, 1848, carried an article by Georg Weerth under the heading "Die Steuerverweigerung in England bei Gelegenheit der Reform-Bill im Jahre 1832"
     p. 19

33 This article is a report from Berlin worked up by the *Neue Rheinische Zeitung* editorial board. The most important information was as in this volume printed in larger type and worded by the editors accordingly. The entire conclusion was

written by Marx. The rest of the text (published here in small type) contains emphasis by the editors.

This was the first time that the *Neue Rheinische Zeitung* called on the population to refuse to pay taxes in reply to the coup d'état begun by the Prussian counter-revolutionary forces. p. 20

[34] The *Köllnische Rathaus* (Cologne Town Hall) was situated in the centre of Berlin which in the middle of the nineteenth century was still called Kölln or Altkölln (Old Cologne). p. 20

[35] In the Freiburg (Fribourg) and other Swiss cantons the Government made recognition of the cantonal Constitution one of the conditions for voting at the elections to the Federal Assembly. In Freiburg this measure was directed against clergymen who tried to get their deputies elected to the National Council.

Many members of the National Council, however, regarded this as a violation of the universal suffrage introduced by the 1848 Constitution and managed to have the elections in the Freiburg canton annulled (for details see this volume, pp. 42-43). Subsequently this decision was reviewed and the annulment of the Freiburg elections reversed (see this volume, pp. 57-58). p. 22

[36] Under pressure from Radetzky, commander-in-chief of the Austrian army in North Italy, the *Vorort* Berne sent its representatives and a military detachment to Tessin, a canton bordering on Italy, where Italian refugees who supported the insurgent movement against Austria had found asylum. The representatives demanded that all the Italian refugees should be deported from Tessin into the interior of the country. The Tessin Government refused to fulfil this demand and agreed to deport only those Italians who had taken a direct part in the insurgents' movement. The conflict was discussed in the columns of the *Neue Rheinische Zeitung* for several months. Engels gave details of the debate on it in the new Swiss Federal Assembly in his article "The National Council" (see this volume, pp. 138-53).

The *Vorort* (the main canton)—the name given to a Swiss canton in whose capital the Diet, and later the Federal Assembly, held its sittings before Berne was proclaimed the Swiss capital. In 1803-09, there were six main cantons—Freiburg, Berne, Solothurn, Basle, Zurich and Lucerne; in 1815 their number was reduced to three: Zurich, Berne and Lucerne, and the seat of the Diet changed every two years.

Until the Constitution of 1848, the *Vorort* authorities to a certain extent fulfilled the functions of the country's Government and its representative was President of the Diet. p. 22

[37] Marx wrote "Cavaignac and the June Revolution" as an editorial introduction to a series of articles published under the title "Herr Cavaignac" in the *Neue Rheinische Zeitung* No. 142 (second edition), No. 145 (special supplement), No. 146, No. 147 (second edition), No. 157 (supplement) and No. 158, November 14, 17, 18 and 19, December 1 and 2, 1848. These articles were reprinted (with certain changes) from the newspaper *La Presse* where they were published from November 7 to 11, 1848, under the general title: "M. Cavaignac devant la Commission d'Enquête sur l'insurrection du 23. juin", their author being Émile Girardin, editor of the newspaper, republican and later follower of Bonaparte. p. 23

[38] "*Little constable*" (*kleiner Konstabler*)—an ironical paraphrase of "little corporal", a nickname given to Napoleon I by the French soldiers in allusion to the fact that, while in emigration in England, Louis Bonaparte joined the detach-

ments of special constables used to break up the Chartist demonstration of
April 10, 1848.   p. 23

[39] An allusion to General Cavaignac's part in the conquest of Algeria and his
behaviour as Governor there in 1848 when he brutally suppressed the Arab
national liberation movement. It was these "exploits" of Cavaignac that gave him
the reputation of a reliable "limb of the law" in the eyes of the French bourgeoisie.
                                                                          p. 23

[40] The Central Commission of representatives of the three democratic organisations
of Cologne—the Democratic Society, the Workers' Association and the Association for Workers and Employers—was set up at the end of June 1848 by decision
of the First Democratic Congress in Frankfurt am Main; Marx was a member of
the Commission. Until the convocation of the Rhenish Congress of Democrats,
this Commission functioned temporarily as the District Committee. The First
Rhenish Congress of Democrats, which was held in Cologne on August 13 and 14,
1848, with the participation of Marx and Engels, confirmed the composition of the
Central Commission of these three Cologne democratic associations as Rhenish
District Committee of Democrats. Besides the President, lawyer Schneider II, it
included Marx, Schapper and Moll. The activities of the Committee covered not
only the Rhine Province but also Westphalia. The Congress adopted a decision on
the necessity to carry on work among factory workers and peasants.

On November 14, 1848, at the beginning of the counter-revolutionary coup
d'état in Prussia, the Rhenish District Committee of Democrats called on the
population to refuse to pay taxes, even before the Prussian National Assembly had
adopted a decision to this effect. Until the Assembly recognised this slogan and the
campaign for the refusal to pay taxes developed in other provinces, Marx judged
it necessary to temporarily restrain the people from forcible resistance to the
collection of taxes. However, he put the slogan of armed resistance on the agenda
when, on November 15, the Assembly at last adopted a decision on the refusal to
pay taxes as of November 17. From November 19 to December 17 the *Neue
Rheinische Zeitung* carried the slogan "No More Taxes!!!" on its front page.

There was a wide response to the appeal in the Rhine Province (see this volume,
pp. 39-40).

In English the text of the appeal was first published in the collection: Karl Marx
and Frederick Engels, *Articles from the "Neue Rheinische Zeitung". 1848-49*,
Progress Publishers, Moscow, 1972.   p. 24

[41] At its sitting on November 13, 1848, held in the Berlin shooting-gallery, the
Prussian National Assembly approved the report of a special commission
describing the Brandenburg Ministry's actions as acts of high treason. The
Assembly decided to publish the report and convey it to the Public Prosecutor for
him to take action (see *Verhandlungen der constituirenden Versammlung für Preussen.
1848*, Bd. 9, Suppl.-Bd.).

This article was published in English for the first time in the collection: Karl
Marx, *On Revolution*, ed. by S. K. Padover, New York, 1971, and then in the
collection: Karl Marx and Frederick Engels, *Articles from the "Neue Rheinische
Zeitung". 1848-49*, Progress Publishers, Moscow, 1972.   p. 25

[42] The reference is to the law safeguarding personal freedom passed by the Prussian
National Assembly on August 28, 1848, and signed by the King on September 24.
It was called the Habeas Corpus Act by analogy with the English Writ of Habeas
Corpus. The law was published in the *Preussischer Staats-Anzeiger* No. 148,
September 29, 1848.

A *Writ of Habeas Corpus* is the name given in English judicial procedure to a document enjoining the relevant authorities to present an arrested person before a court on the demand of persons interested to check the legitimacy of the arrest. Having considered the reasons for the arrest, the court either frees the person arrested, sends him back to prison or releases him on bail or guarantee. The procedure, laid down by an Act of Parliament of 1679, does not apply to persons accused of high treason and can be suspended by decision of Parliament. p. 25

[43] This refers to the editors' introduction to the "Appeal of the Rhenish District Committee of Democrats" published in the *Kölnische Zeitung* No. 308 on November 16, 1848. p. 29

[44] An allusion to the similarity between the measures proposed by Hansemann, the Prussian Minister of Finance (i.e. a compulsory loan as a means to stimulate money circulation), and the views of Pinto, the eighteenth-century Dutch stockjobber, who regarded stockjobbing as a factor speeding up money circulation. Cf. the article "The Bill on the Compulsory Loan and Its Motivation" (present edition, Vol. 7, pp. 278-86). p. 30

[45] The Auerswald-Hansemann Government (the so-called Government of Action) was in power from June 25 to September 21, 1848 (see Note 153).

Besides the ordinary police, a body of armed civilians was set up in Berlin in the summer of 1848 for use against street gatherings and mass demonstrations and for spying. These policemen were called constables by analogy with the special constables in England who played an important part in breaking up the Chartist demonstration of April 10, 1848. p. 30

[46] *Santa Casa* (the Sacred House) — headquarters of the Inquisition in Madrid. p. 31

[47] The *Prussian Brumaire of 1848* — an ironical comparison of the counter-revolutionary coup d'état in Prussia with that in France on the 18th Brumaire (November 9), 1799, as a result of which the dictatorship of General Bonaparte was established in the country.

In the Middle Ages people used to believe that there was special wisdom in the works of the Roman poet Virgil. They regarded his poems as divinely inspired and treated him as an oracle. p. 31

[48] *Dissenters* or *dissidents* — members of religious trends and sects not belonging to the established church; in this particular case adherents of various Protestant sects who did not recognise orthodox Lutheranism. p. 31

[49] *Potsdam* — a town near Berlin, the residence of the Prussian kings where military parades and reviews of the Prussian army were held. p. 34

[50] In English this article was published in the collection: Karl Marx, *On Revolution*, ed. by S. K. Padover, New York, 1971, and in the collection: Karl Marx and Frederick Engels, *Articles from the "Neue Rheinische Zeitung". 1848-49*, Progress Publishers, Moscow, 1972. p. 36

[51] The *Privy Councillors' quarter* (*Geheimratsviertel*) — a district in the south-west of Berlin inhabited mainly by Prussian officials. p. 36

[52] On October 31, 1848, a mass demonstration was held in Berlin in protest against the cruelty with which the Austrian counter-revolution crushed the Vienna uprising. The demonstration ended when unarmed engineering workers were attacked by the 8th Battalion of the bourgeois civic militia. This incident provided

the Prussian reaction with an excuse for replacing the Pfuel Government by the openly counter-revolutionary Brandenburg Government. p. 36

[53] The majority of the National Assembly adhered to the tactics of passive resistance in their struggle against the counter-revolutionary actions of the Brandenburg Government when it began the coup d'état. These tactics amounted to not obeying the Government's orders, including the one on the transfer of the Assembly from Berlin to Brandenburg. The Assembly refrained from more effective forms of resistance to the counter-revolutionary forces, and only after much procrastination did it adopt the decision on the refusal to pay taxes, interpreting it, moreover, in the spirit of passive disobedience to the authorities. Even the Left-wing deputies did not dare call on the people to arm and deal an open blow against reaction, which the *Neue Rheinische Zeitung* saw as the real means of struggle against the coup d'état. As a result of the tactics of passive resistance the Government—which on November 10 brought the troops of General Wrangel into Berlin and declared a state of siege there—managed, by force, arrests and intimidation, to make the Assembly cease its work in Berlin. Then, on December 5, after the resumption of its sittings in Brandenburg in early December 1848, the Government issued orders dissolving it altogether and introducing a Constitution imposed by the King.
p. 38

[54] The *Neue Rheinische Zeitung* published the messages of support for the National Assembly in Berlin on November 21, 25 and 26 (Nos. 148, 152 and 153).
p. 39

[55] This appeal gave the Prussian authorities a pretext for instituting legal proceedings against Marx, Schapper and Schneider II, who were members of the Rhenish District Committee of Democrats. The trial took place on February 8, 1848, and ended with the jury returning a verdict of not guilty (see this volume, p. 520).

In English the appeal was first published in the collection: Karl Marx and Frederick Engels, *Articles from the "Neue Rheinische Zeitung". 1848-49*, Progress Publishers, Moscow, 1972. p. 41

[56] This report did not appear in the *Neue Rheinische Zeitung*.

In accordance with the new Constitution of the Swiss Confederation adopted on September 12, 1848, members of the Federal Court were elected at a joint sitting of the two Chambers of the Federal Assembly: the National Council and the Council of States. The eight members elected earlier were: Johann Kern (canton of Thurgau), Kasimir Pfyffer (Lucerne), Migy (Berne), Rüttimann (Zurich), Brosi (Graubünden), Zenrufinen (Wallis), Favre (Neuenburg) and Blumer (Glarus).

The Federal Court was responsible for the speedy settlement of conflicts which the Diet (see Note 9) had formerly taken years over, and for passing sentence on persons who were charged with high treason but still remained unpunished.
p. 42

[57] See Note 35. p. 42

[58] For the *rebellion of the Bishop of Freiburg* see Note 15.
For the *Sonderbund* see Note 10. p. 43

[59] On October 25, 1848, Bishop Marilley was arrested. On October 30, a diocesan conference of representatives of the Freiburg, Berne, Vaud, Neuchâtel and Geneva canton governments was held in Freiburg (Fribourg). It decided to set the bishop free but to prohibit his stay and activities on the territory of these five cantons. The opening of this conference was announced in the *Neue Rheinische*

Zeitung No. 136, November 7, 1848. Possibly Engels wrote about the conference decision in the above-mentioned report, which did not appear in the newspaper (see Note 56).   p. 43

60   The reference is to the Second Rhenish Congress of Democrats, which was held in Cologne on November 23, 1848. It discussed questions connected with the tax-refusal campaign and also the question of drawing the peasants into the struggle against the counter-revolution. Marx took part in the deliberations of the Congress, which approved his slogans of action and the tactics of active struggle against the coup d'état in Prussia. For reasons of security the newspaper did not cover the sessions of the Congress and gave only extremely laconic reports on its decisions. Thus, the second edition of the *Neue Rheinische Zeitung* No. 153, November 26, 1848, carried the following item: "The Congress of Rhenish democrats, held on November 23, approved the decisions adopted by the District Committee.—Detailed instructions will be communicated by the delegates to their associations."   p. 46

61   On July 5, 1848, the *Neue Rheinische Zeitung* No. 35 published the article "Arrests" giving details of the arrest of Gottschalk and Anneke, then leaders of the Cologne Workers' Association (see present edition, Vol. 7, pp. 177-79). This article served as a pretext for charging the editors with insulting Chief Public Prosecutor Zweiffel and the police officers who made the arrests. Public Prosecutor Hecker sent a letter to the newspaper refuting the article "Arrests" and threatening the editors. Marx published the letter in the *Neue Rheinische Zeitung* and called the Cologne Public Prosecutor's office a "nèw, promising contributor" to that newspaper (see the article "Legal Proceedings against the *Neue Rheinische Zeitung*", present edition, Vol. 7, pp. 186-88).   p. 48

62   The *German National Assembly* which opened on May 18, 1848, in St. Paul's Church, in the free city of Frankfurt am Main, was convened to effect the unification of the country and to draw up its Constitution. Among the deputies elected in various German states late in April and early in May there were 122 government officials, 95 judges, 81 lawyers, 103 professors, 17 manufacturers and wholesale dealers, 15 physicians and 40 landowners. The liberal deputies, who were in the majority, turned the Assembly into a mere debating club. At the decisive moments of the revolution—during the September crisis connected with the signing of Prussia's armistice with Denmark to the detriment of Germany's national interests, during the October uprising in Vienna and the coup d'état in Prussia—the liberal majority helped the counter-revolutionary forces. Thus, the German National Assembly disavowed the decision of the Prussian National Assembly on refusal to pay taxes by 275 votes to 150. The decision referred to in this article was adopted by the Frankfurt National Assembly on November 20, 1848.

In writing this and other articles on the debates in the Frankfurt National Assembly, Marx and Engels made use of the shorthand reports of its sittings which later appeared as a separate publication, *Stenographischer Bericht über die Verhandlungen der deutschen constituirenden Nationalversammlung zu Frankfurt am Main*, Frankfurt am Main, 1848-49.   p. 51

63   The *Federal Diet*—the representative body of the German Confederation, that ephemeral union of German states founded by decision of the Vienna Congress in 1815. Consisting of representatives of the German states, the Federal Diet had no

real power and served as a vehicle of feudal and monarchist reaction. After the March 1848 revolution in Germany the Right-wing circles tried in vain to revive the Federal Diet and use it to undermine the principle of popular sovereignty and prevent the democratic unification of Germany. p. 52

[64] Marx refers to the rejection by Prime Minister Brandenburg of the petition presented by a delegation from the Cologne Municipal Council and other Rhenish delegations asking to be given an audience by the King. When the delegates said that in case of refusal they would suspend payment of taxes, the Prime Minister threatened to resort to bayonets. p. 53

[65] This rumour was based on the conflict between the German Central Authority, or the so-called Imperial Government (see Note 23), which acted in the name of the Frankfurt National Assembly, and the Swiss authorities. Early in October the Imperial Government sent a Note to Berne demanding the cessation of the actions of the German republican refugees and their expulsion from the cantons bordering on Germany. This and the next Note, of October 23, contained both demands and threats, which, however, were rejected by the Swiss Government. The conflict accompanied by frontier incidents continued. Its essence was revealed by Engels in his article "The German Central Authority and Switzerland" (see this volume, pp. 66-74). p. 55

[66] See Note 36. p. 57

[67] A few days before the publication of this report, the *Neue Rheinische Zeitung* No. 198 of November 21, 1848, carried the following report marked with two asterisks:
"*Berne*, November 16. I hasten to inform you of the results of the elections to the executive Federal Council held at today's joint sitting of the National Council and the Council of States. The following were elected:
"President: Burgomaster Furrer, of Zurich;
"Vice-President: State Councillor Druey, of Waadt;
"Members: Colonel Ochsenbein, of Berne;
          Colonel Franscini, of Tessin;
          Herr Munzinger, of Solothurn;
          Herr Näff, of St. Gallen;
          Herr Steiger, of Lucerne.

"The moderate party which has an overwhelming majority in both Councils also had its candidates elected against the candidates of the radical party: Eytel, Stämpfli, Luvini etc."
This information, probably supplied by Engels, contained certain inaccuracies which can be explained by the fact that the Federal Council had not finally constituted itself by that time. Instead of Ochsenbein, Steiger was elected President of the National Council; and the seventh member of the Federal Council was Frey-Hérosé of Aargau. For the details see Engels' article "Personalities of the Federal Council" (this volume, pp. 83-87).
The Federal Council was the supreme executive body of the Swiss Republic. The President of the Republic, elected from among the Council members, was also President of the Federal Council. p. 57

[68] See Note 35. p. 57

[69] See Note 10. p. 58

[70] See Note 36. p. 58

[71] According to the Constitution of the Swiss Confederation of 1848, Swiss citizens had the right to vote after three months' permanent residence.   p. 59

[72] The following report from Berne, dated November 23, 1848, appeared in the supplement to No. 154 of the *Neue Rheinische Zeitung* but it elucidated other questions ("Raveaux's Resignation.—Violation of the Swiss Frontier", see this volume, pp. 63-64). Engels gave detailed information about the debates in the National Council on the Tessin conflict in his article "The National Council", published in the *Neue Rheinische Zeitung* on December 10, 1848 (see this volume, pp. 138-53).   p. 62

[73] The *Barataria's Reich*—an ironical name which Engels gave to the future united German state for which the members of the Frankfurt parliament were drafting a Constitution; an allusion to the imaginary island of Barataria of which Sancho Panza was made Governor in Cervantes' novel *Don Quixote*.   p. 64

[74] During the coup d'état in Prussia the Frankfurt National Assembly undertook to settle the conflict between the Prussian National Assembly and the Crown. For this purpose, first Bassermann (one of the liberal leaders) and then Simson and Hergenhahn went to Berlin as imperial commissioners. In mid-November the Frankfurt National Assembly adopted a decision calling on the Central Authority to help, through the imperial commissioners in Berlin, to form a Ministry which would enjoy the confidence of the country, that is a Ministry more acceptable to the Prussian bourgeoisie than the obviously counter-revolutionary Brandenburg-Manteuffel Ministry. However, this decision proved ineffective because the Frankfurt Assembly's liberal majority openly disapproved of the campaign for refusal to pay taxes as a means of struggle against the coup d'état. The mediation of the imperial commissioners proved to be helpful to the counter-revolutionaries since it diverted the democratic forces in the German states from real support of the Prussian National Assembly in its struggle against the Brandenburg-Manteuffel Ministry.   p. 65

[75] The reference is to the armistice between Denmark and Prussia concluded in the Swedish city of Malmö on August 26, 1848. Though the Prussian ruling circles waged the war against Denmark over Schleswig and Holstein in the name of the German Confederation, they sacrificed general German interests to dynastic and counter-revolutionary interests when they concluded the armistice. They were moved by the desire to release troops for the suppression of the revolution in Prussia, and also by pressure from Russia and Britain, which supported Denmark. Besides a ceasefire between Prussia and Denmark, the armistice provided for the replacement of the provisional authorities in Schleswig with a new government, to be formed by the two contracting parties (representatives of the Danish monarchy were dominant in it), separation of the Schleswig and Holstein armed forces and other harsh terms for the national liberation movement in the duchies. The revolutionary-democratic reforms which had been introduced were now virtually eliminated.

The Malmö armistice and its ratification by the Frankfurt National Assembly caused popular dissatisfaction and protests in Germany.   p. 67

[76] The *Holy Roman Empire of the German Nation* was founded in 962 and lasted till 1806. At different times it included German, Italian, Austrian, Hungarian and Bohemian lands, Switzerland and the Netherlands, forming a motley conglomeration of feudal kingdoms and principalities, church lands and free cities with different political structures, legal standards and customs.   p. 67

[77] Maximilian Gagern's journey to Berlin and Schleswig, made on instructions from the Government of the Imperial Regent John to take part in the armistice negotiations with Denmark in the summer of 1848, ended in a complete failure since both Prussia and Denmark ignored the representative of the impotent Central Authority.

Engels compares this fruitless journey of Gagern's with that of the heroine in Johann Hermes' novel *Sophiens Reise von Memel nach Sachsen* which was popular in Germany at the end of the eighteenth and the beginning of the nineteenth century: after spending more than ten years on her journey she failed to reach her destination.   p. 67

[78] In April 1848 Baden was the scene of a republican uprising led by the petty-bourgeois democrats Friedrich Hecker and Gustav Struve. It started with republican detachments invading Baden from the Swiss border. But this poorly prepared and poorly organised uprising was crushed by the end of April.

p. 67

[79] The first Note to the *Vorort* (main canton) Berne (see Note 36), dated October 4, 1848, and signed by Franz Raveaux, an imperial commissioner in Switzerland, was published in several German newspapers including the *Preussischer Staats-Anzeiger* No. 163 of October 14, 1848. The same day, the *Neue Rheinische Zeitung* (in the supplement to issue No. 116) carried a report from Berne dated October 8 setting forth the content of the Note from the main canton Berne written in reply to the imperial Note. The full text of the Note, dated October 5, was reproduced in the *Frankfurter Oberpostamts-Zeitung* on October 10 (No. 275, second supplement) and October 11, 1848 (No. 276).

A new Note of the German Central Authority, dated October 23 and also signed by Raveaux, was published in the *Frankfurter Oberpostamts-Zeitung* No. 298 on November 6, 1848. An announcement about its delivery to the Berne authorities appeared in the *Neue Rheinische Zeitung* No. 140, November 11. The main canton Berne's reply of November 4 was published in the *Frankfurter Oberpostamts-Zeitung* No. 304 and in the first supplement to it on November 13, 1848. The *Neue Rheinische Zeitung* likewise published the text of this Note in its issue No. 143, November 15, 1848.   p. 68

[80] See Note 73.   p. 68

[81] An allusion to the special troops supplied by the so-called Military Border Area—i.e., military settlements formed in the southern border regions of the Austrian Empire between the sixteenth and nineteenth centuries. The inhabitants of these regions—Serbs, Croats, Rumanians, Szeklers, Saxons, and others—were allotted plots of land by the state, for which they had to serve in the army, pay taxes and fulfil certain public duties. While serving in the army they wore red coats and caps. In 1848 they formed part of the counter-revolutionary army of the Croatian Ban Jellachich deployed against revolutionary Vienna and Hungary.

The names of these border regiments and battalions derived either from the names of the regions where they were formed, the names of the central towns of the corresponding border areas, or the nationality making up the majority of the military unit.   p. 68

[82] See Note 9.   p. 68

[83] After the defeat of the Baden republican uprising in April 1848 (see Note 78), one of its leaders, Friedrich Hecker, emigrated to Switzerland and lived in Muttenz (Basle canton) until September 1848, when he left for America.   p. 72

84 The reference is to the invasion of Baden from Swiss territory by detachments of German republican refugees led by Gustav Struve on September 21, 1848, following the news of the ratification by the Frankfurt National Assembly of the armistice in Malmö and the popular uprising in Frankfurt in reply to it. Supported by the local republicans, Struve proclaimed a German Republic in the frontier town of Lörrach and formed a provisional government. However, the insurgent detachments were shortly afterwards scattered by the troops, and Struve, Blind and other leaders of the uprising were imprisoned by decision of a court martial (they were released during another republican uprising in Baden in May 1849).

p. 74

85 The words "citizen and communist" were taken by Marx from the address of General Drigalski, commander of a division quartered in Düsseldorf, to the population. The address was published in the *Düsseldorfer Zeitung* No. 311, November 24, 1848. The *Neue Rheinische Zeitung* reprinted it immediately after this article. Drigalski said in the address:

"As a communist truly devoted to God and my King, I declare hereby that for the benefit of my poor brothers of the Düsseldorf commune I shall, as long as I live here, pay yearly the sum of thousand talers by monthly instalments to the city poor fund through the Government's central treasury.... Fellow citizens, follow this example and be communists in the noble sense of this word and soon here, as everywhere else, there will be calm, peace and confidence.

"Düsseldorf, November 23, 1848

Citizen *von Drigalski*"

p. 75

86 The state of siege in Düsseldorf was declared on November 22, 1848, the order of Spiegel and Drigalski to that effect being published in the *Kölnische Zeitung* No. 314 (second edition), November 23, 1848.

p. 75

87 Pfuel's speech in the Prussian National Assembly on September 29, 1848, was connected with the declaration of a state of siege in Cologne on September 26. The Cologne authorities had been scared by the growing revolutionary-democratic movement and the campaign of protest against the Prussian-Danish armistice concluded in Malmö and ratified by the Frankfurt Assembly. Pfuel tried to justify this measure, but general indignation against the actions of the Cologne authorities and their condemnation by the Left deputies in the Assembly compelled the Government to issue an order lifting the state of siege in Cologne as of November 2, 1848.

p. 75

88 The *Penal Code* (*Code pénal*), adopted in France in 1810 and introduced into the regions of West and South-West Germany conquered by the French, remained in effect in the Rhine Province even after its incorporation into Prussia in 1815. The Prussian Government attempted to reduce the sphere of its application and by a whole series of laws and orders to reintroduce in this province Prussian Law designed to guarantee feudal privileges. These measures, which met with great opposition in the Rhine Province, were annulled after the March revolution by the decree of April 15, 1848.

p. 76

89 The law of April 6—"Decision on Some Principles of the Future Prussian Constitution" ("Verordnung über einige Grundlagen der künftigen Preussischen Verfassung")—was adopted by the *Second United Diet*, an assembly of representatives from the eight provincial diets of Prussia. Like the provincial diets, the United Diet was based on the estate principle. It sanctioned new taxes and loans, discussed new Bills and had the right to petition the King.

The *First United Diet* opened on April 11, 1847, but was dissolved in June because it refused to grant a new loan. The Second United Diet met on April 2, 1848, after the revolution of March 18-19 in Prussia. It adopted decrees, decisions and a law on the elections to the Prussian National Assembly, and sanctioned the loan, following which its session was closed. p. 77

90 The *Civic Militia Law* was adopted on the basis of the Bill introduced in mid-July of 1848 by the Auerswald-Hansemann Ministry. It reflected the desire of the Prussian liberals to prevent the masses from joining the civic militia formed after the March revolution in Prussia, and to convert it into a purely bourgeois military organisation. (For the criticism of it by the *Neue Rheinische Zeitung* see the article "The Civic Militia Bill", present edition, Vol. 7, pp. 256-65.) The law in effect abolished the militia as an autonomous armed organisation and subordinated it to the King and the Minister of the Interior. This dependence of the civic militia on the Government was utilised by the counter-revolutionary forces during the coup d'état in Prussia. p. 77

91 The reference is to a statement made by the Düsseldorf Chief Postmaster (*Oberpostdirektor*) Maurenbrecher on November 21, 1848, and published in the *Kölnische Zeitung* No. 314 (second edition) on November 23. This statement accused a group of officers of the Düsseldorf civic militia of "sacrilegiously" violating the secrecy of the postal service and correspondence because they tried to find out at the post-office whether postal orders for large sums of money had arrived from the *Regierungspräsident.* p. 77

92 For the *law safeguarding personal freedom* see Note 42. Below Marx quotes Paragraph 9 of this law. p. 78

93 In addition to the proceedings instituted earlier against the editors of the *Neue Rheinische Zeitung,* the Cologne Public Prosecutor Hecker gave instructions, in the autumn of 1848, to bring to court the editor-in-chief Karl Marx and the responsible publisher Hermann Korff, for publishing in their newspaper a number of items which were not to the liking of the authorities, including the proclamation "To the German People" by the republican Friedrich Hecker. Although the examining magistrate declared in October 1848 that there were no serious grounds for prosecution, the Public Prosecutor insisted on his former accusations and even advanced new ones.

In his article "Public Prosecutor 'Hecker' and the *Neue Rheinische Zeitung*" (see present edition, Vol. 7, pp. 485-89), Marx sharply criticised the Cologne Public Prosecutor's office, using the coincidence of the names of the Public Prosecutor and the republican to call the former either "simple Hecker" (" *tout bonnement*") (" *C'est du Hecker tout pur*"—"it's genuine Hecker", as he wrote in French) or "the dichotomous Hecker". This was the "second crime" of the *Neue Rheinische Zeitung* (see this volume, p. 82). p. 81

94 The *Neue Rheinische Zeitung* was accused by the Cologne authorities of insulting police officers and Public Prosecutor Zweiffel in the summer of 1848, by publishing the article "Arrests" exposing the repressive measures against Gottschalk and Anneke, leaders of the Cologne Workers' Association (see present edition, Vol. 7, pp. 177-79). Later this accusation was made at the trial of Marx and Engels (see this volume, pp. 304-22, 511 and 517). p. 81

95 *In partibus infidelium*—literally: in parts inhabited by unbelievers. The words are added to the title of Roman Catholic bishops appointed to purely nominal dioceses in non-Christian countries. p. 81

[96] The *Disch Hotel* was in Cologne; the *Mielentz Hotel*—a hotel in Berlin where the Prussian National Assembly, driven out of its former premises, held its sitting on November 15, 1848.   p. 81

[97] At the end of September 1848, the Imperial Minister of Justice, Kisker, demanded that the Cologne Public Prosecutor should institute legal proceedings against the *Neue Rheinische Zeitung* editors for publishing a series of feature articles which ridiculed Prince Lichnowski, a reactionary deputy of the Frankfurt National Assembly, under the name of the knight Schnapphahnski. Written by Georg Weerth, the feature articles "Leben und Taten des berühmten Ritters Schnapphahnski" were published unsigned in the *Neue Rheinische Zeitung* in August, September and December 1848 and in January 1849.   p. 82

[98] Concerning the *Vorort* see Note 36.
Concerning the Swiss *Diet* see Note 9.   p. 83

[99] On September 6, 1839, the canton of Zurich was the scene of a putsch organised by conservatives and clericals which led to the overthrow of the liberal Government formed on the basis of the 1831 Constitution and brought the conservatives to power. This conservative Government was in turn replaced when the liberals won the elections in 1845.   p. 83

[100] See Note 10.   p. 84

[101] The reference is to the party of moderate republicans headed by Armand Marrast which formed around the newspaper *Le National* in the 1840s; it was supported by the industrial bourgeoisie and a section of the liberal intellectuals connected with it.   p. 84

[102] The draft Constitution for Tessin was approved by the people of this canton on July 4, 1830, three weeks before the July revolution in France which led to the overthrow of the Bourbons and exerted a great influence on Switzerland.
December 1839 saw the revival of the liberal and radical movement in Tessin. As a result of the popular uprising on December 8 a provisional government was set up and the Great Council of Tessin was replaced by a new one with the radical Stefano Franscini at its head. The attempts of the conservative party to take the lead were finally defeated after the elections of November 15, 1840, which brought victory to the liberals.   p. 85

[103] Munzinger and Escher, the main canton Berne's representatives in Tessin at the time of the so-called *Tessin conflict* (see Note 36), insisted that all Italian refugees in Tessin and their families should be removed into the interior of the country. Their demand was contrary to the principle of sovereignty of the cantons.
                                                                                     p. 86

[104] *Commission du pouvoir exécutif* (the Executive Commission)—the Government of the French Republic set up by the Constituent Assembly on May 10, 1848, to replace the Provisional Government which had resigned. It existed until June 24, 1848, when Cavaignac's dictatorship was established during the June proletarian uprising. The majority in the Commission were moderate republicans, Ledru-Rollin being the only representative of the Left.   p. 87

[105] The reference is to an anonymous patriotic pamphlet, *Deutschland in seiner tiefen Erniedrigung* (Nuremberg, 1806), directed against Napoleon's rule. For the

publication of this pamphlet the bookseller Johann Philipp Palm was shot by the
French authorities.   p. 88

[106] See Note 75.   p. 88

[107] The full title of this report in German is "Bericht des Ausschusses für die
österreichischen Angelegenheiten über die Anträge der Abgeordneten Venedey,
Heinrich Simon, Wiesner und Bauernschmied, sowie über mehrere die österreichischen Angelegenheiten betreffende Petitionen". It was published in the
book: *Verhandlungen der deutschen verfassunggebenden Reichsversammlung zu Frankfurt am Main*, Bd. 2, Frankfurt am Main, 1848-49, S. 602-19. The report was read
out by Deputy H. Löwe, of Posen, at the 119th sitting of the Frankfurt National
Assembly on November 20, 1848. Appended to it were letters of the two imperial
commissioners Welcker and Mosle to the Imperial Minister Schmerling and the
Austrian Prime Minister Wessenberg; these letters are repeatedly quoted in this
article. Subsequently, touching on Welcker and Mosle's mission when dealing with
the October uprising in Vienna in his work *Revolution and Counter-Revolution in
Germany*, Engels wrote: "The travels of Don Quixote and Sancho Panza form
matter for an Odyssey in comparison to the heroic feats and wonderful
adventures of these two knights-errant of German Unity.... Their dispatches and
reports are perhaps the only portion of the Frankfurt transactions that will retain
a place in German literature; they are a perfect satirical romance, ready cut and
dried, and an eternal monument of disgrace for the Frankfurt Assembly and its
government" (see present edition, Vol. 11).   p. 88

[108] *Eisele* and *Beisele*, here nicknames for Welcker and Mosle, are comic characters
from a pamphlet by Johann Wilhelm Christern published anonymously, *Doctor
Eisele's und Baron von Beisele's Landtagsreise im April 1847. Genrebilder aus der
neuesten Zeitgeschichte*, Leipzig, 1847. These names also appeared in the Munich
Fliegenden Blättern in 1848.   p. 89

[109] *Die Jobsiade. Ein komisches Heldengedicht*—satirical poem by Karl Arnold Kortum
published in 1784 and repeatedly reprinted in the nineteenth century. The comic
travel map attached to it was a closed labyrinth.   p. 89

[110] An allusion to the uprising in Frankfurt am Main which broke out following the
ratification of the Malmö armistice by the majority of the National Assembly on
September 16, 1848. Next day, there was a mass meeting of protest in the suburbs
of Frankfurt attended by the inhabitants of the city and the neighbouring towns
and localities who demanded the dissolution of the Assembly and the formation of
a new representative body. The Imperial Government called in Prussian and
Austrian troops. When an uprising flared up on the following day, the poorly
armed people were defeated after stubborn barricade fighting. There was
popular unrest in many parts of Germany in response to the Frankfurt events.
                                                                                 p. 92

[111] See Note 81.   p. 93

[112] The Austrian troops of Windischgrätz and Jellachich which suppressed the
Vienna uprising were mostly recruited from the South-Slav peoples.
    Serezhans—special units in border regiments (200 men per regiment) recruited
in the Serbian and Croatian regions of the Military Border Area (see Note 81). In
peacetime they protected the frontier and in wartime fulfilled vanguard, outpost
and patrol duties.

Raizes (Raizen, Razen, Rascier)—the name given to the Orthodox Serbs and often used for Serbs in general. It is apparently derived from the name of one of the first settlements of Serbian tribes, the ancient town Rassa, centre of the Raschka region.   p. 94

[113] A reference to the documents relating to the activities of the German refugees in the border cantons of Switzerland published in the *Frankfurter Oberpostamts-Zeitung* No. 301 (special supplement), November 9, 1848.   p. 98

[114] See Note 74.   p. 99

[115] By decision of the Vienna Congress (1814-15) the lands on the left and the right banks of the Rhine were incorporated into Prussia, and among other titles bestowed on the King of Prussia was that of Archduke of the Lower Rhine. In his manifesto of April 5, 1815, issued on the occasion of the incorporation of this territory into Prussia, Frederick William III promised to introduce representative institutions in the Rhine Province and throughout the country.   p. 99

[116] An English translation of this article was first published in the collection: Karl Marx and Frederick Engels, *Articles from the "Neue Rheinische Zeitung". 1848-49*, Progress Publishers, Moscow, 1972.   p. 101

[117] On *April 10, 1848*, a Chartist demonstration in London was broken up by troops and special constables; the purpose of the demonstration was to present the third Chartist Petition to Parliament.

On *May 15, 1848*, the bourgeois national guard suppressed the revolutionary actions of the Paris workers.

On *June 25, 1848*, the rising of the workers of Paris was crushed.

On *August 6, 1848*, Milan was occupied by Austrian troops, who suppressed the national liberation movement in North Italy.

On *November 1, 1848*, the troops of Windischgrätz took Vienna.   p. 101

[118] As a result of the revolutionary actions of the masses in Vienna, primarily of the workers and students, on May 15 and 16, the Imperial Government was forced to give up the idea of creating an elective two-Chamber parliament and to introduce changes into the electoral law, adopted shortly before that, by extending the franchise. The armed people also secured the abrogation of the order of May 14 dissolving the Central Committee of the national guard and the Academic Legion (see Note 26).

On May 15, 1848, a popular uprising in Naples caused by King Ferdinand's infringement of constitutional rights was brutally crushed, the *lazzaroni* (see Note 25) taking an active part in its suppression.   p. 102

[119] This refers to the suppression of the popular uprising in Frankfurt am Main on September 18, 1848 (see Note 110).   p. 103

[120] On July 25, 1848, at Custozza (North Italy), the Austrian army under Radetzky defeated the Piedmont troops. This was followed by the capture of Milan on August 6 and the conclusion on August 9 of an armistice between Austria and the Kingdom of Sardinia under which the latter was to withdraw its troops from the towns and fortresses of Lombardy and Venice and to hand them over to the Austrians.   p. 103

[121] The uprising in Leghorn (Grand Duchy of Tuscany) began at the end of August 1848 and ended on September 2 with the rout of the government troops. Fearing that the uprising might spread all over Tuscany, the Grand Duke Leopold II

dismissed the moderate liberal Government of Capponi. On October 27 a democratic government of Tuscany was formed headed by Montagnelli. It was he who put forward the slogan of convening an Italian Constituent Assembly (Guerazzi became a member of the Government).

The victory of the people in Tuscany called forth mass demonstrations in Rome (Papal states) demanding the convocation of an Italian Constituent Assembly, resumption of the war with Austria, formation of a provisional democratic government, and social reforms. On November 16, in response to the attempts of the Papal Swiss Guard to disperse the demonstration, the people erected barricades near the Vatican and attacked it. Pius IX yielded, and a new government was set up in Rome with the participation of Left liberals and democrats.   p. 104

[122] *"Troppo tardi, santo padre, troppo tardi!"* ("Too late, Holy Father, too late!") cried the revolutionary-minded people of Rome when Pius IX, after much procrastination, issued an edict on March 15, 1848, introducing a watered-down Constitution of the Papal states.   p. 107

[123] See Note 59.   p. 109

[124] Fearing the growth of the revolutionary movement in Rome (see Note 121), Pius IX fled from Rome on the night of November 24, 1848, and took up residence in the Neapolitan fortress of Gaeta. Meanwhile a struggle flared up in the Papal states between the revolutionary democrats who stood for the proclamation of a republic and the liberals who sought to bring back the Pope to Rome and get his sanction for certain constitutional concessions. In the course of this struggle the liberals were defeated and on February 9, 1849, a Roman Republic was founded.
                                                                           p. 109

[125] The reference is to the treaty (drawn up by the Swiss Diet in 1814 and approved by the Vienna Congress in 1815) which acknowledged Switzerland's permanent neutrality. Under this treaty the Swiss Confederation was defined as a federation of 22 cantons. When a Constitution was introduced in 1848, this treaty became invalid.   p. 119

[126] Concerning the position of Escher and Munzinger as the representatives of the Berne canton in Tessin during the so-called Tessin conflict, see Note 36.
                                                                           p. 119

[127] In 1848-49 moderate bourgeois constitutionalists in Germany called the republican democrats "*agitators*" (*Wühler*) and these in turn called their opponents "*wailers*" (*Heuler*).   p. 120

[128] The articles "The French Working Class and the Presidential Elections" and "Proudhon" were written by Engels in early December 1848 during his stay in Switzerland and were intended for the *Neue Rheinische Zeitung*. However, they were not published and came down to us in manuscript form.   p. 123

[129] In view of the presidential elections in France scheduled for December 10, 1848, the party of the petty-bourgeois democrats, which had formed a bloc for a time with the petty-bourgeois socialists (Louis Blanc and others) and grouped round the newspaper *La Réforme* (its representatives in the Constituent and later in the Legislative Assembly called themselves Montagnards or the Mountain by analogy with the Montagnards in the Convention of 1792-94), nominated its leader, Ledru-Rollin, as a candidate for the presidency. The proletarian socialists,

however, preferred their own candidate, Raspail, a well-known scientist and revolutionary with communist views. Proudhon's followers, grouped round his newspaper *Le Peuple*, also supported Raspail.

The differences between the supporters of these two candidates revealed the internal contradictions among the revolutionary democrats. To characterise these differences Engels made use of the material published in the French democratic and socialist periodicals, in particular, the article "Encore et toujours la présidence" in *La Réforme*, November 14, 1848, and the leading article in *La Révolution démocratique et sociale* No. 10, November 10, 1848.   p. 123

[130] By the "pure" (or tricolour) republicans are meant members of the *National* party (see Note 101).   p. 124

[131] See Note 104.   p. 124

[132] For the revolutionary events in Paris on May 15, 1848, see Note 117.

The *June insurrection*—the proletarian uprising in Paris on June 23-26, 1848 (see present edition, Vol. 7, pp. 124-28 and 130-64).   p. 124

[133] *Equitable Labour Exchange Bazaars or Offices* (the name is given in English in the German original) were founded by the workers' co-operative societies in various towns of England in 1832. This movement was headed by Robert Owen, who founded such a bazaar in London. The products of labour at these bazaars were exchanged for a kind of paper "money" issued as labour "tickets", a working hour being the unit. These bazaars were an attempt by the utopians to organise exchange without money in the conditions of capitalist commodity production and soon proved to be a failure.   p. 130

[134] Concerning this speech of Proudhon's in the French National (Constituent) Assembly on July 31, 1848, see the article "Proudhon's Speech against Thiers" published in the *Neue Rheinische Zeitung* (present edition, Vol. 7, pp. 321-24).
                                                                           p. 132

[135] The royal order dissolving the Prussian National Assembly was issued on December 5, 1848. In the Ministry's explanation accompanying the order the Assembly was accused of having disregarded the royal decree of November 8 ordering it to move from Berlin to Brandenburg, a measure allegedly designed "to protect the deputies' freedom of deliberation from the anarchistic movements in the capital and their terroristic influences".

The imposed Constitution came into force on December 5, 1848, simultaneous-ly with the dissolution of the Assembly. This Constitution provided for a two-Chamber parliament. By means of age and property qualifications the First Chamber was made a privileged "Chamber of the Gentry", while under the electoral law of December 6, 1848, a considerable part of the working people was excluded from the two-stage election to the Second Chamber. According to this Constitution, in case of war or "disorders" "guarantees" of personal freedom, inviolability of the home, freedom of the press, assembly and association etc. were suspended. Wide powers were assumed by the King: he had the right to convene or dissolve the Chambers, to appoint Ministers, to declare war or conclude peace; he had the executive power entirely in his hands, while sharing the legislative power with the Chambers. All this, together with the direct proviso that the King could review the Constitution on his own initiative, played into the hands of the counter-revolutionaries.   p. 134

[136] See Note 2.   p. 134

[137] An English translation of this article first appeared in the collection: Karl Marx and Frederick Engels, *Articles from the "Neue Rheinische Zeitung". 1848-49*, Progress Publishers, Moscow, 1972.   p. 135

[138] See Note 135.   p. 135

[139] The *Vorort*—see Note 36.
Concerning the *Struve campaign* see Note 84.   p. 136

[140] See Note 9.   p. 140

[141] See Note 10.   p. 142

[142] See Note 10.   p. 146

[143] The reference is to the anti-constitutional coup d'état in the Wallis (Valais) canton in May 1844, when the Upper Wallis opponents of bourgeois reforms, instigated by the Jesuits and the clergy, overthrew the liberal Government and annulled the cantonal Constitution of 1840. In a battle at Pont-de-Trient on May 21, 1,500 men of Lower Wallis headed by Maurice Barman were defeated by the 8,000-strong army of General Kalbermatten. With the change of government the Wallis canton joined the Sonderbund (see Note 10) in June 1844.   p. 148

[144] In October 1848 there was an uprising in North Lombardy (Veltlin and other places) against the Austrian occupation troops of Radetzky. Giuseppe Mazzini, who had emigrated to Switzerland after Milan was occupied by the Austrians in September 1848, issued an appeal to the insurgents and tried to help them by organising an expedition of Italian refugees who had settled in the Swiss frontier canton of Tessin.
Crossing the frontier at Valle Intelvi the members of the expedition joined the insurgents, but the uprising was soon crushed and the surviving refugees returned to Switzerland. This provided Radetzky with a pretext for demanding from the Swiss Government the deportation of all Italian refugees, but the Tessin authorities refused to satisfy this demand. The *Neue Rheinische Zeitung* published a number of reports on the course of the uprising in Lombardy (in the section "Italy").   p. 152

[145] The second article in the series "The Bourgeoisie and the Counter-Revolution" (of December 11, 1848) was first published in English in the book: Marx and Engels, *Selected Works* in two volumes, Foreign Languages Publishing House, Vol. I, Moscow, 1950. The series was first published in full in English in the collection: Karl Marx, *On Revolution*, ed. by S. K. Padover, New York, 1971, and then in the collection: Karl Marx and Frederick Engels, *Articles from the "Neue Rheinische Zeitung". 1848-49*, Progress Publishers, Moscow, 1972.   p. 154

[146] Below Marx quotes "Decision on Some Principles of the Future Prussian Constitution" ("Verordnung über einige Grundlagen der künftigen Preussischen Verfassung") and the electoral law for the convocation of the National Assembly adopted by the Second United Diet (see Note 89) on April 6 and 8, 1848. Both documents were published in the book *Verhandlungen des zum 2. April 1848 zusammenberufenen Vereinigten Landtages, zusammengestellt von E. Bleich*, Berlin, 1848.   p. 154

[147] This refers to the Constitution imposed by the Prussian King on December 5, 1848, simultaneously with the publication of the order dissolving the Prussian National Assembly (see Note 135).   p. 154

[148] See Note 109.   p. 154

[149] *Trop tard!* (too late!)—apparently by analogy with *Troppo tardi!* Cf. Note 122.
p. 157

[150] During the March revolution of 1848 the Prince of Prussia fled to England, but on June 4, aided by the Camphausen Ministry, he returned to Berlin. At the sitting of the Prussian National Assembly on June 6 Camphausen sought to present this cowardly flight of the Prince as a journey undertaken for educational purposes.
p. 157

[151] After the March revolution of 1848 in Germany an insurrection of the Poles broke out in the Duchy of Posen for their liberation from the Prussian yoke. The mass of the Polish peasants and artisans took part in it together with members of the lesser nobility. The Prussian Government was forced to promise that a commission would be set up to carry out the reorganisation of Posen: creation of a Polish army, appointment of Poles to administrative and other posts, recognition of Polish as the official language etc. On April 14, 1848, however, the King ordered the division of the Duchy of Posen into an eastern Polish part and a western "German" part, which was not to be "reorganised". During the months following the suppression of the Polish insurrection by the Prussian military, in violation of all agreements with the Poles, the demarcation line was pushed further and further east and the promised "reorganisation" was never carried out.

Under the impact of the March revolution, the national liberation movement of the German population in the duchies of Schleswig and Holstein, which had been incorporated into the Kingdom of Denmark by decision of the Vienna Congress (1815), grew in strength and became radical and democratic, forming part of the struggle for the unification of Germany. Volunteers from all over the country rushed to the aid of the local population when it rose in arms against Danish rule. Prussia, Hanover and other states of the German Confederation sent to the duchies federal troops under the command of the Prussian General Wrangel. However, the Prussian Government which feared a popular outbreak and an intensification of the revolution sought an agreement with Denmark at the expense of the general German interests. The situation was complicated by the intervention of Britain, Sweden and Tsarist Russia in favour of the Kingdom of Denmark. The seven months' armistice concluded between Prussia and Denmark at Malmö on August 26, 1848 (see Note 75), in fact preserved Danish rule in Schleswig and Holstein. The war, resumed at the end of March 1849, ended in 1850 with the victory of the Danes and the two duchies remained part of the Kingdom of Denmark.   p. 157

[152] On September 15, 1848, General Wrangel, who was associated with the reactionary Court clique, was appointed Commander-in-Chief of the Brandenburg military district, which included Berlin. The *Markgrafschaft* (Marches) of Brandenburg, the original core of Prussia, consisted in the Middle Ages of two parts, the Kurmark and the Neumark, hence the title of the general: "Commander-in-Chief of the two Marches."   p. 157

[153] Concerning *Hansemann-Pinto* see Note 44.

The "Government of Action" which succeeded the Camphausen Government was in power from June 25 to September 21, 1848, Auerswald being formally its head. Hansemann, Finance Minister as in the Camphausen Ministry, actually directed the Ministry's activity.   p. 157

[154] Marx refers to the revolution in the Netherlands in 1566-1609 which was a combination of the national liberation war against absolutist Spain and the anti-feudal struggle of the progressive forces. The revolution ended with the victory of the north, where Europe's first bourgeois republic—the United Provinces (the Dutch Republic)—was established, and with the defeat of the southern provinces, which remained under Spanish rule.   p. 161

[155] An allusion to Camphausen, who was formerly an oil and corn dealer, and to Hansemann, who started as a wool merchant.   p. 163

[156] Early in June 1848, the Prussian National Assembly, under pressure from the Government and the moderate constitutionalists, rejected a resolution giving due credit to the participants in the revolution of March 18-19, 1848, in Prussia. After long debates (described by Engels in his article "The Berlin Debate on the Revolution", present edition, Vol. 7, pp. 73-86), the Assembly decided by a majority vote to proceed to the next items on the agenda. The Assembly's renunciation of the March revolution aroused the indignation of the Berlin workers and artisans who, on June 14, took the arsenal by storm to arm themselves and defend their revolutionary gains. The uprising was put down by the army and the bourgeois civic militia.   p. 165

[157] Marx refers here to the numerous promises of the kings of Prussia to introduce a Constitution and representative bodies in the country. On May 22, 1815, a decree was issued by the King in which he promised the setting up of provincial diets of estates, the convocation of an all-Prussia representative body, and a Constitution. Under the National Debt Law of January 17, 1820, state loans could only be issued with the consent of the provincial diets. But these promises made under pressure from the bourgeois opposition movement remained a dead letter. All that happened was that a law of June 5, 1823, established provincial diets with restricted advisory functions.

Financial difficulties compelled Frederick William IV on February 3, 1847, to issue an edict convening the United Diet (*Vereinigte Landtag*), a body consisting of representatives of all the provincial diets of Prussia. The United Diet refused to grant a loan to the Government and was soon dissolved. The electoral law of April 8, 1848 (Marx quotes it above, on p. 154 of this volume), promulgated as a result of the March revolution, provided for the convocation of an Assembly to draft a Constitution by "agreement with the Crown". The two-stage system of voting established by this law secured the majority for the representatives of the bourgeoisie and the Prussian officials.   p. 166

[158] By *Prussian Law* is meant the *Allgemeines Landrecht für die Preussischen Staaten* approved and published in 1794. It included the criminal, constitutional, civil, administrative and ecclesiastical law and was strongly influenced by feudal ideas in the sphere of jurisdiction.

Code pénal—see Note 88.
Constables—see Note 45.   p. 171

[159] On August 21, 1848, Berlin was the scene of mass meetings and demonstrations in protest against attacks on members of the Democratic Club by reactionaries in Charlottenburg, a Berlin suburb. The demonstrators, who demanded the resignation of the Auerswald-Hansemann Ministry, threw stones at the building where Auerswald and other Ministers were staying. The Government replied to the August events with fresh repressive measures.   p. 172

[160] The Belgian Constitution of 1831 adopted after the victory of the bourgeois revolution of 1830 established a high property qualification, thus depriving a considerable part of the population of the suffrage.   p. 173

[161] The reference is to the *Preussische Seehandlungsgesellschaft* (the Prussian Maritime Trading Company)—a trade and credit society, founded in 1772 and enjoying a number of important state privileges. It granted large credits to the Government and actually played the part of its banker and broker. In 1904 it was made the official Prussian state bank.   p. 173

[162] A Bill abrogating exemption from graduated tax payments for the nobility, officers, teachers and the clergy was submitted by Hansemann to the Prussian National Assembly on July 12, 1848. A Bill abrogating exemption from the land tax was tabled on July 21, 1848.   p. 174

[163] At the sitting of the Prussian National Assembly on July 21, 1848, the Bill introduced on the basis of Deputy Hanow's motion of June 3, 1848, was voted down and considered for the second time on September 30. Accepted this time, the Bill was approved by the King on October 9.   p. 175

[164] Nenstiel's motion was introduced as early as June 2, 1848, and the decision mentioned by Marx, which in effect postponed indefinitely the abolition of peasant labour services, was adopted on September 1, 1848.   p. 175

[165] The reference is to the Congress of big landowners which met in Berlin on August 18, 1848. It was convoked by the leaders of the Association for the Protection of Property and the Advancement of the Well-Being of All Classes of the Prussian People. The Congress changed the name of the Association to: Association for the Protection of the Interests of Landowners; the Congress became known as the "Landowners' Parliament".   p. 176

[166] On July 31, 1848, the garrison of the Silesian fortress of Schweidnitz fired at a demonstration of the civic militia and local population protesting against the provocative actions of the military; 14 people were killed and 32 seriously wounded.

The Schweidnitz events served as a pretext for a discussion of the situation in the army by the Prussian National Assembly.

On August 9, 1848, the Assembly adopted the proposal of Deputy Stein, with amendments by Deputy Schultze, requesting the Minister of War to issue an army order to the effect that officers opposed to the constitutional system were bound in honour to resign from the army. Despite the Assembly's decision Schreckenstein, the Minister of War, did not issue any such order. Stein therefore tabled his motion for the second time at the sitting of the National Assembly on September 7, 1848. As a result of the voting, the Auerswald-Hansemann Ministry had to resign. Under the Pfuel Ministry which followed, the order, though in a milder form, was at last issued on September 26, but this also remained a dead letter. Earlier, on September 17, General Wrangel issued an army order which made it clear that the military intended to launch an open offensive against the revolution. It urged the maintenance of "public order", threatened those "who were trying to entice the people to commit unlawful acts", and called upon the soldiers to rally round their officers and the King.   p. 176

[167] A reference to the speech from the throne made by Frederick William IV at the opening of the United Diet on April 11, 1847. The King said he would

never agree to grant a Constitution which he described as a "written scrap of paper".   p. 177

[168] Article 14 of the Constitutional Charter Louis XVIII granted in 1814 read: "The King is the head of the state."   p. 177

[169] *Magna Charta Libertatum*—the charter which the insurgent barons forced King John of England to sign in 1215. It limited the powers of the King in the interests of the feudal lords, and also contained some concessions to the knights and burghers.   p. 177

[170] An allusion to the attempts made by the European counter-revolutionary forces in 1848-49 to restore the Holy Alliance, a league of European monarchs set up in 1815 on the initiative of Austrian Chancellor Metternich and Russian Tsar Alexander I to put down the revolutionary movement.   p. 180

[171] See Note 84.   p. 180

[172] The reference is to the agreements concluded from the fifteenth to the mid-nineteenth century between Swiss cantons and European states for the supply of Swiss mercenaries. In many West-European countries the mercenaries were used by the counter-revolutionary monarchist forces.   p. 183

[173] The King's guard consisting of Swiss mercenaries and *lazzaroni* (see Note 25) took an active part in suppressing the popular uprising in Naples on May 15, 1848 (see Note 118). *Lazzaroni* and soldiers broke into the houses of the people of Naples, including foreigners, looted them and committed violence.   p. 183

[174] *Burghers' communes* (*Bürgergemeinden*) came into being at the end of the Middle Ages. They granted their members certain economic and political privileges including exemption from a number of duties and tax payments, the right to use the commune's property and advantages in filling lucrative government offices. One became a member of the commune either by birth or by living in a given place for a definite period of time and possessing immovable property, or by paying an admission fee.

In the course of time it became more and more difficult to enter a commune, which led to the division of the Swiss population into citizens (*Bürger*) and residents (*Einwohner*), the latter being deprived of the above-named privileges. Within the burghers' commune there appeared a still closer corporation of representatives of the old patrician families who in fact established a monopoly of practically all the major government posts. Abolition of the privileges of the burghers' commune began during the Helvetian Republic in 1798-99, when all the Swiss were made equal in rights and political power was transferred to the residents' commune (*Einwohnergemeinde*), which was declared to be the holder of sovereignty in the name of the entire nation. The Federal Constitution adopted in 1848 enlarged still more the rights of the residents' commune while the burghers' commune only retained philanthropic functions and power over its own property.
                                                                             p. 182

[175] This address was written by Engels, as a member of the Central Commission, on the instructions of the First Congress of the German Workers' Associations in Switzerland which took place in Berne between December 9 and 11, 1848. The Congress was attended by representatives from democratic and workers' associations in a number of Swiss towns. It adopted the rules of the Union of German Associations of Switzerland. In accordance with these rules, a Central

Association (the Berne Workers' Association was elected as such) was to be at the head of the Union, and current leadership was to be exercised by a Central Commission consisting of five members. Engels was a member of the Commission elected on December 14.

Differences arose at the sitting on December 10 when the Congress discussed the question of the attitude towards the March Association. A delegate of the Berne Association spoke against establishing contacts with this non-republican organisation. Nevertheless, the majority of delegates were in favour of an address proposing to the March Association to keep up correspondence. The text of the address was approved by the Congress on December 11. When Engels compiled it he had to take into account the Congress decision. However, in the text of the address written in the name of the Central Commission he managed to reflect the views of the proletarian revolutionaries who regarded this Association only as a fellow traveller in the German revolution and thought that co-operation with it was possible only within strict limits.

The *March Association*, which had branches in various towns of Germany, was founded in Frankfurt am Main at the end of November 1848 by the Left-wing deputies of the Frankfurt National Assembly. Fröbel, Simon, Ruge, Vogt and other petty-bourgeois democratic leaders of the March associations, thus named after the March 1848 revolution in Germany, confined themselves to revolutionary phrase-mongering and showed indecision and inconsistency in the struggle against the counter-revolutionaries, for which Marx and Engels sharply criticised them.   p. 185

176 By 1848, the Berne Association became one of the biggest and most influential German workers' associations in Switzerland. Its members held democratic republican views and were considerably influenced by Weitling and Stephan Born. It disintegrated in the spring of 1849.   p. 185

177 According to Article 1 of the Rules of the Union of German Associations in Switzerland adopted at the Berne Congress, the aim of the new organisation was "to educate members of the Union in the socio-democratic and republican spirit and use all legal means at its disposal so that socio-democratic and republican principles and institutions would be acknowledged by the Germans and put into practice".   p. 185

178 The so-called *Risquons-Tout trial*, held in Antwerp from August 9 to 30, 1848, was a fabrication of the Government of Leopold, King of the Belgians, against the democrats. The pretext was a clash which took place on March 29, 1848, between the Belgian republican legion bound for home from France and a detachment of soldiers near the village of Risquons-Tout not far from the French border. The bill of indictment was published in the *Neue Rheinische Zeitung* No. 45, July 15, 1848, No. 47, July 17, 1848, No. 49 and in the supplement to this issue, July 19, 1848. Mellinet, Ballin, Tedesco and other main accused were sentenced to death, but this was commuted to 30 years imprisonment; later they were pardoned.

See Engels' article "The Antwerp Death Sentences" in Vol. 7 of the present edition, pp. 404-06.   p. 189

179 The *Cologne Workers' Association* (*Kölner Arbeiterverein*)—a workers' organisation founded by Andreas Gottschalk on April 13, 1848. The initial membership of 300 had increased to 5,000 by early May, the majority being workers and artisans. The Association was headed by a President and a committee consisting of representa-

tives of various trades. The *Zeitung des Arbeiter-Vereines zu Köln* was the Association's newspaper, but on October 26 it was replaced by the *Freiheit, Brüderlichkeit, Arbeit.* There were a number of branches. After Gottschalk's arrest Moll was elected President on July 6 and he held this post till the state of siege was proclaimed in Cologne in September 1848, when he had to emigrate under threat of arrest. On October 16, Marx agreed to assume temporary presidency at the request of the Association members. In November Röser began to fulfil the duties of President, and on February 28, 1849, Schapper was elected to the post and remained in it until the end of May 1849.

The majority of the leading members (Gottschalk, Anneke, Schapper, Moll, Lessner, Jansen, Röser, Nothjung, Bedorf) were members of the Communist League.

During the initial period of its existence, the Workers' Association was influenced by Gottschalk, who shared many of the views of the "true socialists", ignored the historical tasks of the proletariat in the democratic revolution, pursued sectarian tactics of boycotting indirect elections to the German and Prussian National Assemblies and came out against support of democratic candidates in elections. He combined ultra-Left phrases with very moderate methods of struggle (workers' petitions to the Government and the City Council etc.), and supported the demands of the workers affected by artisan prejudices etc. From the very beginning, Gottschalk's sectarian tactics were resisted by the supporters of Marx and Engels. At the end of June under their influence a change took place in the activities of the Workers' Association, which became a centre of revolutionary agitation among the workers, and from the autumn of 1848, also among the peasants. Members of the Association organised democratic and workers' associations in the vicinity of Cologne and disseminated revolutionary publications, including the "Demands of the Communist Party in Germany". They carried on among themselves education in scientific communism through the study of Marx's writings. The Association maintained close contact with other workers' and democratic organisations.

With a view to strengthening the Association Marx, Schapper and other leaders reorganised it in January and February 1849. On February 25, new Rules were adopted according to which the main task of the Association was to raise the workers' class and political consciousness.

When in the spring of 1849 Marx and Engels took steps to organise the advanced workers on a national scale and actually started preparing for the creation of a proletarian party, they relied to a considerable extent on the Cologne Workers' Association.

The mounting counter-revolution and intensified police reprisals prevented further activities of the Cologne Workers' Association to unite and organise the working masses. After the *Neue Rheinische Zeitung* ceased publication and Marx, Schapper and other leaders of the Association left Cologne, it gradually turned into an ordinary workers' educational society.   p. 189

[180] The reference is to the trial of A. Brocker-Evererts, owner of the printshop which printed the *Zeitung des Arbeiter-Vereines zu Köln* (published from April to October 1848 and edited first by Andreas Gottschalk and from July to September by Joseph Moll). The trial took place on October 24, 1848. Brocker-Evererts was accused of printing in issues 12 and 13 of the newspaper (July 6 and 9, 1848) the articles "Arrest of Dr. Gottschalk and Anneke" and "Arrests in Cologne" insulting Chief Public Prosecutor Zweiffel and the police. The jury sentenced him to a month's imprisonment and laid down that if the newspaper resumed

publication he would have to pay a big fine. Beginning from October 26 the Cologne Workers' Association published the newspaper *Freiheit, Brüderlichkeit, Arbeit.* p. 189

[181] The laws promulgated by the French Government in September 1835 restricted the rights of juries and introduced severe measures against the press: increased money deposits for periodicals and large fines and imprisonment for the authors of publications directed against property and the existing political system. p. 190

[182] The *First Democratic Congress* was held in Frankfurt am Main from June 14 to 17, 1848. It was attended by delegates of 89 democratic and workers' associations from different towns in Germany. The Congress decided to unite all democratic associations and to set up district committees headed by a Central Committee of German Democrats with its headquarters in Berlin. Fröbel, Rau and Kriege were elected to the Central Committee and Bairhoffer, Schütte and Anneke their deputies. However, due to the weakness and vacillations of the petty-bourgeois leaders, even after the Congress the democratic movement in Germany still lacked unity and organisation. p. 190

[183] At the close of its sitting on July 4, 1848, the Prussian National Assembly decided to grant unlimited powers to the committee investigating the Posen events (see Note 151). In violation of parliamentary rules, the Right attempted to have a motion voted to limit the committee's powers. The Left walked out of the Assembly in protest and the Right took advantage of this and carried a motion prohibiting the committee from travelling to Posen and interrogating witnesses and experts on the spot, thereby unlawfully annulling the Assembly's original decision. This incident is described in Engels' article "The Agreement Session of July 4" (present edition, Vol. 7, pp. 200-07). p. 193

[184] Concerning the union of the three democratic associations in Cologne—the Democratic Society, the Workers' Association and the Association for Workers and Employers—see Note 40. p. 195

[185] After keeping Gottschalk and Anneke in prison for almost six months, the authorities were compelled to release them when the assizes acquitted them on December 23, 1848. p. 196

[186] An excerpt from this article was first published in English under the title "The Prussian Counter-Revolution and the Judiciary" in the collection: Karl Marx, *On Revolution*, ed. by S. K. Padover, New York, 1971. p. 197

[187] The report on the decisions of the Courts of Appeal in Ratibor (Racibórz), Bromberg (Bydgoszcz) and Münster and the decision of the Berlin Supreme Court were printed in the *Neue Rheinische Zeitung* No. 174, December 21, 1848. p. 197

[188] *French parliaments*—judicial institutions which arose in the Middle Ages. The Paris Parliament was the supreme appeal body and at the same time performed important executive and political functions, such as the registration of royal decrees, without which they had no legal force, etc. The parliaments enjoyed the right to remonstrate government decrees. In the seventeenth and eighteenth centuries their members were officials of high birth, representatives of the so-called silk gown nobility. The parliaments, which finally became the bulwark of

Right opposition to absolutism and impeded the implementation of even moderate reforms, were abolished in 1790, during the French Revolution.   p. 198

[189] The reference is to the edict of the Berlin Supreme Court of December 16, 1848, signed by Mühler and published in the *Preussischer Staats-Anzeiger* No. 229 on December 19, 1848.   p. 198

[190] The reference is to the transfer of the sittings of the Prussian National Assembly from Berlin to Brandenburg. This was the beginning of a counter-revolutionary coup d'état in Prussia which ended with the dissolution of the National Assembly and imposition of a Constitution by the King.   p. 200

[191] An allusion to a German legend according to which the souls of the dead, led by the "wild hunter", fly about shrieking fearfully at night. People who meet these ghosts are doomed to wander with them for ever.   p. 200

[192] See Note 89.   p. 201

[193] In December 1848, the counter-revolutionary Austrian Government was not supported by the Imperial Diet on the question of the compulsory loan and asked the bank for a loan. However, it succeeded in obtaining a loan only after threatening the bank with confiscation of all its ready cash.   p. 201

[194] The reference is to the attempt by Gustav Struve and other political refugees to organise an uprising in Baden in September 1848 (see Note 84).

The *"Hilf Dir" military association* was founded in the autumn of 1848 by Johann Philipp Becker, a leader of the democratic and working-class movement. With its Central Committee in Biel (canton of Berne), it united societies consisting mainly of artisans formed in various towns in Switzerland.

The "Hilf Dir" military association pursued a democratic policy and aimed at uniting all German volunteer units in Switzerland for the purpose of establishing a republic in Germany. It was organised as a secret conspiratorial society, on the lines of those in France and Italy. The Swiss authorities, under pressure from German counter-revolutionary circles and the Imperial Government in particular, instituted proceedings against Becker and other initiators of the military association. Becker was sentenced to expulsion from the Berne canton for twelve months.   p. 204

[195] The *republican uprisings in Baden in April and September 1848*—see Notes 78 and 84.

The uprising in Val d'Intelvi (Lombardy) and the part played in it by refugees living in Switzerland—see Engels' article "The National Council" (this volume, pp. 138-53) and Note 144.

The *Lucerne campaigns* were organised in response to the decision adopted by the reactionary Great Council of the Lucerne canton in October 1844, granting unlimited powers to the Order of Jesuits in matters of religion and public education. The liberal circles of the canton made an attempt to overthrow the Government, organising on December 8 a campaign of volunteer detachments against Lucerne. The insurgents were dispersed by government troops. The second campaign, organised for the same purpose from the territory of the neighbouring cantons on March 31, 1845, also proved a failure.   p. 204

[196] In its letter of December 7 to the forthcoming First Congress of the German Workers' Associations in Berne (see Note 175), the Association in Vivis objected to a number of proposals advanced by the democratic German National Associa-

tion in Zurich, suggesting in particular that the new Union should be headed by
the "Hilf Dir" military association in Biel (see Note 194). The letter was discussed
at the Congress sitting of December 10, 1848. The Congress directed the
Central Commission, formed to exercise current leadership of the Union of
Workers' Associations in Switzerland (with Engels as its secretary), to answer the
letter and persuade the Vivis Association to renounce its demands and join the
Union.   p. 207

197 The reference is to the German National Association in Zurich founded in April
1848, a democratic organisation of German intellectuals and workers living in
Switzerland. It was influenced by petty-bourgeois democrats: Fröbel, Ruge and
others. In the summer of 1848 the National Association joined the Union of
Democratic German Associations founded by the First Democratic Congress in
Frankfurt am Main (see Note 182). In August 1848 the National Association
appealed to all the German associations in Switzerland to convene a congress and
unite. Its representatives took an active part in the First Congress of German
Associations in Switzerland held from December 9 to 11, 1848.   p. 207

198 On December 8, 1848, the Lausanne Workers' Association sent Engels a mandate,
delegating him to the Congress (see this volume, pp. 505-06). The leaders of this
Association, G. Schneeberger, Chr. Haaf and Bangert, wrote in this connection to
the Berne Workers' Association on December 8, 1848: "We cannot send a
delegate because of the inactivity of the Vivis Association (which recognises only
the Association in *Biel* as the central body). Therefore we have decided to
authorise our friend *Engels.* If, however, he cannot attend, our friend Frost will act
as our delegate."   p. 208

199 The *Central Committee of German Democrats* (d'Ester, Reichenbach, Hexamer) was
elected at the Second Democratic Congress held in Berlin from October 26 to 30,
1848.
     The *Central Committee of German Workers* in Leipzig, headed by Stephan Born,
was elected at the Workers' Congress held in Berlin from August 23 to September
3, 1848. At this Congress the Workers' Fraternity, a union of workers' associations,
was founded. Its programme was drawn up under the influence of Born and was
concerned only with narrow craft-union demands, thereby diverting the workers
from the revolutionary struggle. A number of its points bore the stamp of Louis
Blanc's and Proudhon's utopian ideas. Marx and Engels did not approve of the
general stand taken by Born, but they refrained from publicly criticising his views,
bearing in mind his endeavour to unite the workers' associations.   p. 208

200 See Note 170.   p. 211

201 An excerpt from this article was first published in English in the journal *Labour
Monthly*, London, 1923, Vol. 5, No. 1. Another excerpt appeared in the collection:
Karl Marx, *On Revolution*, ed. by S. K. Padover, New York, 1971. An English
translation was first published in full in the book: Karl Marx and Frederick
Engels, *Articles from the "Neue Rheinische Zeitung". 1848-49*, Progress Publishers,
Moscow, 1972.   p. 213

202 The reference is to the manifesto published on February 10, 1848, by Pius IX,
who had previously carried out a number of liberal reforms and sanctioned the
formation of a secular government. In the manifesto the Pope gave the blessing of
the Church to the Italian people. Although the manifesto hinted that Pius IX
disapproved of the demand for a Constitution, it was interpreted as an approval of
the movement for constitutional reforms which had developed after the popular

uprising in Sicily in January 1848 against the rule of the Bourbons of Naples.

Under the impact of the French revolution in February 1848 Pius IX was compelled to issue a decree on March 15, 1848, introducing a moderate Constitution in the Papal states.   p. 213

203 After the popular uprising in Rome on November 16, 1848 (see Note 121), Pius IX fled on November 24 to the fortress of Gaeta in the Kingdom of Naples.
                                                                    p. 213

204 The *Mountain*—see Note 129.

The *party of the "National"*—see Note 101.

The *dynastic opposition*—an opposition group headed by Odilon Barrot in the French Chamber of Deputies during the July monarchy (1830-48). It expressed the views of the liberal industrial and commercial bourgeoisie and favoured a moderate electoral reform, regarding it as a means of preventing revolution and preserving the Orléans dynasty. The dynastic opposition was close to the monarchist pro-Orleanist bourgeois politicians headed by Thiers, whose mouthpiece was the newspaper *Constitutionnel*. Until February 1848 this group stood for a monarchy with republican institutions and subsequently for a republic with monarchical institutions.

The *legitimists*—supporters of the Bourbon dynasty, which was overthrown in 1830. They upheld the interests of the big hereditary landowners.   p. 213

205 In the summer of 1848, the anti-feudal movement and the struggle for complete liberation from the rule of the Turkish Sultan gained strength in the Danube principalities of Moldavia and Wallachia, which formally remained autonomous possessions of Turkey. The movement in Wallachia grew into a bourgeois revolution. In June 1848, a Constitution was proclaimed, a liberal Provisional Government was formed and George Bibesco, the ruler of Wallachia, abdicated and fled from the country.

On June 28, 1848, a 12,000-strong Russian army corps entered Moldavia and in July Turkish troops also invaded the country. The Russian and Turkish intervention helped restore the feudal system and the subsequent entry of Turkish troops into Wallachia with the consent of the Tsarist Government brought about the defeat of the bourgeois revolution there. There were bloody reprisals against the population in Bucharest. A proclamation of the Turkish government commissioner Fuad-Effendi declared it necessary to establish "law and order" and "eliminate all traces of the revolution".   p. 214

206 *Pandours*—irregular infantry units of the Austrian army recruited mainly in the South-Slav provinces of the Austrian Empire.

Serezhans—see Note 112.   p. 214

207 See Note 172.   p. 216

208 The reference is to the Swiss citizens living in the Kingdom of Naples who suffered maltreatment and material losses as a result of the suppression of the popular uprising in Naples on May 15, 1848 (see Note 118), and the fierce four-day bombardment and plunder of Messina early in September 1848, after it had been captured by the royal troops sent by Ferdinand II to crush the revolutionary movement in Sicily.   p. 217

209 An English translation of this article was first published in the collection: Karl Marx and Frederick Engels, *Articles from the "Neue Rheinische Zeitung". 1848-49*, Progress Publishers, Moscow, 1972.   p. 218

[210] *"To my dear Berliners"*—an appeal of Frederick William IV published in the morning of March 19, 1848, during the people's uprising in Berlin.

"To my people and the German nation"—an appeal of Frederick William IV published on March 21, 1848.

"To my army"—a New-Year message of Frederick William IV signed by him in Potsdam on January 1, 1849, and published in the *Preussischer Staats-Anzeiger* No. 3, January 3, 1849.   p. 222

[211] *Friedrichshain*—a park in Berlin where the insurgents killed on the barricades during the uprising on March 18, 1848, were buried.   p. 223

[212] On April 8, 1848, during his secret mission on behalf of the King of Prussia, Major Wildenbruch handed a Note to the Danish Government which stated that Prussia was not fighting in Schleswig-Holstein to rob Denmark of the duchy but merely to combat "radical and republican elements in Germany". The Prussian Government tried every possible means to avoid official recognition of this compromising document.   p. 223

[213] See Note 75.   p. 224

[214] The reference is to the battle at Miloslaw on April 30, 1848, during the national liberation insurrection in the Duchy of Posen (see Note 151). As a result, the Polish insurgents commanded by Mieroslawski forced the Prussian troops under General Colomb to retreat.   p. 224

[215] The reference is apparently to the battle at Sokoluv, near Wreschen (Września), where on May 2, 1848, a 3.000-strong Prussian detachment under General Hirschfeld attacked the insurgents commanded by Mieroslawski, who was leading them north to Kujavia intending to continue the struggle there. The insurgents beat off the Prussian attacks and continued their march northwards. But owing to the enemy's superiority in manpower and armaments and disagreements among the commanders, the insurgents were compelled to capitulate on May 9, 1848.
                                                                                   p. 224

[216] See Note 5.   p. 225

[217] The reference is to the popular uprising in Naples on May 15, 1848 (see Note 118).   p. 225

[218] The reference is to the suppression by Windischgrätz's counter-revolutionary troops of the uprising in Prague on June 12-17, 1848, directed against the arbitrary rule of the Austrian authorities (see Engels' articles "The Prague Uprising" and "The Democratic Character of the Uprising", present edition, Vol. 7, pp. 91-93 and 119-20), and also of the uprising in Vienna in October 1848. In December 1848 Windischgrätz's army, which included the troops of the Croatian Ban Jellachich, intervened in Hungary to suppress the national liberation movement and seized Pressburg (Bratislava) and other towns.

Serezhans—see Note 112.

Ottochans (*Ottočans*)—soldiers of the Austrian border regiment formed in 1746 and stationed in Ottočac (Western Croatia).   p. 225

[219] The Imperial Government formed by the Frankfurt National Assembly and headed by Archduke John of Austria took over from the former Federal Diet (see Note 63) its functions of suppressing the revolutionary movement, particularly in

South Germany, with military support from a number of German states including Prussia. p. 225

[220] On July 25, 1792, the Duke of Brunswick, who was Commander-in-Chief of the Austro-Prussian army fighting against revolutionary France, issued a manifesto threatening the French people to raze Paris to the ground. p. 226

[221] This article was first published in English in the book: Karl Marx, *The Revolutions of 1848, Political Writings*, Vol. 1, London, Penguin Books, 1973. p. 227

[222] The reference is to Austria's participation—along with Prussia and Russia—in the first (1772) and third (1795) partitions of Poland. The third partition led to the liquidation of the Polish state. The Austrian Empire annexed a considerable part of Southern Poland and Western Ukraine (Galicia) hitherto belonging to Poland.
p. 229

[223] The reference is to the events in early 1846. In February an unsuccessful attempt at a national liberation uprising was made in the Polish lands. Only in the Republic of Cracow, which from the Vienna Congress of 1815 had been under the joint control of Austria, Russia and Prussia, did the insurgents seize power on February 22 and create a National Government, which issued a manifesto abrogating all feudal obligations. The uprising was suppressed in early March 1846 and Cracow was again incorporated into the Austrian Empire. During the uprising the Austrian authorities provoked clashes between Ukrainian (Ruthenian) peasants and detachments of Polish insurgents, taking advantage of the oppressed peasants' hatred of the Polish nobility. But when the uprising was crushed, the participants in the peasant movement in Galicia were subjected to severe repressions.

The *Ruthenians*—the name given in nineteenth-century West-European ethnographical and historical works to the Ukrainian population of Galicia and Bukovina, which was separated at the time from the bulk of the Ukrainian people. p. 230

[224] Engels expressed this point of view more precisely in his articles written in the spring of 1853 on the prospects of the national liberation struggle of the Slavs and other peoples of the Balkan Peninsula against the oppression of the Turkish Empire. He supported the right of the Southern Slavs in the Balkans to form their own independent state (see Frederick Engels, "What Will Become of European Turkey?", present edition, Vol. 12). p. 231

[225] The *Hussite wars*, named after the Czech patriot and reformer Jan Huss (1369-1415), began with a popular uprising in Prague on July 30, 1419. The revolutionary wars of the Czech people against feudal exploitation, the Catholic Church and national enslavement continued until 1437 and ended in the defeat of the Hussites. p. 231

[226] In the battle at Poitiers (Central France) in 732, also known as the battle of Tours, the Franks led by Charles Martel, the actual ruler of the Frankish state of the Merovingians, defeated the Arabs who had invaded France from Spain.

In 1241 the German and Polish knights were defeated by the Mongolian invaders near Wahlstatt (Dobře Pole) in Silesia. But the Mongols, having sustained heavy losses in this battle and the previous campaigns, were forced to cease their advance westward from conquered Moravia, Hungary and Dalmatia and return to their East-European and Asian possessions. p. 232

[227] See Note 10. p. 233

[228] The reference is to the *Slav Congress* which met in Prague on June 2, 1848. It was attended by representatives of the Slav regions of the Austrian Empire. The Right, moderately liberal wing, to which Palacký and Šafařík, the leaders of the Congress, belonged, sought to solve the national question through autonomy of the Slav regions within the framework of the Habsburg monarchy. The Left, radical wing (Sabina, Frič, Libelt and others) wanted joint action with the democratic movement in Germany and Hungary. The radical delegates took an active part in the popular uprising in Prague (June 12-17, 1848) and were subjected to severe reprisals. On June 16, the moderately liberal delegates declared the Congress adjourned indefinitely.

The *Sabor* (Diet) *of the Southern Slavs* opened in Agram (Zagreb) on June 5, 1848. It was attended by delegates from the Croats, Serbs of the Voivodina, Slovenes and Czechs. Representatives of the liberal landowners and the top sections of the commercial bourgeoisie in Croatia prevailing at the *Sabor* expressed their loyalty to the Habsburgs and restricted the national programme to the demand of autonomy for the united Slav territories within the Austrian Empire. Only a small group of democratic delegates connected the struggle for the national cause with the revolutionary struggle against feudal monarchist regimes.   p. 233

[229] See Note 172.   p. 239

[230] See Note 10.   p. 240

[231] On November 19, 1842, the democratic poet Georg Herwegh was received by Frederick William IV. Disappointed with the outcome of the audience, Herwegh wrote a letter to the King accusing him of violating his promise to introduce freedom of the press. The letter was published in the *Leipziger Allgemeine Zeitung* on December 24, 1842, and later in other German and foreign newspapers. To counteract the influence of this letter on public opinion Frederick William IV ordered the semi-official newspapers to publish articles discrediting Herwegh.

After the publication of this article of Engels' in the *Neue Rheinische Zeitung*, Lohbauer sent a statement to its editorial board in which he rejected suggestions of his involvement in publication of the feuilletons against Herwegh on the grounds that before his arrival in Berlin he had served in the General Staff in Württemberg and had nothing to do with Herwegh's expulsion. His statement was published in the supplement to the *Neue Rheinische Zeitung* No. 199, January 19, 1849.   p. 240

[232] See Note 194.   p. 242

[233] The reference is to the bourgeois revolution in Neuchâtel (principality of Neuenburg) in February 1848, which put an end to its vassal dependence on the Prussian King and proclaimed Neuchâtel a republic (see Note 4).   p. 244

[234] See Note 88.   p. 246

[235] The *Swiss Croats in Italy*—an ironical allusion to the Swiss mercenaries in the service of counter-revolutionary governments in a number of Italian states.
Enlistment agreements—see Note 172.   p. 247

[236] The *Ur-cantons*—see Note 10.   p. 248

[237] See Note 14.   p. 248

[238] The continuation of this article was never written. Engels wrote two more small reports on the Swiss affairs, which were published in the same issue (No. 197) of

the *Neue Rheinische Zeitung* (see this volume, pp. 251-53). The publication of his reports from Switzerland ceased because in mid-January 1849 Engels returned to Cologne and worked as an editor of the *Neue Rheinische Zeitung*. p. 250

[239] Ferdinand II of Naples earned the derisive nickname "King Bomba" after he had ordered the savage bombardment of Messina (Sicily) by a punitive force in September 1848 (see Note 208). p. 251

[240] This article was first published in English in the collection: Karl Marx and Frederick Engels, *Articles from the "Neue Rheinische Zeitung". 1848-49*, Progress Publishers, Moscow, 1972. p. 254

[241] The supplement to the *Neue Rheinische Zeitung* No. 197 of January 17, 1849, carried an item in the section "Neueste Nachrichten" to the effect that the leaflets addressed to the voters had been reprinted from the *Neue Preussische Zeitung* at the printing-press of the *Kölnische Zeitung* and distributed throughout the country by the citizens' associations (see Note 245), which sponsored the *Kölnische Zeitung*. p. 254

[242] The reference is to the Prussian Association for a Constitutional Monarchy founded in June 1848 and its local branches. They were composed of Prussian landowners who had adopted bourgeois methods and customs and members of the bourgeoisie. The Association and its branches supported the counter-revolutionary policy of the Government and were labelled in the democratic press "societies of denunciators". p. 254

[243] Marx refers to the addresses to the primary electors regularly published in the *Kölnische Zeitung* in January 1849 (Nos. 10-18) in connection with the primary elections to the Prussian Lower Chamber fixed for January 22 (the elections were in two stages: those elected at the primary elections were to elect deputies on February 5). Some of the addresses contained direct attacks on the communists (e.g. No. 14 of January 17, 1849) and the *Neue Rheinische Zeitung* (first supplement to No. 15, January 18, 1849, and No. 17, January 20, 1849).
Quoted below is the address "To the Primary Electors", published in the *Kölnische Zeitung* No. 11, January 13, 1849. p. 255

[244] *Morison pills*—pills invented by the English quack James Morison and widely advertised as a cure for all illnesses in the mid-1820s. Their main ingredient was the juice of certain tropical plants. p. 255

[245] *Citizens' associations (Bürgervereine)*, consisting of moderate liberal elements, appeared in Prussia after the March revolution. Their aim was to preserve "law and order" within the framework of a constitutional monarchy, and to combat "anarchy", i.e. the revolutionary-democratic movement.
The last article of the Constitution imposed on December 5, 1848, and the decree on the convocation of the Chambers provided for a revision of the Constitution by the two Chambers before it was finally accepted and sworn to. The Prussian ruling circles subsequently availed themselves of this provision to revise the Constitution along the lines of extending royal prerogatives and the privileges of the aristocracy and the junkers. p. 255

[246] The reference is to one of the Prussian associations founded by the Right forces after the March 1848 revolution in Germany. These associations functioned as organs of the junkers' counter-revolution (see Note 242).

"With God for King and Fatherland"—a phrase from the decree on the organisation of the army reserve promulgated by Frederick William III on March 17, 1813.   p. 256

[247] An allusion to the suppression of the Silesian weavers' uprising in June 1844.
p. 257

[248] An allusion to *Wühler* (agitators) and *Heuler* (wailers) (see Note 127).   p. 259

[249] In their works of the 1840s and 1850s, prior to Marx's elaboration of his theory of surplus value, Marx and Engels used the terms "value of labour", "price of labour", "sale of labour" which, as Engels noted in 1891 in the introduction to Marx's pamphlet *Wage Labour and Capital,* "from the point of view of the later works were inadequate and even wrong". After Marx had shown that the worker sells to the capitalist not his labour but his labour power, Marx and Engels used more precise terms—"value of labour power", "price of labour power" and "sale of labour power".   p. 259

[250] *Code civil (Code Napoléon)*—French Civil Code published in 1804. It was introduced by Napoleon in the conquered regions of West and South-West Germany and remained in force in the Rhine Province after its incorporation into Prussia in 1815.   p. 262

[251] In Britain Charles Stuart (King Charles I) was executed in 1649 and James Stuart (King James II) fled in 1688.
In France the Bourbons were overthrown twice, in 1792 and in 1830.
In Belgium William of Orange, King of the Netherlands, was overthrown in 1830 and Belgium was proclaimed a kingdom independent of Holland. p. 263

[252] An allusion to the words from Frederick William IV's speech on March 6, 1848,at the last sitting of the United Commission of the Estates formed of representatives of the provincial diets: "Stand like a mighty wall, united by your confidence in Your King, Your best friend."   p. 264

[253] The trade agreement which Prussia (on behalf of the German Customs Union) concluded with the Netherlands on January 21, 1839, established low import duties on Dutch sugar, thus causing considerable harm to the Prussian sugar industry and the trade of German towns.   p. 264

[254] The reference is to the joint actions of Austria, Prussia and Russia against the Cracow Republic during the national liberation uprising in the free city of Cracow, and the agreement concluded by these powers on incorporating Cracow into the Austrian Empire (see Note 223).   p. 265

[255] The *Neue Rheinische Zeitung* No. 203, January 24, 1849, carried an item "'My Army' in Cologne" dealing with the outrages committed by the Prussian soldiery. At the end of it a question was put to Colonel Engels, the second commandant of Cologne, whether he had really replied to the demands of the owners of houses destroyed by the soldiers that "in one of those houses 11 talers were stolen from a soldier" and that therefore he believed that "not enough by a long chalk has been done to these houses by the soldiers".   p. 268

[256] The *German Confederation*—an association of German states formed by the Vienna Congress on June 8, 1815. It initially included 34 states and 4 free cities with a feudal-absolutist system of government. The Confederation consolidated

the political and economic fragmentation of Germany and retarded its development.   p. 269

257 The reference is to the refugees who fled to Prussia from the free city of Cracow and from Galicia, which was under Austrian domination, after the suppression of the Cracow uprising and of the Ukrainian peasant movement in Galicia in 1846 (see Notes 223 and 254).   p. 270

258 Engels refers to the Polish national liberation insurrection of 1830-31. The majority of its participants were revolutionary nobles and most of its leaders came from the aristocracy. The insurrection was suppressed by Russian troops, with the support of Prussia and Austria. After the troops sent by Nicholas I captured Warsaw in September 1831, the remnants of the insurgent army crossed the Prussian and Austrian borders early in October and were interned there.
                                                                      p. 270

259 The Hungarian plains between the Danube and the Theiss.   p. 270

260 *Schilda*—the name of a town whose inhabitants, portrayed in the sixteenth-century popular German satirical book *Schildbürger*, typified philistine narrow-mindedness and dullness.   p. 271

261 The electoral law of April 8, 1848, established a procedure of elections "to the Assembly for an agreement on a Prussian Constitution" on the basis of universal suffrage, which was, however, restricted by the system of *indirect* (two-stage) *elections*. The electoral law of December 6, 1848, promulgated immediately after the imposed Constitution, retained the two-stage elections to the Lower Chamber but gave the franchise only to "independent Prussians", which allowed the Government arbitrarily to limit the electorate.   p. 271

262 *Nothing learnt and nothing forgotten.* This phrase is commonly thought to have been coined by Talleyrand in reference to the Bourbons. Its origin, however, goes back to Admiral de Panat who, in 1796, said about the royalists: "*Personne n'a su ni rien oublier ni rien prendre*" ("Nobody has been able to forget anything or learn anything").

For the *wailers* mentioned above see Note 127.   p. 279

263 On January 26, 1849, Faucher, Minister of the Interior in the Government of the liberal monarchist Odilon Barrot, submitted to the Constituent Assembly a draft Bill on the right of association. Its first clause ran as follows: "Clubs are prohibited." Faucher demanded that the Constituent Assembly should immediately discuss his Bill, but the deputies refused. On January 27 Ledru-Rollin, supported by 230 deputies, charged the Government with violating the Constitution and demanded its resignation. However, due to the votes of monarchists and moderate republicans, the draft Bill on the right of association (better known as the draft Bill on clubs) was passed by the National Assembly on March 21, 1849. This was a serious blow to freedom of assembly and association and above all to workers' associations.   p. 281

264 The *mobile guard* was set up by a decree of the Provisional Government on February 25, 1848, to fight against the revolutionary masses. Its units consisted mainly of lumpenproletarians and were used to crush the June uprising of Paris workers. After Louis Bonaparte was elected President (December 10, 1848), the Government, fearing that the mobile guard might side with the republicans, decided to disband it. They curtailed its numbers and deprived it of many privileges: some of the guards were enrolled as soldiers in army units, and

many officers were deprived of their rank. This gave rise to disturbances in the mobile guard, and soon afterwards it was disbanded.   p. 282

265 See Note 104.   p. 283

266 An allusion to the similarity between the schemes for restoring the monarchy in December 1848, when the Orleanist Changarnier assumed command of the national guard and the Paris garrison, and the part played by General Monk in the restoration of the Stuarts in 1660.   p. 283

267 See Note 127.   p. 284

268 The reports of January 29, 1849, from Paris printed with an introductory article by Marx, described the general excitement in Paris caused by rumours that the Government was going to forcibly dissolve the National Assembly. The *Neue Rheinische Zeitung* correspondent wrote that Paris was flooded with soldiers but that the mobile guard had sided with the workers. Louis Napoleon, he reported, had left the palace and joined his troops who received him with a gloomy silence or even exclamations such as "Long live the Red Republic!" Only the bourgeois lst Legion greeted him with "Long live Bonaparte!", "Long live the Ministers!" Everybody was waiting for news from the National Assembly which was to determine the subsequent course of events. The day before, the *Moniteur* had reported that at the session of the Cabinet of Ministers President Louis Bonaparte declared that he fully supported the Government.   p. 285

269 In the *primary elections* to the Second Prussian Chamber on January 22, 1848, the democrats in Cologne won a considerable victory: they made up two-thirds of the electors. They also won in many other towns and rural localities in the Rhine Province. This victory, which proved the correctness of the tactics pursued by the *Neue Rheinische Zeitung*—that of uniting all democratic forces in the elections—aroused apprehensions not only on the part of the authorities but also of the moderate liberals, whose reaction to the elections was reflected in the *Kölnische Zeitung*.   p. 286

270 The reference is to the article "Elections to the First Chamber" published in the *Kölnische Zeitung* No. 24, January 28, 1849. The article expressed an opinion that as opposed to "a somewhat revolutionary-democratic Second Chamber", the First Chamber would be "the pillar of the Crown, law and order and genuine freedom", and called upon the electors to see to it that the "highest culture" and "statesmanly wisdom" should be represented in it by people of really outstanding talent.   p. 289

271 With this article Engels began his series of reports on the Hungarian revolutionary war against the Austrian monarchy. He used army bulletins of the Austrian command published in the official *Wiener Zeitung* and other Austrian newspapers as his main source. In spite of the tendentious and fragmentary character of the information given in them, which Engels himself later emphasised in his letter to Marx on April 3, 1851, he managed to give a fairly exact general picture of the military developments. "At the time," he wrote in this connection to Marx on July 6, 1852, "we presented the course of the Hungarian war in the *Neue Rheinische Zeitung* with amazing correctness on the basis of *Austrian* reports and made brilliant, though cautious, forecasts." Engels also wrote about his reports on the Hungarian war in his letter to H. G. Lincoln, editor of the *Daily News*, on March 30, 1854, offering his services as a war correspondent. In the early 1850s Engels took up a systematic study of military science and the art of war and began to collect

additional material on the Hungarian war (*Memoirs* of Görgey, commander-in-chief of the Hungarian army, biographies of Hungarian generals, the Kossuth Government's official periodicals etc.) with the intention of writing a special work on the history of the revolutionary wars in Hungary and Italy, but these plans did not materialise.

Engels began his reports on the Hungarian events when the situation in revolutionary Hungary was extremely grave. On December 16 Windischgrätz's counter-revolutionary army marched to the south, in the direction of Buda and Pest (two neighbouring towns at the time), and captured them early in January 1849. The Hungarian revolutionary Government (National Defence Committee) headed by Kossuth and the parliament (State Assembly) moved to Debreczin. At the same time counter-revolutionary troops advanced from Galicia (General Schlick's corps), Silesia, the Banat and in other regions. The reactionary German periodicals exaggerated the successes of the Austrian army and foretold a speedy and final defeat of Hungary. Engels, on the other hand, pointed out that Hungary had defence reserves and the possibility to bring about a radical turn in the fortunes of war, which indeed happened soon afterwards.   p. 290

272 The reference is to the Slovak corps formed in 1848 by L. Stur and J. Hurbann under the control of Austrian officers. The corps consisted of Slovak and to some extent Czech students. In 1848-49 it took part in the war against revolutionary Hungary. The corps did not enjoy the sympathy of the people of Slovakia.
                                                                   p. 292

273 The reference is to the civil war in Spain in 1833-40 which was unleashed by the clerical and feudal circles headed by Don Carlos, the pretender to the throne. The Carlist forces commanded by Zumalacarregni and Cabrera-y-Griño operated in Catalonia and the Basque provinces using guerilla methods of warfare. After the 14-thousand-strong army of the Carlists failed to take Madrid in 1837, the Carlist movement declined and was defeated by 1840. In 1848 Cabrera tried to revive it by organising a revolt of the Carlists in Catalonia but was seriously wounded and fled to France.   p. 294

274 The *United Diet*—see Notes 89 and 157.   p. 296

275 See Note 261.   p. 296

276 See Note 150.   p. 296

277 The reference is to the suppression of the Polish national liberation uprising in Posen in April-May 1848 (see Note 151).   p. 296

278 See Note 75.   p. 296

279 The *Government of Action*—see Note 153.
     Constables—see Note 45.   p. 297

280 Johan Tilly, the army commander of the Catholic League during the Thirty Years' War (1618-48), stormed Magdeburg on May 20, 1631, and allowed his soldiers to plunder it. The town was almost completely burnt down and ruined and about 30 thousand people were killed.   p. 297

281 The Prussian Government's Circular Note of January 23, 1849, addressed to all Prussian diplomats in the German states, formulated a plan for restoring the

Federal Diet (see Note 63)—the central body of the German Confederation established by decision of the Vienna Congress in 1815.   p. 297

[282] On September 22, 1848, after the Croatian Ban Jellachich started intervention against revolutionary Hungary, the Hungarian Sejm formed the National Defence Committee headed by Kossuth to exercise control over Count Batthyány's liberal Government. After Jellachich had been defeated and Batthyány's Government had resigned, the National Defence Committee took over the Government's functions on October 8 and Kossuth was vested with extensive powers corresponding to a wartime situation.   p. 299

[283] See Note 223.   p. 303

[284] The trial of the *Neue Rheinische Zeitung* was begun on February 7, 1849. Karl Marx, editor-in-chief, Frederick Engels, co-editor, and Hermann Korff, responsible publisher, were tried by the Cologne jury court. They were accused of insulting Chief Public Prosecutor Zweiffel and calumniating the police officers who arrested Gottschalk and Anneke, in the article "Arrests" published in the *Neue Rheinische Zeitung* No. 35, July 5, 1848 (see present edition, Vol. 7, pp. 177-79).

Though the legal proceedings were instituted on July 6, the trial was only fixed for December 20 and then postponed. Marx's and Engels' defence counsel was Karl Schneider II and Korff's was Hagen. The jury acquitted the defendants.

Marx's and Engels' speeches were published in the *Neue Rheinische Zeitung* as part of a detailed account of the whole trial, which also included the speeches of the Public Prosecutor (not word-for-word but abridged, with references to the publications in the *Kölnische Zeitung*), of all the accused and defence counsels. The account was apparently edited by Marx and Engels, and the texts of their speeches can be considered as their own, as emerges in particular from a comparison of Marx's speech with the preparatory material for it (see this volume, pp. 485-92). The emphasis in the quotations from the articles of the *Code pénal* is the author's. The *Neue Rheinische Zeitung* accounts of this trial and of another, that of the Rhenish District Committee of Democrats, which was held the next day, were published as a separate pamphlet in the spring of 1849.

Marx's and Engels' speeches were not reprinted in Marx's lifetime. They were published in an abridged form shortly before Engels' death in the German Social-Democratic Party papers—the Berlin *Socialdemokrat* No. 37, September 12, 1895, and the *Sächsische Volksblatt* No. 111, September 19, 1895—under the title "Zwei verschollene Vertheidigungsreden von Karl Marx und Friedrich Engels".   p. 304

[285] See Note 88.   p. 304

[286] The reference is to the Prussian law on punishment for written insults which was promulgated on July 5, 1819, for the Rhine and other provinces where the *Code pénal* remained in force after 1815 ("Verordnung wegen Bestrafung schriftlicher Beleidigungen in den Provinzen, wo das französische Strafgesetzbuch vorläufig noch gesetzliche Kraft hat").   p. 307

[287] See Note 158.   p. 309

[288] See Note 245.   p. 315

[289] The reference is to three articles in the *Neue Rheinische Zeitung* denouncing the actions of the prosecuting magistrates against the Cologne democrats, written in connection with the arrest of Julius Wulff (No. 40, July 10, 1848), Falkenheim

(No. 43, July 13, 1848) and Joseph Wolff (No. 62, August 1, 1848). In response to the last article Public Prosecutor Hecker came out with a refutation (*Neue Rheinische Zeitung* No. 64, August 3, 1848), in reply to which the newspaper published the article "Herr Hecker and the *Neue Rheinische Zeitung*" (No. 65, August 4, 1848). p. 316

290 An allusion to the reactionary entourage of Frederick William IV (the Gerlach brothers, Radowitz and others). This Court camarilla was frenziedly counter-revolutionary and played an active part in preparing and staging the coup d'état in Prussia in November-December 1848. p. 321

291 On November 9, 1848, after Prime Minister Brandenburg declared that the Prussian National Assembly had to move to Brandenburg, the Ministers and some of the Right deputies left the sitting. The remaining majority, on the insistence of the Left deputies, decided that the King had no right to adjourn or transfer the Assembly without the consent of the people's representatives. However, despite the National Assembly's decision to continue its session in Berlin, the Government, supported by General Wrangel's troops, who arrived in Berlin the next day, carried out the coup d'état (see also Notes 53 and 135). p. 322

292 The trial of the Rhenish District Committee of Democrats took place on February 8, 1849. Karl Marx, Karl Schapper and the lawyer Schneider II were summoned to the Cologne jury court, accused of incitement to revolt in connection with the Committee's appeal of November 18, 1848, on the refusal to pay taxes (see this volume, p. 41). They were acquitted.

One of the responses to the trial in the revolutionary press was Marx's article published in the *Neue Rheinische Zeitung* on February 10 (see this volume, pp. 340-41).

Marx's speech was included in the general account of the trial published in the *Neue Rheinische Zeitung* Nos. 226 and 231-33 at the end of February 1848; the account also contained the incriminated appeal of November 18, the report of the speech of Public Prosecutor Bölling, and speeches of the other defendants.

In the spring of 1849 this account was published as a separate pamphlet, which also included the account of the trial of February 7 against the *Neue Rheinische Zeitung* (see Note 284). It was not reprinted in Marx's lifetime. In 1885 it was published as a pamphlet, *Karl Marx von den Kölner Geschworen Prozess gegen den Ausschuss der Rheinischen Demokraten wegen Aufrufs zum bewaffneten Widerstand*, Hottingen, Zürich, with a preface by Engels, in the "Social-Democratic Library" series, and reprinted with the other pamphlets of the series in 1887. It was also put out in 1895 in Berlin.

Marx's speech in abridged form or extracts from it were published in Social-Democratic periodicals of the time (*Der Socialdemokrat* Nos. 24 and 26, June 11 and 23, 1885; the Polish journal *Walka klas* No. 517, I-III, 1886) and as a supplement to the Russian edition of *The Poverty of Philosophy* issued in Geneva.

An English translation of Marx's speech was first published in the collection: Karl Marx and Frederick Engels, *Articles from the "Neue Rheinische Zeitung". 1848-49*, Progress Publishers, Moscow, 1972. p. 323

293 See Notes 89 and 146. p. 323

294 See Note 167. p. 329

²⁹⁵ See Note 191. p. 332

²⁹⁶ For *Habeas Corpus* see Note 42.
The *Civic Militia Law* adopted by the National Assembly on October 17, 1848, made the civic militia completely dependent on the Government (see Note 90). Despite this, the counter-revolutionary government circles considered the existence of the civic militia to be dangerous and on November 12, 1848, after Wrangel's troops arrived in Berlin, it was disarmed. p. 333

²⁹⁷ See Note 166. p. 334

²⁹⁸ Marx refers to the reform movement in England. As a result of this movement the British Parliament passed the Reform Act of 1832, which extended the franchise and put an end to the old and corrupt constituencies ("rotten boroughs"). In protest against the opposition to the Reform Bill on the part of the Tories and the House of Lords, the participants in the movement organised mass meetings and advanced the slogan "No Bill, no taxes!" Political unions of the bourgeoisie also called for refusal to pay taxes and withdrawal of deposits from the banks. After the House of Lords rejected the Bill for the third time in March 1832, and Grey's Whig Government, which had proposed the Bill, resigned, the Tories headed by Wellington (Prime Minister in 1828-30) failed to form a government. The King was compelled to turn to the Whigs, who by threatening to pack the House of Lords with new peers succeeded in carrying through the Bill. p. 338

²⁹⁹ Lassalle was arrested in Düsseldorf on November 22, 1848, on the charge of incitement to arming against the Government during the campaign for refusal to pay taxes. The judiciary of the Rhine Province used all means to drag out his case. On Lassalle's request, expressed in his letters to Marx and Engels, the *Neue Rheinische Zeitung* came out in his defence and that of other persecuted Düsseldorf democrats. It carried a number of articles exposing the abuses and illegal actions of the judiciary and the prison authorities against Lassalle (see this volume, pp. 344-46, 474-76). An article on Lassalle, written later on, is published in Vol. 9 of the present edition. Marx and Engels also participated in the steps taken by the Cologne democratic organisations to induce the judiciary to speed up the investigation of the case. In particular they were among the deputation who visited Prosecutor-General of the Rhine Province Nicolovius on March 3, 1849, and protested against the protraction of Lassalle's case (see this volume, p. 344). The trial was held on May 3 and 4; Lassalle was acquitted. p. 341

³⁰⁰ *Pennsylvanian prisons*—solitary confinement prisons. The first such prison was built in Philadelphia (State of Pennsylvania) in 1791. In the nineteenth century this system of confinement was widely used in Europe; in Germany it was applied in 1844 in the Moabit Prison in Berlin and in several others. p. 343

³⁰¹ The reference is apparently to the law of March 29, 1844, on judicial and administrative and criminal court procedure in bringing an action against officials. p. 345

³⁰² The reference is to the Government of the Austrian Empire. During the popular uprising in Vienna in October 1848 the Emperor and his court left the capital on October 7 and moved to the provincial town of Olmütz (Olomouc) in Moravia. Olmütz became the centre of the counter-revolutionary forces. Soon after the fall of Vienna in November 1848 a new government was formed of representatives of the landowning aristocracy and the counter-revolutionary bourgeoisie headed by Prince Schwarzenberg. Ferdinand II abdicated and his nephew Franz Joseph acceded to the throne on December 2, 1848. p. 347

[303] *Tchaikists* (or *tchaikashi*) — Austro-Hungarian infantry who served on small sailing vessels and rowing boats (*tchaikas*) in the Military Border Area making pontoon bridges and transporting troops along the Danube, Theiss and Sava. They were recruited mainly from the Serbs inhabiting the Tchaikash Area in Slavonia. From 1764 they formed a special battalion.   p. 348

[304] The war between the Serbs and the Magyars began in May 1848 over the conflict between the Hungarian Government and the Serbian national movement which demanded autonomy for the Voivodina. The movement was not homogeneous in its social composition and political tendencies. Liberal bourgeois (Stratimirovich and others) and more reactionary landowners prevailed in it, which made it possible for the Austrian ruling circles to use it against the Hungarian revolution. On the other hand, the Hungarian revolutionaries, by refusing to meet the national demands of the Serbs and other Slav nationalities incorporated in the Hungarian state, contributed to making them side with the Habsburgs. It was only on July 28, 1849, i.e. on the eve of its fall, that the Hungarian Republic officially proclaimed the equality of all nationalities inhabiting Hungary.

Having consolidated their domination to a considerable degree with the help of the Croats, Serbs of the Voivodina etc., the ruling classes of the Austrian Empire, far from fulfilling their promises and granting autonomy to the Slav and other peoples of the multinational state, pursued a still more rigid policy of centralisation, abolishing all remnants of self-government in the national regions.
                                                                                p. 348

[305] The reference is apparently to the *Limes Romanus*, a system of fortifications built along the frontiers of the Roman Empire, mainly during the rule of Emperor Hadrian (117-138). Remnants of the *Limes Romanus* still survive. Part of it ran through Western Hungary and the South-Slav border regions of the Austrian Empire.   p. 348

[306] In the battle at Grokhov (Grokhuv) on February 25, 1831, the Polish insurgent troops halted the offensive of the Tsarist army commanded by Diebitsch which had been sent to suppress the Polish insurrection of 1830-31 (see Note 258).
                                                                                p. 349

[307] *Szeklers* — an ethnic group of Hungarians, mostly free peasants. In the thirteenth century their forefathers were settled by Hungarian kings in the mountain regions of Transylvania to protect the frontiers. The region inhabited by them was usually called Szekler land.

The majority of Szeklers sided with the Hungarian revolution.   p. 351

[308] The reference is probably to the appeals of Jozef Madarasz, a Left-winger in the State Assembly of the Hungarian Republic in Debreczin, published in the newspaper *Debreczenski Lapok*. He called on the people to struggle not only against the Austrians but also against the agreers in the Assembly, demanded that the Assembly should be dissolved and new elections declared, and pointed to the need to organise an insurrectionary movement and render all possible assistance to the Hungarian revolutionary army.   p. 351

[309] *Komorn* (*Komárom*), a fortified camp and fortress in North-Western Hungary, remained in the hands of the Hungarians in the rear of the Austrian army during its offensive in late 1848 and early 1849. Subsequently the fortress held out against several sieges by the Austrian forces and played an important part in the operations of the Hungarian revolutionary army.   p. 351

[310] See Note 282.   p. 351

[311] An allusion to the trials of the *Neue Rheinische Zeitung* and of the Rhenish District Committee of Democrats which took place on February 7 and 8, 1849 (see this volume, pp. 304-39).   p. 354

[312] The reference is to the series "Politische Gespräche" by Levin Schücking published in the *Kölnische Zeitung* Nos. 29, 30, 34 and 35 on February 3, 4, 9 and 10, 1849. Wagner, a character in these "Conversations", says to Professor Urian: "You have always played the part of Mephistopheles a bit."   p. 354

[313] See Note 242.   p. 357

[314] An English translation of this article was first published in the collection: Karl Marx and Frederick Engels, *The Russian Menace to Europe*, London, 1953.

p. 362

[315] See Note 228.   p. 363

[316] The reference is to the war of 1846-48 between the United States of America and Mexico, as a result of which the USA seized almost half of Mexico's territory, including the whole of Texas, Upper California, New Mexico and other regions.

In assessing these events in the article Engels proceeded from the general conception that it was progressive for patriarchal and feudal countries to be drawn into the orbit of bourgeois relations because, he thought, this accelerated the creation of preconditions for a proletarian revolution. In subsequent years, however, he and Marx fully understood the deplorable consequences of colonial conquests and the subjugation of backward countries by large states. In particular, having made a thorough study of the history of US aggression in Mexico and other countries of the American continent, Marx in his article "The Civil War in North America" (1861) described it as expansion in the interests of the then dominant slave-owning oligarchy in the Southern States and of the bourgeois elements in the North which supported it, as a policy aimed at seizing new territories to spread slavery.   p. 365

[317] The reference is to Marx's and Engels' criticism of bourgeois cosmopolitanism and their substantiation of the internationalist position of the working class in the national question set forth in the proletarian and democratic newspapers (the Chartist newspaper *Northern Star*, the *Brüsseler-Deutsche-Zeitung*, the French *La Réforme*), in particular their speeches "On Poland" (November 29, 1847) and "On the Polish Question" (February 22, 1848), Marx's "Speech on the Question of Free Trade", and Engels' articles "The Anniversary of the Polish Revolution of 1830", "Reform Movement in France.—Banquet of Dijon" and "Louis Blanc's Speech at the Dijon Banquet" (see present edition, Vol. 6, pp. 388-90, 545-52, 450-65, 391-92, 397-401, 409-11).   p. 366

[318] See Note 206.   p. 367

[319] *Shokazians*—the name of Catholic Serbs.   p. 367

[320] *Morlaks*—one of the nationalities inhabiting Dalmatia, descendants of the Romanised Illyrian tribes which lived in Northern Dalmatia (Split and Zadar regions) and Southern Istria and subsequently merged with the neighbouring Serbs; they were mostly Catholics.   p. 368

[321] See Note 354.   p. 369

322 These are the languages of the West-Slav tribes which in the Middle Ages lived between the Elbe, Saale and Oder.

Wends—originally a general name given in Germany to different Laba (Elbe) Slavs, one branch of which was the Sorbs or Lužice Serbs.

Obodrites (Bodryci)—the largest tribe of Laba Slavs living in the region of the Lower Elbe and Mecklenburg Bay. They made up the core of the Wendish Power, an early feudal national Slav grouping formed in the 1040s. In the middle of the twelfth century, as a result of the German feudalists' expansion to the east accompanied by the extermination or enslavement of the local population, the Wendish Power broke up and the Laba Slavs were subjugated and Germanised. Only the Lužice Serbs have preserved their language and national features.

p. 369

323 *Avars*—a union of tribes in which nomadic Turkic tribes dominated. Coming from Asia, the Avars established themselves in the sixth century in the eastern regions of Central Europe and in the Balkans and formed their state, the Avar Khaganate, constantly waging wars with the Slavs, Germanic tribes and Byzantines. However, as a result of the risings of the subjugated Slav tribes and the blows struck by the Byzantines and Franks, the Avarian state was weakened.

In the 790s the Avars were utterly defeated by Charlemagne's Frankish army and later on fully assimilated by the peoples of the Western Black-Sea regions and the Danube area.   p. 370

324 *Ogulians*—reservists from the inhabitants of Ogulin (Western Croatia) registered with the Karlstadt (Karlovac) infantry regiment formed by the Austrian authorities in the mid-eighteenth century to guard the frontiers; the headquarters of the regiment was in Ogulin.

Serezhans—see Note 112.   p. 371

325 See Engels' articles "The State of Germany", "German Socialism in Verse and Prose", his speech "On Poland", "Three New Constitutions" and "A Word to the *Riforma*" (present edition, Vol. 6, pp. 15-33, 235-73, 389-90, 540-44 and 553-55).

p. 372

326 An allusion to the changed nature of the Czech national movement after the suppression of the popular uprising in Prague on June 12-17, 1848. In its first stage—from the beginning of the March events to the Prague uprising—the Czech revolutionary democrats played a prominent part in the movement, and the Czech peasants and the urban lower strata, including the working class, actively participated in the struggle against feudalism and absolutism. This struggle was fully in the interests of the European revolutionary movement and was vigorously supported by the *Neue Rheinische Zeitung* directed by Marx and Engels (see the articles "The Prague Uprising" and "The Democratic Character of the Uprising", present edition, Vol. 7, pp. 91-93, 119-20). In the summer of 1848 the Czech liberals, representing the bourgeoisie and the landowners, took the lead of the national movement which they turned into an instrument against the revolutionary-democratic forces of Germany and Hungary, and a prop for the Habsburg monarchy and, indirectly, for Russian Tsarism. The orientation of the new leaders of other Slav peoples in Austria towards supporting the Habsburgs and the Tsar so as to secure the satisfaction of their national demands also ran counter to the interests of the revolution. For this reason the *Neue Rheinische Zeitung* denounced the Austrian Slavs' movement in its new stage.   p. 374

327 The *Slovanská Lípa*—a Czech national society founded at the end of April 1848. The leadership of the society in Prague was in the hands of moderate liberals (Šafařík, Gauč), who joined the counter-revolutionary camp after the suppression of the Prague uprising in June 1848, whereas the provincial branches were mostly led by representatives of the radical Czech bourgeoisie.   p. 375

328 *Svornost*—the Czech national militia formed after the revolutionary events of March 1848 in the Austrian Empire. It was recruited mainly from among students. Its main detachment guarded the Czech Museum in Prague, where the Slav Congress was in session in June 1848. During the popular uprising in Prague, this detachment was disarmed. The Austrian troops disarmed the national militia despite the fact that it was commanded by moderate representatives of the Czech movement who disapproved of the insurgents.

Burschenschaften—German students' associations which sprang up under the influence of the liberation war against Napoleon. They advocated German unification. However, alongside progressive ideas extremely nationalistic ideas were widespread in the *Burschenschaften.*

The *Wartburg Festival* was organised by German students' associations on October 8, 1817, to mark the 300th anniversary of the Reformation and developed into a demonstration for the unification of Germany and of protest against the reactionary policy of Metternich and the ruling circles of other states of the German Confederation. At the same time the festival revealed strong nationalistic and pan-German sentiments.   p. 376

329 The *commissions of the estates* of the provincial diets, whose competence was limited to local economic and administrative problems, were instituted in Prussia in 1842. They were elected from among the members of the provincial diets on the estate principle and formed a single advisory body known as the "united commissions". With the help of this institution, which was but a make-believe representative body, Frederick William IV hoped to introduce new taxes and obtain a loan.

p. 379

330 The minutes of the First United Diet (see Note 89) cite the "Uebersicht von den Resultaten der Finanzverwaltung in den Jahren 1840 bis einschliesslich 1846" presented by the Prussian Government (see *Der Erste Vereinigte Landtag in Berlin 1847*, 1. Teil, Berlin, 1847). Marx probably bases his calculations on data from this survey. Some inaccuracies in the tables cited in this article are corrected on the basis of the book *Preussens Erster Reichstag*, 7. Th., Berlin, 1847.   p. 380

331 In 1841 Frederick William IV donated 430,000 marks to establish an English-German Protestant Bishopric in Jerusalem.

Papers of Frederick II were published in Prussia from 1846.   p. 385

332 See Note 245.   p. 390

333 See Note 206.   p. 394

334 On February 16 and 17, 1849, the Cologne court tried Gottfried Kinkel, the editor of the democratic *Neue Bonner Zeitung*. The indictment against him was that in describing in 1848 the outrages of the Prussian soldiery in Mainz in his newspaper (then called *Bonner Zeitung*), he had insulted the Prussian garrison of the town. The court sentenced Kinkel to a month's imprisonment.   p. 396

335 See Note 258.   p. 399

[336] The reference is to the Hungarian State Assembly evacuated from Pest to Debreczin during the advance of the Austrian army in December 1848. Some Right-wing deputies went over to Windischgrätz. p. 399

[337] The reference is to Austrian Prime Minister Prince Schwarzenberg's Note of February 4, 1849, addressed to the Frankfurt National Assembly, in which, in the name of his Government, he opposed the formation of a united German state. The Note was published in the *Wiener Zeitung* No. 39, February 15, 1849. p. 402

[338] *Magyarisers*—a group of influential aristocratic landowners in Croatia, Slavonia, the Serbian Voivodina and other ethnic regions who advocated Magyarisation of the population in these areas. The narrow selfish interests of this group had nothing in common with the Hungarian revolution. They proved to be a cause of the Hungarian Government's nationalist mistakes. p. 409

[339] The reference is to the *chief committee governing the Serbian Voivodeship* or *Chief Odbor*—an executive body formed by the Assembly (*Skupština*) of representatives of the Serbian communities in the South-Slav border regions of the Austrian Empire in May 1848. The Assembly proclaimed the Voivodina an autonomous region within the Empire.

The chief committee was the scene of struggle between the liberal group headed by Stratimirovich, who was elected President, and the clerical-feudal group who professed loyalty to the Habsburgs and opposed liberal reforms. Early in 1849 the second group, headed by Patriarch Rajachich, prevailed. It directed the national movement of the Voivodina Serbs towards still closer collaboration with the Austrian counter-revolutionary Government. The latter, however, after using the Serbs to fight revolutionary Hungary, broke its promises and refused, in March 1849, to grant them autonomy. p. 409

[340] The reference is to the decree sent to Croatia by Count Moritz Almásy, head of the Hungarian Provisional Finance Chamber formed under the auspices of Windisch-grätz in Pest after the Hungarian revolutionary army left the town. The *Deutsche Allgemeine Zeitung* No. 45 of February 14, 1849, reprinted the following note to the text of this decree from the Agram newspaper *Slavenski jug*: "We publish this new act of Austrian politics without comment. The Croatians who have learned that loyalty to our Emperor and King and our Habsburg-Lotharingian Royal House is paid for with blood and money, must now also learn to understand such decrees in Magyar." p. 410

[341] The reference is to the cruel suppression by the Austrian reactionaries headed by Windischgrätz of the popular uprising in Prague in June 1848 (see Note 218). p. 411

[342] As a result of the popular uprising Pius IX was compelled to give his consent to the establishment of a temporal Ministry and the convocation of a Constituent Assembly on the basis of universal suffrage on November 16, 1848. The subsequent development of the bourgeois-democratic revolution led to the election of the Constituent Assembly on January 21, 1849, which on February 9 deprived Pius IX of his temporal power and proclaimed a republic. The Roman Republic existed until July 3, 1849, when it was crushed by foreign intervention.

In English this article was first published in the collection: Karl Marx and Frederick Engels, *Articles from the "Neue Rheinische Zeitung". 1848-49*, Progress Publishers, Moscow, 1972. p. 414

343 According to the convention in 1753 the 20-gulden or conventional system of money circulation was introduced in Austria and Bavaria: 20 guldens were to be coined out of one Cologne mark of pure silver (approximately 234 grams). Since then silver and gold money was called conventional money (C.M.). By the beginning of the nineteenth century metal money was practically replaced by paper money, called "Vienna currency", and the coining of metal money almost ceased. But the conventional system was still preserved. As the amount of paper money in circulation increased, especially during the 1848-49 revolution, the rate of the conventional money constantly rose, which prompted the population to hoard gold and silver coins.   p. 416

344 *Urbar duties* (*Urbariallasten*)—duties of the feudal-bound peasants registered in the *Urbars*, inventories of feudal land possessions. Beginning with the thirteenth century they also included taxes and other incomes as provided by law. p. 416

345 In June 1848, at the time of the conflict between the Croatian nationalists and the Austrian Government which refused to meet their demands, the *Sabor* (Diet) meeting in Agram (Zagreb) (see Note 228) vested the Croatian Ban Jellachich at first with dictatorial powers. However, Jellachich, who represented the Croatian nobility, quickly came to terms with the Austrian Court and used his dictatorship to suppress the peasant movement in Croatia. The Austrian Government, which had dismissed Jellachich from the post of Ban during the conflict, reinstated him at the beginning of September 1848 and appointed him commander of the imperial troops in Hungary. Placing Croatian formations at the service of the Austrian reaction, Jellachich took part in the counter-revolutionary campaign against Hungary and in suppressing the popular uprising in Vienna.   p. 417

346 As to the source of the data on the finances of the Prussian monarchy between 1840 and 1846 and in 1847 used in this article, see Note 330.   p. 418

347 Issue No. 3 of the *Revue rétrospective ou Archives secrètes du dernier Gouvernement*, published by Jules Taschereau, carried a list of the secret funds of the July monarchy's Foreign Ministry for 1840, 1842, 1844-47 in which the annual pension of the editor of the *Frankfurter Oberpostamts-Zeitung* Karl Berly, a secret agent of the Guizot's Government, was mentioned.   p. 421

348 *Peterwardein border guards*, like Serezhans, Ottochans and other South-Slav army formations, guarded the Austro-Turkish border (the so-called Military Border Area). They were named after their respective regimental or company districts and communities (see also Notes 81, 112 and 218).   p. 423

349 See Note 307.   p. 425

350 Cavalry units in the Austrian army included not only squadrons but larger tactical formations—divisions which usually consisted of two squadrons.   p. 427

351 *Cumans*—descendants of Polovtsi (Kumans), a Turkic nationality. They appeared on the territory of Hungary in the ninth century together with the Magyars, but the bulk settled there in the thirteenth century, fleeing from the Mongolian yoke after the battle on the Kalka River.

   Jazyges (*Iazyges, Jaszok*)—descendants of the Sarmatian tribes. They first appeared on the territory of Hungary about the eleventh century.

   Cumans and Jazyges, who had been granted land by the Hungarian kings, formed two independent districts between the Theiss, Danube and Gran. For their special services to the Hungarian Crown a large part of the population were granted nobility. Palatin, the imperial governor in Hungary, was their supreme judge and ruler. p. 428

352 The *Treaty of Pressburg* (Bratislava) signed on December 26, 1805, between Austria and Napoleonic France put an end to the war of the Austrian monarchy against Napoleon within the third anti-French coalition (Britain, Austria, Russia and Sweden). The signing of the treaty was preceded by the capitulation of the Austrian army at Ulm (October 17-20) and the defeat of the Austrian and Russian forces at Austerlitz (December 2). p. 429

353 In this article Engels pays special attention to the condition in Transylvania at the turning-point of the revolutionary war in Hungary. In January and February 1849 the Hungarian revolutionary troops checked the Austrian offensive on almost all the fronts and, harassing the Austrians by repeated attacks and continuous fighting, prepared for the decisive battle in April 1849.

In Transylvania as in other national regions which were part of Hungary at the time, the struggle was waged in the conditions of sharp national contradictions. The majority of its motley population—Rumanians, Hungarians including Szeklers, and Germans, mostly from Saxony—were Rumanian peasants exploited by the Hungarian landowners and Austrian officials. Though the advanced part of the Rumanian bourgeoisie and intelligentsia welcomed the Hungarian revolution of 1848, the Austrian agents using social and national antagonisms organised an uprising of the Rumanians against revolutionary Hungary in September 1848. The Rumanian legions under Colonel Urban fought against the Hungarians together with the Austrian troops of Baron Puchner. However, the Polish refugee Bem, appointed commander of the Hungarian army in Transylvania in December 1848, prevented Puchner from entering Hungary via Transylvania and during January-March 1849 managed to inflict several serious blows upon the counter-revolutionary forces in Transylvania proper.

A small contingent of Russian troops sent to Puchner's aid by Lüders, the commander of the Tsarist expeditionary corps in Wallachia, failed to stop Bem's advance and by the end of March the latter had practically driven the enemy out of Transylvania. Bem's success was furthered by his desire to reconcile the national contradictions between Hungarians and Rumanians notwithstanding the resistance of the representatives of the Hungarian Government, who expressed the interests of the Hungarian nobility. (Later Engels specially emphasised this in his article "Bem" written for the *New American Encyclopedia*.) The Rumanian democrat Bălcescu also called for joint action by the Rumanians and Hungarians against the Habsburgs. Janku, the leader of the insurrectionary movement of the Rumanian poor peasants, held similar views.

However, the Hungarian revolutionaries among the bourgeoisie and the nobility realised too late that co-operation with the downtrodden nationalities was necessary. This made it possible for the Austrian ruling circles to use the Rumanian national movement in Transylvania, headed by the clerical-aristocratic clique, as a weapon against revolutionary Hungary. After the suppression of the Hungarian revolution in Transylvania, the Austrians established a regime of ruthless national oppression there despite all their demagogic promises. p. 432

354 After agreeing on the possibility of joint action against republican France in July 1791, Austria and Prussia signed a treaty in February 1792. The Austro-Prussian alliance encouraged by Tsarist Russia became the core of the first anti-French coalition, which by March 1793 was joined by Britain, Russia, Sardinia, Naples, Spain, Holland and some of the German principalities. In 1795 the coalition broke up.

The suppression by the Tsarist army of the 1794 Polish uprising led by Kosciuszko is connected with the first anti-French coalition. The insurgents demanded that the Constitution which had been proclaimed by the Four Years' Sejm (1788-92) should again come into force. The adoption of the Constitution had been used as a pretext for the occupation of Poland by Prussia and Russia in 1793 and led to the second partition of Poland (the first was carried out by Prussia, Russia and Austria in 1772). After the suppression of the Kosciuszko uprising a third partition of Poland between Austria, Prussia and Tsarist Russia took place in 1795 and the Polish state ceased to exist.   p. 438

[355] See Note 170.   p. 438

[356] See Note 303.   p. 441

[357] *Arians*—a trend in Christian religion which was widely spread among several German tribes in the fourth and fifth centuries. Arian heresy was condemned by the official church in 381.   p. 442

[358] See Note 319.   p. 442

[359] *Honvéd*—literally: defender of the homeland; the name given to the Hungarian revolutionary army of 1848-49, which was set up by decision of the Hungarian revolutionary Government on May 7, 1848, on the formation of ten battalions of the Honvéd.   p. 444

[360] The original text of the speech from the throne made by Frederick William IV at the inaugural sitting of the Prussian Diet was published in a special supplement to the *Neue Rheinische Zeitung* No. 233, February 28, 1849. In the text of the speech published after this article in the *Neue Rheinische Zeitung* No. 234, March 1, 1849, this passage was changed as follows: "To my greatest regret a state of siege had to be proclaimed in the capital and its immediate environs to restore the rule of law and public safety. Corresponding proposals will be presented to you, gentlemen, without delay." Below in the article the speech from the throne is cited from the latter publication.   p. 445

[361] The reference is to the draft laws on clubs and meetings, posters and the press which were being prepared by the Government (on this see Marx's article "Three New Draft Laws" published in the *Neue Rheinische Zeitung* on March 13, 1849, present edition, Vol. 9). These drafts are compared with the reactionary press laws passed in France in September 1835 (see Note 181).   p. 445

[362] The reference is to the speech from the throne by Frederick William IV at the inaugural sitting of the Second United Diet (see Note 89) on April 2, 1848; the text of the speech was prepared by the Camphausen Ministry.   p. 446

[363] The *White Hall*—a hall in the royal palace in Berlin where the first joint sitting of the two Chambers of the newly convened Prussian Diet was held on February 26, 1849.   p. 446

[364] On March 21, 1848, Frederick William IV, frightened by the barricade fighting in Berlin, issued an appeal "To my people and the German nation" (see Note 210) in which he promised to set up a representative institution based on the estates, grant a Constitution, make Ministers responsible, introduce jury courts etc.   p. 447

[365] The reference is to the two decrees on amending the old trade statute — introducing chambers of commerce (*Gewerberäte*) and trade courts (*Gewer-*

begerichte)—which were issued by the Prussian Government on February 9, 1849.   p. 448

[366] *Gagging laws*—the name given to the six exceptional laws passed in England in 1819 after the cutting down by hussars and yeomanry of participants in a mass meeting for electoral reform at St. Peter's Field, Manchester (the so-called battle of Peterloo); the laws restricted freedom of assembly and the press.   p. 448

[367] See Note 348.   p. 453

[368] Taking advantage of the forthcoming expiration of the seven months' armistice signed by Denmark and Prussia at Malmö (see Note 75) the Prussian ruling circles refused to prolong it with a view to raising the prestige of the Prussian monarchy by waging the war, which was very popular in Germany, and realising their aggressive plans. Military operations were resumed in March 1849 and proceeded with varying success. Eventually, under pressure from the Great Powers, Prussia signed a peace treaty with Denmark in Berlin on July 2, 1850, temporarily renouncing its claims to Schleswig and Holstein and treacherously leaving the population of these duchies to continue the war alone. The Schleswig-Holstein troops were defeated and compelled to cease resistance. As a result both duchies remained within the Kingdom of Denmark.   p. 456

[369] The moderate liberal Gioberti who headed the Piedmont Government strove to use the movement which had spread in Italian states for an all-Italy Constituent Assembly and unification of the country in a democratic way in order to carry out the plan of establishing a federation of Italian states which was in the interests of the Savoy dynasty. After the proclamation of a republic in Rome on February 9, 1849, and the beginning of a campaign for a republic in Tuscany, Gioberti made efforts to restore the power of Pius IX and Grand Duke Leopold II with military aid from Piedmont. Such a policy and his refusal to carry out progressive reforms in Piedmont made Gioberti extremely unpopular and led to his resignation on February 21, 1849. Under mass pressure and apprehensive over the future of the Savoy dynasty in the impending crisis in Italy, the Piedmont ruling circles were compelled to declare on March 12, 1849, the resumption of the war against Austria. However, the Piedmont army, which was poorly prepared for the war and led by monarchist generals who were afraid to impart a really popular character to the war, was soon routed by the Austrians. On March 26 the new King of Sardinia, Victor Emmanuel, was compelled to sign an armistice with Austria on more onerous terms than in August 1848.   p. 456

[370] The reference is to the failure of the counter-revolutionary General Laugier, supported by the Piedmont ruling circles and the Austrians, to interfere with the development of revolutionary events in Tuscany and prevent the abdication of Grand Duke Leopold II and the proclamation of a Tuscan republic. On January 30, 1849, the Grand Duke fled to Siena, and later to Gaeta, the residence of Pius IX. On February 18, a republic was proclaimed at a popular meeting (official introduction of the republican system was postponed till the convocation of a Constituent Assembly, which never took place due to sabotage by the moderate wing of the movement).   p. 456

[371] The information reproduced by Engels from a French newspaper was not entirely correct. However, the events which marked the beginning of the culminating stage of the struggle between the revolutionary movement in Sicily and the Government of King Ferdinand of Naples provided a basis for rumours about the

proclamation of a Sicilian republic. On February 25, 1849, Ferdinand sent the Sicilians an ultimatum. Though promising to sanction the restoration of the 1812 Constitution he demanded disarmament and consent to occupation of the major parts of the island by Neapolitan troops. The refusal of the Sicilians to accept the ultimatum led to fierce fighting; although the Neapolitan forces were superior in numbers and arms, the Sicilians offered resistance until the beginning of May 1849.   p. 456

372 The thoughts expressed here show Engels' keen insight into future military developments in Hungary. Indeed, the general counter-offensive of the Hungarian revolutionary army was launched in the mentioned region at the beginning of April 1849. On April 2, the revolutionary army won a major victory at Hatvan, followed by a series of strong blows at the enemy. Thus, Engels' forecast did not come true so far as the time of the offensive was concerned, but was quite correct in respect of the place of concentration of the main Hungarian forces for a decisive blow and its direction.   p. 457

373 A major part of the urban population in Transylvania was made up of Germans (Saxons) who constituted about 16 per cent of the region's total population.
                                                                                                     p. 461

374 On November 22, 1848, Lassalle delivered a speech at a popular meeting in Neuss (near Düsseldorf) in which he called upon the people to offer if necessary armed support to the Prussian National Assembly. Lassalle was arrested on the same day. On the legal proceedings against Lassalle see Note 299.   p. 463

375 Here and elsewhere, the reference is to the articles of the *Code pénal* (see Note 88).   p. 463

376 *Code d'instruction criminelle*—the French Criminal Code in force in the Rhine Province of Prussia. Further Article 360 of this Code is cited.   p. 464

377 The *Neue Rheinische Zeitung* No. 186, January 4, 1849, carried information about the deputation of sixteen Düsseldorf citizens to Prosecutor-General Nicolovius among whom were members of the Cologne Workers' Association and the Democratic Society. The deputation handed in a petition signed by 2,800 Düsseldorf citizens, the text of which the newspaper appended to the report.
                                                                                                     p. 474

378 *Kameralgüter*—landed estates which passed into the ownership of the Crown after the death of the last descendant of a feudal family, confiscated lands etc. The *Kameralgüter* also gave the owner the right to collect taxes and other privileges, and were managed by a special administration directly subordinated to the Hungarian Royal Chancellory in Ofen.   p. 479

379 This note was probably written as a rough draft (many words and sentences are crossed out in the manuscript) of a report for the *Neue Rheinische Zeitung*, but no item on this subject appeared in the newspaper.

The occasion for writing this note was a clash of the Workers' Association (see Note 179) and the democratic organisations in Cologne with the police and military authorities who wanted to prevent the people's procession on the occasion of the release from prison on December 23 of Gottschalk, Anneke and others acquitted by the jury after six months of imprisonment. The acquittal was seen by the masses as a victory of the democratic movement, which they wanted to celebrate by procession. The authorities prohibited this procession and it did not take place.   p. 483

380 This fragment is apparently part of the draft of the fourth article in the series "The Bourgeoisie and the Counter-Revolution" which dealt with Hansemann and the Government of Action (see Note 153) he in practice headed. Some of the ideas were reflected in the published version of the article (see this volume, pp. 168-70).

p. 484

381 The extant part of the draft of a speech at the trial of the *Neue Rheinische Zeitung* held on February 7, 1849 (see Note 284), refers to that part of Marx's speech in which, on the basis of a legal analysis of the relevant articles of the French *Code pénal*, he refutes the accusation levelled at the newspaper's editors of insulting Chief Public Prosecutor Zweiffel and calumniating the police officers. To what extent Marx used this draft in the speech itself can be seen by comparing it with the published text (see this volume, pp. 304-17). The manuscript of the draft has come down to us in an incomplete and rough form, indecipherable in some places.

p. 485

382 Marx was summoned before the examining magistrate on November 14, 1848, after the *Neue Rheinische Zeitung* published the second article in the series "Counter-Revolution in Berlin" containing a call to refuse to pay taxes as a measure against the counter-revolutionary coup d'état in Prussia (see this volume, pp. 16-18). However, fearing the people's reaction to the persecution of the editors of a popular newspaper, the authorities confined themselves to confirming one of the charges brought against the *Neue Rheinische Zeitung* earlier, after it had published the appeal "To the German People" by the republican Friedrich Hecker (see Note 93).

p. 495

383 Engels wrote this petition when he arrived in Berne about November 9, 1848, as a political refugee. On the reasons for his departure to Berne see Note 3. The warrant for his arrest and trial, mentioned in the petition, was issued by the Cologne judiciary, who, on the demand of the Imperial Minister of Justice, instituted proceedings against him and a number of other persons for their speeches at the public meeting in Cologne on September 26, 1848. Later, the judicial authorities found it expedient to annul the case, and this was officially announced at the end of January 1849, when Engels, who had returned to Germany, was summoned before the examining magistrate (see this volume, p. 516).

p. 497

384 The People's Committee was elected on November 13, 1848, at a public meeting in Cologne held in protest against the transfer of the Prussian National Assembly from Berlin to Brandenburg. It consisted of 25 representatives of Cologne democratic and proletarian circles, among them Marx, Beust, Nothjung, Weyll and Schneider II. The Committee became one of the organising centres of the people's struggle in the Rhine Province against the coup d'état in Prussia. It sought to rearm the civic militia, which was disarmed in September 1848, when a state of siege was declared in Cologne, and reorganise the army reserve on a democratic basis; it carried out agitation among soldiers and attempted to create a workers' volunteer detachment. Taking part in the tax-refusal campaign, the People's Committee tried to draw into it peasants from the neighbouring localities.

p. 501

385 Article 209 of the *Code pénal* (see Note 88) concerns resistance to the representatives of state power, and Article 217, incitement to rebellion. p. 501

[386] Marx, Korff and others were accused by the Imperial Ministry of having libelled deputies of the Frankfurt National Assembly in: 1) Georg Weerth's series of feuilletons *Leben und Taten des berühmten Ritters Schnapphahnski* directed against Lichnowski, a Right-wing deputy, and published anonymously in the *Neue Rheinische Zeitung* in August, September and December 1848 and January 1849; 2) a report from Breslau in the *Neue Rheinische Zeitung* No. 95 for September 6, 1848, about Prince Lichnowski's machinations in the electoral campaign; 3) a report from Frankfurt am Main in the *Neue Rheinische Zeitung* No. 102 for September 14, 1848, exposing false information in the report by Stedtmann, deputy to the Frankfurt National Assembly, concerning the vote on the armistice with Denmark; 4) a resolution of a public meeting in Cologne published in the *Neue Rheinische Zeitung* No. 110 for September 23, 1848, in which the deputies of the Frankfurt National Assembly who had voted for the armistice with Denmark were accused of having betrayed the nation (see present edition, Vol. 7, pp. 588-89).   p. 504

[387] The trial of the *Neue Rheinische Zeitung* fixed for December 20, 1848, was postponed and was heard on February 7, 1849 (see this volume, pp. 304-22 and Note 284).   p. 504

[388] The First Congress of German Workers' Associations and Democratic Organisations of Switzerland was held in Berne on December 9-11, 1848. On the work of the Congress and Engels' participation in it see Note 175.   p. 505

[389] The reference is to the Central Committee of German Workers in Leipzig (see Note 199).   p. 505

[390] Marx's and Engels' defence counsel, lawyer Schneider II, demanded that the proceedings be adjourned in view of the fact that the accused had not been informed of the trial in due time (ten days prior). The trial took place on February 7, 1849.   p. 511

[391] When the *Zeitung des Arbeiter-Vereines zu Köln* (see Note 180) ceased to appear, the newspaper *Freiheit, Brüderlichkeit, Arbeit*, which began publication on October 26, 1848, became the organ of the Cologne Workers' Association (see Note 179). The publisher was Röser, Vice-President of the Cologne Workers' Association, and the responsible editor was W. Prinz. At the end of December 1848, as a result of Gottschalk's interference in the paper's affairs, its publication was interrupted. From January 14, 1849, the newspaper *Freiheit, Arbeit* began to appear, its publisher being the printer Brocker-Evererts. Prinz, its responsible editor and a supporter of Gottschalk, pursued the policy of splitting the Cologne Workers' Association. He refused to submit to the editorial commission which had been appointed at the committee meeting of the Cologne Workers' Association on January 15 and consisted of Schapper, Röser and Reiff; therefore the committee meeting of January 29 resolved that the *Freiheit, Arbeit* could not be regarded as the Association's newspaper and that the *Freiheit, Brüderlichkeit, Arbeit* should resume publication; Christian Joseph Esser was appointed its editor. The *Freiheit, Brüderlichkeit, Arbeit* reappeared on February 8 and continued publication up to the middle of 1849. The *Freiheit, Arbeit* continued to appear until June 17, 1849. It sharply attacked Marx and the *Neue Rheinische Zeitung's* editorial board and published various malicious insinuations against them.   p. 513

[392] After December 23, when the members of the Cologne Workers' Association, Anneke, Esser and Gottschalk, were acquitted, the last-named tried to keep aloof

from the Association (at first he went to Bonn, and later to Paris and Brussels); at the same time, he endeavoured, through his associates, to cause a split in the ranks of the organisation and again impose a sectarian policy on it. In a statement written in Brussels on January 9, 1849, and published in the *Freiheit, Arbeit* on January 18, Gottschalk explained his "voluntary exile" by the fact that, despite the acquittal, many of his fellow citizens remained convinced of his guilt. He declared that he would come back only "at the call of the hitherto supreme arbiter in the country" (an allusion to Frederick William IV) or "at the call of his fellow citizens". For an appraisal of this ambiguous statement see the decision of Branch No. 1 of the Cologne Workers' Association (present edition, Vol. 9). p. 513

[393] According to the decree of December 5, 1848, the elections of electors were fixed for January 22, and the election of deputies to the Second Chamber of the Prussian Diet for February 5, 1849. p. 514

[394] The Democratic Society in Cologne was set up in April 1848; it included workers and artisans as well as small businessmen. Marx, Engels and other editors of the *Neue Rheinische Zeitung* who directed the Society's activity wanted to orientate it towards a resolute struggle against the counter-revolutionary policy of the Prussian ruling circles and exposure of the liberal bourgeoisie's policy of agreement. In April 1849, Marx and his followers, who had practically begun to organise an independent mass proletarian party, considered it best to dissociate themselves from the petty-bourgeois democrats and withdrew from the Democratic Society. Meanwhile they continued to support the revolutionary actions of the German democratic forces. p. 514

[395] The passport which Engels produced to obtain a residence permit for the canton of Berne was issued by the Government of the French Republic on March 30, 1848. At that time Marx and Engels were preparing to go to Germany, intending to take a direct part in the German revolution. On April 6 they left Paris for their native country. p. 515

[396] Lieutenants Adamski and Niethake took part in the September events in Cologne and in November 1848 were elected to the People's Committee (see Note 384). When the threat of arrest arose, they fled to Belgium, but were arrested there and deported to France. On December 14, after their voluntary return to Germany, they were court-martialled. On May 29, 1849, the court martial deprived Adamski of his commission and sentenced him to nine months' imprisonment in a fortress. p. 521

[397] The banquet in Mülheim on the Rhine described here was one of the first democratic banquets arranged in the Rhine Province to mark the anniversaries of the February revolution in France and the March revolution in Germany. Considering these banquets as a form of revolutionary education of the masses, Marx and Engels took part in some of them. p. 522

[398] The new Statute of the Cologne Workers' Association was adopted on February 25, 1849. According to it, the Association's main task was to raise the workers' class and political consciousness and it was to be built not on the guild principle as before, but on a territorial basis; consistent democratisation was to apply in the internal life of the organisation, and simultaneously the authority of its elected leading body—the Committee—was to increase. Nine branches were set up as planned. All this contributed to extend popular support for the Association and to enhance its political influence. p. 524

³⁹⁹ See Note 127.   p. 525

⁴⁰⁰ See Note 75.   p. 525

⁴⁰¹ After the flight of Grand Duke Leopold II on January 31, 1849, and the establishment on February 8 of the radical Government (triumvirate) consisting of Guerazzi, Montagnelli and Mazzini, the movement for a republic and unity with the Roman Republic intensified in Tuscany. The radicals regarded this as the beginning of a democratic achievement of Italian unity. On February 18, 1849, a public meeting in Florence proclaimed the foundation of a Tuscan republic. However, under pressure from the liberals and moderate democrats the Guerazzi Government postponed the formal proclamation of the republic until the convocation of the Tuscan Constituent Assembly. As moderate elements dominated the Assembly, the triumvirate again postponed the establishment of a republic on March 27, 1849. The republic had not yet been officially proclaimed when a counter-revolutionary revolt on April 11, 1849, brought Leopold II back to power. Guerazzi's policy of yielding to pressure from the moderates also upset the plan for uniting Tuscany with the Roman Republic.   p. 526

⁴⁰² On his arrival in Cologne on April 11, 1848, Marx, who was compelled to renounce his Prussian citizenship in 1845, petitioned the Cologne City Council to grant him the right of citizenship and received a favourable reply. But this decision had to be confirmed by the royal provincial government, which early in August 1848, after four months of delay, informed Marx that his petition had been turned down. Marx lodged a complaint with the Minister of the Interior, Kühlwetter, but on September 12, 1848, the latter confirmed the decision of the provincial government (see present edition, Vol. 7, p. 581). Though the campaign of protest prevented the reactionaries from immediately carrying out all their intentions towards the editor of the *Neue Rheinische Zeitung*, the threat of expulsion from Prussia as a foreigner hovered over him. Later the Prussian Government expelled Marx from Prussia under the pretext that he "had abused hospitality". Due to this act and repressions against other editors, the newspaper ceased publication in May 1849.   p. 527

⁴⁰³ On February 27, 1849, the *Kölnische Zeitung* carried a report on the banquet of February 24. The item said in particular: "Deputy Gladbach especially distinguished himself among the orators by his thunderous speeches against the House of Hohenzollern, Count Brandenburg and others."   p. 529

⁴⁰⁴ The reference is to the group of participants in the Baden uprising of April 1848 who emigrated to Besançon (France); later, under the name of the Besançon company and headed by Willich, they took part in the Baden-Palatinate uprising of 1849.   p. 529

⁴⁰⁵ See Note 178.   p. 530

NAME INDEX

pated in the war against revolutionary Hungary in 1848-49.—423, 478

Leopold I (1790-1865)—King of Belgium (1831-65).—307

Leopold II (1797-1870)—Grand Duke of Tuscany (1824-59).—456, 526

Lessing, Gotthold Ephraim (1729-1781)—German writer, critic and philosopher of the Enlightenment.—225

Lessner, Friedrich (1825-1910)—prominent in the German and international working-class movement; member of the Communist League; took part in the 1848-49 revolution; prosecuted at the Cologne communist trial in 1852; member of the General Council of the First International; friend and comrade-in-arms of Marx and Engels.—525, 529

Leuthaus—Prussian judiciary official; examining magistrate in Cologne in 1848.—46, 192

Lichnowski, Felix Maria, Prince von (1814-1848)—Prussian army officer; deputy to the Frankfurt National Assembly (Right wing); killed during the Frankfurt uprising in September 1848.—82, 504

Lohbauer, Rudolf—Prussian journalist; in the early 1830s radical, then emigrated to Strassburg; professor in Berne from 1835; in the 1840s returned to Berlin where he contributed to Prussian government and pietist periodicals.—239, 240

Louis XI (1423-1483)—King of France (1461-83).—228

Louis XVI (1754-1793)—King of France (1774-92); guillotined during the French Revolution.—15

Louis Bonaparte—see Napoleon III

Louis Napoleon—see Napoleon III

Louis Philippe I (1773-1850)—Duke of Orleans, King of the French (1830-48).—129, 131, 275, 307

Löwenfels, T. W.—German writer; a refugee in Switzerland; participated in the republican uprising in Baden in September 1848.—204

Lubomirski, Jerzy, Prince (1817-1872)—participant in the Slav Congress in Prague; deputy to the Austrian Imperial Diet in 1849.—377

Lubomirskis—family of Polish princes.—229

Lucas—member of the Workers' Association in Mülheim (Rhine Province) in 1849.—522

Lüders, Alexander Nikolayevich, Count (1790-1874)—Russian general, in 1848 commander of the occupation corps in Moldavia and Wallachia; in 1849 fought in the war against the Hungarian army in Transylvania.—436, 472

Ludwig Joseph Anton (1784-1864)—Archduke of Austria.—212

Lusser, Florian (1820-1889)—Swiss Public Prosecutor; deputy of the Uri canton to the National Council (1848-60).—108

Luther, Martin (1483-1546)—leader of the Reformation; founder of Protestantism (Lutheranism) in Germany; ideologist of the German burghers.—35

Lutter—Prussian official; police inspector in Cologne in 1848.—190

Luvini, Giacomo (1795-1862)—Swiss colonel of Italian descent, radical politician, lawyer; in 1847 fought in the war against the Sonderbund; deputy of the Tessin canton to the National Council from 1848.—114, 115, 118, 140, 141, 144, 145, 146, 147, 148, 152

M

Madarasz, Jozef—Hungarian politician and lawyer, editor of Left newspapers; during the 1848 revolution the Left-wing leader of the Hungarian State Assembly.—351

Malkowsky von Dammwalden, Ignaz (1784-1854)—Austrian general of Polish descent; participated in the war against revolutionary Hungary in 1848-49.—472, 473, 478

Malten, H.—German conservative journalist; editor of the Frankfurter Oberpostamts-Zeitung (1848-49).—421

P

Wrangel, Friedrich Heinrich Ernst, Count von (1784-1877)—Prussian general, participant in the counter-revolutionary coup d'état in Berlin and the dissolution of the Prussian National Assembly in November 1848.—17, 18, 51, 75, 157, 223, 261, 296, 321, 334, 357, 447

Wrbna-Freudenthal, Ladislaus, Count (1795-1849)—Austrian major-general; took part in the war against revolutionary Hungary in 1848-49.—351, 412, 460

Wulff, Julius—German democrat; President of the People's Club in Düsseldorf (1848); took part in the Baden-Palatinate uprising in 1849.—315

Wysocki, Józef (1809-1874)—Polish politician and general, participant in the insurrection of 1830-31; during the 1848-49 revolution in Hungary commander of the Polish legion in the Hungarian revolutionary army; took part in the Polish uprising in 1863-64.—443

Wyss, Franz Salomon (1796-1849)—Austrian major-general; took part in suppressing the October uprising in Vienna (1848) and in the war against revolutionary Hungary in 1848-49.—120, 121, 137

Wyss—architect in Berne, brother of General Franz Wyss.—137

Z

Zayas, Juan Antonio—Spanish ambassador in Switzerland (1848-49).—137

Zeisberg, Karl von (1788-1863)—Austrian major-general, subsequently lieutenant-field marshal; fought in the war against revolutionary Hungary in 1848-49.—466

Ziegler, Paul Karl Eduard (1800-1882)—Swiss politician, participant in the war against the Sonderbund (1847); deputy to the National Council (1848).—60, 61, 149

Zweiffel—Prussian official; Chief Public Prosecutor in Cologne; in 1848 deputy to the Prussian National Assembly (Right wing).—30, 46, 48, 49, 81, 82, 304, 307, 311-13, 317, 486, 491, 501, 511, 517, 518

Y

Yelena Pavlovna (*Fridericke Charlotte Marie*) (1807-1873)—Russian Grand Duchess.—212

INDEX OF LITERARY AND MYTHOLOGICAL NAMES

Achilles—hero of Homer's *Iliad*; in Greek mythology, one of the Greek leaders in the Trojan War.—394

Ajax—a character in Shakespeare's drama *Troilus and Cressida*.—139, 149

Beisele—see *Eisele and Beisele*

Cassandra (Gr. Myth.)—a daughter of Priam (King of Troy), prophetess; a character in Aeschylus' tragedy *Agamemnon*.—356-58

Don Quixote—title character in Cervantes' novel.—68

Dottore Bartholo—a character in Beaumarchais' comedies *Le Barbier de Seville* and *La folle journée, ou le mariage de Figaro*.—148

Eisele and Beisele—main characters in an anonymously published satirical pamphlet by Johann Wilhelm Christern, *Doctor Eisele's und Baron von Beisele's Landtagsreise im April 1847*.—89

Figaro—main character in Beaumarchais' comedy *La folle journée, ou le mariage de Figaro*.—262

INDEX OF QUOTED
AND MENTIONED LITERATURE

WORKS BY KARL MARX AND FREDERICK ENGELS

Prussian Financial Administration under Bodelschwingh and Co. (this volume)
— Preussische Finanzwirtschaft unter Bodelschwingh und Konsorten. In: *Neue Rheinische Zeitung* No. 224, February 17, 1849.—418

Public Prosecutor "Hecker" and the "Neue Rheinische Zeitung" (present edition, Vol. 7)
— Der Staatsprokurator "Hecker" und die "Neue Rheinische Zeitung". In: *Neue Rheinische Zeitung* No. 129, October 29, 1848.—81-82, 304, 496

The Tax-Refusal Trial (this volume)
— Der Steuerverweigerungsprozess. In: *Neue Rheinische Zeitung* No. 218, February 10, 1849.—344

The Trial of Gottschalk and His Comrades (this volume)
— Prozess gegen Gottschalk und Genossen. In: *Neue Rheinische Zeitung* Nos. 175 and 176, December 22 and 23, 1848.—210, 474

The Victory of the Counter-Revolution in Vienna (present edition, Vol. 7)
— Sieg der Kontrerevolution zu Wien. In: *Neue Rheinische Zeitung* No. 136, November 7, 1848.—23

Engels, Frederick
The Armistice with Denmark (present edition, Vol. 7)
— Der Waffenstillstand mit Dänemark. In: *Neue Rheinische Zeitung* No. 52, July 22, 1848.—223

Bulletin No. 22 (this volume)
— Das Zweiundzwanzigste Bulletin. In: *Neue Rheinische Zeitung* No. 225 (supplement), February 18, 1849.—401

[*Debate in the National Council*] (this volume). In: *Neue Rheinische Zeitung* No. 153 (second edition), November 26, 1848.—136, 141-42

Debate about the Existing Redemption Legislation (present edition, Vol. 7)
— Debatte über die bisherige Ablösungsgesetzgebung. In: *Neue Rheinische Zeitung* No. 67, August 6, 1848.—175

Duel between Berg and Luvini (this volume)
— Duell zwischen Berg und Luvini. In: *Neue Rheinische Zeitung* No. 160, December 5, 1848.—147

Elections.—Sydow (this volume)
— Die Wahlen.—Sydow. In: *Neue Rheinische Zeitung* No. 153 (supplement), November 26, 1848.—58, 113, 136, 141

Elections to the Federal Court.—Miscellaneous (this volume)
— Wahlen für das Bundesgericht.—Verschiedenes. In: *Neue Rheinische Zeitung* No. 150, November 23, 1848.—95

The Ex-Principality (this volume)
— Das Exfürstentum. In: *Neue Rheinische Zeitung* No. 140, November 11, 1848.—245

The First Trial of the "Neue Rheinische Zeitung". Speech by Frederick Engels (this volume)
— Der erste Pressprozess der "Neuen Rheinischen Zeitung". In: *Neue Rheinische Zeitung* No. 221, February 14, 1849.—485, 520, 521

The Frankfurt Assembly Debates the Polish Question (present edition, Vol. 7)
— Die Polendebatte in Frankfurt. In: *Neue Rheinische Zeitung* Nos. 70, 73, 81, 86, August 9, 12, 20, 26, 1848.—230

From the Theatre of War in Transylvania and Hungary (this volume)
— Vom ungarischen und siebenbürgeschen Kriegsschauplatze. In: *Neue Rheinische Zeitung* No. 235 (special supplement), March 2, 1849.—440

The German Central Authority and Switzerland (this volume)
— Die deutsche Zentralgewalt und die Schweiz. In: *Neue Rheinische Zeitung* No. 153, November 26, 1848.—88

German Socialism in Verse and Prose (present edition, Vol. 6)
— Deutscher Sozialismus in Versen und Prosa. In: *Deutsche-Brüsseler-Zeitung* Nos. 73 and 74, September 12 and 16, 1847; Nos. 93, 94 and 95, November 21, 25 and 28, 1847; Nos. 96, 97 and 98, December 2, 5 and 9, 1847.—372

Joint Sitting of the Councils.—The Federal Council (this volume)
— Vereinigte Sitzung der Räthe.—Der Bundesrath. In: *Neue Rheinische Zeitung* No. 156, November 30, 1848.—113, 180

Latest News of the Magyars.—Victory on the Theiss.—Brutality of the Austrians.—State of War in General (this volume)
— Neueres über die Magyaren.—Sieg an der Theiss.—Brutalität der Österreicher.—Lage des Krieges im Allgemeinen. In: *Neue Rheinische Zeitung* No. 231, February 25, 1849.—443

The Magyar Struggle (this volume)
— Der magyarische Kampf. In: *Neue Rheinische Zeitung* No. 194, January 13, 1849.—366

Measures against German Refugees.—Return of Troops from Tessin.—The Patricians' Commune (this volume)
— Die Massregeln gegen deutsche Flüchtlinge.—Die Truppen aus Tessin zurück.—Die Patriziergemeinde. In: *Neue Rheinische Zeitung* No. 180, December 28, 1848.—250

Measures Concerning the German Refugees (this volume)
— Massregeln wegen der deutschen Flüchtlinge. In: *Neue Rheinische Zeitung* No. 165, December 10, 1848.—180, 204

[*More News of the Magyars*] (this volume). In: *Neue Rheinische Zeitung* No. 231 (supplement), February 25, 1849.—428, 443

The National Council (this volume)
— Der Nationalrat. In: *Neue Rheinische Zeitung* Nos. 165 and 165 (second edition), December 10, 1848.—59, 136, 179

News from Switzerland (this volume)
— Verschiedenes. In: *Neue Rheinische Zeitung* No. 151 (supplement), November 24, 1848.—58

On the Polish Question (present edition, Vol. 6)
— Reden über Polen. In: *Deutsche-Brüsseler-Zeitung* No. 98, December 9, 1847.—371-72

[*Raveaux's Resignation.—Violation of Swiss Territory*] (this volume). In: *Neue Rheinische Zeitung* No. 154 (supplement), November 28, 1848.—98, 119

[*Result of the Elections to the National Council*] (this volume). In: *Neue Rheinische Zeitung* No. 152, November 25, 1848.—59

WORKS BY DIFFERENT AUTHORS

[Hermes, J. T.] *Sophiens Reise von Memel nach Sachsen,* Bd. 1-6, Leipzig, 1778.—67

Hildebrandt, C. *Kuno von Schreckenstein, oder die weissagende Traumgestalt,* 2. Aufl., Bd. 1-3, Quedlinburg und Leipzig, 1840.—168

Hobbes, Thomas. *Elementa philosophica. De cive,* Basileae, 1782.—165

Horatius Flaccus, Quintus. *De Arte Poetica,* 139.—290, 401
— *Carminum,* Ode 3. In: *Q. Horatii Flacci opera omnia poetica,* Halae, 1802.—143
— *Epistolae,* Liber primus, Epistola II.—68

Kamptz, K. A. *Jahrbücher für die Preussische Gesetzgebung, Rechtswissenschaft und Rechtsverwaltung,* Bd. 37, Berlin, 1831.—382

Kortum, K. A. *Die Jobsiade. Ein komisches Heldengedicht.*—89, 154

Lessing, G. E. *Minna von Barnhelm* (comedy in five acts).—225

[Löwenfels, T. W., Neff, F. u. Thielemann, G.] *Die zweite republikanische Aufstand in Baden,* Basel, 1848.—204

Marseillaise.—530

[Maurenbrecher, P. W. *Die Erklärung des Düsseldorfer Oberpostdirektors Maurenbrecher.*] In: *Kölnische Zeitung* No. 314 (second edition), November 23, 1848.—77

Milton, J. *Paradise Lost.* A Poem, in twelve books.—88

Molière, J.-B. *George Dandin ou le mari confondu* (comedy in three acts).—356
— *Le bourgeois gentilhomme* (comedy in three acts).—164

Mourir pour la patrie (*Les Girondins*).—530

Patow, E. R. von. *Promemoria, betreffend die Massregeln der Gesetzgebung, durch welche die zeitgemässe Reform der guts- und grundherrlichen Verhältnisse und die Beseitigung der noch vorhandenen Hemmungen der Landeskultur bezweckt wird,* Berlin, June 20, 1848. In: *Stenographische Berichte über die Verhandlungen der zur Vereinbarung der preussischen Staats-Verfassung berufenen Versammlung,* Beilage zum *Preussischen Staats-Anzeiger,* Bd. 1, Berlin, 1848.—175

Proudhon, P.-J. *Argument à la Montagne.* In: *Le Peuple* No, 5, November 15-21, 1848.—123
— *Qu'est-ce que la propriété? Ou recherches sur le principe du droit et du gouvernement,* Paris, 1841.—129
— *Système des contradictions économiques, ou philosophie de la misère,* T. I-II, Paris, 1846.—129

Rossini, G. *Tancredi* (opera).—91

Rotteck, K. von. *Allgemeine Geschichte vom Anfang der historischen Kenntniss bis auf unsere Zeiten. Für denkende Geschichtsfreunde,* Freiburg und Konstanz, 1813-1818.—157
— *Staats-Lexikon oder Encyklopädie der Staatswissenschaften, in Verbindung mit vielen der angesehensten Publicisten Deutschlands,* Bd. 15, Altona, 1843.—89

Schiller, F. von. *An die Freude.*—213
— *Die Jungfrau von Orleans.*—17
— *Der Taucher.*—89

Schücking, L. *Politische Gespräche.* In: *Kölnische Zeitung* Nos. 29, 30, 34 and 35, February 3, 4, 9 and 10, 1849.—354

Shakespeare, W. *As You Like It.*—163
— *Hamlet.*—34, 198
— *King Lear.*—83
— *Troilus and Cressida.*—18, 139

A Thousand and One Nights (Arabian tales).—287

Unruh, H. V. von. *Skizzen aus Preussens neuester Geschichte,* Magdeburg, 1849.—334

[Vulpius, Ch. A.] *Rinaldo Rinaldini, der Räuber Hauptmann.* Eine romantische Geschichte unsers Jahrhunderts in Drei Theilen oder neun Büchern, 2. Aufl., Th. 1-3, Leipzig, 1799.—69

[Weerth, G.] *Leben und Taten des berühmten Ritters Schnapphahnski.* In: *Neue Rheinische Zeitung,* August, September and December 1848 and January 1849.—504
— *Die Steuerverweigerung in England bei Gelegenheit der Reform-Bill im Jahre 1832.* In: *Neue Rheinische Zeitung* No. 142 (second edition) and No. 143, November 14 and 15, 1848.—19

DOCUMENTS

Allerhöchste Kabinetsorder an das Staatsministerium, betreffend den Staatshaushalt und das Staatsschulden-Wesen. De dato den 17ten Januar 1820. In: *Gesetz-Sammlung für die Königlichen Preussischen Staaten,* 1820, No. 2.—382, 383, 388

Allgemeiner Etat der Staats-Einnahmen und Ausgaben für das Jahr 1844. In: *Gesetz-Sammlung für die Königlichen Preussischen Staaten,* 1844, No. 9.—380

Allgemeines Landrecht für die Preussischen Staaten, Berlin, 1817.—172, 296, 315, 381, 382, 388, 389

An meine lieben Berliner [des Königs Friedrich-Wilhelm IV. von Preussen vom 19. März 1848]. In: *Allgemeine Preussische Zeitung* No. 80, March 20, 1848.—222

An mein Volk und an die deutsche Nation [des Königs Friedrich-Wilhelm IV, Berlin, den 21. März, 1848]. In *Allgemeine Preussische Zeitung* No. 82, March 22, 1848.—222, 447

An sämtliche Königlichen Regierungen. In: *Preussischer Staats-Anzeiger* No. 200, November 20, 1848.—47

17. Armee-Bulletin. In: *Wiener Zeitung* No. 19, January 23, 1849.—290-91

18. Armee-Bulletin. In: *Wiener Zeitung* No. 24, January 28, 1849.—291, 294, 302

19. Armee-Bulletin. In: *Wiener Zeitung* No. 27, February 1, 1849.—300, 303

20. Armee-Bulletin. In: *Wiener Zeitung* No. 30, February 4, 1849.—401

21. Armee-Bulletin. In: *Wiener Zeitung* No. 30, February 4, 1849.—401

22. Armee-Bulletin. In: *Wiener Zeitung* No. 38, February 14, 1849.—401, 402, 404-08

23. Armee-Bulletin. In: *Wiener Zeitung* No. 42, February 18, 1849.—423-26, 468

24. Armee-Bulletin. In: *Wiener Zeitung* No. 45, February 22, 1849.—437, 459

25. Armee-Bulletin. In: *Wiener Zeitung* No. 51, March 1, 1849.—478, 480

Armee-Befehl von F. H. E. Wrangel, Potsdam, September 17, 1848. In: *Neue Rheinische Zeitung* No. 109, September 22, 1848.—176, 261, 334

Patent die ständischen Einrichtungen betreffend. Vom 3. Februar 1847. In: *Gesetz-Sammlung für die Königlichen Preussischen Staaten,* 1847, No. 4.—166, 387

Patent über die Publikation des Reichsgesetzes, betreffend das Verfahren im Falle gerichtlicher Anklagen gegen Mitglieder der verfassunggebenden Reichsversammlung. Vom 14. Oktober 1848. In: *Gesetz-Sammlung für die Königlichen Preussischen Staaten,* 1848, No. 46.—201

[*Petition des Kölner Gemeinderats an den König.*] In: *Kölnische Zeitung* No. 311 (second edition), November 19, 1848.—45, 53

Die Proklamation [*des Königs Friedrich-Wilhelm IV. von Preussen vom 11. November 1848*]. In: *Neue Preussische Zeitung* No. 116 (special supplement), November 12, 1848.—20

The Statutes of the United Kingdom of Great Britain and Ireland, 60 Geo. III. and 1 Geo. IV. 1819-1820. And 1 Geo. IV. 1820, London, 1820.—448

Stenographische Berichte über die Verhandlungen der zur Vereinbarung der preussischen Staats-Verfassung berufenen Versammlung, Beilage zum *Preussischen Staats-Anzeiger* (Marx and Engels used this report as published in the newspapers).—75, 99, 154, 169-77, 223, 296, 334

Stenographischer Bericht über die Verhandlungen der deutschen constituirenden National-Versammlung zu Frankfurt am Main, Bd. 1-9, Frankfurt a. M. und Leipzig, 1848-1849 (Marx and Engels used this report mainly as published in the newspapers).—51-52, 65, 68, 99

Traité de commerce entre la Prusse, la Bavière, la Saxe, le Wurttemberg, la Bade, la Hesse-Electorale, la Hesse-Grand-Ducale, les Etats commant l'union de douanes et de commerce, dite de Thuringe, le Nassau, et la ville libre de Francfort, d'une part, et les Pays-Bas, d'autre part, le 21. Janvier 1839. In: *Gesetz-Sammlung für die Königlichen Preussischen Staaten,* 1839, No. 10.—265

Uebersicht von den Resultaten der Finanz-Verwaltung im Jahre 1847. In: *Vorlagen an die National-Versammlung,* 1848.—383, 388

Verfassungsurkunde für den Preussischen Staat, December 5, 1848. In: *Gesetz-Sammlung für die Königlichen Preussischen Staaten,* 1848, No. 55.—134, 154, 177, 201, 255-57, 259-67, 287, 289, 323, 328, 346, 391, 447, 448

Verhandlungen der constituirenden Versammlung für Preussen. 1848, Bd. 9 (Suppl.-Bd.), Leipzig, 1849.—19, 25, 36, 38, 41, 48, 50, 200, 323, 333, 338, 339

Verhandlungen des zum 2. April 1848 zusammenberufenen Vereinigten Landtages, Berlin, 1848.—446

Verordnung, betreffend die Auflösung der zur Vereinbarung der Verfassung berufenen Versammlung. Vom 5. Dezember 1848. In: *Stenographische Berichte über die Verhandlungen der zur Vereinbarung der preussischen Staats-Verfassung berufenen Versammlung,* Beilage zum *Preussischen Staats-Anzeiger,* Bd. 3, Berlin, 1848.—134, 135

Verordnung, betreffend die Ausführung des Gesetzes über die Errichtung der Bürgerwehr. Vom 17. Oktober 1848. In: *Gesetz-Sammlung für die Königlichen Preussischen Staaten,* 1848, No. 47.—77-79

Verordnung, betreffend die Errichtung von Gewerberäthen und verschiedene Abänderungen der allgemeinen Gewerbeordnung. Vom 9. Februar 1849. In: *Gesetz-Sammlung für die Königlichen Preussischen Staaten,* 1849, No. 6.—449

Verordnung über die Bildung des Vereinigten Landtages. Vom 3. Februar 1847. In: *Gesetz-Sammlung für die Königlichen Preussischen Staaten,* 1847, No. 4.—166

Verordnung über die Errichtung von Gewerbegerichten. Vom 9. Februar 1849. In: *Gesetz-Sammlung für die Königlichen Preussischen Staaten,* 1849, No. 6.—449

Verordnung über die zu bildende Repräsentation des Volks. Vom 22ten Mai 1815. In: *Gesetz-Sammlung für die Königlichen Preussischen Staaten,* 1815, No. 9.—166

Verordnung über einige Grundlagen der künftigen Preussischen Verfassung. Vom 6. April 1848. In: *Gesetz-Sammlung für die Königlichen Preussischen Staaten,* 1848, No. 11.—77, 154, 201, 323-29, 339

Verordnung wegen Bestrafung schriftlicher Beleidigungen in den Provinzen, wo das französische Strafgesetzbuch vorläufig noch gesetzliche Kraft hat. Vom 5ten Juli 1819. In: *Gesetz-Sammlung für die Königlichen Preussischen Staaten,* 1819, No. 15.—307

Verordnung wegen der künftigen Behandlung des gesammten Staatsschulden-Wesens. Vom 17ten Januar 1820. In: *Gesetz-Sammlung für die Königlichen Preussischen Staaten,* 1820, No. 2.—166

Vorläufiger Entwurf einer Verordnung zur Ergänzung der Allgemeinen Gewerbe-Ordnung vom 17. Jan. 1845. In: *Kölnische Zeitung* No. 24 (first supplement), January 28, 1849.—265-66

Wahlgesetz für die zur Vereinbarung der Preussischen Staats-Verfassung zu berufende Versammlung. Vom 8. April 1848. In: *Gesetz-Sammlung für die Königlichen Preussischen Staaten,* 1848, No. 12.—154, 166, 271, 296, 323-29, 339

Wahlgesetz für die zweite Kammer. Vom 6. Dezember 1848. In: *Gesetz-Sammlung für die Königlichen Preussischen Staaten,* 1848, No. 55.—271

[*Zirkularnote der preussischen Regierung vom 23. Januar 1849.*] In: *Kölnische Zeitung* No. 25 (special supplement), January 30, 1849.—297

[*Die Zustimmungs-*] *Adressen* [*an die Nationalversammlung in Berlin*]. In: *Neue Rheinische Zeitung* No. 148, November 21, 1848.—39

[*Zweite Antwortnote des Vororts Bern vom 4. November 1848.*] In: *Frankfurter Oberpostamts-Zeitung* No. 304, November 13, 1848.—68

[*Zweite Note der deutschen Zentralgewalt an den Vorort Bern vom 23. Oktober 1848.*] In: *Frankfurter Oberpostamts-Zeitung* No. 298 (supplement), November 6, 1848.—68

ANONYMOUS ARTICLES AND REPORTS PUBLISHED
IN PERIODIC EDITIONS

Allgemeine Zeitung No. 38, February 7, 1849: "Pesth, 1. Febr." and "Wien, 3. Febr."—368

Deutsche Allgemeine Zeitung No. 48 (supplement), February 17, 1849: "Prag, 13. Febr."—410
— No. 54, February 23, 1849: "Nota des Grafs Almásy."—431

Düsseldorfer Zeitung No. 311, November 24, 1848: "Düsseldorf, vom 22. November."—79

— No. 336, December 23, 1848: "Münster, vom 20. Dez."—200

Frankfurter Oberpostamts-Zeitung No. 314 (supplement), November 24, 1848: "Die Fortdauer der Ueberstände an der Schweizergrenze."—117

Grazer Zeitung No. 54, February 23, 1849: "Temesvár (Correspondenz)."—461
— No. 54, February 23, 1849: "Bulletin" (report).—468
— No. 56, February 25, 1849: "Ungarischer Kriegsschauplatz: Sieg der Russen in Siebenbürgen."—454
— No. 59, February 28, 1849: "Officieller Bericht über das Gefecht bei Kronstadt."—472

Kölnische Zeitung No. 11, January 13, 1849: "An die Urwähler."—255
— No. 24, January 28, 1849: "Die Wahlen zur ersten Kammer."—289
— No. 25, January 30, 1849: "Die Wahlen."—286
— No. 25 (supplement), January 30, 1849: "Ungarn (Von Kriegs-Schau-platz)."—290
— No. 35 (first supplement), February 10, 1849: "Ungarn" (report).—347
— No. 40, February 16, 1849: "Kein Zentrum."—392
— No. 41, February 17, 1849: "Der ungarische Krieg."—398

Der Lloyd No. 84 (morning edition), February 18, 1849: "Pesth, 15. Februar."—426
— No. 99 (evening edition), February 27, 1849: "Pesth, 24. Februar."—471

Neue Preussische Zeitung No. 110, November 5, 1848: "Das Ministerium Brandenburg."—3
— No. 113, November 9, 1848: "Berlin, den 8. November."—14,16
— No. 115, November 11, 1848: "Aus Breslau, den 8. November."—39
— No. 115 (supplement), November 11, 1848: "Der Bericht der Zentral-Abteilung über Kirche und Schule."—30
— No. 118, November 15, 1848: "Ob Königtum, ob Republik."—32

Neue Rheinische Zeitung No. 48, July 18, 1848: "Bürgerverein" (Düsseldorf).—314
— No. 74, August 13, 1848: "Die Sitzung der Nationalversammlung vom 7. und 8. August."—390
— No. 95, September 6, 1848: "Breslau" (Lichnowski).—504
— No. 102, September 14, 1848: "!!! Frankfurt a. M. den 11. Septbr. 1848. 75. Sitzung der National-Versammlung."—504
— No. 211, February 2, 1849: "Wien, 28. Jan."—291

Die Presse No. 50, February 28, 1849: "Kronstadt, den 5. Februar."—472
— No. 51, March 1, 1849: "Offizielle Nachrichten. 25. Armee-Bulletin."—479

La Presse No. 4517-4521, November 7-11, 1848: "M. Cavaignac devant la Commission d'Enquête sur l'insurrection du 23. juin."—23

Revue rétrospective ou Archives secrètes du dernier Gouvernement No. 3, 1848. [Review of secret archives of the Foreign Ministry of the July monarchy for 1840, 1842, 1844-47.]—421

Schweizerisches Bundesblatt No. 6, March 17, 1849: "Angelegenheit der italienischen Flüchtlinge im Kanton Tessin."—141-53

La Suisse No. 291, December 6, 1848: [Circular to the cantonal governments].—180

Wiener-Zeitung No. 32, February 7, 1849: "Proclamation des F. M. G. Puchner.—Nachrichten von Kriegsschauplatze."—350
— No. 33, February 8, 1849: "Fünfter Armeebericht des F. M. L. Schlick."—360
— No. 40 (evening supplement), February 15, 1849: "Ungarn. Pest, 13. Februar. (Amtliches.) Proclamation." [Windischgrätz's proclamation.]—415
— No. 44, February 21, 1849: "Siebenbürgen" (report).—432

INDEX OF PERIODICALS

SUBJECT INDEX

22 *

T

GLOSSARY OF GEOGRAPHICAL NAMES [a]

Agram	Zagreb	Leopoldstadt	Leopoldov
Breslau	Wrocław	Leutschau (Löcse)	Levoča
Bromberg	Bydgoszcz	Marienburg (Földvar)	Feldioară
Eperies	Prešov	Mediasch	Medias
Erlau	Eger	Misox (Moesa)	Mesocco
Esseg (Eszék)	Osijek	Myslowitz	Mysłowice
Fiume	Rijeka (Rieka)	Neheim	Neheim-Hüsten
Fünfkirchen	Pécs	Neuhäusl	Nové Zámky
Gleiwitz	Gliwice	Neutra	Nitra
Gran	Esztergom	Oberlausitz (Lausitz)	Upper Lusatia
Grosswardein	Oradea	Ödenburg	Sopron
Hermannstadt	Sibiu	Ofen	Buda
Karlowitz (Karlovce)	Karlovci Sremski	Olmütz	Olomouc
		Oppeln	Opole
Karlsburg	Alba Julia	Pancsova	Pančevo
Karlstadt	Karlovac	Peterwardein	Petrovaradin
Kaschau (Kassa)	Kosiče	Plattensee	Balaton
Klausenburg (Kolozsvár)	Cluj	Posen	Poznań
Komorn (Komarno)	Komárom	Pressburg (Pozsony)	Bratislava
Kosel	Koźle	Raab	Györ
Kronstadt	Braşow	Rátibor	Racibórz
Lemberg	Lvov	Rimaszombat	Rimavská Sobota
		Schemnitz (Selmeczbanya)	Banska Štiavnica

[a] This glossary includes geographical names occurring in Marx's and Engels' articles in the form customary in the German press of the time but differing from the national names or from those given on modern maps. The left column gives geographical names as used in the German original (when they differ from the national names of the time, the latter are given in brackets); the right column gives corresponding names as used on modern maps and in modern literature.— *Ed.*

Schweidnitz	Swidnica	Waag (Vag)	Váh
Semlin	Zemun	Waitzen (Vácz)	Vác
Stettin	Szczecin	Weisskirchen	Bela Crkva
Szegedin	Szeged	Werschetz (Versecz)	Vršac
Szeretfalva	Sereth	Wreschen	Września
Temesvár	Timişoara		